In Defence of
BRITAIN'S
MIDDLE EASTERN
EMPIRE

A Life of Sir Gilbert Clayton

"General Gilbert Clayton played a central part in the war against the Ottoman Empire and the subsequent partition of the Middle East. This is a full, critical, and original account not only of a key personality but also such major issues as the Sykes–Picot agreement and the Balfour Declaration. Even on such well-known figures as T.E. Lawrence, Timothy Paris provides valuable and persuasive assessment. A masterly work." WM. ROGER LOUIS, University of Texas, past-president of the American Historical Association and editor-in-chief of the *Oxford History of the British Empire*

"Sir Gilbert Clayton was only 53 when he died suddenly in Baghdad in September 1929, a few months after arriving there as ambassador, but, as this admirably comprehensive biography shows, he had already spent some more than 30 years in the Middle East. Clayton was a principled pragmatist, one of a growing band of latter-day servants of empire whose practical experience gradually led him to conclude that direct rule, or even enlightened indirect rule, over colonial territories, was becoming less and less of a practical proposition. Basing his account on official and private papers, Dr Paris' account ably traces Clayton's singular, if largely unacknowledged, contributions to 'Britain's moment in the Middle East'." PETER SLUGLETT, Director of the Middle East Institute at the National University of Singapore

"Gilbert Clayton's career in the Middle East spanned over thirty years, most notably as head of British intelligence in Cairo during World War I. A key figure in British policy during the war and after, his role has never been fully acknowledged in previous scholarship. Thanks to Tim Paris, we now have a deeply researched, analytical study of Clayton's life and work in the service of the British Empire in the Arab world at a key transitional moment, based largely on numerous archival sources. This book will serve as a major resource for scholars of the period." CHARLES D. SMITH, Professor Emeritus of Middle East History, University of Arizona

In Defence of
BRITAIN'S MIDDLE EASTERN EMPIRE

A Life of Sir Gilbert Clayton

TIMOTHY J. PARIS

sussex
ACADEMIC
PRESS
Brighton • Chicago • Toronto

2 4 6 8 10 9 7 5 3 1

First published 2016 in Great Britain by
SUSSEX ACADEMIC PRESS
PO Box 139
Eastbourne BN24 9BP

and in the United States of America by
SUSSEX ACADEMIC PRESS
Independent Publishers Group
814 N. Franklin Street, Chicago, IL 60610

and in Canada by
SUSSEX ACADEMIC PRESS (CANADA)

British Library Cataloguing in Publication Data
A CIP catalogue record for this book is available from the British Library.

Library of Congress Cataloging-in-Publication Data
Applied for.

ISBN 978-1-84519-758-2 (hardcover)

Typeset and designed by Sussex Academic Press, Brighton & Eastbourne.
Printed by TJ International, Padstow, Cornwall.

Contents

Acknowledgments

Fifty years ago one of Sir Gilbert Clayton's friends described him as a man who 'had a talent for keeping his own counsel'. That was perhaps a desirable trait in a man who served as director of British Intelligence in the Middle East during the Great War, and as one of Britain's pre-eminent political officers and diplomats in that region in the years following. For the biographer, however, the reticence of one's subject is not a helpful characteristic. Still, owing to the help I received from so many individuals and institutions, I encountered no great difficulties in coming to an understanding of Clayton or his views on the varied and complex issues he confronted in his professional life, a career that spanned thirty-three years and encompassed no fewer than ten different Middle Eastern countries and territories.

I must begin with the Clayton family who extended their kind hospitality and provided much information about Sir Gilbert without in any way attempting to restrict or influence this work. Dr John P. Clayton, C.V.O., met with me in York, London, Windsor and Wiltshire, answered numerous questions and provided a wealth of anecdotal information concerning his father. Sir Gilbert's grandson, also known as Bertie Clayton, and his wife Rosalind, welcomed me into their home and shared with me an unpublished family history prepared by Sir Gilbert's father, W. L. N. Clayton, as well as photographs and memorabilia associated with Sir Gilbert's career. David Thorne and his wife Susannah, Clayton's great-granddaughter, also supplied information and photos and I learned much from David's researches in family history as reflected on his helpful website. I must also thank Perry and Gyr King, grandsons of Sir Gilbert's brother, Admiral John Clayton (1888–1952), who allowed access to their grandmother's diaries. And Gyr and his wife Nicola, kindly invited me into their home for a few days while I read them. Clayton's niece Margaret, and her husband Professor Justin Gosling, provided a typescript of the unpublished memoir of Sir Gilbert's brother, Sir Iltyd Nicholl Clayton (1886–1955).

A number of academics answered enquiries concerning this project. Among these, I owe a special debt to Professor M. W. Daly, who allowed me to draw on his extensive knowledge of Middle Eastern history and very generously provided documents from his own collections, including copies of papers relating to Clayton kept at the Weizmann Archive in Rehovot, Israel. Professors Charles D. Smith, Peter Sluglett, Charles Tripp and William Roger Louis also answered queries or provided helpful information, as did Dr Toby Dodge and Dr Yigal Sheffy and Professor Eugene Rogan of the Oriental Institute and St. Antony's College, Oxford. Sir Roger Tomkys, who has taken an interest in my work for more than twenty years, also advised me on this project, read a draft of the entire manuscript and offered helpful suggestions for its improvement. I must thank the Master and Fellows of Pembroke College, Cambridge, who extended their hospitality to an Old Member. Sir Richard Dearlove, former Master of the College, also kindly assisted with an enquiry. Several local historians on the Isle of Wight provided helpful information. Most importantly, Sister Eustochium of St. Cecilia's Abbey at Ryde – former site of the Isle of Wight College – supplied plans of the old College grounds and information concerning Clayton's time at the College. Patrick Nott, Diana Wood, Kate McDonnell, Gillian Burnett, Ann Barrett and Sheila Caws answered questions concerning the Isle of Wight, as did Chris Yendall of the Carisbrooke Castle Museum. Mr. R. E. Brinton supplied documents and a Nineteenth Century prospectus of the Isle of Wight College.

I must also thank the archivists of some twenty different institutions where I conducted research for this book. Jane Hogan of the Sudan Archives, Durham University, where the Clayton and Wingate papers are kept, was especially helpful and I owe much to her and the staff of that archive for their patience and assistance provided during the many weeks I spent there. Debbie Usher, archivist of the Middle East Centre at St Antony's College, Oxford helped me navigate through the many important collections of private papers held at the Centre. For assistance and permission to quote from unpublished collections of papers I must thank the staff of the Royal Archives, Windsor and Her Majesty Queen Elizabeth II for permission to quote from papers in the Archives, the staffs at the National Archives (formerly the PRO) at Kew, the Imperial War Museum and the National Army Museum (London), the Royal Artillery Museum, Woolwich, the Rhodes House Library, Mr Randle Meinertzhagen and the Trustees of the Richard Meinertzhagen Estate, the Bodleian Library at Oxford, the Parliamentary Archives, London, Carisbrooke Castle Museum on the Isle of Wight, the Trustees of the Liddell Hart Centre for Military Archives, Kings College, University of London, the British Library, the Birmingham University Library, the Pembroke College Library and Churchill Archives Centre, Churchill College, Cambridge, the Syndics of Cambridge University Library, Newcastle University Library, the Firestone Library of Princeton University and the University of Arizona Library in Tucson. Permission to quote from the Weizmann papers was kindly granted curtesy of Yad Chaim Weizmann, the Weizmann Archive, Rehovot, Israel.

On the home front, Leo Beus, provided that most valuable of all commodities – time – in the form of relief from my paying work, which enabled me to complete this book. My brothers Joe and Dan read a draft of the entire work and provided helpful comments from the educated, non-expert perspective. Joe also helped draw the maps appearing in this book. Finally, I must thank my wife Annette for her patience and understanding over the course of the six years that it took me to complete my research and writing. I must add that none of the above bears any responsibility for errors of fact or interpretation that may appear in this work.

List of Maps and Illustrations

Maps (after page xii)
The Red Sea and western Arabia, 1914–1928.
Egypt and the Sudan, *c.* 1900.
The Levant, 1925–1926.
The Modern Middle East.
The Sykes–Picot Agreement, 1916.

The author and publisher gratefully acknowledge permissions received to reproduce illustration copyright material. Every attempt has been made to identify copyright owners. The author and publishers apologize for any errors or omissions and would be grateful to be notified of any corrections that should be incorporated in the next edition or reprint of this book.

Plate section (after page 192)
1 Bertie Clayton and his father, William Lewis Nicholl Clayton, *c.* 1876 (courtesy of David Thorne).
2 Bertie Clayton and his sister Ellinor, *c.* 1879 (courtesy of David Thorne).
3 The Isle of Wight College, from a prospectus of the 1880s (courtesy of R.E. Brinton).
4 Clayton's plan of the Battle of the Atbara, 8 April 1898 (Clayton family and Sudan Archives, Durham University).
5 Maxim guns arrayed before the Battle of Omdurman, 2 September 1898 (The Image Works).
6 Clayton's 'Birdseye View' of the Battle of Omdurman, showing his position during Phases 1 and 2 of the battle (courtesy of the Clayton family and Sudan Archives, Durham University).
7 Clayton and his pet lion cub, at Wau, Bahr al-Ghazal Province, Sudan, 1903 (Clayton Family).
8 Commandant's office, Wau, Bahr al-Ghazal Province, Sudan, 1902 (courtesy of David Thorne).
9 Field Marshal Lord Kitchener (Bain Collection, Library of Congress).
10 The Governor-General's Palace, Khartoum (Matson Collection, Library of Congress).
11 Sir Francis Reginald Wingate (Bain Collection, Library of Congress).
12 Hussein ibn Ali (Lowell Thomas Collection, Marist College Archives and Special Collections).

List of Abbreviations

AIR	Records of the Air Ministry, at TNA.
Arbur	The Arab Bureau, Cairo.
BL	British Library, London.
BUL	Birmingham University Library.
CAB	Records of the Cabinet, at TNA.
CIGS	Chief of the Imperial General Staff.
CID	Committee of Imperial Defence.
C-in-C	Commander-in-Chief.
CO	Records of the Colonial Office, at TNA.
C.P.	Cabinet Paper.
CP	Clayton Papers, at SAD.
CPO	Chief Political Officer.
CSC	Records of the Civil Service Commission, at TNA.
CUL	Cambridge University Library.
DBFA	*Documents on British Foreign Affairs, the Foreign Office Confidential Print.*
DBFP	*Documents on British Foreign Policy.*
DMI	Director of Military Intelligence.
DMO	Director of Military Operations.
EEF	Egyptian Expeditionary Force.
FO	Records of the Foreign Office, at TNA.
GHQ	General Headquarters.
GOC	General Officer Commanding.
Green Book	An unpublished, partial Clayton family history, by W. L. N. Clayton (1845–1927), father of Sir G. F. Clayton.
IO	India Office.
IWM	Imperial War Museum, London.
KV	Records of the Security Service, at TNA.
LHCMA	Liddell Hart Centre for Military Archives, King's College, University of London.
MECOX	Middle East Centre Archive, St. Antony's College, Oxford.
SAD	Sudan Archives, Durham University.
TNA	The National Archives of the United Kingdom, Kew, London.
WA	Weizmann Archives, Rehovot, Israel.
WO	Records of the War Office, at TNA.
WP	Wingate Papers at SAD.

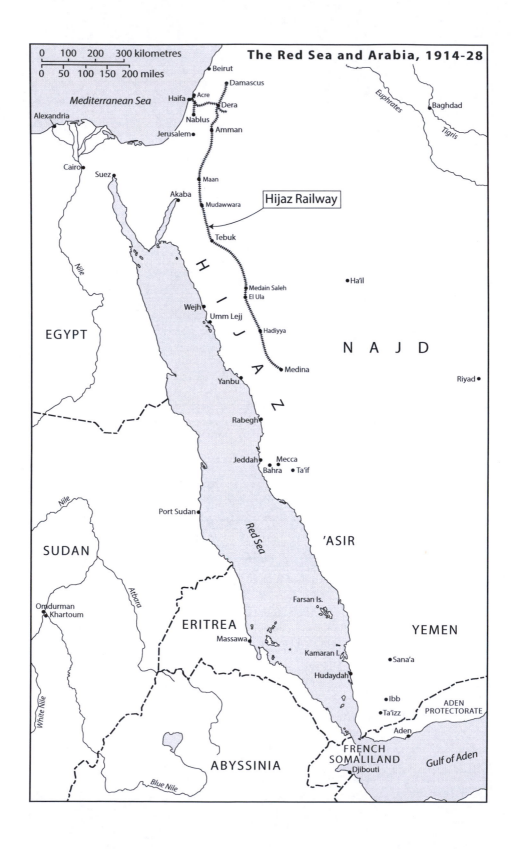

The Red Sea and Arabia, 1914–28

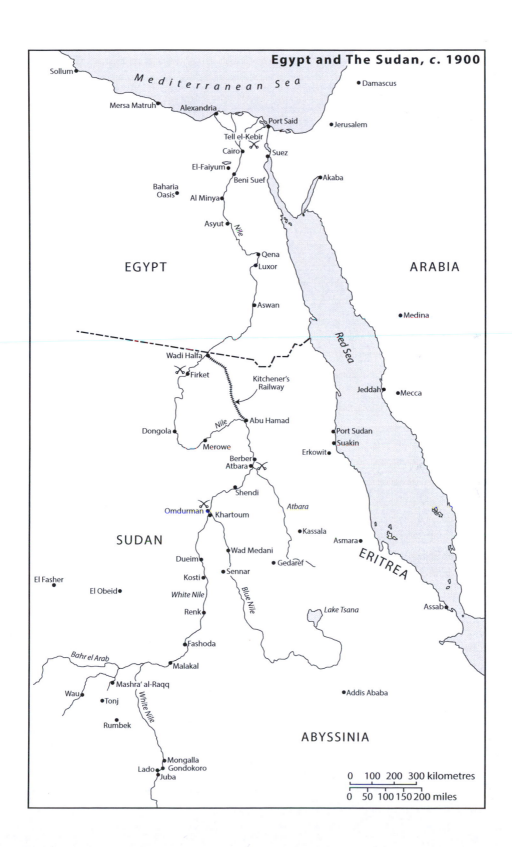

Egypt and The Sudan, c. 1900

Mediterranean Sea

Sollum
Mersa Matruh
Alexandria
Port Said
Tell el-Kebir
Cairo
Suez
El-Faiyum
Beni Suef
Baharia Oasis
Al Minya
Asyut
Nile

Damascus
Jerusalem
Akaba

EGYPT

Qena
Luxor

Aswan

ARABIA

Medina

Red Sea

Wadi Halfa
Firket
Kitchener's Railway

Jeddah
Mecca

Dongola
Nile
Abu Hamad
Merowe
Berber
Atbara

Port Sudan
Suakin
Erkowit

Shendi

Omdurman
Khartoum
Atbara

SUDAN

Kassala
Asmara
ERITREA

Dueim
Wad Medani
Gedaref

El Fasher
Kosti
Sennar

El Obeid
White Nile
Blue Nile

Renk
Lake Tsana
Assab

Fashoda

Bahr el Arab
Malakal
Mashra' al-Raqq
Addis Ababa

Wau
Tonj
White Nile

Rumbek

ABYSSINIA

Mongalla
Lado
Gondokoro
Juba

0   100 200   300 kilometres
0   50 100 150 200 miles

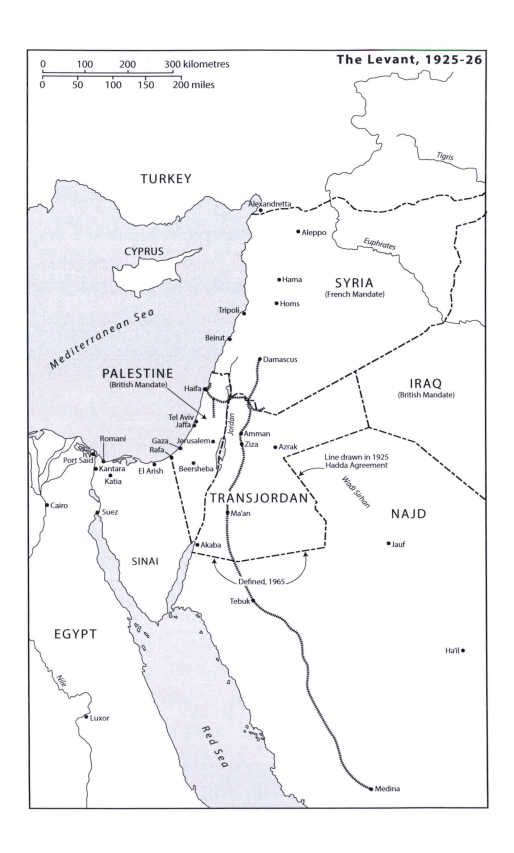

The Levant, 1925-26

0 100 200 300 kilometres
0 50 100 150 200 miles

TURKEY

CYPRUS

Alexandretta

Aleppo

Euphrates

Tigris

Mediterranean Sea

Hama

Homs

SYRIA
(French Mandate)

Tripoli

Beirut

Damascus

PALESTINE
(British Mandate)

Haifa

IRAQ
(British Mandate)

Jordan

Tel Aviv
Jaffa

Amman
Ziza

Azrak

Romani

Gaza
Rafa

Jerusalem

Line drawn in 1925
Hadda Agreement

Port Said

Kantara

El Arish

Beersheba

Wadi Sirhan

NAJD

Katia

Cairo

TRANSJORDAN

Suez

Ma'an

Jauf

SINAI

Akaba

Defined, 1965

EGYPT

Tebuk

Nile

Ha'il

Luxor

Red Sea

Medina

The Modern Middle East

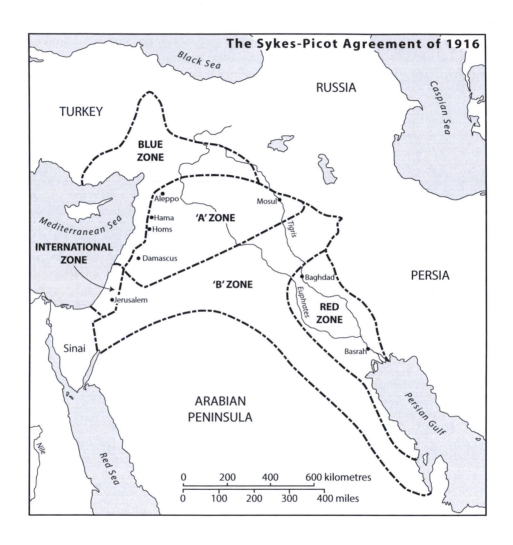

The Sykes-Picot Agreement of 1916

PART ONE

PREPARATION

1

Introduction: Following the Furrow

8.30 a.m., Saturday, March 2nd 1929
Ziza Aerodrome, Twelve Miles south of Amman, Transjordan

It was a large assembly for such a small party. Five aeroplanes of the Royal Air Force sat quietly on the dirt airstrip as their crews scrambled about, readying the machines for the 550-mile flight to Baghdad. Three of the aircraft were to be flown in escort. The fourth was loaded with baggage and supplies. Only the fifth was to carry passengers and then only four, two men and two women, who now stood together at the airstrip's edge, huddled against the early morning desert chill. Their eyes were fixed on the fifth plane, the latest model of the Vickers Victoria, a twin-engine biplane, normally used to ferry troops and supplies along the Cairo to Baghdad desert air route. The pilot, oblivious to his passengers, sat bent over his instruments, curiously exposed in an open cockpit atop the Victoria's large bulbous nose.

As the planes were not yet ready to depart, Lady Clayton returned to conversation with her maid. Lady Clayton was no stranger to the Middle East. For nearly seventeen years she had followed her husband round the region, to Khartoum and Cairo, Jerusalem and now Baghdad. Next to her stood Commander A. P. Thorowgood, her brother, recently seconded by the Royal Navy to serve as private secretary to the man with whom he was now engaged in deep discussion. General Sir Gilbert Falkingham Clayton, KCMG, KBE, CB, had been Britain's pre-eminent man on the spot in the Middle East for years. A small man, perhaps five feet six inches tall and weighing little more than eleven stone, Sir Gilbert's slight stature belied his importance. A few senior British officials could boast of service in the region longer than Sir Gilbert's thirty-three years, but none could point to a more varied experience. He had served in the Sudan and Egypt, in Palestine and in Transjordan. He had influenced the course of events in Libya, in Syria and in the Lebanon. He had negotiated with Arab rulers in Cairo, in the deserts of Arabia and in the Yemen. From Aleppo to Aden, Benghazi to Baghdad, Sir Gilbert Clayton was the best known British official in the Middle East, a man on familiar terms with kings and sultans, amirs and imams, prime ministers and prelates and – unusually for a man of his eminence – with peasants and peanut vendors. And now, at the age of fifty-three, Sir Gilbert was about to take up his final post, the culminating appointment of his career, as His Majesty's High Commissioner for Iraq.

The pilot now looked up and signalled his passengers with a wave of his hand. Soon they were aboard and Sir Gilbert pulled the door shut behind them. Within a minute, the two Napier Lion 570 horsepower engines roared to life and the Victoria began her slow progress, throwing up large clouds of dust as she groaned into the air just short of the airstrip's end. Once airborne, the Victoria described a fat, lazy arc to the northeast, as the pilot, straining at the controls, slowly brought the plane to its cruising altitude of just over two miles. After a short while, he began peering over the edge of his cockpit at the featureless desert below, as if he had dropped something on an earlier flight and was now anxious to locate it. After another ten minutes, he did find it – a thin, nearly imperceptible line, scratched into the hard-pan desert floor a mile or so off the Victoria's left wing. It was the furrow, a two-metre wide line ploughed into the desert in 1921, when Britain's desert air route was established. The air route – a vital thread connecting Britain's Middle Eastern empire – originated at the RAF aerodrome in the Cairo suburb of Heliopolis and stretched some 870 miles to the RAF station at Hinaidi, near Baghdad. Flying the Cairo to Amman leg, the pilots had no difficulty finding their way, as the landscape was punctuated by many familiar landmarks. But the stretch between Amman and Baghdad was different; here, the vast and vacant high Arabian desert was nearly featureless and if a pilot lost his way or, as was fairly common in the early 1920s, if he went down, the furrow would provide the necessary guidance for wayward or distressed aircraft.

Since 1921, aeroplane reliability had been improved greatly and, with three escorts and the accompanying baggage plane, the Clayton party had little concern that they would not reach Baghdad safely. But it was, even then, a long flight. At best, the Victoria could manage only 110 miles per hour and, even with the typically favourable tailwind of the eastern journey, it would take about six hours to reach Baghdad. Inside the cabin, designed to accommodate twenty-four troops and their gear, the small party sat together, Sir Gilbert by one of the Victoria's portside windows. Conversation was nearly impossible over the din of the engines and the party soon fell silent, each absorbed in thought. Staring out at the desert emptiness, the new High Commissioner's mind drifted back to other deserts, other posts, other challenges. . . .

Nothing in Gilbert Clayton's family history had presaged a Middle Eastern career. His ancestors had distinguished themselves in the Royal Navy, not in Eastern adventures, and that may have been the reason why Gilbert's great-grandmother, herself the widow of a Navy captain, had established herself on the Isle of Wight in 1830. Located just across the Solent from the great naval base at Portsmouth, the island was a popular residence for current and retired officers. But Bertie, as he was known to family and friends throughout his life, would follow a different course. Encouraged by the example of his father, a colonel in the Isle of Wight militia, Bertie was determined to become a 'gunner' in the Royal Artillery. Like so many boys of his era, he was inspired by stories of Empire, of India and the Far East and of Egypt and the Sudan, where that iconic hero of Empire, General Gordon, had met his end at the hands of the dreaded Mahdi. Even at the Isle of Wight College, where he received his first formal schooling, Bertie had pursued, and excelled in, the Army and Navy curriculum designed to prepare boys for military careers. At the age of fourteen he had taken the preliminary examination for the Royal Military Academy at Woolwich, where boys were trained for careers in the artillery and the engineers. It took Bertie three tries to pass the difficult final entrance exam for Woolwich, but he did pass and rose in his class to finish tenth.

By January 1896, only six months after his twentieth birthday, Bertie was in Egypt, assigned to an artillery battery at Alexandria. Two years later he was on his way south, into the deserts of the Sudan, where General Kitchener was about to take on the Khalifa, successor to the Mahdi, whose Dervish armies had laid waste to the country for a decade. Placed in charge of a machine gun battery, Bertie twice faced the Dervish onslaught. At the Atbara, the Anglo-Egyptian army won a hard-fought victory in April 1898; five months later, on the plain at Omdurman, a Sudanese force of perhaps 60,000 was obliterated by Kitchener's artillery and machine guns – not a battle, but an execution, wrote one reporter. Bertie had done well against the Dervishes, well enough to be recommended for a prized position in the Egyptian Army. All the senior officers in that Army were British soldiers, seconded from their British army billets under ten-year contracts with the Egyptian government. For a young subaltern like Bertie Clayton, the prospect was tantalizing. Not only would his pay quadruple, he would rise overnight from lieutenant to major – *bimbashi* – and the opportunities for adventure in the Sudan, where he was posted, were infinitely greater than in the regular army.

For the next thirteen years Clayton would work in the Sudan. He thoroughly enjoyed his early experiences in the country – training his Egyptian and Sudanese troops, leading patrols into the Sudanese jungles, and hunting big game. In 1902, he accepted a new challenge at Wau in Bahr al-Ghazal province, deep in the jungles of southern Sudan. It was a difficult post. The climate was deplorable, alternating between insufferable heat and torrential downpour. Disease was common, and often fatal. And the loneliness – at times Clayton was the only European within 400 miles of Wau – sometimes drove men mad. Yet, he valued his experience at Wau. It was there that he learned the fundamentals of administration, for he was put in charge of everything – finances, agriculture, food supply, security, provincial development and justice. And it was at Wau that he learned how to treat with the local populations, acquiring a tolerance and understanding that would later serve him well. By 1906, Clayton had become a favourite of the governor-general who brought him to Khartoum in that year as his private secretary. For seven years he would work in the Sudanese capital for Sir Reginald Wingate. At times he thought he was only bottle-washing for 'Master', as the governor-general's subordinates referred to their chief. But during those seven years, Clayton learned much of colonial administration and, as he gained the confidence of Wingate, he was given ever more responsibility, eventually advising the governor-general and the authorities in London on the Sudan's development and relations with its colonial neighbours.

As the Victoria droned on towards Baghdad and Sir Gilbert reflected on those happy, easy days in Khartoum, he looked across at his wife with an affectionate smile.

He had met Enid in 1911 and they married the following year, while he was still working as Wingate's private secretary. Unlike the wives of many British officials serving in the East, Enid insisted on accompanying her husband to his various posts. She had always made the most of her experiences. And, unusually for British wives of the time, she took an interest in the people of the region, mingling with the ladies of the harem and even learning some Arabic. True, there had been some grim times. Bertie and Enid had lost two of their children in the East, one a victim of infection, the other of plague. But the early years of their marriage had been filled with optimism and enthusiasm as Clayton steadily advanced in government service. In 1913, Wingate appointed him Sudan Agent and Director of Intelligence for the Egyptian Army. Working in Cairo, Clayton was the face of the Sudan Government in the Egyptian capital, acting as Khartoum's representative to the Egyptians and to the large European community there. As Intelligence Director, he was the 'eyes and ears' of the Sudan in Egypt, gathering information not only on the Egyptians, but also on any Europeans whose activities might affect the Sudan government.

Clayton had not served a year as Sudan Agent before the European war broke out in 1914. He immediately offered his services to General Sir John Maxwell, commander of the British Force in Egypt, who promptly appointed him Director of Intelligence for the Force. Only thirty-nine at the time of his appointment, Clayton faced a daunting task. Many assumed the Turks would enter the war on the side of Germany and Austria-Hungary, and when they did so, in November, he had to scramble to assemble an Intelligence organisation. Few men with experience were available, but Clayton did his best, assembling a group of amateurs – foreign correspondents, archaeologists, travellers with Eastern experience – anyone who knew some Turkish or Arabic and could be of use. The War Office in London even managed to scrape together a small contingent and send them out, one of whom, T. E. Lawrence, would later earn fame from his exploits in Arabia. Clayton's immediate concern was with the Ottoman army. Did they intend to move on Egypt? If so, when and where? He began gathering Intelligence from every available source. Refugees, deserters, travellers and diplomats from neutral countries were interrogated. Agents were dropped by sea on the coasts of Syria, Palestine and Arabia. Aerial reconnaissance, then in its early stages, was used in Sinai. By late 1914, he had gathered enough information to predict the timing and magnitude of a Turkish attack on the Suez Canal, a critical link in Britain's Imperial communications that must be protected at all costs. His information proved good enough and the Turkish attack of February 1915 was successfully repelled by Imperial troops.

No less troubling to Clayton than the enemy's military advance was the Turkish Sultan's call to *jihad*. If the Turks were able to unite Islam in a holy war against the Entente of Britain, France and Russia, the position in the Middle East would be made incomparably more difficult. In Clayton's view, the key to splitting the solidarity of Islam lay in Arabia. Somehow Britain must prevent the Arabs from joining the *jihad* and going over to the Turco-German alliance. As early as the fall of 1914, he focused on the pre-eminent Arab family in Islam, the Hashemites. Every effort, Clayton thought, should be made to win over Hussein, Amir of Mecca who, as descendant of the Prophet and guardian of the Holy Places of Mecca and Medina, could prevent a unified Islam being ranged against the Entente. It was a struggle; London was unconvinced, apathetic even, and the Government of India positively hostile to an Anglo-Arab alliance. But, in 1915, he was able to persuade Sir Henry McMahon, the British High Commissioner for Egypt, of the importance of co-opting the Arabs. It was Clayton who inspired and oversaw Sir Henry's 1915–16 correspondence with Hussein, letters which convinced the Amir to abandon his Turkish overlords and join the Entente.

To the west of Egypt, he faced yet another problem. There, German and Turkish agents were busily at work trying to convince the Sanusiyya, an Islamic sect domi-nant in Libya, to join the Central Powers and attack Egypt. Throughout 1915, Clayton forestalled the Turco-German efforts, preventing the western desert of Egypt from becoming a battleground at a time when Britain, already stretched to the limit by the campaign against the Turks at Gallipoli, could not spare a man or a gun for another fight. Not only did he have to contend with hostile Turks, Germans and Libyans, he had also to resist Italian efforts to implicate Britain in the fight in Libya. Italy had been at war with the Sanusiyya since 1911, and was still fighting them when the war broke out in 1914. And they badly wanted British assis-tance. London was inclined to give it, for the Italians were neutral in the European war until May 1915, and the Foreign Office was loathe to adopt any policy that might estrange the Italians and push them into the German embrace. Somehow Clayton managed to assure London, placate the Italians, and forestall the Germans, the Turks and the Sanusiyya until 1916, when Britain was able to contend with the threat in the west.

In the distance, Clayton could just make out the desert station at Rutbah Wells, an isolated outpost, roughly marking the mid-point between Amman and Baghdad. Again, he drifted back to that miserable year of 1916. Clayton was by this time over-whelmed. In addition to directing the British Intelligence effort, he was still acting as Wingate's Sudan Agent, was responsible for the administration of Martial Law in Egypt, was acting as British liaison to the Egyptian Sultan and was made responsible for a new unit, the Arab Bureau, charged with assimilating and coordinating British Intelligence throughout the Middle East. And, just as the Arab Revolt against the Turks broke out in June 1916, his relations with his chiefs, Wingate in the Sudan, and General Murray, the new commander of the Egyptian Expeditionary Force, began to deteriorate. Murray was deeply suspicious of the Arab Bureau which reported to the Foreign Office in London, not to his headquarters, and Wingate came to disagree fundamentally with Clayton's views on the strategic direction of the Revolt. Crushed by overwork, illness, and the strain of trying to satisfy too many masters, he collapsed in the autumn and was removed as Director of Intelligence, just as his son Thomas, not yet a month old, succumbed to infection.

But Clayton's colleagues knew full well that he was too knowledgeable, too valu-able, to be shunted aside and, early in 1917, his fortunes revived as he was appointed Chief of Staff, Hijaz Operations by his old chief, Wingate, who had now arrived in Cairo as the new High Commissioner for Egypt. Clayton worked closely with his men in Arabia, especially Lawrence, as he planned strategy for the Revolt. At the same time, a new commander was appointed in the region, General Sir Edmund Allenby, 'the Bull', as he was called by those familiar with his ferocious temper. Clayton quickly gained the new chief's confidence. In the fall, Allenby appointed him Chief Political Officer of the Egyptian Expeditionary Force and, as the British army fought its way north to Jerusalem at year's end, Clayton was put in charge of the civil administration of all territory liberated from the retreating Turkish army.

That autumn of 1917, was a watershed for Clayton, for it marked his transition from the military to the political and diplomatic arena. By early 1918, he was reporting directly to the Foreign Office, as the military direction of the Revolt was transferred to others, and Clayton became absorbed in the emerging political problems in Palestine and Syria. They were formidable. Not only were the Arabs and the French now at loggerheads over the future of Syria, a new problem had appeared in the form of the Balfour Declaration, Britain's recent proclamation of support for the Zionist programme by which the Jews sought to establish a national home in Palestine. Clayton smiled ruefully as he recalled the question-begging instruction sent to him by the Foreign Office regarding the Zionists; he was to promote their programme 'on right lines'. What did that mean? A Jewish State in Palestine? And if not a State, then how was he to promote a national home for the Jews in a country where 90 per cent of the inhabitants were Arabs?

Throughout 1918, he wrestled with the growing problem of Jewish–Arab relations, advising the Foreign Office to proceed slowly with the Zionist programme. Whatever the merits of the programme – and Clayton saw several – Britain could not afford to antagonize the Arabs by overtly promoting a Jewish national home in Palestine at a time when Allenby was about to mount his great assault against the Turks in Syria and needed Arab support. And what of McMahon's letters of 1915, letters which Clayton helped prepare? They appeared to pledge British support for Arab independence in Palestine and, to many in England and the East, could not be reconciled with the promise of a Jewish national home in the same country. If the Jewish problem was not enough, the Arabs had also just learned of Britain's secret 1916 pact with the French – the Sykes–Picot Agreement – in which the parties divided up the Arab lands of the Ottoman Empire in anticipation of an Entente victory. Syria was to go to France under Sykes–Picot, but Clayton knew that most Syrians wanted nothing to do with the French and were sure to resist them when Allenby reached Damascus. Again and again he advised the Foreign Office to secure a public promise from the French that they did not intend to annex Syria. But when the Middle Eastern war ended in late October 1918, the political fights were only beginning.

By March 1919, Clayton was ready to throw his hands up. The Foreign Office in London seemed unwilling, maybe even incapable, of resolving the pressing problems in Palestine and Syria. For their part, the Zionist leaders were angry that their programme was not being implemented to their satisfaction and turned on the British administrators in Palestine, including Clayton, accusing them of indifference, even hostility, to their plans. And then, just when it seemed he could do no more, Clayton was confronted with yet another crisis. In March 1919, the Egyptians, infuriated by the British refusal to abolish the Protectorate they had established over Egypt in 1914, rose in violent revolt. Rampaging mobs surged through the streets, trains were burned, houses ransacked, Europeans murdered. Inevitably, Clayton was drawn into the maelstrom. Allenby, now the hero of the Middle Eastern campaign, was made High Commissioner for Egypt as the hapless Wingate was sent home. Everyone thought that 'the Bull' would restore order by crushing the Egyptians. But he did not; he turned instead to his chief adviser on Eastern politics and Bertie Clayton had a very different view of the Egyptian situation.

Clayton was convinced that the Egyptian revolution was not the work of a few extremist instigators, but a truly national movement, one that transcended class, religion, even gender. He proposed what he believed was the only viable, long-term solution – a policy of conciliation, of devolution, of handing over the running of Egypt to the Egyptians. At the same time, he insisted that Britain need only ensure her vital interests in Egypt: protection of the Suez Canal, the Nile waters and the welfare of the large European population in the country. Within weeks, Allenby appointed Clayton Adviser to the Egyptian Ministry of the Interior, perhaps the most important position held by a foreigner in the Egyptian government. For three years Clayton pursued his devolution policy in Egypt with the full support of Allenby. But there was formidable opposition; the Anglo-Egyptian community felt their position, their very livelihoods, imperilled and the British Cabinet were adamantly opposed to handing over internal autonomy to the Egyptians, unless it was done in the context of a fully-negotiated treaty in which British interests were acknowledged. The Egyptian nationalists would not concede a treaty. Stalemate ensued. Finally, in early 1922, Clayton and Allenby appeared in London, intent on a showdown with the government; Britain must issue a unilateral declaration of Egyptian independence, or they would resign. The Cabinet conceded, a qualified declaration of Egyptian independence issued and Clayton, who had proposed the elimination of his own position as Adviser, was out of a job.

Within weeks of his return to England, he accepted a new position, Chief Secretary – the number two man – in the British Mandate government in Palestine. Once again, Clayton found himself in the position of trying to reconcile the irreconcilable, of trying to persuade the Arabs to accept the Zionist programme in Palestine. He soon found himself in disagreement with the High Commissioner, Sir Herbert Samuel, who believed the Palestinian Arabs could be persuaded to cooperate with the Mandate government. While serving in Jerusalem, Clayton was also placed in charge of the new Arab government across the River Jordan. Although Transjordan was formally part of the Palestine Mandate, it was not made subject to the Zionist programme. Instead, the country was ruled by an Arab Amir, Abdullah, son of King Hussein, Britain's war-time ally in the fight against the Turks. But Abdullah proved a poor ruler; he was uninterested in the thinly-populated and resource-poor country and squandered the small British grant he had been given to maintain order there. In 1924, Clayton reluctantly issued an ultimatum to the Amir; reform Transjordan's government, or leave. Abdullah decided to mend his ways.

And, in 1929, he was still in Amman, as Clayton's plane made its way to Iraq, where the Amir's brother, Faisal, was king. But the limited success Clayton had achieved in Transjordan was not enough to cause him to stay on in Jerusalem. In May 1925, he resigned, sadly disillusioned by the British government's Palestine policy. He left many friends behind, so many that had the Colonial Office in London accepted the recommendations of both the Arabs and the Zionists, Clayton would have succeeded Samuel as the next High Commissioner.

A man of Clayton's experience, however, would not remain idle for long. Four months after his departure from Jerusalem, he was on his way back to the Middle East, this time as British plenipotentiary to the new power in Arabia, Ibn Saud, Sultan of Najd. Ibn Saud had emerged in the early 1920s, just as old King Hussein, embittered by London's post-war Middle Eastern policies, had fallen out of favour with the British. But the Sultan posed problems of a different sort for England. In pursuing an aggressive, expansionist agenda in the Arabian peninsula, he had pushed up against Britain's Mandated territories in Transjordan and Iraq. Clayton was sent out to curtail the Sultan's ambitions, and, in November 1925, he concluded two treaties with Ibn Saud. In one, Clayton restrained the Sultan in the East, regulating the movement of tribes along the Iraq–Najd boundary. In the second, he defined the Sultan's border with Transjordan, conceding large tracts to Ibn Saud in the deserts to the east and south of Amman, but preventing the expansion of Najdi territory in the north, up to the Syrian border. There must be no separation, Clayton insisted, between the Mandated territories of Iraq and Transjordan. The desert air route, tying together Britain's Middle Eastern empire, and over which Clayton was now flying, must pass over British-controlled territory.

Even before he could return to England, Clayton received new instructions from the Colonial Office. He was to proceed to the British port of Aden in the southwest corner of the Arabian peninsula and from there to travel inland to Sanaa, in the Yemen, to confront the Imam Yahya. The Imam's forces had penetrated into Britain's Aden Protectorate, the territory above the port of Aden, which was populated by tribes in treaty relationship with the British. The expense of ejecting Yahya from the Protectorate by force was prohibitive in that time of post-war economy. Yet, Britain could not allow him to remain in the Protectorate, flouting international law and perhaps endangering the vital port of Aden. The only solution was a negotiated treaty providing for his withdrawal. Over the course of three weeks in February 1926, Clayton attempted to persuade the Imam to withdraw. He could not. Yahya held the upper hand and he knew it.

Like other Arabian rulers, the Imam was also shrewd enough to understand that he could confound British objectives by playing them off against their colonial rivals in the region. In August 1926, he concluded a pact with the Italians who now appeared to threaten Britain's position in the southern Red Sea. Italian ambitions might have been prompted by commerce – they had, after all, colonies on the East African coast in Eritrea and Somaliland – but Britain could not allow another European Power to establish itself in the Red Sea or to threaten Aden, both critical links in Imperial communications with India and the East. So, in early 1927, the

Foreign Office called on Clayton to negotiate with the Italians. As a result of his discussions, both parties agreed to keep the southern Red Sea free of military or naval bases and to allow freedom of commerce in the region. That was good enough for London and Clayton was credited with another diplomatic success.

By this time, Sir Gilbert was widely regarded as Britain's greatest authority on the Middle East and it came as no surprise when, just after his Rome negotiations were concluded, he was again called upon to negotiate with Ibn Saud. Talks in late 1926 for an Anglo-Saudi treaty had failed. In Clayton's view, the London authorities were seeking to accomplish too much by the treaty they had presented the Arab ruler. With greatly reduced expectations, Clayton returned to Arabia in May 1927, and, after three weeks of discussion, produced the Treaty of Jeddah, which would form the basis of Anglo-Saudi relations for a generation.

Even after Jeddah, Sir Gilbert was not finished with Ibn Saud. In May 1928, only nine months before his journey to Baghdad, he was called in by the Colonial Office to once more treat with the Arabian ruler. Trouble had again risen in the east, along the Najd–Iraq border, where Arab tribes had swept out of the desert and attacked police posts 70 miles inside Iraq. Clayton suspected that Ibn Saud had no control over the attacking tribes, that they represented a dissident faction in Arabia. If he was correct and Ibn Saud capitulated to British demands that he respect the Iraqi border and punish the attackers, then the king might very well lose whatever authority he still held in eastern Arabia. Sir Gilbert travelled to Arabia twice in 1928, but could not convince the King to back down. Even now, as the Victoria was approaching the Euphrates River at Ramadi, Clayton continued to wrestle with the problem of Ibn Saud.

Soon the High Commissioner's plane was over Ramadi, now joined by another RAF escort of five planes. Baghdad lay only about fifty miles away, to the east and south, on the Tigris. They had left the furrow now; it was no longer necessary in the familiar Iraqi landscape. But as they approached the city, Sir Gilbert reflected on that line in the desert. It was a literal guide across the desert, but in many ways it was also a metaphor of his professional life, a career devoted to the preservation of those vital lines of Imperial connection. During the war it had been the Eastern Mediterranean, the Suez Canal and the Red Sea. And now, in the aviation age, the desert air route could be added to the list. Slowly the Victoria began its descent to the Baghdad West aerodrome. As the pilot made one pass over the landing field, Sir Gilbert looked down and saw the assembled guards of honour, the military bands and a carpet of Imperial red slowly being unrolled in the sand to herald the arrival of the new High Commissioner.[1]

2

Vectensian: Youth, 1875–1895

The Romans called it Vectis. Why they should have referred to a diamond-shaped island lying just off the south coast of England by a word meaning 'lever' or 'crow bar' is something of a mystery. Perhaps they meant that once the island had been taken, as it was in AD 43, the Romans could use it as a tool, a lever, to prise open the door to the riches of England. No one knows. Later, it would become known as the Isle of Wight, a name of equally uncertain origin. And, while the latter name persisted, inhabitants of the place would often, and oddly, be referred to on the basis of the earlier name, as Vectensians. But however they were called, there were few people or events in the island's past that also figured prominently in the history of England. It was once said that the island had never produced 'a good horse, a wise man, or a pretty woman'.[1] For centuries, the Isle of Wight sat insignificantly, just off the bottom of England, rather like the footnote it was in the book of British history. True, Charles I had been imprisoned there, more or less, for a year at Carisbrooke Castle in 1647–8, preliminary to his removal and eventual execution; but this hardly rendered the island important. Most of its 380 square kilometers was taken up by farm land, the towns were small and lightly populated and island commerce, such as it was, centred largely on the smuggling of contraband items from the Continent, a boom industry in the eighteenth century.

But in the nineteenth century change came to the Isle of Wight. Mainlanders – 'Overners', as they were called – began to appreciate the beauty and temperate climate of the place and, more important, came to have the money to make the short journey across the Solent to enjoy both. It certainly helped that Queen Victoria herself was one of the first holiday-makers. Having visited the island in the early 1830s, the Queen so enjoyed herself that she and Prince Albert eventually decided to construct a major residence there. In 1845, they purchased Osborne House in the north of the island from Lady Isobelle Blachford and bought extensive surrounding grounds owned by Winchester College.[2] The Prince, who saw the Solent as something like the Bay of Naples, envisioned an Italianate design, Palladian in style, complete with loggias and a campanile. The first phase of the new Osborne House was completed in 1846. It was expanded over the years and even after the Prince died in 1861, the Queen continued to spend her summers and Christmas holidays on the island until her own death. Inevitably, others followed the Queen's lead and by the 1870s the Isle of Wight had become a tourist destination. Even before this, the island had begun to attract serving and retired naval officers and their families, owing to its close proximity to the great naval base at Portsmouth.[3] It was certainly close; on a clear day a person standing in the town of Ryde on the northeast shoulder of the island could, with a good telescope in hand, read the time of day on the Portsmouth town clock some four miles away across the Solent.[4]

On the 28th of May 1830, Phoebe Clayton, herself of a distinguished naval family, and the widow of a captain in the Royal Navy, made the short journey across the Solent from Portsmouth to establish her new home in Ryde.[5] No one would have questioned the naval credentials of Phoebe's family. Her paternal grandfather, John Falkingham (1707–77), had been a captain in the Royal Navy and his life story read better than fiction. He had served in both the East and West Indies, had participated in various 'secret expeditions' against the French, and had fought in several fierce actions at sea against the French and Spanish. He had been shipwrecked, captured by a Spanish privateer, imprisoned and then made a daring escape across France. Eventually, he retired to Barbados 'which was his native country and where he inherited very good possessions.'[6] John's younger brother Edward Falkingham (1709–83), achieved even greater prominence, commanding several ships of the line during the mid-century war against the French, and retiring a rear-admiral. Edward and John's uncle, also named Edward (1679–1757), had started the great tradition. Commanding Royal Navy vessels for thirty years, including nearly a dozen different ships of the line, he had captained the *Oxford* (70 guns) in Admiral Byng's squadron during the battle off Cape Passaro in July/August 1718, where seven Spanish ships, including three flagships were captured.[7] Later appointed Governor of Newfoundland, a Commissioner of the Royal Navy and, ultimately, its Comptroller, he retired in 1756, as an Admiral of the White.

It was hardly surprising then that Phoebe would marry into a naval family. Her husband, Captain Thomas Wittewronge Whitwell Clayton (1766–1806), had been taken aboard his father's ship as a nine year old midshipman, and most of his life had been spent at sea. In 1805, he was put in command of the 'Sea Fencibles', a naval militia formed in the late eighteenth century to fend off an anticipated Napoleonic invasion of England. Thomas commanded the Fencibles in the west of Ireland, where he died from illness at Dingle near Bantry. Thomas' father, Admiral Samuel Wittewronge Clayton (1734–95) was even better known in the Royal Navy, having commanded in the Falkland Islands and fought against the American revolutionaries in the waters off New England (1778–81). In 1780, he was appointed captain of what would become the most famous of all British fighting ships, HMS *Victory*, later Lord Nelson's flagship at Trafalgar (1805). Of Samuel's father little is known, except that he lived in Barbados, married Thomasina Wittewronge on that island in 1729 and died there six years later.[8]

Of all the Clayton forebears, the Wittewronges appear to have been least inclined towards naval or military careers. They had, however, distinguished themselves in trade in their native Flanders. Jacques Wittewronge (1531–93) was born in Ghent in that country and, as his grandson Sir John Wittewronge explained in a family history written in 1664, Jacques left Flanders in a 'hott time of persecution' to 'enjoy his conscience, and made shipwreck of his outward estate to preserve his inward peace'.[9] He settled in London and soon began to resurrect the family's fortunes in the more congenial climate of religious tolerance then enjoyed by Protestant dissenters. The family's prospects were enhanced by Jacques' astute son Jacob (1558–1622), who amassed a considerable fortune in a brewery partnership and, even more, by marrying well. Jacob's son John (1618–93), author of the 1664 family history, continued the family business, outlived three wives, was knighted in 1640 and created baronet in 1662. How John's grandson Thomas came to reside in Barbados is unknown, but it was the latter's daughter, Thomasina, who married Samuel Clayton on that island in 1729.[10] And, it was their son, Samuel Wittewronge Clayton, who came to captain the *Victory* fifty years later.

Whether through Falkingham, Clayton or Wittewronge good fortune, or some combination of all of them, by the time Phoebe and her youngest son arrived on the Isle of Wight in 1830, the Clayton family was sufficiently well-off that none of Phoebe's three sons was required to work for a living. The source of the family's wealth is unclear, but in a later family history an oblique reference suggested that the Claytons had amassed a 'considerable interest' in the Bank of England. In any event, neither Phoebe's eldest son, Thomas (1799–1875), nor her youngest, Samuel (1803–75) pursued any profession.[11] Thomas suffered from chronic ill health and it was to her youngest son, Samuel that Phoebe left her 'considerable property' when she died in 1841. Samuel, it seems, was content simply to manage the family's affairs, though he did play 'a prominent part in the public business of the island'.[12] In 1835 he built the family's residence, Eastfield House, in Dover Street in Ryde, and, eight years later, married another island resident, Anna Maria Nicholl (1823–1904). Anna Maria's father, of an old Welsh family, had moved to the island in 1830, the same year as Phoebe, and had become good friends with Samuel.

Samuel and Anna Maria prospered in Ryde, and had ten children, eight of whom, unusually for the age, lived to adulthood. Their eldest, William Lewis Nicholl Clayton was born in January 1845. Like his father, he followed no profession, remained at home and interested himself in the family's affairs. And, just as his father had, he took an active role in the 'public business' of the island, serving on various local and district councils and as a guardian of the nearby parish of Brading for more than twenty years. His three younger brothers took degrees at Cambridge and Oxford and two of them were ordained in the Church of England. William's interests, however, were of a decidedly more martial character. But family obligation, and possibly poor health, prevented him from joining the navy – his first choice – or the army, and he contented himself with service in the local Isle of Wight Artillery Militia.[13] William served in the local Militia for more than thirty years, leaving in 1900 as a lieutenant-colonel at the mandatory retirement age of fifty-five.

Just across from Eastfield, in Dover Street, was Loudon House, the residence of Edward Williams Pilkington (1803–67), a retired navy captain, and his large family. Not surprisingly, the Claytons and Pilkingtons became well-acquainted and, in due course, William became engaged to Captain Pilkington's sixth daughter, Maria Martha. Their wedding was delayed for a time, though, as the Pilkingtons regarded William as 'rather fast', particularly disapproving of his habit of riding a bicycle about the streets of Ryde.[14] Despite these reservations, William and Maria Martha were married on September 3, 1874. For a time after their marriage the couple continued to live in Ryde and it was there, at Fitzharding Lodge, 20 West Street, that their first child, Gilbert Falkingham Clayton, was born on the 6th of July 1875. Soon after Gilbert's birth the family moved to a rented house called Hill Grove in the village of Bembridge, a short seven miles from Ryde and their numerous Clayton and Pilkington relatives. While at Hill Grove, two daughters, Ellinor Maria (1878–1969) and Mary Frances (1881–1903) were born. Shortly after Mary's birth William purchased a house on the shore at Bembridge called West Cliff and here the Claytons lived until 1891. The Claytons had two more children while living at West Cliff, Edward Nicholl, who was born in1884, but lived less than a month, and Phyllis Rachel (1885–1938). Gilbert's two surviving brothers, Iltyd Nicholl (1886–1955) and John Wittewronge (1888–1952) were born at nearby Sandown, while the family lived at Bembridge. The Claytons' last child, Norah Beryl (1895–1969) was born after the family moved to Sandown in 1891.

Although Iltyd was born eleven years after his brother Gilbert, his recollections – set down more than fifty years later in an unpublished memoir – provide good insight into island life in the last decade of the nineteenth century.[15] Bembridge, he recalled, was 'a gem of a place', then just a tiny village with 'not more than a half-dozen of the "gentry" in residence'. His parents lived 'a very happy life' in the town and West Cliff made an ideal home for the children. On one side of the house were two small ponds, on another a walled garden, and on a third, a grass terrace that ran down to a seawall and the waters of the English Channel. In the summer, the children would cross the terrace to the half-mile wide beach and the sea where they would paddle about and, at low tide, collect cockles and play in the sand. The children had a nurse and, for a time, a French governess, employed to instruct them in the language. Iltyd could 'remember no unhappiness as a child'. Even Sundays, though 'kept fairly strictly', were enjoyed by the children. They had to memorize the 'collect' for each Sunday, and repeat it to their mother, but they took pleasure in the familiar hymns and 'all the games played in church by . . . every child'. The children had two dogs and numerous toys and they delighted in communicating with the young girls next door by means of a 'telephone' consisting of 'a string stretched between the two houses with, as microphone, a tin, through the lid of which [it] was fastened, and into which the conversationalist spoke.'

William sold West Cliff in 1891, and the family moved to a new house he built and called Harpenden, located just five miles down the coast in Sandown.[16] Sandown was by now a popular tourist destination, featuring a large esplanade, which the Claytons frequented in the summer months when the pierrot concert parties and Punch and Judy shows were performed on the beach. By this time the family's financial position appears to have been in some decline; Iltyd observed that 'money was scarce' and that 'luxuries . . . had to be severely rationed'. But, in that simpler era the family found delight in simpler pleasures. Sandown, like most towns on the island, employed a couple of 'coaches and four' for island tours and the children often took seats in the coach from which they enjoyed a leisurely tour of the island's sights. Occasionally, they would walk to the train station and travel to Ryde by the cheap return (6*d*), where they would visit for the day their Eastfield Grannie (Clayton), their Loudon House Grannie (Pilkington) or their many aunts and uncles. There was of course no cinema yet, but a primitive precursor called Poole's Diorama came to the island every year and the children got 'a great thrill' from watching a succession of scenes painted on cloth and rapidly wound from one roller to another across the stage. Years later Gilbert laughingly described his memories of the time in a letter to his mother. Ryde was 'not what you would call a tearingly exciting place,' he noted. 'Still it gives several points to Sandown, where "Readings and Music" by the "Merry Little Layman" constitute the acme of dissipation, not to say debauchery'.[17]

The Clayton children revered their parents and Iltyd recalled that they always formed 'a remarkably united family'. As the children grew older, the closeness continued: 'It was notorious,' Iltyd added, 'that if we went to a dance together we would always be found crowded together between dances with our partners dragged willy nilly into the circle.' He attributed these strong familial ties to his mother whom he admired greatly, not only for her 'unerring taste in everything' and her remarkable memory, but also for her 'keen sense of humour and fun' on the one hand, and her 'deep piety' on the other. William, like most Victorian fathers, was a slightly more remote figure and, especially when dressed in the uniform of an artillery officer, a subject of some awe. The children were very impressed with his martial bearing and every May when the Isle of Wight Artillery Militia conducted its annual training in Newport, the family took rooms in the village to observe the drills. For young Gilbert – 'Bertie' as he would be known to family and friends for his entire life – this was a time of great excitement. Every morning, as he heard the Militia's band strike up in the distance, he would race out to the raised footpath beside the road and march beside the regiment as it passed by on its way to Carisbrooke Castle. There, the regiment would conduct their drill and fire the guns from the castle ramparts.[18] Small wonder that from an early age, Bertie, and later Iltyd, both aspired to be 'Gunners' in the Royal Artillery. Only John would follow a different path and, like so many of his Falkingham and Clayton ancestors, join the Royal Navy.

All the Clayton children were educated at home by William, until they were ten or eleven, when the boys were enrolled at the Isle of Wight Preparatory College at Ryde. Bertie, of course, was the first, 'having gained a scholarship of £15 per annum, tenable for 3 years from Sept. 1885'.[19] The Isle of Wight College had been created only six years earlier, when the 'Mansion and grounds of Apley House, Ryde' were acquired by the founders.[20] The notion of the founders was that the new college would provide an education 'free from the prevailing strict and somewhat narrow traditions of the British public schools, while keeping the best, and at a cost which could be afforded by parents of very moderate means, whose sons, by character, could be expected to show results; in particular sons of yeomen, clergy and men of the services.'[21] The College was situated on more than twenty acres of beautiful grounds in Ryde, bordering on the Solent. The main College building, Apley House, had been built in about 1724, purportedly by one David Boyce, a notorious smuggler, who ended his days in Fleet Prison in 1740.[22] The property was now expanded, school rooms were added, a chapel and gymnasium were built, and cricket pitches, racquet and fives courts constructed. A prospectus from the 1880s described the course of instruction as divided into two departments – one, 'the Classical and Mathematical with special reference to the universities,' the other, 'the Modern adapted to Pupils preparing for the Army, Navy and Civil Services, and other professions'.[23] The latter curriculum, almost certainly followed by Bertie Clayton, encompassed instruction in divinity, mathematics, Latin, physical science, modern languages, English history, literature and composition. 'There are special classes,' the Prospectus added, 'for the Woolwich, Sandhurst, Cooper's Hill and Indian Civil Service Examinations.'[24] Instruction was provided by the Headmaster – during Bertie's time, the redoubtable Canon F. D. Teesdale – assisted by a Second Master, two Assistant Masters and six instructors. Tuition fees were based on a boy's age (those under twelve paid £6/year less) and on whether a boy lived at the College in one of the three houses on site, or was a 'day boy'. Boarders under the age of twelve were assessed a fee of £24 per annum and paid a boarding fee of £50–65 per year. At least for a time, Bertie was likely a boarder. A decade later, when Iltyd started at the College, and John later joined him, the younger boys lived at home and took the fifteen minute train ride from Sandown to Ryde every day during the school term.[25]

The provision of so-called 'Army classes' at the College was not unusual.[26] Many public schools offered them in the last quarter of the century and they focused on training the boys for entrance into the military academies – Woolwich for the artillery and the engineers, Sandhurst for the infantry and cavalry. Admission to both was by examination and the competition was stiff, particularly for the more academically demanding academy at Woolwich. Advertisements for the Isle of Wight College invariably emphasized the provision of 'army and navy classes' and there is little doubt that many boys, including Bertie Clayton, pursued that course.[27] Just how well Bertie performed in his work at the College is unclear, as the academic records were lost or destroyed at some point after the College closed in 1905. However, he did win several awards, including book prizes for achievement in Classics, German, Latin Prose and English, as well as a prize for freehand drawing. He contributed essays and poems to the school magazine, *The Vectensian*, and did well enough in his studies to pass 'twentieth into Woolwich' in 1893. However, as will be seen, he needed some extra preparation to do so.[28]

Iltyd later observed that by the time he began at the College in 1897, it was already 'in a rather decaying condition', but when Bertie was a student 'it had been quite flourishing'.[29] Indeed, Bertie would later look back fondly on his time at the College. In 1898, while a subaltern in the Anglo-Egyptian army marching on Khartoum, Bertie would host an 'Old Vectensian' dinner, entertaining three former school-mates, two brothers named Farmar and Cyril Wilson, who would later report to Bertie from Arabia during the Great War.[30] And, after Bertie distinguished himself in the Battle of the Atbara, in April 1898, he was delighted and amused to read a story written about him for 'The Vec': '[I]t is very well got up and reflects great credit on the compiler,' he wrote from the Sudan, 'although to read it I might be Wellington at least'.[31]

It was at the Isle of Wight College that Bertie also acquired his life-long enjoyment of sport. Team sport had become an important feature of public school life in the second half of the century; rugby and cricket were thought to develop important physical attributes – health, strength, coordination and quickness – and, even more significantly, to form character by inculcating discipline, team spirit and loyalty.[32] The spacious College grounds were ideally suited to rugby and cricket and Bertie played both and, it seems, with great energy; he had his collar bone broken and a few teeth knocked out playing 'rugger'.[33] Since the College was situated at the water's edge, swimming was also popular and the College regulations specified that each boy was 'required to learn swimming'.[34]

Despite its promising beginnings, the experiment of the Isle of Wight College did not persist. As a result of declining enrollment and consequent financial distress, the College grounds were given up in 1902, and four years later the property was purchased by a community of Benedictine nuns who still occupy the grounds, now named St. Cecilia's Abbey. Little evidence remains of the College or of those boys who passed through it for a quarter of a century, save for a stained glass window depicting the College, donated by a few Old Vectensians, and installed in St. John's Church, Ryde, in 1933. Yet, the most careful observer can still find one small vestige of Bertie Clayton's time at the College. On a window-pane in an old schoolroom that 125 years ago looked out to the north, to the College lawns and across the Solent, a few students had scratched their names into the glass, and, near the top of the pane, in uneven block letters, one can just make out – faint but still perceptible – the name 'G. F. Clayton'.[35]

In December 1889, Bertie passed the Preliminary examination for admission to the Royal Military Academy at Woolwich.[36] Entrance to the Academy had been determined by competitive examination since the 1850s, but it was not until 1870, when they were turned over to the Civil Service Commissioners, that the entrance exams assumed a more formal aspect. Admission now involved a two-step process. The 'Preliminary' could be taken by a boy, like Bertie, as young as fourteen, and was not very demanding; no marks were given and a boy had only to 'satisfy the Commissioners' as to his basic competence in mathematics, geography, geometrical drawing, Latin, French or German and 'writing English correctly in a good legible hand from dictation'.[37] But the 'Further' examination, taken two or three years later, was far more rigorous. After first passing a detailed physical exam, the candidate had to produce legal proof that he was between sixteen and eighteen years of age, provide a certificate showing his passing of the 'Preliminary' and another, signed by the head of his school, certifying as to his 'good moral character'. The subjects on which the boy was then examined included required papers in mathematics, Latin and French or German, any two optional papers in higher mathematics, German or French (that not taken in Part I), Greek, English history, chemistry, physics or physical geography and geology. A third class of subjects included English composition, freehand and geometrical drawing.[38] Bertie sat for the 'Further' at Portsmouth in June 1892 'but failed to get in'. He went up again in December and came just short, placing fifty-fourth on the list from which only fifty were taken.[39]

Bertie's failures were by no means unusual; most candidates for Woolwich, and even the less demanding Royal Military College at Sandhurst, found the 'Further' too difficult. As a result, a 'class of special tutors called "crammers" had arisen'.[40] They had been preparing boys for decades by the time Bertie took the exam. In the 1860s sixty-five percent of the Sandhurst candidates and ninety-seven percent of those sitting for Woolwich had attended crammers' courses.[41] An 1868–9 Royal Commission, appointed to assess the state of military education in the country, criticized the influence of crammers and found it 'prejudicial', but they persisted and even flourished. The best known and most successful of them was Captain Walter H. James whose establishment, known by his many students as 'Jimmy's', was located in Lexham Gardens, just off the Cromwell Road in Kensington.[42] William Clayton, determined to give his son every opportunity of becoming a Gunner, promptly arranged for Bertie to join Jimmy's spring course in 1893. Years later Bertie recalled that among the boys at Jimmy's in that spring of 1893, was a candidate preparing for his third go at the Sandhurst exam. The boy's manner was so annoying to his tutors and fellow students that he had to sidle along the perimeter of the classroom with his back to the wall in order to reach his place without getting his bottom kicked by the other students. Young Winston Churchill had thoroughly exasperated Captain James who found the boy 'distinctly inclined . . . to teach his instructors instead of endeavouring to learn from them'.[43]

Churchill may have antagonized his fellow students and driven Captain James to distraction, but he fully appreciated the value of Jimmy's which, 'for at least two decades' had 'held the Blue Ribbon among the crammers'. Jimmy's was not interested in deep learning or in thorough knowledge of a subject, but only in achieving marks sufficient to gain admission. Churchill described the approach: 'It was said that no one who was not a congenital idiot could avoid passing thence into the Army. The Firm had made a scientific study of the mentality of the Civil Service Commissioners. They knew with almost Papal infallibility the sort of questions which that sort of person would be bound on the average to ask on any of the selected subjects. They specialized on these questions and on the answering of them.'[44]

The system worked for both Bertie and Winston. At the June 1893 examination Bertie passed twentieth on the list of fifty successful candidates. He scored well in mathematics, less so in Latin and his French and German (optional) scores were good and roughly the same. Of the optional papers Bertie chose higher mathematics and though his score was low, he compensated with good marks in English composition and freehand and geometrical drawing.[45] Churchill just squeezed by in his examination for Sandhurst, finishing ninety-fifth on the list. Passing too low to qualify for the infantry, he was allotted a place in the far more expensive ranks of the cavalry.[46] On September 28, 1893 Bertie arrived at the Royal Military Academy, Woolwich, known to generations of Gunners and Sappers (Engineers) simply as 'The Shop'.

The Shop had been created by Royal Warrant in 1741, to instruct 'the raw and inexperienced people belonging to the Military branch . . . in the several parts of Mathematics necessary to qualify them for the service of the Artillery and the business of the Engineers'.[47] Until the late nineteenth century, though, the record of The Shop, and that of the Royal Military College at Sandhurst, founded sixty years later, was an uneven one. The prevailing ethos was against professionalism generally and military education specifically. The Duke of Wellington thought all formal military education the greatest nonsense and the fusty old Duke of Cambridge, who served as commander-in-chief of the Army for nearly forty years during the second half of the nineteenth century, held that 'a man who will stick to his regiment will learn his profession in that regiment much better than in any college'.[48] The British military academies did not purport to provide a university education like the U.S. academy at West Point or the French at St. Cyr. They were, instead, directed to studies that had a practical application. But even this pragmatic approach could not defeat the 'spirit and fashion' of the time, which, as reflected in a 1902 report on the academies, was 'rather not to show keenness' regarding one's military education.[49] This attitude was much more evident at Sandhurst which was severely criticized by the 1868 Royal Commission and the 1902 committee.

While it may have been fashionable for the Woolwich or Sandhurst cadet to display indifference to his military studies, he was nevertheless said to have exhibited a 'restless and unruly spirit' and was often involved in local disturbances. At Woolwich there were occasional dust-ups with local townsfolk and there was even a 'mutiny' of sorts in 1861, when most of the company of cadets refused to obey orders. Bullying was also a chronic problem until late in the century. The newly joined gentlemen cadets – 'neux' and later, 'snookers', as they were called – were often subjected to acts of 'downright cruelty' by their seniors. Even in Bertie's time, snookers might be called to 'give an angle of 45°' which required the cadet to put his head against the wall and place his feet as far away as possible, so that when the body was rigid it formed an angle of almost 45° with the floor. The snooker's feet were then kicked out from beneath him. Or, the new cadet might be required to 'look out for squalls' which entailed climbing to an open window, putting one's legs and arms through the bars of the grating, and remaining there, even in winter, with little or nothing on. A 'third diversion' involved placing two stools, one on top of the other and both atop a barrack room table. The neux was ordered to the top and the bottom stool kicked from under him. The injuries resulting from these punishments were sometimes severe enough that the responsible cadets were rusticated.[50] But the compilers of the Academy's *Historical Records* thought the effects on the victims not at all bad, as such practices induced 'habits of strict and unquestioning obedience to those of higher rank'.[51]

By the time of Bertie's arrival at the Academy in 1893, the course of instruction had been fixed at two years, each of two terms, with the first running from September to February, and the second, March through July. In 1889 the Academy adopted a new curriculum for the 'scientific corps', designed to more closely tailor the course of study to the two fields of speciality, artillery and engineering. The new programme, called 'bifurcation', provided that all cadets pursue the same course work during their first year. This encompassed strong doses of mathematics, either French or German, and chemistry and physics. Military courses included fortification, military topography, drawing and model drawing. A physical component involved battalion and squad drill, gymnastics and riding and gun drill. Cadets passing highest on the list at the end of the first year were then given the choice of 'bifurcating' – pursuing a course of study in their second year more suited to the engineers. The remainder were attached to the Artillery Division. During their second year at the Academy the engineers continued their mathematical work, and studied some artillery, but devoted more time to fortification and landscape drawing, while the Gunners emphasized artillery, gave less time to fortification and had the option of landscape drawing. Cadets in both divisions continued their work in chemistry and physics, topography and drill and both took a year-long course in tactics, military administration and law.[52] Upon leaving the Academy after the second year, both artillery and engineering cadets received commissions as second lieutenants, but the engineers proceeded to the engineering school at Chatham for two further years of instruction.

Bertie improved his position during his time at the Academy, and when he left in the autumn of 1895, passed out tenth in his class. Whether he was offered a position in the Engineers after his first year is unknown; the numbers required for the Engineers varied from year to year and no record appears to have been kept of the number of positions offered or to whom offers were made. But Bertie had always wished to become a Gunner and he was certainly in the Artillery Division during his second year.[53] One may be equally certain that Bertie enjoyed his time at Woolwich, just as he had at the Isle of Wight College. Many years later a classmate recalled Bertie's good humour and spirit and his participation in 'rags of the milder kind', like the demonstration he organized, in nightshirts and top hats, against 'Lights out' at ten o'clock. 'As a student Bertie never "mugged-up stuff", never burned the midnight oil. He had the mind that seizes facts, pigeonholes them, and brings them out at the opportune times.'[54] His ability to retain and apply factual detail and his good humour were two attributes which would serve Bertie well in later years and go far toward explaining his success as an administrator and diplomat.[55] No doubt Bertie endured his share of bullying at the hands of 'old cadets' and, like all his fellow classmates, occasionally had to suffer through 'hoxters', as the early-morning defaulters' drill was called. Still, he found time to continue his participation in team sport and, although he later complained that sport 'was a department in which I never shone much', Bertie did earn his 'colours' by representing the Academy in the annual cricket match against Sandhurst.[56] The 1895 team on which he played 'did badly on the whole', but Bertie's batting statistics for the season were third best on the Woolwich side: 13 innings, 1 time 'not out', 295 runs, a high score of 109 and an average of 24.6.[57]

On August 2, 1895, Bertie passed out of the Academy and two months later was gazetted a second lieutenant in the Royal Artillery. The Artillery was then organized into Garrison, Field and Horse batteries. Upon leaving the Academy most cadets were placed in the Garrison batteries and although most Garrison units were posted abroad – nearly two-thirds of them were sent to India or the colonies – they received slightly higher pay. But the Garrison Artillery was not favoured among officers; there was little *esprit de corps*, the turnover rate was high and most sought transfer to the 'smarter mounted branches' where they had better opportunity for active service and promotion.[58] However, in the autumn of 1895, these do not appear to have been concerns of Bertie Clayton, as he was posted to No. 16 Company, Eastern Division, and sent to Shoeburyness to undertake the obligatory gunnery course. He had at last realized his dream of becoming a Gunner in the Royal Artillery.

3

The Lion and the Sphinx: The British Empire and the Middle East

'I will try dearest mother, by God's grace, to lead the life of a true soldier in every sense of the word.'[1] With these words, hurriedly scratched in a note written aboard the P & O liner *Britannia*, Bertie Clayton sailed from Southampton on the 15th of January 1896, bound for Egypt. Clayton's reference to a 'true soldier' was doubly allusive and would have been readily understood as such. As a true soldier of Christ, he was undertaking to lead an honourable, even virtuous life, a sentiment sure to appeal to his devout mother. But, equally, he was a soldier in the army of the world's greatest empire and was thus imbued with a profound sense of duty, of obligation, to spread the benefits of Pax Britannica. In late nineteenth century Britain this latter sentiment, this sense of imperial mission, was one shared by more than just soldiers. Less than two years after Bertie's departure a young reporter for London's *Daily Mail*, G.W. Steevens, also boarded the *Britannia*, also bound for Egypt. At first unimpressed, Steevens reported that after only two days 'the ship grows on you'. The *Britannia* was 'miraculously clean', the officers 'point device in their manners and courtesy'. As you dress 'decorously for dinner', he informed his readers, 'you begin to realize that you are going to a part of the world where your people are sahibs, to be treated as such, and to behave as such'. He was particularly struck by the 'family aspect' of the ship:

> When the mothers bring the babies up on to the promenade-deck you get an illustration of the continuity of the British Empire — continuity in space and continuity in time. These toddling nuisances are quite at home at sea . . . their home from birth up is the world, wherever there may be work to do. Many of them, you know, will go on living until they die on ships and in queer torrid corners of the world. They will die earlier than we stay-at-homes . . . But they will not die, we hope, till they have got other infants to make themselves a nuisance about promenade-decks; and, die soon or late, it is odds on their having done a decent bit of work for their country and themselves.[2]

Steevens was perhaps justified in ruminating on the temporal and spatial continuity of the empire. By the time of Queen Victoria's Diamond Jubilee – which fell between the voyages of Clayton and Steevens, on June 22, 1897 – the British Empire covered a quarter of the earth and a quarter of its population. There was nothing to compare to it. The Roman Empire, at its greatest reach, comprised two and one-half million square miles and perhaps eleven million people; the Queen's Diamond Jubilee telegraph message reached out to 372 million of her subjects in domains spanning eleven million square miles. It is true that the Empire had not yet reached its greatest extent – that would not come until 1933. But the 1897 Jubilee did represent the Empire at 'full flush', at its very apogee in terms of pride, energy and enthusiasm for the great civilizing mission that Britain had undertaken. And these feelings percolated down to the barracks, the music halls and the school rooms, where world maps depicted British possessions in bold red. Of course there were the 'white settlements', the nearly independent countries of Canada, Australia, New Zealand and South Africa. And India was, and would remain for another half-century, the most prominent jewel in the crown. But bits of imperial red appeared all over the world map. In Asia, the British were in Burma, Malaya, North Borneo and Sarawak, in New Guinea and in Hong Kong. In Africa, along the eastern seaboard, Britain ruled in Somaliland and in Uganda and exercised a protectorate over British East Africa. In the west of the continent, Gambia, the Gold Coast, Sierra Leone and most of Nigeria were in British hands. In the south, the British Cape Colony and Natal resided uneasily next to the Boer Republics of the Transvaal and the Orange Free State. The British were also in South America in British Guiana, and along the Central American coast in Honduras. Most of the islands of the Caribbean had been held by Britain for a century or more. In the South Pacific, too, the British controlled, in one form or another, hundreds of islands, many of them so remote and unfamiliar that even the experts at the Colonial Office had to resort to the atlas to find them. And, most gratifying to the Queen-Empress – and indeed to many Britons not half her age – was the knowledge that this great efflorescence of empire had occurred in barely a generation's time. The annual Colonial Office List, containing the names and positions of British officials throughout the Empire, numbered only 152 pages in 1862; by 1897 it had ballooned to 562 pages.[3]

The glue which held the Empire together was the Royal Navy. Effectively unchallenged since Trafalgar, the Navy had adopted its famous 'Two Power Standard' in 1889: The British fleet would always be 'at least equal to the naval strength of any other two countries'.[4] By the time Clayton left for Egypt in 1896, the Navy maintained a fleet of 330 ships, manned by 92,000 sailors. Britain's nearest naval rival, France, had ninety-five ships afloat, the United States, a distant fifth, only fifty-six. The Royal Navy seemed unassailable and a sampling of its wonderfully-named fighting ships – *Thunderer, Devastation, Colossus, Hannibal, Mars, Hecate* and *Cyclops* – suggested that Britain would brook no opposition in maintaining her command of the sea routes to Empire. Imperial thinking also dictated naval strategy. Advocates of the 'Blue Water' policy asserted that Britain and its possessions were best defended by a widely dispersed navy. 'It was the ubiquity of the British presence, in all five continents, that was the strength of the island kingdom.'[5] The policy was best exemplified by the Navy's great bases spread across the globe, at Gibraltar, Malta and Aden, in Trincomalee, Hong Kong, Esquimalt and Halifax.

The British Army, however, did not compare so favourably with the Navy. And, stacked against its continental rivals, it appeared pitifully small and dangerously out-of-date. In 1895, there were only about 210,000 men in the regular Army and the Artillery in which Clayton served manned only some 700 guns. A quarter of a century earlier, the Prussians had put 880,000 men under arms against the French. The Army was still organized on the antiquated regimental system and British regiments, though long on tradition and *esprit de corps*, were short on modern technology, tactics and advanced weaponry. Indeed, the Army had no general staff until 1906; every other European army had one by 1890. The state of British military thinking at the beginning of the century was best illustrated in a letter written by the Secretary of State for War to the Prime Minister in 1903: 'I do not find that any definite instruction exists as to what is the exact purpose for which the army exists and what duties it is supposed to perform.'[6]

The Army was just as slow in adopting new technology. It was the last force in Europe to abandon muzzle-loading canon and although the American inventor Hiram Maxim had successfully tested his prototypical single-barreled machine gun as early as 1884, the Army promptly rejected it as too expensive. The Army's cadre of officers was also weak. In 1870, a gentleman could still purchase a commission in a cavalry or infantry regiment, even though it had long been recognized that financial means was hardly good qualification for service as an officer. Even after the government eliminated the purchase system in 1871, a young officer still could not survive in the Army without a private income. Clayton's pay as a subaltern in the Royal Garrison Artillery was only 5*s*. 7*d*. per day – £100. 10*s*. 0*d*. per year – perhaps slightly augmented by his service abroad.[7] And, with this, he was required to purchase his uniforms, pay his mess bill and buy most of his kit. Not surprisingly, until he joined the Egyptian army in late 1900, Clayton, like many other young officers, required an allowance from his father – probably between £60 and £100 per year – to make ends meet.[8]

Despite the disadvantages of Army life, Clayton arrived in Egypt in January 1896, full of enthusiasm for his new career. With two other lieutenants he was assigned to No. 16 Battery at Alexandria, then under the command of Major J. H .L. Dallas and Captain W. C. Hunter Blair.[9] Although fifteen years older than Clayton, Walter Hunter Blair would become a mentor and life-long friend. It was a good connection. Not only was Hunter Blair a brother-in-law of the Seventh Earl of Glasgow, he would rise to Major-General in the Army and always had sound advice for Bertie and later for his brother Iltyd, who would be commissioned in the Artillery in 1906.

The Egypt in which Clayton arrived in 1896 occupied an anomalous position in the British Empire. It might be coloured pink, or demarcated by striped diagonal lines on the world map, but not in solid, imperial red, for British rule in the country was not formalized by any treaty, decree or proclamation. It was, rather, informal and had evolved in a slow and reluctant fashion, driven by financial worry and strategic imperative. The origins of British rule can be traced to the Napoleonic invasion of the country in 1798, generally regarded as marking the beginning of modern Egyptian history. The country was then – and would be until 1914 – a province of the Ottoman Empire, its governor owing allegiance to the Turkish Sultan at Constantinople. The French army left Egypt in the early 1800s, not long after Nelson's great victory at Abukir Bay, and were then supplanted not by the British but by a Balkan adventurer, Muhammad 'Ali (r.1805–1849). A man of great energy and determination, Muhammad 'Ali looked west, to London and Paris, not north to Constantinople. His western predilections brought a modern administrative system to Egypt. He dug canals, brought steam travel to the Nile and increased foreign trade ten-fold during his reign. Improvements in irrigation carried out during his rule brought large areas under cultivation that had been wasteland or desert. His development of the Egyptian army along western lines was so successful that European coalitions had to be assembled to stop his advances in Greece and Syria. Muhammad 'Ali's successor, 'Abbas I (r.1848–54), departed from his grandfather's plans and pursued a retrograde policy, dismissing his western advisers and reducing the size of the army. But Muhammad 'Ali's son Sa'id, (r.1854–63), who succeeded 'Abbas, returned to his father's modernization policies. European educated and French-speaking, Sa'id again turned to the west. One of his closest friends was a Frenchman, Ferdinand de Lesseps, the prime mover behind a scheme to dig a canal through the desert connecting the Mediterranean with the Red Sea. The Suez Canal was not completed until 1869, during the reign of Sa'id's successor, Isma'il (r.1863–79). But, ominously, Sa'id was the first modern Egyptian ruler to incur European debt – to the tune of £7,000,000 – used, in part, to finance the Canal.

The opening of the Suez Canal was a watershed in modern Egyptian history. Prior to 1869, many European investors had interests in Egypt, particularly in cotton, the country's primary export. But after the Canal opened, Egypt assumed a new and strategic significance out of all proportion to the country's economic importance. The sea voyage from London to Bombay was now cut by fifty-one percent and it very soon became a guiding principle of Britain's eastern policy that no foreign power should control the Canal.[10] Consistent with this policy, British Prime Minister Benjamin Disraeli purchased Egypt's shares in the Canal Company (about 40% of the total, the balance being held by French investors) in 1874 for a mere £4,000,000. The reason Isma'il sold the Egyptian Canal shares was all too apparent; he had been incurring debt at an alarming rate. By the time he was deposed at the demand of his European creditors, he had run up a staggering debt of £98,500,000. In fairness to the Khedive – as the Egyptian ruler was now called – much of this money was expended on the improvement of Egypt: 5,000 miles of telegraph cable, 1,000 miles of railway and 8,000 miles of irrigation canals were built during Isma'il's reign, in addition to many roads, bridges, docks and lighthouses. He tripled the value of Egypt's exports, improved Alexandria's harbor and opened more than 4,000 schools. Yet, Isma'il also squandered a great deal of borrowed money. Construction of Cairo's famous opera house was a debatable investment, but the many palaces he built, the Khedival yacht and other personal extravagances could hardly be justified as a public charge. The resulting debt was not only extraordinarily large for a country with so little ability to meet its obligations, it was also securitized, tiered and layered in such byzantine complexity that very few had a comprehensive understanding of it. One who did, though, was Major Evelyn Baring, sent out from London in 1876, as Britain's representative on the *Caisse de la Dette Publique*, a commission of European creditors established to administer the Egyptian debt. Three years later, in the face of yet another budget crisis, complete control of Egypt's revenue and expenditure was turned over to two 'controllers', one British, the other French. Baring, scion of the great London banking house of Baring, was again the British nominee.

Isma'il's successor, Taufiq (r.1879 - 92) now faced a dismal situation. Not only had he been deprived of control over the country's economy, he was soon facing an insurrection mounted by a clique of disgruntled Egyptian army officers, led by colonel Ahmad Urabi, who vowed to wrest control of Egypt from the European financiers. But Urabi underestimated British, if not French, resolve. The French would later regret their failure to respond to Urabi's challenge, a failure largely attributable to domestic French politics. The British, however, quickly rose to the occasion. On September 13, 1882, a British army met Urabi's force at Tell el Kebir to the north-east of Cairo. In thirty-five minutes it was over; British primacy in Egypt was assured. A year later, Baring was appointed British Agent and Consul-General. Still, no formal change occurred in Egypt's status. The country was still an autonomous Turkish province. British relations with Egypt still came under the jurisdiction of the Foreign Office, not the Colonial Office and, officially, Baring's status was still no greater than that of any other European consul in Cairo. But no one doubted that Baring – Lord Cromer from 1892 – ran Egypt. He would do so from 1883 until 1907. Imperious in style, abrupt in manner, Cromer was rarely challenged in Egypt, or in England. In Cairo, subordinates described him simply as 'the Lord', and the British Agency, from which Cromer directed the affairs of the country, was referred to by the Egyptians as *bayt al-lurd*, house of the Lord. Steevens of the *Daily Mail* succinctly described his position: 'In theory, he has no more right to tell the Khedive what is, or is not, to be done than you have. He just happens to give advice, and the Khedive happens to take it.'[11]

One hundred forty miles to the north-west of the *bayt al-lurd* lay Egypt's second city, Alexandria. Stretched out in a thin arc along the Mediterranean shoreline, the city seemed to direct its gaze north to the European continent rather than inwards towards Egypt. The focus was not surprising. With its large continental population – mostly Greek and Italian – its beautiful Italianate buildings, French street names, European clubs and its popular opera, Alexandria appeared more European than Egyptian. As a result, it held little appeal for the western tourist seeking something of the exotic East or of Egypt's ancient past. In fact, almost nothing remained of Alexandria's halcyon days when it was the greatest centre of learning in the ancient world. Thomas Cook, who had been organizing Egyptian tours for thirty years, curtly dismissed the city in one of his travel brochures: 'After briefly scanning

Alexandria, which is a sort of Oriental-European conglomerate with but few attractions, we hasten to modern Egypt – Cairo – which represents a combination of ancient orientalism with Parisian innovations.'[12] The assessment was accurate. But while Alexandria lacked tourist appeal, it more than compensated as a trading entrepôt. Steevens reported that Alexandria cleared nearly a million tons of goods from its docks in 1896, the year of Bertie Clayton's arrival, and the customs valuation for that year's exports exceeded £13,000,000. Cotton dominated the Egyptian market; nearly 600,000 bales were shipped from Alexandria in that year, more than half of them bound for English mills.[13]

A few hundred yards from the Alexandria docks, the city's commercial life was centred on its great square, dominated by a triumphal bronze statue of Muhammad 'Ali. On one side stood the Cotton Exchange, on another the bourse – the stock exchange, Egypt's most important financial institution – and on a third the law courts. The Place Muhammad 'Ali, as it was then known, was also the hub of the city's European quarter. The British community and its church of St. Mark was just to the north, the French and Greek communities to the south and the Armenians and the Italians to the west.[14] The streets round the periphery of the square were crowded with small Greek and Italian shops bearing such names as 'Pharmacie Hippocrate', 'Cornucopia Grocery', 'Ceres Corn-Chandlery' and 'Reliance Ironmongery'.[15] Alexandria's social season peaked during the summer months when the stifling heat and dust of Cairo drove the government and the European diplomatic missions north to the Mediterranean. European consuls could mix with their colleagues at the Muhammad 'Ali Club, located just to the south-east of the square, or attend the races or play tennis at the Alexandria Sporting Club. In the evenings, the opera at the Zinzinia Theatre was a popular choice. And nearly every night one could find the best of the European community down along the Mahmudia Canal, which defined the city's southern edge, attending a formal dinner or a ball at one or another of the great mansions owned by the city's merchant millionaires. By the 1870s some of the city's prominent Europeans began moving their homes out of the city to the suburb of Ramleh, located about five miles to the east of the Place Muhammad 'Ali. There was no road yet along the shore, but a tram-line was run out from the centre of the city to Ramleh, the stations along the way bearing the names of many of Alexandria's prominent European families. The substantial British community in Ramleh lived much as they would have at home, organizing their amateur theatrical groups, holding recitals, hosting dances, 'at homes' and tennis tournaments. A group of officers from the nearby British garrison even imported hounds from England and established a hunt in Ramleh. But the dogs found the climate uncongenial and when they died so too did the hunt.

The British garrison was stationed at the Mustapha Barracks, situated about half-way between Ramleh and Alexandria. It was here that Clayton learned his trade as a 'gunner'. Although he kept no diary for 1896–7, it appears from later diaries and correspondence that he and his fellow lieutenants regularly made the short tram ride into the city. Like most of the officers in the British garrison, he frequented the Alexandria Sporting Club. In his 1902 diary he described a brief stop in Alexandria on his way home on leave when he paid a visit to the Club and saw 'all the old crowd'. He also seems to have made friends from among the European community there, one of which – described only as 'Cavafy' in Clayton's later diaries – may have been related to the great Greek poet, Constantine Cavafy (1863–1933).

In the fall of 1897, Clayton was granted his first leave and returned to England for three months.[16] By November he was back in Egypt. As enjoyable as his new career was, Clayton, like most young subalterns, yearned for action, for combat. During his first two years in Egypt he had seen none, even though during that time 'small wars' were in progress in the south of Africa – in Matabeleland (1896), and in Bechuanaland (1896–7) – the Benin expedition was underway in west Africa, as was the Third Ashanti War (1896–7), and hostilities had resumed on the northwest frontier of India (1897–8). Of far greater interest to Clayton than all these wars, though, was the conflict going on 1,000 miles to the south, in the Sudan, where Sir Horatio Herbert Kitchener, the Sirdar – commander – of the Egyptian army, was engaged in a fight with the forces of the Khalifa. It was a popular campaign, for most Britons believed it would lead to a vindication of the death of the age's greatest imperial hero, General Charles Gordon.

It would have been difficult to find a British citizen in the last twenty years of the nineteenth century unfamiliar with the story of Charles George Gordon. Born at Woolwich in 1833, Gordon seemed destined for a military career. His father was an artilleryman and a lieutenant-general and Charles naturally attended the Military Academy at Woolwich. Soon after leaving the Academy, he distinguished himself in the siege of Sebastopol during the Crimean War. By the early 1860s Gordon was in China, where, at the age of thirty, he was made a general by the Chinese, placed in command of an army, and charged with suppressing the infamous Taiping Rebellion. He did so in such a decisive fashion that he was made a Companion of the Bath on his return to England, where he became known as 'Chinese Gordon'. Not content with a conventional army career, though, Gordon eventually found his way to Egypt, where he was appointed by the Khedive as Governor of Equatoria Province, deep in the southern Sudan. Three years later, in 1877, he was made governor-general of the entire country, only to resign in 1879, shortly after the deposition of Isma'il. For the next four years Gordon bounced round the empire as if looking for his next great mission. He did not find it in Abyssinia, India, Mauritius or Palestine.

Gordon's sense of mission was accentuated by his deep Christian faith, a faith that apparently arose from a sort of epiphany experienced during an attack of small pox in China, an event, he said, which 'brought me back to my Saviour'. But Gordon's faith was not of any traditional variety; it was, rather, of a 'mystical, fatalistic . . . [and] highly unconventional' turn.[17] Ultimately answerable only to the will of God, Gordon immersed himself in biblical studies and adopted a life-style of asceticism and self-abnegation. Whatever abilities he possessed as a commander or leader, it was his peculiar sense of religious mission – of apocalyptic destiny – and his consequent disregard for authority, that rendered Gordon unsuitable for a responsible imperial assignment. The great Conservative Party leader Lord Salisbury once remarked that Gordon was 'the last possible man to be entrusted with any sort of diplomatic mission'.[18] Yet, within four years of his departure from the Sudan events in that country had taken such a remarkable turn that Gordon was again being considered as the leader of a mission to Khartoum.

Egyptian rule in the Sudan had always been deeply unpopular amongst the Sudanese. The Egyptians were seen as oppressors who imposed an inequitable system of taxation, undermined the economy of the country by suppressing the slave trade, and played favourites, showing partiality to a few, select Sudanese tribes, and alienating nearly all others. Egyptian administrators posted to the country could not even reach their Sudanese subjects on a common ground of ethnicity; they spoke not Arabic, but Turkish, an alien language in the Sudan, and they were contemptuously referred to as 'Turks'. Indeed, the period of Egyptian rule in the Sudan (1825–85) is generally described as the era of *al-Turkiyya al-sabiqa*, 'the former Turkish government', or simply as the *Turkiyya*. Despite widespread discontent with Egyptian rule, though, Sudanese unhappiness lacked any focal point round which feelings of opposition could coalesce. That focal point was provided in 1881, with the sudden emergence of Muhammad Ahmad, known generally as the Mahdi – the guided one. The period of his brief ascendancy, and the longer rule of his successor, the Khalifa, 'Abdallahi ibn Muhammad (r.1885–98), would become known as the *Mahdiyya*. Muhammad Ahmad was born in Dongola Province in 1844, and early on gravitated towards a religious life. As a young man he became an adherent of a Sufi order of Islam. Leading a life of abject humility, rigorous discipline and self-denial, he sought only the spiritual path that would lead him to a mystical union with God. In the 1860s be began travelling about the Sudan on religious missions, gradually gained a following, and, in 1870, settled on Aba Island in the White Nile south of Khartoum. Intensely personal as his faith was, Muhammad Ahmad's religious ideas could hardly be characterized as an organized and coherent system of beliefs; they were, rather, a 'deposit of ideas and hopes'.[19] On a personal level one aspired to a union with God by leading a simple, humble, devout life and rejecting wealth, pleasure and excess in any form. But Mahdism also exhibited a political aspect; in its desire to return to the purity of Islam, it emphatically rejected all impediments to that goal and that, of course, included contemporary governments, most especially that of the 'Turks', who were denounced as *kufara*, infidels. This reactionary and militant aspect of Mahdism was by no means unique. It also appeared in the Sanusiyya of North Africa and among the Wahhabis of central Arabia. Later in his career, Clayton would be called upon to contend with both sects.

In early 1881 Muhammad Ahmad experienced a series of visions, revealing that he was the expected one, the Mahdi, and, on June 29, the manifestation – the declaration – of the Mahdi was made on Aba Island. The government in Khartoum was well aware of these developments and reacted quickly. But the forces they sent to take the Mahdi were inadequate. In two sharp actions in August and December 1881, the Mahdi and his Ansar warriors defeated the Egyptians.[20] The governor-general sought reinforcements from Cairo but none were available as Egypt was then fully absorbed with the Urabi rebellion. By 1882 the Mahdi was on the offensive.

More battles were fought and won and not until September 1882 did the Mahdists suffer a serious reverse at El Obeid, in Kordofan Province, to the southwest of Khartoum. But by the end of the year, the Dervishes – as Europeans referred to the Ansar – were unvanquished and Mahdism, if anything, was gaining in strength. The Egyptians appealed to the British for help. Having just crushed the Urabists at Tell el Kebir, though, the government were interested only in consolidating the British position in Egypt preparatory to a withdrawal from the country which, Prime Minister Gladstone hoped, would occur sooner rather than later. In fact, the government much preferred that the Egyptians evacuate the Sudan altogether, and no one in London was interested in another military adventure, particularly one that would occur 1,000 miles away in the desert wastes south of Cairo.

The Egyptians, however, took a different view and were determined to crush the Mahdi and reassert their authority in the Sudan. An Egyptian force of 10,000 men was quickly assembled, placed under a British commander, Colonel William Hicks, and sent south in mid-1883. On November 5, Hicks' army confronted the Dervishes at Shaykan, to the south of El Obeid. The Egyptian force was obliterated; only 250 soldiers walked away from the battle and Hicks was not among them. Swelled by his triumph at Shaykan, the Mahdi soon extended his rule, eliminating the Egyptians in Darfur, to the west, and in the Bahr al-Ghazal in the far south. In eastern Sudan the military results were more mixed, but by early 1884, government forces were effectively pinned down to the coast at the Red Sea port of Suakin.

This then was the situation in January 1884, when the British government approached Gordon concerning his possible return to the Sudan. It did so with grave reservations. Baring, now British Agent in Cairo, was cabled twice with the suggestion of Gordon's appointment. Twice he flatly rejected it. Only after a third request did he grudgingly acquiesce and then only on the understanding that Gordon expressly pledge himself to carry out the government's policy – the evacuation of the Sudan.[21] But the Gladstone government issued Gordon ambiguous written instructions – he was ordered to the Sudan only to report, preliminary to an eventual evacuation – and it failed later to insist that he evacuate the country, even though Gordon later observed he understood that was why he had been sent. No sooner did he depart on his mission than Foreign Secretary Lord Granville was left wringing his hands. 'Are you sure', he asked a colleague, that 'we did not commit a gigantic folly?'[22] Within days Granville's fears proved amply justified, for, soon after Gordon reached Cairo, the Foreign Secretary learned that the Khedive Taufiq had happily signed a letter, prepared by Gordon, appointing him governor-general of the Sudan 'so that good government may be restored'.[23]

On February 18, 1884, Gordon arrived in Khartoum. Within a few weeks he was advocating postponement of the evacuation and a 'smashing of the Mahdi'. Meanwhile, the Mahdi was closing in. By May, Khartoum was surrounded and Gordon was in very serious trouble. Forgetting that in December 1883 they had clamoured for Gordon's dispatch to Khartoum, the British press now demanded that an expedition immediately be sent to relieve him. Gladstone was loathe to send any such force. He prevaricated. Two months passed. Finally, on August 5, Parliament voted £300,000 for the purpose. But it was not until January 1885 that the Gordon relief force actually arrived in northern Sudan. The Dervishes could have taken Khartoum weeks, if not months, earlier. But the Mahdi was no fool and certainly understood that the death of Gordon at his hands might very well provide the British a *casus belli*. So he spent weeks sending messages to the governor-general asking for his surrender. Gordon, perhaps resigned to his destiny, refused them all. It was now a race against time for the relief force. On January 28, 1885, two steamers carrying an advance party from the force at last reached Khartoum. They were too late. On the 26th Khartoum had been overwhelmed and, despite the Mahdi's likely orders to the contrary, Gordon was killed, and beheaded, by the rampaging Dervishes. The relief force retired to the north. Six months later the Mahdi himself died, in less heroic circumstances, probably succumbing to typhus.

The ensuing outcry, the fury of the press and public with Gladstone and his ministers for allowing the death of Gordon, was unbounded. The government only just survived, by fourteen votes, in the House of Commons. And the formidable Lord Salisbury, moved a vote of censure in the Lords. Salisbury had, in fact, been a severe critic since the Gordon mission had been made public, roundly accusing the government of 'not impolicy, but imbecility'.[24] Yet, the Liberal government survived and prevailed again in a November 1885 election. It did not fall until July 1886, and that failure had little, if anything, to do with the demise of Gordon. Still, after his death, something of a Gordon cult swept over Britain. He was commemorated in poetry and prose, in stage-plays and in oil paintings, busts and statues. His image was emblazoned on everything from water jugs to bookmarks. Headmasters at many of England's great public schools – Harrow, Marlborough, Winchester and Eton among them – held Gordon up as the paradigm of Christian virtue, honour, and selfless duty to empire.[25] The reality, of course, was something else and a generation would elapse before Lytton Strachey would take much of the wind from the sails of the Gordon myth in his iconoclastic masterpiece, *Eminent Victorians*.

It is doubtful whether the Gordon myth or the public sentiment for vengeance much affected government policy. Lord Salisbury, for all his criticism of Gladstone's handling of the Gordon affair, did nothing to reverse the government's hands-off Sudan policy when he served as Prime Minister from 1886 to 1892. Nor was he motivated in the slightest to take any measures against the Mahdi's successor, the Khalifa, to avenge Gordon's death. When he returned to the Premiership in 1895, following another Gladstone ministry, Salisbury again showed little interest in the Sudan. However, in the following year his Sudan policy would change. This had nothing to do with Gordon, and much to do with European politics. On March 1, 1896, the Abyssinian Emperor Menelik annihilated an Italian army of 5,000 at Adowa. The Italian government fell in the wake of the disaster and the new prime minister urgently requested British aid in the Sudan. The Italians pleaded for an Anglo-Egyptian attack on the Dervishes who, it was feared, were plotting an alliance with Menelik to take the Italian outpost at Kassala in eastern Sudan. Of no less concern to Salisbury than the Italian predicament was the news that the French government had recently approved an expedition to the upper Nile from west Africa, under the command of Captain Jean-Baptiste Marchand. Both concerns were somewhat unfounded. The Khalifa was not particularly interested in an alliance with the Christian Abyssinians and the French did not care much about the upper Nile, although they were keen to give that impression, as it might prompt the British to enter into talks to resolve a wide range of issues pending between the two Powers. Finally, as will be seen, Salisbury was also worried about the aspirations of Leopold, King of the Belgians and ruler of the so-called Congo Free State, who *did* wish to establish himself on the upper Nile. With these considerations in mind, on March 11–12 the Cabinet authorized Anglo-Egyptian operations to secure Dongola Province in northern Sudan and perhaps 'to plant the Egyptian foot farther up the Nile'.[26]

On March 18, 1896, shortly after Bertie Clayton's arrival at Alexandria, the Egyptian army began its advance. The army of 9,000 was commanded by the Sirdar, General Kitchener. The senior officers of the force were all British, the junior officers and troops nearly all Egyptian and Sudanese. As the army moved south along the Nile, the railway was extended with it from Wadi Halfa. The Khalifa was well aware of the advance and small Dervish forces skirmished with the invaders along the way. But only one significant clash occurred, on June 7, at Firket, where the Dervishes sustained more than 1,000 casualties and the Egyptians and Sudanese only twenty-one killed and ninety-one wounded. During the summer months the army halted due to an outbreak of cholera and to the seasonal drop in the Nile which prevented passage of the expedition's steamers. But on September 23, Dongola was occupied without opposition. Having attained his authorized objective, Kitchener returned to London to secure Cabinet approval for a further advance. He received it, along with a promise of British troops should he require them.

On his return to the Sudan, Kitchener faced a difficult decision. He knew his further advance would require more troops because, inevitably, as the army moved deeper into the Sudan, the Khalifa would make a stand, at some point, with all the forces at his disposal. Just as clear, in order to supply his larger force, Kitchener would need to extend the railway. If the railway progressed on its present course – along the giant southwestern bulge of the Nile between Wadi Halfa and Abu Hamed – Kitchener's engineers would encounter extraordinarily difficult terrain. And if the railway ground to a halt, his steamers would have great difficulty in traversing the cataracts between Merowe and Abu Hamed. Kitchener decided on a radical change in course, a change dictated by the only feasible alternative: a new railway would be built on a direct line across the Nubian Desert between Wadi Halfa and Abu Hamed. In the opinion of a young subaltern who would soon join Kitchener's force, and who doubled as a correspondent for *The Morning Post*, 'no more important decision was ever taken by Sir Herbert Kitchener, whether in office or in action.' 'The Khalifa', young Winston Churchill added, 'was conquered on the railway'.[27] Despite Churchill's hyperbole, there was considerable truth in his suggestion that once the railway reached Abu Hamed and Kitchener could supply and arm as large a force as the government would allow him, the Dervishes were doomed. The first sleepers for the 235 mile line were laid on January 1, 1897. Abu Hamed, already secured by a 'flying column' from Kitchener's force in early August, was reached on October 31, 1897. He was now poised to launch the second phase of his plan for the reconquest of the Sudan.

4

'A Smack at the Khalifa': The Sudan Campaign, 1898

On February 28, 1898, Clayton received orders to join Kitchener's army in the Sudan. He was not among the first; British troops had already begun arriving at Abu Hamed in January. The 1st battalions of the Warwicks, Lincolns and Cameron Highlanders – all from the British Army of Occupation in Egypt – arrived first, along with an Artillery detachment, trailing two large field pieces, six 5-inch howitzers and six Maxims. As additional support, the 1st battalion of the Seaforth Highlanders were moved from Malta to Egypt and it was this force that Clayton joined at the end of February. He left Alexandria on March 3, unable to conceal his excitement: 'I am so delighted at getting up at last,' he wrote to his mother, 'that I feel quite mad and ready to do anything. . . Tell Dad I am beginning to soldier now'.[1] He travelled in a baggage train with three other officers and twenty-five men of the Seaforths. One of the officers, Angus McNeil, would become a good friend and, a quarter-century later, would serve under Clayton in Palestine. Clayton had taken considerable care in preparing for the journey south and proudly described his kit to his mother: a bed valise 'which forms a bed, and then rolls up with all one's bedding in it'; an 'ordinary valise' for all his things; a small bag for the journey; a basket 'containing all necessaries for meals'; a tin basin, with leather cover, 'containing toilet apparatus'; and two cases of stores 'containing food of all sorts, such as tinned meats and soups, vegetables, tobacco and everything of that kind'. Clayton knew he would be unable to take most of this sizable kit with him to the front; marching-order baggage south of Abu Hamed would be limited to twenty-seven pounds. But he informed his mother of a 'rather neat thing' he had devised. All his stores were packed in two cases 'with equal quantities of each thing in each case'. If he had to leave one case behind, he would still have one case with 'a certain amount of everything with me'.

On March 6, Clayton reached Khizam, north of Luxor, where he left the train and boarded a post-boat for the journey to Assouan (Aswan). The journey seemed rather like a luxury tour, as the boat was a well-appointed Cook's steamer in which Clayton had his own cabin, 'a great score', he noted. At Luxor the boat stopped and the passengers, which included civilian travelers, disembarked for a moonlight tour of 'a magnificent old Egyptian temple'. Clayton thoroughly enjoyed the journey, though he found the people on board 'a very queer lot, except Lady Randolph Churchill and her son who are very nice'.[2] Again, on the 7th, the steamer stopped at Edfu, where, Clayton reported, 'we walked up and saw a most splendid old temple over 2000 years old, which was most interesting'.[3] The next day the steamer arrived at Aswan where he boarded a train for the short ride to Shellal 'to get over the cataract' and then embarked on an Egyptian government steamer bound for Wadi Halfa.

The signs of war were everywhere apparent now. At Shellal, Clayton observed the stark contrast between the island of Philae 'with the ruins of a most beautiful temple' and the nearby wharf 'with piles of coal and stores of all kinds lying about and gangs of convicts in chains unloading them from the trains and putting them on to barges'.[4] South of Aswan the landscape, too, changed dramatically. The river-fringe of vegetation had all but disappeared and the 'rocky, barren hills' now came right down to the river bank. By day, Clayton added, the scenery is 'arid and ugly, but the sunsets and sunrises are beyond anything you can imagine . . . and everything becomes tinted with the gorgeous colouring of the sky'. As if in acknowledgment of the contrast, the Army proclaimed that that all British troops south of Aswan would be considered on 'active service'. But the time soon began to drag for Clayton as the steamer, burdened by two massive barges attached to either side and heavily laden with stores, made very slow progress. Occasionally, and despite its shallow, thirty-inch draft, the boat ran aground on the Nile's sandbanks, further delaying the journey. An Egyptian major was on board and the young British officers amused themselves 'by learning some Arabic from him, which', Clayton added, 'is not only useful, but serves to pass the time'.[5]

On March 12 Clayton arrived at Wadi Halfa. He was met by Lieutenant Edouard Percy Girouard of the Royal Engineers, a French-Canadian who, though only thirty, had been put in charge of the construction of the desert railway. Clayton was assigned a 'curious little room with mud walls and roof . . . that abounds in scorpions and tarantulas'. His spirits picked up, though, when he was invited to dine with General Leslie Rundle, Kitchener's Chief of Staff, who was 'most kind and nice' to him. On the 14th, just as he was to leave on the desert railway for Abu Hamed, he received some exciting news – all troops were to push up quickly to the front; Mahmud Ahmad, the Dervish commander, was reported to be advancing from the south in the direction of Berber. Clayton travelled with eleven other officers in a 'saloon carriage', the men in 'covered trucks', as the train pushed across the burning Nubian Desert towards Abu Hamed. Like most British officers, he was also accompanied by a servant and a syce (groom), who had been sent on with his horse the day before.

Arriving at Abu Hamed on the 15th, the train stopped only briefly and continued on to the end of the line, which had now reached about half-way to Berber. At line's end Clayton boarded a sternwheeler and steamed for six hours to a point just north of the fifth cataract of the Nile. He and his fellow officers were now down to the last of their food, which, to his annoyance, had to be shared with another officer, 'a stupid ass who had brought nothing'. Tinned beef, some ration biscuit and 'muddy, dirty water' made their final meal. In order to circumvent the cataract, the party then mounted camels for a seven hour ride. Clayton enjoyed a good laugh at the expense of the Seaforths who cursed and groaned in anguish 'as the saddles were all very rough baggage packs and the Highlanders . . . don't wear anything under their kilts!'[6]

Finally, on March 17, two weeks after he had left Alexandria, Clayton reached the front at Berber. A 'very warlike place', Berber was enclosed by a *zareba* – a densely constructed wall of thorn bush – and was just seven miles north of the British camp at Kenur. As Clayton and the remaining Seaforths approached the camp they were delighted to find 'the road lined by Soudanese troops who cheered like anything' at the British advance. The Anglo-Egyptian camp had now swollen to about 14,000 men,[7] and the whole force at Kenur was in a tense state of readiness. The officers were ordered to 'sleep fully dressed with sword and revolver' at their sides, for, as Clayton noted, 'no one knew when the Dervishes might appear'. Kenur was located a mere five miles north of the junction of the Nile and the Atbara, a smaller river which, during the rains, flowed into the Nile from the south-east. It was now mostly dry. On the 20th Kitchener informed the troops that Mahmud Ahmad had left Shendi, far south on the Nile, had crossed east to the Atbara, and was now on that river, about twenty miles to the south. The order was given to 'march out and fight him'. However a five-hour march produced no sign of the enemy and the Anglo-Egyptian force ground to a halt at El Hudi, some five miles up the Atbara, where it erected a new *zareba* and encamped for the night. They next day the army moved another seven miles up river to Ras El Hudi, encamped again and constructed yet another *zareba*. Mahmud was said now to be only ten or fifteen miles away. Yet nothing happened; nor would anything happen for the next two weeks.

Kitchener would not have delayed the battle had he known that the Dervish army was then experiencing serious problems. The Khalifa's initial plan of defence had been formulated the previous summer: Mahmud had been ordered to reinforce Berber and to stop the invaders there. But he delayed, protesting to the Khalifa that his army was unwilling to march. On September 6, 1897, Kitchener seized the initiative and occupied Berber before Mahmud could rally his forces. It was the first in a succession of Dervish mistakes; had Mahmud acted quickly and reinforced Berber before Kitchener's force could move on the village, he might just have held up the Anglo-Egyptian advance. Now, the Khalifa began to experience supply problems, exacerbated by famine and a consequent failure of morale which, in turn, resulted in desertions from Mahmud's force. The Khalifa's logistical problem was to prove insoluble. He maintained a large force in Omdurman – more than 40,000 men – but once away from their base, the Ansar could not be supplied. Despite these problems, Mahmud was determined to move against the 'Turks'. The Khalifa agreed and ordered that Mahmud's force be strengthened by another commanded by 'Uthman Diqna (Osman Digna). But the young Mahmud and the wily veteran Digna disagreed on strategy. More time was lost while the dispute was referred to the Khalifa for resolution. Eventually, in February 1898, the combined Dervish force of Mahmud and Osman Digna moved east, arriving on the Atbara on March 19 in a much depleted and weakened state. They constructed a *zareba*, dug trenches and waited.[8]

By March 21, Kitchener knew precisely where the Dervish force was encamped, yet made no move to attack. It appears that despite his outward display of magisterial self-assurance, the Sirdar was undergoing a crisis of self-confidence. He pondered his options. He sought advice from Cromer who, in turn, consulted the War Office in London. Telegrams flew between Cairo, London and the front. But everyone, including Kitchener, knew that only he, the man-on-the-spot, could decide what to do. Kitchener's lack of resolve was nothing new to Cromer. Five months earlier the Sirdar had been strained to the breaking-point and had even tendered his resignation to 'the Lord'. Cromer ignored it. Now, while Kitchener wrestled with the course of action he should pursue, the troops at Ras El Hudi sweltered in the 'beastly hot' sun during the day and 'shivered with cold' every night. Kitchener tried to draw Mahmud into action; nearly every day British or Egyptian cavalry units were sent out and they often skirmished with Dervish patrols. On the 29th the British brigade were ordered to march out 'to try and engage the Dervishes, but they were not to be tempted'. On the same day they learned that two Egyptian battalions and an artillery battery that had been sent eighty miles up the Nile to Shendi, had taken the place and thus cut off Mahmud's line of retreat.

By this time Clayton had been joined by Lieutenant Owen, from his battery in Alexandria, and by Hunter Blair who would command Clayton's four-gun Maxim battery. Although he was pleased to see them, Clayton was getting fed up with Kitchener's inertia: 'We are all getting very sick of these continual alarms which come to nothing and everyone is longing to get at Mahmud and smash him . . . I do hope we shall come to fisticuffs with [him] as it will buck every one up and make them feel we have not come up here for nothing.'[9] Still the army sat. The ubiquitous George Steevens, who had joined the army to report for the *Daily Mail*, reported the effect: '[A]s lazy day seated after lazy day, the whole camp and the whole army began to dim into the phantom of a dream'.[10]

Unable to draw the Dervishes out, the Sirdar finally decided to move. On April 4, the force marched five miles closer to Mahmud's position. The next day a reconnaissance in force encountered a large Dervish contingent and got into a 'very tight place', barely managing to retire intact. Then, on the afternoon of the 6th Clayton and his fellow officers received their orders; they were to attack on the morning of April 8, Good Friday, at dawn. On the 7th the force again moved, to Um Dabia, a mere seven miles from the Dervish camp. Clayton looked forward to the battle with a mixture of light-hearted excitement and dim foreboding. 'I am in excellent health', he wrote home, 'my only ailment being a couple of boils (Ahem!) where I sit down.' But he fully expected the fight would be 'a precious tough job . . . I am afraid that we shall lose a good many men, as their position is very strong. However, we are all delighted to have got at them at last and everyone is eagerly looking forward to tomorrow'. In a postscript, he added: 'If anything should happen, after all it is better so, than in any other way.'[11]

At 6 p.m. on the 7th the army started. Two hours later they halted, ate some of their rations and rested until 1 a.m. on the 8th, when the march resumed. At 6 a.m. they arrived at a ridge, just 1,000 yards from Mahmud's *zareba*. The Dervish commander had constructed a large, oval enclosure, facing north with its back to the dry river-bed of the Atbara. The ground in front, cleared of scrub in anticipation of the attack, rose gradually to the ridge on which the Anglo-Egyptian force was now poised. The Sirdar's force formed up into a wide arc of some 1,500 yards facing the *zareba*. The British brigade, under General William Gatacre, comprised the left. Here, the Cameron Highlanders stood in front, in double-line formation. Behind them, in columns of companies, the Warwicks were on the left, the Seaforths in the centre, and the Lincolns on the right. To the right of the British, three brigades of Sudanese and Egyptians completed the arc. Interspersed among the infantry brigades were various units of artillery, including Maxims, Krupp and Maxim Nordenfelt quick-firing guns. As the infantry moved into position, at 6:20, the artillery opened fire. For an hour and twenty minutes the guns pounded the *zareba*. The Dervishes had a few of their own guns, but almost none were able to answer the crushing bombardment. Soon a fire broke out within the enclosure and the Dervish cavalry shot out on the British left but, as described by Steevens, 'tut-tut-tut-tut went the Maxims' and the Dervish horsemen turned away to the south in the direction of the riverbed.

At 7:40 the order to attack was issued. The drums began to beat, the pipes skirled and cries of 'remember Gordon' rose from the British attackers. Gatacre drew his sword and moved forward on foot, the Camerons in line just behind. The Dervish defence appeared formidable. Behind the wall of thorns was a stockade, then a triple line of trenches. Within the enclosure itself, perhaps 10,000 Dervishes lay low in a honeycomb of foxholes and rifle pits. On the right front of the *zareba*, opposite the Camerons' left, was a heavily reinforced stockade. Facing this defence work, to the left of the Camerons, stood Hunter Blair and Clayton with four Maxims. Behind them, next to the Warwicks, Owen commanded two more. As the Camerons began their deliberate march towards the *zareba*, a staff officer galloped up behind their line and shouted in the direction of Hunter Blair's Maxims. Clayton described the action from that point:

> When the line advanced we were told to go out and cover the attack so we ran out to a little hillock about 100 yards ahead of the line and about 300 yards from the enemy. Here we found out what it was like being under fire with a vengeance, for the bullets came buzzing round like anything. I noticed one plough up the dust between my feet and plenty whizzed round one's ears. We opened fire on the part that the Camerons were advancing on, and all the time were well peppered from the stockade on the enemy's right. Presently the Camerons got too close for us to go on firing across their front, so we turned our attention to our friends in the stockade and fairly peppered them. Presently they could stand it no longer and bolted out across open ground on the right to gain the bush – very few of them reached it however, as immediately they got out into the open we got on to them and shot nearly all.[12]

The Dervishes had nothing to answer the Maxim. Weighing only forty pounds, the gun was highly mobile and could be pulled quickly into position on its two-wheeled carriage. It was capable of firing ten rounds per second over a range of 2,500 yards, and, at the close range used at the Atbara, its effect was devastating.[13] Each gun was operated by only two men and, as Clayton noted, 'they were more or less protected by shields, so that . . . the officers are the only ones really exposed'.

Cutting across the front of the Maxims, the Camerons soon reached the *zareba*, pulled it apart at points, and streamed through. On the right, the Egyptians and Sudanese carried the wall at about the same time. The Dervishes fought bravely for a time, but were soon in full retreat, falling back towards the riverbed. The attackers showed no mercy; fleeing and wounded Dervishes alike were shot or bayoneted. 'Even Dervishes holding out the traditional mimosa sprig of submission were ruthlessly shot, bayoneted or clubbed. "Tommy was as bad as the Blacks"', added the Sirdar's brother, Walter Kitchener.[14] Clayton, who followed the Camerons through the *zareba*, but did not fire again, provided a reason why even the wounded were killed: 'You had to keep your eyes well skinned going through their camp . . . as they were hiding about and taking pot shots at you and also the wounded would stick a spear into you if you were not careful.'[15]

From the start of the Camerons' advance until the cease-fire sounded only forty minutes had elapsed. The British lost three officers and twenty men who were killed or later died of wounds; eighty more were wounded. The Egyptian and Sudanese units suffered fifty-eight killed and some 400 wounded. As for the Dervishes, Clayton reported that '3,000 dead or wounded were counted in and round the *zareba* and in the river'. It was, he concluded, 'a very warm affair while it lasted'. The Anglo-Egyptians remained on the battlefield 'til 4 p.m. in a blazing sun, no shade, with the most fetid smell pervading the whole place'.[16] They then marched back to camp. Clayton was 'fairly done', having gone thirty-six hours without sleep and eighteen without food. The first major fight in the reconquest of the Sudan was over.

On April 12, Clayton and the British brigade arrived at Darmali on the Nile, fifteen miles north of the junction with the Atbara. Here, the brigade went into summer quarters, sitting for four months, waiting for another British brigade to be assembled in Cairo and for the seasonal rise in the Nile which would allow passage of the force's gunboats up river for the final assault on Omdurman. Clayton was relieved to be able to stand down from the state of readiness the force had been in for weeks. 'I got my underclothes washed,' he wrote to his mother, 'and not before they wanted it, as I had not even had them off for eight days and they were to say the least "unsavoury".'[17] Darmali was a miserable place, treeless, unbearably hot and very dusty. The officers and men were quartered in mud huts and each officer had a small tent as well. The force was 'fairly hard up for something to do'. Life in camp was 'more than monotonous,' Clayton complained; 'it is but an existence and every day the programme is the same': reveille was at 5 a.m.; 'then parade, whether fatigues or a short march out'. Breakfast was at 8, stables from 9.30 till 10, 'then sit in our mud hut and read or write'. The mules were watered at 12, lunch was at 1, and then 'again sit indoors till 4'; then tea and, at 4.30, water and feed mules; 'then out for a ride or a walk – come in and have bath and shave – dinner at 7 and bed at 8.30'.

'This happens every day without variation and I fear that by the time our three months here is over we shall we shall have degenerated into Soudanese vegetables.'[18] The officers were offered a one month leave, which they could take in Cairo or even Constantinople or Athens. But Clayton, always conscious of unnecessary spending, decided to stay in camp and 'stick it out'.

The men tried to devise ways to amuse themselves in the 'dead alive hole' of Darmali. Clayton first inventoried his 'loot' from the Atbara – two very good *jibbas* (white Dervish shirts with coloured, sewn-on patches) and six spearheads – and sent them down to Wadi Halfa 'to avoid losing them'. The officers then began cutting out pictures from the illustrated papers and pasting them up on the walls of their huts. On April 1, Clayton started a diary, though he frankly admitted there was not much worth recording in it. Still, he asked his mother to save all his letters, as he was 'dependent on them for writing up all the earlier part of the campaign at a future date'.[19] There was little in the way of hunting round the camp; the weekly 'bag' consisted only of doves and sand grouse. Because there was no cover in the arid land-scape, the few gazelles in the area could not even be approached for a rifle shot. Gymkhanas were organized on a regular basis and every conceivable sort of horse, donkey and camel race was devised. Clayton entered for a pony race, 'but one had to ride over 11 stone 7 lbs and, saddle and all, I could not make myself more than 11 stone 2lbs, so I could not run'. The men also put on concerts and acted in farces, some of which, Clayton reported, were 'distinctly risqué'. The officers played polo 'of sorts' in the desert, and fished in the Nile. Clayton would have enjoyed a regular dip in the river, but swimming was allowed at only one place which was 'always crowded with highly scented and twotty Tommies', so he went only once.[20]

Every young officer coveted the honour of being mentioned in a despatch, but Clayton knew he would not be mentioned in the Sirdar's despatch describing the battle; he had not been long enough with the expeditionary force for that. He was delighted to learn, though, that the Khedive had sanctioned the issue of a Sudan medal, with clasp 'the Atbara'; 'so I have got one medal at any rate', he informed his mother. Although he had little of interest to report, Clayton dutifully wrote home every week and, while he did not hesitate to describe the discomforts of Darmali, his letters were tempered with unfailing good humour. In a June letter he provided the menu for a dinner he hosted with Russell, a fellow officer: soup, partly tinned, partly ration beef; fish, 'caught by Russell in the river'; 'jugged hare, shot by Russell'; beefsteak and preserved vegetables, from rations; 'sandgrouse, shot by me'; corn-flower, strawberries and stewed dates; 'slices of bologna sausage on toast'; Pilsner beer, whiskey and soda and rum (from rations); coffee; cigarettes and cigars.[21] An argument with his syce provided Clayton the opportunity for more humour and hinted at his growing store of Arabic:

> I . . . managed to explain matters, by dint of summoning my entire Arabic vocabulary of bad language (which is extensive) to my assistance. . . I proceeded to inform him that his ancestors had been "like pitch", that he was the same and that his descendants would be the same. I also explained that

he and all his were "dogs and sons of dogs" and that they would probably be buried "in a dunghill" and various other pleasantries. He then retired with a kick (not on the back but near it!) and profuse apologies, calling down every blessing on the heads of me and my family.[22]

Although Clayton decided not to take any leave that summer, he did enjoy a three day barge trip down the Nile, along with seven other officers and some seventy men. The trips were organized every week to provide some relief from the monotony of Darmali. Towed by a sternwheeler, the barge stopped at Berber, Abadir and Quininetti, north of which the party moored at a spot with large palms and grassy banks and enjoyed a day of swimming and shade. By this time, early July, the Nile had already started to rise and Clayton's thoughts turned to the resumption of the campaign: 'I hope that another six weeks will see us on the march . . . There is some talk of the Khalifa having evacuated Khartoum or being about to do so – if this is true we may possibly go on almost at once, but I think it is only a rumour. Personally, I hope the whole thing does not fizzle out, as it would be very mortifying not to have a smack at the Kahlifa after we have been stewing up here all summer.'[23]

On July 6, Clayton celebrated his twenty-third birthday and stood two of his fellow officers – 'and myself by the way' – each to a pint of champagne at dinner. The next day he was delighted to receive a 'splendid birthday budget of letters' from England. Clayton eagerly looked forward to letters from home and took the keenest interest in family news. He was pleased to learn that his sisters, Ellinor, Phyllis and Mary were being sent abroad for a year, but warned his mother that 'if they come back with spectacles, banded hair, bloomers and no waists, I shall disown them, also I will not be corrected when I make slight mistakes owing to a deficient education!'[24] He often sent his sisters Egyptian stamps, and cautioned them to save those with 'Soudan' printed across them, as, he thought, they were sure to become valuable. Unusually, he received a letter from his father, who 'provided particulars about how we stand in money matters'. He promptly reminded his mother that he was due to be promoted lieutenant on November 2 – the third anniversary of his commission – when he would receive a pay increase of 1/3d per day, 'which comes to £22.10.0d per annum, so that next year he [his father] must knock that amount off my allowance'.[25]

By mid-July the troops had eagerly begun preparations for the advance on Omdurman. Orders had been issued directing the newly assembled British brigade, the 2nd, to leave Cairo for the Sudan. This would bring British units in the Sudan to 8,200 men, and raise the total force to 25,800. Three new gunboats had also been ordered and shipped in pieces to Berber where they were assembled for the advance. Clayton enjoyed seeing Kitchener pass Darmali on one of them, the *Melik*, which looked 'exactly like a miniature man of war. The Sirdar was standing up on board, smiling away, as pleased as Punch, and letting off the steam syren, just like a child with a new toy'.[26] And then, only three weeks before his battery was to break camp and join the advance, Clayton fell ill. On July 22, he began to feel 'very queer' with a high temperature, 'splitting head, and acute diarrhoea'. Two days later he was moved to hospital. The doctors feared enteric fever – typhoid. They had good reason; fifty British deaths were ascribed to typhoid in the Nile camps that summer and several more probably occurred among soldiers sent home with the disease. But slowly Clayton recovered, deeply grateful that the doctors had got to him early on, for he well knew that had he contracted enteric fever, 'it would have been Good-bye to Khartoum'.[27] On July 30, 'weak as a cat', he was released from hospital and, twelve days later, left Darmali with his battery. The final campaign had begun.

The British brigade travelled by steamer to Wad Habashi, a camp on the Nile 120 miles south of the junction with the Atbara and only sixty miles north of Omdurman, the Dervish capital. The Egyptians and the Sudanese were already there, awaiting the British and the artillery. 'We all seem to have perked up and taken a new lease of life now that we are going on', he wrote to his mother. His kit was limited; besides what he stood up in, he took only his bed valise in which was rolled up one shirt, three pairs of socks, one pair of drawers, one spare pair of breeches, one spare jacket, a toilet hold-all, his writing case and 'two cholera belts'.[28] By August 22, the Anglo-Egyptian force of nearly 26,000 was fully assembled just south of Wad Habashi. The combined fire power was imposing: forty-four guns and twenty Maxims among the land force and thirty-six guns and twenty-four Maxims installed on ten gunboats.

On August 25, the army began the march south. During the next two days they marched some twenty miles round the Shabluka (6th) cataract, arriving at El Hajir on the 27th. At Shabluka the Khalifa missed another opportunity to stop, or at least impede, the invading force. At points round Shabluka the Nile narrows to a mere 100 yards and well-positioned defenders could have created severe problems for the Sirdar.[29] Recognizing this, the Dervishes had earlier constructed five forts in the narrow defiles surrounding the river. Inexplicably, they had been abandoned and now Kitchener's gunboats passed without resistance through the narrows to the open waters south of Shabluka. Here, Clayton fell ill again with diarrhea and 'a slight touch of dysentery', but not enough to cause him to fall out.[30] The march continued. By August 30 they were within twenty-five miles of Omdurman. On September 1, the army halted at Kereri, just six miles north of the city. The Dervishes were reported nearby, so a *zareba* was hastily constructed on the west bank of the river at the village of Egeiga. The British and Egyptian infantry brigades were formed into a 2,000 yard arc inside the perimeter of the *zareba*, facing west, with their backs to the river. The gunboats had already moved six miles up river to Omdurman where they began pounding the city. Six 5-inch howitzers, firing fifty pound shells with the new lyddite explosive were landed on the east bank, opposite the city, and joined in the bombardment. A few shells found the great white conical dome of the Mahdi's tomb, a symbol of Mahdist inviolability, now crumbling.

Towards nightfall on September 1, the gunboats turned back to the north, taking up positions for the night next to the Anglo-Egyptian army and playing their powerful searchlights across the plain of Kereri looking for any Dervish movement. The Khalifa's army was there, waiting, four or five miles to the west of Egeiga. Its total strength was – and is – unknown. Estimates range from 35,000 to 60,000; the official post-battle report reckoned the total at 52,000. Whatever the true Dervish strength, and to the Sirdar's great good luck, they did not move that night when the Anglo-Egyptian force was most vulnerable. General Archibald Hunter, in command of the British division, later described his fear of a night attack: 'So long as [the] enemy came on in daylight I had no fear. But my conviction till I die will be that if he had attacked us in the dark before dawn, with the same bravery he attacked us next day by daylight we should have been pierced, divided, broken and rolled into the river.'[31] But the Dervishes were not known for night attacks; the commanders were unsure of their ability to control the Ansar in the dark. Also, it is possible that the Khalifa was uncertain about the exact location of the Anglo-Egyptian army; he may have thought the force at Egeiga was an advance post and that the main force was behind the Kereri hills to the north-west of the village. This thinking may have explained the Khalifa's election to forego a night attack; it does not support his decision to attack across the open plain of Kereri – where the full and devastating effect of superior British firepower could be brought to bear – instead of in the streets and alleys of Omdurman. As Hunter observed, a 'house-to-house defence . . . would have been quite another affair'.[32]

The Dervish attack began just before 6 a.m. on Friday, September 2, 1898, when Clayton first saw the advance of 'about 35,000 or 40,000 strong in three huge lines stretching as far as the eye could see, cheering and shouting with banners waving'. At 6.15 the artillery opened up on the advancing Ansar at 3,000 yards. The infantry and Maxims joined in at 1,400 yards. The Dervishes had their own artillery, but the shells they sent over 'nearly all burst a shade too high and hit the ground behind us'. Clayton continued:

> At this juncture a large force poured over the hills to our left and advanced to attack but were checked by the artillery fire, so [they] marched across our front and joined the centre attack, suffering heavy loss. The centre column consisting of thousands of men still pushed on with marvelous bravery in spite of the terrific fire and enormous losses . . . Meanwhile a fierce attack had been delivered on the Soudanese from the hills on the right, the enemy getting within 200 yards in places; it was however eventually beaten back by the fire of the Soudanese and Egyptians assisted by the gunboats from the river, and they retired along the hills. At 8 a.m. the "Cease Fire" sounded.[33]

Clayton's battery alone had loosed off 36,000 rounds in this first phase of the battle and, he said, 'made some good practice'. But the battle was not quite over. After the cease-fire, the 1st British brigade had been ordered to march on Omdurman and was moving along the river across a low range of hills when, Clayton added, 'we heard a terrific fire going on, on the right'. A large force of Ansar had streamed out of the Kereri hills to the north and attacked the right flank of General Hector MacDonald's Egyptian and Sudanese brigade. The 1st British brigade, with Clayton's Maxim battery, 'at once wheeled to the right and advanced at the double over the hill and down on to the plain'. Here, 'the bullets were flying pretty thick' and several of the Cameron Highlanders fell close to Clayton. But when the Dervishes saw the relief arrive, they drew off. Only one Ansar warrior 'got up to the bayonets' of the Sudanese. Clayton's Maxims, however, were 'hedged off by the Egyptians and had to advance behind them, so that we did not get in a shot, which was very annoying as we were losing men from the enemy's fire as they retired'.[34]

Clayton did not witness what has become the best known action of all the Sudan campaigns – the charge of the 21st Lancers, made famous by its most famous participant, Winston Churchill, in *The River War*. But this cavalry charge into a ravine concealing some 3,000 Dervishes, including hundreds of Osman Digna's infamous Fuzzy Wuzzy warriors, was as ill-advised as it was costly. Fully forty percent of the Anglo-Egyptian casualties at Omdurman were sustained by the 21st Lancers, and even that arch-defender of imperial warfare George Steevens thought the charge a disregard of orders and a 'gross blunder'.[35] Still, three British soldiers were awarded the Victoria Cross for conspicuous acts of heroism exhibited during those few minutes of savage hand-to-hand fighting in the ravine, and it is for this reason that the charge of the Lancers is often regarded as one of the last great cavalry engagements in British history.

By 10.30 a.m. Omdurman was over – 'not a battle,' Steevens noted, 'but an execution'.[36] The total Anglo-Egyptian losses were lighter than the Atbara; fifty-one dead and 382 wounded. The Mahdist casualties were stunning by comparison: 10,800 dead, at least 16,000 wounded and 4,000 taken prisoner. The Khalifa only just escaped. Mahdism was dead. On Sunday the 4th, Clayton, Owen and a few representative officers and men from each Anglo-Egyptian unit boarded boats for the three mile trip up river to Khartoum, where they attended the Gordon Memorial Service. The Dervishes had abandoned Khartoum in 1885, leaving the symbol of imperial decadence to rot in the Sudanese sun. But now, amid the ruins of the former governor-general's palace, the avengers assembled to pay a long-overdue homage to the great imperial martyr. They bowed their heads in prayer, listened to a funeral march and the hymn 'Abide with Me', after which the British and Egyptian flags were hoisted, 'God Save the Queen' and the Khedivial anthem were played and the guns fired a salute. The troops then fell out and wandered about the old palace ruins and the weed-choked gardens. Clayton climbed to a balcony on the top of the house and was shown 'the exact spot where Gordon had been killed'.[37]

That afternoon he was back in Omdurman where he toured the Mahdi's tomb and the Khalifa's house with Friedericks, a colleague from the Engineers. They 'got the *yuzbashi* [captain] of the Egyptian regiment there to collect us some loot, including two marble inscriptions from the walls of the tomb'. The next morning the British division was ordered to parade through the streets of Omdurman. But that afternoon Clayton and Friedericks returned to the tomb 'to fetch our loot and found that the *yuzbashi* had made a very nice collection & put it by for us, but unfortunately the Sirdar had been round that morning and happened to see it and had collared the lot. It was very mortifying as, if there had been no parade in the morning, we should have fetched it then.'[38] This would not be the last time that Kitchener would make off with property intended for Clayton.

On September 7, a Dervish steamer arrived from the south, surrendered to the Sirdar and reported that the French were now at Fashoda. Clayton did not accompany the Sirdar on his subsequent trip south for the tense meeting with Captain Marchand that came to symbolize Great Power rivalry in the 'scramble for Africa', a meeting that nearly brought the British and French to war over that tiny village in the middle of a swamp. In 1902, Clayton would himself visit the place and puzzle over its significance. But now he received orders to return to Egypt with his battery. He left Omdurman on September 9, and arrived in Cairo nine days later. He was soon enjoying dinner at the Turf Club and playing squash racquets and cricket at the Gezira Sporting Club. Immediately applying for leave, Clayton received an 'indulgence passage' on the *Dilwara*, bound for Southampton, and reached England on October 7. Although he would later rise to the rank of brigadier-general in the army, his fighting days were over.

5

Bimbashi: Clayton in the Egyptian Army

The next year passed uneventfully for Clayton, but just as he was preparing to depart for England on his autumn 1899 leave, exciting news arrived from home: War with the Boer Republics now seemed certain and the Cabinet had decided to send British troops to South Africa. For a twenty-four year old subaltern in the Artillery, a South African war offered great opportunities for adventure and glory and Clayton eagerly looked forward to his expected reassignment to the Cape. It did not come. As the weeks passed, the need for soldiers in South Africa steadily increased as the British learned that the well-organized and determined Boers presented an adversary far different from the primitive Ansar warriors of the Khalifa. During the 'Black Week' of mid-December 1899, British troops were defeated by the Boers in three separate actions, sustaining losses of 7,000 in killed, wounded and missing. Returning to Egypt in January 1900, Clayton still held out hope for new orders. All round him soldiers who had been deployed in the fight against the Khalifa were being dispatched to the Cape. Yet, as it became increasingly clear that he would not be among them, a new opportunity appeared for Clayton – the Egyptian Army.

Among the many men leaving Egypt for South Africa were several British officers employed by the Egyptian Army and the need to replace them soon became pressing. The modern Egyptian Army had existed since the days of Muhammad Ali, when it formed a formidable fighting force. But after the rout of the Egyptians by British forces at Tell el-Kebir in 1882, the Army was disbanded and then re-formed under British leadership. From 1883, all the senior positions were held by British officers and appointment to the Egyptian Army soon came to be regarded as something of a 'plum job'. In the early days, their numbers were small – only twenty-six at first and, ten years later, just sixty-four. But the officers who joined saw the opportunity for enhanced pay, increased responsibility and little risk of jeopardizing their long-term prospects. They were not required to relinquish their commissions in the British army, but were instead 'seconded' for up to seven years (after 1902, for ten years), serving under a series of contracts each signed by the commander – the Sirdar – of the Egyptian Army on behalf of the Khedive. Career risk was further minimized by a rule that allowed the seconded officer to resign on three months notice if he found that Egypt did not suit him. Failing that, he would revert to his British regiment at the expiration of his contract without loss of prospect or promotion.[1] Only if he stayed on in Egypt after ten years would an officer lose his claim to regimental promotion, relinquish certain pension rights and be relegated to 'half-pay' status. An Egyptian Army position was sought after for another reason. A young British lieutenant or captain was immediately vested with significant responsibility; he entered the force as a *bimbashi*, the equivalent of a major in the regular army. But the most appealing feature of Egyptian Army service was an immediate and substantial increase in pay. Frank Stirling, a Sudan colleague of Clayton who joined in 1905, described his experience:

> The system of selection for the Gyppy [Egyptian] army had been established by the Sudan. A candidate might be strongly recommended by the Commander-in-Chief [of the British army] . . . but he had no hope of getting in unless he was vouched for by an officer already in the Egyptian service. Once appointed he would be taken on in a series of four contracts, two of two years and two of three, making a total of ten. Should he in his first contract prove undesirable, both he and his backer would be dismissed at the end of their respective contracts. Consequently officers in the Egyptian Army were extremely careful in adopting a nominee. I was fortunate enough to be selected at the end of my first year in Alexandria. It was a most welcome rise in pay, from £10 a month as a lieutenant in the British Army to £50 a month as a *bimbashi* in the Egyptian, and now that my financial problems were beginning to be solved I became confirmed in my belief that life was worth living.[2]

For Clayton there was still another reason for joining. Unlike Stirling, he had been commissioned in the Royal Garrison Artillery and '[t]he prospects of the R.G.A. had become hopeless. . . , as they had fallen several years behind their Field Artillery contemporaries in the matter of promotion'.[3] Doubtless Clayton took all these factors into consideration. And he did not need to search for a sponsor. Major Malcolm Peake, a fellow veteran of the River War, warmly recommended him and on November 12, 1900, Clayton signed his first contract with the Sirdar. Now a *bimbashi* in the service of the Khedive, he would receive £E540 per year, subject only to a three-month probationary period at £E440.[4]

Within three weeks of signing his contract, Clayton found himself on a train bound for Khartoum. There was no surprise in this. With the elimination of Mahdist rule after Omdurman, it was decided that the British and the Egyptians would jointly govern the Sudan, a new form of imperial rule with a new name – the Condominium. Fully sixty-five percent of the Egyptian Army was stationed in the Sudan, as was Clayton's commander, Major Peake, and the reasons for deploying the bulk of the Army there were obvious. The British government was very reluctant to incur *any* expense relating to the Sudan after the 1896–98 campaigns and had grudgingly consented to a British garrison of only six infantry companies in the whole country. Since the Egyptian Army was paid for by Egypt, the obvious solution was to use that army for defence and the maintenance of order in the Sudan. This well suited Lord Cromer. He was very doubtful about the efficacy and loyalty of the Egyptian Army anyway, holding the opinion that many young native officers had imbibed too deeply at the wellspring of Arab nationalism and could not be trusted in their Egyptian stations. He was happy for them to be stationed a thousand miles away in Khartoum. 'The best thing to do with the Egyptian army in time of war, as also in time of peace,' he wrote, 'is to keep the greater portion of it in the Sudan'.[5] Sir Reginald Wingate, who, since December 1899, held the dual positions of Sirdar of the Egyptian Army and governor-general of the Sudan, was in full agreement with this policy. And, he agreed for another reason that had nothing to do with Egypt. British officers in the Egyptian Army provided a ready source of manpower for the new Sudan administration he was developing. Of the sixty-seven British officials in the Condominium government at the end of 1901, forty-six came from the Army. And all the provincial governors were military men, as no civilian was appointed to such a post until 1909.

The reconstruction of Khartoum was still in its early stages when Clayton arrived in December 1900. He was stationed at Halfaya, on the east bank of the Nile, just north of the city and the junction of the White and Blue Niles. His house, shared with another British officer, was 'quite a nice one, as houses go here,' he wrote to his mother, 'but is of course entirely built of mud with no windows or doors or plaster, or any such products of civilization'.[6] But Clayton was not by nature a complainer and he enjoyed his new work. After his house-mate was reassigned at the end of December, he was left in command of two field batteries, each comprised of six 75-millimeter Maxim Nordenfelt guns and two horse artillery 'galloping Maxims'. He also was put in charge of two garrison company depots. He enjoyed his new responsibilities and by January, was already settling into a routine of a type enjoyed by many British officers across the Empire. Rising early, he would attend parade and drill, instructing his junior officers and men in the operation and maintenance of the guns. He kept three horses and once a week after morning drill he would join his men in tent-pegging, racing across the desert at a gallop, lance in hand, plucking small targets out of the sandy landscape. After a quick breakfast, he then would join Major Peake for two or three hours of office work. But from noon or 1 p.m., the remainder of his day was free. Afternoons might find him across the river at Omdurman, enjoying four chukkas of polo with his fellow officers. On other days he would play tennis in Khartoum, shoot sand grouse outside the city, or even get up a foursome for a round of golf on the local course scratched out of the desert. Clayton's diaries for 1901–2 were also filled with dinner engagements with the few dozen British officials stationed in Khartoum. On other evenings he would dine with friends at the all-British Sudan Club in Omdurman, usually staying afterwards to play bridge. The Sudan was already becoming a tourist destination for those interested in extending their Egyptian holidays for a trip further up the Nile or for big-game hunting and Clayton would often meet or see-off the 'tourist train' at its terminus in Halfaya. Sometimes, he was invited to the governor-general's Palace in Khartoum and occasionally even joined Lady Wingate for breakfast or dinner. And every Sunday, unless out on patrol or prevented by weather, he would attend services, then held at the Palace, as there was no Anglican church yet in Khartoum.

Because the British community in Khartoum was so small, Clayton inevitably got to know well all the important men in the Sudan administration. After Wingate himself, the most important and certainly the best-known figure in the country was the Inspector-General, Rudolf Slatin or, to give his full name, Baron Sir Rudolf Karl von Slatin Pasha. An Austrian, Slatin had come to the Sudan in 1878, served under Gordon and was captured by the Mahdi's army in 1884. Imprisoned for eleven years at Omdurman, he escaped in 1895, and became Wingate's assistant in the Intelligence Department of the Egyptian Army. In 1896 he published a widely read account of his exploits, *Fire and Sword in the Sudan*, and two years later he was with Kitchener at Omdurman, savouring the crushing defeat of the Khalifa. A life-long friend of Wingate, he was appointed Inspector-General in the Condominium government three months before Clayton arrived. Slatin seemed to go where and when he pleased in the Sudan and it was widely recognized that no European possessed a more thorough knowledge of the country and its peoples. Clayton first met him during the 1898 campaign and it was Slatin who, after Omdurman, had shown Bertie the spot where Gordon had been slain by the Dervishes. Their paths crossed often in the following years, until his Austrian citizenship debarred Slatin from returning to the country after the outbreak of war in 1914. Clayton also soon came to be on familiar terms with Wingate's three most important advisers, the financial, legal and civil secretaries, who formed the inner circle of the Sudan government.

Clayton's appearances at the Palace inevitably put him into frequent contact with the Sirdar and governor-general himself, Sir Francis Reginald Wingate. In one capacity or another he would work for Wingate for the next eighteen years and there is no question that Wingate was the most important and influential figure in Clayton's early career. Born in 1861, into a middle-class Scottish family, Wingate, like many of his subordinates, had graduated from the military academy at Woolwich. He joined the Egyptian Army in 1883, and, nine years later, was appointed its Director of Intelligence. He served in the 1898 campaign in that role, was present at Omdurman and at Fashoda and, a year later, was deputed by Kitchener to track down the Khalifa. Wingate found him on November 24, 1899 at Umm Diwaykarat, 180 miles south of Khartoum. The remnants of the Mahdist army were routed by Wingate's force; the Khalifa was found dead, his face pointing towards Mecca.

Kitchener had served as the first governor-general of the Sudan after Omdurman, but when he was ordered to South Africa in December 1899, Wingate was appointed to succeed him, both as Sirdar and as governor-general. There seems little doubt that Clayton got on well with Wingate from the start. On May 9, 1901, only six months after joining the Egyptian Army, he was ordered by the Sirdar to assume temporarily the duties of Staff Officer for the Khartoum district, while the officer regularly holding that position went on extended leave. Clayton's delight at the appointment springs from the pages of his diary, even though he noted it would mean relinquishing a scheduled visit to England: 'My leave done for!'[7] In fact, the staff officer position in Khartoum – if occupied even on a temporary basis – held out great promise, for it was recognized as a stepping stone to the post of deputy assistant adjutant general, one of only two positions held by *bimbashis* on the headquarters' staff of the Army.[8] Clayton received more good news when he learned that he had been promoted to the rank of captain in the Garrison Artillery. Still conscious of his position in the British army, he promptly sent in his application to Peake for transfer from the Garrison to the Field Artillery where, as noted, the opportunities for promotion were much better.[9]

Despite his enhanced responsibilities as a temporary staff officer, Clayton's social activities continued undiminished, interrupted only occasionally by distant rumblings of possible revivals of Mahdism in the shape of various 'false Mahdis' and by the violent, periodic summer storms known as haboobs. A new and formidable Mahdi never appeared, but the storms were real enough. Arising quite suddenly on the horizon, a great cloud of dirt and dust, sometimes miles across and thousands of feet high, would sweep across the desert, so well-defined that it appeared like a solid wall moving inexorably towards the city. The force of the wind, often accompanied by torrential rain, was so great that it brought life in Khartoum to a stand-still. 'Had to spend two hours holding doors and windows to prevent their blowing in,' Clayton noted after a June 1901 haboob; 'everything flooded'.[10] He was caught outside when another haboob struck later in the summer and was so blinded by the storm that he lost his way, something then difficult to do in a town so small as Khartoum.

The leisurely pace of life in Khartoum was also broken by numerous holidays – eighteen of them were celebrated annually by 1914. And, in deference to the Muslim population, every Friday was observed as a 'holiday' and all government offices were closed. Although no Egyptians occupied the higher ranks in the Sudan government, the dual nature of Anglo-Egyptian rule was accorded a nod by celebrating the Khedive's birthday every year on September 15. This also provided one of the very few occasions on which British soldiers mixed with their Egyptian subordinates – they were invited to breakfast. At the time, the gulf separating Briton and 'native' was taken for granted. It would have been regarded as unusual, and undesirable, were the British and the Egyptians – far less the Sudanese – to mix socially. In part, this was a product of the insularity that characterized British communities throughout the Empire. No doubt it was also an inevitable aspect of empire: the British were rulers, the Egyptians and the Sudanese the ruled. And perhaps it was in some measure a result of what would later be called ethnocentrism. It is hardly surprising then that, at the turn of the nineteenth century, the vast majority of Britons (and there is nothing in Clayton's papers to suggest that he was not among them) never reflected on the issue at all.

In September 1901, Clayton's brief tenure as staff officer ended when he was ordered to lead a patrol into the eastern Sudan. Army patrols were a common feature of British rule in the first decades of the Condominium. They served a variety of purposes. Some were punitive, like that undertaken in January 1902, when a British officer, Captain Scott-Barbour, was ambushed and killed by a Dinka tribe near Rumbek in the Bahr al-Ghazal. Wingate reacted quickly. Two patrols were immediately sent into the area. More than a hundred Dinka were killed, tribal leaders were executed and 'not more than a dozen houses [were] left standing in the district'.[11] Other patrols were exploratory, as vast areas of the Sudan were still unknown to Europeans at the turn of the century. In 1904, *bimbashi* D. C. E. ffrench Comyn led an expedition into the upper reaches of the Pibor River, a tributary of the Sobat, which, in turn, flowed into the Nile. Penetrating further than any previous explorer, ffrench Comyn later published his maps with the Royal Geographic Society.[12] Still other patrols were made in conjunction with survey parties, often undertaken jointly with neighbouring colonial powers, for the purpose of delineating the Sudan's eastern, southern and western borders, large segments of which were still undefined. Finally, and most frequently, patrols were sent out simply to 'show the flag'. In the early years of the Condominium there were so few government officials in the provinces, and the area over which their responsibility stretched so vast, that many inhabitants had never laid eyes on a British government inspector or an Egyptian or Sudanese provincial official (*ma'mur*), much less the governor, the *mudir,* of the province.

The patrol led by Clayton during October – December 1901 was of this last variety. Traveling north from Halfaya by train, he assembled his patrol at El Damer on the Nile. In addition to Clayton and another British officer, Bulkeley Johnson, the patrol consisted of several Egyptian officers, twenty NCOs and men, twenty-seven horses, a detachment of cavalry (50 horse), one donkey, two Maxim guns and fifty-four transport camels. For the next three weeks the patrol moved south and east, generally following the course of the Atbara and covering 15–20 miles per day. Typically rising at 4 a.m., the men would march from 5 till noon. Afternoons were reserved for resting and hunting. Game was plentiful, if unremarkable, and Clayton carefully recorded the contents of his 'bag': guinea fowl, hare, gazelle, ariel and dik-dik. The trip was otherwise largely uneventful, the territory covered by no means *terra incognita*. At specified points the patrol came upon dumps of rations and forage, delivered for them in advance. Twice they even received mail, delivered from Kassala, a large town and provincial headquarters to the south-east. And the local sheikhs they encountered, well familiar with a government presence, were all friendly, frequently supplying the officers with fresh meat, milk and eggs. Not until October 30 was there any change in this pleasant routine. On that day it was reported that two gunners and a cavalryman had stolen sheep from a nearby village. Clayton presided over the ensuing court martial and summary justice was rendered: 'Gave them 30 lashes each', he tersely recorded in his diary.[13]

Near Sofi, a small village 340 miles from their starting point, the Atbara was joined by the Setit, a river flowing in from the east. Leaving most of the patrol to rest for a week, Clayton and Bulkeley Johnson headed up the Setit with a handful of Egyptian officers, a cook, four local guides, two camelmen and some pack animals. This was more difficult country, featuring dense jungle and more varied wild life, including lions which at night were kept at bay by maintaining a large fire till dawn. After fifty miles, they stopped, just short of the village of Umbega, 'beyond which,'

Clayton noted, 'is debatable land, the Abyssinian frontier not yet having been settled'.[14] Returning to the Atbara at Sofi, Clayton gained the admiration of the local natives by shooting a hippopotamus. He later described the scene to his mother: 'You should have seen the natives cutting him up and quarreling over the meat. They were all crawling about inside the huge carcass, almost naked and smothered in blood and gesticulating and jabbering like a lot of monkeys.'[15] The patrol then left the river and proceeded west, some 110 miles, to Howata on the Rahad, a tributary of the Blue Nile. Following the Rahad in a north-westerly direction they soon arrived at Wad Medani, a large town near the junction of that river with the Blue Nile. From Wad Medani, Khartoum was little more than 100 miles further down the Blue Nile, and in seven days the patrol was back in Halfaya. In total, they covered nearly 1000 miles in 55 days. Clayton thoroughly enjoyed his first patrol. He returned 'fit as a fiddle' and, he recorded, 'what with the regular open-air life and hard exercise, I was as hard as a nail'.[16] Although great fun and good exercise for Clayton, and perhaps good training for the men under his command, it is difficult to see what the patrol accomplished for the Sudan government. There was no need to pacify any of the tribes in the areas covered by the patrol. Nor was it apparent that any needed to be convinced or even reassured as to the existence or primacy of the British position in the country. Yet patrols such as that undertaken by Clayton continued to be a regular feature of the Condominium government for years to come.

Clayton resumed his regular duties and in January 1902, took his battery up the Nile to the Egyptian Army artillery training camp at Wad Ban Naqa, near Shendi, for a month of exercises. But by mid-February he was on the march again. From Shendi he proceeded to the Atbara and on the 26th he camped in the 'old British Maxim battery lines of '98' where four years earlier he and his fellow gunners had made short work of the Dervish army. He then proceeded to Berber where he was to be posted with his battery for the next two years. However, while dining with friends at the provincial headquarters on the evening of March 3, Clayton fell ill. Feeling 'seedy', he stayed in bed the next day. Now seriously ill with headache, severe back pain and a temperature of 103°, he was dosed with quinine and phenacetin, medications typically used to treat malaria. The local Egyptian doctor came to see him on the 8th and administered more of the same. Neither worked and the following day his temperature rose to 104°. Two days later he was carried to the station and placed on a special train for Halfaya. There, he was put in bed at the home of a friend and a nurse was sent over from Khartoum. It was touch-and-go for Clayton, but by the 13th his condition slowly started to improve and his temperature was down. Two days later he was able to eat solid food, his first in twelve days. On the same day, friends cabled Clayton's parents to let them know he was recovering. There seems little doubt that Clayton had suffered a recurrence of the malaria he had likely first contracted in 1898, after the Atbara. At intervals, the disease would continue to plague him for the rest of his life.

On February 17, his illness now behind him, Clayton received welcome news. Peake had granted him four months leave. Clayton left El Damer by train on the 28th, arriving the next afternoon at Halfa, just short of the Egyptian frontier. Here, the Nile traveler had to proceed north by steamer, as the railway had not yet been completed to Shellal, two hundred miles to the north. Clayton boarded the steamer *Toski* and reached Shellal on the evening of April 1. Here he again caught a train, arriving in Cairo twenty-four hours later on the evening of April 3. His total journey of nearly five days was then typical for a traveler making the slightly longer trip from Khartoum to Cairo. After dining with the Sirdar and Lady Wingate – also on their way home – Clayton travelled to Alexandria the next day where he 'saw all the old crowd at the club' and found time to visit his former billet at the Mustapha Barracks, just outside the city.[17] On the 5th he boarded the S.S. *Bohemia* of the Austrian Lloyd line for Trieste. The voyage was a pleasant one, interrupted only at Brindisi, on the heel of the Italian boot, where all passengers were subjected to the standard and compulsory quarantine inspection. But they were soon on their way, and reached Trieste on April 9. Proceeding overland by train, Clayton travelled to Vienna and then through central Europe to Brussels. Crossing from Ostend to Dover, he at last arrived at Charing Cross Station, London on April 11. He had made good time, his journey from El Damer to London lasting just two weeks.

Clayton relished his leaves in England and spared no expense on either himself or his family and friends. Although he spent most of his time during the next fourteen weeks at Sandown with his family – meticulously totaled at the back of his 1902 diary at fifty-three days – he also enjoyed thirty-four days in London. There he took a room in Jermyn Street, attended several plays and dined at some of the city's most fashionable clubs and restaurants, including the Trocadero, the Savoy and the Café Royal. He met his fifteen year old brother Iltyd in London, put him up in a room next to his in Jermyn Street, treated him to breakfast at the Primrose Club and then showed him round 'the Shop' at Woolwich. He also took his brother John (Jack), just turned fourteen and already decided on a navy career, to Portsmouth where they toured the great naval yard. And Clayton had plenty of time to spend with his sisters, Phyllis and Mary and, later, Ellinor, who arrived home from a holiday in Malta in early June. He visited his 'Eastfield Granny' several times in Ryde and took the train, or bicycled, round the island to visit his many aunts and uncles. A far less pleasant feature of his 1902 leave involved ten separate trips to a London dentist where, in early May, he 'had the remainder of his teeth out', and two months later was fitted with a plate.

Conspicuously absent from Clayton's diary is any mention of a romantic interest. He did spend four days in Ireland in late May at Kilmannock near Waterford visiting with Violet Barrett-Hamilton and her family. And Violet's name and address appear as the very first entry in the 'addresses' section of his 1902 diary, but whether she was anything more than a good friend to Clayton must be left to speculation. Clayton also found time to visit his old headmaster from the Isle of Wight College, Canon Teesdale. And his diary is filled with bicycling, cricket and golf engagements. Of official obligations there is almost no mention, although this would change significantly during leaves taken in later years. Early in his holiday he did meet with an officer in charge of the Sudan section of the Intelligence Division at the War Office, but Clayton provided no description in his diary of the nature of their talk. He also attended the Royal Artillery's annual regimental dinner in June and visited the London club of the Artillery, but neither was obligatory and both more likely just provided enjoyable evenings in town. On July 28, Clayton spent his last day in England with Iltyd, who showed him round his school, Lancing College, and who had the pleasure of receiving three school prizes, handed out by the Bishop of Rochester, in the presence of his elder brother. The next day he boarded the train at Victoria Station, bound for the Sudan.[18]

Clayton arrived at Berber in northern Sudan on August 11, and would have started for Halfaya the following day but 'a very bad haboub' came up, sections of the railway were washed out, and he was delayed in returning to his battery until the 15th. During the next several weeks he returned to his familiar schedule: duty in the morning, afternoons occupied by polo, tennis or golf, and evenings by dinner and bridge at the club in Omdurman. But on October 7, 1902, this pleasant routine came to an abrupt halt. 'I was asked,' he noted in his diary entry for that date, 'if I would accept a billet in the Civil [government] in the Bahr el-Ghazal and I accepted.'[19] For the remainder of the month Clayton busied himself with preparations for his new assignment. He consulted Slatin on life in the south, sold his ponies to friends, discharged his three servants and his syce, and engaged a 'black boy' as a new servant. On November 1, 1902 he boarded the Nile steamer *Dal* for the south.

6

'It Ain't All Violets Here': Inspector in the Southern Sudan, 1902–1903

In 1902, the southern Sudan comprised roughly twenty-five percent of the entire country, perhaps 250,000 square miles. Although it was not in any way politically distinct from the rest of the Sudan, the region still exhibited many differences. It was generally regarded as consisting of those lands between the Great Lakes of Central Africa in the south and the east-west running stretches of the Bahr al-Arab, Bahr al-Ghazal and Sobat rivers in the north. It might be said that to the south of those rivers, Africa started. To the north of them, the country was generally arid, the people Arab and Muslim. To the south, the climate was tropical, the population black and mostly pagan. The north was predominantly Arabic-speaking; in the south some eighty different languages were spoken. 'Culturally the north [was] linked to Egypt and the wider Arab world, the south to Africa and the cultures of the peoples of the Congo, Uganda and Kenya.'[1]

The south was first penetrated by the Egyptians in 1840, during the *Turkiyya* (1825–85), when Egypt held sway over the Sudan. But the Egyptians could hardly be said to have established firm control over the region. That much was apparent because the area was dominated from the 1850s by traders, first in ivory and then in slaves. In the 1860s the Khedive Isma'il sought to reassert Egyptian authority over the area and to crush the slavers, first by employing the explorer Sir Samuel Baker and then through Gordon, as governor of Equatoria, in the far south of the region. The large slave traders were effectively stopped. But, on the strong insistence of his European creditors, the Khedive abdicated, Gordon resigned and the southern Sudan reverted to its traditional ways. The *Mahdiyya* arrived in 1884, but it too was unsuccessful in subjugating the south. At first the Mahdi's forces scored some notable successes, but they were soon repulsed in Equatoria and, despite periodic attempts to re-establish their authority, never came close to controlling the region. Nor did Islam hold the slightest appeal for the local population, much less the militant and messianic brand of Islam espoused by the Mahdi.

By the 1880s the southern Sudan had become a chessboard on which the European Powers played their game for control of the headwaters of the Nile. At various times, the Germans, Italians, French and Belgians all contemplated moves on the Upper Nile. But the Germans dropped out in 1890, the Italians in 1891, and, as seen, the French retired near the end of the decade after the Fashoda crisis. This left only the Belgians in the game with their king, Leopold, well positioned to the south-west in the Congo Free State. Although a determined player, Leopold could acquire only one piece, a small wedge of territory on the Upper Nile near Uganda called the Lado Enclave. And this was acquired only as the result of an uncharacteristic diplomatic gaffe by the British, usually adroit players in the 'scramble for Africa'. Still, the lease of the Lado Enclave created only a life estate in Leopold; when he died in late 1909, the Enclave reverted to Britain and the Belgian gambit ended.

Although the Belgians were not as much of a threat as the British imagined, it was the incessant scheming of Leopold that precipitated the British advance into the Bahr al-Ghazal in December 1900. Initially, the area was designated a military district, but on January 1, 1902, the Bahr al-Ghazal province was formed. To the east, another *mudiria* was created a year later, from the Fashoda military district, and denominated the Upper Nile province. A chunk of the latter province was broken off in 1906 and reconstituted as the Mongalla *mudiria*. With the transfer of the military districts to civil jurisdiction, the officials posted to these provinces assumed civilian designations identical to those used in northern *mudirias*. A British *mudir* was assisted by one or two British inspectors who, in turn, supervised the work of the lowest-ranking officials, the *ma'murs*, these lower posts being held by Egyptians. Before Clayton left Khartoum in the *Dal*, he was designated an inspector and transferred from the Army to the 'Civil', a step simply accomplished by a stroke of the governor-general's pen. The transfer had no effect on his status or rank in the Army: 'Peake has said that he will always take me back into his Artillery again,' he assured his mother, if 'I want to go back'.[2] Such transfers were, in fact, commonplace and the pages of the *Sudan Gazette* – the official record of the government's proceedings – are filled with the names of officers oscillating back and forth between the Army and the 'Civil'.

A posting to the Sudan's southern provinces was one to which few, if any, British officers looked forward. Although the average tour of duty in the Bahr al-Ghazal has been reckoned at twenty-nine months, it was probably considerably shorter in the early years of the century. Turnover among *mudirs* was equally rapid; seven governors served in the province between 1902 and 1914.[3] For Clayton, the assignment was 'quite an experiment' and 'a new move and entire change of life and work'.[4] This was considerable understatement, as he would soon learn. The combination of danger, disease and climate made appointments to the southern Sudan one of the most challenging assignments in the Empire. The chance of being murdered was fairly slim, although Scott-Barbour's death at the hands of the Dinkas occurred just a few months before Clayton left Khartoum. But disease was common, and the Sudan had experienced all of the most virulent epidemics – small pox, cholera and typhoid. Dysentery and malaria were familiar maladies. Captain W. H. Hunter, who had led one of the punitive expeditions following the murder of Scott-Barbour, was himself felled by the dreaded blackwater fever, a fatal complication arising from repeated malarial attacks, only four months before Clayton arrived in the province. The man who reported Hunter's death, *kaimakam* (lieutenant-colonel) E. H. Armstrong, was killed by an elephant the following April.[5] If these facts of life in the south were not daunting enough, the climate was sure to give any prospective official pause. It was miserable; insufferable heat and humidity alternated with four or five months of unremitting rain. Camels and horses could not live in the Bahr al-Ghazal at all, and two British officials in the province chose to resign, 'rather than face another rainy season'.[6] The effects of the enervating climate were compounded by loneliness. As Clayton himself would experience, it was not uncommon for a British official to spend weeks, even months, away from his colleagues. In 1906, Wingate received an alarming report concerning a Captain Logan who had been 'all the summer practically alone at Mongalla'. It was reported that 'he did not look well, that he had "a wild look in his eyes" and . . . was suffering from African irritability in a high degree'.[7] On top of all this, there was not a single improved road in the province and in 1902, the telegraph line from Khartoum stopped at Renk, more than 400 miles to the north of Wau, the provincial headquarters.

As he left Khartoum on the *Dal* Clayton had some notion of the conditions he would face, but had no idea yet of his ultimate destination. That would be decided by the *mudir*, *kaimakam* W. S. Sparkes, when Clayton reached the provincial head-quarters at Wau, 900 miles to the south. His boat, the *Dal*, was an old, paddlewheel steamer. Used in the River War, it had delivered Kitchener to his 1898 confronta-tion with Marchand at Fashoda and was now employed for transport and river-clearing operations. Attached to the *Dal* was a barge bearing a large store of rations, thirty Sudanese soldiers, eleven mules, Clayton's donkey and fifty civilian native men, women and children. Adding to the cacophony emanating from this crowd, the *Dal*'s labouring engines caused the boat to throb and shake so much that Clayton, describing his journey in a letter home, found that he could not manage at a table, but had to write on his knee. Pouring with perspiration from the heat, he was able to write only by placing a handkerchief over the paper to 'prevent it from becoming pulp'. Anticipating the difficult times to come, Clayton was travelling light, only 'taking the oldest of things' with him. Apart from his few necessities, he had ordered a camera from Cairo and had purchased a '.450 cordite double barrel big game rifle', necessary, he wrote, 'for beasts like lions and elephants. . . [F]or big game hunting one wants the very best article'.

Already, the country through which the *Dal* moved was changing. Just south of Khartoum the flat banks of the Nile were covered with coarse yellow grass and mimosa scrub, giving way a little back from the river to 'the inevitable desert'. But within a day or two the banks, though still flat, were getting 'green and fresh looking', and there was 'any amount of geese, duck, teal and water fowl of all descrip-tions to be seen'.[8] By November 6, the *Dal* reached the village of Renk, a non-descript place, notable for Clayton only because it marked the first appearance of the seroot fly: 'He is an awful brute about the size of a wasp, and just as you are thinking of nothing in particular, he settles on you and digs his proboscis into you, which feels just like a red-hot needle going into your flesh and raises a most painful blister.'[9] As soon as the seroot fly retired for the evening, the mosquitoes appeared, in droves, and dinner had to be finished and the mosquito netting brought out, before nightfall.

Two days later the *Dal* arrived at Fashoda, a site already famous in Anglo-French relations. Clayton was unimpressed, but appreciated the significance of the spot. 'It does not appear to the casual observer to be a place worth making much fuss about,' he wrote, 'but of course its possession, and that of the country above it [i.e., to the south], means the control of the Nile basin which is everything to Egypt and the Sudan.'[10] At Fashoda Clayton also encountered the Shilluk, one of the three great tribes of the southern Sudan, the others being the Dinka and the Nuer. He could not say much about their clothing, 'conspicuous by its absence', but was struck by their hair 'trained into the most extraordinary shapes . . . and plastered with mud to keep it in shape'. Some of the Shilluk, he added, 'improve (?) their appearance by plastering themselves with [a] sort of white clay, which gives them a most ghastly appearance'.[11]

Just south of Taufiqia, which the *Dal* reached the next day, the Nile seemed to split, as the Sobat flowed in from the east and Bahr al-Ghazal from the west, the latter river being augmented by two rivers flowing down from the south, the Bahr al-Jabal and the Bahr al-Zaraf. To the east and south of Taufiqia was the country of the Nuer and Clayton took an impish delight in titillating his family with the danger he faced. 'Although a fine tribe', he wrote, the Nuer were 'unfriendly to the government'; they 'have a playful habit of skinning people alive when they catch them and making their skins into drums, so that they are to be treated with reserve'.[12] The *Dal*, however, turned west, reaching the mouth of the Bahr al-Ghazal on November 11.

Here, Clayton had his first experience with sudd. As he described it, 'the sudd is a great [floating] tangle of vegetation which forms on the river in the upper reaches. . . and gets so thick, if allowed to remain, that it completely blocks the channel and becomes like the land'. The sudd formed formidable barriers on most of the great rivers of the southern Sudan. In places it was so thick that trees grew on it and even the largest game, elephants and hippos, could traverse it. One giant block of sudd on the Bahr al-Jabal measured more than twenty-two miles in length and four separate sudd-clearing expeditions, spanning several years, were required to clear the obstruction. The sudd was the greatest impediment facing any outside power wishing to exert its authority over the region. It had impeded the Egyptians and defeated the Mahdists. The British persevered, and prevailed, only after years of costly and dangerous sudd-clearing operations. As early as December 1899, Clayton's commanding officer, Malcolm Peake, had begun sudd-clearing on the Bahr al-Jabal, opening more than eighty miles of the river. The methods used to clear sudd were simple, if laborious. A steamer encountering a block would first raise a full head of steam and ram the obstruction head-on in an effort to force its way through. This method worked for the *Dal*, which encountered blocks only 100–200 yards in length on the Bahr al-Ghazal during Clayton's journey south. If ramming failed, though, the crew would unpack shovels, axes, picks and saws and assault the obstruction by cutting down through four-yard square portions of the sudd block. The cut section was then circled with a wire hawser attached to the steamer, which would reverse its engines and pull the section free, allowing it to float down river.[13] But here there was risk, for, as Clayton observed, '[t]he danger is that if you fail to force through, the sudd may close in behind you and you cannot get either way'.[14] In such a remote area as the southern Sudan this posed a serious danger; as late as 1915, forty people starved to death on a steamer trapped in the sudd.[15]

On November 13, the *Dal* reached Mashra' al-Raqq, a pestilential island of mud situated in the middle of a swamp that stretched in every direction as far as the eye could see. The *Dal* could proceed no further, there was no British officer at the place, and Clayton had to wait four days before a smaller steamer, the *Tamai* arrived from Wau to collect him. Meanwhile, he slept aboard the *Dal* which 'lay in a stagnant, stinking backwater, which breeds so many insects and mosquitoes that they fairly jostle one another'. 'The first night I did not sleep a wink', Clayton added, 'as I had unwittingly left a small chink in my mosquito curtains and in a twinkling the mosquitoes were in full possession and I was almost eaten alive'.[16] Finally, the *Tamai* arrived on the 16th and Clayton left the following day, travelling forty miles north to the mouth of the Jur. This river posed problems no less formidable than the Bahr al-Ghazal. During its first eighty miles on the Jur, the *Tamai* crept through an immense swamp, and the channel of the river was narrower and more winding than the Bahr al-Ghazal. Since there were no trees in the swamp and since the wood-fired steamers could not carry a sufficient supply of fuel to reach Wau, the journey south had to be completed in stages. Leaving the last wood station, on the Bahr al-Ghazal, the steamer would travel fifty miles south on the Jur, where it would stop and everyone would disembark and transfer to small native boats which would take them another twelve miles along to a barge anchored in the stream. Here, they would await a steamer approaching from the opposite direction, carrying just enough wood to reach the passengers on the barge, turn round and return to the first wood station south of the swamp.

Cumbersome though this process was, it paled in comparison to the problem of proceeding down the Jur itself. The stream was so narrow and featured so many sharp corners, that the steamer was often unable to negotiate the turns and the crew was forced to jump into the river and swim to the reeds lining the river's edge. They would then tie ropes to clumps of vegetation and use the steamer's winch to pull the boat through the turn. Often the process had to be repeated several times to get through a particularly acute angle in the river. On November 22, despite working all day, the crew of the *Tamai* was able to travel only eight miles up the Jur. Three days later the barge was reached, but no steamer had arrived from Wau to collect them. For six days Clayton sat on the barge, waiting. He could not go ashore; there was none, only 'interminable swamp', the view of which soon got 'monotonous and depressing'. He was 'getting very sick and bored of it' when yet another problem arose – the river began to fall rapidly. The rainy season now over, the Jur would soon drop to a point that it would be impassable. Clayton recognized that 'matters will be serious if [the] steamers don't come soon'.[17] Leaving the river was impossible; there was no way to get through the swamp. If the steamer did not arrive, they would be trapped until the river rose again, months later, by which time their rations might be exhausted. But finally, on December 1, and to his great relief, Clayton saw in the distance the smoke from a steamer. It was the *Warrana* from Wau. 'The most cranky little craft you can possibly imagine', the *Warrana* had somehow been cobbled together from two aluminum barges that Marchand had abandoned when he left Fashoda in 1898. Twice during the next few days the boat sprang leaks that quickly had to be plugged with rags and cement. Clayton, jammed on board with forty natives who had been marooned with him on the barge, described the conditions:

> If you go from one side of the boat to the other, the mere fact of shifting your weight across makes her heel till you think she must capsize . . . [I]f you stay on the lower deck it is impossible to get more than a yard or so from the boiler and furnace and you are almost roasted alive, while if you go up above there is no shade. And in addition there is always a rain of sparks and chunks of burning wood from the funnel. All our clothes were burnt all over in great holes! In addition the steam pipe runs along the deck with nothing to cover it up and if you are strange to the construction of the animal, you are apt to rest some portion of your body on it and burn yourself badly as I did the first day! To crown all she makes such an infernal panting and puffing that you can hardly hear yourself speak.[18]

The *Warrana* had other problems. One-half her stern-wheel was broken, making a straight course – had one been available – impossible. And she encountered the same difficulties as the *Tamai*, particularly the challenge of negotiating the endless turns and corners of the Jur. But, at last, on December 3, they escaped the swamp, reached land and tied up at a wood station where they stayed for four days. Here, Clayton found relief as he was able to go ashore, exercise and hunt, the jungle teeming with wildlife – hippos, crocodiles, duck, geese and 'cranes of all kind'. By December 7, they were underway again. But the river was continuing to fall and several times the crew had to be turned out to fasten ropes to the steamer and drag it over sandbanks, a particularly dangerous operation because at this point the Jur was 'swarming with crocodiles'. Clayton shot at several, wounding them. But the many hippos he saw in the same area he left undisturbed for fear that if he merely wounded one, it would charge the boat and capsize it. On the 10th the steamer ran aground again and, despite six hours of effort, they were unable to haul the *Warrana* over the sandbank. There was no choice; they decided to send her back downstream to Mashra' al-Raqq, and to walk the remaining eighty miles to Wau. But on the 12th, as they were about to leave the river, a native sailing boat, a *felucca*, arrived on its way down from Wau. Some of the party, including Clayton, went aboard the *felucca*, the remainder proceeding on foot. Still, even the smaller *felucca* had to be hauled over sandbanks several times.

Finally, on December 18, Clayton arrived at Wau. The 900 mile journey from Khartoum had taken him exactly seven weeks. His first impressions of his new post were favourable:

Wau is such a pretty place – you would almost imagine yourself in England. It stands on the left bank of the Jur River and is just a clearing in the forest, which encloses it on three sides. On the opposite bank of the river is a large grass plain extending for about a mile back from the river and beyond that is forest again. . . To look at it one could not imagine it anything but the healthiest of places, but I believe fever is prevalent during the rainy season, probably owing to the large amount of vegetation.[19]

Colonel Sparkes was in charge at Wau and when Clayton arrived he found two other British officers there, Sanders, who commanded a detachment of Sudanese troops, and Nickerson, a doctor. Clayton spent the next few days unpacking, exploring the immediate countryside and learning his new duties. On the 24th he shot three guinea fowl for the station's holiday dinner, but noted the next day that it 'was not a very exciting Christmas'.[20]

Clayton's duties as inspector were hardly well-defined. Several years later a provincial administrator described an Inspector's duties as covering 'taxation to prisons . . . municipal improvements to supervising schools'.[21] But in 1903, the Bahr al-Ghazal had no prisons or schools and taxes would not be levied in the province for another seven years. Municipal improvement was a dream for the future. Clayton's job could better be described as 'doing whatever needed to be done' and, as Sparkes was leaving soon on an extended patrol, Clayton reported that he 'has handed practically everything over to me'. Among other responsibilities, he was charged with securing food supplies for all officials and troops in the province, preparing the *mudiria's* budget, monitoring the rubber and ivory trade, constructing and repairing bridges and roads, administering the law, inspecting and maintaining government property and running the 'city' of Wau.

Like most inspectors in the early years of the Condominium, Clayton was ill-equipped by either training or experience to perform any of these tasks. Yet, he undertook his new responsibilities with characteristic brio, as he described in a letter home:

The "city" of Wau has to be looked after and one is a sort of mayor, district council and sanitary authority all in one. Among other trifles two stores and four houses have to be built and nearly all the houses re-thatched before the rains. There are of course besides any number of small things to keep an eye on, such as the station garden, cattle, etc. You will see from this that one has plenty to occupy oneself and even if one were absolutely alone, one would never be dull.[22]

Since Sparkes was about to leave, he also turned the budget over to Clayton, who had never before prepared one. He had 'something like £20,000 to be accounted for under various votes – rations, transport, personnel, etc.'.[23] And he was left in sole charge of the province's office. Sanders, in command of the Sudanese troops, 'had nothing to do with any of the civil work', and, as Clayton was left with 'only a very second-rate Syrian clerk', he had 'to do almost everything'.[24] 'Almost everything' included considering the divorce petition of a Sudanese soldier:

> A gentleman came up the other day and asked to be divorced from his wife (a native of this place). I asked his reasons and he said that (1) she was getting old and ugly – he was right! (2) she wouldn't work and make bread or marissa [beer]. (3) He was tired of her and wanted to marry someone else. (4) She was a shrew and always nagging. My own senses assured me on point (1). The native officer corroborated on the score of point (2), and, as the lady burst into a flood of abuse and recrimination directed at everyone indiscriminately, point (4) seemed to be established. DECREE NISI granted, but man forfeits her dowry, which he had paid to her people (£1.)! All parties satisfied and man marries again next Day! Such is the simplicity with which the Gordian Knot is severed in these parts.[25]

Clayton's legal training was limited to one course in military law given at Woolwich and, in deciding cases, he could draw upon only his considerable reserves of common sense and an innate sense of fair play. Both were brought to bear when he presided over a baffling murder trial in February 1903:

> A man came in the other day to the native officer at Tonj and complained that a Sheikh had killed his mother, so O[fficer] C[ommanding] Tonj sent them both in here. When I interviewed the Sheikh, he said "Oh yes, I killed her, but she was a witch and killed two of my children and various other people by her enchantments." He then gave a very detailed account of the various enchantments which she had used. I then turned to the plaintiff and he said "Yes, he is quite right – she was a witch and killed several people by sorcery. I am sorry I said anything about it and I think the Sheikh did quite right and I hope you won't do anything to him." He even refused to take five cows from the Sheikh, which is the price of a life according to native custom. I was then rather defeated, so I fined the Sheikh five cows (equivalent to about £25) as a warning and told him that if he ever did anything of that kind again he would probably be shot. He was most apologetic and said that he was very sorry, but he had not understood the new arrangements quite, but would be careful not to do such a thing again.[26]

Of greater concern to Clayton than his judicial, office and town work was the responsibility of ensuring an adequate food supply for the people in his charge. 'My chief anxiety here is whether I can get enough for everyone to eat. The staff of life here is dhurra (a sort of Indian corn). Out of this the blacks make their bread and their marissa (a sort of beer), so if it runs short it simply means starvation.'[27] By May he had secured enough dhurra to last through July, but needed another 30,000 pounds for August and September, and could not secure it. There was food in some places in the far reaches of the province, like Shambe, but that was 250 miles away and transport was not available. More than 200 transport camels had been sent down the previous autumn, but every one had died by March. Mules were in short supply and, in any event, could not travel during the rainy season. Nor could he pay for native carriers; they were busy planting their crops and would not be available till June at the earliest. He continued to wrestle with the problem throughout the spring.

Although his numerous duties as inspector kept Clayton busy, he still had free time, especially during the rainy season which started in May. In February his camera arrived and he enjoyed taking pictures of Wau, the flora and fauna of the area and the natives ('unfit for publication', he cautioned his family, as 'all the people are stark naked'). Hunting, a pre-occupation of all British officers serving in the southern provinces, also took up much of Clayton's time. By May, he had specimens of bush-buck, waterbuck, roan antelope, reedbuck, white-eared Kob, tiang (antelope), oribi (a small gazelle), Jackson's hartebeest, wild pig and giraffe, in addition to a wide variety of birds. He had plenty of time to read, too. Books were abundant, as officers passing through Wau customarily left in the mess-hut the volumes they had finished. Clayton enjoyed historical biography and military history, particularly accounts of nineteenth-century conflicts. He also took several papers and nearly every mail brought issues of the *Weekly Times, Punch, Sketch, World, Army and Navy Gazette, Field, Nineteenth Century, Review of Reviews* or *Spectator*. Although *The Times* arrived at least six weeks after publication, even when he received several issues in one mail, he would read only one per day, in strict chronological order.

By May 1903, Clayton had also assembled a large selection of pets to keep him company. He described the 'menagerie' to his mother:

> First there are my two little anthropoid apes or "dog-faced" baboons. One of these is perfectly tame and the other very fairly so. The tame one rushes to me whenever I go near and clings tightly round my leg, screaming with rage whenever I go away. Then there are two kittens which I have got up from Meshra with some difficulty, as there are none in the country and these are imported. I want to get them tame and let them live in my house and the mess, as the place swarms with mice and rats. Thirdly, there is a leopard cub, which I got not long ago – he is a jolly friendly little beast and will play with me as long as I like to keep it up. Last but not least there is a huge great brute of a chimpanzee, which was brought in the other day from away down South. He is hardly to be called a pet yet and, as he is somewhat uncertain in temper, I am rather afraid of him. He is immensely powerful . . . so he is a nasty customer to get the wrong side of. Last night he got his rope entangled round one of the posts of the verandah and when I and my servant tried to extricate him, he got furious and seizing my servant by the hand, bit his finger to the

bone with his great strong teeth. At other times he is perfectly friendly and quiet and lets one scratch him and pull him about. He is more horribly and weirdly human than you can possibly imagine, as he does not leap and run about like other monkeys, but walks about in an upright position or just sits down and gazes round with a bored expression. There are none of them about anywhere near here and the natives never tire of looking at him and most of them honestly think he is a human being. He certainly looks like a little old man, and when he and a hideously unintelligent looking black, who does odd jobs for me here, are squatting on their "hunkers", side by side, one looks every bit as human as the other – In fact I think that of the two, the "chimp's" face is the more intelligent and has more expression.[28]

Apart from his hobbies and his pets, Clayton was conscious of the importance of getting on well with the natives. He had no trouble in resolving their various disputes and was certain 'they realize perfectly that one tries to be absolutely just and impartial'.[29] And he was careful not to interfere in their activities. Every Thursday night he was kept awake by the native men, drunk on marissa, and 'tom-toming' and 'yelling' well into the early morning hours. On March 10, 1903, the first day of the Muslim festival of Lesser Bairam, he was besieged by 'all sorts and conditions of people. They all express the wish that I shall very shortly be made a pasha, and expect to be tipped for the kindly thought'.[30] Yet, despite his good relations with the natives, Clayton was always aware of his own vulnerability in the country, particularly when alone and venturing outside Wau: 'One always goes about armed and with an escort when outside the Government stations. Not that anyone is likely to attack one, except in the very out-of-the-way places, but still these blacks are not to be trusted and if they thought they had a good chance of knocking one on the head and looting one, they might do so.'[31]

Although he enjoyed his hunting, reading, photography and pets, and his good relations with the natives, Clayton's greatest joy came in the shape of letters from home. Mail was delivered to Wau once per month and, by 1903, every two weeks, if the boats and carriers could get through. A letter posted from Sandown usually took about six weeks to reach Wau. When mail came by carrier, the men came out of the forest and across the plain on the other side of the Jur, and Clayton was glued to his telescope, focused on the forest's edge, awaiting their arrival. When the mail was due and 'day after day goes by and it does not turn up', he found it 'maddening in the extreme'.[32] When the mail arrived and he received nothing from home, he was cruelly disappointed. But he usually got a 'full budget' of letters from his mother, brothers and sisters. He replied only to his mother because 'I really cannot screw up enough news in this somewhat dead-alive spot for more than one family letter.'[33] As seen though, Clayton took pains to make his letters interesting to those at home, filling them with vivid and entertaining accounts of Wau and his experiences there. In style, they were similar to letters that many young British officers wrote from their imperial postings, expressed with bonhomie and a light-hearted insouciance that often masked the difficult conditions of life in challenging and dangerous regions. Clayton also took a keen interest in events at home, and especially in the efforts of Iltyd and Jack to pass their exams for entrance into the Artillery and Naval academies. And, since his pay was now substantial — £E660 per year as an Inspector in the Civil, with an additional £E6 per month in 'climate pay' – he was happy to send money home and even to pay allowances to his sisters. He also sent generous cash presents to the entire family at Christmas and even loaned his father £100.

Occasionally, though, the unpleasant realities of life in the Bahr al-Ghazal crept into Clayton's letters. Wau was only about seven degrees of latitude above the equator and it seemed always to be hot. In early April he reported a high temperature of 103°F and a low of 84°. The day-time heat was similar to that of Khartoum, but the nights were hotter and 'very much damper'. Later in April, the rains began and, by May, it began raining hard and nearly every day. There was no escaping it, for even the best-thatched roof leaked. He had to interrupt a May 10 letter because 'a smart shower was falling inside my house'.[34] And, as Clayton had earlier observed, the rainy season also meant sickness. Even before the 1903 rains arrived, Sparkes, Nickerson and Sanders were all down with fever and Clayton was himself feeling very 'seedy'. In early March he had a 'go' of fever. But the fever was different from that he had experienced in the north. It came on very suddenly, knocked him flat for two or three days, and then he was up again 'except for feeling that I had been well beaten all over'. Every attack – and he was to suffer them every two or three weeks for the remainder of his time in Wau – was exactly the same, but 'no apparent evil effects remain[ed]'.[35]

Clayton seemed to be bothered less by these recurrent bouts of fever than by the solitude he now had to endure. Soon after Sparkes left in mid-January, the doctor, Nickerson, was called away and then Sanders 'had to go off to Rumbek at a moment's notice'. He was slightly unnerved at first, writing to his mother that there was 'no Englishman or white man of any kind within 200 miles of me'. But, typically, he made light of the situation: 'I have been alone here for nearly a fortnight and to tell you the truth I am getting a little "fed up" with my own society – charming though no doubt it is'.[36] Soon, consumed with his solitude, he began to analyze it:

> I always find that one rather enjoys the first week or so when one is alone; then
> for the next fortnight or so it becomes more unbearable every day until one
> feels that one would embrace a crossing-sweeper if he came along – After that
> it begins to get better and one settles down with oneself, so to speak, until
> finally, after a month or two one looks upon the arrival of a fellow creature as
> almost an intrusion and quite resents it.[37]

By the middle of May 1903, the rain, the periodic fevers, the loneliness and resulting boredom were beginning to take a toll on Clayton. After recounting all these problems in an uncharacteristically revealing letter, Clayton summarized life in Wau for his mother – 'You will gather from this that it a'int all violets here'.[38] But at the end of his letter, Clayton left a tantalizing clue of changes to come; a new *mudir* had been appointed to temporarily relieve Sparkes, and 'I expect him up here in about a week, when I shall leave almost at once and take ship to Khartoum'. The next day he wrote to his father with the exciting news – he had been appointed deputy assistant adjutant general on the headquarters staff of the Egyptian Army. This was a 'plum billet' for a *bimbashi*, as the only other Major on the staff was the Sirdar's aide de camp. In 1901, he had served only a few months as staff officer in the Khartoum district – the traditional stepping stone to the DAAG position – but now he had 'jumped straight into the coveted place without ever dreaming of getting it'. True, his annual pay would be reduced from the £E732 per year he was receiving as an inspector in the Bahr al-Ghazal, to £E660 as a staff officer in Khartoum (and even £E60 less while serving in Cairo), 'but there is no comparing the two jobs from the point of view of advancement'. He had some regrets. He would like to have stayed on in the south until 1904, perhaps to shoot a couple of elephants and buffalo and to take part in 'one or two punitive expeditions next winter'. Most important, Clayton appreciated that his experience had been 'invaluable and such as few men get'. After all, 'practically the whole time I have been here', he informed his father, 'I have been running the whole show'.[39] He was certainly correct to emphasize the value of his experiences; they would stand him in good stead in later years. But it was with few real regrets that he boarded a north-bound steamer at Wau on June 5, 1903.

7

Master: Private Secretary to Wingate, 1907–1913

After suffering through a journey nearly as arduous as that taken eight months earlier on his way south, Clayton arrived in Khartoum on June 24, only to learn that his sister Mary had died at home three days earlier. Only twenty-one, she had fallen ill with appendicitis and had succumbed to peritonitis. As Iltyd later recalled, Mary's death was 'a great grief to us all as she was a very loveable person'.[1] Clayton immediately left for England and did not return until October, when he took up his new duties on the headquarters' staff of the Egyptian Army. He was first posted to the Army's Cairo headquarters and then, in February 1904, to Khartoum, where he continued to serve until the fall of 1905. Clayton had taken his usual summer leaves in England the previous two years, but his 1905 leave began later, in the autumn, the delay having been caused by a bout of Malta fever.[2] Although he doubtless benefitted from his work on the headquarters staff, Clayton's belief that the appointment would accelerate his advancement in the Army proved to be incorrect. In a Note describing his Sudan service he later complained that while serving on the adjutant's staff he had been 'passed over' by three of his contemporaries.[3] But he was not long disappointed. On returning to Cairo after his 1905 leave, Clayton learned that the he had been promoted *kaimakam* – lieutenant colonel – and given command of the 2nd Infantry Battalion at Khartoum.[4]

By this time Clayton had been in the East for ten years and for a man yet to reach his thirty-first birthday, had not done badly at all. He had been promoted captain in the British Army and lieutenant colonel in the Egyptian. He had fought in a major military campaign, been mentioned in a despatch (Omdurman) and received a medal. He had served as a government administrator, and acquitted himself well in difficult circumstances. He was well liked and respected as a soldier and, it appears, had become proficient in Arabic. His papers contain no record of his having taken formal instruction in the language, but by April 1906, he was sitting as 'president' of a local examination board for intermediate Arabic. He was also now a familiar figure in Khartoum and was pleased to learn shortly after his return that he had been elected Secretary of the Sudan Club. And Clayton's 1906 diary contains the first mention of his activities as a Freemason. He may have joined before 1906, but whenever he became a member, and for whatever reason, it was a move that could only help his career; two of his later chiefs, Wingate and Kitchener, were both active Masons.

Yet even though his recent promotion suggested that Clayton's career was proceeding satisfactorily, it seems that by 1906 he had begun to lose enthusiasm for army life. Whether he was disappointed at being earlier 'passed over', or had become bored with the routine of life in a peacetime army, or simply desired a greater challenge elsewhere, is unclear. But on May 24, 1906, Clayton sent in his application for an appointment in the 'Civil'. His original plan was to rejoin the Sudan Civil Service in the Bahr al Ghazal, a choice that must have surprised those of his colleagues familiar with the difficulties Clayton had experienced in the province only three years earlier. But, for some reason, his application was never forwarded, the position at Wau was filled, and, on re-application, Clayton was appointed senior inspector, Kassala Province, on August 28, 1906.[5] He likely applied for this specific post as he had just spent two months at the provincial headquarters in the town of Kassala with two companies of his 2nd battalion and found it 'a charming little place'.[6] He described his new appointment to his mother:

Every province has a Governor, a Senior Inspector and three or four Junior and Deputy Inspectors. The Senior Inspector, if a soldier, is always a kaimakam, his Junior Inspectors bimbashis and the Deputy Inspectors are all young civilians forming the nucleus of a future Sudan Civil Service. The Junior Inspectors and some of the more experienced Deputy inspectors are each in charge of a district in which they live and for the administration of which they are responsible. The Senior Inspector may have an unimportant district, but is seldom there as he is par excellence the Governor's deputy, acts for him when away, takes his leave when the Governor is in the province and when they are both in the province assists him by inspecting out districts, etc. As Senior Inspector I have the powers of a 1st class magistrate; i.e., I can give up to 5 years penal servitude, and when the Governor is away his powers devolve on me and I can give any punishment though of course death and long sentences of penal servitude must be confirmed by the Gov. General. They pay, and very well — £800 a year, but of course the expenses are great as one has to keep up about 10 animals . . . and a pretty large staff – the minimum being 1 cook, 1 body servant, 1 syce, 1 assistant syce, 3 camel men and probably 1 gardener . . .[7]

Before Clayton could take up his new post he was ordered to Sennar Province, up the Blue Nile, to take over temporarily for the Governor, his old Isle of Wight College school-mate, Cyril Wilson, who was then on leave. The provincial headquarters was then at Singa, a village located on the Blue Nile, 220 miles southeast of Khartoum. Clayton enjoyed his time there, though the rainy season was much the same as in the Bahr al Ghazal. 'When it comes down it makes no mistake about it and . . . the place becomes a sea of mud'. He toured the district, made a short visit further up river to Rusayris (Roseires), and presided over a two day murder trial. He was relieved to be able to convict the defendant of the lesser charge of culpable homicide, rather than murder, 'as it is unpleasant having to sentence a man to death and still more so having to superintend the carrying out of the sentence'. Despite his understandable unease with capital cases, on the whole, Clayton enjoyed provincial administrative work, particularly in what he called the 'out provinces' like Sennar. 'It is most varied and interesting,' he wrote to his mother, 'and one is always having to think out things for oneself and act quickly on one's own initiative in important matters, where a mistake may have serious consequences'.[8]

In early November Clayton left Singa, proceeding in the direction of Kassala to Gedaref, 150 miles to the northeast, where he had been ordered to act temporarily for the senior inspector who was then away. He did not finally arrive at his new post at Kassala until Christmas day 1906. But sudden personnel changes in the Condominium government under Wingate were common and Clayton had barely settled into his work there before he received a wire from Khartoum offering him the position of assistant private secretary to the governor-general. This he correctly saw as a great opportunity. He accepted immediately and, on March 3, 1907, left Kassala, travelling east through Italian Eritrea, to the port of Massawa, where he sailed for Suez. From Suez he journeyed by train to Cairo where he stayed for a fortnight, and then left on his annual leave. Clayton's appointment as assistant private secretary must have come as a surprise to him, particularly since there was no such position in the Sudan Government. And because no provision had been made for the position in the Government's budget, Clayton was re-transferred to the Egyptian Army for a year so that he could be paid and, at the same time, work on the Sirdar's staff. Wingate's private secretary was then Lee Stack and when Stack was promoted to the dual position of Sudan Agent and Director of Intelligence the following February, Clayton took over his position as private secretary.[9] It seems likely that Clayton was brought to Khartoum in 1907 for the specific purpose of being trained in the duties of private secretary in anticipation of Stack's promotion.

To those unfamiliar with the workings of the Condominium government, the post of private secretary may have seemed insignificant. In practice, though, the governor-general's private secretary was an important figure in Khartoum. In large measure he controlled access to his chief, as the communications, reports and returns of provincial governors and the heads of departments passed through his hands. He also 'drafted replies, minutes, proclamations' and other documents for Wingate. He could more accurately be described as the Sirdar's assistant.[10] Indeed, the governor-general worked with his private secretary nearly every day, and even during their long summer leaves in England, Wingate and Clayton could often be found working in London or at the Sirdar's home near Dunbar in Scotland. And when they were apart, the letters and telegrams flew between the two. Because of his close proximity to the seat of power, the private secretary was carefully selected by Wingate. In 1903, when the position was just evolving, Wingate stipulated that his private secretary had to be a 'fairly senior officer . . . in the closest touch with everything civil or military'.[11] No less important, he had to be completely trustworthy, know the Sirdar's mind, be skilled at organisation and willing to work hard.[12] From the private secretary's standpoint, the position was equally significant. His advice was sought on important issues and he was involved in decision-making at the highest level. Harold MacMichael, who began his thirty-year career in the Sudan in 1905, once identified Wingate's four confidants during this period and three of them were private secretaries – Stack, Clayton and Stewart Symes, the latter succeeding Clayton in the post in 1914.[13] Only Slatin figured more prominently in the Sirdar's inner circle. And, since appointment and promotion in the Sudan lay almost exclusively in the hands of the governor-general – who took the keenest interest in personnel matters – proximity to Wingate invariably meant advancement for the assiduous private secretary. Stack and Clayton were both promoted to the position of Sudan Agent and Director of Intelligence. Later, Stack and Symes would both rise to the governor-generalship of the Sudan.

In many ways Clayton was an obvious choice for private secretary. Although fourteen years Wingate's junior, his background exhibited some striking similarities to the Sirdar's. Both hailed from comfortable, but by no means affluent families; both were graduates of the Royal Military Academy – each passing out tenth in his class – and served in the Royal Artillery; both joined the Egyptian Army and served under Kitchener in the Nile campaign of 1898; both were proficient in Arabic; both were avid Freemasons; and both believed deeply in Britain's imperial mission. Clayton first met Wingate during the 1898 campaign and saw the Sirdar on a regular basis after he joined the Egyptian Army and was posted to the Sudan in December 1900. From the outset, he enjoyed good relations with Wingate. If not for the disparity in their ages and positions, one might even have said they were friends. Wingate quickly came to appreciate Clayton's 'good and hard work' as private secretary, but it was also clear that the Sirdar and Lady Wingate simply enjoyed his company. Lady Wingate was particularly fond of Clayton. She gladly accepted the role of godmother to Clayton's second child, Jane, in 1914, wrote to Clayton promptly on learning that his sister Ellinor had contracted scarlet fever in 1911, and was delighted to receive a recommendation from Clayton's mother concerning an appropriate school for her young daughter, Victoria. And, when the Sirdar was away from Khartoum in 1911, she and Clayton played 'strenuous bridge every night' at the Palace.[14]

The Sirdar, too, soon developed a fondness for Clayton. When his brother Iltyd sought a position in the Indian Army in 1910, Clayton asked Wingate if he would write on Iltyd's behalf. 'I hate to be one of the crowd asking for chits,' he wrote, 'but as my father is now old, I feel somewhat responsible for my younger brothers'. Having met Iltyd during a 1908 visit to Khartoum, the Sirdar was happy to oblige and used the opportunity to express his high regard for Clayton: 'I formed an excellent opinion of your brother when I saw him and if he is like his elder brother, I have no hesitation in strongly backing his application.' When Wingate's son was about to enter The Shop in September 1911, the Sirdar was delighted that Clayton, then in London, had offered to take him to the Academy. 'Nothing could have pleased me more,' he wrote, 'than that Malcolm should have been taken to Woolwich by yourself.'[15] The good relations between Clayton and the Wingates appear to have extended even to their families who must have had some contact during this period.

Clayton's youngest sister Norah asked him to 'send her love to Victoria', Wingate's young daughter, when he next wrote to the Sirdar.[16] With such a good relationship as a foundation, it hardly seems surprising that Wingate's confidence in Clayton increased over the years. In 1913, when he chose Clayton to succeed Stack as Sudan Agent, Wingate wrote to him expressing his 'entire confidence' in Clayton's 'wisdom and common sense'.[17]

The governor-general was not, however, an easy chief to serve. Wingate ran the Sudan as if it were an eighteenth century monarchy. He took little interest in the details of administration, but loved the status of his position. The Sirdar revelled in pomp and state, travelling about the country on frequent and often unnecessary tours of inspection with an absurdly large retinue of soldier-escorts, aides and assistants. Fundamentally insecure in his own position, Wingate was jealous of his own authority and reluctant to delegate any portion of it to his subordinates.[18] Although he appeared to be absorbed in work, Wingate actually spent little time on government business. Indeed, he lived only about half of every year in the Sudan, the balance being spent in Egypt, Europe and Britain. Most of his time was taken up by a staggering volume of personal correspondence, much of it with socialites, European royalty and officials who, despite their frequent and costly visits to the Sudan, had nothing whatever to do with the governance of the country. Cromer had detected Wingate's regal pretensions early on and sought to curb them. He rejected the Sirdar's proposal to purchase a 'State Coach' as 'utterly unsuitable' and 'ridiculous', and was equally critical of the governor-general's constant pandering to European royalty, arguing that they were troublesome and expensive, that 'they certainly do no good, and may even do harm'.[19] Yet Wingate continued to entertain them, often lavishly and always expensively, and the practice increased after the Lord's departure from Egypt in 1907.

The Sudan had by now become fashionable, a popular winter destination for the smart set. Between 1900 and the outbreak of war in 1914, the list of visitors entertained by the Sirdar included a dazzling array of royalty, many of whose titles have long since been consigned to the dustbin of European history: Prince George William of Brunswick, Prince d'Arenberg, the King of Saxony, Count Berchen, the Duchess d'Aosta, Prince Leopold, Prince Lichtenstein, the Duke and Duchess of Schleswig-Holstein, Count Hunyady, Princess Schonburg, Prince Windischgratz, Count Plater, the Marchesa Gentile-Farinola, the King of the Belgians, Princess Henry of Battenberg, Lady Desborough, the Dowager Duchess of Roxburgh, the Princess Royal and the Duke of Fife, the Duke of Connaught and King George V. Non-royal visitors included Lord Roberts, Winston Churchill and the former American president Teddy Roosevelt.[20] When Roosevelt stopped in Khartoum in March 1910, after a hunting trip in the south, Wingate was ill and undergoing medical treatment in Cairo. The presidential reception was entrusted to Clayton, who assured the Sirdar that every detail had been seen to, that everything was 'maksoot' – just what was wanted. Clayton won high praise from Roosevelt and seems also to have impressed the former president's eighteen year old daughter Ethel, who later corresponded with him.[21]

In entertaining such lofty personages, Wingate imported many of the forms of European court society to Khartoum. The Palace became the scene of levees, formal dinners, teas, garden parties and fêtes – all of them 'stilted, sticky' and more than a little anomalous in such a poor, undeveloped country as the Sudan.[22] Although Wingate may have viewed the Sudan as his own satrapy, the country was, in fact, dependent on an annual grant from Egypt to meet its expenses. It was not until 1913 that revenue exceeded expenses in the Sudan – and then only just – and the Egyptian subvention was stopped. Wingate disliked the reality of dependence, but, as Cromer pointed out, 'those who pay the piper have a right to call the tune'.[23] When the Sirdar later chafed at the visit of an Egyptian minister to the Sudan, Cromer's successor, Sir Eldon Gorst, brought him up short: 'We cannot object to Egyptian Ministers taking an interest in Sudan affairs if we are continually asking the Council of Ministers to provide money for the development of the country.'[24] But throughout his time as governor-general Wingate resisted Egyptian control. While Cromer sat in Cairo, he had little to say; the Lord would decide every major point of Sudan policy and administration, and a good many minor ones. In contrast, Gorst usually confined himself to the big questions and was content to defer to Wingate in matters of detail. Kitchener, appointed British Agent on Gorst's death in July 1911, had the dominating personality of Cromer, but lacked the Lord's interest in administration and attention to detail. And, with the exception of financial issues, Kitchener and the governor-general agreed on most matters affecting the Sudan. As a result, Wingate enjoyed more latitude under his former chief.

If Wingate occasionally had to defer to the Egyptian government, and more often to the British Agent in Cairo, his authority in Khartoum was rarely challenged. If any rivals to his authority appeared, as they did in the early years of the Condominium, Wingate adroitly eliminated the competition. This rather ruthless streak was well recognized by the Sirdar's subordinates. In early 1917, after Wingate had moved to Cairo as the new High Commissioner, the powerful British Adviser to the Egyptian Ministry of Finance, Lord Edward Cecil, soon left the country. This came as no surprise to Lee Stack, Clayton's predecessor as private secretary: 'It looks as if, like [in] the Sudan, the elimination of outstanding personages [is] . . . beginning.'[25] In fact, the governor-general's personality flaws were all too obvious to those in frequent contact with him. But, it must also be said that Wingate exhibited countervailing traits – sound judgment in most matters, sympathy, generosity and unfailing support of those loyal to him. His papers are filled with requests made to the Home authorities for recognition and honours for his subordinates. And those honours that were effectively in his own gift – such as the Turkish Orders of Osmanieh and Medjidieh, nominally awarded by the Khedive – were liberally dispensed by the Sirdar to Britons serving in the Sudan government and the Egyptian Army. Clayton himself was invested with the 4th Class of the Order of Osmanieh in 1908, soon after he began work as private secretary.[26] And, while recognizing that the style of Wingate's governor-generalship was pretentious and often ludicrous, most of his civil servants also readily acknowledged that the Sirdar had accomplished much for the Sudan. He brought order, system and some sense of security to the country in the aftermath of the comparative chaos of the *Mahdiyya*. A modern infrastructure was initiated, even if enabled by Egyptian loans; railway and telegraph systems were begun or expanded and a new deep-water harbour, Port Sudan, was constructed on the Red Sea. A modern legal system was put in place and land settlement issues largely resolved. Wingate also prevented a recrudescence of Mahdism, not just by military action, but more effectively by encouraging a Sunni orthodoxy in the country.[27] Among his many subordinates who appreciated these accomplishments and, at the same time, laughed at the governor-general's regal style, Wingate seemed to have well earned the intentionally ambiguous sobriquet 'Master'.

Clayton was among those who referred, privately, to Wingate as 'Master'. And he later stated that during the time he served as private secretary he often felt that he was merely 'bottle-washing and devilling' for the governor-general. But, he also admitted that his years in Khartoum gave him a keen insight into certain issues important to his later career, particularly those involving relations with Egypt's and the Sudan's often troublesome neighbours and with Britain's allies France and Italy.[28] In fact, some of Clayton's work *was* little more than bottle-washing. He had to treat with such mundane matters as applications for British citizenship, the Sudan cattle trade, and writing notes of thanks to friends of the Sirdar, including one to a cleric who had sent Wingate a pamphlet on 'Thrift'. He wrestled with a dispute concerning an unpaid bill for polo sticks and balls incurred by the Club at Khartoum, sat on a committee to consider the closure of Khartoum's skating rink, and immersed himself in the knotty issues surrounding a postal convention between the Sudan and the Belgian Congo.[29] And, like the Sirdar, he spent an inordinate amount of time on personnel matters, recommending and opposing men for a wide variety of positions, and, always sensitive to Wingate's own views, was careful not to support applications from '*mazlum* men', those who felt they had been wronged or ill-treated.[30]

Clayton also handled the large volume of correspondence from men seeking positions in the Condominium, invariably rejecting all but experienced soldiers, engineers, physicians and veterinarians. And, in 1912 and 1913, he sat on the Sudan Selection Board which convened every summer in London to interview young men for entry-level positions in the Sudan. The Sudan Civil Service had received its first recruits in 1901. It had not been established because either Cromer or Wingate particularly desired a civilian administration in the country, but because the soldier-administrator, whom they both preferred, could not be depended upon for long-term service. He could be called back to the army on short notice – as happened between 1899 and 1901, during the Boer War – and many returned to the army in regular course when their periods of secondment ended after seven (later, ten) years. Thus, the civilian corps was begun in 1901, as an attempt to create stability in the civil service. There was no competitive examination for such posts; rather, young men, mostly Cambridge and Oxford graduates, first sought placement through their university's appointments board and were then interviewed in London by senior officials in the Sudan and Egyptian governments. Once selected, the candidate spent another year, at either Cambridge or Oxford, studying Arabic and then took up his position. In the Sudan, the recruit began his career as a deputy inspector. Their numbers were small – up to 1914, only eighty-eight men joined the service – and those chosen exhibited remarkably similar backgrounds and characteristics.[31]

Although the Service would later acquire the aura of an elite corps, it was not so regarded during its early years. Even the few senior civilian employees in the Sudan government believed that many of those selected were of indifferent quality, and they refused to sit on the Selection Board because they believed the civilians then serving in the Sudan were being given short shrift. That was why Clayton was asked to serve on the Board in 1912 and 1913. He once described the vague criteria used by the selectors: consideration was given to 'character, literary ability . . . physical fitness' and an 'aptitude for . . . administrative work'. He added that men who had distinguished themselves athletically, those who had obtained 'Blues', were often chosen because in their school, university and private life [they have] shown the above characteristics'.[32] These rather questionable criteria were applied for years, so much so that it was later said that the Sudan was 'a country of Blacks ruled by Blues'.

As Wingate gained confidence in Clayton he gave him greater responsibility. In 1910, he was appointed secretary to the Governor-General's Council. The Council then served only an advisory function; Wingate would not allow it any executive authority. But Clayton still benefitted from his work on the Council, becoming well acquainted with the significant issues affecting the Sudan and the major personalities involved in solving them. He was also charged with drafting portions of the Sudan's yearly report which was, in turn, incorporated into the British Agent's annual report for Egypt. These were important tasks, but, oddly, it was while he was away from the Sudan, on leave in England, that Clayton enjoyed his greatest responsibilities. Wingate spent much of his own leave time at his home in Scotland and while there delegated authority to a few, trusted Sudan officials to work with those London departments of the Home government involved in Sudan affairs. The issues, varied and sometimes trivial, generally came under two heads – the Sudan's external relations (including its frontiers) and the country's economic development. As early as 1909, Clayton was deputed by Wingate to visit the Foreign and Colonial Offices to plead the Sudan's position concerning Abyssinia. He argued Wingate's ideas for suppressing the arms traffic from that country and for rectifying the Sudanese-Abyssinian boundary. The Sirdar concluded that Clayton had taken 'quite the right line' in resisting the Colonial Office's competing view as to the correct location of the boundary.[33] Wingate also suspected the Italians of fomenting trouble in Abyssinia directed against the Sudan and Clayton was again dispatched to the Foreign Office to persuade officials there of Italian duplicity.

During his 1911 leave he was once more sent to the Foreign Office, this time concerning the Sudan's western boundary, as the French were insisting on placing three towns in the far west in French territory and not where they belonged, in Darfur, in western Sudan. On this issue, though, Clayton displayed a growing sensitivity to the wider, international situation, arguing for an accommodation with France: 'The present Moroccan crisis seems to make it inadvisable for Great Britain and France to fall out in the face of German ambition', he suggested to the Sirdar.[34] In the summer of 1912, Clayton again appeared at the Foreign Office, this time advancing the Sudan position concerning the Mahagi Strip, a small slice of territory deep in the southern Sudan, the boundaries of which required clarification in the face of Belgian claims emanating from the adjacent Congo. Even the Uganda Boundary Delimitation Commission was a matter of interest to the Sudan and to Clayton, though Uganda, then a British protectorate, hardly represented a threat. Still, the governor-general thanked Clayton for his 'excellent letter . . . explaining the various points in connection with . . . the rectification'.[35]

In 1909 Clayton had the opportunity of more direct diplomatic work when he accompanied Wingate on an investigative mission to British Somaliland. Located in the horn of Africa, at the southern end of the Red Sea and just across from Aden, the Somaliland Protectorate had been established twenty-five years earlier to protect the sea route to India. In recent years the country had been the scene of some turmoil caused by a Somali renegade, Sayyid Muhammad Abdalla Hasan, widely known as the 'Mad Mullah'. But if the Mullah was mad, it was only in the sense that he was angry, not insane. He had received a thrashing at the hands of the British in 1905, retreated to the south and east into Italian Somaliland, and, for the last year or so, had been causing no end of trouble for the British, Italians and Abyssinians. When the Mullah was not engaged in pillaging and plundering British- and Italian-protected tribes, he was preoccupied with various intrigues calculated to sow dissension between his European overlords. Unpleasant questions had been asked in the House of Commons in March 1909, and the Colonial Office urged the Foreign Secretary, Sir Edward Grey, to send Wingate over from the Sudan to the Somali port of Berbera to investigate and suggest a solution.

On April 18, 1909, Wingate left Port Sudan with Slatin, Clayton and a typically large entourage. After a week at Aden, the party arrived in Berbera, on the 26th. Wingate was not in the country for a week before he began reaching some sweeping conclusions as to the causes of the recent trouble. He first fixed blame on the British Commissioner, Captain Cordeaux who, he concluded, had antagonised the Mullah and the Somali tribes. Wingate made no attempt to conceal his disapproval of Cordeaux's conduct with the result, as the Sirdar noted in his diary, that the Commissioner became 'so annoyed that he could scarcely speak'. Cordeaux felt that Wingate had completely undermined his position in the country, declined to coop-erate with him and even threatened to resign. Wingate next threw stones at the Italians. It was in their interest, he concluded, 'for us to be embroiled with the Mullah'. At the same time, they were 'doing their best to induce the British Government to pull the chestnuts out of the fire for them, whilst doing little or nothing to assist in that operation themselves'. Finally, the Sirdar complained of the 'utter want of comprehension of the facts of the case on the part of the Home Government'.[36]

Wingate consulted with Clayton, and especially Slatin, on the Somali situation, but how much Clayton shared the opinions of Master, or influenced them, is unknown. In a letter home, he noted only that 'the situation is a most complicated and difficult one' and that he was fully absorbed with 'reading up the situation and taking notes'.[37] In any event, neither Clayton nor Wingate ever clapt eyes on the Mullah; he was over 200 miles away, deep in the interior, and had enough sense to stay there. He did answer a letter from the mission, which Wingate found 'not satisfactory'. Having accomplished nothing, the party left the next day. All that came of the two-month mission was a report which, with 'Appendices and Annexes, numbered some 270 pages'. There really was no satisfactory solution to the Somali problem. Britain could not abandon the Protectorate; everyone acknowledged it was strategically important to Imperial defence. 'From a purely military point of view', Wingate argued, the best policy would be to crush the Mullah once and for all'.[38] But that would be prohibitively expensive. The only viable solution was to continue the present policy; that is, to do nothing except maintain the British presence along the Somali coast and defer the *dénouement* with the Mullah to a later date. And that was the course chosen. Not until after the War, in 1920, would the Mullah be crushed. These forays into the diplomatic world and visits to the Foreign and Colonial Offices were important to Clayton, not so much in their details, or even in how the problems posed were solved, but rather because they exposed him to issues that required study, reflection, subtlety and often a broad perspective, to resolve. All were attributes he would draw upon in his career after leaving the Sudan.

The development of the Sudan was the other major topic with which Wingate and Clayton were absorbed in the early years of the century. Economics was not the Sirdar's métier, but, to his credit, Wingate realised the importance of attracting British capital to the Sudan in order to accelerate the country's development and he involved his private secretary in the effort. He asked Clayton to explain 'in strict confidence' to Slatin, Phipps, Civil Secretary to the Sudan Government, and Bonham Carter, the Legal Secretary, his general views on the development of the Sudan:

> It is quite clear that the present attitude of the [Egyptian] Nationalists and the Legislative Council is to prevent any Egyptian money being expended in the Sudan; the attitude of the Home Government is also one of "hands off" in regard to their Sudan responsibilities and I am confident that any effort to obtain money from the British Government for Sudan development at the present time is certain to meet with an absolute refusal. As Egypt has no money whatever to spare for the Sudan and still less now that there is every possibility that the new Suez Canal Convention will be thrown out, we shall very soon be on our beam ends financially and therefore it is a matter of most vital importance to do all we possibly can to induce British Capital and thus the British Capitalist to have a vested interest in the country. This can only be done by getting powerful men on to our side. . . .[39]

Despite this laudable goal, it proved difficult to interest British capital in the Sudan. Government concessions could be offered to the developer, but investment in such a remote and undeveloped country was risky and agriculture, specifically, cotton, was the only commodity that suggested profit for the entrepreneur. In 1904, a cotton and wheat concession was granted to an American to develop land at Zeidab, near Damer on the Nile, but the venture met with little success. Reorganised in 1907, as the Sudan Plantations Syndicate, the company eventually generated a small profit. But, by 1911, the Syndicate had turned its attention to the Gezira – the fertile plain lying between the White and Blue Niles south of Khartoum – where it began planning a vast, irrigated development. However, not until Kitchener took an interest in the project and secured a British guarantee for a loan of £3 million to help finance the Gezira Scheme, did the project take wing.[40] By the summer of 1913 Clayton had become something of a student of the Scheme and of the Syndicate. He delivered 'sound criticisms' on the correspondence between Wingate and the Syndicate and met frequently with the company's managing director, A. P. MacGillivray, to sound him out on the details of an agreement with the government. 'My impression is that the Syndicate are keen on the agreement,' Clayton wrote in August 1913, 'and will put up £500,000 at par, provided they can obtain a satisfactory renewal clause. . . .'[41]

By now, Clayton had become the governor-general's right hand man; he was an expert on the Sudan's personnel, its economic development and relations with its colonial neighbours. He had no particular desire to leave the Sudan service, but Clayton realized that he had outgrown his job as private secretary. And then, just as he began to weary of his position, a new opportunity appeared in the north, in Cairo.

8

Sudan Agent: Cairo, 1913–1914

By 1913, Clayton was ready to move on from his work as private secretary. He did not, however, contemplate a return to the Army. As early as January 1910, he had written to the Sudan Government advising them that, under his Egyptian Army contract, his ten years of seconded service were due to expire on November 12, 1910, and that he intended to retire from the British Army, in the hope of working permanently in the Sudan service. His application was promptly approved by Wingate on January 30, and in November 1910, he retired from the British Army on 'half-pay' at £120 per year.[1] He certainly did not suffer financially as a result of the decision; by 1911 he was earning £E960 per year, with a 'special executive allowance' of £E120 per annum for serving as secretary to the Governor-General's Council, far more than he would have made in the British Army. Promotion and honours followed. In early 1912, he was promoted 'temporary Miralai' (colonel) in the Egyptian Army and in the following year was awarded the 3rd Class of the Order of the Medjidieh.[2]

Despite feeling that he was at times only 'devilling' for the Sirdar, Clayton appreciated that his work as private secretary was rarely exacting, the pay was excellent, and the three or four months of annual leave-time more than generous. And, although he had to be available during his leaves if called upon by the governor-general, he still had plenty of leisure time. Every summer he spent several weeks with his family at Sandown and he always found time to visit his former commanding officer from the Atbara, Walter Hunter Blair. He and Hunter Blair had been friends since 1896, and Clayton was especially delighted to learn that Iltyd, upon passing out of The Shop in the fall of 1906, was assigned to Hunter Blair's battery at Guernsey. From the summer of 1908, Clayton also spent at least two weeks of every leave in Scotland. In part, this was because it was necessary for him to visit Dunbar to meet with Wingate on Sudan government business. But, beginning in 1908, he also paid an annual visit to Kelburn Castle in Ayrshire, home of David Boyle, the 7th Earl of Glasgow and his wife, Countess Dorothea Elizabeth Thomasina Hunter Blair, the elder sister of Walter Hunter Blair. Clayton had likely been introduced to 'the Glasgows', as he called them, by his former commanding officer, and looked forward to his annual visits to Scotland. Not only did Kelburn offer good opportunity for outdoor sport – fishing, shooting, golf and sailing – Clayton had also formed a close friendship with the Glasgows' son, Alan Boyle. An enthusiastic aviator, Alan founded the Scottish Aeroplane Syndicate in 1909, and developed the first British-built monoplane, the 'Avis'. But it was Alan's mother who would play the more important role in Clayton's life. The Countess, it seems, enjoyed a well-deserved reputation in British society as an accomplished match-maker, and before long saw an opportunity in Bertie Clayton. Her cousin, Elizabeth Thorowgood (neé Hunter Blair), was a frequent visitor to Kelburn and the Countess soon fixed on Elizabeth's second daughter, Enid, as a possible match for Clayton.

Enid Caroline was born in Madras, India in 1886. Her father, Frank Napier Thorowgood, was a civil engineer who had been involved for years in the design and construction of Madras harbour. The Thorowgoods returned to England in 1888 and, six years later, moved to Montreux in Switzerland. There Enid learned French and German and also shared her father's interests in painting and natural history. By the time the family returned to England in 1901, Enid had begun to study art seriously. After further training in Paris and London, she became an accomplished water-colourist, exhibited her work and was even able to sell many of her pictures. In the summer of 1911, Enid was invited by the Countess to Kelburn, coincidentally, at the same time Clayton was making his fourth summer appearance at the castle. One day, shortly after his arrival, Clayton was standing near the foot of the castle's great staircase when he saw a woman descending. Enid fixed her gaze on him, paused two steps from the bottom and then jumped to the floor. Struck by the young woman's appearance and impish behaviour, Clayton resolved to himself on the spot: 'I am going to marry this woman'.[3]

Enid and Bertie met again at Kelburn in the summer of 1912, became engaged, and, to everyone's surprise, announced their intent to marry that same summer. 'Your letter of the 27th July came as a great surprise,' Wingate wrote, 'for of course I had calculated on your marriage not taking place – as you said – until this time next year. . . .'[4] They were married on Wednesday, September 18, 1912 at St. Peter's Church, Cranley Gardens, London, by the Bishop of Khartoum. Clayton's friend from the Egyptian Army, Captain C. H. Townsend served as best man, but, 'the bride was unattended by either bridesmaids or pages'. Among those in attendance was the matchmaker, the Countess of Glasgow, and Clayton's good friend from the Sudan, Lee Stack. After a reception at the home of Enid's mother, the couple left for their honeymoon at Kelburn Castle, 'lent by the Earl and Countess of Glasgow'.[5] Bertie and Enid immensely enjoyed their week-long stay at Kelburn 'an ideal place to honeymoon in', he informed Wingate.[6] But they could not stay long; the couple left Ayrshire on the 26th and, on October 2, Clayton departed for Egypt. Enid came out later, her usually laconic husband noting in his diary for November 26: 'E. arrives Port Said ! ! ! ! ! ! !'[7] Enid stayed with Bertie in Khartoum until the following March when she returned to England, now pregnant with the couple's first child. In June 1913 Clayton left the Sudan to join her, noting with some annoyance in a diary entry for July 1: 'Sirdar arrives London. Consequently I neglect my wife.'

On August 13, 1913, after some considerable difficulty for Enid, the Claytons' first child, Patience, was born at the home of Enid's mother in London. Just seven weeks later Enid and Patience left England to join Bertie in Egypt. Unlike the wives of many British soldiers and civil servants working in the East, Enid insisted on living abroad with her husband and she could be quite 'scathing' in her criticism of those British wives who refused to do the same. Enid lived with Bertie in Khartoum, and later in Cairo, Jerusalem and Baghdad. Unusually for the time, she also mixed with the local women in each of those places, taking part in local causes and frequently inviting them to tea. She even studied Arabic and gamely spoke the language, though sometimes baffling the 'ladies of the harem' when she unconsciously lapsed into German.[8]

Enid's autumn 1913 journey terminated not in Khartoum, but in Cairo, to which Clayton had been re-assigned upon being appointed Sudan Agent and Director of Intelligence. Exactly when Wingate decided to make the appointment is uncertain, but it likely came about in the summer of 1913 as a result of the intended retirement of P. R. Phipps, Civil Secretary in the Condominium government. Stack was named to succeed Phipps and Stack's job as Sudan Agent fell vacant. Clayton's formal appointment to the post would not occur until the spring of 1914, but he was signing papers as 'Sudan Agent' as early as October 1913. Wingate was sorry to see him go: 'I cannot tell you with what regret I view your departure from myself . . . but it was your really good work as P[rivate] S[ecretary] that enabled me to unhesitatingly select you for your new appointment . . . I shall feel very acutely your absence – not only as a most capable P.S. but as a tried old friend and comrade and one who never abused a confidence.'[9] As a sign of his gratitude for Clayton's nearly seven year tenure as his private secretary, Wingate arranged for him to receive the Order of Medjidieh, 3rd Class, which was conferred on Clayton on November 9 by the Khedive.

The position of Sudan Agent and Director of Intelligence was among the most important in the Condominium government. There had been only four Agents since the post was initiated in 1901, and among its prior occupants was Count Gleichen, a cousin of Queen Victoria, and Lord Edward Cecil, a son of the former Prime Minister, Lord Salisbury. A 1903 Note described the Sudan Agent as 'the channel of communication between the outer world and the Civil Administration of the Sudan Government'. This included communications between the Sudan and the various Egyptian Ministries and the British Army of Occupation in Egypt. And, 'except on purely financial matters' the Sudan Agent was to be 'the sole channel' between the Sudan government departments and the British Agent in Cairo. Most important, in Wingate's view, the Sudan Agent was to be 'the exponent in Cairo of the views of the Sudan Government' – that is to say, of Wingate's views.[10] For the governor-general, who took the greatest interest in any sort of Egyptian intrigue, whether in British or Egyptian circles, and who always wanted the latest gossip – 'gup' as he called it – the Sudan Agent was to be his 'eyes and ears in Cairo'.[11]

The Agent's duties as Director of Intelligence were less clearly defined. Most Intelligence work relating to the Sudan was undertaken in Khartoum by an assistant director working under the supervision of Slatin. Much of that work focused on assessing the state of public opinion in the country which was gleaned from the periodic reports of provincial governors and from the department's own agents.[12] Still, the Sudan Agent undertook his own Intelligence gathering and took particular interest in the activities of the foreign diplomatic missions in Cairo and in those native officers in the Egyptian Army who were thought to be the source of seditious conduct, some of it directed towards the Sudan. As the European situation deteriorated in 1914, the Intelligence activities of the Agency were to increase significantly.

In many respects the issues with which Clayton was concerned did not change after he arrived in Cairo and took up the duties of Sudan Agent in October 1913. He still worked on the Gezira scheme. He continued to be absorbed in the Sudan's relations with its neighbours, the Italians and Abyssinians in the east, the French in the west. The Italians Clayton found to be 'slippery customers', reflecting in part no doubt the Sirdar's views and also perhaps his own experiences from the 1909 mission to Somaliland. Relations were better with the French. He reported in January 1914 that he had already 'established a regular "Entente Cordiale" with the French Agency' in Cairo.[13] Clayton was now treating directly with the French and Italians, through their Agencies in Cairo; he was, in a very real sense, the Sudan's diplomatic Agent in Egypt. These diplomatic chores, interesting though they were, meant a significant increase in Clayton's work, for he now had to report, in writing, at least once and often two or three times a week to the governor-general. And this was in addition to the dozens of telegrams that passed between Cairo and Khartoum every month. Obsessed with secrecy, Wingate's letters to Clayton bore a bewildering array of designations to which not even Clayton could ascribe any corresponding significance: 'private', 'very private', 'strictly private', 'private and confidential', 'very private and personal', 'personal and decipher yourself' were just a few of the twenty or more phrases written by Wingate across the top of his letters to his Sudan Agent to indicate levels of confidentiality. Annoyed that Clayton later designated a letter to him as 'for your eyes only' and then also sent the same information to the Sirdar's private secretary, Wingate required all such future letters to be emblazoned with 'a prearranged sign . . . Solomon's seal'. So, after August 1915, such top secret letters between Clayton and Wingate were marked at the top with a circle enclosing a six-pointed star.[14] Clayton was also instructed to open the Sirdar's letters to Kitchener and to other British officials in the Egyptian government, study their contents, reseal and deliver them and then pretend unfamiliarity with their contents. This enabled Clayton to fully comprehend and then to reiterate and support the governor-general's views on any topic as if they were his own.[15] Despite these measures, he had to reassure Wingate continually that he was mindful of the need to always promote the Sudan's interests: 'I know how necessary it is in my present post,' he emphasised to his chief, 'to keep oneself "purely Sudan" and to try to look at every question from that point of view'.[16]

Clayton had also to report to Wingate on domestic Egyptian politics, an area with which he then had less familiarity. In April 1914, there was a ministerial crisis in Egypt, the prime minister resigned and was replaced by Hussein Rushdi. Detailed information concerning such changes was important to the Sudan; as a partner in the Condominium arrangement, Egypt was entitled to a voice in Sudan affairs and the views of Egyptian ministers concerning the Sudan varied. So Clayton routinely reported on Egyptian political developments, though he was reluctant to approach the British Agency directly for information because, he said, 'it is not my business'.[17] This did not, however, prevent him from acquiring information from other sources, and he soon established good relations with the two most important British officials in Egypt outside of the British Agent himself – Ronald Graham, Adviser to the Egyptian Ministry of the Interior, and Lord Edward Cecil, now Adviser to the Finance Ministry. Clayton's 1913–14 diaries contain notes of frequent golf and dinner engagements with both men and he surely learned much about the Egyptian political scene from them.

Wingate appreciated Clayton's efforts to keep him apprised of Egyptian developments and was especially pleased that he was getting on well with his old chief Kitchener, who had been British Agent in Cairo since July 1911. 'Clayton is doing very well and has evidently got the confidence of the Agency, which is a great point,' the Sirdar wrote to Stack in mid-1914. 'He is working capitally and both he and his wife are, I think, socially appreciated.'[18] The governor-general was, in fact, somewhat suspicious of his former chief. It was all the more important therefore that Clayton gain the confidence of Kitchener so that he could report fully on any issue affecting the Sudan that Kitchener might have under consideration. Wingate offered his Sudan Agent good advice for dealing with the Field Marshal: 'As you gradually find your feet and establish confidence between him and yourself, you will find that it will generally be best policy to talk matters over with him in the first instance before getting too immersed in purely Egyptian aspects of the various cases.'[19]

This was sound advice, but Clayton was probably no less suspicious of Kitchener than was Wingate. Perhaps he remembered Omdurman, when Kitchener had 'collared' his loot after the battle. But there was an even more recent example of Lord K's conduct that may have given Clayton pause. Among the many friends made by Clayton during his time as private secretary was Professor John Garstang, an archaeologist on the faculty of the University of Liverpool. In 1910, while conducting excavations at Merowe on the Nile, some 120 miles north of Khartoum, Garstang unearthed a magnificent bronze head of the Roman Emperor Caesar Augustus. Back in London, he had three plaster casts of the head made; one was intended for the governor-general's palace in Khartoum, the second for the Cairo Agency, and the third for his friend Bertie Clayton as a present on the occasion of Clayton's wedding in September 1912.[20] Shortly after the casts were made, Kitchener, who fancied himself something of an antiquary, came across them in a London shop. Immediately drawn to the mesmerizing stare of the emperor so faithfully reproduced in the casts, the Field Marshal asked what was intended for them. When informed that one was destined for Captain Clayton, Kitchener promptly announced that he was returning to the East shortly, that he knew Clayton, would take the cast, and see that it was delivered to him. Some months later, and well after he and Enid were married, Clayton encountered Garstang in the lift at Shepheard's Hotel in Cairo. Clayton sensed a certain coolness in Garstang's manner and asked if anything was troubling him. With some asperity, Garstang replied with his own question: Had not Clayton received the wedding present he had sent to him? Clayton expressed complete surprise; he knew nothing of Garstang's gift. Of course, Clayton never mentioned the incident to Kitchener and, most likely, Lord K's apparent perfidy was unknown to anyone save Bertie, Enid and Garstang himself. Then, in January 1915, Sir Henry McMahon was appointed to Cairo in succession to Kitchener, now in London as Secretary of State for War. Some time after his arrival in Cairo, MacMahon invited the Claytons to dinner and Enid recounted the story of the missing head to the High Commissioner. Sir Henry was appalled and told Enid she must return to the Residency and take that copy of the head which had been prominently displayed there for the last two years or more.[21]

Whether Clayton was troubled by Lord K's conduct, was indifferent, or simply found it amusing, is not recorded in his diaries or surviving papers, but he soon found the Agent a master no less demanding than Wingate. Of course, Kitchener was not, strictly speaking, Clayton's chief; the Sudan Agent was employed and paid by the Sudan government. But this mattered little to Lord K; he called on anyone – including Clayton – who he thought could be useful, and those calls came to the Sudan Agent frequently in 1914. Clayton was soon enlisted to act as an intermediary in the ongoing negotiations between Kitchener and MacGillivray of the Gezira syndicate.[22] At the same time, 'Lord K' kept Clayton busy for days working on a draft Abyssinian treaty and a secret 'partition map' of that country, in addition to devising a plan for heading off Italian schemes to co-opt the Abyssinians. Meanwhile, the Italian Agent in Cairo was a frequent visitor at the Sudan Agency, trying – vainly – to pump Clayton for information. Although there was a chancery at the British Agency in Cairo that handled communications with London, Kitchener directed Clayton to prepare despatches concerning Abyssinia to the Foreign Office. In addition to the time consumed by this work, Kitchener declined to read cables or letters from Khartoum, insisting instead that Clayton summarize and verbally explain to him all the important points in the documents.[23]

Kitchener also drew Clayton into the difficult issues relating to the Sanusi tribesmen in the western desert of Egypt. Although the Sanusi would become a thorn in the British side in 1915, it appears that Clayton was already well familiar with the complex questions swirling round the Sanusi, their Italian adversaries and the British, for his April 1914 Note on the subject was incorporated by Kitchener into a despatch sent to the Foreign Office.[24] Clayton was also drawn into Lord K's dispute with the War Office in London regarding a dangerous shortfall of British officers in the Egyptian Army, an issue of equal concern to Wingate. 'I allude to it pretty well every day I go to the Agency', he assured the Sirdar. A meeting with Kitchener on the issue on the morning of April 8, 1914, points up the difficulty Clayton experienced in serving two such dominating personalities and also reveals how adroit he was becoming in working with both men. Acknowledging that the Sudan was becoming dangerously short of British officers, Lord K suggested that, instead of taking on more civilians, the Sudan ought to offer permanent employment to a certain number of officers whose temporary contracts had expired. Clayton disagreed, pointing out that 'there would certainly be an outcry from the civilians now serving, who would inevitably complain that their prospects and those of future candidates were being ruined'. Kitchener 'saw the force of this' and it was at this point that a novel idea popped into Clayton's head, one about which he had not previously written to Wingate:

> It struck me that it might be possible to begin forming what might be called "The Sudan Political Service", recruiting it on the line suggested by Lord K and using it to supply the staff for those outlying provinces which are already laid down as requiring Military Governors. This Service could be quite distinct and under different conditions to the present Civil Service which would remain as the "Administrative" Service – in fact it would be on very similar lines to the Political Service in India which are recruited from selected officers from the Indian Army. I suggested this to Lord K and he seemed much taken with it and told me to go into the question and to write privately to you about it.

At this point Clayton had pointed out a flaw in Kitchener's thinking on a difficult issue and suggested a viable alternative that still incorporated elements of Lord K's idea. He had now only to disarm the inevitable criticism from Wingate that he had made a major policy proposal without securing the Sirdar's prior approval. But, since Lord K was already amenable to the idea, this was not difficult; he had only to assign credit: 'I think the scheme is rather an attractive one and, as I told Lord Kitchener, the idea of starting the nucleus of a "Political Service" is one that you have had in your mind for some time.' [25]

Clayton would not work much longer with Lord K. Kitchener left Cairo in the spring of 1914, for his annual leave and, save for a brief visit in late 1915, never set foot in Egypt again. As he was about to embark on his return voyage to Cairo in August 1914, Europe flared into war and he was called back to London and to the War Office where he would serve as Secretary of State. That Lord K left Egypt with a high opinion of Clayton cannot be doubted. When Clayton was suggested as the Director of Intelligence for British forces in Egypt in the autumn of 1914, Kitchener did not hesitate to approve the appointment. And when Clayton was recommended for his first British honour, the CMG, in 1915, his name appeared not on the list of Wingate or Sir Henry McMahon, then British representative in Cairo, but on that of Lord Kitchener of Khartoum.

PART TWO

WAR

9

Intrusive: Organizing a Middle Eastern Intelligence, 1914–1915

Clayton's summer 1914 leave would be his last for more than four years. When he and Enid arrived at Sandown in early July, the storm clouds had already gathered over Europe. The European Powers had been moving into their respective opposing camps for a decade or more and the assassination of the Austrian Archduke Franz Ferdinand at Sarajevo on June 28 served merely to provide the spark that ignited the conflagration. Britain had resolved most of her problems with France in 1904, by the so-called Entente Cordiale, and with Russia in a 1907 Agreement that settled disputes between the two in Persia. In opposition, long-time allies Germany and Austria-Hungary appeared defiant and increasingly bellicose. Less certain was the position of the lesser European countries and particularly those on the Near Eastern periphery. No one knew whether, in the event of war, Italy, Greece, Rumania, Bulgaria and, even more critical to the region, the Ottoman Empire, would side with the Entente of France, Russia and Britain or would join the Central Powers, Germany and Austria-Hungary. 'Things look bleaker than ever in Europe today', Clayton wrote to Wingate on July 31. 'From our smaller and local standpoint,' he added, 'hostilities with Italy should free our hands to some extent in regard to Abyssinia & Tripoli [North Africa] though it may complicate the issues.' One of the complicating issues, of course, was the position of Egypt. Nominally still subject to Ottoman suzerainty, Egypt could itself adopt a hostile attitude towards its actual ruler, Great Britain. Clayton favoured foreclosing the possibility of Egyptian opposition by annexation. 'I hope some good may arise and that we shall definitely take Egypt – it will be difficult to run the show there at all in such troublous times if we don't.'[1]

Clayton's leave was to have lasted until the end of August, but by midnight on August 4, Europe was at war. Three days later the P & O liner *Mooltan*, 'virtually commandeered for Egyptian officials', left England for Port Said. Ronald Storrs, Oriental Secretary at the British Agency in Cairo since 1909, was aboard and later described his fellow passengers in his memoir, *Orientations*. Among them was the Sirdar and 'an unassuming Captain Clayton, soon to become one of the best known figures in the Near East'.[2] The great rush of British officials to return to the East appeared unnecessary, for the outbreak of hostilities in Europe had little effect in

Egypt. The vast majority of Egyptians were indifferent, even oblivious, to the war. No threat had materialised in the Middle East and many men in the substantial British community in Egypt immediately sought appointments in the British Expeditionary Force, which left England for France on August 12. The Turks were officially neutral and it was not at all clear that they would abandon their neutrality and side with Germany. And, even if they did, few were convinced that the Turks would be a formidable opponent.

For a century or more, with only occasional departures, British policy had been to buttress the crumbling foundations of the Ottoman state. Throughout the nineteenth century the Empire had been seen as a useful impediment, a sort of buffer, against Russian irredentism. A decisive military defeat of the Ottomans, it was thought, would provide the Russians with access to the Mediterranean in which the British had held a predominant position since the Napoleonic wars. There was good cause to worry about the ambitions of the Czars; there had been Russo-Turkish wars in 1768–74, in 1787–92, in 1806–12, and again in 1828–29. It was after the last of these conflicts that Britain came to see Russia as its greatest threat in the Near East. The Crimean War (1854–56), though it again pitted Russian against Turk, was more a European conflict than a battle for primacy in the region. But the Russians were forced to climb down by the Treaty of Paris (March, 1856) and the European Powers guaranteed the independence and territorial integrity of the Ottoman Empire. Yet, each of these conflicts seemed to underscore Ottoman military inadequacy in the face of Russian aggrandisement.

The last thirty years of the century brought a new factor into the shifting dynamic of the Near East – the emergence of national movements in the Ottoman provinces of south-eastern Europe. In the Eastern Crisis of 1875–78, risings in Bosnia and Herzegovina, in Bulgaria, Serbia and Montenegro resulted in yet another Russo-Turkish war, one that again appeared likely to embroil the European Powers. By January 1878, with the Russians poised on the European approaches to Constantinople, the British ordered a fleet to the Straits connecting the Black Sea with the Mediterranean and a European war again appeared likely. But the crisis was averted, defused diplomatically at the Congress of Berlin (1878). This time the Ottoman Empire was the big loser, as Montenegro, Rumania and Serbia gained independence from their Turkish overlords. At the same time, Bosnia and Herzegovina passed from Ottoman to Austrian 'protection'. Bulgaria was sliced into three portions, the northern falling under Russian control, a southern piece remaining with the Turks and a third portion accorded some measure of independence. Of all her European territories, the Ottoman Empire retained full control over only Macedonia.

Until the crisis of 1875–78, the 'Eastern Question' as it was called, was viewed largely as a Russo-Turkish contest, albeit one that often had significant ramifications for the European Powers. But after the Congress of Berlin, European concerns focused more on the effects of Balkan nationalism and on the instability of the region caused by the effective removal of the Turks from Europe. The Ottoman Empire now seemed less relevant and especially so to the British. Since the opening of the

Suez Canal in 1869, and the occupation of Egypt in 1882, the strategic focus appeared to move south, from Constantinople to Cairo. This shift in focus did not mean, however, that Britain had abandoned her policy of supporting the Ottoman Empire. That policy persevered – though perhaps not with the enthusiasm shown earlier – and was pursued also by France and Austria.

The nineteenth century also saw significant changes in the Ottoman government itself. Springing partly from a recognition that they had fallen far behind their European contemporaries in the matter of modern government, Ottoman intellectuals initiated a period of widespread reform in Constantinople during the years 1839–76, the period generally referred to as the *Tanzimat* (reorganisation). Proclamations issued in 1839 and 1856, resulted in reforms in Ottoman taxation, education, law and military conscription and, most important, these reforms were applied to all Ottoman subjects, Muslim and non-Muslim alike. The idea that allegiance to the Empire was defined by Ottoman citizenship, rather than by religion or ethnicity, came to be called 'Ottomanism'. In 1876, a new constitution was adopted that embodied these concepts and provided for a legislative assembly that was, at least in part, representative. But in 1878, Sultan Abdulhamid II (r. 1876–1909) dissolved the assembly, suspended the constitution, and returned the country to the autocratic rule of his predecessors. The advent of Hamidian rule also marked the collapse of Ottoman finances. By 1874 the Turks had run up a staggering debt – nearly £200 million – and interest payments on foreign loans consumed fully 60% of state expenditure. In 1876 the government defaulted and the Ottoman Public Debt Administration (OPDA), a committee of foreign creditors not unlike the *Caisse de la Dette* in Egypt, was established to administer the debt. The Ottoman Empire, like Egypt, had relinquished its financial independence to European creditors.

The reign of Abdulhamid has been characterized generally as retrograde, repressive, and cruel. The Sultan was vilified by Europeans as a tyrant, a murderer of Christians, who had well-earned the sobriquets 'Abdul the Damned' and 'the Red Sultan'. There were some grounds to support these views. Suspicious to the point of paranoia, the Sultan established a secret police and a spy network so thorough that it sniffed out, and crushed, nearly every embryonic reform movement and current of dissent at home or abroad that posed a challenge to his rule. But the Sultan was not the unmitigated villain suggested by his European detractors; he had a human side, was skilled in wood-working and took the greatest pleasure in having the stories of Sherlock Holmes read to him at bed-time. He was also a clever man – perhaps shrewd would be more appropriate – an able diplomat and an adroit politician. Above all, he was resilient; he survived every insurrection, scheme, plot and stratagem thrown at him for thirty-three years. By the time he finally was deposed in 1909, only two Sultans in Ottoman history had enjoyed longer reigns.

One technique that enabled Abdulhamid to cling to power was his invocation of Pan-Islamism, a doctrine that, as will be seen, would cause endless worry among British authorities in Cairo and London during the war years. The notion that Islam could be used as a unifying force had both foreign and domestic implications. Within the Empire, appeals to Islamic unity had a cohesive effect; Muslim subjects of the Empire would bond together in defence of the state. Of course, in this sense, Pan-Islamism was antithetical to Ottomanism, an essentially secular doctrine founded on the idea that all citizens of the Empire were to be treated equally, irrespective of their religion, and owed allegiance to the state based on their Ottoman citizenship alone. But, as the Empire was progressively truncated in the latter nineteenth century, losing ever more European territory to Russian aggrandisement and Balkan nationalism, the proportion of non-Muslims in the Empire decreased correspondingly, and the appeal of Pan-Islamism widened. In the foreign context, Pan-Islamism was invoked by the Sultan to enlist the allegiance and support of Muslims outside, or on the periphery of, the Empire. Abdulhamid was able to do this by emphasising his role as the Caliph of Islam.

As a viable political force, the Caliphate had been in decline well before the Mongols eliminated the last Abbasid Caliph in 1258. But the title persisted over the centuries – even if it was little more than a title – and came to reside in the Egyptian Mameluks. When Egypt was conquered by the Ottomans in 1517, Sultan Selim I assumed the title of Caliph. But the Sultans did not make use of the title in any political way until 1774, when it first appeared in a treaty with the Russians. The Sultan there advanced a new idea; as Caliph, he held religious authority over all Muslims, even in those territories lost to the Russians in battle. Historically, and theologically, the idea was flawed. Although traditionally styled as defender of the faithful, the Caliph had never possessed a religious or spiritual authority. He was never regarded as the repository of divine truth. He did not define religious dogma or promulgate it. He possessed no sacerdotal or 'priestly' functions at all. Yet, the characterization of the Caliph as the supreme religious functionary of Islam, as a kind of Islamic Pope, gained wide currency in Europe from the late eighteenth century. Abdulhamid and his successors exploited this European misconception of the Caliphate. In a series of treaties with the Austrians (1909), Italians (1912), and the Bulgarians and Greeks (1913), the Ottomans were able to retain some vestige of control by asserting the Sultan-Caliph's rights as the supreme arbiter in religious matters involving Muslims in lands lost to those countries by war or treaty. For the colonial powers, especially Britain, Pan-Islamism was a vaguely ominous concept. By 1914, there were nearly one hundred million Muslims in the British Empire, seventy million in India alone. If the Ottomans joined the Central Powers, and the Sultan-Caliph appealed to all of Islam to join the struggle, what the reaction of the British Empire's immense Muslim population would be was anybody's guess.

Whatever their domestic or international implications though, notions of Muslim solidarity embodied in Pan-Islamism were by no means adequate to curtail opposition to Hamidian rule from within the Empire. There had always been opposition to Abdulhamid, but in the last decade of the century, three distinct strands began to coalesce to form the Young Turk movement, formally known as the Committee of Union and Progress (CUP). The first strand was comprised of Turks living abroad, most of them in Paris, and many of whom had been exiled in 1895, when the Sultan's spies uncovered their secret society. A second group emerged from disaffected civil servants and students. The third, and most formidable, opposition faction came from officers in the Ottoman army, particularly a group of young officers stationed at Salonika, who were dismayed by the declining state of the army in the early years of the new century. None of these groups proposed radical reform; their common programme called for restoration of the 1876 constitution and a resumption of the legislative assembly that that had been suspended by Abdulhamid in 1878. In the summer of 1908, a group of army officers revolted and demanded that the Sultan restore the constitution. Unwilling, or unable, to challenge a rising from within the army, he relented and the constitution was restored. Still, not all Turks were enamoured with the new constitutional regime. A counter-coup, perhaps approved by Abdulhamid, was launched in April 1909. The CUP responded quickly, crushed the protestors and deposed the Sultan, exiling him to Salonika, headquarters of the CUP.

Despite their reforming efforts, the CUP could do little to arrest the continuing deterioration of the Empire. The restoration of constitutional government could not forestall Bulgaria's 1908 declaration of independence or Austria's annexation of Bosnia in that year. In 1911, the Italians invaded the Ottoman North African province of Tripoli and a year later the Turks were forced to cede the province to Italy in the face of further threats in the Balkans. The 1912 threat came in the form of a coalition of Bulgaria, Greece, Serbia and Montenegro, whose combined forces drove the Turks out of Europe altogether. In that same year, Albania declared its independence. But the Balkan coalition fell apart in 1913, and in the ensuing Second Balkan War, the Ottomans were able to regain a toe-hold in Europe, securing portions of Thrace. However, overall, the results of the Balkan Wars were devastating; the Empire lost nearly 55,000 square miles of European territory and 4.2 million subjects.

The poor performance of the Ottoman army in North Africa and in the Balkan Wars suggested that the army would pose no serious threat to Russia or to Britain should the Turks join the Central Powers in 1914. But the CUP moved quickly to address Turkish military inadequacies. Already, in 1913, a forty member German military mission under Liman von Sanders was sent to Constantinople to reform the army and, by August 1914, the German mission had swollen to 2,000 men. This was not as alarming a development as it appeared. Prussian officers had been advising the Turks since the 1830s, and in 1882, the Germans had undertaken a complete overhaul of the Ottoman army at the request of Abdulhamid. Moreover, the German military presence in Constantinople did not necessarily imply a political alliance between Germany and the Ottoman Empire. Far from it; if recent events were any indication, such an alliance was unlikely. True, the Kaiser had made well-publicised visits to Constantinople in 1889, and again in 1898, and the Germans had obtained Ottoman concessions for the fabled Berlin to Baghdad railway in 1899. On the other hand, Berlin had supported Austria-Hungary's annexation of Bosnia in 1908, and in the First Balkan War of 1912, not only did the Germans decline to back the Turks, they infuriated the Sultan by approving the Greek seizure of Ottoman islands in the Aegean Sea. And, with one very important exception – Enver Pasha, Minister of War from January 1914 – none of the CUP leaders was particularly inclined toward an alignment with Germany.

None of this is to suggest, however, that the British did not foresee the Ottoman Empire as a potential enemy. As early as 1906, London began to consider a possible Turkish threat to Egypt. In that year a disagreement arose between Turkey and Britain concerning the Palestine-Egypt boundary in Sinai, a dispute known as the Taba Affair. Although it generated a fair amount of sabre-rattling on both sides, the Affair was resolved diplomatically, and its most important effect from the British perspective was to prompt a reconsideration of the Ottoman Empire as a potential adversary. Still, a December 1906 study concluded that 'the defence of Egypt in the event of trouble with the Ottoman Empire . . . gives at present no ground for concern'.[3] A further assessment, made in 1907 by the Committee of Imperial Defence (CID), again found a Turkish invasion of Egypt through Sinai to be unlikely, but considered a raid on the Canal to be quite possible. Most dangerous of all though was the possibility that the Turks might foment a popular insurrection against British rule in Egypt.[4]

The Taba Affair and the resulting 1906–7 assessments also prompted consideration of Britain's Intelligence-gathering capabilities in the Middle East. Since the Ottomans had not been seriously considered as antagonists until Taba, the collection of Intelligence on Turkish intentions and military preparedness had been unsystematic, ad hoc, inadequate. London and Cairo depended largely on the reports of British diplomatic representatives and military attachés in Constantinople, on information provided by members of the Levant Consular Service and even on the accounts of British travellers in the region. A handbook on the Turkish army had first been published in 1877, but badly wanted updating. Six revisions would be produced by the time war broke out in 1914. Information was lacking even on the immediate approaches to Egypt through Sinai. Surveys of Sinai and southern Palestine were thus undertaken in 1910 and in early 1914 to remedy the information void.

British military and Intelligence services also appear to have shown little interest in the Middle East in the immediate pre-war period. The British army had never been keen on Intelligence and was slow to develop such a function. There was no permanent Intelligence section in the War Office until 1873, and even in August 1914, British field commands and expeditionary forces, such as the Army of Occupation in Egypt, had no standing Intelligence sections. Armies in the field had always established Intelligence units when hostilities commenced and disbanded them when the fighting stopped. Since no fighting was going on in Egypt, the Army of Occupation relied on the Egyptian Intelligence Department for information on the Ottoman Empire.[5] The army's discomfort with Intelligence gathering was not surprising; the sentiment in the British army had always been that it was unsporting, ungentlemanly even, to spy on one's potential enemies. The prevailing attitude was best described by the official historian of the Crimean War: 'The gathering of knowledge by clandestine means', he wrote, 'was repulsive to the feelings of an English Gentleman'.[6] That attitude seemed to be confirmed when the British Expeditionary Force crossed to France in August 1914; its hastily assembled Intelligence Corps was so ill-equipped it had to requisition mounts from the Grafton Hunt for transport.[7]

Unlike the Army, the British Intelligence services, the precursors of MI5 and MI6, certainly had no qualms about spying on one's potential enemies, but they had only been established in October 1909 and, quite naturally, were more interested in German intentions than in a possible Turkish threat. Little is known about Intelligence gathering in the region prior to 1914, probably because little Intelligence was gathered. The Foreign Office, which had for years administered a secret service vote, allocated a meagre £1,000 to the British embassy in Constantinople in 1908, but how even this small amount was expended is unknown.[8] However, as will be seen, both the Security Service and the Secret Intelligence Service would take a greater interest in the region in 1915.

Owing largely to the lack of an organised Intelligence-gathering capability in the Middle East, estimates of Turkish strength in the event of hostilities were little more than guesswork. A January 1911 assessment reflected the view that the Turks could amass as many as 100,000 men in forty-five days along the Sinai-Palestine border and as many as 20,000 of these could reach the Canal in a fortnight. Similarly, a May 1912 study concluded that the Ottoman army could allocate 100,000 men for operations against Egypt without depleting Turkish forces in Europe or on the Caucasus frontier.[9] By the autumn of 1914, then, the British had come to acknowledge the Ottoman threat, had studied, in some detail, the approaches the Turks might take in the event of an attack on Egypt, and had reached some very general conclusions as to the numbers and quality of the opposition forces that could be deployed for the purpose. Clayton, upon whom would fall the burden of Middle Eastern Intelligence during the first two years of the war, later summed up the state of affairs:

> Previous to the war there was in existence no general and organised system of Intelligence in the area . . . Such activities as existed were local, and restricted to certain areas, and they were concerned with but a small portion of the large number of subjects contained in [Intelligence and Counterintelligence] . . . activities. Great difficulty was consequently experienced after the outbreak of war in building up an organisation which should be both thorough and, at the same time, closely inter-related in all its parts.[10]

As this assessment suggests, upon his arrival in Cairo in mid-August 1914, Clayton was immediately confronted with an array of difficult questions. What would the Ottomans do now that Germany had declared war and commenced operations in Europe? If Turkey followed suit, where would she direct her armies, to the Balkans, towards Russia in the Caucasus, or against Egypt? And if the Turks joined Germany, what would the Arabs in Syria, Palestine, Arabia and Mesopotamia do? No less important, what actions would be taken by the Arabs in North Africa? Would the Sanusi tribesmen on Egypt's Western border join their co-religionists in an assault on Egypt? And, of most immediate importance to Clayton, how would the Egyptians themselves react? A War Office analysis of February 1914, while reasoning that the Turks could bring no more than 23,000 men to the Canal within a month after mobilisation, still concluded that Egypt might very well rise up against British rule in the event of a Turksish attack.[11]

The British were then unaware that a pro-war party in the CUP, led by Enver, had concluded a secret alliance with the Germans on August 2, calling for reciprocal military support against Britain's ally, Russia. Sir Louis Mallet, British ambassador in Constantinople, would not learn of it for nearly three months. But, just as Clayton was arriving in Egypt, the British did learn, from their embassy in Petrograd, that the CUP leaders had issued an August 8 order to the Ottoman Second Army in Syria to begin planning for a possible attack on Egypt. Still, nearly all British authorities in the East believed the Turks were 'fence-sitting', for, in the words of Wingate, they would 'be committing political suicide' if they joined the Germans.[12] Until mid-October, Clayton shared this view. In late August he instructed his men in Sinai to stop sending patrols east of the Canal, 'urging the vital importance of doing nothing that would cause alarm or give rise to misconception on the part of the Turks'.[13] Again, on September 9, he concluded that a Turkish mobilisation in Syria was defensive only.[14]

Until hostilities began in the region at the end of October, Clayton had available to him two primary sources of Intelligence – reports from consular officials and information from Arab agents deployed in Sinai. An October survey of British consular officials in Beirut, Aleppo, Damascus and Jerusalem disclosed little Arab enthusiasm for a Turkish war against Britain, but yielded scant information on Ottoman war preparations.[15] Unusually, Clayton appears to have side-stepped diplomatic channels and obtained these reports directly.[16] At the same time, he was receiving periodic reports from the governor of Sinai, Alwyn Jennings-Bramly and his assistant, Charles Barlow, who were running Arab agents throughout the peninsula. However, the quality of the Arab reports was indifferent, at best, and, until reconnaissance flights were begun in Sinai in late November, the reports were not subject to corroboration. Inevitably, reliance on the Arab agents led to mistakes. In an early September 'Appreciation', Clayton's Intelligence department reported that 'it seems almost certain' that Hussein Ibn Ali, Amir of Mecca, 'has now definitely thrown in his lot with Turkey'. Two weeks later the same conclusion was reached regarding Ibn Saud, Amir of Najd in Central Arabia. Neither was correct.[17]

Although Allied consuls and Arab agents provided Clayton's main sources of Intelligence, he took information from wherever he could get it. On September 7, he reported that the British censor at Alexandria had discovered, and taken over, a wireless station there. Two days later, he added that the censor was using the apparatus to send 'trap messages' from a Russian steamer in Alexandria harbour 'to see if they get into circulation through unauthorised channels'.[18] The results, if any, were not reported, but it seems unlikely that any messages were intercepted; the Turks were known to have only one wireless station, set up in Constantinople in 1911, and, indeed, the British had only one, owned and operated by Lloyd's, at Port Said.[19] A variety of information was also obtained from unspecified agents and from 'an arrival from Syria' who reported on the Turks' efforts to commandeer grain and transport (camels), and the call-up 'of all men between 20 and 40' for military service in Syria.

In September, Sir Julian Byng, commanding the Army of Occupation – soon to be renamed the Force in Egypt – was replaced by General Sir John Maxwell. Clayton may have known Maxwell prior to his arrival in Cairo. The general had commanded the Army of Occupation from 1908 to 1912, and, like Clayton, had fought in the Sudan campaigns of 1898, when, as a colonel, he commanded native brigades at the Atbara and Omdurman. He certainly knew Wingate very well, and within a fortnight of his arrival in Cairo, Maxwell sent his former colleague an unexpected note: 'Clayton is very helpful and good', he wrote, and 'I have handed over to him all Intelligence work'.[20] To his former, and current, chief, Lord Kitchener, Maxwell clarified Clayton's new role: 'I have closed down all intermediary Intelligences and concentrated everything in Clayton's hands, and he keeps both the [British] Agency and myself informed.'[21]

In some ways, Maxwell's decision to put Clayton in charge of Intelligence for the army was questionable. Clayton was only thirty-nine at the time of his appointment and had acted as head of the Egyptian Intelligence department for less than a year, during which time the scope of his responsibilities had been much more limited than those now placed upon him. But, as noted, the Egyptian department had long provided Intelligence services for the Army of Occupation which, like other expeditionary forces in the British army, had no standing Intelligence section. It must also be said that Maxwell had little in the way of options. There was a great demand for officers on the Western Front and, as he complained to Wingate, 'I get telegrams all day ordering people home'. With the exception of one colonel, he lost his entire staff to France and had to assemble a completely new staff 'who do not know either their Division or anything about the country'.[22] Clayton did know the country; he had worked in Egypt and the Sudan for eighteen years and likely seemed to Maxwell to be the obvious and best choice.

At the end of September Clayton summarized the results of his Intelligence efforts during the preceding six weeks in a letter to Wingate, for whom he was still acting as the Sudan's representative in Cairo:

[The Turks] are undoubtedly actually preparing for some sort of action against Egypt in the event of the war party gaining the ascendant, and if they do declare war there seems little doubt that they will make a move in this direction. On the other hand there is a strong peace party in Constantinople so it just depends whether they will be able to control Enver and his pro-German hot-heads or not. There is no doubt that German influence is paramount in . . . [Constantinople] and only success of the Allies in Europe can defeat it. It is a very anxious time & becoming a strain so that sometimes one longs for it to be settled, even if it is the wrong way it would be a relief in a certain way.

In adding his praise for the handful of men in his department, Clayton also hinted to the Sirdar that he had himself proposed to Maxwell that he take over Intelligence work for the Force in Egypt:

> Many thanks for your . . . kind appreciation of the work of the Intelligence staff here. The people in my office are certainly doing splendidly and there is never a grumble at the abnormally long hours. We have certainly reaped the reward of offering to take over all the Intelligence work, in that the various Ministries and Departments seem to act on the principle "when in doubt send to the Intelligence" and we get bombarded with every kind of conundrum.

He concluded with a slight criticism of his new chief, who seemed not to take the Turkish threat seriously enough:

> General Maxwell seems very calm . . . I am not sure he is not a little too calm & inclined to take things too easily in regard to a Turkish advance. But . . . I daresay he adopts that attitude purposely in order to keep people from getting excited & talking nonsense.[23]

By mid-October Clayton was convinced the Turks were preparing for a major assault on the Canal. 'The Turkish situation looks to me daily more menacing and there is but little doubt that an advance on the Canal is more than probable in the near future.' Based on the 'methodical and thorough preparations' that the Turks were making, he concluded that 'it is not now a sudden dash across Sinai to the Canal which is the scheme, but a much larger and comprehensive plan'. No less worrisome, Clayton had been 'finding out a good deal about the ramifications of German-Turkish plots in this country for engineering risings and trouble & I trust . . . that forewarned is forearmed'.[24] Although Cairo had been instructed earlier to refrain from soliciting Arab support in Turkish-controlled territory, the Agency had at last received approval to begin efforts to enlist the Arabs as allies. Foreign Secretary Sir Edward Grey instructed the Acting British Agent, Milne Cheetham, to inform Syrian notables in Cairo that 'Britain has no quarrel with the Arabs . . . [and] will not consider that the Arabs are involved in this war, unless they by overt acts take part in assisting the German-Turkish forces . . . .' Despite the rising tension in Cairo, Clayton must have smiled when he read Grey's further suggestion to Cheetham for co-opting the Arabs: 'You should give them some presents', the Foreign Secretary added.[25] Clayton may not have distributed any presents, but he lost no time in reacting. 'The Arab policy recommended has now been approved from home at last', he informed Wingate, 'and I am sending out all the agents I can get hold of from anywhere.'[26]

The pace of events now quickened. On October 21, Maxwell warned the War Office that a Turkish-sponsored Bedouin raid in Sinai was imminent, and the next day Kitchener ordered the evacuation of the peninsula, a move consistent with the War Office plan for a static defence of Egypt along the Canal. On the same day, in

Constantinople, Enver issued secret orders to the Ottoman Navy, now under German command, to attack the Russian fleet and Black Sea ports. On the 23rd, Mallet, British ambassador to the Porte, finally learned of the Turco-German treaty of August 2. Six days later, the Turkish fleet opened up on the Russian Black Sea ports and, at the same time, the Bedouin force of 2,000 launched their raid in Sinai, now rendered unnecessary by the British evacuation of the peninsula. On November 2, Russia declared war on the Ottoman Empire and Britain announced the imposition of Martial Law in Egypt. Three days later, Britain and France announced a state of war with Turkey. On November 11, Sultan Mehmed V declared war on Britain, France and Russia and, on the 14th – confirming Britain's Pan-Islamic fears – he proclaimed a *jihad*, a holy war, against the Empire's infidel opponents. The fight for the Middle East was on.

Clayton was already busy. During the last week in October he had got his hands on three sets of cyphers from the Turkish Commissariat in Cairo, procured at considerable expense, and only for a few hours, so that they could be photographed. But the results were disappointing, for intercepted telegrams that were decoded using the cyphers did not disclose 'any of the schemes which we know have been set on foot in Turkey by German influence'.[27] What might have been an Intelligence coup of the highest order was short-lived anyway, as Turkish officials in Egypt were sent packing on the declaration of war and the Commissariat was closed.

With the outbreak of hostilities, Clayton quickly realised that the Intelligence Department for the Force in Egypt would have to be expanded and its specific responsibilities better defined. The most immediate need was to organise the Intelligence for the Middle Eastern theatre on strategic and tactical lines. Maxwell had established a defence force on the Canal and Jennings-Bramly was appointed its Intelligence chief at Ismailia, assisted by Barlow in the northern Canal sector and by A. C. Parker, a nephew of Lord Kitchener and an authority on Sinai, in the south. These three would be responsible for tactical Intelligence along the Canal – running Arab agents in Sinai, organising ground and air reconnaissance, and, later, interrogating prisoners. Establishment of the Ismailia Intelligence unit enabled Clayton to reduce his daily involvement in tactical military Intelligence, and free up time for his much wider responsibilities in Cairo.[28] Not only did he remain in charge of political Intelligence in Egypt, the Sudan and the Arab Middle East (except for Mesopotamia, which then fell under the jurisdiction of the Government of India), he was also responsible for counter-intelligence, propaganda and, later, Egyptian censorship, and he was charged with ascertaining the intentions of the Sanusi in the Western Desert. On top of all this, he continued to act as Sudan Agent and as Maxwell's liaison with the British Agency. In recognition of Clayton's enhanced duties, and his 'very useful work', Maxwell arranged with the War Office for him to be given the local and temporary rank of lieutenant-colonel. Clayton mistakenly attributed the promotion to Wingate, an error that the Sirdar made no effort to correct.[29]

Now that the war had started, Clayton's primary concern was with the Ottoman army order of battle: what was the precise composition of that army, in men and materiel, and where, when and how would it be deployed? One source of Intelligence had already been lost when all of the Entente consulates in Ottoman territory were closed in early November. Some information could be gleaned from neutral countries whose diplomatic and consular officers still resided in the Empire – the Greek Consul at Beirut was identified as one such source – but documentary evidence of Intelligence from this source is sparse, no doubt because such countries were leery of generating any sort of record that could jeopardise their neutrality. Some information was also provided during the early months of the war by refugees and former residents of Turkish territories, 6,000 of whom descended on Egypt during the first ten weeks of the war. Among them were railway officials, ship captains and 'good or fairly good English and French missionary' sources who provided a report on Turkish artillery in Palestine.[30] But these people had not been trained to identify military equipment, to follow troop movements, or to ascertain their strengths or intentions, and the information provided was generally unhelpful. One surprising source was a man named Webb, described as an English waiter at the Hotel Fast, headquarters of the German staff at Jerusalem, who reported – erroneously – that Turco-German forces would be approaching the Canal on January 10, 1915.[31]

Another source, used extensively by Clayton until March 1915, when the Turks tightened their control of the Levantine coast, was provided by agents dropped by ship. Initially, the system worked well. Agents were inserted along the entire coastline from Alexandretta (Iskenderun) in the far north to Akaba in the south, and Clayton was not above employing some fairly dubious characters to implement the scheme:

> Quite a number of agents I sent over to Palestine some weeks ago have succeeded in getting through and getting safely back – some with quite good information. We have also a regular system in conjunction with the Navy by which agents are landed on the Syrian coast & picked up again by native boats. I find the hasheesh smugglers at Alexandria & Port Said most useful in this respect. I am afraid I am laying up a store of trouble for myself when the war is over by the rascals I am in with now![32]

Clayton also set up 'a system of agents in connection with the ships, run by Stirling, up the Gulf of Akaba'.[33] Stirling, a former Egyptian Army colleague of Clayton, described the system:

> We would steam down the Red Sea in a cruiser, keeping well out of sight of land, till about noon, when we would lower a cutter in which I would push off with the spy who was due to land that night. We would sail till we raised land, from then on had to row; we dared not risk having our sails observed from the shore, and would reach the coast some time after dark. I would land my agent, telling him when to return to the shore again and how to signal his position; then we would lie up on one of the small islands along the coast

until it was time to creep in, again under cover of darkness, and take our agent off.[34]

The quality of information extracted from these agents, or spies, as Stirling called them, was generally regarded by Clayton as poor. Putting aside the general caveat that the product of secret Intelligence is 'uncertain information from questionable people', he was more concerned that their information was nearly always 'vague as regards numbers or military details'.[35] Although Clayton continued to drop agents along the Syrian and Palestine coasts, by March 1915, Maxwell was complaining that 'though we get agents in, we can't get them out. The Turks take very good care we don't and anyone the least suspicious is at once arrested'. Clayton soon began to despair of even landing the agents: 'The restrictions are now very severe and . . . posts have been placed all along the coast, so that it is very difficult to land agents surreptitiously now. I know that at least two of my agents have been caught and I fear that both have been hanged, so that no one is very keen on going.'[36]

Because of their vagueness and unreliability, agent reports, when they could be obtained, were rarely relied upon without some sort of corroborating information. In Syria, this was often impossible to secure, but in Sinai, and to a lesser extent, Palestine, agent reports could be tested by means of aerial reconnaissance. The use of airplanes for this purpose was fairly new; the Italians had first flown reconnaissance flights over Libya during the Turco-Italian war of 1911–12. But by November 4, 1914, Kitchener had dispatched three planes from England and Clayton found three more in Egypt, one confiscated from a German citizen.[37] The first flight of a Royal Flying Corps (RFC) detachment occurred on November 27, and was immediately seen by Clayton as inadequate. 'The aeroplanes sent out from home are not really of much use,' he complained, 'as they are small machines with a radius of only 50 or 60 miles'. More useful were the five Nieuport seaplanes, hydroplanes as they were then called, sent out on the French seaplane carrier *Foudre* at the beginning of December.[38] No airplane could then be considered reliable, but at least the Nieuports had the advantage of mobility; they could be launched from any point their carriers could reach and, by the end of 1914, were reconnoitring from El Arish to Beirut and flying inland as far as Beersheba, thirty miles from the Mediterranean coast. Their value was soon apparent. On December 12, a hydroplane flight along the coast between Gaza and El Arish estimated the number of Turkish troops in the area, based on a count of tents, at one-eighth the number provided by Arab agents. The British Navy also deployed two cruisers to patrol the coast, each capable of carrying a hydroplane, and two German freighters, *Anne Rickmers* and *Rabenfels*, commandeered at Port Said in August, were refitted to carry two seaplanes each. The Intelligence gathered from them came only in the form of pilot reports, as aerial photography would not be used in the theatre until August, 1915.[39]

In addition to using these varied sources to learn of the plans and movements of the Turks, Clayton was also preoccupied with counter-intelligence matters. There were still some 7,300 Germans and Austrians residing in Egypt in September 1914, many masquerading as citizens of neutral countries, and only after Maxwell's arrival did the British begin rounding them up.[40] Clayton was convinced that German and Turkish agents in Egypt were scheming, planning to engineer a rising in the country and an attack by Sanusi tribesmen in the western desert, both timed to coincide with a Turkish attack on the Canal. Another source of potential trouble was the Khedive himself, Abbas Hilmi II (r. 1892–1914). Abbas had made no secret of his dislike of British rule and routinely consorted with Egyptian nationalists or Turkish plotters, as the mood suited him, to undermine British authority. Regarded by the British as 'trickier than a Stuart king', Abbas was fortuitously visiting Constantinople when war broke out. He would never return. On December 18, after much debate in London and Cairo, Britain declared a protectorate over Egypt and, two days later, Abbas was deposed, replaced by his uncle, Hussein Kamil, a more pliable man from the British perspective, who took the title 'sultan'. Well before the protectorate was declared, Clayton saw to it that 'several prominent sedition-mongers of the Khedivial party' were arrested and deported or interned.[41]

These moves, however helpful, did not eliminate all internal threats. Clayton still believed that there were 'a lot of dangerous people about', and that 'continual vigilance' was required. Indeed, Cheetham reported to the Foreign Office on November 10, that the Advisers of Finance (Lord Edward Cecil) and Interior (Ronald Graham) and Clayton, 'in whose hands military and civil Intelligence have been centralised, hold very strongly that the Turks and Khedive have been working secretly for months to prepare a religious outbreak in Egypt itself and to incite the western Bedouins and the Senoussists to move in the name of Islam along the western borders'. 'We believe', he added, 'that we ought to be adequately prepared . . . and that . . . no expense or inconvenience should be allowed to stand in the way of insurance against a fanatical outburst . . . The crucial point will be when it is known that a Turkish army is actually engaged on or near the Canal'.[42] In light of the Turkish *jihad* proclamation of November 14, Clayton was also greatly concerned about the two divisions of Indian troops that formed the bulk of the Canal defence force and which contained significant Muslim elements. In mid-December two small parties of Baluchis (thirteen men in all) stationed at Suez deserted. Clayton left immediately for the Canal to 'organise a regular system of secret service in order to prevent the spread of propaganda amongst the Mohammedan troops'. He also decided 'to put the whole Canal zone under military control', a decision endorsed by Maxwell on December 19.[43] As will be seen, Clayton would be involved in counter-intelligence work throughout his time as Director of Intelligence and, as late as June 1916, would initiate a series of important, and controversial, deportations of European undesirables from Egypt.

With the outbreak of fighting in early November Clayton knew he could no longer rely on the handful of men in the Egyptian Intelligence to meet the vastly increased demands of his office. To their credit, the War Office came to the same conclusion in London and on November 6 offered to send a group of seven young officers to Cairo to fill the void. The only regular army officer in the group was Captain Stewart F. Newcombe, just recalled from France, whom Clayton had known from his Sudan work since as early as 1910. Clayton's plan was that the group, which arrived in Cairo in mid-December, would form a new Military Intelligence section in his office:

> I have now got Newcombe, Aubrey Herbert, George Lloyd – also Woolley & Lawrence (of the Palestine Survey) – under me and I am at last able to start a proper Military Intelligence Section. There is a mass of stuff to do and I have not up to date had the time or staff to do more than collect a certain amount of information. It now all requires collating and putting into proper form. Then there are all the various schemes to be worked out and times and distances to be calculated, etc., etc. All this I have now given over to them under my supervision and I hope that it will mean a great deal more can be done in the more military line, which was impossible before. They are all a bit raw at the work at present except Newcombe (and even he is a bit wild), and want a lot of supervision, but they will learn.[44]

Clayton also made a few local acquisitions. Kinahan Cornwallis, yet another former Sudan colleague, was lent indefinitely to Clayton in December by the Egyptian Ministry of Finance. Philip Graves, former Constantinople correspondent for *The Times* of London was already preparing a detailed report on the Ottoman army in early November and would join the new section in January, along with his uncle, Robert W. Graves, who had worked in the Ottoman civil service.[45]

On paper, the group assembled in Cairo in December seemed promising. George Lloyd was a Member of Parliament, had previously worked as an honorary attaché in Constantinople, knew Turkish and some Arabic and would later serve as Governor of Bombay and High Commissioner for Egypt. But he did not get on well with his new chief, Newcombe, and a friend who visited him only nine days after his arrival found him 'very discontented, already working to get home, thoroughly restless'. Lloyd longed for a front-line position. 'He wants to be shot at', his friend concluded. In April 1915, he got his wish, having secured a position with the British force at the Dardanelles.[46] Aubrey Herbert, also an MP also knew Turkish and Arabic, and, like Lloyd, had served in Constantinople as an attaché. Despite his extreme short-sightedness, Herbert would later achieve fame with the Albanians, who twice offered him their throne, and was said to be the model for the fictional hero of John Buchan's espionage thriller *Greenmantle*. Herbert found Clayton 'a very nice fellow', but disliked Newcombe, whom he described as a 'vain ambitious inarticulate man'. He too left Cairo for the Dardanelles in April 1915.[47]

Leonard Woolley and T. E. Lawrence were archaeologists who had worked at excavations in northern Syria and had accompanied Newcombe on a survey of Sinai in early 1914. Most recently, Lawrence had worked in the geographical section of the War Office, writing up his report on the Palestine survey. Woolley, who spent his time in Cairo 'writing windy concealers of the truth for the press', would soon move to Port Said where he organised the dropping of agents into Syria and Palestine. His Intelligence work would end in August 1916, though, when his vessel struck a mine and sank off Alexandretta. He was picked up by the Turks and imprisoned for the duration.[48] Newcombe worked for less than a year in Cairo, leaving in early September 1915, also for the Dardanelles. Lawrence was to serve longer in the Military Intelligence section than any of the group dispatched from London in December and did not leave Cairo for Arabia until the autumn of 1916. Although he disparaged his early work as a 'bottle-washer and office boy pencil-sharpener and pen wiper', Lawrence would become one of Clayton's most astute and incisive analysts. In addition to preparing maps of the region, and occasionally interrogating prisoners of war, he would spend much of his time compiling and editing the daily Intelligence bulletins that the section began issuing in April 1915.

The short tenures of Lloyd, Herbert, Woolley and Newcombe were unfortunately typical in Clayton's Intelligence Department and, later in the Arab Bureau, formed in early 1916. It was a problem he would have for his entire time in Cairo; officers were transferred from one post to another, from the Western Front to the Middle East and back again so often that it was impossible to maintain a stable, knowledgeable Intelligence cadre at all. At no time were any of his offices adequately staffed. This would have serious professional and personal ramifications for Clayton as the war dragged on. Still, the Military Intelligence section did develop a certain camaraderie, a sort of esprit de corps, epitomised by the telegraphic address later adopted by the section. 'We called ourselves "Intrusive",' Lawrence later wrote in his classic *Seven Pillars of Wisdom*, 'for we meant to break into the accepted halls of English foreign policy and build a new people in the East, despite the rails laid down for us by our ancestors'.[49]

Contrary to his hopes, the new section did not even temporarily lighten Clayton's work-load:

> I thought that the establishment of a separate Military Intelligence section would reduce the calls on my time but up to the present the reverse has been the case as there has been a great deal to think of and arrange in order to get the Section started on sound lines. Also, with the exception of Newcombe, they are all amateurs and require a good deal of watching to begin with. However they are all tumbling to the job well and I think we have really begun to get a move on & have already got a good deal of useful material.[50]

The new section was involved in every aspect of Intelligence, including the recruitment and handling of agents, interrogation of refugees and prisoners, construction and continual revision of the Turkish order of battle, preparation of maps, guides and handbooks on the region, counter-intelligence and the preparation and dissemination of propaganda. Much of the work, of course, was undertaken to determine Turkish intentions.

What were the Turks up to? On December 6, Jemal Pasha, Minister of the Ottoman Navy, had arrived in Damascus with a plan to lead the Turkish Fourth Army in an assault on Egypt. The plan was to move an actual attacking force of some 25,000 troops along a route from Beersheba through the centre of Sinai towards Ismailia on the Canal, with diversionary columns deployed along the northern and southern approaches through the peninsula. Clayton's Intelligence, bombarded by inconsistent reports, over-estimated the Turkish strength from the start. A December 15 analysis put the Ottoman force at 60,000, 'of whom 40,000 may be effective'.[51] The French and English missionaries, mentioned earlier, estimated this force as bearing ten heavy guns, eighty quick-firing field guns and howitzers and thirty-one machine guns, although Intelligence believed the actual numbers to be 'very much greater'.[52] A year-end report, based on 'good and recent local authority', put the number of Turkish troops 'mobilising in the South' at 120,000, but added that 'good sources' reported not more than 15,000 to 20,000 men south of Jerusalem. 'Reliable English and American sources' accounted for some 70,000 Turkish soldiers, but acknowledged that troops from Syria could be transported only as far as the railhead in central Palestine, well to the north of Bersheeba; thereafter, the attacking force would be diminished as it could travel by road only and was dependent on camel transport. The same report also described dissension within the Turco-German force. German officers were said to be complaining bitterly of 'Turkish incompetence' and insisting that the attack could not succeed with fewer than 100,000 men. For their part, the Turkish officers were pessimistic, grumbling that they were being made the 'catspaws of the Germans'. Neither Turks nor Germans were said to have any trust in the Arab officers among them. Nevertheless, it was thought that the attack would be pushed through because Jemal 'himself has always been ardently desirous of recovering Egypt, his pet scheme'.[53] At the same time, Clayton learned that the Turks were concentrating at Hebron and expending 'great energy in completing the route to Beersheba'.[54] At year end, he was certain that the 'Germans and their Turkish pupils' were going to attack Egypt through Sinai.[55]

By early January Clayton's frustration with the often wildly disparate estimates of his human Intelligence sources was beginning to creep into his office's reports: 'It is extremely difficult to estimate with any accuracy the mobility of the Turkish troops, or even . . . to determine their whereabouts . . . as these are constantly governed by local and political reasons, which have nothing to do with strategy or tactics'. 'Turkish vagueness and the difference in terminology between the various sources of information', he added, 'put yet another obstacle in the way of accurate tabulation of the troops'.[56] He was sure of the Turkish concentration, but flights over Gaza could not confirm it: 'South of Jerusalem very large numbers of troops are reported, principally at Hebron and Gaza, estimates are given of any numbers up to 70,000 (!) but actual numbers are quite unknown. Aeroplane reconnaissance at Gaza has failed to discover signs of soldiers or civilians there, but this is inconclusive as many thousands could be billeted in the town without betraying their presence'. Still, he concluded that 'no large bodies of troops have advanced South of [the line] Gaza-Beersheba'.[57] And, although he was confident of Jemal 'being able to collect something approaching 100,000 men for the invasion of Egypt', he still had little idea of the actual size of the invading force.[58] Estimates of the pace of the Ottoman advance were to prove more accurate; a January 10 analysis concluded 'that from the date of the first movement of troops from Beersheba to an attack on the Canal' – a distance of 155 miles – 'only 14 days are necessary for 100,000 men'.[59]

Just when Clayton needed aerial reconnaissance the most, the planes were grounded by bad weather, between January 5 and 16, 1915. However, sorties made on January 17, 18 and19, provided estimates of 25,000 to 33,000 Turkish troops in Sinai.[60] Projections of the date of the attack also varied. On January 14, Clayton reported, correctly, that it had been postponed until early February, but on the 25th he informed Wingate that 'it was said to be fixed for Jan. 27th'.[61] Also on the 27th, Intelligence finally concluded that the attack would be directed at the central sector of the Canal, between Lake Timsah and the Great Bitter Lake. But the Canal defence force did not credit the report, persisting in their belief that the Turks would attack from along the northern, coastal route.[62]

The Ottoman attack that finally occurred on the night of February 2–3, 1915, fell like a damp squib. The Turks actually had available only about 25,000 men for the assault, far less than the number required to carry the Canal and overcome its 30,000 defenders. The attack was easily repulsed and it soon became apparent that the Turks had lacked sufficient troops, artillery and bridging equipment to prevail. Both Ottoman (200 killed, 700 prisoners) and British (30 dead) losses were light. On the afternoon of February 3, Jemal ordered his forces to withdraw, a general retreat that Clayton appears to have misread. Although he recognised that the Turk 'retirement from the Canal has been very complete', he also thought the attack might very well have been 'merely a reconnaissance in strong force, as at least half their force including their best troops were not engaged . . . I am inclined to think that they will try and make another attempt in the near future with a large force and fresh troops in the firing line'.[63]

Clayton did not escape criticism for his Intelligence work before, and immediately after, the attack. Some members of the War Council in London thought that the British defenders had been surprised, a criticism that Kitchener addressed by explaining that the unusually wet weather, and resulting available water in Sinai, enabled the Turks to advance more quickly than expected, and at the same time hindered reconnaissance efforts.[64] But neither Maxwell – who praised the RFC and French hydroplane pilots – nor Wilson, the commander on the Canal, expressed displeasure with the Intelligence. Other contemporaneous accounts saw little to complain of regarding Clayton's group.[65] Scholarly assessments are mixed. While the late identification of the Turkish point of attack in the Canal's central sector and the consistent over-estimates of the total strength of the invading force have been identified as Intelligence shortcomings, the most thorough analyst concludes that Clayton's work, although it resulted in a brief, tactical surprise for the defenders, 'provided enough accurate information to meet the early-warning needs of the Egypt command'.[66] And, to his credit, Clayton erred on the side of caution; failure to detect enemy plans, or to under-estimate their scope, might have had disastrous results. In the event, the inflated numbers given by Clayton for the attacking force did not cause the imperturbable Maxwell to apprise the War Office of any inadequacy in his defensive force or to ask for reinforcements. And, although Clayton was convinced the Turks and Germans were plotting for a rising in Egypt to coincide with the assault on the Canal, he concluded well before the attack that 'the bulk of the [Egyptian] people' would cause no trouble, thus removing the need to garrison troops throughout the country, troops that could better be deployed along the Canal.[67] More than a year would pass before the Turks would finally give up on their hopes of conquering Egypt, but as 1915 wore on, Clayton's attention began to focus less on the Canal and more on a region where, he came to believe, the sultan's call to *jihad* could best be defeated – Arabia.

10

Our Friends Across the Water: Origins of the Anglo-Arab Alliance

Clayton waited till well after dark on the evening of October 26, 1914, before leaving his office for a secret meeting in the nearby Cairo suburb of Heliopolis. There he met Colonel Aziz Bey al-Masri, a founder of *al-'Ahd* (the Covenant), a secret society of Arab officers in the Ottoman army. Clayton knew all about al-Masri. Until recently, the colonel had enjoyed a successful career in the army, including distinguished work leading the Sanusi against the Italians in the Libyan war of 1911–12. But shortly after forming *al-'Ahd* in 1913, he had been arrested in Constantinople, threatened with execution, and then exiled to Egypt. Two months earlier, Clayton's assistant in the Intelligence Department, Captain R .E. M. Russell had met with al-Masri, who told him that *al-'Ahd* – which only a year earlier had advocated a sort of dual Turco-Arab empire, along the lines of Austria-Hungary – was now intent on creating a new order, 'a united Arabian State, independent of Turkey and every other power except England, whose tutelage and control of foreign affairs they invite[d]'.

Al-Masri and his co-conspirators envisioned a state 'totally independent of religion' defined as 'the land of Arabic speaking people bounded on the North by the line Alexandretta–Mosul–Persian Frontier'. Mere British goodwill was of no interest to al-Masri; *al-'Ahd* needed 'money and armaments' to start their revolt against the Turks.[1] Russell had been unimpressed with al-Masri and so too was Clayton. He listened patiently to the colonel's plan to organise a revolution in Mesopotamia from among a nucleus of Arab officers stationed there and to his requests for money, arms and artillery. But he quickly dampened al-Masri's enthusiasm; Britain was not at war with Turkey and it was 'very improbable' that London would even consider such a scheme. To Milne Cheetham, Acting British Agent in Cairo, Clayton reported that not only was al-Masri's plan 'vague and the details . . . not thought out , . . to support it would be to give pledges the extent of which it would be difficult to estimate'.[2]

Al-Masri's *al-'Ahd* was among the most recent of several Arab societies that had begun to form around the time of the CUP revolt in 1908. Some of these groups were open societies, formed by young Arabs seeking only to foster Arab culture and identity within the Ottoman polity. Others, like *al-'Ahd* and *Jam'iyyat al-Umma al-'Arabiyya al-Fatat* (the Society of the Young Arab Nation), known simply as *al-Fatat*, were secret societies, founded to protect the 'natural rights of the Arab nation'.[3] Until Turkey's declaration of war appeared imminent, none of these societies espoused Arab independence. Like *al-'Ahd*, they sought merely to raise the standing of Arabs within the Ottoman Empire. Although a great deal of scholarly effort would later be expended on unearthing the origins and agendas of these various Arab nationalist movements, it seems most unlikely that they had much of an effect on the Arab population of the Empire before the war. Of the few hundred students, intellectuals and discontented army officers who represented their total membership, open or secret, they formed 'only a drop in the ocean of the five million Arab inhabitants of the Ottoman Empire'.[4]

Despite his dismissal of al-Masri, Clayton had for some time been interested in the Arabs as a possible counterpoise to the Turks. As noted earlier, he had misgauged the sympathies of various Arab chiefs for the Turks – notably Hussein, Amir of Mecca, and Ibn Saud of Najd – but he remained concerned that 'a general pan-Islamic movement, engineered from Constantinople' would have an effect in Arab territories harmful to the Entente and was anxious that the movement be countered.[5] Clayton's concerns were shared by Ronald Storrs, Oriental Secretary at the British Agency. With Clayton's approval, Storrs sent a private letter to his former chief Lord Kitchener at the War Office, suggesting that an overture be made to Hussein to learn whether Britain could 'secure not only the neutrality but the alliance of Arabia in the event of Ottoman aggression'.[6] Kitchener, who already had Clayton's September 6 'Appreciation' in hand, responded on the 24th: 'Tell Storrs to send secret and carefully chosen messenger from me to Sherif Abdullah [Hussein's second son] to ascertain whether, should present armed German influence at Constantinople coerce Sultan . . . to acts of aggression and war against Great Britain, he and his father and Arabs of Hejaz would be with us or against us'.[7] While waiting for Abduallah's reply to Kitchener's message, Clayton was approached by 'responsible adherents of the Pan-Arab movement living in Cairo' concerning Britain's attitude in the event Turkey declared war. These Arabs, who expected nothing more from Britain than a 'benevolent attitude towards their aspirations for self-government', had already sent letters to Arab notables in Syria, Palestine and Arabia urging them to refrain from joining with Turkey. At the same time, and with Clayton's approval, they dispatched agents to Beirut, Jeddah and the Persian Gulf, presumably with the same message.[8]

On October 30, Abdullah's reply to Kitchener's overture was received in Cairo. Abdullah proposed a 'more close union with' Britain, 'so long as she protects the rights of our country' and the rights of his father 'against any foreign aggression, and in particular against the Ottomans'.[9] Kitchener responded the next day: 'If the Arab nation assists England in this war that has been forced upon us by Turkey, England will guarantee that no internal intervention takes place in Arabia, and will give [the] Arabs every assistance against external foreign aggression.' And then, from out of the blue, Kitchener added: 'It may be that an Arab of true race will assume the Khalifate at Mecca or Medina and so good may come by the help of God out of all the evil that is now occurring.'[10] This unsolicited reference to an Arab – as opposed to a Turkish – Caliphate, would cause no end of trouble for the British in the future. But the reply sent by Abdullah's father, Hussein, simply restated his friendliness towards Britain and added that due to his position in Islam and to conditions in the Hijaz, he could not yet break with the Turks.[11] There the correspondence ended. It would not be revived for another eight months.

Kitchener's approaches to Hussein could have come as no surprise to Clayton, for Hussein was head of the most prominent Arab family in the Ottoman Empire. Appointed Amir of Mecca by the Sultan in 1908, he was descended from the Prophet's tribe, the Quraysh, and could follow his lineage back to Hashim, the great-grandfather of Muhammad. The ascendancy of Hussein's Hashemite ancestors over the *Haramain* – the holy places of Mecca and Medina – could be traced to the tenth century, and he was responsible for the conduct of the *hajj*, the annual pilgrimage to the holy places. In his effort to bring the Arabs to the British side, then, Kitchener's solicitation of Hussein was grounded in sound logic.

Hussein ibn 'Ali was born in Constantinople in 1853, but spent his early years in the Hijaz, the long strip of the Arabian peninsula running along the eastern edge of the Red Sea from Akaba in the north to 'Asir, a small, undefined territory above Yemen, in the south. As a young man, he learned much from three of his uncles who had served as Amirs of Mecca during the last half of the century. But, in 1893, he was ordered to Constantinople, where he remained as the 'guest' of the Sultan for the next fifteen years. Hussein's appointment to Mecca in 1908 coincided with the advent of CUP rule in Constantinople and the Amir would never be on good terms with the Unionists. The CUP advocated two principles of governance that were anathema to Hussein, as both could be applied to undermine his authority in the Hijaz. Until 1914, the CUP pursued a policy of secularisation in government, a policy in which the authority of the state was held to emanate not from Islamic doctrine, but from constitutional government modelled on western lines. Hussein's authority in the Hijaz, by contrast, was based largely on religious principles; quite apart from his ancestry, he had, after all, direct responsibility for the *Haramain* and the *hajj*. He was not the least inclined to apply constitutional government in the Hijaz. Not only was such government incompatible with the religious traditions that had underlain the Amirate for centuries, Hussein saw constitutionalism as a dangerous innovation that could be invoked to curtail his own authority. Even more troubling was the CUP policy of centralisation, a programme calculated to bring the empire's far-flung provinces under tighter central government control. In March 1913, the Ottomans proposed a new Provincial law, the Law of the *Vilayets*. Ostensibly, the proposal was a *de*centralising measure, calling for continued authority of the *vali* (governor) in the provinces in conjunction with locally-elected councils. But the practical effect of the law was to promote local decision-making favourable to the central government at the expense of traditional Arab leaders.

There were also more practical manifestations of CUP interference that troubled Hussein. In 1910, the Ottoman government modified the status of Medina from an administrative division of the Hijaz *vilayet,* to an independent entity, answerable directly to the Ministry of the Interior in Constantinople. The administrative change concerning Medina underscored the importance of that city to the Porte. Not only was Medina the second city of Islam – the burial place of Muhammad – it was also a point of strategic significance. Only three months before Hussein's arrival in Mecca, the first train had steamed into Medina, now the southern terminus of the Hijaz railway. Construction of the line was begun in 1900, as a favourite project of Abdulhamid. But the Young Turks, too, were well aware of the railway's importance and early on announced their intention of extending the line south to Mecca and then west, to the port of Jeddah. The advantages of the extension were obvious. It would provide a fast, efficient and economic means of transporting pilgrims from the Balkans, Anatolia and the Levant to the holy places and, no less important, it would enable the government to send troops and materiel to the Hijaz, quickly if necessary, in order to maintain its authority and control over the region. For precisely the same reasons, the line represented a threat to Hussein. His acknowledged jurisdiction covered the tribes of the Hijaz and the livelihood of many tribes, in turn, depended on supplying and protecting (or, occasionally, looting) the camel caravans from the north. The railway, if extended, would disrupt this historic arrangement. And, of course, the ability to rapidly transport troops from the north by train would make Hussein far more vulnerable to government control. Between 1908 and 1914, the Amir came under persistent pressure from Constantinople to acquiesce to the extension. In early 1914, he was offered one-third of the line's anticipated revenues – 250,000 guineas – and even more enticing, a guarantee of the Amirate in Hussein for life and in his family in perpetuity. He refused, well aware that the line would irrevocably impair his authority as Amir.

By early 1914, Hussein and the Ottoman government had been at odds over these issues for nearly six years. During the eight year period 1909–16, no fewer than six *valis* were removed from the Hijaz. Not all these changes could be attributed to Hussein, but it was abundantly clear that the Amir did not get on well with the Turkish governors. The imperial government soon became exasperated with him and it appears that as early as 1911 the CUP seriously entertained the idea of removing Hussein from the Hijaz. But the plan was stopped by some of Hussein's few remaining friends among the old guard at the Porte. Again, in 1914, the CUP appointed a strong *vali*, Vehib Bey, to govern the province. Hussein reacted quickly, mobilising the tribes and townsmen of the Hijaz to resist what the Amir represented was a CUP attempt to invade their traditional rights, including the exemptions from taxation and military conscription that the *vilayet* had long enjoyed. With the townsmen and the Bedouin united in their opposition to the *vali* and to the proposed Law of the *Vilayets*, it appeared that the Hijaz was very near to revolt. But, another costly military adventure, it was thought, would further undermine Ottoman finances and the CUP backed down. A proposed military expedition to the province was cancelled, Vehib Bey was recalled, and the plan to implement the provincial law was halted. Hussein had again prevailed, but only just.

The crisis of early 1914 must have convinced Hussein that his position at Mecca was in serious jeopardy. That may explain why the Amir's second son, Abdullah, stopped in Cairo on his way to Constantinople in February 1914. Abdullah met with

Kitchener, then still the British Agent, and asked him whether Britain would assist his father in the event he decided to resist further Turkish moves against him in the Hijaz. Kitchener could offer no encouragement; Britain would not interfere in the internal affairs of the Ottoman Empire, he explained, with whom the British then had friendly relations. Two months later, on his return journey, Abdullah met with Storrs. As the Oriental Secretary described the meeting, Abdullah again raised the issue of British assistance, requesting an agreement that would guarantee the status quo in Arabia against 'wanton Turkish aggression'. Storrs politely declined, insisting, like Kitchener, that Britain was still on friendly terms with the Turks.[12] As seen, five months later, their roles now reversed, Kitchener would approach Abdullah with an offer of assistance. If nothing else, the events of 1914 demonstrated that Anglo-Arab cooperation, based on an arrangement with the Hashemites, presented possible advantages for both sides.

With these recent events well in mind, on November 13, Clayton persuaded Cheetham to send the Foreign Office a telegram he had drafted calling for a statement of British policy concerning the Arabs. After noting that 'the leaders of the Arab movement' in Cairo had suggested that the Arabs might be suspicious of British plans to annex territory in Arabia, Clayton proposed that 'an excellent effect would be produced by a definite statement on the part of [the] British Government that there was no intention to undertake any naval or military operations in Arabia except for [the] protection of Arab interests against Turkish or other aggression, *or in support of {an} attempt by the Arabs to free themselves from Turkish rule*'. Although he had disparaged Aziz al-Masri's plans only three weeks earlier, with war now declared, Clayton also included a description of the colonel's plan to foment an Arab rising in Mesopotamia, and added a specific request for instructions: 'Is any further action now desirable here in connection with [the] Arab movement as a whole?'[13] The Foreign Secretary responded the next day, leaving it to Cheetham to decide whether to send al-Masri to Mesopotamia and authorising £2,000 for the purpose. Grey added: 'You can give the assurance you suggest in the name of the British Government. The Arab movement should be encouraged in every way possible.'[14] As a result of Clayton's cable, Kitchener's October 31 guarantee that foreign aggression against the Arabs would not be tolerated by Britain had now been transformed into an affirmative pledge of military support for Arab efforts to free themselves from Turkish rule. Again, on the 16th, Clayton drafted a telegram, sent in Cheetham's name to the Foreign Office, promoting al-Masri's plan for an Arab rising in Mesopotamia.[15] Clayton and Storrs had been irked by official foot-dragging in securing an Arab policy from London, but Clayton was now pleased that 'our efforts in Arabia and Syria are bearing as good a fruit as can be expected considering how long they took in making up their minds'.[16]

As Clayton's November 13 telegram suggested, Aziz al-Masri was not the only Arab in Cairo concocting plans for Arab opposition to the Turks and enlisting British support for them. He also had frequent contacts with a number of Syrians resident in the city who advocated British action in their home country. Most prominent among them were Muhammad Rashid Rida, a well-known Syrian intellectual and reformer, and Dr Faris Nimr, a native of the Lebanon and proprietor of the Cairo newspaper, *al-Muqattam*. Dr Nimr's views, characterised by Cairo as those of 'a leading and representative Syrian Christian', were pitched on strategic lines. England, he argued, had an obligation to fill the void that would be created by a Turkish defeat. Although Britain might be tempted to accord France a dominant position in northern Syria in order to create a buffer between British Egypt and the Russians to the north, this would be a mistake as it would 'break up the natural unity of the Syrian Arabs'. Two-thirds of the Syrian population, he argued, were opposed to the French, whose interest in the country was based merely on sentiment. The vast majority of Syrians hoped for an English occupation on the Egyptian model. So, he continued, Britain should compensate France with colonial possessions elsewhere, Egypt and Syria should be united under the Egyptian Sultan, and both countries accorded some measure of autonomy. If Britain allowed Syria to be fractured into French and British spheres, he warned, this would fan the flames of Pan-Islam and *jihad*. Dr Nimr's views were not entirely shared by Syrians of the so-called Pan-Arab Party in Cairo, led by Rashid Rida. He claimed to represent 'the feelings of Mohammedans in general and Arabs in particular' in advocating the 'complete independence of Islam' in the Arabian peninsula, an area he defined roughly in the same way as Aziz al-Masri – bounded by the Persian Gulf in the east, the Indian Ocean to the south, the Red Sea, Egypt and the Mediterranean on the west and Asia Minor in the north. In order to effectuate this grandiose plan, he asserted, 'the Arabs of Syria and Mesopotamia are ready to take charge of an independent government on the principles of decentralisation or confederation'.[17]

Clayton was deeply sceptical of all these utopian schemes. 'I confess that I cannot see any practical possibility of the formation of an Arab Empire (temporal) such as Sheikh Rashid Riza and his friends dream of. The idea is an attractive one but the necessary elements appear to be lacking.'[18] Although Rashid Rida came often to Clayton's office to profess his pro-British sympathies and promote his ideas, the Intelligence Director was not taken in. He found the sheikh 'well-educated and intelligent', but also a 'fanatical Moslem of the anti-Christian school'. 'I do not delude myself that Rashid Rida is in the least pro-English except in so far as friendship with England can further his aims and those of his . . . party.'[19] He did not, however, reject the Syrian approaches; that would risk 'throwing them into the arms of the Pan-Islamic party'. He always met with them, but offered no encouragement; he was, he said, 'safe and non-committal'. 'I have to be very guarded in addressing the Syrians', he added, and 'I always take up the line that it is of no use for them to attempt to force England's hand but, if they want England's help, they must be patient and wait until England can give it in her own good time . . . .'[20] More important, Clayton fully realised that the views of Nimr, and more so Rashid Rida, went 'a great deal further than our Govt is likely to follow'. In a February 7, 1915 Note to the British representative – now called the High Commissioner, after declaration of the protectorate – Clayton advocated a waiting policy: 'It would appear most undesirable at the present moment to give any assurances in regard to Syria or to take any action in that country which would commit England to a definite policy and thereby tie her hands in the future. Any military action on the coast of Syria which cannot be justified on purely military strategical lines is to be deprecated. . . .'[21]

Clayton's February 7 Note was directed to the new High Commissioner in Egypt, Sir Arthur Henry McMahon. Most people thought McMahon a poor choice to succeed Kitchener. He knew little of Egypt or the Arabs and spoke neither Arabic nor French, the diplomatic lingua franca of the time. Wingate would have been a better choice, but does not appear to have been considered. Cheetham, who had acted in the role since Kitchener's departure from Egypt in the spring of 1914, was also lightly regarded. Storrs found Cheetham 'quite incapable of making a plan or giving an order', and Gertrude Bell, who would join Clayton's Intelligence Department in late 1915, later described him as 'a typical F[oreign] O[ffice] man of the bloodless type'.[22] McMahon fared no better. He had served his entire career in India, where he last worked as foreign secretary to the Government of India. Kitchener selected him for Cairo in December 1914, probably because he eventually intended to return to Egypt himself and did not want a strong personality in the post in the interim. The Viceroy, Lord Hardinge, thought McMahon 'dreadfully slow of mind', and Ronald Graham, Adviser to the Egyptian Ministry of the Interior, wrote that he was 'quite the laziest man I have met'.[23]

Clayton – who would work closely with McMahon during the most critical period in the history of Anglo-Arab relations to date – initially shared these views. He first met with the new High Commissioner on January 22, 1915, when he, Maxwell and Parker 'fully explained' to him the 'action taken as regards Arabia'.[24] He found McMahon to be 'very retiring', a 'man of few words; . . it is difficult to know what his real thoughts are'. To Wingate, he described McMahon as 'close as an oyster'. And Lee Stack, on a visit to Cairo in 1915, wrote that 'the High Commissioner does nothing . . . Clayton finds the Residency very difficult to deal with'. Wingate, who spent far too much time on his correspondence, was frustrated that McMahon did not bother to respond to his many letters. Clayton offered an explanation:

> It is I think largely a question of extreme caution which avoids any action or even any expression of opinion until absolutely certain of its ground – add to this a great disinclination to putting pen to paper at all, and you have the reason . . . A personal interview is generally satisfactory & gives good results but to endeavour to get anything in writing is rather like attempting to extract blood from a stone.[25]

Most important to an understanding of McMahon's work on the Arab question are the views of Mervyn Herbert, whose brother Aubrey was then working in Clayton's Intelligence Department. Mervyn, a career diplomat, arrived in Cairo in March 1915 to work in the Chancery attached to the British Residency. It must be said that he did not get on well with McMahon; he thought him an incompetent and lazy man who had alienated the Chancery staff. He believed that McMahon did 'next to nothing' in Cairo, although he was interested in the 'furtherance of Arab aspirations in return for their support'.[26] '[A]ll other work & all other questions' he 'practically excluded from his mind', Herbert confided to his diary. Yet, 'even in the Hedjaz question' Herbert concluded, 'there was a pitiful lack of control [and] coordination', as McMahon operated in the belief 'that there was a man running it who had definite views, alternative plans in other words who really understood it all'. The man to whom Herbert referred was made clear in a diary entry of the same date: 'His system here, if one can so call it, has been to rely on 2 or 3 people entirely & blindly – in practice they have been Edward Cecil [Finance Ministry Adviser], Brunyate [Legal Adviser] and Clayton to the exclusion of all others'.[27] On the eve of the Arab Revolt, in early June 1916, when Clayton dispatched two of his staff to Jeddah, Herbert noted that 'the fruits of Clayton's policy – which will in future no doubt be called McMahon's – ought to appear now any day if the [Arab] movement is successful as it should be'.[28]

Clayton's influence with McMahon in early 1915 was nothing like that described by Herbert later in that year or in 1916. But both Clayton and McMahon did advocate early on a plan that was inextricably bound up with Arab aspirations for Syria. This was the suggestion of a landing at Alexandretta (Iskenderun), a Syrian port in the north-east corner of the Mediterranean. On January 3, 1915, already aware that the Turks were assembling an army for an assault on Egypt, Clayton suggested a British offensive, initiated by a landing at the port. The strategy had several points to recommend it. Alexandretta had a good, deep-water harbour, the best in the eastern Mediterranean, and a landing there would 'completely cut off the Syrian army from its base' in Turkey and would sever the Ottoman lines of communication, 'not only with Syria, but also with Bagdad'. Clayton also had reason to believe – perhaps based on his talks with Faris Nimr and Rashid Rida – that 'a large portion of the population of Syria and Palestine would welcome the advent of a British force and it . . . would encounter but slight resistance from [the] inhabitants and might even be actively assisted'.[29] Two days later an even more elaborate argument for the scheme issued from Clayton's Intelligence Department. The unsigned memo – likely drafted by Lawrence, a proponent of the plan – put forth the argument that 'within the last few years the Arab National feeling has developed in an astonishing degree' and that 'a general Arab revolt directed by the Pan Arab military league would be the immediate result of an occupation of Alexandretta following on a defeat of the Turkish forces in the South'.[30] On the February 7, yet another Note issued from Clayton. As described above, in this paper Clayton stressed that a landing at Alexandretta should proceed only if justified on 'purely military strategical lines', not in support of Syrian nationalism.

The Alexandretta proposal was not novel; Maxwell had pushed for a landing there a month earlier. However, what neither Maxwell nor Clayton reckoned on was the extent of French interest in the project. Both Cheetham and, later, McMahon cabled the Foreign Office in support of the plan, but Grey was already committed to advising France on any contemplated landing in Syria.[31] In a Minute attached to Clayton's January 3 Note, the Foreign Secretary observed that 'the French must be asked to associate themselves in any operation against Syria'.[32] Still, the Cabinet discussed the proposal on January 13, and both Kitchener and General Charles Callwell, the Director of Military Operations, were in favour of it. But by mid-February, in the face of French opposition and a lack of available transport, the plan was dead.[33] Lord Cromer, still interested in Arab affairs in his retirement, summed up the resolution: 'There cannot be the smallest question of our going to Syria. We do not want it, and . . . any attempt in that direction on our part would lead to a serious quarrel with France'.[34]

In proposing a landing at Alexandretta and in promoting an Arab policy to London, Clayton had moved from a purely Intelligence function to the role of a policy advocate. One historian of the period would later severely criticise Clayton for 'consistently and systematically' flouting 'the rule that intelligence and policy must be kept apart'.[35] But the criticism is unwarranted for several reasons. First, it is doubtful there was any such 'rule' in 1915, and, if there was, it was likely observed more in the breach than in application. Also, the criticism fails to take into account that Clayton was not just the Director of Intelligence; he also acted as Sudan Agent, liaison between the High Commissioner and the Force in Egypt, and as an acknowledged expert on Eastern affairs. Third, Clayton's views were routinely requested by his chiefs, requests he could hardly ignore. As he explained to Wingate: 'my personal views are often asked both by the G.O.C. [Maxwell] and the High Commissioner on various subjects, embracing a very wide field. The High Commissioner especially seems to regard me as his Director of Intelligence for Egypt in addition to my other duties'.[36] Fourth, even if a line of demarcation between Intelligence-gathering and policy-making was observed in London, this was not always the case when it came to the Empire. In part, this was because there were few men in London who were well-versed in Eastern matters. Cromer – who did understand Egypt, better than anyone in England – observed that 'no member of the Government . . . really has a grasp of Eastern questions . . . Sir Edward Grey, in spite of many good qualities, does not possess it in the smallest degree'.[37] As a result, the home departments involved in Imperial matters – the Foreign, India, Colonial and War Offices – were inclined to defer to the opinions of their experienced men on the spot, quite regardless of what positions they held abroad. When, for example, a crucial letter from Hussein arrived in the Foreign Office in August 1915, George Clerk, head of the war department in the Office, noted that 'Sir H. McMahon and his advisers are in a better position than anyone else to gauge the Sherif's sentiments'. Austen Chamberlain, the Secretary of State for India and a harsh critic of the Cairo authorities in 1915, observed years later that 'in dealing with these Oriental countries one must trust one's experts and the man on the spot'. Again, in early 1916, when the CID resolved to establish an Arab Bureau – an Intelligence office in Cairo headed by Clayton – it concluded that the Bureau's 'first function' was to 'harmonise British political activity in the Near East' – hardly a brief limited to Intelligence-gathering.[38] Finally, even if Clayton did cross some shadowy line separating Intelligence from policy, there is no evidence that anyone at the time criticised him for doing so. Certainly, various policies advanced by Clayton were criticised, occasionally severely, but not because they issued from the Director of Intelligence.

The most severe critics of the Arab policy developing in Cairo were the Government of India and its governing London department, the India Office. India's opposition to Cairo's Arab policy sprang in some measure from a sense of territoriality; the Indian government had exercised authority over the Persian Gulf, Aden and Arabia for decades. India concluded the first treaties with the Gulf sheikhs in 1820, and had assumed control over Aden in 1839. No one questioned India's jurisdiction. Indeed, in Mesopotamia, the Government of India landed its own army in the south of the country in early November 1914. Inevitably, the sudden intrusion of Cairo into what was seen by Delhi as an Indian bailiwick prompted opposition, particularly from the Viceroy, Lord Hardinge. Already, in December 1914, India had quashed Clayton's proposal to send Aziz al-Masri to Mesopotamia.[39] Again, in early 1915, India asserted its jurisdiction over the Red Sea ports of Arabia and claimed authority over British approaches to Arab chiefs in the region, including the Idrisi of 'Asir and Hussein. 'Aden have grabbed most of the Red Sea coast – indeed all that is of any importance – into their sphere', protested Clayton in late February.[40] In March, after the Turks confiscated a shipload of durra intended for pilgrims in the Hijaz, India imposed a commercial blockade of Jeddah, a move Clayton would fight until the blockade was lifted in May. Even more important for Clayton, the 'Arab question', as he complained 'seems now to be definitely placed in the hands of the Indian Government'.[41] Eventually, Cairo won a qualified victory; it was decided that the Red Sea would be divided into two 'spheres', India controlling relations with the Arabs in Aden, the Yemen, and 'Asir – to be administered through the British Resident at Aden – and Cairo receiving authority from Jeddah northwards. Cairo's irritation with India, however, did not prevent Clayton from assisting the Resident at Aden in concluding a treaty with the Idrisi of 'Asir in April 1915; he provided £200 pounds to a relative of the Idrisi, then residing in Egypt, who travelled to Aden and proved instrumental in completing the treaty.

As seen, on February 14, 1915, the Foreign Office had agreed to Clayton's proposal of armed support of Arab efforts to free themselves from Turkish rule. But India persisted in objecting to the policy:

> [T]he policy of His Majesty's Government should be to encourage the Grand Sharif [Hussein] by all possible means short of military intervention to throw off the Turkish yoke, and to support him against Turkey (subject to the same limitation) as independent ruler of the Hedjaz, using their good offices with other Arab chiefs whom they can influence (such as the Idrisi Saiyid and the Amir of Nejd) to encourage him in that capacity . . . [I]t would not be politic for His Majesty's Government to give the Grand Sharif more than diplomatic assistance. Material assistance might conflict with the obligations . . . to maintain the independence of other Arab chiefs. For this and other reasons it appears desirable to leave the Arabs to manage their own affairs.[42]

The Government of India were particularly sensitive to any policy statement concerning Mesopotamia. They were bent on outright annexation of the Basra *vilayet* in the south of the country 'as absolutely necessary to safeguard the future of our position in the Persian Gulf'. The Viceroy stressed that India did not want 'to take Baghdad at all', but neither did they wish to see a 'Turkish or any other hostile administration there'. As for Arabia, he repeated that 'our wisest course seems to me to be to let the Arabs in Arabia work out their own salvation'.[43]

No less worrisome to India was the question of the Caliphate. It will be recalled that, in October 1914, Kitchener had gratuitously suggested an Arab Caliphate to Hussein, a rather transparent hint that the Amir's assumption of the office would be regarded favourably by Britain. For Delhi – which governed some seventy million Muslims – this was a dangerous proposal, no less so because until fairly recently India had promoted Indian Muslim loyalty to a *Turkish* Caliphate as means of countering Russian pretensions in Central Asia. Yet, Kitchener's hint of an Arab Caliphate was embodied in a private, even secret, message. Britain's public stance on the issue had been consistent, as described by Clayton in early 1915: 'any proposal as regards an Arab Khalif should come from the Arabs themselves'.[44] Grey was 'strongly opposed to any interference in the religious question' and, in April 1915, the Foreign Office clarified that Britain would 'make it an essential condition in any terms of peace that the Arabian peninsula, and its Mohammedan Holy Places, should remain in the hands of an independent sovereign state'. If the Muslims decided on an Arab Caliph, Grey added, 'their decision would . . . be respected by His Majesty's Government, but the decision is for the Mohammedans to make'.[45]

Despite Grey's unambiguous statement, both Wingate and Clayton advocated a more aggressive approach as part of their effort to bring the Arabs to the British side. To McMahon, Clayton argued that 'the Moslem world was undoubtedly looking for some sign as to our intentions regarding the Khalifate', and he suggested that 'it might not be a bad thing to hint to [Hussein] . . . "very secretly" that he would not be considered an unsuitable candidate by HMG should the Moslem world select him'.[46] For his part, Wingate bombarded Grey, Cromer, Hardinge and McMahon with memoranda concerning the Caliphate written by the Grand Qadi (judge) of the Sudan and Sayid Ali al-Mirghani, the leading religious figure at Khartoum. The Qadi advocated the termination of the Turkish Caliphate and al-Mirghani openly backed Hussein as the best choice for a new, Arab Caliphate. Hardinge agreed that Hussein would be a suitable Caliph in succession to the Sultan, but insisted that it was too soon to even consider the question: 'we must wait until Constantinople has fallen and the Sultan has been driven out'. To Chamberlain, Secretary of State for India, he complained that 'McMahon and Wingate are much too anxious to interfere, or rather to promote intrigue, in connection with the Khalifate'.[47]

Clayton's views on the Caliphate and on British support of the Arabs were crystallized in a Note written near the end of July, 1915. In light of the critical events that were about to unfold in Cairo, it warrants extensive quotation:

> The Sherif of Mecca is undoubtedly the candidate for the Khalifate who is
> most suitable from the British point of view, and he has also the advantage
> of possessing most of the attributes which are considered essential by Moslem

opinion. He is a member of the Koreish [Quraysh] family and he is the actual keeper of the Holy Places of Islam. There are, however, difficulties and pitfalls in the path of his election and the greatest care must be taken to avoid making a false step. Firstly, it is vital that Great Britain should give no indication publicly of favouring the Sherif's claims. His Majesty's Government have declared that the selection of the Khalifa is a matter for the Moslems alone, without any interference by Christian Powers, and no action should be taken which can be interpreted as being contrary to this declaration. Secondly, the idea of the Khalifa as not only the religious head but also the greatest temporal power in Islam appeals to a large selection of Moslems who dream of a mighty Mohammedan Empire once more taking the lead in the world . . . Consequently nothing less than the real independence of the Khalifate will satisfy them and any shadow of protection by a Christian Power would be fatal. It is therefore essential that no action on the part of Great Britain should give any hint of protection. An early proclamation of the independence of Arabia will go far towards increasing the claims of the Sherif to the Khalifate, especially if British influence is exerted in his favour with other Moslem Chiefs who are friendly to Great Britain. Respect [Hussein's] wishes, consult him on all matters concerning the pilgrimage, facilitate the payment of all religious dues from States under British rule – all actions such as this will also help to prepare the way. But material assistance, especially in the form of military aid or any definite alliance between the Sherif and . . .[Britain] would tend to give rise to the idea, which would be sedulously fostered by our enemies, that he was under British protection. There is one other point of primary importance. One of the results of peace with Turkey should be if possible the voluntary renunciation by the Sultan of the Khalifate. If this could be brought about many difficulties would be avoided.[48]

In view of his earlier appeals to the Foreign Office, it is difficult to escape the conclusion that Clayton's July Note was written, at least in part, to disarm India's opinion that Cairo had been far too aggressive in supporting Arab aspirations. Wingate, who was in almost daily contact with Clayton by wire, had been making similar efforts from the beginning of 1915. In January, he wrote to the Viceroy stressing 'the unlikelihood that a single Arab State could ever become a serious menace or danger to our Imperial interests', as Hardinge believed. '[B]y upholding the principle of Arab nationality', Wingate argued, 'we shall be not merely creating an efficient counterpoise to Turkish pan-Islamism, but will pave the way to control, by agreement, those districts where Turkish ascendancy has hitherto proved a stumbling block to all progress'.[49]

Hardinge disagreed, but at least he listened. London, on the other hand, had not sought Wingate's advice and the Sirdar was frankly miffed that neither Cheetham nor McMahon solicited his views on the Arab question. In early 1915, he repeatedly advised Clayton not to proffer his opinions to the Residency, advice that, as seen, Clayton did not follow. The Sirdar felt, with some justification, that he was better

positioned than India to direct Arab affairs, not only by reason of geographic proximity, but also because of his own considerable experience. Not until late February
did he decide to drop his 'dog-in-the-manger attitude & let . . . the authorities have
our views for what they are worth'.[50] Wingate's opinions were, if anything, stronger
than Clayton's when it came to British support for 'our friends across the water', as
he referred to the Arabs of the Hijaz. True, like Clayton, he thought Rashid Rida a
'visionary' in asserting that the Arabs could form an empire when, in fact, 'they are
scarcely an embryo'. And he did not see how the various Arab tribes 'with their innu-
merable divisions and internal hostilities . . . [could] be combined in any satisfactory
way against our common enemy'. But that did not prevent him from concluding
that the Arabs should 'be told authoritatively that we shall support them through
thick and thin'.[51] For Wingate, there was no inconsistency in this thinking because
British support for Arab goals, regardless of their merits, would have the practical
effect of preventing them from joining the Turks. 'All these plans for the formation
of an independent Arab sovereign State and Khalifate are, I fully admit, Utopian at
. . . present', he explained to Cromer. 'But the more we can keep the better educated
Moslems busy with their plans for their Utopian kingdom and Khalifate, the less
likely they are to imbibe the vile lies and poisonous propaganda' of pan-Islam. To
Hardinge he argued that 'in the theory of Arabian union, and by concessions to the
pan-Arabian ideal, may lie . . . a partial solution of many of our present difficulties'.
And he urged the Foreign Secretary that Britain should take the lead in 'showing
sympathy with Arab aspirations' so as to 'consolidate on our side the divergent views
of the various Moslem nationalities and communities'.[52] Years later, after the war,
Wingate offered Hardinge a candid explanation of his thinking:

> I admit to having been sufficiently opportunist to take the fullest advantage
> of the situation to treat the Sherif's revolt rather as a really useful war measure
> than as a means to an end for the renaissance of a great united Arab Empire.
> [A]s long as the movement served the purpose in knocking out one or two of
> the stones of the arch of the Central Powers I am satisfied that its object . . .
> has been achieved.[53]

To the extent Wingate's ex post facto explanation of his policy was accurate, it may
be criticised as cynical, manipulative, even duplicitous. But whether it was effective
would be determined by events that began to unfold in Cairo in July 1915.

11

Clayton and the Pledge: The McMahon–Hussein Correspondence

While Cairo and Delhi were squabbling over Arab affairs during the first half of 1915, Hussein's position in the Hijaz continued to deteriorate. In February, the Sherif's eldest son 'Ali uncovered a Turkish plot to depose his father. Hussein decided to send his third son Faisal to confront CUP leaders with documents evidencing the plot and to secure removal of the Turkish *vali* from the Hijaz. But Faisal was given other, secret instructions by his father; he was directed to make contact with *al-Fatat* leaders in Damascus on his way to Constantinople. Hussein already knew *al-Fatat's* agenda. He had been approached by an emissary of the secret society in January who informed him of their intent to start a revolt in Syria and asked the Sherif to lead the cause. Faisal arrived in the Syrian capital on March 26, and met with members of *al-Fatat* and *al-'Ahd*. Hussein had been non-committal when earlier approached by *al-Fatat* and Faisal, having learned more of the Syrians' plans, was unconvinced of the scope and strength of their movement. He believed that in order for the conspirators to succeed, the assistance of one of the Allied Powers was essential. Arriving in Constantinople in April, Faisal was left equally uneasy by his talks with Turkish officials who assured him that Hussein need have no concern for his position in the Hijaz, but that, rather more ominously, his public proclamation of support for the *jihad* was essential.

On his return journey Faisal again stopped in Damascus. Now, the *al-Fatat* and *al-'Ahd* leaders provided him with a document outlining their programme. If Britain would recognise Arab independence in a defined area – identical to that described by Aziz al-Masri and Rashid Rida in Cairo, except that the Syrians excluded British-controlled Aden – then 'the future independent Arab State' would enter into a defensive alliance with, and accord economic preference to, Britain. This document, later called the Damascus Protocol, was presented to Faisal along with a pledge of the societies' leaders to recognise Hussein as 'King of the Arabs' or (accounts differ) as 'spokesman of the Arab race'. Faisal was sworn in as a member of both organizations, the Protocol was then 'written out in Lilliputian characters' and sewn into the lining of a servant's boot, and Faisal returned to the Hijaz.[1]

Hussein was now presented with a dilemma. If the Turks could be trusted, he could solidify his position in the Hijaz by publicly backing the *jihad* and assisting the Ottoman war effort. But this might expose him to hostile action by Britain, which was undeniably master of the Red Sea. On the other hand, Kitchener's messages of the previous autumn suggested that a declaration in favour of Britain and against the Turks would likely secure British protection and, quite possibly, support for an independent Arab state with Hussein at its head. Still, alliance with a Christian state against the Sultan-Caliph might compromise his position in the Islamic world. And, most important, it was by no means certain who would win the war. Yes, Britain had beaten back the Ottoman assault on Egypt in February, but the success of the British campaign at the Dardanelles, launched just that April, was far from assured; nor was it at all clear that the Anglo-Indian army would prevail in Mesopotamia. The Sherif's sons were no help. Abdullah favoured an armed revolt, but 'Ali was opposed and Faisal, though committed to a revolutionary solution, thought it premature to make any move. After much deliberation, Hussein finally decided to join the British and tentatively set the date for an armed rising for the following winter. At the same time, he decided to renew his contacts with the British to learn what price he could extract for the promise of an Arab alliance.

On July 14, Abdullah thus wrote the first in a series of letters that the pre-eminent scholar of the correspondence has noted 'haunted Anglo-Arab relations' for 'half a century'. It was an exchange in which Clayton's role would prove critical, for by the time of Abdullah's letter, Clayton had come to hold a 'crucial position . . . in the direction of the war in the Middle East'.[2] Years later, in 1923, Clayton confirmed his role in the correspondence, stating that he 'was in daily touch with Sir Henry McMahon throughout the negotiations with King Hussein, and made the preliminary drafts of all the letters'.[3] Because of the importance of the correspondence, particularly with regard to the (non-)treatment of Palestine, Clayton's participation must be examined in some detail.

In his July 14 letter Abdullah – in effect, Hussein – purported to be writing on behalf of 'the whole of the Arab nation' in proposing a fifteen year treaty with Britain. He called upon the British to acknowledge the independence of the Arab countries in an area identical to that set forth in the Damascus Protocol, even down to the exclusion of Britain's Aden protectorate. Both contracting parties, he added, were to 'offer mutual assistance' to 'face any foreign power which may attack either party' and, if either party 'enters upon an aggressive conflict' then the other would 'assume a neutral attitude', unless it opted to join. England was also to agree to the 'abolition of foreign privileges in the Arab countries'. This was a reference to the Capitulations, a series of centuries-old concessions made by the Turks that accorded citizens of various western countries economic and legal preferences in Ottoman territories. Echoing Kitchener's suggestion of the previous October, Abdullah added that England was to 'approve the proclamation of an Arab Khalifate of Islam'. In return for British agreement to these provisions, 'the Arab Government of the Sherif' was to award Britain 'preference in all economic enterprises in the Arab countries'.[4] To all this Abdullah requested a reply within thirty days.

In Clayton's opinion, Hussein was overreaching. '[H]e opens his mouth pretty wide', he informed Wingate, 'and his demands are so suspiciously like those of

Rashid Riza's party that I think they must have been in communication with him . . . The High Commissioner will have to send a vague reply saying it is early days to begin negotiating agreements, the first thing being to oust the Turks from Arabia'. Storrs agreed, and also thought the Sherif presumptuous: 'It may be regarded as certain that that he has received no sort of mandate from other [Arab] potentates. He knows he is demanding far more than he has the right, power, or hope to expect.'[5]

McMahon concurred in these views and proposed to send a reply stating that the discussion of boundaries was premature, especially since the Turks 'have not been expelled from much of the area in question'. After all, the Arabs 'in some parts' – he was doubtless thinking of Mesopotamia – 'are still . . . working for [the] Turks and Germans'. Surprisingly, the India Office, which reviewed Abdullah's letter, disagreed with the proposed reply. While Hussein's terms were probably dictated 'by extreme Pan-Arab aspirations' and were 'obviously unacceptable', they thought that McMahon's reply would 'not only not engage him for our cause, but may lead [Hussein] to think that we were not serious in our overtures'. India proposed a reply suggesting that the Sherif send an emissary to Cairo, perhaps Abdullah, to 'negotiate a preliminary agreement for securing the independence, rights and privileges of the Sheriffate'. Foreign Secretary Grey adopted the India Office suggestion, instructing McMahon to add it, if he thought it advisable. As far as the Caliphate was concerned, the Foreign Secretary proposed a restatement of Kitchener's intimation of the previous autumn; if Hussein was proclaimed Caliph 'with the consent of his co-religionists', Britain would welcome the resumption of an Arab Caliphate. Although Grey was content to leave McMahon discretion in his response, both he and Sir Arthur Nicolson, permanent under-secretary at the Foreign Office, wanted an immediate reply. 'This matter is very urgent', Nicolson minuted. Grey added: 'Send off the telegram now'. But McMahon declined to adopt London's suggestions. He would not ask Hussein to send anyone to Cairo, concluding that 'the moment . . . has not arrived when we can usefully discuss even a preliminary agreement . . . .'[6] Thus, in McMahon's August 30 reply to Abdullah, he reiterated Kitchener's 1914 message regarding an Arab Caliphate, but declined to discuss 'questions of limits and boundaries' as premature, especially since Arabs in parts of the proposed Arab State were 'lending their arms to the German and the Turk'.

Contrary to his 1923 statement that he prepared drafts of all of McMahon's letters to Hussein, Clayton informed Wingate that he was not involved in drafting McMahon's August 30 reply: 'I was not in the show at all from beginning to end – it was apparently run by Storrs, so I know no more than what I have sent you copies of.' Those copies did not include McMahon's letter, which Clayton did not obtain until the end of September. 'I imagine', he then added, that Storrs is the author'.[7] Wingate would have preferred that Clayton take a more active role, as he did not agree with McMahon's reply to the Sherif. 'I cannot too strongly urge that some more definite encouragement should be given . . . .' And, if Clayton was correct that Rashid Rida was in contact with Hussein, then he should not discourage the Syrian. 'We have need of all our Arab friends', he added, 'and I think you would do well to give him at least the impression that you view his project with some degree of sympathy . . . It is very desirable not to throw overboard Arab Union projects'. Clayton's reply discloses the fine line he was trying to walk along with the Arabs and his doubts about supporting them. As noted earlier, he was sceptical of their plans, and so refrained from encouraging them:

> On the other hand, one does not want to discourage the Arab movement in any way; nor have I done so. It may be a very useful card and the only one we can play against Pan-Islamism. There is one point however that has always struck me about the Arab movement – . . . If it is not going to be a big success well and good, but if it were really to succeed should we have not created rather a Frankenstein! Islam is always Islam and Great Britain is after all one of the great (indeed the greatest) champion of Christendom, and can never really be a Moslem power in the eyes of the Moslems (and God forbid that she should). Hence a mighty Mohammedan Empire in the heart of the British Empire is a questionable advantage.[8]

Hussein's reply to McMahon, dated September 9, was received in Cairo about the middle of October. The Sherif was struck by the tone of 'coolness and hesitation' displayed in McMahon's letter on the question of boundaries of the proposed Arab state. Hussein stressed that he was not personally seeking 'these limits' but that they reflected the proposals of 'our people' who believe the boundaries essential for economic life. The success of his negotiations, he emphasised, depends on whether Britain admits or rejects the proposed frontiers. As for the Caliphate, he said only 'may God have mercy on its soul and comfort Moslems for their loss'. Although Hussein was clear in his insistence on the boundaries described in the July 14 letter, no time limit was specified for a reply to his latest letter and no sense of urgency was suggested. But by the time his September 9 letter was received in Cairo a new development had transpired that would completely alter the complexion of the negotiations.

In late August 1915, Muhammad Sharif al-Faruqi, a twenty-four year old lieutenant in a Turkish infantry division at the Dardanelles, crossed over to the British lines under a white flag. The young deserter had an interesting story to tell and London decided he should be sent to Cairo where his bona fides could be tested by Colonel Clayton.[9] By his own account, Faruqi was born of a distinguished Arab family in Mosul, in northern Mesopotamia, in 1891. He was educated at the military school in Constantinople and spoke Turkish and French in addition to his native Arabic. Now in the Ottoman army, on the outbreak of war Faruqi joined the secret al-'Ahd and later, after being transferred to Aleppo, the civilian society, al-Fatat. Instrumental in uniting the two societies, Faruqi claimed that by the time he joined al-Fatat, the leadership had already sworn allegiance to Hussein as 'Khalifa'. Al-'Ahd, he continued, had also sent an emissary to Hussein who learned from the Sherif that the British were willing to support Arab claims to independence. Faruqi informed Clayton that he would travel to Mesopotamia and 'bring over a great number of officers and men' to the Arab cause. After all, he claimed, 90% of Arab officers in the Ottoman army were already members of *al-'Ahd*. Members of the secret society, Faruqi added, desired a 'friendly treaty with the English'. The new government they envisioned would be 'national and not religious. It will be an Arab not a Moslem Empire'. The various Arab countries in the new polity would be governed by 'principles of decentralization', but would adhere to a central government headed by Hussein as Caliph and Sultan.[10]

Clayton appears to have had more than one discussion with al-Faruqi during the first week in October, talks he described in a letter to Wingate on the 9th. Although the 'pan-Arab party' of which Faruqi was a member had the same goal as Rashid Rida, Clayton thought their specific aims 'much more moderate and practical', definitely not 'tinged to the same extent by Moslem fanaticism'. Faruqi's military party, Clayton held, was not 'carried away by the dream of an Arab Empire' and 'are fully aware of the fact that the elements of such an Empire do not exist among the Arabs'. As Clayton described them, Faruqi's party had three general requests: 'a general recognition of their aspirations by England'; the 'promise of a fair measure of self-government in the various countries concerned'; and, the 'guidance and support of England – but of no other power'. The last point, Clayton thought, was obviously 'the crux' of the matter, 'owing to French claims to Syria'. He then added a quote from Faruqi that was troubling: 'We would sooner have a promise from England of half what we want than a promise from Germany and Turkey of the whole, but if England refuses us we must turn to Germany and Turkey.' Maxwell had asked Clayton to prepare a Note for him summarizing his talks with Faruqi. Clayton promised Wingate that in writing it he would 'take the opportunity of rubbing in the fact that if we definitely refuse to consider the aspirations of the Arabs, we are running a grave risk of throwing them into the arms of our enemies which would mean that the jehad which so far has been a failure would probably become a reality'.[11]

In his October 11 memorandum describing his talks with Faruqi, Clayton did rub it in.[12] He began with a repetition of Faruqi's statements concerning the aims of *al-Fatat* and *al-'Ahd*, including their desire to 'establish an Arab Caliphate in Arabia, Syria and Mesopotamia' and to secure a British 'promise to assist them to obtain a reasonable measure of independence and autonomous government in those Arab countries where England can fairly claim that her interests are greater than those of her Allies'. Clayton continued his description with a recitation of Faruqi's statements, interlaced with his interpretation of them:

> Al-Faruqi states that a guarantee of the independenceof the Arabian peninsula would not satisfy them, but this together with the institution of an increasing measure of autonomous Government under British guidance and control in Palestine and Mesopotamia would probably secure their friendship. Syria is of course included in their programme . . . El Farugi declares that a French occupation of Syria would be strenuously resisted by the Mohammedan population.

And then Clayton added his own gloss on these points:

> [B]ut they must realize that France has aspirations in this region. They would however no doubt seek England's good offices towards obtaining a settlement of the Syrian question in a manner as favourable as possible to their views and would almost certainly press for the inclusion of Damascus, Aleppo, Hama and Homs in their Arab confederation.

He then reverted to a description of Faruqi's statements. 'In El Farugi's own words "our scheme embraces all the Arab countries including Syria and Mesopotamia, but if we cannot have all, we want as much as we can get".' Clayton was again repeating Faruqi's words in reporting that Turkey and Germany 'have already approached the leaders of the Young Arab Committee and . . . have gone so far as to promise them the granting of their demands in full'. That was a remarkable statement and, if true, elevated the correspondence with Hussein to a new level of urgency. Clayton thought he had some evidence to support it: 'The German Counsul at Aleppo has been especially active in this matter and a recent report of the despatch of very large sums of money from Constantinople to Baghdad and neighbourhood for the purpose of buying over the local chiefs is significant'.[13] But evidence of Turco-German attempts to buy Arab cooperaton is not quite the same as an agreement to meet the demands of *al-Fatat* and *al-'Ahd* 'in full', and it appears that there is no evidence in the German archives to support Faruqi's extravagant claim.[14]

Following his apparently fabricated report of a Turco-German promise to support Arab demands, Faruqi delivered a threat: His party were 'convinced that they can no longer remain neutral and, unless they receive a favourable reply from England within a few weeks, they have decided to throw in their lot with Turkey and Germany and to secure the best terms they can'. Clayton concluded that his 'very thorough discussion' with Faruqi, 'together with the experience of the past year, during which there have been considerable opportunities of studying the pan-Arab movement, lead to the conviction that the proposals now put forward are of very grave and urgent importance'.[15] He added that the Sultan's call to *jihad* 'so sedu-lously preached from Constantinople has been a failure . . . largely due to the attitude of the Arabs, which has been passively hostile towards Turkey'. He stressed, too, that Hussein's recent proposals were 'very similar' to those advanced by Faruqi and that McMahon's reply to the Sherif had elicited an expression of surprise at the 'hesi-tation of the British authorities'. A statement of British intentions was therefore required, and soon. 'That the attitude of the Sherif is that of the majority of the Arab peoples there can be little doubt.' If Clayton was referring to Hussein's attitude concerning the nature and scope of Arab aspirations, there was little basis for such a sweeping conclusion.

Clayton advised that a favourable reply to the Arab proposals, even if it did not meet all their demands 'would probably put the seal on their friendship'. His description of the alternative scenario shows that he appeared to believe Faruqi's threat: 'On the other hand, to reject the Arab proposals, or even to seek to evade the issue, will be to throw the Young Arab Party definitely into the arms of the enemy. Their machinery will be at once employed against us throughout the Arab countries and' – he concluded, with another unfounded statement – 'the Arab chiefs who, are almost to a man, members of or connected with the Young Arab Party, will be undoubtedly won over'. In fact, no 'Arab chiefs' were known to be members of the Young Arab Party, and the only one who was 'connected with' that party was Hussein and, apart from a similarity in their territorial demands, the extent to which the Sherif identified himself with them was far from clear. There is little evidence in the documentary record of the time demonstrating that other 'Arab chiefs' had exhibited the slightest interest in, or were even aware of, the agenda of *al-Fatat* and *al-'Ahd*. Indeed – although Clayton did not know it – Ibn Saud, then dominant in central Arabia, had rejected an overture from *al-Fatat* in 1914, before they approached Hussein.[16]

Clayton's October 11 memorandum has baffled historians; most have concluded that his statements concerning Faruqi and the Arab movement are inconsistent with those of the otherwise level-headed and cautious Intelligence Director. Some have argued that he was simply duped by Faruqi, others that he was self-deluded, or the victim of his own faulty Intelligence, or even that he fell prey to a personal desire to influence policy.[17] He certainly did exaggerate. Yet, there is evidence Clayton genuinely believed that the Arab question had reached a crisis point. As he informed Wingate, 'the matter is . . . very urgent and every day of importance'. McMahon, he added, 'seemed inclined to think that he was being a bit rushed! . . [but] the "rushing" was being done by forces over which we unfortunately have no control'. Clayton was not alone in thinking the matter pressing. Storrs wrote to Kitchener's private secretary: 'I gather from the Sherif, as does Clayton from Faroki, that they feel, rightly or wrongly, that the time has come to choose between us & Germany . . . I have thrashed the thing out at great length with Clayton & beg you to give all possible prominence to the Note [Clayton's of October 11] being sent home by . . . [Maxwell] in this week's bag'. Storrs also suggested that the sense of urgency was necessary to counter foot-dragging by the Residency. 'If you knew the difficulty Clayton and I had all last autumn in getting Sir Milne [Cheetham] to make any proposal about, or take an interest in, the Arab question, you would understand our difficulty.'[18] Wingate, too, believed immediate action was necessary. 'We must now hope and pray it is not too late', he wrote. And to the Director of Military Operations in London he stressed that 'the matter is of the very greatest importance at the present juncture'.[19] The Sirdar heartily approved of Clayton's Note and praised him for making Faruqi's story 'a peg on which to hang a despatch' from Maxwell to the War Office. But Wingate had independent grounds for thinking the Arabs were at a crossroads; an agent had just arrived at Khartoum from Arabia carrying a message from Hussein to Ali Mirghani in which the Sherif had emphasised the urgency of a British commitment, failing which the Arabs might be driven into the enemy camp, and the Ottoman declaration of *jihad* become effective.[20]

Clayton's October 11 Note did not reach London until the 25th, but his message of urgency arrived on the 12th. On that day, or perhaps earlier, he discussed with

Maxwell the terms of two telegrams his commanding officer was sending to London. In the first, Maxwell noted he was sending Clayton's paper and that the Arab question was 'of great importance and requires immediate consideration'. In the second, Maxwell conveyed Faruqi's hyperbolic statements, as repeated in Clayton's Note:

> [T]he Arab question is now very pressing. A powerful organization with considerable influence in the Army and among Arab chiefs, viz: — the Young Arab Committee, appears to have made up its mind that the moment for action has arrived. The Turks and Germans are already in negotiation with them and spending money to win their support. The Arab party however is strongly inclined towards England but what they ask is a definite statement of sympathy and support even if their complete programme cannot be accepted. [The] Sherif of Mecca, who is in communication with the Arab party, also seems uneasy and is pressing for a declaration of policy on the part of England. If their overtures are rejected or a reply is delayed any longer the Arab party will go over to the enemy and work with them, which would mean stirring up religious feeling at once and might well result in a genuine Jehad. On the other hand, the active assistance which the Arabs would render in return for our support would be of the greatest value in Arabia Mesopotamia Syria and Palestine.[21]

The language tracks the October 11 Note; Clayton's imprint is unmistakable. On the same day, the 12th, despite feeling 'rushed', McMahon sent Clayton's Note to the Foreign Office. In yet another cable, of the 16th, Maxwell again stressed that 'time is of the greatest importance'; it was 'urgent to waste no time'. And, he added, specific proposals must be made to Hussein; 'time is past in my opinion for vague generalities'. Even if the British insisted on retaining the Basra *Vilayet*, 'the rest of Mesopotamia must be included in the negotiation', and, with regard to Syria, the Arabs would 'insist on Homs, Aleppo, Hama and Damascus being in their sphere'. On the 18th, McMahon jumped on the bandwagon: 'Arab party are at a parting of the ways and unless we can give them immediate assurance . . . they will throw themselves into the hands of Germany'.[22]

There seems little doubt that Clayton, Storrs, Wingate, Maxwell and McMahon all genuinely believed that Germany was on the verge of co-opting the Arabs, that the Arab party could be bought by Germany and that a critical point in Anglo-Arab relations had been reached. Apart from the India Office, which remained sceptical, London hardly needed convincing. Kitchener had been in favour of an Anglo-Arab alliance for more than a year and, as shown, the two top men at the Foreign Office, Grey and Nicolson, were convinced that the Arab question was urgent in August, when they received Abdullah's July 14 message. Before concluding, though, that everyone in Cairo, and many in London, had been bamboozled into thinking that the Arab question had reached a crisis, some attention must be paid to the context in which the Clayton–Faruqi talks occurred.

In October 1915, the Allied position in the Middle East was far from encouraging. Already, in September, many were beginning to see that the Allied campaign in the Dardanelles was doomed to fail. Clayton realised that if the Allies abandoned Gallipoli, Turkey would be able to reinforce its Syrian army and renew the threat to Egypt. A mid-October report listed eight solid pieces of evidence leading Intelligence to conclude that '[e]verything points to the fact that a new offensive is contemplated by the Turks in Sinai'.[23] Clayton was not alone. General Archibald Murray, then Chief of the Imperial General Staff, observed that '[i]f Gallipoli goes, Egypt will be attacked early next year and this time it will be no feeble attack, as the railway will be completed for the last 60 miles. We cannot afford to let the Turks join hands in Egypt with the Arabs. . . .'[24] And then there were the German *agents provocateurs*. As described in the next chapter, the Intelligence reports for 1915 were filled with confirmed accounts of German agents running up and down the country from Aleppo to Jeddah 'preaching union of the Mohammedans under the Turks and Holy War'.[25] The Germans may not have promised to meet the Arab party's demands for independence, but they were most certainly making an effort to promote pan-Islam and the *jihad*. And, as seen, Clayton was deeply concerned with the threat of pan-Islam. At the remove of a century, it is easy to dismiss the Turco-German appeal to a universal *jihad* as illusory, risible even; Islam is now seen as diverse, as variegated, as other major religions. But to criticise Clayton and his Cairo colleagues on this basis, is to impart contemporary understanding to people living, and making decisions, one hundred years ago, surely an illegitimate approach.

If the stalemate at Gallipoli, the threat of a renewed attack on Egypt, and the increasing menace of *jihad* were not troubling enough, more disturbing news had just been received in September 1915, when the Bulgarians came into the war on the German side, a move that would lead to the reopening of the Berlin to Constantinople railway in January 1916, enabling the Germans to freely supply their ally. Then, on October 5, an Austro-German force, soon to be joined by the Bulgarians, invaded Serbia. On the same day, Wingate received news that the Imam of Yemen had joined the Turks.[26] Small wonder Cromer was pleased that 'the whole Arab question has now come to a head and . . . a decision is imminent . . . The whole situation looks very bad and it may be that the Germans before long will have practically raised the whole East against us'.[27] Faruqi's report of an imminent Arab agreement with the Turks and Germans was false, and Clayton and his colleagues may justly be criticised for claiming that a crisis in Anglo-Arab relations was imminent when there was very little credible evidence to support it. But they were perhaps justified in thinking that, in view of the deteriorating Allied position in the East, an Anglo-Arab alliance should be pressed on London.

This then was the context in which Clayton prepared his October 11 Note. Two months earlier, it had been 'early days to begin negotiating agreements' with Hussein. But now, it was 'pretty evident' to Clayton that the Sherif would expect 'some fairly definite statements of the views of H.M.G. regarding Arab aspirations'. Convinced that a critical point had now been reached, he admitted to overstating his case in order to persuade his chiefs in Cairo and the authorities in London to reach an accord with the Arabs. 'I have put the issues rather forcibly perhaps but it does not seem to me to be a time when we can afford to mince words or gloss over truths because they are unpalatable. Facts are facts and H.M.G. should be put in possession of them.'[28] As shown above, Clayton did not propose a definite response to Arab demands because he believed in Arab nationalism or in the viability of a future Arab state. To the contrary, he was deeply sceptical of both. And, even if an Arab State did result from British sponsorship, he was very doubtful that it would prove beneficial to the British Empire. Nor did he think that an Arab rising against the Turks would be militarily significant. The advantages he anticipated were of a decidedly different character:

> There appears some misapprehension with regard to the strength of the Arab movement. It has never been contended that this movement is going to be of extreme value from the offensive point of view . . . the vital point is that if the Arabs are not for us, they will be against us . . . [I]n considering the Arab movement, too much attention has been given to its possible offensive value, and it has to some extent been forgotten that the chief advantage to be gained is a defensive one, in that we should secure on their part a hostile attitude towards the Turks, even though it might only be passively hostile, and rob our enemies of the incalculable moral and material assistance which they would gain were they to succeed in uniting against the Allies the Arab races and, through them, Islam.[29]

This message, of the defensive value of an Arab alliance, would be repeated many times by Clayton over the ensuing months in light of the letter that Cairo was about to send to Hussein.

On October 24, McMahon completed his response to Hussein's demands. He repeated the statement, made in April, that Britain would guarantee the Holy Places against all external aggression and would recognise their inviolability. In addition, Britain was 'prepared to recognise and support the independence of the Arabs in all the regions within the limits demanded by the Sherif'. But that broad pledge was qualified in four important respects. First, the 'two districts of Mersina and Alexandretta [in the far northwest of the area demanded in Hussein's July 14 letter] and portions of Syria lying to the west of the districts of Damascus, Homs, Hama and Aleppo cannot be said to be purely Arab and should be excluded from the limits demanded'. Second, Britain's assurances could be given only to the extent that she was 'free to act without detriment to her ally France'. Third, Britain had already made agreements with various Arab chiefs; the pledge to Hussein would have to be subject to those existing treaties. Finally, the Arabs must recognise that in the Baghdad and Basra *vilayets* in Mesopotamia 'the established position and interests of Great Britain necessitate special administrative arrangements in order to secure these territories from foreign aggression, to promote the welfare of the local populations and to safeguard our mutual economic interests'. Though not a territorial limitation, McMahon added that in the independent Arab areas, Britain would give her advice and assistance in as much as 'the Arabs have decided to seek the advice and guidance of Britain only'.

Who wrote the October 24 letter? Certainly, McMahon took responsibility. He had received Foreign Office authorisation to give the pledge and it was sent over his signature. And the Foreign Office was well aware of the terms of the letter. Grey had received a draft from McMahon on October 19, and commented on it. He did not like the provision regarding Arab use of only British advisers, as he thought it would lead the French to believe that Britain was making a bid for control of Syria. But McMahon explained that this had been specifically requested by the Arabs in order to forestall French control. On the recommendation of the India Office, the Foreign Secretary also instructed McMahon to extend the 'sphere of British control' in Mesopotamia to include the Baghdad as well as the Basra *vilayet*, and to add the qualification concerning existing Arab treaties. Grey also would have preferred adoption of the India Office suggestion, made in August, that Hussein be invited to send an emissary to Cairo to discuss the boundaries of the proposed Arab State. But, time did not allow for protracted negotiation. '[I]f something more precise than this is required, you can give it.' '[T]he important thing', Grey added, 'is to give our assurances that will prevent Arabs from being alienated, and I must leave you discretion in the matter, as it is urgent and there is not time to discuss an exact formula'.[30] The general terms, though not the exact language, of McMahon's letter were thus approved by the Foreign Office.

It is also possible that Storrs prepared the October 24 letter, as, according to Clayton, he had likely drafted McMahon's August 30 message. And, of course, Clayton himself may have drafted it. As noted, he claimed, in 1923, to have written drafts of all McMahon's letters to the Sherif, and there is a draft of the letter written on Intelligence Department paper, though that draft could have been prepared by McMahon or Storrs, or, indeed, by Clayton, Storrs and McMahon. On October 24, Clayton reported to Wingate that a formula submitted by the Sirdar (a draft that was not used and that is broader in both its promise of British support and in its qualifications to that support) had been seen by McMahon who 'has now decided on the terms of his reply'. The evidence is inconclusive, but even if Clayton did not prepare the October 24 letter, he was certainly involved. The letter incorporates points made in Clayton's October 11 memorandum. And, on the 25th, when the messenger left Cairo with the letter, a Note in the Residency's files states that '[a] few special points, some contained in the letter & others not important enough to warrant their inclusion, were verbally impressed on [the messenger] by the Residency & the Intelligence Dept.'[31]

Whoever drafted it, the October 24 letter is a masterpiece of circumlocution and raises more questions than it answers. What were the 'special administrative arrangements' contemplated for the Basra and Baghdad *vilayets*? What were the interests of France in Syria and what territories did those interests encompass? And what was meant by the 'districts' of Damascus, Homs, Hama and Aleppo? The Arabic word *wilaya* (Tukish, *vilayets*) was used for 'districts'. It means an administrative district headed by a *vali* – a province. It may also be used, more generally, to describe a region or an area. There were certainly *vilayets* of Baghdad, Basra, Syria and Aleppo. But Damascus, although often referred to as a *vilayet*, was not one. And Homs and Hama certainly were not *vilayets*. So, McMahon (or Storrs, or Clayton) must have been using the word in the generic sense to mean some undefined regions surrounding the four specified cities. Indeed, McMahon soon clarified that he was referring to the four towns, not to any *vilayets*.[32] The question is not merely academic. The Arabs would later claim that Palestine – not mentioned in the correspondence – was intended to be within the area of Arab independence offered by McMahon because Palestine did not lie 'to the west of the districts of Damascus, Homs, Hama and Aleppo'. If 'districts' meant the four towns and their surrounding environs – and, so the argument goes, it could mean nothing else, since there were no *vilayets* of Homs, Hama and Damascus – then Palestine was well to the south of them.

This issue, which would engender decades of argument, ill will and scholarly debate, cannot be resolved because of the more general reservation concerning French interests. At the time, no one knew the scope of French claims in the Middle East. In December 1915, and at least until the following spring, the French *did* claim that Palestine was in their sphere of interest. And that may explain Clayton's 1923 statement that 'it was never the intention that Palestine should be included in the general pledge given to the Sherif'.[33] In making that statement, Clayton may have been referring to the general reservation concerning French interests and not to the exclusion pertaining to the 'districts' of the four Syrian towns, for in an April 1916 Note prepared by the Arab Bureau (headed by Clayton) it was stated that the area of Arab independence was bounded in the west by the Red Sea and the Mediterranean 'up to about Lat. 33°'. That latitude lay very near the northern boundary of what was regarded as historic Palestine, thus placing that territory within the area McMahon intended to be part of an independent Arab state.[34] As will be seen, in November 1917, the British would announce their support for a national home for the Jewish people in Palestine. If Britain had intended in 1915 that Palestine be included in the area of Arab independence, how could that intent be reconciled with a national home for the Jews in the same territory? Competing answers to that question would bedevil Anglo-Arab relations for a generation.

Palestine may have been in Hussein's mind when he responded to McMahon's letter on November 5. The Sherif conceded the Mersina and Adana *vilayets* in the far north, but insisted that the '*vilayets* of Beirut and Aleppo (both actual Turkish provinces) and their sea coasts' are 'purely Arab *vilayets*' and should be included in the area of Arab independence. The Beirut *vilayet* included much of Palestine. Similarly, the Mesopotamian *vilayets* 'are parts of the pure Arab Kingdom' and must also be included, though he was prepared to leave them under British administration 'for a short time . . . and against a suitable sum paid as compensation'.

While Cairo was pondering a response, trouble was brewing in Whitehall. 'India are furious & making every difficulty', Clayton reported. He was right. Chamberlain had been consulted, verbally, before McMahon's October 24 letter was sent, and had insisted on the reservations regarding the Baghdad *vilayet* and existing Anglo-Arab treaties. But he had not seen the final letter before it was dispatched. Owing to the supposed urgency of the reply, no one in London had. For his part, the Viceroy, Hardinge, could 'not get over McMahon's fatuous proceedings in giving away . . . all the gains of our hard earned victories in Mesopotamia . . . It is one of the most deplorable performances I have ever known'. '[W]e and the India Office are perfectly furious with McMahon', he added, and 'the really absurd idea of the creation of an independent Arab State stretching from the north of Syria to the Persian Gulf, which McMahon and Maxwell are pressing for all they are worth with the Grand Sherif as head and Kahlif'. The Viceroy was also convinced that McMahon was 'abandoning enormous potential sources of revenue' in Mesopotamia, which he saw as a potential 'field for commercial expansion and [Indian] emigration'. Chamberlain concurred: 'Mesopotamia has been regarded as India's reward for her exertions'. Moreover, he saw Hussein as 'a nonentity without power to carry out his proposals'. The Arabs, he wrote, were 'without unity and with no possibility of uniting and I disbelieve in the reality and efficacy of the suggested Arab revolt in the Army and elsewhere'.[35]

Grey, who understood what Cairo was trying to achieve, had little sympathy for India's imperial designs: 'Our primary and vital object is not to secure a new sphere of British influence, but to get the Arabs on our side against the Turks'.[36] As for India's disbelief in Arab unity, Clayton exposed a logical flaw in their thinking:

India seems obsessed with the fear of a powerful & united Arab State, which can never exist unless we are fools enough to create it. On the other hand, they talk of the lack of unity among the Arabs, whereas this is the main safeguard against the powerful state which they say they dread. I don't for a moment deny the menace that would arise were such a state to be created as the Arabs dream of, but I shouldn't have thought that anyone would consider it within the bounds of practical politics & it will have to be our business to see that it does not ever become a possibility owing to our backing one horse to the exclusion of the others.[37]

This argument was not, however, communicated to India and Indian objections to the Cairo policy were having an effect. 'There is a feeling', Parker reported from London, 'that the Arab movement is unreal, shadowy and vague; and that it cannot, on account of its incoherence, be of any value to us'.[38] London's growing scepticism doubtless had an effect on McMahon's next letter to Hussein, dated December 14. With regard to the Beirut and Aleppo *vilayets*, McMahon delayed any further commitment or clarification: 'as the interests of our ally France are involved in them both, the question will require careful consideration and a further communication will be addressed to you . . . .' Similarly, British interests in the Baghdad *vilayet*, 'and the adequate safeguarding of those interests call for a much fuller and more detailed consideration than the present situation and the urgency of these negotiations permit'. McMahon added that Britain had no interest in urging the Sherif to 'hasty action which might jeopardise the eventual success' of his plans, but 'you should spare no effort to attach all the Arab peoples to our united cause and urge them to afford no assistance to our enemies . . . It is on the success of these efforts and on the more active measures which the Arabs may hereafter take in support of our cause, when the time for action comes, that the permanence and strength of our agreement must depend'.

Clayton's involvement in McMahon's December 14 letter is again unclear. When he sent a copy of the letter to Wingate on the 21st, Clayton noted only his thought that McMahon 'has made as good a job of it as possible'.[39] In addition to India's vigorous opposition, McMahon had adopted a cautious and non-committal stance with Hussein because the Alexandretta scheme had been revived, and again rejected, after the Allied failure at Gallipoli. It was rejected by the Cabinet, even though Kitchener, Maxwell, McMahon and Clayton all argued strongly for an assault on the port with the troops removed from Gallipoli.[40] In addition to the inevitable French objections, the 'Westerners' in London – those who believed that all effort should be concentrated on the Western Front and not on another frolic and detour in the East – were now in the ascendant. The rejection of the Alexandretta proposal undermined the idea of sponsoring an Arab movement, because an Arab revolt could not succeed without British military assistance, and the best way in which that assistance could be given – an Alexandretta landing – had again been turned down. The movement must 'go by the board', Clayton wrote, 'as we cannot encourage them & then leave them to the tender mercies of the enemy'. But, as he reflected on the matter, Clayton concluded that 'it is still more important than ever to win over the Arabs. If we had adopted the forward [Alexandretta] policy they might have come over anyhow but now they are extremely likely to go over to the enemy unless we can gain their sympathy by promising something approaching to what they want'.[41]

Hussein's January 1, 1916 reply to McMahon's December letter disclosed that while the Sherif was not prepared to compromise further concerning Arab territories, he would not press his position to the point of impasse. Regarding Mesopotamia, he would leave the amount of compensation to be paid by England – to which McMahon had never agreed, even in principle – to the 'wisdom and justice' of Britain. About Syria, the Sherif was less amenable: 'it is impossible to allow any derogation that gives France, or any other Power, a span of land in those regions'. At the same time, Hussein had no interest in impairing Franco-British relations. So, he added, 'at the first opportunity after this war is finished, we shall ask you (what we avert our eyes from to-day) for what we now leave to France in Beirut and its coasts'.[42]

McMahon's reply of January 25, 1916 was the last that addressed territorial issues. The Baghdad *vilayet*, McMahon repeated, would be further considered only after Turkey had been defeated. As for Syria, he merely expressed satisfaction that Hussein would not insist on anything that might injure the alliance of Britain and France. What 'more decided measures' the Sherif might now take 'in this great cause [with which] Arabia is now associated', he left to Hussein's discretion. Clayton wrote the January 25 letter, the only one in the series for which there exists solid evidence of his authorship. 'I was asked to draft a reply at very short notice – having only a couple of hours to do it in – and I have tried to steer clear of the various quicksands and yet to say something that would satisfy the Sherif'. Clayton continued to worry about the likelihood of an eventual dispute between the French and Arabs over Syria, but one of his primary objectives had been achieved. 'I feel sure that our efforts have gone a long way to counteracting German Pan-Islamic propaganda amongst the Arabs'. He was still concerned with 'the people in India [who] cling so firmly to the wrong end of the stick'. But three days after McMahon's letter left Cairo, Clayton took steps to address those concerns by sending Gertrude Bell to India. The Arabian traveller and writer who had been working in the Intelligence Department since November 1915, was a good friend of the Viceroy, and Clayton was convinced Bell was in complete agreement with Cairo's policy and that she might 'succeed in inducing a better impression of what the Arab question really means'.[43]

Since there is strong evidence that Clayton drafted only one of McMahon's four letters treating Britain's pledge to Hussein and definitely did not draft another (that of August 30, 1915), some explanation must be offered for his 1923 statement that he prepared drafts of all of them. Of course, the absence of evidence does not prove that Clayton did *not* draft them, although, as seen, his letters to Wingate – the best indication of Clayton's actions during this period – at least suggest that he did not draft the two as to which his participation is unclear. And, it will be recalled, Wingate had proposed language for McMahon's critical letter of October 24, in which the British pledge was given. Wingate's formula was not adopted by McMahon and if Clayton prepared the October letter, he would not likely admit in a letter to the Sirdar that he, Clayton, had prepared a draft that did not adopt Wingate's language. Clayton was, after all, still employed and paid by the Sudan Government and Wingate, his long-time mentor, was still one of his chiefs, the others being Maxwell and McMahon. Indeed, only two months before the letter was sent, Wingate admonished Clayton to ensure that any statements he made on the Arab question must 'synchronize' with Wingate's. Especially, in treating such issues as the Caliphate or 'the general partitioning [of the Ottoman Empire] after the war' it was critical that 'our statements should not vary'.[44] What can be said with confidence, though, is that even if Clayton did not actually draft all of McMahon's letters to Hussein, they are suffused with his ideas. As he wrote in 1923, he was 'in daily touch' with McMahon and one need only compare the October 24 letter with Clayton's October 11 memorandum – the four Syrian cities, the Basra *vilayet,* the reservation regarding French interests – to conclude that Clayton's influence was significant, if not decisive.

What of Clayton's declaration in that same 1923 statement that it was not intended that Palestine be included in the area of Arab independence? As noted, this plausibly could be based on the general reservation concerning French interests; Britain could make no pledges that trenched on French claims and those, it was thought, would, or might, include Palestine. Clayton believed that the reservation regarding French claims encompassed Palestine. Also, he made his 1923 statement within a week of his arrival in Jerusalem as Chief Secretary in Palestine, the number two man in Britain's Mandate government in that country. Only ten months earlier, in June 1922, a White Paper had been published confirming British support for a Jewish national home in Palestine. In his new position, Clayton could hardly have undermined the White Paper policy by issuing a statement that Britain had pledged

Palestine to the Arabs in 1915. Of course, he could have made no statement at all. But that might have placed him at odds with his new chief, Sir Herbert Samuel, High Commissioner of Palestine and a confirmed Zionist. It is clear that Samuel asked Clayton to provide the statement because the High Commissioner was then deeply troubled by opposition in England to the national home policy. Shortly after the 1922 White Paper was published, a motion was carried in the House of Lords that the Palestine Mandate was 'inacceptable' in its endorsement of the Jewish national home policy because, for among other reasons, it violated the 1915 British pledge to the Arabs. Samuel doubtless thought that the man involved in drafting that pledge could clarify the intent behind it. It will be shown later that Clayton was not an opponent of the Zionist policy and believed that Britain's 1915 pledge could, and should, be reconciled with that policy.

The controversy concerning the 1915 pledge and Palestine can never be satisfactorily resolved because of the intentionally ambiguous nature of the October 24 letter. Still, a few general points concerning the exchange of letters can be made. Although many would refer to the McMahon–Hussein correspondence as a treaty or an agreement, it was neither. No understanding was reached between the parties concerning Mesopotamia, Palestine or Syria. And, even had it been, Hussein had no authority from the inhabitants of those regions to bind them to any sort of agreement; the Sherif's jurisdiction did not extend beyond the Hijaz, as Clayton well knew.[45] True, Hussein professed to write on behalf of the 'Arab Nation' and the 'Arab Kingdom' in his letters, but these entities existed only in the minds of Arab nationalists, not on any maps of the region. The British did pledge themselves to support Arab independence, but even that promise was conditioned, at least implicitly, on a general Arab rising against the Turks, and Hussein did not bring about anything like an effective, widespread Arab revolt. In Arabia, local rulers were either pro-Turkish or, like Ibn Saud, pro-British, but inactive. The Arab populations of Mesopotamia and Palestine were largely indifferent to the revolt that Hussein would launch in June 1916. In Syria, the small, nascent Arab nationalist movement was ruthlessly crushed by Jemal Pasha, even as Hussein and McMahon were corresponding. No Syrian rising ever occurred.

On these bases, some have argued that the correspondence created no obligation on the part of the British at all, that the letters were nothing more than an informal exchange of ideas and aspirations that entailed no binding commitment. But this essentially legal argument left many uneasy and, to their credit, no post-war British government denied that a pledge had been given to the Arabs. No amount of interpretive gymnastics could be applied to the letters that negated the facts that Britain *did* promise to support Arab independence and, in return, Hussein *did* revolt against the Turks. Whatever one might say about the territorial scope of Britain's promise, or about the extent and efficacy of Hussein's revolt, those facts had to be admitted. Clayton himself did not know what the ramifications of the correspondence would be, but the limited objective he sought by the pledge had been achieved: 'the Sherif has definitely decided that his interests lie with the Allies and not with the Turks', he wrote, 'and, whatever may be the outcome of the negotiations, it seems that they have at least had the effect of preventing him from throwing in his lot on the side of our enemies.'[46] And, for Clayton, that was enough.

12

Like Permeating Oil:
Counter-Intelligence

There was something fundamentally wrong with the Sultan's November 1914 call to *jihad*. It was not flawed in the declaration of a holy war itself; the Ottomans had been proclaiming such wars against the Russians since the 1770s, and as recently as 1897, against the Greeks. So the 1914 proclamation against the infidel Christian Entente of Britain, France and Russia was hardly novel. But the instigators of the new *jihad*, the Germans and Austrians, were themselves mostly Christian, as were the citizens of then neutral countries like America and Italy, whom the Turks had no wish to alienate. The Empire also encompassed significant Christian and Jewish populations. The five *fetvas* (formal legal opinions) that preceded the *jihad* ceremony of November 14, then, had to carve out all these peoples from the scope of the holy war based on some fairly strained interpretations of Islamic law. To those Muslims who cared to think about it – and not many did – the Sultan's selective *jihad* must have seemed logically flawed, if not downright ludicrous.[1] Clayton saw cracks in the foundations of the *jihad* in early 1915, as the Germans and Turks were then making serious efforts to draw the Sanusi into the war on Egypt's western border. Only three years earlier, the Sanusi had joined their Turkish co-religionists in a war to repel the Italians from the North African provinces of Tripoli and Cyrenaica. Now they were being asked to join a holy war against Christian infidels, a holy war from which Christian Italy was 'carefully excluded'.[2]

The doctrinal weaknesses inherent in the *jihad* did not, however, prevent the Turks and Germans from expending great effort and substantial funds to co-opt the Arabs, east and west of Egypt. In August 1914, even before the *jihad* proclamation, Otto Mannesmann, a German resident in Morocco, was dispatched by the Germans to Tripoli and later, in May 1915, to Ahmad al-Sharif, leader of the Sanusi, to enlist him in the holy war. Ahmad declined – at least for the time – not because he thought the *jihad* conceptually flawed, but because he was unconvinced the Germans would support him in a manner adequate to take on the British in Egypt. Mannesmann would be the first of many agents recruited by the German Foreign Office to ignite the fires of holy war throughout the Islamic world from Tunisia to Afghanistan.

The German *jihad* campaign was directed from Berlin by Baron Max von Oppenheim. Born in 1860 into a prominent banking family, Oppenheim took advantage of his family's wealth to travel extensively in the Middle East from his early twenties. He followed no definite profession, but his explorations and archae-ological work provided cover for his real passion – spying. In 1896 Oppenheim secured a post at the German consulate in Cairo, where he worked until 1909, pro-ducing hundreds of reports to the German Foreign Office on Middle Eastern topics, many of them espousing the benefits of pan-Islam and dripping with anti-British vitriol. So well-known was Oppenheim's predilection for intrigue that he was referred to by the British in Cairo simply as 'the Spy'.[3] Just before the outbreak of war in Europe, Oppenheim was summoned to the Foreign Office in Berlin's Wilhelmstrasse and charged with organizing the *jihad* campaign against the Entente powers.

In addition to producing anti-Entente propaganda for dissemination throughout the Middle East, the Baron began recruiting agents for work in the region, agents who would spread the message of pan-Islam and incite anti-colonial uprisings in Entente-controlled territory. Shortly after sending Mannesmann to North Africa, Oppenheim put together a team for a mission to Afghanistan to convince the Amir, Habibullah Khan, to assemble an army for the invasion of India. At the same time, the Baron's man in Constantinople, the oriental scholar Curt Prüfer, was instructed to send a German agent named Robert Mors to Alexandria, where he had served before the war in the Egyptian police. Mors arrived there in mid-September 1914, in a ship crammed with propaganda pamphlets and explosives, the latter to be used in sabotaging the Canal while the Ottoman army approached through Sinai. Mors was captured within a month of his arrival, but the Afghan mission, led by Oskar von Niedermayer, did get through to Kabul, with the British hot on their heels. In January 1916, the German mission even induced the Amir to sign an agreement calling for an armed attack on India in return for a stupendous bribe of £10 million. But the agreement came to nothing; even if the money had been paid, it was impos-sible to supply the Emir with the arms and equipment necessary for an assault on the sub-continent.

Again, in October 1914, Oppenheim agreed to support the mission of the Austrian orientalist Alois Musil to central Arabia where he planned to persuade the paramount tribal leaders Ibn Rashid of Ha'il, and his rival for Arabian supremacy, Ibn Saud, to join the Turks. But the Arabian chiefs were more interested in fighting each other than the British, and Musil's mission achieved nothing. While Musil was roaming about in the wastes of central Arabia, Oppenheim dispatched yet another agent to the region, the African explorer and anthropologist Leo Frobenius. The plan was for Frobenius, a recent convert to Islam, to travel south through the Hijaz, cross the Red Sea to Massawa in Italian Eritrea, and then proceed to Abyssinia and the Sudan, where he would assemble dissident tribes for an African *jihad* aimed at the underbelly of Egypt. Frobenius did reach Massawa in March 1915, but the Italians, now close to an alliance with the Entente (which they would join in May), offered no encouragement to the German. News of his mission soon hit the Italian newspa-pers, the German Foreign Office failed to offer support, and the Italians deported him at the end of March.[4]

Clayton was aware of all these German expeditions and knew also that the holy war programme was being 'organised from Berlin and Constantinople' by Oppenheim.[5] Indeed, the Baron's passion for the *jihad* and the pan-Islamic idea was so great that he could not resist returning to Constantinople himself to continue the effort on the spot. But his propaganda was not well received among the religious communities there. Cairo Intelligence attributed this to Oppenheim's 'Jewish origin' rather than to the anomalous nature of the selective *jihad* or to the lack of interest in pan-Islamism.[6] Still, the Baron's movements were followed closely by Cairo from June 1915, when he left Constantinople for Damascus.[7] Now in the Syrian capital, he laid a wreath on Saladin's tomb 'on behalf of the Kaiser', and afterwards made a stirring speech at the Umayyad Mosque. The Syrians, however, were no more taken with Oppenheim than the Turks. He was heckled by the 'head sheikh' and his attempted rejoinder was 'laughed down' by the Arab crowd. 'He is not a very adroit intriguer', Intelligence observed, as 'his pronounced Jewish manner and appearance are much against him . . . It would take far more than his influence to raise an anti-Christian movement in Syria'.[8] Oppenheim was assisted, not very ably, by the German vice-consul at Haifa, Loytved von Hardegg, who distributed hand-bills urging 'all good Muslims to kill each at least two French or British subjects'. At Mount Carmel, von Hardegg had the graves of French soldiers opened and he 'defiled their bones in the traditional and disgusting manner'. Rumours were also put about that the Kaiser had converted to Islam. But Clayton's Intelligence found no evidence that these heavy-handed measures were having any effect on the Muslim populations of Palestine and Syria.[9]

Undeterred by his failures in Syria, Oppenheim was soon on his way to the Hijaz. Having earlier met both Hussein (1908) and Faisal (April 1915), the Baron anticipated a favourable reception. But, on his arrival at Medina, Oppenheim was promptly expelled.[10] Quite apart from Hussein's unwillingness to allow any Christian into the sacred regions of Mecca and Medina, he was not about to receive the German *provocateur* or to answer the Sultan's call to *jihad*. That would have committed him to the Turco-German cause and the Sherif was then in the middle of his correspondence with McMahon, an exchange of letters that, as seen, would lead to a British alliance. Even before the appearance of Oppenheim in the Hijaz, Hussein had consistently rejected all German overtures. Since November 1914, any German who turned up in the country, whether by design or accident – such as the survivors of the German vessel *Emden*, sunk in the Indian Ocean – were turned away or attacked by Hijazi Bedouin. Intelligence confirmed in September 1915, that 'the Arabs are intensely hostile to the Germans and have killed several who have attempted to land on the coast'.[11] By February 1916, his correspondence with McMahon now reaching its inconclusive end, Hussein was sending his British allies secret messages providing them details for capturing German agents he had professed to help reach the African coast.[12]

The failures of Oppenheim and his *jihad* agents were, for the most part, well known to Clayton and his department. What these failures did not reveal, though, was that the Turks and Germans were not agreed on an Arab policy. Both Berlin and Constantinople saw the importance of enlisting Hussein's support for the holy war, and for precisely the same reasons that Clayton and his Cairo colleagues saw for *preventing* that support – a public declaration for the *jihad* issuing from the Amir of Mecca, protector of the *Haramain* and the *hajj*, might have a galvanizing effect throughout Islam. But Enver was deeply suspicious of the German *jihad* campaign. He curtailed German propaganda efforts in Arabia, refused to allow the establishment of a German consulate at Jeddah, and flatly rejected Berlin's proposals to bribe the Sherif. For their part, the Germans were divided over the Arab question. Hans von Wangenheim, German ambassador to the Porte, held that the failure to secure Hussein's backing of the *jihad* would completely undermine the pan-Islamic programme. But others considered the Hashemites unreliable or politically insignificant. Von Wangenheim's successor at Constantinople even proposed giving up on Arabia altogether. And no one in Berlin appears to have seriously considered backing Arab schemes for independence. When Aziz al-Masri approached the Germans in May 1915 – his plans for fomenting a Mesopotamian uprising having been quashed by India – he was promptly turned away.[13] The Germans would not, in fact, give up on Arabia until Hussein launched his revolt in June 1916, but they never made the slightest inroad in the country.

If the Germans wandering about in the Hijaz made obvious and easy targets for the Arabs, the Turkish agents of Enver's shadowy *Teşkilat-ı Mahsusa* (Special Organization) were much less conspicuous and rather more effective than their German counterparts. The *Teşkilat-ı Mahsusa* was Enver's Intelligence agency, unaffiliated with either Ottoman military Intelligence or the Interior Ministry's secret police. Modelled on western lines and complete with an administrative hierarchy, secret budget, headquarters and field directors, the organization was engaged in everything from propaganda to para-military sabotage operations. That Enver's spy network was able to maintain secrecy cannot be doubted; it does not appear, by name, in Clayton's papers or in the records of the Arab Bureau or military Intelligence. Yet, it was said to have had thousands of members, to have recruited Ahmad, the Sanusi leader in Cyrenaica, and Ibn Rashid in central Arabia and, at one point – rather improbably – to have between 500 and 600 agents in Egypt.[14] Certainly, some prominent figures who were later claimed as members of the organization, were known to the British. Sheikh 'Abd al-'Aziz Shawish, the reputed director of the Cairo cell before the war, had been an instructor in Arabic at Oxford and was a vocal and virulent opponent of British rule in Egypt before decamping to Constantinople on the outbreak of fighting. Enver's brother Nuri, who would command the Sanusi army in 1915, was the principal *Teskilat-ı Mahsusa* agent in Cyrenaica and his movements were closely followed by Clayton from the time of his arrival in North Africa.

Despite their purported numbers, the agents of Enver's Special Organization had no success in Egypt. Clayton's administration of martial law, his deportations of enemy subjects and internment of native dissidents, and his tightening of the Egyptian censorship effectively quelled Turkish clandestine efforts in the country. And, for the most part, the Egyptians were not amenable to Turkish subversion anyway. Just like the Germans, the Turks over-estimated the appeal of pan-Islam and the call to *jihad*. Egyptian dislike of British rule was evident enough, but that sentiment did not translate into a desire to replace British with Turkish rule.

While Clayton may not have described the *Teşkilat-ı Mahsusa* by name, he was acutely aware of the presence of Turkish spies in Egypt and his counter-intelligence efforts were directed toward their elimination. But he did not have exclusive control over Egyptian counter-intelligence; he shared that responsibility with the Egyptian police which was controlled by the Interior Ministry's Department of Public Security. The police maintained large offices in the major cities – Cairo, Alexandria and Port Said – and smaller ones in the Canal Zone, and in each province. However, each of these units worked in 'watertight compartments' and did not share information or coordinate their efforts with British Intelligence.[15] Moreover, the Cairo police, the largest and most important office in the department, were 'inclined to run jealous and to resent anyone giving them clues or making suggestions'.[16] Even more troubling, Clayton was convinced that the Egyptian police, perhaps infiltrated by Turkish agents, were not to be trusted with 'any really secret work'.[17] The police were unable to prevent two attempts on the Egyptian Sultan's life, in April and June, 1915, attempts that Clayton was convinced were backed by the 'ex-Khedive's organization', the CUP, and 'German gold'. By July 1915, in the wake of the second attack on the Sultan, he was complaining that the police 'don't seem to have caught anyone much yet'.[18] In August he proposed a complete reorganization of the police, but, as anticipated, faced 'strenuous opposition' from the Ministry of the Interior, advised by his friend, Ronald Graham.[19] The reforms proposed by Clayton did not occur, but he was encouraged in early 1916 by the arrival in Cairo of representatives of London's Security and Secret Intelligence Services, who, as will be seen, proposed to extend their system to Egypt – 'and not before it is wanted,' Clayton added, as he was convinced they would 'soon expose some of the flaws in the Egyptian police'.[20]

Clayton could do little in the way of reforming the Egyptian police, but he was able to reorganize, and improve, another aspect of counter-intelligence, the censorship. As early as the autumn of 1914, he was directing the censor to 'knock out' various articles in the press containing false, misleading or inflammatory information damaging to the Entente war effort. Like the police, the censorship was controlled by the Ministry of the Interior and it too wanted reorganization. This time, Clayton undertook the job himself: 'When I tell you that there were about six different censorships, all under different people,' he wrote to Wingate, 'it will show you how necessary some sort of coordination had become. It was rather looked upon by some as interference on my part I fancy, but I can't help that as something had to be done and no one seemed inclined to do it!'[21] In fairness, the Egyptian censorship was undermanned and staffed with men not quite up to the task. And because of the cosmopolitan population of war-time Cairo, men capable in a wide variety of languages – Arabic, Turkish, Italian, Greek, French, even Armenian – had to work long, tedious hours to staunch the flow of undesirable information. Even after his reorganization, Clayton still had to write to Graham complaining of the continued publication of controversial material.[22] Graham, however, was unwilling or unable to solve the problem, so, in November 1915, Clayton brought the censorship under direct military control by establishing a new 'D' section in military Intelligence responsible for the task.[23]

Clayton also had considerable success in shutting down enemy trading from Egypt. As previously noted, hundreds of prominent Europeans in Egypt, some of German origin, were able to remain in the country after the war started by asserting their citizenship of neutral countries. Because the Capitulations were still in effect in Egypt, these Europeans, and their businesses, were effectively immune from unilateral Egyptian action to expel them. The correspondent, G.W. Steevens, mentioned earlier, provided a succinct description of the practical effect of the Capitulations: 'If I were to go out of the hotel now and shoot an Egyptian, and then go into a Frenchman's house, the Egyptian police could not enter the house without the presence of the French Consul, and could not arrest me without the presence of the English Consul; and by him I . . . [must] be tried.'[24] So, legal cases, backed by competent evidence, had to be brought against the neutrals in order to stop their trading with enemy firms. In April 1915, the first cases had been prepared against three such firms who were brought up for trial before a special military court. By the end of the year Clayton had established an enemy trading section within the censorship and assigned George Lloyd, now returned to Cairo after Gallipoli, the task of 'closing down enemy firms for good & all'.[25] In January 1916, Lloyd submitted a damning report of enemy trading in Egypt, laying heavy blame on the Egyptian government for its failure to curtail the trade.[26]

Clayton's actions in stopping enemy trading from Egypt and his counter-intelligence efforts inevitably brought him into conflict with Europeans resident in the country. He took it all in stride. 'I am having a jolly time with various Consuls General on account of the arrests of suspects, enforcing of military restrictions, etc.', he reported to the Sirdar in May 1916; 'I had three in, one after another, this morning – each one trying a ramp'.[27] But the ramps of the European consuls were nothing compared to the firestorm that was about to sweep through diplomatic circles when Clayton decided to clean the Egyptian house of European suspects in May 1916. He confessed that he was 'worried . . . to fiddlestrings' by the situation in the country in the spring of that year:

> The troops are leaving Egypt fast [for the Western Front] & we shall soon be down to the irreducible minimum. I am therefore urging much more stringent measures against potential spies & enemy agents . . . We cannot afford to run risks and it is far better to intern a few innocent persons than to take any chances. The difficulty is, of course, that all enemy agents masquerade under neutral nationality &, moreover, are often of high standing. It is therefore certain that diplomatic representations will be the result of drastic action in the absence of definite proof, which is seldom obtainable. However, I am all for facing protests – we are up against it now & the sooner we realize it and take off the gloves the better. I am no pessimist but if we go fiddling

along listening to the lawyers' and the diplomats' talk, we shall likely find one day that we have lost the war.[28]

General Archibald Murray, the former CIGS, now commanding in Egypt, fully concurred in Clayton's plan. Murray believed the situation in Egypt was 'analogous to the condition of Ireland before the late rebellion'. He agreed that Egypt was 'full of rich German and Austrian spies', and wrote to his replacement as CIGS, General William Robertson, that he was 'hard at work on the subject with Clayton'.[29] General Arthur Lynden-Bell, Murray's chief of staff, knew that there would be 'a rumpus about sending these people home without direct proof', but concluded, like Clayton, that 'we cannot afford to take any risks, . . For the safety of Egypt, these people should be removed'.[30]

On June 1, 1916, seventeen Europeans, nearly all of Swiss nationality, were rounded up and put aboard a ship bound for England. Clayton admitted he had no direct evidence against any of them, only 'strong presumptions', and worried that the ensuing 'racket will inevitably fall on my head'. He was prepared to face the racket, though, for he was convinced that there was a hostile organization in Egypt 'with the Germans at the back of it'. He was not so much concerned about the possibility of an armed uprising in the country; that would likely be futile, he thought, and 'easily quelled'. But the political effect of any such rising would be 'disastrous in Egypt and very serious in the Sudan'. In implementing his deportation policy, Clayton was well aware he was taking some personal risk. He was particularly concerned about his relationship with Murray, who agreed to the deportations, but 'is distrustful now & thinks perhaps he has been rushed and that all is well, so that I am going to bear the brunt of it all'. He even asked Wingate to write 'in very general terms' to Murray in support of his action. As will be described in chapter 16, Clayton would experience difficulties with Murray, and more so his staff, in 1916, but the arrests of June 1916 do not appear to have been the cause. As expected, after the June deportations, Murray was bombarded by protests from the European diplomatic community in Egypt. If his letters to London are any indication, though, he fully supported Clayton's measures.[31] For his part, Clayton took responsibility for the deportations and the resulting diplomatic fall-out. As was the case with his over-estimation of enemy strength prior to the February 1915 Turkish assault on the Canal, he had taken a cautious approach. But, as he informed Wingate, he would 'sooner make a mistake on the right side than the wrong'.[32]

Clayton's counter-intelligence efforts were largely successful. There were no insurrections in Egypt during the war and the German spy missions, entertaining though they were, accomplished nothing. In fact, the German *jihad* programme was a failure in every sense but one; British time, effort and money had to be expended in tracking the movement of enemy agents and, in some areas, most prominently southern Persia, in chasing them about the country. Clayton followed the exploits of the Germans with interest, but he was far more preoccupied with conventional Intelligence, especially information concerning the continued Turkish presence in Sinai. The Turks had not abandoned the peninsula after their failed February 1915 attack. But, in April, following on the Entente landings at the Dardanelles, they began moving troops north to contend with the new threat. At the same time, they floated rumours of another Canal attack, rumours that Intelligence concluded were 'designed to cloak the Northward movement of troops'.[33] By late May, Clayton's men were convinced that the Turk presence in Sinai was nothing more than bluff. 'They have no camels, no stores and no troops with which to begin a new offensive on the Canal, but they intend that the Canal should be disturbed at odd moments by the sham attacks of small patrols and by rumours of great things impending. If in this way their petty garrisons in the desert can contain a [British] fleet and an army of 15,000 men on the Canal they will be doing more than their duty to their fellows on the Dardanelles . . . The bluff then in Sinai becomes the Turkish main line of defence.'[34]

In August 1915, Intelligence reported that the Turks had no more than 2,000 men in 'Sinai proper', a number that could hardly do anything more than 'escort a mining-party to within reach of the Canal'. But two months later, with the Entente campaign at Gallipoli hopelessly stalled and the Bulgarians now in the camp of the Central Powers, Clayton's Intelligence believed that 'everything points to . . . a new offensive . . . by the Turks in Sinai'. And, in November, several reports established that the road and railway were being 'pushed vigorously' into Sinai by the Turks.[35] Indeed, in early December, Clayton reported to Wingate that a renewed attack on the Canal was expected about the end of January 1916.[36] Yet, conflicting reports were being received from unnamed sources in Constantinople. These sources reported that the Turks would postpone action in Sinai and instead mount an offensive against the British in Mesopotamia. Clayton was unsure; such reports could not be confirmed until Turkish troops actually reached Aleppo in northern Syria. Only then could it be determined whether they were moving south toward Sinai, or east to Mesopotamia.

Not until late December did Clayton come round to the view that the Turks would direct their efforts toward Mesopotamia, not Egypt.[37] And, in February 1916, Cairo Intelligence concluded that an Ottoman 'campaign for the conquest of Egypt will not be undertaken this year'. There were good reasons supporting this conclusion. With the Entente evacuation of Gallipoli, completed in January 1916, there were now more than 300,000 troops in Egypt and another Turkish assault on the Canal would have little chance of success. Also, the Turkish railway – critical to the transport of heavy guns through the sands of Sinai and the supply of a large invading force – was still 150 miles from the Canal. Nor had the Turks completed any roads through the peninsula; the nearest was still seventy miles from Ismailia on the Canal. Based on these facts, Intelligence were convinced that the Ottomans could not attack with more than 40,000 troops, a number certainly insufficient to overwhelm the British defenders. At the same time, rumours were spread – probably by Clayton's department – of an impending Entente landing somewhere on the Syrian or Palestine coast. In order to address that contingency, the Turks had to spread their forces throughout the Levant, thus preventing a concentration in Sinai.[38] Finally, on February 16, the Russians dealt the Turks a severe blow at

Erzerum in Eastern Anatolia, a defeat, Clayton concluded, that 'ought to put a final stopper on any invasion of Egypt on a large scale'.[39] In fact, by January 1916, the Turks and Germans had returned to their old game of bluff: Jemal intended only to keep a 'sufficient force' in Sinai and Palestine 'to prevent us from withdrawing troops from the Canal Zone'.[40]

In reaching these conclusions Clayton again had to rely heavily on human Intelligence, much as he had a year earlier, before the February 1915 assault on the Canal. And, once again, agent reports were wildly inconsistent. A December 1915 report, based on information from Arab agents, put the Turkish garrisons in Sinai at 15,000 men, but Clayton's analysts were sceptical: 'The actual figures are of course conflicting, as any reports from Arab agents must be'. In January 1916, revised estimates of Turkish forces in Sinai varied from 26,000 to 32,000 men, though aerial reconnaissance again suggested that 'agents have exaggerated' the number of enemy troops.[41]

Arab agents were not, of course, Clayton's only source of human Intelligence. He continued to gather information from a wide variety of sources, among them ship captains and passengers, Americans working in Turkey, the Russian military attaché in Sofia, letters intercepted by the censors, and Ottoman army deserters and prisoners, like the Turkish ADC to a German colonel whose information was shown to be false by an Arab prisoner taken from the same unit. He also received Intelligence from clerics resident in Ottoman territory, such as a Father Buono at Nazareth and Father Poli, the 'Guardian of Aleppo', and from Italian consuls in Syria and Beirut, until they were sent home in June 1915, shortly after the Italians joined the Entente. In addition, he placed agents in the Egyptian *suqs* (markets), and in certain Cairo cafes frequented by native officers in the Egyptian Army, some of whom were suspected of treasonous activity.[42] Until early 1916, Clayton also continued to supervise the dropping of agents into Ottoman territory, but, as described earlier, he considered them 'unreliable at best' and, in any event, they were often captured. In January 1916, he learned that 'three good agents whom I had in Syria & from whom I expected much have been arrested and I presume hanged! Bad luck!'[43]

This necessary reliance on human intelligence lent a certain cloak and dagger atmosphere to British Intelligence during the Great War, an atmosphere that would later be brilliantly depicted in the stories of Somerset Maugham and John Buchan and the non-fiction accounts of the novelist-turned-spy, Compton Mackenzie, who worked for the SIS in Greece during 1915–17. Another Intelligence officer, the young John deVere Loder, posted to the Intelligence unit at Port Said, described life in his office in 1916:

> Life is really quite like a page out of a novel . . . The air vibrates with hushed whispers, the stairs leading to the office resound with the stealthy tread of stage villains, corpulent Egyptians with tarbooshes, down-at-heel Greeks, Syrian refugees and terrified enemy aliens. Rifles, revolvers and ammunition pass in and out disguised as rations, in the office we keep invisible ink, secret drawers and insoluble ciphers. Letters arrive by special messengers enclosed

in two or three envelopes covered with mystical seals, while the least member of the organization is known by a number and the greatest by a single letter. Meanwhile we pass to outsiders as ordinary staff officers about whose occupation the civilian may speculate, but only superficially fathom. Little do they realize that their every movement is watched, and that, as we sit in the hotel bars of an evening, we are gathering the threads of a case into our hands, which will convict the wealthy Greek contractor of undermining the integrity of the British merchant service, the erstwhile Austrian (now a protected Russian subject) of disseminating propaganda inimical to our interests and the humble fisherman of passing information to submarines![44]

Loder doubtless meant to amuse his family with his description but, in those days before sophisticated electronics, spy satellites and computers, there was much truth in it. His concluding reference to submarines would certainly have caught Clayton's eye. In mid-1915, there were reported to be no less than twenty-seven German and Austrian submarines lurking in the Mediterranean and they were playing hell with Entente vessels, civilian and military alike. Clayton again looked to the 'great hashish smugglers' for a solution. He had used them before, in support of his sea-drops of agents on the Syrian coast. Now, he proposed to Maxwell and Kitchener that he select one or two of the largest smugglers, 'buy them and their whole organization lock, stock and barrel for the period of the war', and then pay them £10,000 or £15,000 'for every submarine captured or destroyed using their information & so much for every gallon of petroleum seized. You would thus have at your disposal', he added, 'the finest Intelligence service possible for the purpose'. The timing of Clayton's plan was perfect, for the British then had 'the biggest smuggler of the lot under sentence of deportation' and 'he was working every string to get off'. The scheme was evidently approved because he reported only three weeks later that it was 'already bearing fruit and the first instalment of information is distinctly useful'.[45]

More reliable than information acquired from agents was that obtained by the interception of wireless messages. By May 1915, the Turks had established wireless stations at Jerusalem – which could receive messages from Constantinople and Berlin – and Damascus.[46] Smaller stations were also set up at Beersheba and Medina. But these stations were apparently used sparingly, for there is no evidence that the British were intercepting messages in 1915. However, by February 1916, Intelligence from wireless intercepts was regularly appearing in reports, typically disguised as information from POWs or from an 'absolutely reliable source'. Shortly thereafter, the Arab Bureau got their hands on the Ottoman code book used by Turkish commanders in Palestine, Mesopotamia and the Hijaz.[47] Still, the information obtained was incomplete because in operations, such as those in Palestine in 1916–17, the Turks relied primarily on land-lines, using wireless only as a back-up. Also, those messages that were intercepted could only be decrypted in London, where cryptanalysis was conducted in MO5e (later, MI1(b)) of the War Office and in a small section in the Admiralty, later known as Room 40. Not until October

1916 was a cryptanalysis unit sent to Egypt. The War Office acted more promptly in establishing interception stations in the region. During March – June 1916, a Special Wireless Section (SWS) established interception stations in Salonika, Cyprus and Egypt, where the Section erected its primary antenna atop the great pyramid at Giza. As a result of these measures, from April 1916, Ottoman and German wireless messages were routinely intercepted from the Caucasus, Syria, Palestine, Sinai and the Hijaz.[48]

By early 1916, Clayton had, rather unobtrusively, taken his place among the handful of men on the spot directing the British war effort in the Middle East. T. E. Lawrence later described his influence in the Intelligence department:

> Nearly all of us rallied round Clayton, the Chief of Intelligence, civil and mili-
> tary, in Egypt. Clayton made the perfect leader for such a band of wild men
> as we were. He was calm, detached, clear-sighted, of unconscious courage in
> assuming responsibility. He gave an open run to his subordinates. His own
> views were general, like his knowledge; and he worked by influence rather
> than by loud direction. It was not easy to descry his influence. He was like
> water or permeating oil, creeping silently and insistently through everything.
> It was not possible to say where Clayton was and was not, and how much
> really belonged to him. He never visibly led; but his ideas were abreast of
> those who did: he impressed men by his sobriety, and a certain quiet and
> stately moderation of hope. In practical matters he was loose, irregular,
> untidy, a man with whom independent men could bear.[49]

Allowing for some literary flourish, there was much truth in Lawrence's description. Clayton was 'calm' and 'detached' and he rarely issued specific orders to his subordinates, preferring to work, as Lawrence observed, by influence. Many of the men who worked directly under Clayton were highly educated, experienced and influential personalities, most of them with decided opinions, accustomed to ventilating their own views and having them seriously considered. In dealing with such men, Clayton was certainly wise to at least appear to lead without 'loud direction', in a 'loose, irregular, untidy' fashion. And Lawrence was correct in suggesting that his chief's influence was pervasive, yet difficult to discern. Although very few were probably aware of the full extent of Clayton's responsibilities, by the spring of 1916, the list was impressive. In addition to his work as Director of Military Intelligence, he was still acting as Sudan Agent, and was responsible for the Arab Bureau and for the administration of martial law throughout Egypt. He directed Anglo-Egyptian relations with the Sanusi and, as has been seen, was instrumental in devising and effectuating policy with the Arabs of Syria and the Hijaz. He also acted as liaison between the High Commissioner and the British commanders in the Middle East, first Maxwell and then Murray, between Wingate and McMahon and between Wingate and the Egyptian Sultan, Hussein Kamil, with whom he met nearly every week during the first half of 1916. Clayton was, as Lawrence wrote, 'creeping silently and insistently through everything'.

In other respects, Lawrence's description of Clayton was inaccurate. Neither his views nor his knowledge could fairly be described as 'general'. To the contrary, his knowledge encompassed a stupendous mass of detail and, as seen, his opinions and objectives concerning British policy in the region and Anglo-Arab relations were specific, uncomfortably so for some, such as those in India. Nor was it impossible to say – in a literal sense, at least – 'where Clayton was and was not'. Just the opposite; everyone seemed to know where Clayton was; from December 1915, he could be found in his office at military headquarters in Cairo's Savoy Hotel where he worked, usually fourteen hours a day, and was 'bombarded' by letters, petitions and interviews with persons of every stripe, from the native agent spying in the Cairo *suqs* to the French Minister, complaining of British intentions regarding Syria. In this last respect, Storrs' assessment was more accurate than Lawrence's: By 1916, Clayton had 'become one of the best known figures in the Near East'.[50]

13

Reorganizing the Intelligence, 1916

If Storrs was correct that Clayton had become one of the best known figures in the Near East, it was because of the many responsibilities he had undertaken during the first eighteen months of the war. Yet, his duties in Cairo's Intelligence Directorate were altered in the early months of 1916, as a result of two developments – the failure of the Entente campaign at the Dardanelles and a major reorganization at the War Office in London. In December 1915, the CIGS, Archibald Murray, was replaced by Lieutenant-General William Robertson and Murray was appointed commander of the Mediterranean Expeditionary Force (Medforce), then engaged in evacuating the Gallipoli Peninsula. In the same month, Kitchener removed the War Office Intelligence sections from the Directorate of Military Operations (where they had resided since 1901) and created a new Directorate of Military Intelligence under Brigadier-General George Macdonogh, an experienced officer who had run the Intelligence functions of the Operations Directorate before the war. This reorganization also encompassed the Intelligence Services – the predecessors of MI5 and MI6 – who would soon appear in Egypt.

Before the war, the Security Service operated within the War Office's Operations Directorate as MO5(g) under Major Vernon Kell, who had run the Service since its inception in October 1909, and would continue as its chief until 1940. Working with a staff of only eighteen in August 1914, Kell's group would swell to 844 by war's end, and already, in 1915, was highly regarded as a counter-espionage unit. By June of 1915, German espionage activity in Britain had been effectively crushed. The Secret Service (later known as SIS, the Secret Intelligence Service) had a different experience. It too had been founded in October 1909, but its functions were not formally differentiated from Kell's Security Service until May 1910, when its brief was limited to the acquisition of foreign Intelligence, as distinct from the counter-espionage mission of Kell's MO5. The SIS chief, Mansfield Cumming – referred to simply as 'C', the designation by which the head of SIS is known to this day – had a more difficult path to follow. Before the war, his group was also placed under the Operations Directorate of the War Office. But Cumming was a naval officer and took much of his direction from the Director of the Intelligence Division (DID) at the Admiralty, the formidable Captain (later Admiral, Sir) William Reginald

'Blinker' Hall. Adding to the confusion, the SIS was funded by the Foreign Office, through its 'Secret Vote', and the Office naturally demanded some control over Cumming's activities. As part of Kitchener's December 1915 re-ordering, the Intelligence sections of the old Operations Directorate assumed 'MI' designations and Kell's Security Service became MI5, a designation still used. And in April 1916, the SIS moved from MO6 authority, to a newly-created MI1(c), headed by Colonel C. N. French, where it resided until the end of the war.[1]

Cumming's SIS had been operating in the Near East since February 1915, when he appointed Major Rhys Samson, former British Consul at Adrianople and, most recently, liaison to France's Duxième Bureau (Military Intelligence), to lead an espionage/counter-espionage group in Athens focused on Turkey and the Balkans. It was Samson's group, then referred to informally as the 'R Organisation', that the novelist Compton Mackenzie joined in the autumn of 1915. Although it has been argued that 'a close working relationship developed between Athens . . . and Cairo' in 1915, there is little in the way of documentary evidence that reveals the nature or extent of the collaboration.[2] Only one letter from Clayton to 'C', and one memorandum by Clayton concerning the R Organisation could be found, both strongly recommending its continuance in the Middle East after the war.[3] The War Office's Intelligence files, the papers of the Cairo Residency and those of the Arab Bureau contain few and only cryptic references to the R Organisation, even after it moved to Alexandria in December 1915.

In 1997, MI5 released an administrative history of its Middle East unit, but the records of MI6 – in any event, not open to examination – likely contain little information on SIS operations in the region from this period.[4] The official historian of the SIS for the period 1909–49 has noted that the Service 'had only a tenuous involvement with the Middle East' during the war, largely because once Egypt became a British protectorate in December 1914, the SIS, with its brief limited to foreign Intelligence, 'could have no direct responsibility there'.[5] Still, there are hints of collaboration between Cairo and the SIS operation in Athens by the summer of 1915. It has been disclosed that the R Organisation was then investigating the system of supply for enemy submarines operating in the Eastern Mediterranean and it seems likely that this work was related to, or was even the same operation as, that which Clayton had proposed for using hashish smugglers to acquire information regarding submarine supply and movements. Other evidence of SIS–Cairo collaboration appears in the visit of Lawrence to Athens in August 1915, probably at the request of Samson, to help get the R Organisation's 'dislocation in order'. However, the claim by Lawrence's authorised biographer that Lawrence became 'Samson's representative in Cairo' has been questioned.[6]

In December 1915, most of the R Organisation moved from Athens to Alexandria, leaving a small group in the Greek capital under Mackenzie. Samson's move was prompted in part by the Entente evacuation of Gallipoli – the Intelligence focus was now shifting from Turkey and the Balkans to Egypt – and partly by the political instability in Greece where King Constantine I was pro-German, but the Prime Minister, Eleutherios Venizelos, stood firmly in the Entente camp. Just as

Samson was completing his move to Egypt, a letter was sent from Military Intelligence in London to Clayton, a letter it was said, that 'informed Colonel Clayton of the existence of the Central Special Intelligence Bureau in London [MI5 and SIS]. . . and asked him to approach General Sir John Maxwell . . . with a view to cooperation'.[7] That Clayton, the director of Military Intelligence in Cairo, was then unaware of the London Intelligence agencies some sixteen months after the war had started, is most unlikely, particularly since he had been working with the R Organisation for months and must have known something of the authority under which R worked. In any event, the lack of coordinated Intelligence between Cairo and London was evident enough, and Clayton jumped at the offer of cooperation. Macdonogh, the DMI, responded promptly by sending Major Eric Holt-Wilson of MI5 to Egypt to 'see what could be done in the matter'.

Already, before Holt-Wilson's arrival in early February 1916, Clayton had prepared a memorandum for Macdonogh outlining his proposals for a major reorganization of Britain's Middle Eastern Intelligence. He was critical of the previous division of effort, where the R Organisation had been confined to the operational area of Medforce (the Dardanelles) and the Balkans, and Cairo was assigned 'the remainder of Turkey and the South'. He argued for collaboration between the two organizations, a collaboration focused on four of the 'greater political questions' in the region: the political aspirations of the Balkan countries in the Balkans, the Aegean and Western Turkey; the activities of the CUP, particularly with regard to sedition in India and nationalism in Egypt; the Arab question in Turkey, Arabia, North Africa and Egypt; and, finally, the 'growing organisation of Islam', which, he added, 'will need to be treated with the utmost care . . . to prevent its becoming a powerful instrument in the hands of those hostile to British Imperial interests'. For Clayton, these questions were closely inter-related. 'The scenes may shift' and some players 'appear in one act [and] some in another', he argued with theatrical metaphor, yet 'there is but one stage and one play', and 'the company is one'. So too, he concluded, 'should be the management'. Clayton made no distinction in his proposed reorganization between war-time and post-war conditions; to the contrary, the post-war period would see 'increased political activity', thus warranting continuation of the combined organization. Cairo, he continued, should be the centre of a single, coordinated Intelligence treating these great issues. To initiate the amalgamated organization, Clayton proposed that the counter-Intelligence function of GHQ Medforce, now in Egypt, should be combined with the R Organisation and both 'should be affiliated to the Intelligence Bureau at Cairo in the same manner as the "Arab Bureau" now under consideration, and that such organisation should continue its activities after the War'.[8]

The ideas set forth in Clayton's memorandum were largely endorsed by Holt-Wilson, who agreed that counter-intelligence work in the region suffered from a lack of centralized control. He proposed to Macdonogh that the counter-intelligence section of Clayton's department be consolidated with Medforce's similar section (already handed over to the R Organisation in January) and that both be placed under Samson in a new unit called the Eastern Mediterranean Special Intelligence Bureau

(EMSIB). The proposal was immediately accepted by Macdonogh, Kell and French, who also agreed, doubtless with C's concurrence, that the EMSIB would 'contain both MI1(c) and M.I.5 elements'.[9] Locally, the proposals were endorsed by McMahon, Maxwell and Graham, Adviser to the Egyptian Ministry of the Interior. However, Clayton's further suggestion, supported by Holt-Wilson, that the new EMSIB should be of a permanent character, was deferred by the Foreign Office for further consideration after the war.[10] Clayton must also have expressed to Holt-Wilson his unhappiness with the Egyptian police, as described above, for in his memorandum on counter-espionage in Egypt, sent to MI5 on February 17, Holt-Wilson appended a supplementary note to Macdonogh in which he argued that the new EMSIB should have both MI5 and SIS elements because of the 'weakness of the local police in European personnel capable of making judicious enquiries regarding Europeans'.[11]

Consistent with the proposal that the new unit contain both Intelligence and counter-espionage elements, Holt-Wilson suggested that the EMSIB be divided along those lines into 'A' and 'B' branches, with the staff of 'A' branch to be appointed by, and to receive 'general instructions' from MI1(c) in London, while the staff of 'B' branch should 'continue to be provided and appointed by the British Military Intelligence Directorate at Cairo [Clayton] in consultation with the Bureau Director [Samson], through whom all executive instructions shall issue . . . .'[12] 'B' branch was specified as serving an information-collecting function; without civil or military police duties, 'B' branch would assemble the materials 'necessary for the successful prosecution of a case' and then transfer them to the legal authorities. The geographic scope of the EMSIB was a wide one and was to include Egypt and the Sudan, Abyssinia, North Africa, Tripoli, the Turkish Empire, Persia, all the Balkan countries, and the Aegean and Eastern Mediterranean islands.

Although the odd bit of information may occasionally come to light, it is unlikely that a clear picture of the nature and measure of success of EMSIB's work will ever emerge. In the autumn of 1918, EMSIB was swallowed up by the Egyptian Expeditionary Force, then in Palestine, and ceased to have a separate existence. Its records were not sent to Britain after the war and, most likely, were destroyed.[13] Still, the EMSIB must have been a very busy agency indeed. By October 1916, it had as many as 300 'staff and agents' in Egypt, making it SIS's largest overseas operation.[14] If any conclusions can be drawn from the absence of war-time trouble in Egypt from the spring of 1916, it might be argued that the counter-espionage efforts of EMSIB were successful there. For Clayton, the EMSIB reflected at least a partial attainment of his goal of consolidating Middle Eastern Intelligence and, on a personal level, it relieved him of some of the crushing burden of work by placing counter-espionage work in Samson's hands.

While the EMSIB was formed to address problems arising from the lack of coordination in Britain's Middle Eastern Intelligence, the Arab Bureau was founded, at about the same time, to contend with two different, but related, problems perceived by Clayton – the absence of an organized effort to combat Turco-German propaganda and the need to harmonize the various and often conflicting British policies in the region.[15] Throughout 1915, British efforts to disseminate pro-Entente propaganda had been limited largely to dropping leaflets by air over Palestine and Arabia and to the publication of articles favourable to the Entente in pro-British Arabic publications such as Faris Nimr's *al-Muqattam*. The lack of coordination in British policy-making was a far more serious problem. Everyone with a hand in Middle Eastern issues – at least twenty different authorities, by one account – seemed to be following an independent course. Telegrams between London and the Middle East were said to be 'a perfect babel of conflicting suggestions and views which interweave and intertwine from man to man and place to place in an almost inexplicable tangle'.[16] The differences between Egypt and India and, by extension, their home government sponsors, the Foreign and India Offices, have already been described. But the lack of coordination, and cooperation, also extended to the War Office and the Admiralty in London and, in the region, to the separate commands in Egypt, the Dardanelles and Mesopotamia. Clayton had offered the services of his department to Medforce even before the initial landings on the Gallipoli Peninsula in April 1915, but they 'made no attempt to avail themselves' of the Intelligence and help which Clayton was 'anxious and willing to give'. He still sent his information to the Dardanelles command, but received 'little or nothing in return'. Clayton also wrote to offer an exchange of information with the British residency at Aden, controlled by the Government of India, but they 'never even had the courtesy to acknowledge' his letter.[17]

Just as the War Office reorganization and the Dardanelles evacuation prompted a re-evaluation of the Intelligence, so did those events instigate a reassessment of British policy-making for the region. Already, in late November 1915, the War Office dispatched a Brigadier-General Malcom to Cairo to assess the situation. As a result of talks with Maxwell and Malcolm, Clayton reported to Wingate that Cairo will now be 'the centre of everything . . . [A] very large Intelligence system including a Near Eastern Bureau and a naval branch is to be attached to my present office, or rather added on to it. Apparently it is decided that I am to run it all'.[18] The particular idea of a Near Eastern bureau was one that immediately appealed to Clayton, as he saw that such a bureau could address the problems of Turco-German propaganda and the lack of policy coordination he had identified four months earlier. However, the General Staff appears to have envisioned creation of the bureau in London, a notion that Clayton strongly opposed, as he described in a letter to Kitchener's nephew, A. C. Parker, then attached to the War Office:

> With regard to the Section which it is apparently proposed to form at the War Office, I am very strongly of [the] opinion that this Section should be formed here, and attached to the Intelligence Department. It is only by working on the spot, where they would have the full benefit of all the detailed information which we get, and have the opportunity of seeing all the various people who gravitate to Cairo, that they would be able to get a really clear grasp of the whole situation . . . Another strong reason for having a section, or bureau, here is that I think any such bureau should include in its sphere

the institution of an offensive propaganda to meet that of the Pan-Islamic Bureau that has its headquarters in Berlin. Up to the present we have been content with a purely defensive attitude in this matter (and in many others) and I feel very strongly that we should have some organisation by which we could strike back.

While Clayton believed the proposed bureau would prove instrumental in countering Turco-German propaganda, he also saw that it could be useful as a mechanism for coordinating British policy in the region. In his view, the bureau should have 'correspondents' in India, Aden and Mesopotamia for the exchange of information on issues of mutual interest, and a 'liaison office' in London that would 'keep all the Government offices concerned fully informed'. As if to pre-empt War Office action in establishing a bureau in London, Clayton informed Parker that he had 'already formed a small nucleus here [Cairo] in anticipation of the regular bureau', and that both McMahon and Maxwell agreed with his plan.[19] Clayton was not interested in establishing a Near Eastern bureau in Cairo in order to promote his own role in Middle Eastern policy-making; he believed that he and his colleagues in the Intelligence were simply better suited to the task. 'I can see such a bureau in London', he warned the Sirdar, 'crammed with all the "cranks" who dabble in Near Eastern affairs & imagine themselves experts on the strength of a tourist visit to Jerusalem or Constantinople'.[20]

Although he had good reasons for promoting a Near Eastern bureau and for locating it in Cairo, Clayton did not yet possess sufficient influence with the London departments to bring his plan to fruition. For that he needed help and he received it in the form of Sir Mark Sykes, who appeared in Cairo just as the scheme for a bureau was being discussed by Maxwell, McMahon and Malcolm of the War Office. By all accounts, Mark Sykes was an interesting character. He had, within the span of a year, achieved a prominent position in British Middle East policy-making. Like George Lloyd and Aubrey Herbert, he was born into a wealthy family, travelled widely in the East before the war, written books on the region, and become a Member of Parliament. Never short of opinions, and often inclined to express them forcefully, Sykes soon came to the attention of Kitchener who arranged a seat for him on the Committee of Imperial Defence, where he advanced the Field Marshal's (and his own) views on Eastern affairs. Clayton had met Sykes four months earlier when he stopped in Cairo as part of a tour to learn the views of the men on the spot in Egypt, Mesopotamia and India.[21]

Sykes would come to exercise a significant influence on British Middle Eastern policy during the next three years, until he fell victim to the great influenza epidemic which swept the globe in 1919. Everyone seemed to recognize his abilities and, as a keen wit and brilliant caricaturist, he made for good company. But Sykes was a creature of sudden enthusiasms who would fix on an idea or a principle, advance it in hyperbolic and often outlandish ways, and then fire off in a different direction when some new notion caught his attention. His modern biographer tellingly sub-titled his life of Sykes 'portrait of an amateur', perhaps because Sykes possessed neither the attention to detail nor the perseverance to ensure that his ideas were fully matured.[22] For his part, Clayton was pleased that Sykes was sympathetic to many of his own ideas concerning Eastern policy, but somewhat uneasy that he would not represent them correctly in London. Sykes 'seems to have frightened the people somewhat at home', Clayton later wrote to a War Office acquaintance, 'but I think his various schemes are taken somewhat too seriously. He is apt to enlarge on schemes which are at bottom extremely sound and make them appear fantastic'. But, characteristically, Clayton found something good to say of anyone he criticized. Sykes would still 'be of great use', he added, 'as he is full of energy and knowledge'.[23]

Sykes was of great use in advancing the proposal for a Near Eastern bureau. After discussions with Clayton, Maxwell, McMahon and Malcolm, he cabled the Foreign Office his view that a new bureau to be established 'under D.M.O. and [my]self' was the 'best means of co-ordinating an Arabian and Islamic Intelligence'. And, like Clayton, he urged that the bureau's headquarters should reside not in London, but in Egypt, from where the 'German Pan-Islamic bureau', which was 'making considerable headway in all fields', could best be countered.[24] But by mid-December, Sykes, now in London, was concocting an elaborate structure for the bureau, to be placed 'nominally' under the Foreign Office, with himself as head, unless Clayton wished him to be his 'receiver' in London, where he could 'put the case for you to the statesmen'. Still, Sykes's view of the functions of the new bureau were similar to Clayton's – to 'harmonise British political activity in the Near East' and 'to co-ordinate propaganda in favour of Great Britain among non-Indian Moslems'.[25]

Anticipating that Sykes would enlarge on his plan to the extent of alarming the London authorities, Clayton wrote to Kitchener, to the Foreign Office and to Blinker Hall at the Admiralty. He stressed to the Foreign Office that the purpose of the new bureau was merely 'to study all Near Eastern questions' and, though he hoped that it would be 'endowed with a considerable measure of independence', the bureau would work 'under the control of the High Commissioner of Egypt', who, of course, worked at the direction of the Foreign Office. Hall, at the Admiralty, was quickly won over after reviewing Clayton's proposal. 'I am delighted to do anything to get the closest co-ordination between all our Intelligence . . . [and] am entirely at your service in the matter'. The Admiralty Intelligence director added that, like Clayton, he did not wish to 'centralise Intelligence on the Near East in London, but to feed you with everything we get, and regard you as the principal Intelligence centre for that part of the campaign'.[26] In a further letter to Hall, Clayton emphasized that his ideas for the bureau differed from those of Sykes:

> Sykes . . . may have perhaps alarmed the various authorities at home, and led them to think that a more far-reaching organisation is contemplated than might be desirable. My ideas are somewhat different than those of Sykes, in that what I want to start is a Bureau here which will be a centre to which all information on the various questions connected with the Near East will gravitate. My idea is to have a staff here of men who are competent to sift and

catalogue this information and to bring it into a form in which it is easily digested by those who may not be experts in the various questions . . , its object being merely to collect and collate information on all subjects and to advise all concerned when required.

As if anticipating Lawrence's later assessment of his administrative style, described above, Clayton opposed Sykes' idea of laying down a definite structure for the bureau at its inception. As the men of the bureau 'work and gain experience, the various lines on which the Bureau would proceed will become apparent, and the organisation can be built up . . . It is no use trying to sketch out in too much detail the programme of work and the system of organisation. The Bureau will be quite a new child and must be allowed to grow up and expand in the direction indicated by experience'.[27]

By early January 1916, Clayton had begun to distance himself from Sykes as well as from his ideas. He advised Hall that it would perhaps be unnecessary to tie Sykes down as a 'permanent member of the Bureau', as 'he would be more useful as a free-lance, available to go wherever it was necessary to obtain information'.[28] Wingate had suggested that Sykes head the London liaison office of the bureau, as a section of the Directorate of Military Operations.[29] Clayton disagreed, arguing that the bureau's London representative should be a 'suitable official' on the staff of the Intelligence Division of the Admiralty; that is, an officer under Hall.[30]

On January 5, 1916, the Prime Minister directed that an inter-departmental conference of the Committee of Imperial Defence be convened to consider the establishment of an 'Islamic Bureau at Cairo'. The conference was held two days later and included representatives of the Foreign and India Offices, as well as the directors of Military (Macdonogh) and Naval (Hall) Intelligence, the Director of Military Operations (General Frederick Maurice), the War Office liaison with the SIS (Lt. Col. French), Kitchener's representative (Lt. Col. O.A. FitzGerald) and Sykes himself. Using Sykes' plan as a starting point, the conference quickly decided that, due to objections to the suggested title of 'Islamic'– doubtless from the India Office – the new bureau 'would be concerned only with Arabs' and thus styled 'either Arab or Arabian'. The conference also agreed, as Sykes proposed, that the first function of the bureau would be 'to harmonise British political activity in the Near East' and to keep all concerned government departments 'informed of the general tendency of Germano-Turkish policy'. This was arguably a wider responsibility than Clayton envisioned. He saw the bureau merely as a co-ordinator of Eastern policy; 'harmonize' implied a more active role in ensuring that divergent policies were reconciled. Clayton's idea was slightly more limited: the bureau should 'furnish information . . . rather than express views, though I presume it would naturally draw conclusions from the information it obtained'.[31]

The conference adopted the view of Sykes and Clayton that the second function of the bureau would be to 'coordinate propaganda in favour of Great Britain and the Entente among non-Indian Moslems', the latter reference an obvious concession to the Government of India. The actual work of the bureau was enumerated in nine, separate paragraphs, but generally involved supplying periodic reports to the

Foreign Office for circulation to other interested departments, supplying pro-Entente propaganda to the Foreign Office and to India (to be used at its discretion), stimulating pro-Entente and anti-German feeling in the Middle East, and keeping in close touch with French authorities in the region.[32]

Conspicuously absent from the CID report was any mention of the structure and personnel of the bureau as elaborated by Sykes. FitzGerald later explained to Clayton that 'many details of the working of the Bureau which Mark Sykes put up . . . were all left over to be arranged by you and him [Sykes] after the Bureau was working'. This conclusion coincided precisely with Clayton's view that the details of bureau organization and staffing should not be laid down until the bureau had been up and working for some time. Nor did the conference's report specify the authority under which the bureau was to operate. FitzGerald again clarified for Clayton that 'it was to be a branch of your office in Cairo [and] was to be controlled by you'.[33] The Foreign Office attendee underscored that 'the whole sense of the Committee was that it should be under . . . [McMahon] and under his subordinate Capt. Clayton'.[34]

The London conference thus accepted Clayton's views as to the functions of the Arab Bureau – as it was now called – but rejected his idea that it should be only 'nominally' under the Foreign Office, with its London liaison on the staff of Hall's Admiralty Intelligence Division. That proposal was firmly rejected by the India Office whose agreement to the new unit was conditioned on the Bureau's control by the Foreign Office. For India, the work of the bureau was 'much too important & delicate a business . . . to be controlled by any body except that which is officially responsible for the foreign policy of H.M.G.'.[35] The India Office were not, however, opposed in principle to an Arab Bureau. Chamberlain acknowledged that there was a 'clear need for greater activity and close cooperation' which could be met by the creation of the bureau.[36]

By February 1916, the Arab Bureau had 'suddenly materialized' in Cairo, and, as Clayton noted, 'very much along the lines I had hoped'.[37] He immediately began staffing the new agency. The unanimous choice for the director was David G. Hogarth, a prominent archaeologist of the Near East and keeper of the Ashmolean Museum at Oxford, where he had mentored Lawrence before the war. Clayton also drew heavily from his Intelligence department, enlisting the services of Kinahan Cornwallis, who would assume responsibility during Hogarth's frequent absences and eventually took on the directorship, in addition to Lawrence, Philip and Robert Graves, George Lloyd and A. C. Parker. Gertrude Bell would soon begin work in Basra as the Bureau's Mesopotamian correspondent. India had no correspondent, but sent a man to Cairo, Arthur Brownlow fforde, who reported regularly to Delhi. But, like Clayton's Intelligence department, the composition of the Bureau changed constantly, in a kaleidoscopic fashion. Some men were assigned to other theatres. Others worked for the Bureau on an ad hoc basis, returning to their regular duties when specific tasks were completed. Still others performed Bureau work, but were never formally assigned to it. As was the case with the Intelligence department, the failure to maintain a stable, long-term staff would undermine the Bureau's effectiveness.

The Arab Bureau would have many critics among contemporaries and historians alike, some of whom depicted it as an assemblage of dilettantes, amateurs dabbling in matters of high policy. Others, like Gertrude Bell, saw the Bureau as comprised of a 'brilliant constellation' of clever, talented personalities. But, however its staff is characterized, it would be a mistake to describe the Arab Bureau as possessing anything like a single, over-arching outlook or policy. And the conventional historic treatment of the Bureau as a sort of renegade group of pan-Arab visionaries has been substantially revised. The only historian to study the Bureau in detail has concluded that it had no 'monolithic' perspective, that it was pragmatic in its approach to Middle Eastern problems, and 'more often worked in pursuit of policy directives from London . . . than in contradiction of them'.[38]

Although Clayton did not formally serve as the Bureau's director – his responsibilities were much wider and more varied – he was the 'ex-officio head of the agency' from its inception. It was, 'Clayton's show', concludes the historian of the Bureau, and, for this reason, it was identified 'closely with Cairo's view of the Arab world'.[39] Cairo's view of the Arab world was constructed largely by Clayton, Wingate and Maxwell. For McMahon, now, in 1916, increasingly reliant on Clayton, the views of the Bureau were regarded as those of Clayton. As A. B. fforde observed, McMahon 'only worked through Clayton and did not even send for Hogarth'.[40] As described in the following chapters, the Arab Bureau's effectiveness would later be undermined by the Egyptian command, but, according to the Bureau's historian, whatever success it did experience during the war was 'due to Clayton's adroit management of sensitive relations between Khartoum, the residency and the Egyptian high command'.[41]

The actual work of the Arab Bureau was varied. Consistent with his original plan, Clayton immediately began an 'Anti Pan-Islamic Section' of the Bureau which prepared and disseminated propaganda.[42] But the work also encompassed the preparation of handbooks on various regions of the Middle East, surveys of prominent Arab personalities, trade reports and Intelligence summaries. The Bureau translated correspondence, monitored wireless intercepts and assembled a reference library on Middle Eastern topics. As envisioned by Clayton, it became something of an 'analytical clearinghouse' for information regarding the Arab world.[43] Consistent with this vision, from June 1916, it produced a secret, periodic report, the *Arab Bulletin*, which summarized Intelligence from Tunisia to Afghanistan and was provided to a select group of government authorities interested in the region. And, as will be seen, the Bureau would take an active role in the Arab revolt, arranging supplies for the Sherifian forces, monitoring their progress and proposing courses of action.

Clayton regarded the creation of EMSIB and the Arab Bureau as positive developments; both, he thought, would bring badly needed order to the chaos of Middle East Intelligence and policy-making. The same could not be said of the appearance of Medforce in Egypt in early January 1916. Following the Dardanelles evacuation, some fourteen divisions of Entente troops descended on Egypt. The country was teeming with soldiers. And Cairo's famous Shepheard's Hotel was said to be overflowing with Generals, 200 of them by one account.[44] The Egypt command was reorganized, and a general headquarters, 'similar to that of an army echelon' was created in Cairo, where it was installed in the Savoy Hotel.[45] In view of the plan for an increased Staff, including Intelligence, Clayton's position was 'regularised' in the new structure and he was made a General Staff Officer, first grade (GSO1).[46] In light of Clayton's increased responsibilities, Maxwell now wished to remove him from Sudan Agency work and restrict his duties to GHQ, Intelligence. 'I do not think that Clayton can possibly continue in his dual capacity', he advised Wingate. '[H]e will have to shed Soudan affairs; he very nearly broke down with overwork a few days ago'.[47] But Wingate did not agree and Clayton continued his work as Sudan Agent.

The appearance of Medforce in Cairo, along with its own Intelligence unit and its new commander, the former CIGS Archibald Murray, created an awkward situation. There were now two commanders in Egypt. 'The reorganization of command is still unsettled', Clayton reported near the end of December. 'Some say that Sir A. Murray will command on the Canal under Sir J. Maxwell . . . others that Sir A. Murray will be in command in the . . . fighting areas . . . while Sir J. Maxwell will continue as G.O.C. Egypt. The first course appears sound and practical, but the second must lead to confusion, loss of efficiency and overlapping'. Clayton was right about the confusion, for it soon became apparent that Medforce had arrived in Cairo 'under the impression that they were to take over'.[48] Maxwell confessed that he was 'very hurt' by the decision to send out Murray and complained bitterly to Robertson and Kitchener that the dual command in Egypt was 'absurd, wasteful and unnecessary'. As an example, he exclaimed that there was now in Egypt 'no less than four Intelligence Departments!!'[49]

Maxwell was baffled by the decision to place two commanders in Egypt. 'I suppose in the shuffle of Robertson to CIGS they felt bound to do something for Murray, but why at the expense of Egypt!' Clayton offered an explanation that was nearer the mark: 'I have little doubt from what I have heard privately that it is all part of the movement in high places at home to get rid of Lord K. from the W[ar] O[ffice]. I am told that a considerable section of the Cabinet are bent on this . . . As Sir John [Maxwell] is one of Lord K's men, . . there is reason to think that they meant to get him out if they could . . . The idea . . . was to put all military operations . . . under Sir A. Murray and to relegate Sir John Maxwell to a mere Military Governorship'.[50]

While the powers in London wrestled over Egypt's command structure, Clayton was left wondering about the scope of his own Intelligence duties. The idea of a greatly expanded Intelligence, placed under him, that had been mooted at the end of November, now seemed increasingly doubtful. Initially, he 'suffered very little interference', as the commanders, he claimed, left his department 'practically untouched'.[51] But Clayton well understood that Murray might end up as sole commander in Egypt and he was anxious to be on good terms with Medforce Intelligence. When he learned of Murray's intention to relocate Medforce to the Canal Zone, Clayton offered to turn over to him the tactical Intelligence unit run by Jennings-Bramly and Barlow in Sinai.[52] This was no great concession because, as described earlier, Clayton had relinquished day-to-day responsibility for Bramly's operation to the Canal defence force a year earlier. Still, he foresaw difficulties ahead. Murray's GHQ had 'no conception of the various problems of administration' in Egypt, and he was justifiably worried about 'Medforce Intell. trying to butt in and interfere in matters of which they know little or nothing'.[53]

Clayton had good cause for concern. Murray, and more so his staff, held the Force in Egypt in low regard, as described by Medforce's Chief of Staff, General Arthur Lynden-Bell:

> The whole of our troubles out here are connected with Maxwell . . . He is no soldier, as is clearly shown by the fact that, although he was in Egypt for a whole year, he made not the slightest attempt to arrange for the defence of the country, and further, the fact that he has no idea of making any preparations for offensive fighting.

Lynden-Bell's criticism extended to Clayton:

> We were told that the Egyptian Intelligence was most astonishingly efficient and that the astounding work they had done should be talked of with bated breath. On examination, however, it is quite clear that this is an absolute myth. Their intelligence is mainly confined to harem gossip and politics. There is not the slightest thought in any of the intelligence reports I have seen of anything connected with the enemy or fighting. My own intelligence fellows, I find, have in a fortnight amassed far more knowledge of the Sinai Peninsula than has ever been produced by the Egyptian Intelligence Department.[54]

Lynden-Bell was too quick to throw stones, particularly since he and Murray were living in a glass house. In February 1916, they estimated that the Turkish force in Palestine amounted to 250,000 men, a figure five or six times greater than the actual number. An historian of Intelligence operations in the Palestine theatre has concluded that 'Medforce's inexperienced intelligence section erred in a basic overestimation of the Ottoman strength, while its counterpart in Cairo was more cautious'.[55]

On January 22, 1916, GHQ Medforce, including 'the whole of its Intelligence', moved from Cairo to Ismailia on the Canal. 'We are delighted', Lynden-Bell reported, 'to get away from the hopeless atmosphere of Cairo and to get clear of Maxwell'.[56] Meanwhile, Clayton continued to cooperate with Murray's command. Parker, who had returned to Cairo from London, was sent to Ismailia, primarily because of his knowledge of Sinai, and, in return, Clayton received Captain Wyndham Deedes. Fluent in Turkish and experienced in Intelligence work, Deedes was a 'first rate fellow' who would prove a valuable addition to Clayton's staff and would also work in the newly-formed Arab Bureau.[57]

Clayton also relinquished to Medforce his control of Syrian Intelligence, including the sea-drops of agents along the Syrian coast. 'I have found it quite unsound to attempt to continue running the Syrian Intelligence system under present conditions and have suggested handing it over to M.E.F.', he informed the Sirdar in February. He could not 'help feeling sorry at handing over one's own child', but felt that 'as the information primarily is intended for M.E.F., they should have control of the system'. Lynden-Bell was delighted. Medforce had now got Maxwell 'clear of everything East of the Canal. He [Maxwell] was meddling about in Syria and also playing about with the French Navy, but we have arranged that he has nothing to do with Syria and that we collect all the intelligence regarding Syria . . .'[58] In fact, Clayton's Syrian Intelligence system, including infiltrated agents, was soon handed over to the EMSIB, just as the new MI5/SIS operation had taken over Medforce's counter-espionage work. When Leonard Woolley went down off Alexandretta in August 1916, he was then working for the EMSIB, not Murray's GHQ.[59]

By late February 1916, the division of command between Medforce on the Canal and Maxwell in Cairo had become unworkable. 'In Intelligence matters', Clayton complained, 'it is almost impossible to know where Egypt leaves off and M.E.F. begins'.[60] Finally, on March 10, Maxwell was recalled and the Force in Egypt was consolidated with Medforce in a new, Egyptian Expeditionary Force (EEF), and placed under Murray. Although pressure was now applied to Murray to return to Cairo – chiefly by the foreign consuls in Egypt – he refused. Concerned that he would 'be immersed in politics and social functions and constant visits from foreign representatives', he remained at Ismailia.[61] Clayton did not join him. '[H]eadquarters of the Intell. is to stay here [Cairo]', he informed Wingate, 'as I pointed out that it was impossible to move'.[62]

Clayton's description was inaccurate; Cairo was no longer 'headquarters' of the Intelligence. By late March 1916, Murray's Intelligence had expanded significantly. Now led by Colonel Godfrey Holdich, it included eighteen staff officers and handled order-of-battle and topographical Intelligence as well as aspects of clandestine Intelligence-gathering. Clayton's Intelligence section continued, denominated as the 'Cairo Branch', but, with only seven officers, was regarded as the 'rear intelligence component of EEF'.[63] Just as the EMSIB had reduced, if not entirely eliminated, Clayton's work in counter-intelligence, so did the new EEF Intelligence relieve him of Intelligence-gathering East of the Canal.

The absence of a commander in Cairo meant that some of the work previously performed by Maxwell, including the administration of martial law and looking after developments in the Western desert, was left unattended. The man that Murray and Kitchener intended for these responsibilities could not be spared from the Western Front. So Kitchener asked McMahon for suggestions for the post, recognizing that 'Clayton would do, but he has his hands full'. McMahon, who was probably unaware of the full range of Clayton's responsibilities, discussed the matter with Murray and both agreed that Clayton 'would admirably fulfil all duties of the proposed appointment. Clayton has up to now had a very large share in the administration of martial law . . . in Egypt and also in [the] Intelligence work of the Western [Libyan] front'. The High Commissioner then added another course to

Clayton's already full plate: Murray and he would also 'both welcome him as liaison officer' between EEF and the Residency.[64] Clayton was now busier than ever. As he informed Wingate at the end of March, Murray has 'appointed me his staff officer for all matters concerning the civil government of the country and of martial law and for purposes of liaison between himself and the High Commissioner'. Murray gave Clayton a 'very free hand' in dealing with 'local matters', which Clayton thought appropriate for 'a new General who knows nothing of local conditions and is not even resident in Cairo'.[65] Clayton's work as liaison between McMahon and Murray would cause him significant problems as 1916 wore on and relations between the civil and military chiefs deteriorated. But, of more immediate concern was the situation on Egypt's western border, for the Sanusi leader, Ahmad al-Sharif, had now jumped down from the fence on which he had been sitting for the last year and gone over to the Turks.

14

Egypt's Little Wars: The Conflicts in Libya and Darfur

The request that landed on Clayton's desk in early December 1914 was a peculiar one: drums, brass band instruments, a rifle and 'some pairs of white buckskin shoes'.[1] Odd though the request was, Clayton acted promptly to meet it, for it had been made by Ahmad al-Sharif, the Grand Sanusi of the Sanusiyya Brotherhood, located just across Egypt's western frontier in Cyrenaica. An Islamic reform movement, the Brotherhood exercised a preponderant political and spiritual influence over the tribes in Cyrenaica and western Egypt. With the war against the Turks just a month old and Clayton already suspecting an Ottoman advance on the Canal, the risk that the Sanusi would simultaneously move on Egypt from the west had to be minimized. As noted earlier, in late 1914, the British Force in Egypt was losing men every day to the European theatre, Egypt was thinly defended, and the possibility of a two-front war could not be easily dismissed. No one knew whether Ahmad was swayed by the Ottoman Sultan's call to *jihad*. But it was well known that he had fought alongside his Turkish co-religionists just three years earlier against the Italians. Indeed, he was still fighting the Italians and only recently had pushed them back to Tripoli on the Mediterranean coast. The Sanusi's regular army of trained and uniformed soldiers – the *muhafiziya*, as they were called – was small, perhaps only 3,000 men; but the Brotherhood had several thousand adherents in Egypt itself, in the country's western desert, and, if Ahmad brought the *jihad* to Cyrenaica, these Egyptian Sanusiyya might rise as well.[2]

The Sanusiyya were a fairly recent phenomenon in Islam. Based on the teachings of its eponymous founder, Muhammad al-Sanusi (b.1787), Sanusi doctrine was, in some respects, an amalgam of the Sufi mysticism that underlay Sudanese Mahdism and the asceticism of the Wahhabis of Central Arabia. Like the Mahdi, Muhammad had a charismatic personality which won him many adherents, and he also exhibited the peripatetic lifestyle of the Mahdi. He travelled widely, taught in Cairo and Mecca, and eventually settled in the deserts of Cyrenaica, the easternmost province of modern Libya. The basis of the Sanusi system was the *zawiya*, a place of religious instruction, but also a trading and agricultural centre. By the time of Muhammad's death in 1859, the map of North Africa was dotted with these religious settlements.

The Grand Sanusi was succeeded by his fifteen year old son, Muhammad al-

Mahdi, who continued his father's proselytizing mission, establishing *zawiyas* in Arabia and the Sudan and more than thirty in Egypt's western desert. But unlike the Sudanese Mahdi, Muhammad al-Mahdi had no interest in translating his burgeoning religious influence into an anti-imperial political programme. When the Mahdi raised the standard against his Anglo-Egyptian overlords in the Sudan, Muhammad al-Mahdi remained impassive. Yet, he could not avoid bumping up against the imperial powers in North Africa during the late nineteenth-century 'scramble for Africa', and a French attack on a *zawiya* near Lake Chad in 1901 led to sporadic fighting with France that persisted until 1911.[3]

How much of a threat the Sanusi represented to Egypt was a matter of some speculation at the turn of the century. It was estimated that the Sanusi had four, perhaps five million adherents, but by the time of Muhammad al-Mahdi's death in 1902, nothing suggested that any portion of them would, or could, be brought against British Egypt. The sect was thought to be neither 'anti-British nor anti-French, but anti-European and its leaders do not recognise the political frontiers which have been traced on the map of Africa in London, Paris and Berlin'.[4] Muhammad's eldest son, Muhammad Idris, was too young to succeed on his father's death, so the mantle of Grand Sanusi passed to Idris' cousin, Ahmad al-Sharif. When the Italians invaded North Africa in September 1911, Ahmad readily joined the Turks in the fight. Although the Egyptians were clearly sympathetic to the Turco-Sanusi effort, British Egypt was officially neutral and Kitchener, then British Agent in Cairo, made considerable effort to ensure that Egypt was not used as a pipeline for the supply of war materiel to either side. The Turco-Sanusi effort against the Italians achieved some notable successes, due in no small measure to the active leadership provided by Enver Pasha and his younger brother Nuri Bey. The Italians suffered several defeats, but just when a Turco-Sanusi success seemed assured, the First Balkan War erupted in October 1912. The Turks had no choice but to hastily conclude a treaty with the Italians – a treaty that effectively acknowledged the legitimacy of the Italian occupation – and withdraw their troops to southeast Europe to confront the Balkan coalition. Ahmad continued the fight against Italy but, with some justification, felt he had been left twisting in the wind by his Turkish allies.

This, then, was the situation when, two years later, Ahmad al-Sharif's request for brass band instruments and buckskin shoes arrived in Clayton's office. He was well aware that the Turks and Germans were making 'every effort to suborn' Ahmad, and he believed that if 'the religious card is well played' and the Sanusi decides to 'cut up rough, we shall have a much more serious situation and a lot of trouble both inside and out' of Egypt.[5] Yet, in the late months of 1914, Ahmad was showing 'every disposition to be friendly' to the British, an attitude, Clayton reasoned, that was 'entirely due to the fact that it would be against his interest to quarrel with us unless he was certain that we were losing the upper hand in Egypt'.[6] Like Hussein of Mecca, the Sanusi was fence-sitting, waiting to see whether Britain or Turkey would gain the upper hand in the region.

Neither McMahon nor Maxwell took the lead in devising or implementing British policy regarding the Sanusi, so it fell to Clayton to maintain the unsteady equilibrium along Egypt's western frontier and to prepare for hostilities if it was upset. When the Sanusi requested a meeting with Bimbashi Leopold Royle of the Egyptian Coastguard – the agency then responsible for security on Egypt's Mediterranean coast – Clayton brought Royle in and 'primed him well up' on the line he should take with Ahmad. And, just in case Ahmad decided to 'cut up rough', Clayton himself made secret preparations for 2,000 of the Australian Mounted Rifles and a unit of cavalry at Alexandria to move across the frontier and confront the Sanusi. He also drafted the letters and telegrams sent to the Sanusi by Maxwell and McMahon. And, concerned that German and Turkish arms were reaching the Sanusi by sea, Clayton arranged, by 'diplomatic scheming', a meeting with the GOC, the High Commissioner and the British Admiral in command which resulted in a permanent naval patrol of the northwest coast of Egypt by two Royal Navy and two Egyptian Coastguard cruisers. He also had frequent meetings with Muhammad Idrisi, who acted as Ahmad's agent in Cairo and who was thought to be pro-British. And, perhaps most important, McMahon's communications to the Foreign Office regarding the Sanusi were either drafted by Clayton or written after long talks between him and the High Commissioner.[7] Clayton was, in fact, running the show in the west. Wingate fully appreciated how 'delicate' the Sanusi situation was and how successfully Clayton had 'steer[ed] a clear course among so many rocks and shoals'. Maxwell and McMahon, 'as well as the British Government', he added, 'are to be congratulated on having had someone on the spot like yourself who thoroughly understood the question'.[8]

The rocks and shoals to which the Sirdar referred were created by the Italians, who greatly complicated Anglo-Sanusi relations and elevated them to the level of European diplomacy. 'If those wretched Italians weren't mixed up' with the Sanusi, Clayton wrote, 'the problem would be quite simple. A lump sum down and a promise of more to come would do the trick in a moment, but of course we should at once be accused of an unfriendly act' by Italy.[9] McMahon, in fact, did consider subsidizing the Sanusi, but appears to have been dissuaded by Clayton 'in deference to [the] Italians'.[10] Rome was indeed exerting pressure on London and it soon became apparent that the two governments had widely different perspectives. The Italians regarded the Sanusi as a rebel, while Britain treated him as an independent ruler. 'Our dealings with him', reported Foreign Secretary Sir Edward Grey, 'are principally driven by a desire to secure his goodwill so that he can restrain his followers and prevent them from joining a jehad which would be as unwelcome to us as to Italy'.[11] Unpersuaded, the Italians continued their efforts in Rome, where the Colonial Minister called on Rennell Rodd, the British ambassador, and asked for British help in bringing about some sort of compromise with the Sanusi which would acknowledge Italian sovereignty in Libya. Rodd thought the Italian request should be met, for an issue much larger than Italian primacy in Libya was then on the tapis – Italy's entry into the war on the Entente side. If British pressure on the Sanusi could help achieve that goal, then it should be applied.[12]

Clayton saw the force of Rodd's argument. He acknowledged that 'both the Italian Government and press have assumed an attitude of injured surprise at what they insinuate is an unfriendly policy on the part of Great Britain towards Italy in giving material assistance to a Sheikh whom they regard as a rebel'. Yet, he was reluctant to lean on the Sanusi, whose attitude in the spring of 1915 was regarded as 'most satisfactory' by Cairo.[13] Nor did Clayton believe that Ahmad was amenable to a peaceful resolution with Italy anyway. In his view, it was 'exceedingly unlikely' that the Sanusi, whose attitude towards the Italians was one of 'great bitterness', would consider any peace terms that allowed the Italians to remain in Cyrenaica. And, if British pressure was applied to Ahmad, he would likely 'throw himself into the arms of the Pan-Islamic party'. True, he continued, that would represent no great threat to Egypt 'from a military point of view', but any hostilities against him by Britain 'would probably have far reaching effects in regard to Moslem feeling, not only in Egypt and the Sudan, but in Arabia and possibly even in India'. He dismissed Rodd's suggestion that Ahmad could be bought off with a promise of autonomy in three large oases, Kufra and Jaghbub, deep in the Cyrenaican interior, and Siwa, then under Egyptian administration.

The Sanusi already occupied those places – and many more – so the promise of them offered little inducement. Nor could the British act as a 'referee' between Ahmad and the Italians. If Clayton's 1909 experiences with the Italians and the Mad Mullah in Somaliland provided any example, the Italians could not be trusted to live up to any arrangement brokered by the British. The only viable approach to the problem, then, was to tell Ahmad that the Italians had approached the British for assistance and ask the Sanusi what his 'minimum conditions' were. The Italians would then need to state the conditions they would be prepared to offer. Only then could it be seen whether there was any hope of bringing the two parties together. If nothing else, this approach would have 'the advantage of delaying matters somewhat'. Meanwhile, an Entente victory at Gallipoli might make the Sanusi more amenable, as might a successful outcome of negotiations with the Idrisi of 'Asir, who was 'closely connected with the Senussi'.[14]

Two weeks later Clayton prepared another memorandum recommending that 'no stringent measures' be taken regarding the Sanusi. '[A]t the present critical juncture as regards Great Britain and her Moslem subjects it would obviously be undesirable to risk forcing hostilities with the Senussi as, although he is almost negligible from a military point of view and would be speedily crushed between Italy and England, his misfortunes would inevitably be turned to account by the Pan-Islamic party, who would hold him up as an example of British perfidy'.[15] Clayton knew that McMahon would either send his memoranda on to London, or, as happened, repeat their contents in cables to the Foreign Office; so he did not reflect in them his conviction that British policy towards the Sanusi would have no bearing on Italy's decision to enter the war, a belief he later described to Wingate:

It is curious how little the powers that be seem to appreciate the situation. One can understand that they were anxious to placate Italy as much as possible in order to bring her in with us, [but] my small experience of Italian diplomacy has led me to maintain throughout that they would come in when and if it suited their own interests and not otherwise. And she was naturally anxious at the time to drive as good a bargain as possible with England. I have therefore been dead against throwing overboard our present Senussi policy and thereby upsetting all our Moslem friends in order to obtain the help of Italy which we were bound to get if it suited them to give it, and not otherwise. What they have been offered by the Allies in Europe was obviously sufficient to outweigh the offers made by Austria, so why throw the Senussi into the sale as well.[16]

Clayton was correct about the Italians. When they entered into the secret London Agreement with the Entente in late April 1915, the Italians extracted huge territorial concessions as the price for entering the war against the Central Powers. But regarding Libya, the Agreement provided only that 'all rights and privileges' still held by the Turkish Sultan by virtue of the treaty ending the Turco-Italian war of 1911–12 were 'transferred to Italy'. Since Turkey had already conceded Tripoli to the Italians by the 1912 treaty ending that war, the London Agreement expanded little on the Italian claim. And, from the British standpoint, no promise of hostilities against the Sanusi was given.[17]

Throughout the late spring and summer of 1915, Clayton continued his efforts to 'steer a safe course between the Scylla of Italy and the Charybdis of the Senussi'. He was ready for a fight, if it came to that, but his preparations had to be kept secret, as 'any overt defensive or offensive measures would almost certainly precipitate a crisis'. He also 'gingered up' the Italian Navy, having Maxwell, McMahon and the Royal Navy commander wire their Italian counterparts to request an increase in their patrols of the North African coast. Annoyed that McMahon had delayed sending the contents of his April memoranda to the Foreign Office for three weeks, Clayton drafted a wire from the High Commissioner to Ahmad in which he 'dropped a hint of mediation' with the Italians.[18] At the same time, he continued to use Muhammad Idrisi as an intermediary, though 'suggestions of peace with Italy' made through Idrisi had no effect on Ahmad. Still, as the Sanusi was exhibiting no hostility towards Egypt, Clayton continued to advocate a waiting policy and was opposed to any overtures being made 'until an issue is reached at the Dardanelles'. If the Entente were victorious there, he thought, Ahmad would almost certainly be amenable to a resolution with Italy.[19]

Meanwhile, the Sanusi *was* being pressured, but not by the British. The Germans and Turks were both insisting that he take action against Egypt. Although Intelligence concluded in May 1915, that arms traffic to Cyrenaica was continuing 'on a large scale', a British merchant ship captain whose vessel sank in the Gulf of Sidra, reported that Ahmad's forces were poorly armed – many with only old-pattern rifles – that ammunition was short, and food 'very scarce'. Still, the Sanusiyya were strong enough to beat the Italians in an early March fight at Syrt and again push them back to the coast. The captain had seen no more than 5,000 Sanusi troops dispersed throughout the country and predicted that with 'a very few decent troops with machine guns', the British 'could clear the country'. But Ahmad, the captain concluded, was 'by no means inclined to attempt hostilities against Egypt, on which his country is now entirely dependent for food'.[20]

The reported weakness of the Sanusi did not affect Italian diplomacy, even after Italy entered the war on the Entente side in May. Grey was informed by the Italian ambassador that his government 'feel bitterly that we do nothing to discourage the hostile action against them of the Senoussi, that we continue to treat him as a friend, and even encourage him'. The Foreign Secretary concluded that it was 'absolutely necessary to give the Italians some satisfaction' and suggested to McMahon that he ought at least to send Ahmad a message 'pointing out that Italy is our Ally' and 'urging him to make peace'. The matter, he added, 'has become very urgent'. Before replying, McMahon had 'a long talk' with Clayton during which the Intelligence Director 'strongly urged that we should not retreat from the position which we have always maintained and allow ourselves to be made a catspaw of Italian diplomacy'.[21] McMahon followed Clayton's advice; no overtures along Foreign Office lines were made to Ahmad.

Clayton's policy was not driven by a simple desire to avoid being made a 'catspaw' of Italian diplomacy; he also had in mind wider, strategic considerations. By late July 1915, the Force in Egypt had been stripped to the bone by the manpower requirements of the Entente fight at Gallipoli and Maxwell was frankly worried: 'What I fear is the Senussi. I fear him because his influence is far reaching and fanatical. So far he is quiet, but he is surrounded by Turkish and pro-German influences, including Enver's brother [Nuri] . . . [W]hat with the lies of great German successes and the undoubted Russian retreat, and our stalemate at Gallipoli coupled with the constant stream of wounded arriving at Alexandria may tempt the old man to think that the day of Islam has dawned & he may raise the standard of Islam & then the fat is in the fire. I have absolutely no means to cope with him . . . Egypt is overrun with his adherents and . . . if an uprising of pure Islamic origin occurs the attitude of the Mohammedan Indians on the Canal would be doubtful'.[22]

Such a message from the usually imperturbable Maxwell was bound to give London pause. It did. As Clayton reported, 'a very strong wire came from Lord K saying that by no means whatever was the slightest risk to be run of offending the Senussi'.[23] Prompted by Clayton, McMahon followed up with a rejection of yet another proposal by the Italians that pressure be brought to bear on the Sanusi: 'I think that there would be [a] far greater likelihood of its precipitating hostilities with the Senoussi and this in [the] present state of operations in the Dardanelles we are naturally most anxious to avoid . . . [I]t is imperative to our interest and therefore presumably to that of our ally Italy to maintain peace on our western frontier'.[24]

Meanwhile, the Turks and Germans continued to exert pressure on Ahmad. Mannesmann, who had appeared in Cyrenaica in the spring, was busy arranging arms shipments to the Sanusi. He was assisted by a young German adventurer, Baron Otto von Gumppenburg, a veteran of the Turco-Italian war. But, after making a delivery of arms to the Sanusi, Gumppenburg was captured by the British just off the Cyrenaican coast on July 11, 1915. Clayton personally interrogated the young German and succeeded in extracting some information from him 'by means of threats and cajolery', and a hint that he was likely to be treated by the British as a spy. Gumppenburg was not, however, very forthcoming, even after Clayton informed him that unless he could 'produce something better, he must be prepared to take whatever he gets (not improbably a bullet before he has done)'.[25] Despite the capture of Gumppenburg, Turco-German pressure was paying dividends. On August 15, a British submarine was fired on at Sollum, the westernmost port on the Egyptian coast which marked the border with Cyrenaica. Again, on August 25, Sanusi troops 'feinted an attack' on the British fort there, withdrawing the next morning. At the same time Ahmad, now suffering from 'giganticus ego', according to Clayton, dispatched letters to Muslim leaders in Arabia and India, imploring them to join the Sultan's *jihad* against the Entente.[26]

As late as August 1915, Clayton clung to the belief that Ahmad had 'no desire for hostility against England or France'. Yes, he was accepting Turk and German money, arms and training, but, Clayton held, this was 'with the intention of using it against Italy'. However, a month later, with the evidence of a series of Sanusi provocations on the border before him – 'continual pin-pricks', as Maxwell described them – Clayton was beginning to think it likely that Ahmad would jump down from the fence on the Turco-German side.[27] Still, he persisted in his view that the Sanusi should be mollified. 'As a military force', the Sanusiyya were not 'very formidable'. But with Egypt 'so denuded' of troops, he reasoned, 'it is very important to keep him quiet'.[28] Clayton continued to use Ahmad's Cairo agent, Muhammad Idrisi, as an intermediary, sending him to meet with the Sanusi at Sollum. Muhammad was 'a foxy old man' whom he trusted 'no further than I can see him', but Clayton admitted to Wingate 'that our various negotiations through him have very probably saved an explosion'.[29] Despite his absorption in the early October discussions with Faruqi, described earlier, Clayton found time to provide Muhammad with instructions prior to his departure for Sollum and talks with Ahmad.

By late October 1915, it was clear that Clayton's policy of buying time by appeasing the Sanusi had played itself out. In early November Ahmad began probing the British positions round Sollum. Then, on November 10, a German submarine sank a Coastguard cutter in Sollum harbour. On the following day, the British naval tender H.M.S. *Tara* was sunk and 94 British sailors were taken prisoner just east of Sollum. On the 16th, the British fort there came under sniper fire. And, over the next two days, Sanusi troops appeared fifty miles east of Sollum at Sidi Barani where they occupied a *zawiya* and attacked the nearby British post.[30] The telegraph line east of Sollum was cut repeatedly and on the 23rd, 134 officers and men of the Egyptian Coastguard deserted to the Sanusiyya. Most troubling of all, five or six German submarines were reported to be lurking in the Gulf of Sollum; this meant that the British fort there, as well as posts to the east at Bagbag and Sidi Barani, could not be reinforced or supplied by sea. Moreover, the railway from Alexandria stopped more than 100 miles to the east of Sollum and the coast road could not bear heavy traffic. There was no choice: on November 23, it was decided to place a force at Mersa Matruh, 125 miles east of the Cyrenaican frontier at Sollum, and to evacuate Sollum, Bagbag and Sidi Barani.[31]

It was not entirely clear to Cairo Intelligence if the events of November 1915 were directed by Ahmad, who might have been 'trying to regain control of the situation', or engineered by the Turks acting on the orders of Nuri Bey. In fact, by early December Ahmad had disappeared into the desert and the Sanusi forces were under the command of Nuri and Ja'far al-'Askari, a Baghdadi-born officer in the Turkish army. Whoever was directing the Sanusiyya, the time for diplomacy with Ahmad was over. The British had, by this time, assembled a 3,000-man force at Mersa Matruh, supported by reconnaissance airplanes, armoured cars and, just off the coast, the Royal Navy cruiser H.M.S. *Clematis*. The Sanusi force – also about 3,000 men, half of them *muhafiziya* – were engaged on December 11 and 13, near Matruh. But neither action was decisive. British casualties totalled twenty-five killed and some seventy wounded, while Sanusi losses were 120 killed and an unknown number wounded.[32]

The fighting round Mersa Matruh occurred one week before the Entente began evacuating the Gallipoli Peninsula. Nuri was known to be in contact with Constantinople via the German submarines, but it is doubtful that he had any inkling of the Gallipoli evacuations at the time of the mid-December engagements. For Clayton, though, the timing was propitious; as thousands of Entente troops began flowing into Egypt from the Dardanelles, any risk to Egypt from the west disappeared. The feared rising of Sanusiyya in Egypt's western desert never occurred. Nor could it, for just after the mid-December fighting, Maxwell and Clayton began rounding up the Sanusi's 'friends and relations' in Egypt and placing them 'in detention'. The move was not just a security measure; the Sanusi's supporters in Egypt were, in effect, being held as hostages pending release of the sailors taken prisoner from the *Tara*.[33] On Christmas day 1915, the British force at Mersa Matruh went on the offensive, confronting a Sanusi army of equal numbers, some 3,000 men, a few miles from the British fort. The Sanusi, under Ja'far al-'Askari, were soundly beaten – 373 killed and eighty-two taken prisoner, more than ten percent of its total force. British losses were light, with only ten killed and fifty-three wounded.[34]

The actions of December 1915, eliminated the Sanusi threat to Egypt. Both Mannesmann and Nuri had left Cyrenaica before the December 25 battle. Ja'far, who had been in command, was later wounded and captured in February 1916, informing his captors that Ahmad had 'always played us false and always meant to'.[35] Sollum, on the Cyrenaican border, was re-taken by the British in mid-March 1916. In April, Mannesmann was murdered by the Sanusiyya in the Libyan desert. Ahmad was finished. He tried to recover his position by requesting talks with the British, but Clayton would have none of it. No discussions would occur until Ahmad met four conditions: the turn-over of all British, Indian and European prisoners; the removal of all Turks and Germans from Cyrenaica; a ban on all armed men entering Egypt from the west; and Ahmad's own withdrawal to Jaghbub oasis in the interior. The conditions were not accepted, but Wingate was delighted with them, noting that Clayton's 'own hand in [their] concoction was very evident'.[36]

The defeat of the Sanusi did not, however, resolve British differences with the Italians. In early 1916, relations between Rome and London were still said to be 'exceedingly delicate', and Grey was concerned that if Britain made a separate peace with the Sanusi 'behind Italy's back' – thus enabling him to fight on against the Italians without fear of attack from Egypt – Rome might 'consider themselves at liberty to conclude separate arrangements for peace with the Central Powers'. Improbable as that scenario must have seemed to Cairo, Grey informed the Italians that Britain would not make peace with the Sanusi without prior reference to Rome.[37] Meanwhile, Maxwell and McMahon concluded that it was no longer advisable to treat with Ahmad on any basis. Instead, they proposed to negotiate with Ahmad's cousin, Muhammad Idris, who, as the eldest son of Muhammad al-Mahdi, the second Grand Sanusi, was now characterized by Cairo as 'the real Senussi'. Muhammad Idris was reported to disagree with Ahmad's 'offensive policy towards Egypt' and to be amenable to making peace with both Italy and Egypt. The Foreign Office agreed and two months later tripartite talks among Idris, the British and the Italians were begun.[38] The decision to divide the Sanusiyya by treating with Muhammad Idris instead of Ahmad again appears to have been the product of Clayton's discussions with his Cairo chiefs. When Murray took over as GOC in Egypt, he decided to adhere to the four conditions for peace with the Sanusi laid down by Maxwell and he also concurred in the decision to side-step Ahmad and negotiate with Muhammad Idris alone, decisions made after talks with Clayton, 'who had already been in consultation with the British Agency' on those points.[39] The British and Italians did negotiate with Muhammad Idris and, after protracted discussions, concluded peace with the 'real Senussi' in April 1917. Britain's Sanusi policy, largely devised and implemented by Clayton, had won out.

While the threat on Egypt's western frontier had been eliminated by 1916, the wily Ahmad was still capable of causing trouble for the British and Clayton and Wingate were convinced that the rumblings which began to issue from western Sudan in late 1915 were instigated by Ahmad and his Turco-German cohorts. To Wingate's credit, the Sudan had been quiet since the outbreak of the Middle Eastern war; the Sudanese seemed to be more concerned with meeting the requirements of daily life than with news from the remote battlefields of Europe or even the fights of the hated Turks against the Entente. Nowhere was this attitude more apparent than in Darfur, the vast region in western Sudan.

For centuries before the advent of the *Turkiyya* in the Sudan in 1825, the Fur Sultanate in the far west of the country had been one of the great powers in the region. Not until 1874 had it been brought under Egyptian rule and, while the Sultanate was conquered by the Mahdists nine year later, neither regime was able to establish close control over Darfur. In 1890, the Sultan of Darfur was murdered and the Sultanate passed to 'Ali Dinar who spent nearly all his time in Omdurman until the Anglo-Egyptian conquest of 1898. Whether 'Ali Dinar was a true adherent of Mahdism is doubtful, but the Sultan returned to El Fasher, the capital of Darfur, shortly after Omdurman and remained in the province for the rest of his reign. He was content to recognize the Condominium government and to pay a £500 annual tribute as a symbol of his submission. In the early years of the new century, Wingate would have brought Darfur directly under the Condominium, but Cromer rejected the proposal, instructing the Sirdar that 'Ali Dinar should be tethered to Khartoum 'by the lightest of threads'. For the most part, the arrangement worked well before the war. The Sultan, of course, had his grievances; he complained of outstanding debt owed by Khartoum, of the customary cross-border raiding and of the Sudan's provision of safe-harbour to rebellious Darfur tribesmen. But his greatest complaint involved French encroachment on his territory from the west. In 1900, France had established a protectorate over Chad and the easternmost region of that country, Wadai, bordered on 'Ali Dinar's sultanate. After Fashoda (1898), France and Britain agreed that the line dividing their respective spheres of influence in the region would run between Wadai and Darfur. However, despite several false starts, the boundary between those two regions had still not been demarcated by the time war broke out in Europe. In January 1915, the two parties agreed to defer the boundary delimitation until after the war.[40]

During the last months of 1914, and the first quarter of 1915, Wingate, still worried about possible trouble in the Sudan, pursued a policy of appeasing 'Ali Dinar. 'It is vitally important', he wrote to Clayton, 'that at the present time 'Ali Dinar should not be made suspicious of us'.[41] In the spring of 1915, though, the Sultan failed to pay his annual tribute to Khartoum and in April he warned Wingate that he would repel any aggression against Darfur. Still, the Sirdar was unconvinced these developments meant that 'Ali Dinar was contemplating action against the Sudan, and he professed that he was committed to doing his utmost to 'avoid having a Darfur expedition on my hands'. Clayton, however, added to Wingate's unease in May 1915 by sending three letters to his chief, each expressing his conviction that 'the Senussist programme of the German-Turkish agitators embraces Darfur'. Yet, he acknowledged that the enemy would find it 'difficult to keep up communication with ['Ali Dinar] and also to supply him with any material assistance'. And, he thought, there was 'a good deal of bluff' in 'Ali Dinar's letters: '[W]hen it comes down to the point he will probably shrink from overt hostilities just as the Senussi does'.[42]

Clayton's speculations were groundless. He had no evidence at hand suggesting that the enemy's 'Senussist programme . . . embraces Darfur'. Nor had he any evidence of contact between the 'Turkish-German agitators' in Cyrenaica and the Sultan. In fact, two months after Clayton's last May letter to Wingate, McMahon reported – most likely with Clayton's knowledge – that there was no evidence that any 'hostile agents' had arrived in Darfur. Nor was there any 'information of communications between [the] Senussi and 'Ali Dinar'.[43]

On one point, though, Clayton was certainly correct: the Turks and Germans would have found it difficult to supply, or even to communicate with 'Ali Dinar. The Sultan's capital at El Fasher was 1,500 miles from the Mediterranean coast and most of the intervening territory was desert. Unknown to Clayton, Enver *had* written to the Sultan in February 1915, but the letter took more than a year to reach Darfur.[44] And, even had the enemy been able to supply 'Ali Dinar with arms to attack the Sudan, El Fasher was more than 500 miles from Khartoum. So remote was Darfur that the railway running west from Khartoum, stopped at El Obeid in Kordofan, fully 400 miles from El Fasher.

Despite these imposing distances, the Turks and Germans were attempting to suborn the Sultan, although evidence of these attempts did not come to light until much later. In addition to Nuri's letter, in March 1915, the German agent Leo Frobenius, whose abortive African mission was described earlier, attempted to contact 'Ali Dinar, though it is unknown whether he was successful. In August, Nuri, having heard nothing after his February letter, again wrote to the Sultan. And the Sanusi himself, in a series of October letters to the German Emperor, sent via Constantinople, stated that he had written to 'Ali Dinar inviting him to attack the British in the Sudan.[45]

It is unlikely that 'Ali Dinar was much influenced by any overtures that may have reached him in 1915 from the Turks or Germans. Nor were the Sanusi's relations with the Sultan so good as to suggest an alliance in the making. 'Ali Dinar had been involved in a dispute with the Sanusi's agent in Kufra, in southern Cyrenaica, over the failure to deliver ammunition that the Sultan had purchased.[46] Unaware of the dispute, Clayton and Wingate continued to imagine some sort of arrangement between the two leaders. 'There can be little doubt that they are working together', Clayton concluded in October. And, 'if the Senussi goes against us, I take it A[li] D[inar] will attempt to play the fool'.[47]

If the Sultan was inclined to play the fool, it was probably not because he had been suborned by the Turks, Germans or the Sanusiyya. His 'complete renunciation of the authority of the Sudan Government', received in Khartoum in July 1915, was the product of his own programme. At the end of 1915, Clayton learned from Muhammad Idrisi, the Sanusi's Cairo agent, that two months earlier 140 camels carrying 2,000 rifles and ammunition had been sent to Darfur from Cyrenaica. It was unknown whether the shipment had reached El Fasher but, in any event, Clayton thought the number of rifles 'much exaggerated', as 'they did not have that amount to spare'.[48] As 1915 closed, Wingate's man in western Kordofan reported that there was no evidence of war preparations in Darfur; even minor border raids were thought to be unlikely.[49]

Despite the absence of evidence that the Sultan was in league with the Sanusi, or that he had been swayed by Turco-German propaganda, or, indeed, that he had any war-like plans against the Sudan at all, Wingate began preparing for a strike against Darfur in January 1916. Lacking any proof of 'Ali Dinar's war preparations, Wingate now emphasized the loss of prestige the Condominium government would experience among Sudan's western tribes if he remained inactive in the face of the Sultan's 'continued public insults'. The Sultan had been insulting; he wrote to Sudan government officials referring to them as 'infidels and dogs', the 'Governor of Hell' and the 'Inspector of Flames'.[50]

Offensive though the Sultan's messages were, Wingate fully realized that larger issues were in play. He acknowledged that it was not a 'suitable time' for taking on 'the administration of a large new tract of country' such as Darfur. Nor was it 'desirable to increase the already large number of theatres of operations' by precipitating a fight against a remote and obviously weak native ruler.[51] Anticipating objections to his plans from Cairo, he had instructed Clayton to keep British officials there in the dark and for most of 1915, the Sirdar had managed to keep his dealings with Darfur secret.[52] But an assault on Darfur would require approval from Cairo and London, and neither seemed likely to give it. McMahon would not approve of action west of Kordofan without referral to London and Lord Edward Cecil, Adviser to the Egyptian Ministry of Finance, plainly stated his opposition to such a 'costly and troublesome' expedition. For his part, Maxwell, still in Cairo in February 1916, declined to send any troops in Egypt to the Sudan until he received War Office approval.[53] Surprisingly, in mid-February 1916, Wingate did receive approval for Egyptian reinforcements which would enable an advance on Darfur. He had bypassed the sceptics in Cairo by appealing directly to his old chief, Kitchener. Five days after receiving War Office approval, Wingate ordered his 'Darfur Field Force' to advance from El Obeid to Nahud, in western Kordofan. Clayton 'fully explained the situation to the authorities' in Cairo, but, on instructions from Wingate, refrained from telling them of the Sirdar's direct approach to Lord K.[54]

Clayton must have felt uneasy explaining the Sirdar's actions to the Cairo authorities. And, as he later observed to Maxwell – with some understatement – he was 'a little surprised' that the War Council in London had approved Wingate's plan for the conquest of Darfur. But, he added, London doubtless wanted 'a little counter-blast' to the recent and serious defeat that Anglo-Indian troops had suffered at the hands of the Turks at Kut in Mesopotamia.[55] Despite his doubts about the wisdom of the Darfur expedition, Clayton dutifully presented the Sirdar's requests for troops and war materiel to Murray, now in sole command in Egypt. The requests were substantial. No doubt worried about the ramifications that might arise from the failure of another eastern 'sideshow' after the disasters at Gallipoli and Kut, Wingate requested that the Darfur Field Force be supported by additional troops, a flight of planes, armoured cars, ambulances, repair waggons, wireless sets and petrol reserves. Clayton observed that the requests had made Murray's headquarters 'scratch their heads as it is a biggish order at short notice'. At Wingate's prompting, he even made 'private' enquiries about extending the railway 400 miles from El Obeid to El Fasher.[56]

In early April 1916, just as Wingate's force was preparing for the final assault on El Fasher, yet another stumbling block appeared on the road to Darfur. It came again from Cairo, where the French representative, Albert Defrance, informed Clayton that a British attack on El Fasher would represent a 'grave inconvenience' to France. If 'Ali Dinar retreated to the west, into French-controlled Wadai, as a result of the British assault, there would be no way of coping with him as French troops in Chad had been greatly reduced to buttress Entente forces in the Cameroons, in West Africa. Just as the Italians had complicated the situation in Cyrenaica, so now were the French confounding British plans for Darfur. Clayton and Wingate were convinced that the French objections were not military, but political; Paris was worried that the British move on Darfur represented an attempt to grab territory in the still unresolved boundary region between Wadai and Darfur. Clayton was well aware that the British government would 'risk no friction at the present critical moment' with France, for 'one of the great difficulties they apprehend is that of keeping the French & Italians in' the war. So, he 'pitched it mild' to Defrance, assuring him that Britain was animated only by military considerations and had no ulterior motive in moving on Darfur. By mid-April Clayton was able to report that the French were satisfied regarding British plans 'provided we give them ample notice of any decisive action against El Fasher'. Notice was provided and the French actually cooperated with the British plan by making a 'demonstration' in Wadai that precluded 'Ali Dinar from receiving any support from that region.[57]

With all the military, political and diplomatic pieces to his Darfur scheme now in place, Wingate ordered the final assault on El Fasher in early May. On the 22nd, 'Ali Dinar's small force was routed near El Fasher and the city was occupied the next day. The Sultan himself was run to ground in November 1916, when he and two sons were shot dead southwest of the capital. Wingate was delighted, only to have his balloon popped shortly after the May victory when an account of the campaign was published in Cairo's *Egyptian Gazette* under the headline 'Egypt's Little Wars'. 'Don't you think', he wrote irritably to Clayton, 'that you could instil a little more sense into them?'[58]

Why had Wingate undertaken the Darfur expedition? Some of the explanations he offered were obviously meritless. To Cromer, he argued that had he not made the attack 'German and Turkish officers would almost have certainly got into the country, organized the Sultan's army and produced a most dangerous situation on our western flank'.[59] 'The Lord' would certainly have seen this as nonsense; there was not the slightest hint of a German or a Turk within 1,000 miles of Darfur. Kitchener probably found equally implausible the Sirdar's argument that Turco-German propaganda had 'taken possession of Ali Dinar' and that he was caught up in the plan with 'the Senussi . . . to raise trouble on the whole of the Western Frontier of Egypt and the Sudan'. No evidence, then available, supported either contention. Kitchener might, though, have found more credible Wingate's prestige argument, even if it was overstated: If the Sirdar had 'continued to put up with 'Ali Dinar's threats and insolence in silence, the whole Sudan . . . would have lost confidence in the Government'.[60] Whether, during the middle of a world war, when every man was needed on the Western Front, the maintenance of government prestige in a region 1,000 miles deep in the African interior was a sufficient rationale may be doubted, but Lord 'K' approved the plan and Wingate achieved his victory.

Other possible explanations for the Darfur expedition, unrelated to the conduct of 'Ali Dinar, must also be considered. As described earlier, Wingate refused to leave the Sudan after the outbreak of war, arguing that his presence was essential to the maintenance of order in the country. As a result, he had been marginalized by Cairo and London, neither of which had much sought his advice in 1915 regarding important regional issues, such as the Arab question, on which he considered himself an expert. The launch of an expedition to Darfur, however unjustified, might restore the Sirdar to a position of prominence in government consuls. It must also be said that Wingate was an avowed imperialist in an age when such a designation did not carry the negative connotations that it would later. The Sirdar observed in March 1916 that if the Darfur campaign was successful, the British government 'will have added about a half million square miles of valuable territory to their possessions in the cheapest manner possible'.[61]

Whatever the reasons behind Darfur, the campaign there, and in Cyrenaica – Egypt's little wars – consumed a great deal of Clayton's time and effort, adding to his already overwhelming workload. There would be no respite as 1916 progressed, for just as the Darfur campaign was concluding, Clayton learned that Cairo's 'friends across the water' were on the verge of revolt. The solidarity of Islam was about to be broken.

15

Revolt!: The Arab Rising, 1916

On the morning of June 10, 1916 Sherif Hussein ibn 'Ali, Amir of Mecca, descendant of the Prophet and guardian of the Muslim holy places, thrust a rifle through a window of his palace at Mecca and fired a single shot at the Turkish army barracks across the way. The Arab revolt had begun. For Clayton, the Sherif's rifle shot represented the culmination of eighteen months of unremitting effort to strike a blow at the Turks and defeat the Sultan's call to *jihad* – in effect, to undermine the Islamic unity of the Ottoman Empire.

Hussein was animated by more practical considerations. Well before his secret correspondence with McMahon concluded, the Sherif was being subjected to Turco-German pressure to join the war and support the Turks' planned 1916 attack on the Canal. In late February, Enver and Jemal travelled to Medina to appeal directly to Hussein. The Sherif gave his standard, anodyne protestations of loyalty, but on March 16, wired Enver that he would join the Ottoman war effort only if the Ottomans issued a general amnesty for Arab political dissidents, agreed to some measure of autonomy for Syria and Mesopotamia and guaranteed the Amirate in Hussein for life and in his family in perpetuity. Enver rejected Hussein's terms and, about the same time, approved a German scheme to send another mission to the Hijaz, this under Major Othmar von Stotzingen, accompanied by 3,500 Turkish troops. The plan was for von Stotzingen and the Turkish contingent to traverse the length of the Hijaz to the Yemen, where, in the friendly surroundings of the pro-Turkish Imam, they would establish an Intelligence and wireless station capable of communicating with German forces in East Africa. Hussein saw the mission as an obvious threat to his own position. He was further unnerved when, in May, twenty-one Syrian nationalists were executed in Beirut and Damascus on the orders of Jemal. His position in the Hijaz now imperilled, Hussein knew that the time for fence-sitting was coming to an end.

The situation was not promising. The British negotiations had ended inconclusively, his correspondence with McMahon shot through with ambiguities and qualifications that left the future of Syria, Palestine, even Mesopotamia, completely up in the air. And, he must also have entertained doubts about the wisdom of a British alliance. The Turks had, after all, beaten back the Entente assault on the Dardanelles and, just that April, a 12,000 man Anglo-Indian army south of Baghdad – under siege for 146 days – had been forced to surrender to the Turks. But he had little choice and it is likely that his decision to revolt was driven by the legitimate concern of maintaining his own position in the Hijaz. In the event, the von Stotzingen mission came to nothing; it had prompted the Sherif to revolt, but the revolt itself doomed the mission to failure. It ground to a halt in early June outside the Hijazi port of Yanbu, where most of the German party were killed, the major himself lucky to escape to the north.[1]

While the revolt had the immediate effect of defeating the von Stotzingen mission, little planning preceded Hussein's June 10 rifle shot and neither the Sherif nor his British allies had developed a strategy for an Arab insurrection. More important, Hussein had no guns, no trained officer corps and no standing army – and no means to feed or supply one. Hogarth, now directing the Arab Bureau, reported after a brief visit to the Hijaz coast that the revolt was 'genuine and inevitable but about to be undertaken upon inadequate preparation [and] in ignorance of modern warfare . . . In both the organization of the tribal forces and the provision of armament far too much has been left to the last moment and to luck'.[2]

Although the British considered that Hussein had moved prematurely, they were not taken by surprise by the revolt. In mid-April Wingate had received a letter from Hussein's second son, Abdullah, reporting that the revolt would begin in six to eight weeks. Clayton immediately began arranging for the dispatch of rifles and small arms ammunition to the Hijaz.[3] Still, he was not inclined to encourage Hussein to undertake military action. In March, he suggested to Kitchener that Cairo should 'go easy and await developments'. Again, in April, he advised the War Office and the DMI, Macdonogh, against 'moving too fast', and he sent the same message to Wingate.[4] Clayton would have preferred that the Sherif not undertake military action at all, at least for the present. In his opinion, such action was unnecessary; a definite and public declaration of hostility to the Turks would be sufficient to undermine the notion of Islamic solidarity and undercut the *jihad*.[5] And, he believed, any military action Hussein undertook was likely to be ineffective anyway.[6]

There was another reason that Clayton wished to apply the brakes to Hussein: In March he learned that the Sherif and his third son, Faisal, were planning for the Arab rising to begin in Syria. Clayton and McMahon were adamantly opposed to the idea, for the British were in no position to support the Arabs in the north. It will be recalled that, despite Cairo's best arguments, the scheme for a British landing at Alexandretta on the north Syrian coast was rejected by the Cabinet in November 1915, just as it had been in February of that year. Nor was the Syrian nationalist movement in any condition to engineer or support a rising. Jemal's public executions of Syrian nationalists in August 1915 and again, as noted, in May 1916, had eviscerated the movement in the north. And, as a precautionary measure, Jemal had removed Arab units in the Turkish army from Syria and deployed them in other theatres. As Hussein himself admitted, Syria was 'useless for revolutionary purposes'. So, any action by Faisal in Syria was sure to fail.[7] But for Clayton, there was another reason to discourage the Sherifian plan, a reason grounded in Entente diplomacy. '[W]e have definitely surrendered any claims we might have had to Syria,' he observed, 'so that it is very difficult to take any action . . . in that area without incurring a risk of being accused of bad faith towards our allies'. Syria had been 'given entirely over to the French' and Clayton well knew that Britain would 'have serious trouble with France' if an Arab rising there was encouraged by the British.[8]

Wingate departed from Clayton's views – not the last of their disagreements regarding the revolt – and recommended that Faisal 'should be given the means of at once raising the standard of revolt in the Syrian hinterland with a view to cutting the Turkish communications with Baghdad'. The Sirdar agreed that it 'might be more convenient if the Sherif confined his activity to the desert and to southern Arabia', but argued that Hussein's 'desire to strengthen his position in Syria was connected with his aspirations to the Khalifate'. The Sherif, Wingate thought, had his 'heart . . . set on the Syrian project'.[9] But, on May 1, 1916 Clayton informed the Sirdar that Faisal would not initiate the revolt in Syria, a decision that came as a great relief to Clayton, as he repeated that Britain would 'have serious trouble with France if we encouraged any such scheme'.[10]

France's interest in Syria was, of course, no surprise to anyone in Cairo or London. As described above, the British pledge given to Hussein in October 1915 had embodied a general reservation regarding France: Britain could support Arab independence only in those areas wherein Britain was 'free to act without detriment to the interests of her ally France'. Indeed, since January 1915, Clayton had pressed the Foreign Office for 'an early understanding with our Allies in regard to the eventual policy to be adopted in Syria. . . .'[11] The Foreign Office agreed that France had to be associated with any British plans for Syria and Clayton himself concluded, as early as April 1915, that Britain had left Syria to France, acknowledging that the French had 'certain claims [to Syria] – though mainly sentimental – whereas we have none'.[12]

The French were, in fact, very suspicious regarding British intentions for Syria. In early September 1915, the French ambassador in London submitted a Note to Grey complaining of the attitude of the British authorities in Cairo and insinuated that Clayton's Intelligence Department had been encouraging the aspirations of Syrian nationalists in Egypt. Clayton took exception to the French complaint. As described earlier, he had done nothing to encourage the Syrians. Certainly, he had listened to the pro-British faction of Syrians in Cairo; to do otherwise would make them think that Syria had been consigned to the French, and 'push them into the arms of the pan-Islamic party'. But he had also listened to the smaller, pro-French contingent of Syrians resident in the Egyptian capital. He had entertained all shades of opinion, but 'studiously avoided giving any indication of what the future settlement [of Syria] might be' or even his 'personal views on the subject'. Clayton concluded his response to the French complaint with a slight jab at the Foreign Office; his difficulties in dealing with the Syrians had been 'considerably increased' owing to his 'complete ignorance of the lines which the future policy of the Allied Powers was likely to follow'. Grey accepted Clayton's explanation, repeating it to the French ambassador in late October.[13]

The French complaint against Clayton and the ongoing, secret McMahon–Hussein correspondence underscored for Clayton the importance of reaching some sort of understanding with France concerning Syria. 'I am still a little anxious', he wrote the Sirdar in early November 1915, 'as to whether the F.O. will grasp the nettle & come to that definite understanding with France . . . [T]here must be a very generous measure of "give and take" and very complete trust & openness between us & France'. McMahon agreed. On November 2, he met with Defrance, the French minister in Cairo, and, without alluding to his correspondence with Hussein, raised with him the Arab question and the importance attached by the Arabs to the four Syrian cities of Aleppo, Hama, Homs and Damascus. Those four cities and their surrounding environs, it will be recalled, were specifically mentioned as reserved to the Arabs in McMahon's October 24 letter to the Sherif.[14]

The Foreign Office were well aware of the desirability of securing an agreement with France consistent with the pledge made to Hussein. Already, in October, Grey had invited the French ambassador to hold talks on the Arab question.[15] And, in mid-November a British committee, comprised of representatives of the Foreign, War and India Offices, was assembled in London for the purpose of deciding how the French should be approached. An idea that they should be 'bought out' of their claims to Syria was quickly dismissed by Sir Arthur Nicolson of the Foreign Office. Nicolson was deeply sceptical of the Arab movement, arguing that it was 'unreal' and 'incoherent' and, in any event, it had to be accepted that France 'has a rightful claim to Syria'. It was decided, instead, to tell the French 'generally of our dealings with the Arabs' and ask for their cooperation 'in giving similar guarantees as ourselves in the area to be allotted to them'.[16]

On November 23, 1915, the British committee met with the French representative, François Georges-Picot, the former French Consul in Beirut and an ardent imperialist. The French had already gotten wind of Hussein's extravagant territorial demands – although not the British response to them given in October – and Picot was in no compromising state of mind.[17] He took a hard line, stating that 'the French must of course have the whole of Syria and Palestine, and . . . would never consent to offer independence to the Arabs'. He added that the Arab movement 'had been much exaggerated by the Cairo authorities, and that, in reality, it had little or no strength or following'. Picot was equally unimpressed by Nicolson's warning that the Entente's indifference to Arab claims might risk 'inflaming . . . Mohammedan religious feeling all over Arabia, Syria and North Africa'. He foresaw no possibility of trouble arising from pan-Islamism in the region.[18]

A. C. Parker, who had worked for Cairo Intelligence and was now temporarily assigned to the War Office, was a member of the British negotiating team and reported the proceedings to Clayton. As he read Parker's Note on the November 23 meeting, Clayton became convinced that there was no hope of reaching agreement so long as Picot was the French delegate. Picot, noted Clayton, was 'well known as being extreme in his ideas, and completely saturated with the vision of a great French possession in the Eastern Mediterranean'. He also argued that Picot should be made to correctly understand Cairo's view of the Arab movement, as Clayton had already explained it to London: It was not regarded as having great offensive value in the Middle Eastern war; 'the chief advantage to be gained is a defensive one, in that we should secure on . . . [the Arab] part a hostile attitude towards the Turks, even though it might be only passively hostile, and rob our enemies of the incalculable moral and material assistance which they would gain were they to succeed in uniting the Arab races and through them, Islam, against the Allies'.[19] Parker fully understood Clayton's views, but was unable to sway Picot, whom he found 'absolutely uncompromising'. At the suggestion of the Foreign Office, Parker prepared a Note on the Arab movement, signed by Callwell, then the DMO, and himself which stated that the French should be informed that their intransigence on the question of Arab independence might 'endanger all British possessions in the East, and may thus necessitate the removal of a very large part of the British Army from France'.[20]

That remarkable threat, however, was never transmitted to Picot, for when the Frenchman returned to London in December, after consultations in Paris with the French Premier Aristide Briand, it was obvious that French views had changed considerably. The British Committee, recently joined by Mark Sykes, was surprised to learn that the French now 'realized the importance of the Arab movement' and agreed 'to the towns of Aleppo, Hama, Homs and Damascus being included in the Arab dominions to be administered by the Arabs under French influence'. Picot still insisted that Paris would never agree to the Lebanon being placed under a 'Mohammedan Suzerain' and that France should still have Palestine – or, at least 'the whole of the Jordan Valley and the whole of the coast as far as the present Egyptian frontier' – but progress had been made.[21]

After the December meeting it was decided to turn over the detailed Anglo-French negotiations to Sykes and Picot, and, by January 3, 1916, the two had reached basic agreement. France was accorded direct administrative rights over an area – designated the 'Blue Zone' – that encompassed the Lebanon and extended northwards, well into central Anatolia, modern-day Turkey. A similar area of direct administration – the 'Red Zone' – was assigned to Britain and covered the Basra and Baghdad *vilayets*. A future Arab State, or States, was acknowledged in a Zone 'A', which encompassed the four Syrian cities (Aleppo, Hama, Homs and Damascus), ran east to the Persian frontier, and included the northern Mesopotamian city of Mosul. Zone 'A', though nominally independent, was to be within the sphere of French administrative and commercial influence. Zone 'B', the area south of the French sphere, was similarly to be an area of British influence. Britain was also accorded rights in, and access to, the Palestine ports of Haifa and Acre, allowing for British access to the Mediterranean. Palestine itself was coloured brown on the Sykes–Picot map and assigned to future international administration, owing to the multi-national religious interests in that region. The Sykes–Picot agreement was embodied in an exchange of letters approved by the British and French governments in February 1916. Russian acquiescence was obtained later that spring at the expense of Ottoman territory in north-eastern Anatolia.[22] But the agreement was kept secret – Clayton did not learn of its terms until mid-April 1916 – for the obvious reason that it would be seen for what it was – an example of imperial grab which was sure to be characterized as such by the Turks and Germans and, quite likely, by the Arabs.

Although Sykes–Picot would later be characterized by the Arabs as the 'product of greed at its worst' and a 'startling piece of double-dealing', the agreement directly sprang from, and was intended to be consistent with, the McMahon–Hussein correspondence.[23] McMahon had never agreed to an independent Arab state in the Lebanon (that is, in the area 'west of the districts of Damascus, Homs, Hama and Aleppo'), and, more generally, British support for Arab independence in the region was fully qualified by the reservation regarding French interests – Britain could make no promises detrimental 'to the interests of her ally France'. Similarly, no understanding had been reached regarding the Basra and Baghdad *vilayets*, where McMahon had specified 'special administrative arrangements' would obtain. And, as described earlier, Palestine was not mentioned in McMahon's correspondence with Hussein, but *was* an area of French interest; Picot had made that much abundantly clear in his London meetings of November 23 and December 21. That France had now backed off her direct claim to that area by agreeing to an international administration did not undermine the point that, at the time of McMahon's October 24, 1915 letter, Palestine was claimed by France and was thus subject to McMahon's general reservation regarding French interests.

No one in Cairo was informed of the Sykes–Picot negotiations, and Clayton was now concerned that since London had confirmed French entitlement to Syria during the November-December 1915 meetings, Britain would be exposed to a claim of bad faith – this time by the Arabs. '[I]t is hard to see how we can go on negotiating [with Hussein] much longer, without laying ourselves open to a charge of breach of faith, unless we honestly tell the Arabs that we have made Syria over to the French'. He did not believe France would ever limit her claim to Syria and was equally certain that Hussein would regard French pretensions as inconsistent with McMahon's letter pledging British support for an Arab Syria, despite the qualifications accompanying the British promise. '[W]e shall have to try and get the Arabs to take up a reasonable line towards' the French, he wrote, 'as well as endeavour to get the French to see the Arab point of view'.[24]

Not until mid-April did Clayton receive from Sykes the outline of his agreement with Picot, and the full text was not sent until early May, 1916. Clayton did not see Sykes–Picot as inconsistent with McMahon's pledge of the previous October; the two undertakings could be reconciled, particularly in view of the ambiguity and qualifications attached to the pledge given to Hussein.[25] But, equally, his review left him concerned that the spheres of influences outlined in the agreement would be seen by Hussein, specifically, as inconsistent with the McMahon pledge, and by the Arabs, generally, as an egregious example of European imperialism. 'I sincerely trust', he wrote, 'that they will keep the agreement secret at present from our Arab friends or we shall have a certain amount of trouble'. Hogarth agreed and prepared a Note, in which Clayton concurred, criticizing the pact and expressing the hope that it was provisional in nature, allowing for 'considerable revision' at a later date. The Arab Bureau director also saw that it was sure to be objected to by Hussein and by most Syrians, who were vehemently opposed to 'French penetration' in Syria. Moreover, the boundaries drawn by Sykes and Picot did not provide access to the

Mediterranean for the future Arab State in Zone 'A' and were, in any event, 'unscientific', as they did not correspond to the social, economic and ethnographic realities of the region. Later, after meeting with Picot in London, Clayton concluded that the Frenchman realized that while his agreement 'was very useful as a guide to policy & a preventive of any possible friction among the Allies, it would be very inadvisable at present to make it public'.[26] Clayton misread Picot; the Frenchman saw his agreement as far more than a 'guide'. He and his colleagues in Paris would insist on strict adherence to the 1916 agreement, especially so at the post-war peace conference, and Anglo-French relations would become badly strained as the British later tried to modify the pact to meet Arab demands.

As Clayton hoped, the Sykes–Picot agreement was kept secret. Hussein was not formally advised of the Entente pact until May 1917, and the full text was not disclosed until the following autumn, when it was made public by the Russian Bolsheviks in the wake of their November revolution. No doubt Hussein would have objected to Sykes–Picot had he learned of its terms in 1916. It is impossible to know whether he also would have reconsidered his decision to revolt. But, in mid-1916, Hussein was fully preoccupied with other matters, specifically how to confront the two divisions of Turkish troops then stationed in the Hijaz.

Despite the Sherif's lack of preparation, his forces scored several successes in the first weeks of the revolt. Mecca fell on June 15, and the Turkish barracks there were overwhelmed in early July. Jeddah, the Red Sea port nearest Mecca, surrendered on June 16, taken with the help of a British naval bombardment. Other key Red Sea ports at Rabegh and, further north, at Yanbu, capitulated in late July. Ta'if, Hussein's summer residence in the hills east of Mecca, fell on September 22. The capture of Ta'if, made possible by Wingate's dispatch of an Egyptian Army artillery battery, was a major success, as more than 2,000 Turkish officers and men laid down their arms.[27] Medina was another matter. The Arabs first attacked the city, and the Hijaz railway to the north, five days before Hussein's formal commencement of hostilities. But, defended by some 12,000 Turkish troops, well-supplied and equipped with artillery, the city easily repulsed Hussein's Bedouin attackers. Despite further attacks and frequent disruptions of the Hijaz railway – Medina's supply line from the north – the city would hold out until after the war, not surrendering until February 1919.

A week before the revolt erupted in the Hijaz, McMahon received an urgent wire from the Foreign Office relaying a request from the French government that Clayton come to London 'to discuss Arab affairs with M. Picot and the Home Authorities'.[28] McMahon and Wingate agreed that a visit by Clayton to London was an 'excellent move', but the timing could not have been worse. Anticipating the outbreak of the revolt, Clayton had just asked Hogarth and Cornwallis of the Arab Bureau to accompany Storrs on a trip to the Hijaz coast to meet secretly with Abdullah. They were not expected to return for another ten days and McMahon insisted that they be debriefed by the Intelligence Director before he left for London. Nor could Murray allow Clayton to leave; the round-up of suspect European neutrals in Egypt, discussed earlier, was planned for June 1, and Clayton's services were 'urgently' required by the EEF commander. But by mid-June, the Sherif's revolt now a reality, the Foreign Office cabled that it was 'urgently necessary to have . . . [Clayton] here as soon as possible'.[29]

That the French and British governments should have requested Clayton's presence in London to discuss Arab affairs may be taken as some indication of the view that he, rather than his two chiefs, McMahon and Wingate, was the man on the spot driving Britain's Arab policy. However he was regarded, Clayton saw that his visit to London presented an excellent opportunity to explain Cairo's thinking on the Arab question to the Entente's policy-makers. He was unsure from the Foreign Office's cryptic telegrams precisely why he was being called home, but suspected the reason was to discuss 'the final [Sykes–Picot] agreement with Picot and the Russian representative, whoever he may be'. Wingate had higher hopes, suggesting that Clayton do his 'utmost to stir up the Foreign Office or the War Office' and relieve the 'general air of confusion and uncertainty' pervading Whitehall.[30]

Clayton left Cairo on June 19 and, travelling via Marseilles, arrived in London ten days later. His reception was far from favourable, for he arrived in London just as a series of 'alarmist telegrams' were received from the Government of India describing the effect there of the Sherif's revolt. He found the War Office and the Admiralty 'quite all right' about Hussein's rising, but others 'were much alarmed and inclined to reproach all of us out here with having assisted in bringing about a very difficult and dangerous situation – they were very far from enthusiastic in fact, especially the Foreign & India Offices'.[31] Clayton immediately set about calming the home authorities. He had 'personal interviews' with Prime Minister Asquith, Foreign Secretary Grey and Austen Chamberlain of the India Office. He also met with Cromer, still a significant voice in Middle Eastern affairs, and with former Viceroys Lord Curzon and Lord Hardinge who, as seen, had been furious with McMahon over his concessions to Hussein regarding Mesopotamia.[32] How much Hardinge knew of Clayton's involvement in McMahon's correspondence with Hussein is unclear, but the former Viceroy, who had now replaced Nicolson as Permanent Under-Secretary at the Foreign Office, was soon won over by Clayton. He was 'immensely' impressed by the Intelligence Director, who appeared 'thoroughly sensible and comprehending as to what can and cannot be done' in the Middle East.[33] Clayton also met with key figures in British Intelligence. He conferred with Colonel French, head of MI1(c), under whose section Mansfield Cumming of the SIS worked. Meetings with Macdonogh and Hall, with whom he had corresponded, also seem most likely and he certainly worked with Kell's Security Service in developing criteria for applications by foreign nationals wishing to enter Egypt during the war.[34] And Clayton had 'one or two long talks with Mark Sykes and Picot'. He found the Frenchman 'very reasonable' in understanding the need to 'make up with the Moslems of Syria', but, as noted, he was far too optimistic in thinking that the French would regard Sykes–Picot as simply a 'useful guide' to policy, rather than as a binding agreement governing the post-war Middle East.

On July 6, Clayton and Sykes attended a meeting of the War Committee, at which all members of the Cabinet were present. Sykes urged British support for the

Arab revolt and described as a major impediment to that policy 'the jealousy which subsists between Simla [India] and Cairo'. The Government of India, he concluded, was 'incapable of handling the Arab question'. These were controversial points and it took some courage to state them, as Chamberlain and former Viceroys Curzon and Hardinge were present. But, characteristically, Sykes overstated his case, arguing that Percy Cox, then chief political officer in Mesopotamia, be made high commissioner of that country and placed in charge of all Arab areas then under the jurisdiction of India and that Cox himself be placed under the authority of the Foreign Office.[35] Clayton, of course, joined in Sykes' arguments concerning support of the Arab movement, but he knew that the proposal to remove India from all Arab affairs was far too dramatic a change to be endorsed by the Cabinet. After the July 6 meeting, Clayton spoke privately with Chamberlain and volunteered that he was not in favour of the changes Sykes proposed. This was enough for Asquith who, at the next War Committee meeting of July 11 'observed that none of the Committee was impressed by Sir Mark Sykes' proposals'.[36]

Clayton's comments at the War Committee meeting of July 6 were more practical. He urged that Hussein's monthly subsidy should be increased to £125,000, an amount that Grey found excessive. However, Clayton pointed out that the large subsidy was needed not only to fund the revolt, but also to replace the funds previously provided by the Turks for maintenance of the holy places and the security of the *hajj*, the annual pilgrimage. That argument appealed to Curzon and Chamberlain who were concerned that the British position throughout the Muslim world would be undermined if it were found that Britain had done nothing to maintain the *Haramain* and the *hajj*. The Committee authorized only £50,000 per month on July 6, and Clayton and Grey were authorized to prepare a telegram to McMahon reflecting that decision. But, if it was determined that additional funds were required for the purposes described by Clayton, the government would reconsider the proposal. Five days later the Committee, having received cables from McMahon and Wingate underscoring the points made by Clayton, authorized a £125,000 per month subsidy for four months.[37]

On Monday, July 10, 1916 Clayton had the honour of receiving the CMG – awarded to him a year earlier – from King George V at Buckingham Palace.[38] Clayton got on well with the King and, as will be seen, would have audiences with him in the future. After the brief ceremony on the 10th, the King offered Clayton a glass of champagne but, not liking the taste of it, he politely declined. The King agreed, adding that he thought that champagne tasted like rusty nails in cider.[39] Despite his friendly reception, Clayton found the King 'somewhat nervous' about the Arab situation, perhaps because George V's private secretary Lord Stamfordham, was 'distinctly anti-Sherif'. But, in Clive Wigram, the King's assistant private secretary, he found a more congenial ear. Wigram took to Clayton immediately; he found the Intelligence Director 'most interesting' and liked 'his quiet, unassuming manner'.[40] Wigram would correspond with Clayton after his return to Cairo and the two met occasionally after the war, as their sons later attended the same school in England. For his part, Clayton kept Wigram, and the King, current on Middle

Eastern developments by his letters, and even arranged for Wigram to receive copies of the secret *Arab Bulletin* from the Foreign Office. He also sent the King a set of the first issue of Hijaz stamps (His Majesty was an avid stamp-collector) and some rare photographs of Mecca. The King was, in fact, keenly interested in Arab affairs. When Hogarth met with Wigram in the late summer of 1916, he provided him with a copy of a memorandum by Clayton on the revolt and learned that the King had instructed his secretary to 'get all . . . he could' out of the Arab Bureau director concerning the Arab movement.[41]

Having spent ten days in London, Clayton left for Egypt immediately after his audience with the King. By his own reckoning, he had achieved 'nothing epoch-making'. But he did explain the 'whole question as we know it' to the 'powers that be', emphasized the importance of backing the Sherif, and, in some measure, calmed the India and Foreign Offices. Clayton impressed the London departments with his practical and moderate ideas and it appears that he was regarded by them as the leading authority on the Arab movement. He later confessed to being a little surprised 'by the readiness with which some of the suggestions of an unimportant person like myself were adopted in certain cases'.[42]

On returning to Cairo, Clayton found chaos. If the Sherif was ill-prepared to launch his revolt, the British authorities on the spot were equally unprepared to assist it. No decision had been made in London, Cairo or Khartoum concerning British direction of the Arab movement. Even before Hussein fired his fateful rifle shot, Wingate wrote to the CIGS, Robertson, emphasizing that he had 'no sort of political responsibility' for the revolt and would assume none, unless he was given 'dual local political and military' authority.[43] Murray reluctantly offered to assume 'military supervision' of the rising and informed Robertson that Clayton recommended that he do so. But the CIGS rejected the offer, noting that there were 'many interests involved in the Arab movement', including the Foreign and India Offices, as well as the French and Russian governments. For this reason, no 'change as to the general control and supervision' of the revolt would be made. The DMO, General Frederick Maurice, later explained that the 'Government is not anxious to appear to be too concerned in the matter, as it wishes the Sherif to appear to the Mohammedan world as having acted on his own, and for that reason have not agreed to . . . [Murray] being in supreme control of the whole operations'.[44] Having had his offer rejected by London, Murray decided that he would have nothing to do with the revolt, except for providing whatever supplies he could spare. He informed McMahon that Clayton's Cairo Intelligence branch was 'not to touch the question of operations' and that all requests for supplies and munitions must be directed to his GHQ at Ismailia and not to Clayton. In response to Murray's question as to who was supervising or controlling the revolt, McMahon replied that no one was, 'except the Sherif, who is acting on his own initiative'.[45]

On June 26, McMahon informed Wingate of his view that the 'co-ordination of military matters' should be carried out by Murray, but that he, as High Commissioner, must retain control over political issues associated with the Arab movement. But, two days later, after discussions with Murray, Parker and Hogarth

(Clayton was then en route to London), McMahon advised the Sirdar that he, Wingate, should direct military operations from Khartoum, while McMahon continued to exercise political control. Wingate quickly declined: unless he was given 'full discretionary powers', he would assume no responsibility.[46]

By early July no decision had yet been reached as to who was in control. Murray and McMahon were able to work out a *modus vivendi* under which all communications with Hussein would be sent to Hogarth at the Arab Bureau, any requests from the Hijaz for materiel would be forwarded by Hogarth to Murray's headquarters at Ismailia, and all demands by the Sherif relating to personnel were to be sent to Wingate. But Murray continued to worry that his headquarters would be in some way identified with the revolt; he was 'particularly anxious that no officer of the Cairo branch of GHQ Intelligence shall attempt to deal . . . with any communications from the Sherif which may come into his hands'.[47] Parker, now assigned to Clayton's Intelligence staff in Cairo, explained the attitude of Murray and his staff: 'GHQ are inclined to take the line that it was foolish to get the Sherif to come in now – and rather look on it as a mess they do not wish to be mixed up in. I was warned officially that no officer in this office was to assist Hogarth in any way – I managed to get this somewhat modified so that Lawrence assists in all but where action is necessary and Hogarth is permitted to consult me. Also, Cornwallis is being definitely allowed to do Arab Bureau work, so we go on as before.'[48] Parker was correct about Murray; the commander-in-chief continued to insist that 'the operations in and arrangements for the Hedjaz are not in any way under my general direction'. And Murray's CGS, Lynden-Bell, wrote privately to the DMO that '[w]e do not wish at all to run the show ourselves'.[49]

While Murray was careful to avoid any connection with the revolt, Wingate continued to insist that since McMahon would concede no political authority to him, he might act as an adviser, but 'would assume no responsibility whatever. Up to the present I admit no responsibility for what has been done hitherto'. In August, he wrote to Robertson, stating that Murray 'is in charge of all military operations' and that 'I have now no responsibility either military or political in the matter'. Informed by Murray that operations in, and arrangements for, the revolt were not, in fact, under his direction, the Sirdar expressed surprise, and added: 'As you are aware, they are not under mine either'.[50] And, he assured Robertson, 'in the strongest possible manner' that he had 'no aspirations towards the political or military running of the revolt'. His position, he wrote, was that of an 'interested onlooker' and he was 'very anxious that no impression should get abroad that I wished for general control of the Sherif's movement'.[51] For his part, McMahon maintained that political control must remain in his hands, refused to delegate any authority to Wingate, and declined to refer the question of control of the Arab rising to London.[52] Parker thought that Wingate should direct the Arab movement from Khartoum but, after discussions with McMahon, 'was entirely unable to get the H[igh] C[ommissioner] to see it' and became convinced that McMahon was afraid of losing control of the Arab movement.[53] Lynden-Bell added to the criticism, reporting that McMahon and Murray 'do not get on, and I have no hesitation in saying that it is the High

Commissioner's fault'. McMahon, he added, 'wants to keep the thing in his hands and is quite incapable of dealing with it'.[54]

The attitudes of Murray, McMahon and Wingate were, in equal measure, petulant and pusillanimous and the result was that for the first four months of the Arab campaign no direction at all was provided by Hussein's British sponsors. Early on, Clayton saw that the 'whole trouble is want of expert Military control in the hands of one man'. 'The present system,' he added, 'is quite hopeless and everything falls on the wretched Arab Bureau – a body of somewhat shadowy substance with a small staff of no military experience and carrying insufficient weight'.[55]

While the lack of leadership among the top men in the Middle East may be attributed, in significant part, to the personalities of McMahon, Murray and Wingate, it was also apparent that weakness and indecision extended to London. From a purely military standpoint, the Cabinet's decision to create commissions to enquire into the huge military failures at Kut and the Dardanelles was a mistake and should have been deferred until after the war, for however laudable the motives behind them, the commissions had a marked chilling effect on top British military men in the field; careers were certain to be ruined by the governmental enquiries and this made British leaders excessively cautious, wary of any new or problematic military adventure. 'I am afraid that [the] Dardanelles and Mesopotamian Commissions exercise a paralysing effect,' Clayton observed, 'but we shall have much more cause for a commission if Mecca is recaptured by the Turks'.[56]

The debilitating effect of the commissions was compounded by weakness in, and internecine fighting among, the home government departments. Unsurprisingly, the India Office were opposed to the revolt, fearful of the disquieting effect it was thought to have on Indian Muslim opinion. And the Foreign Office, according to Clayton, was a 'weak spot', manned by young diplomats who were 'poorly trained and are dilettantes'. Robertson, who as CIGS was the government's top military adviser, was a confirmed 'Westerner' and viewed any campaign outside of the Western Front as a distracting sideshow. The CIGS was well aware of the differences among the departments and the lack of leadership in the Middle East, but was not inclined to make any decision that might remedy the situation. He was content to leave management of the revolt in the hands of the Arab Bureau which, he wrote to Wingate, was 'working very effectively under Clayton, and, being in Cairo, is better placed for dealing with India, France and Russia, who all have a finger in the pie, than Khartoum would be'.[57] Most of the men on the spot would have disagreed with that assessment, including Clayton, who, as noted, was well aware the Bureau had neither the military expertise to direct a campaign, nor the 'weight' to sponsor policy decisions concerning the Arab movement. 'There seems to be no commanding spirit to formulate a policy and push it through', he complained to Wingate; 'hence the difficulty in getting any policy at all'.[58]

Inevitably, the absence of a 'commanding spirit' who could take charge of the Arab movement created a 'holy muddle' during the first months of the revolt. The Sherif's insatiable appetite for money and supplies – food, arms and ammunition – could hardly be met and he was dismayed when, 'a nought' having been left off one consignment, he received only ten percent of the amounts requested. A large ship-ment of Japanese rifles sent to the Hijaz were found to be useless, as the Arabs could not 'work' them. A battery of howitzers was landed at Jeddah, but could not be moved inland because they lacked 'broad sand wheels' and could not be transported across the desert. Acutely aware of the lack of trained military leadership among the Sherif's forces, Clayton asked Aziz al-Masri to take charge, as he was 'the only man we have available who is in any way competent'. But Hussein declined to accept al-Masri and when he was eventually persuaded to do so, the Sherif's eldest son, Ali, quarrelled with him. Large shipments of supplies were landed at Rabegh, but were never sent inland as the local sheikh there misappropriated them. Clayton sent Parker to the Hijaz in early August to reconnoitre the area round Akaba for a possible landing there, but the mission was not explained to Hussein beforehand and Parker was denied permission to proceed. A flight of planes was despatched from Suez, but on arrival by ship at Rabegh, was promptly ordered by the British to return to Egypt. Just as they left port, a Turkish squadron arrived from the direction of Medina and bombed the town. The Royal Navy, with the concurrence of Aden (run by the Government of India), enabled the Idrisi to occupy Kunfida, a Red Sea port in the undefined borderland between the Hijaz and 'Asir. Informed of the occupation, Hussein promptly dispatched a force to the port to eject the Idrisi, and the British were faced with the absurd prospect of two of its allies in the war against the Turks fighting each other. Eventually, the Idrisi was convinced to climb down and evacuate Kunfida after receiving assurances that the port's status would be reconsidered after the war, but the incident provided yet another example of the problems associated with the 'duality of control' in the Red Sea by India and Egypt.[59]

All these difficulties, though, were nothing compared to the problem of supplying manpower for the revolt. Hussein's forces – they could hardly be called an army – consisted mostly of Bedouin from those tribes whose support the Sherif could enlist by the payment of money. Although quite capable of individual acts of bravery, the Bedouin were, in Wingate's words, little more than 'untrained rabble'.[60] The assault on Medina had demonstrated that the Arabs could not contend with Turk artillery and were no better suited to a confrontation with disciplined, regular Turkish troops. Lawrence and Clayton understood early on that the Arabs could succeed only by a programme of irregular warfare. Clayton argued that 'the Arabs should never risk a serious engagement but should prosecute remorselessly a guer-rilla warfare against the Hejaz railway and the Turkish lines of communications. Once their lines of communication are seriously interfered with really they are done – and this is the style of warfare for which the Arab is eminently well-adapted'.[61] However, there were still thousands of Turkish regular army forces in the Hijaz who could not be dislodged by Bedouin guerrillas and if the Turks counter-attacked, the revolt might very well collapse.

The obvious solution was that British troops should be landed in the Hijaz to confront the regular Turk forces. Yet, during the first three months of the rising no one except Wingate favoured this solution. The most obvious reason was that there were no British troops available for a landing. Murray's EEF had been stripped to the bone by mid-1916, as more than 200,0000 men were shipped from Egypt to the Western Front in order to maximize the effect of the Entente's great summer 1916 offensives there. Murray and Lynden-Bell thus made clear that they would not part with a single man for an Hijaz operation without express orders from the War Office.[62] Such orders were not likely to issue; in the wake of the failures at Kut and Gallipoli, London was not inclined to embark on another costly and doubtful sideshow remote from the decisive theatre in France. Pressed by Wingate to send a British brigade to the Hijaz, Robertson irritably replied that '[w]ith such a scattered Empire as ours, I am constantly being pressed to send troops all over the world on minor enterprises'. He did not share the Sirdar's anxiety about the possible failure of Hussein's revolt and so was 'strongly opposed to sending any troops into the Hedjaz . . . I have none I can free from . . . more important theatres'. Murray concurred. 'I do not think, and Clayton agrees with me,' he wrote to the CIGS, 'that we should send British troops to assist the Sherif, though such action is recommended by the Sirdar'.[63]

The Arab Bureau and Cairo Intelligence also recognized that the use of British or Indian troops to support the revolt was neither likely nor desirable. 'I do not think there is the faintest chance of any expedition being approved either of Indian or of British troops anywhere near the Sherif's country', Parker wrote. And Hogarth was certain that Hussein would never request British troops or, 'under any stress, accept our armed cooperation in the interior of the Hejaz'.[64] The idea of admitting Christian troops to the Muslim holy land was, in fact, anathema to the Sherif. Not only was such a decision abhorrent on religious grounds, the Turks would surely proclaim that Hussein was undermining the sanctity of the *Haramain*; the Sherif, and his movement, would then be irreparably damaged throughout the Islamic world. Clayton recognized the problem from the outset of the revolt. Any action 'by British troops (even Moslem troops) would, I feel sure, arouse feelings of great uneasiness & suspicion', he argued. Moreover, he saw that the majority of the Arab party, though friendly to Britain, were 'distinctly pan-Islamic at heart, and of course the Indian Moslem, who has no particular interest in Arab freedom, thinks only of the integrity of the Holy Places (if he thinks about [it] at all, unless moved by agitators)'. Wingate was unpersuaded. In the event of a Turkish counter-attack from Medina, Hussein would have to choose between British troops in the Hijaz and 'almost certain defeat'. But the Sirdar appeared to have been more concerned about the assessment of responsibility than the success of the revolt when he concluded that if a British offer of troops was refused by Hussein, 'then we are exonerated from all blame for the failure of his movement'.[65] As discussed below, the idea of deploying British troops in Arabia, definitively rejected in the summer, would arise again in the autumn of 1916, as the feared Turkish counter-attack materialized.

If British troops in Arabia was an impossibility, the same objections did not clearly apply to the Egyptian Army. The use of Egyptian troops posed no religious problems, but did raise serious political issues. Wingate, as noted, had dispatched an Egyptian artillery battery to the Hijaz in June, a small unit that proved instrumental in the reduction of the Turk garrison at Ta'if three months later. But the

Sirdar recognized that the employment of Egyptian troops in Arabia 'raises a question of policy'.[66] The first question of policy was created on November 7, 1914, when, on the heels of the declaration of martial law in Egypt, Maxwell had proclaimed that Britain accepted 'the sole burden of the war' and would not call upon the Egyptian people for assistance.[67] The promise was broken almost at once, however, as Egyptian Army artillery was used in the defence of the Canal in the winter of 1914–15. And paid Egyptian civilian labour was used in non-combatant roles – mainly, entrenching and fortification work – at the Dardanelles and, in greater numbers, during British operations in Palestine in 1917–18. But no large contingent of Egyptian Army troops had been deployed against the Turks and, in view of Maxwell's 1914 promise, were not likely to be.

Maxwell's 1914 proclamation sprang from a recognition that the Egyptian people, and particularly the upper class – many of whom were of Turkish ancestry – were, at bottom, pro-Turkish in sentiment, and would likely object to Egyptian troops being used to fight their Ottoman co-religionists. McMahon reported that Hussein Rushdi Pasha, the Egyptian prime minister, only very reluctantly agreed to sending any Egyptian unit to the Hijaz and urged that they be sent as volunteers, dressed in native clothes, and not as a uniformed army contingent. For his part, Hussein Kamil, the Egyptian sultan, while widely – and correctly – regarded as pro-British, advised against sending any Egyptian soldiers to Arabia.[68]

In addition to these political objections, Egyptian troops, just like their Entente counterparts, were in short supply. Wingate was most reluctant to detach any Egyptian soldiers from his Darfur operation and equally loathe to send any from Khartoum. Even a request from the Sherif that Egyptian Army officers be sent to the Hijaz to help train his troops was questioned by Clayton. And, when the Army's officer corps was approached for volunteers, not a single man offered his services, as the Sultan required all officers considering such employment to sign a paper acknowledging the Egyptian government's disclaimer of responsibility for any man hurt or killed in the Hijaz.[69] Despite these problems, by the end of October 1916, thirty-seven officers and 718 NCOs and men of the Egyptian Army were deployed in Arabia, most of them in training roles or in operating the few artillery pieces and machine guns provided to the Sherif.

Now that British, Indian and Egyptian troops had all been ruled out for service with the Sherifian forces, the only remaining option was Arab prisoners of war, taken in Sinai and Mesopotamia. There were then a few hundred Arab POWs in Egypt and some 2,600 in India. In the first week of the revolt, Clayton cabled the Government of India a request that the Arab POWs there be sent to Egypt for eventual deployment in Arabia and, at the same time, he approached the Arabs then imprisoned in Egypt. His plan was that the Arab prisoners from India would form the nucleus of a POW unit in the Hijaz, supplemented by those held in Egypt. The POWs in Egypt initially agreed to go, but then changed their minds, making Clayton doubtful about the whole experiment. He saw that they could 'hardly be trusted with a battery in the face of the enemy, especially as they have given as their reason that, having once fought for the Turks in this war, they do not wish to fight

1 Bertie Clayton and his father, William Lewis Nicholl Clayton, c. 1876.

2 Bertie Clayton and his sister Ellinor, c. 1879.

The Isle of Wight Proprietary College,

3 The Isle of Wight College, from a prospectus of the 1880s.

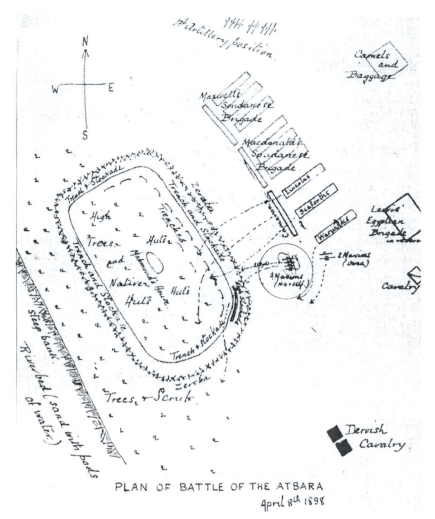

4 Clayton's plan of the Battle of the Atbara, 8 April 1898.

PLAN OF BATTLE OF THE ATBARA
April 8th 1898

5 Maxim guns arrayed before the Battle of Omdurman, 2 September 1898.

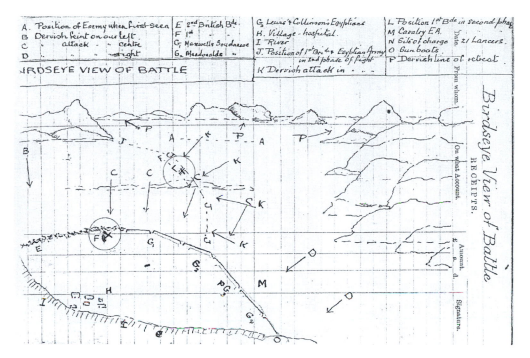

A. Position of Enemy when first seen	E 2nd British Bde.	G₅ Lewis' & Collinson's Egyptians	L Position 1st Bde in second phase
B Dervish feint on our left	F 1st	H. Village - hospital.	M Cavalry E.A.
C " attack " " centre	G₃ Maxwells Soudanese	I River	N Site of charge. Date 21 Lancers.
D " " " right	G₄ Macdonalds "	J. Position of 1st Bde & Egyptian Army in 2nd phase of fight	O Gun boats
		K Dervish attack in " " "	P Dervish line of retreat

IRDSEYE VIEW OF BATTLE

Birdseye View of Battle

RECEIPTS.

From whom.

On what Account.

£. Amount. s. d.

Signature.

6 Clayton's 'Birdseye View' of the Battle of Omdurman, showing his position during Phases 1 and 2 of the battle.

7 Clayton and his pet lion cub, at Wau, Bahr al-Ghazal Province, Sudan, 1903.

8 Commandant's office, Wau, Bahr al-Ghazal Province, Sudan, 1902.

9 Field Marshal Lord Kitchener.

10 The Governor-General's Palace, Khartoum.

11 Sir Francis Reginald Wingate.

12 Hussein ibn Ali.

13 Faisal ibn Hussein.

14 Abdullah ibn Hussein.

15 General Sir Archibald Murray.

16 Port Said, Egypt.

17 General Sir Arthur Lynden-Bell.

18 Sir Henry McMahon.

20 Sir Ronald Storrs.

19 The Savoy Hotel, Cairo.

21 T. E. Lawrence, with D. G. Hogarth and Alan Dawnay, 1918.

22 British Agency, Jeddah.

23 General Sir Edmund Allenby.

24 Sir Mark Sykes, *c.* 1918.

25 Enid, Bertie, Patience, Sam and Jane Clayton, *c.* 1919.

26 Sa'd Zaghlul, Egyptian nationalist leader.

27 Dr.Chaim Weizmann.

29 Sir Gilbert and Lady Clayton, Government House, Jerusalem, 1924.

28 Government House, Jerusalem, 1920.

30 Allenby, Balfour and Samuel, 1925.

31 Lord Curzon.

32 Ibn Saud, c. 1926.

33 Austen Chamberlain, Stanley Baldwin and Winston Churchill, 1925.

35 George Antonius.

34 Leo Amery.

36 Patience, John, Enid, Bertie and Sam Clayton, at Apple Porch, Peaslake, 1926.

37 Enid, John (Jack) and Bertie Clayton, c. 1927.

THE PALESTINE BULLETIN

SUBSCRIPTION RATES:
L.P. 3.— for a year
L.P. 1.500 for half a year
Delivered Home Daily
TELEPHONE: 415
Telegrams: P A L T A G.
Address: JERUSALEM.
JAFFA ROAD, P. O. B. 583.

RISHON-LE-ZION
Carmel Oriental
WINES AND BRANDIES
A Standard of Quality
Throughout the World

PUBLISHED DAILY.
Registered as a Newspaper at the G. P. O. Jerusalem.

VOL. IV.   No. 964.   Jerusalem, Monday, March 19th., 1928.   Copyright,   Price 10 Mils.

CLAYTON TO THE RESCUE
PROCEEDING TO JEDDA TO CONFER WITH IBN SAUD

LONDON, March 18 (P.T.A.)
It is understood on good authority that Sir Gilbert Clayton is proceeding to Jedda, where he will meet King Ibn Saud, with a view to discussing and settling the difficulties between him and Nejd and Transjordan.

IRAQ RAIDS.
JEDDAH (Arabia), Monday.
Ibn Saud, King of the Hedjaz, arrived here to-day from Medina to meet Sir

Ibn Saud.   Brig.-Gen. Sir Gilbert Clayton.
Gilbert Clayton, the British Emissary.—Reuter.

Sir Gilbert Clayton has gone out to Jeddah to discuss with Ibn Saud the question of Iraq frontier raids for which Ibn Saud's tribes are held responsible.

38 Headline from *The Palestine Bulletin*, 19 March 1928.

39 Sir Gilbert arrives at Baghdad as the new High Commissioner for Iraq, 2 March 1929.

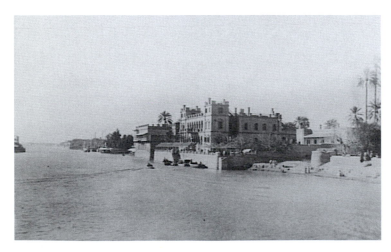

40 The British Residency, Baghdad.

against them'. Yet, in light of the problems faced by the Sherif, Clayton was reluctant to give up on the scheme altogether. He had Faruqi – now Hussein's agent in Cairo – speak to the Arab prisoners and, by the end of July, all but two officers and thirty men agreed to fight with the Sherifian forces. Their attitude was still somewhat doubtful however, and Clayton decided to delay a further request to India to dispatch the POWs there until he was certain that the prisoners sent from Cairo would, in fact, fight for the Sherif. His caution proved justified. On arrival at Jeddah, all the Arabs, save for the officers and twenty-five men, refused to join the fight. The recalcitrant POWs informed Hussein that they had not been told in Cairo that they were being sent to fight the Turks and that Turkish prisoners in Jeddah warned them that if they fought against the Turks, their families would be 'destroyed' and they would be hanged if captured. But Clayton concluded that the 'real reason' the Arabs declined to fight was simply that 'they have had enough of fighting and are not for any more, either on one side or the other'.[70] Whatever the real reason, the plan to use Arab POWs to augment the Sherif's forces had failed. Robertson summarized the British position in October 1916: 'Our military policy with regard to the Sherif should be to avoid any military commitments and to confine our assistance to the supply of Mohammedan instructors, arms and supplies so as to enable him to stand on his own legs.'[71] Hussein was on his own.

The first few months of the Arab revolt had proved distinctly unpromising. None of the top British men in the region had exhibited the least semblance of leadership. The attitude of the London departments ranged from indifference to scepticism to downright hostility. No strategic vision for the rising had emerged. There was no possibility of augmenting the Sherif's undisciplined and inadequate levies. And the provision of food, guns and supplies for the revolt – left to the 'wretched Arab Bureau' – had been erratic and inadequate. Few would have disagreed with Lynden-Bell's late September assessment that the revolt was 'very much a comic opera performance'.[72] Still, the Sherif had experienced no major setbacks, territory had been wrested from the enemy, and a few thousand Turks killed or captured.

In the first week of September, matters took a further turn for the worse. Cyril Wilson, Clayton's former Sudan colleague and fellow graduate of the Isle of Wight College, who had been posted to Jeddah as British liaison with Hussein, reported that the Turks were planning a drive from Medina to retake Mecca. The Turkish *Mahmal* – the ceremonial caravan bearing the *kiswa*, the shroud annually draped round the *Ka'ba* in Mecca – had arrived at Medina from the north, accompanied by Ali Haidar, sherif of a rival Hashemite clan, who was to replace Hussein as Amir when the Turks broke through to Mecca. Wilson recommended the immediate dispatch of two battalions of British troops and a flight of airplanes to block the Turkish advance to Mecca via Rabegh.[73] The annual pilgrimage was scheduled to occur between September 26 and October 8, and, if disrupted by the enemy, would, he believed, cause mass defections of the Arabs to the Turks, the failure of the revolt and a severe blow to British prestige in the East.

Murray and Lynden-Bell thought Wilson's fears unwarranted. Lynden-Bell argued that even if the Sherif was 'swamped' by the Turks, that event would not have 'any effect at all' on the British position in the region. And, Murray had recently spoken to the Egyptian Sultan who was 'strongly opposed' to the presence of any British troops in the Hijaz and believed that British prestige would be harmed if they were sent.[74] On September 12, Murray convened a conference at Ismailia to discuss the Hijaz situation. In addition to the EEF commander, McMahon, Clayton, Lynden-Bell, Cornwallis, Storrs, Wilson and Admiral Roslyn Wemyss, the naval commander-in-chief, East Indies and Egypt station, attended. The hapless Wilson was completely taken by surprise when Murray went after him in an 'absolutely bald-headed' and 'damned caddish manner'. Murray was more than irritated by the revolt and fixed on Wilson as the author of the current difficulties. But relations between the EEF commander and McMahon had also deteriorated badly during the last few months and, as Wilson reported to the Sirdar – who would not leave the Sudan to attend the conference – Murray was really getting at McMahon through Wilson.[75] Wilson gamely argued that the presence of a British brigade at Rabegh, even though it could not be used in the Arabian interior, was supported by Faisal who believed that the 'moral effect' on the disheartened Arabs would be great enough to enable them to resist a Turkish advance on Mecca.

Murray was not swayed. The War Office, he stressed, had decided that Britain would concentrate on the Western Front 'every single man we possibly can'. Further, of the 350,000 men he had under his command in the spring (following on the evacuation of Gallipoli), he had 'despatched every single man' he could to France, and left himself 'some mounted troops and four weak and ill-trained Territorial divisions'. He had been ordered by Robertson to advance to El Arish in Sinai and '[n]othing will induce me to reduce the strength of the troops required to carry on that plan'. Despite this, he emphasized, he had met nearly all requests from the Hijaz – 24,650 rifles, eight machine guns and two artillery pieces (taken from the Turks), as well as tons of food had been sent. He also threw cold water on the request for airplanes. Did not Wilson understand that a request for two planes would mean two more machines and three engines kept in reserve, 212 camels to carry the equipment, the erection of three aerodromes, a hangar and store sheds, not to mention trained pilots? Yet, there were only fifteen working planes in all of Egypt. In short, he would not send one plane or one man to the Hijaz without direct orders from London.

McMahon had little to say by way of rejoinder, except to point out that the revolt was now a 'purely military business' and that he regretted his involvement in the matter. 'It was the most unfortunate date in my life when I was left in charge of the Arab movement', he added. Clayton avoided the political issues and simply noted that Wingate would send an Egyptian Army brigade from the Sudan – say, three or four battalions of Sudanese – provided they were replaced by British troops from Egypt. This, he observed, would answer any religious objections. Murray declined: 'I don't intend to do either'. He would only agree to send McMahon's formal request for troops to London, along with his own statement that he would 'not provide the troops unless I am ordered'.[76]

Clayton was appalled by the 'unjustifiable and most unfair attack on the wretched Wilson', and told him afterwards that 'much the same' had happened to him 'on several occasions'. Yet, while he believed that Wilson had been wrongly assailed by Murray at Ismailia, Clayton agreed with the commander's essential point that British troops should not be sent to the Hijaz. His reasons, though, differed from those of Murray. 'I do not like it myself at all, as I know that whatever the Sherif may himself say, much capital will be made of it against us (it is already the main plank in Ali Haidar's platform[)] . . . but it is a necessity now and we must take the lesser evil'.[77]

The day after the Ismailia conference, Murray duly forwarded McMahon's memo requesting the dispatch of British troops to Rabegh. The memo was likely prepared by Clayton, as it embodied many of his arguments: Britain was 'morally committed' to Hussein, he argued, having pledged to support Arab independence. Moreover, the revolt had 'the sympathy if not the actual support of the majority of the Arab races'. But the Arabs were beginning to doubt British support and to lose heart. If the Turks were now allowed to break through to Mecca, the pilgrimage would be 'severely endangered and the whole Arab movement might collapse'. If that occurred, Britain would suffer 'grave damage' to her 'prestige throughout the Moslem world'. More practically, there would be no impediment to 'Turkish expansion down across the Red Sea'. They would have 'free access to the Eastern shores of the Red Sea' and the situation in Abyssinia and Somaliland would be affected, 'thus jeopardizing the whole military and political situation east of Suez'. Finally, if Britain did not meet the Turkish threat, the French were ready to send French Moslem troops and that would rob Britain of the 'very great political advantages which the Sherif's success will hereafter give us'.[78]

These were all good arguments, if somewhat hyperbolically stated, but not good enough to persuade the War Committee, which turned down the request for a brigade on September 17. Clayton was ambivalent about the rejection. '[O]n the whole, I am not exactly sorry. I fear greatly the bad effect of any intrusion of British troops on Hejaz soil and only very grave risk could justify such a step. In this case I was inclined to think that the risk did justify it, but one is always inclined to be a little local in one's views on the spot'.[79] Despite the Committee's decision against sending a British brigade to Rabegh, four days later the War Office approved the dispatch of a flight of four planes to the port and ordered a brigade to be held in readiness, only to be sent 'as an extreme measure at the very urgent request of the Shereef'. The decision came as a great surprise, particularly because only a day earlier Robertson had submitted to the Cabinet a memo arguing strongly against such a move. Clayton attributed London's 'volte face' to papers he had privately sent to the War Office and Admiralty detailing the von Stotzingen mission, papers which likely arrived in Britain on September 19, two days before the decision was made to send the flight.[80] Clayton's speculation seems warranted, for nothing else transpired in the East or in London which would have prompted the War Office change in policy.

In the event, neither the brigade nor the flight was sent to Rabegh. On September 27, Wilson cabled from Jeddah that the Turkish threat had abated. If a four-gun artillery battery and the flight were sent, he added, the Arabs could counter any Turk move on Rabegh. Three days later, Parker reported from Rabegh that even the flight could be cancelled if the guns were sent.[81] Wilson and Parker and, by extension, Cairo and Khartoum, had under-estimated the formidable transport and supply problems the Turks faced in traversing the 170 miles of rugged country between Medina and Rabegh. And, the fall of Ta'if on September 22 had freed up Abdullah's 5,000-man Arab army which was now available to buttress the Rabegh defences.

The September reprieve was, however, only temporary. During the last three months of 1916, Turkish deployments west of Medina would again produce crises in the Hijaz ports of Rabegh and Yanbu and the debate concerning the use of British forces in Arabia continued in Khartoum, Cairo and London. However, with the immediate threat to Rabegh removed, the War Committee now took a broader view of the revolt and asked McMahon and Murray to consider whether additional troops would be required in Egypt in the event the Arab movement collapsed. McMahon charged Clayton with formulating his response. Clayton's two page memorandum reflected a concise statement of the political and strategic merits of the revolt and, at the same time, disclosed something of his skill in advocating a debatable proposition. Realizing fully that many at home objected strongly to British sponsorship of the Sherif's rising, he began by disarming the opposition with a single sentence that accepted their position: 'There is no reason to think that the collapse of the Sherif of Mecca would affect the situation in Sinai appreciably or that feeling would be roused in Egypt which would necessitate a larger garrison'. Having thus drawn in his opponents with a concession, Clayton then launched a barrage of a dozen separate reasons supporting his more fundamental point that the revolt should still receive British support:

> On the other hand, the fall of the Sherif would give the Eastern coast of the Red Sea to the Turks, thus increasing for the Navy the strain of guarding the sea route to India. It would furnish the Turks with a base in Arabia for military and political activity which might well extend to the Euphrates, Aden, Abyssinia, the Sudan and Somaliland, [and] it would endanger seriously the position of the Idrisi and [Ibn] Saud, with both of which chiefs H.M.G. have signed treaties since [the] outbreak of war. The main factor that recommended the Sherif's revolt was that whether it succeeded or failed our military commitment would be small and we should be able to counteract by diplomacy alone the evil effect in Eastern eyes upon British prestige caused by the [1914] evacuation of Sinai, the . . . [surrender at Kut] . . . and the evacuation of Gallipoli. The Sherif's revolt has shattered the solidarity of Islam, in that Moslem is fighting against Moslem. It has emphasised the failure of the Jehad, and endangered the Khalifate of the Sultan. The gravity of this blow to Turkey can be estimated by the furious protest of pro-Turk Moslem elements. The intrigues of the Committee of Union and Progress and of German Orientalists have been to a large extent counteracted. The agreement [with Hussein] carries on and completes our policy in Arabia, as exemplified in the agreements with the Hadramaut [that area of southern Arabia bordering on the Arabian Sea], Oman, Muscat, Koweit and with [Ibn] Saud. With the last named, it

gives Great Britain a band of influence running across Arabia from [the] Red
Sea to [the] Persian Gulf as a bar to the progress of hostile activity and penetration, it has rendered pro-British a large body of anti-Turk sentiment in
Turkish Arabia, Syria and Mesopotamia and it has impaired the loyalty of the
Arab divisions of the Turkish army. Its effect is continuing and even should
the Sherif only succeed in holding out until peace is declared it will be found
to have had a cumulative effect which may influence greatly the final situation.
Admittedly if we stand on the defensive in the East until peace is made we
profit directly by the Sherif not only in political and religious questions, but
if our credit and prestige (behind which is the existence of our trade and the
maintenance of foreign possessions with minute garrisons) are restored by
offensive action from the Canal we shall find our way made infinitely more
easy by the Sherif, not only in the absence of Arab assistance to the enemy, the
rottenness of the Syrian army, and the block on the Syrian railways, but in the
general support given to us by all classes of the people and the continual menace to our enemies which will be constituted thereby.[82]

Regardless whether one accepted all of Clayton's arguments, the cumulative effect
of his ideas was formidable. He had stated many of these points previously, in earlier
letters, reports and memoranda, but some were new, such as the notion of a band,
or belt, across Arabia formed by Anglo-Arab alliances of which the Hashemite
pledge formed a central strand.[83]

The points Clayton advanced for supporting the revolt did not, however, suggest that he had come round to backing the proposal to land British troops at
Rabegh. He made clear his opposition to that course in an October 12 letter to
Wingate, knowing, of course, that the Sirdar had argued strongly in favour of sending the brigade. Relying on points made by Murray's staff, Clayton observed that
it would take ten days to assemble and embark the brigade at Suez, three days to
reach Rabegh, (assuming shipping were available) and then another week to disembark, settle down and prepare their position before they were ready to engage
the Turks. So, he concluded, 'if we wait until the Turks really make a determined
attack, the brigade will either not be required at all because the Arabs have beaten
the Turks or it will be too late because the Turks have been successful'. The available options, then, were to send the brigade at once, on the chance that it might
be wanted, or to not send it at all and, instead, send Hussein the guns he had been
requesting. Clayton definitely favoured the latter course. Wilson and Parker had
both reported that with three batteries of artillery, 'the Arabs can not only hold the
Turks, but take the offensive'. He also noted that the Hijaz railway had been 'seriously damaged' and the tribes should be paid and trained to continue demolition
work on the line. Further, Murray required the brigade for his contemplated operations in Sinai, operations that would have 'a real and lasting effect on the Hejaz
situation'. No less important, Parker had reported 'the great dislike on the part of
the Arabs to the landing of Englishmen in the Hejaz'. Indeed, Hussein had only
reluctantly asked if the brigade would be available 'if urgently wanted', and if Cairo

waited until they were 'urgently wanted', they would be too late. Finally, Clayton reiterated that a British landing would be 'seized upon at once by the Pan-Islamist propagandists' in India and elsewhere.[84]

Based on these arguments, Clayton urged that the brigade be withheld, that the Sherif be supplied with the requested artillery and technical assistance and that British energies be directed to pushing the Turks in Sinai and at the adjacent port of Akaba. 'A line across from say Gaza to say East of Bir Saba [Beersheba].' he reasoned, 'with its right flank protected by the impassable country West of the Dead Sea and with a flanking force in the Akaba district will . . . (a) [c]ompletely protect Egypt, (b) [m]enace the whole of the Turkish hold on Syria and encourage every disloyal element there, [and] (c) [t]hreaten any force sent to the Hejaz with annihilation.'[85] Two days later Clayton sent the October 12 letter to Lynden-Bell, acknowledging that his views would 'not quite coincide' with the Sirdar's.[86]

Clayton was taking some personal risk in opposing Wingate on the Rabegh issue, because only a week earlier the War Committee decided that military control and supervision of all arrangements for assistance to the Sherif would be vested in Wingate, finally ending the uncertainty that had hampered management of the revolt for four months. McMahon requested reconsideration of the decision, only to receive further instruction from the Foreign Office that he concede to Wingate whatever political control of the revolt was necessary to enable the Sirdar to effectively manage the situation in the Hijaz.[87] But the really crushing blow would be administered to McMahon a week later when Grey cabled Wingate offering him the post of High Commissioner for Egypt. The Foreign Office informed McMahon of the decision in a 'decypher yourself' telegram, 'so that he had the mortification of himself slowly and laboriously, word by word, spelling out a message which must have been as disagreeable a one as is possible for a man to receive'.[88]

The dismissal of McMahon could hardly have come as a surprise to insiders in the East or in London. He had been at cross-purposes with Wingate and Murray for months. Most of those in the Residency's Chancery, including Cheetham and Mervyn Herbert, disliked and disrespected him. He had no allies in the Foreign Office – especially since Hardinge had succeeded Nicolson as Permanent Under-Secretary – and certainly none in the India or War Offices, where highly critical private letters were routinely received from the East. Clayton, however, believed that McMahon had been unfairly treated, doubtless because he knew that McMahon had taken the brunt of criticism for a controversial Arab policy devised, in large measure, by Clayton himself. Ill-suited though McMahon was for the post of High Commissioner, Clayton defended him. '[Y]ou may hear McMahon crabbed a great deal & called lazy & useless', he wrote to Wigram. 'Don't believe it. The best fellows out here don't think so'.[89]

McMahon's dismissal resolved the problems arising from the lack of British direction of the revolt, but not the dispute over strategy. Wingate continued to press for a British brigade to Rabegh; Murray and Lynden-Bell just as strongly argued against it. 'I am bound to say,' Murray wired Wingate, that 'I am and always have been opposed to the despatch of either British troops or aeroplanes to Rabegh'. He complained that he had given the Arabs twenty million rounds of small arms ammunition, and (incorrectly) they had not killed or captured 2,000 Turks. Murray appreciated that if Hussein's revolt was allowed to fail, there might be an 'outcry' in some quarters at home, but 'in view of the practical certainty that we shall be committed to a campaign in Arabia if we land troops at Rabegh, I would accept the risk of the Shereef . . . being deposed and Mecca occupied by the Turks'.[90]

In mid-November 1916, Murray, Lynden-Bell and Clayton were supplied with additional authority for their arguments against sending British troops to the Hijaz. The authority came in the form of twenty-eight year old T. E. Lawrence. Sent to Arabia by Clayton a month earlier, Lawrence submitted a report that effectively demolished Wingate's arguments.[91] Clayton's covering Note described him as 'an officer of great experience and knowledge of Arabs', and Lawrence certainly wrote with the confidence of authority. He began by observing that 'the towns in the Hejaz do not support the Sherif's movement'. Rather, Hussein's strength derived from the tribesmen who had held up the Turks' advance on Mecca for five months. Rabegh itself, he added, 'is not and never has been, defensible with Arab forces'. 'So long as the tribes hold out' in the hills east of Rabegh, a British force was unnecessary. But, 'if the tribes give way, the Turks will reach Rabegh in about four days'. That would not allow time for a British force to be collected, embarked, transported, disembarked and prepared for action. Nor did the tribesmen desire British assistance. They were well disposed towards England, but very fearful of a British landing, for '[w]e have appropriated too many Moslem countries for them to have any real trust in our disinterestedness, and they are terribly afraid of an English occupation of the Hejaz'. So, if a British force were landed, they would 'say "we are betrayed" and scatter to their tents'. The Sherif's strength lay 'only among the tribes' and if they fled upon a British landing 'there is no more "Sherif's movement"'. Lawrence also argued that the Arab objections did not extend to airplanes or to instructors in 'technical matters', such as the operation of artillery, explosives, machine guns and armoured cars. Britain, Lawrence concluded, should supply these items, especially the guns, which, in his opinion, would enable the Arabs 'to hold up the present Turkish forces as long as they require'.[92]

Of course, Wingate was angered by Lawrence's report, particularly so since it was sent by GHQ to London before the Sirdar could comment upon it. On November 6, he had described Lawrence 'as a man who has thoroughly grasped the situation' and, a week later, he admitted to being 'influenced to some extent by what Lawrence told me in regard to the feelings of Feisal's Arabs respecting the landing of any large bodies of foreign troops at Rabegh'. But, by the 23rd, with Lawrence's report now in hand, the Sirdar described him as 'a visionary' whose 'amateur soldiering has evidently given him an exaggerated idea of the soundness of his views on purely military matters'. He was equally disappointed by opposition from the Arab Bureau, which was 'being drifted about by any wind that blows'.[93]

Wingate was, in fact, isolated; no one else of importance in the East supported a British landing in Arabia. McMahon, Clayton, Hogarth, Wemyss, Murray, Lynden-Bell, Lawrence and Aziz al-Masri were all opposed. Even Hussein, though very fearful of a Turkish advance, would not make a definitive, written request for British assistance. In the face of this opposition, and now charged with military and political responsibility for the revolt, the Sirdar himself grew cautious. Soon after accepting that responsibility, he informed Murray that 'if I fail to effect any serious improvement in the Hedjaz situation, I do not think the cause for failure . . . can be fairly laid to my charge'.[94] It was Wingate who ordered the shipment of British planes to Rabegh on October 12, and then recalled them only four days later, as the ships carrying the machines steamed into Rabegh harbour. And, a month later, with the Turkish threat still pending, he conceded that 'from the political and religious standpoint, it would be desirable to delay the despatch of such troops to the last moment. They should be held in readiness at Suez'.[95]

Despite formidable opposition to a British landing from the men on the spot, the issue came repeatedly before the War Committee during the last four months of 1916. The recurring discussions were prompted in large part by significant Turk advances on Rabegh, at the end of October, and on Yanbu, in early December. These movements were enough to persuade one faction in the Committee – Grey, Curzon and, surprisingly, Chamberlain – that a British landing was essential to prevent the collapse of Hussein's rising. They were still strongly opposed by the CIGS, Robertson, who explained his views to Murray on October 16, the day before the Committee again rejected a landing of British troops: 'I had great difficulty in knocking out the Rabegh proposal. It gave me a great deal of trouble. It would undoubtedly have been strategy gone mad . . . My sole object is to win the war and we shall not do that in the Hedjaz nor in the Sudan. It makes one despair to see the short-sighted views of the Sirdar. Our military policy is perfectly clear and simple . . . The policy is offensive on the Western Front and therefore defensive everywhere else.'[96]

Robertson was exasperated by the repeated appearances of the Rabegh question before the War Committee. It was 'a perfect nuisance' for him and he admitted to being 'as stubborn as a donkey' in opposing a British landing in Arabia.[97] In early November the CIGS was directed by the War Committee to attend a Foreign Office meeting where Curzon, Chamberlain and Grey agreed that it was 'of the highest importance to deny Rabegh to the enemy' and asked Robertson to again report to the Committee on the feasibility of a landing. But, by this time, Robertson had secured the opinions of the British commander in Mesopotamia, the Viceroy and Murray, who all sent telegrams stating their opposition to a landing. The Government of India flatly disagreed with Chamberlain, the Secretary of State for India. A British landing, argued the Viceroy, would 'certainly cause general Muslim resentment in India [and] . . . [w]e believe [the] collapse of the Sherif would be less prejudicial to us in India than military intervention in the Hedjaz'. At the invitation of Robertson, Murray also reported that if he were required to detach a brigade from the EEF and send it to Rabegh, he very much doubted his ability to move on El Arish, as previously ordered.[98]

In late November, the DMO, General Maurice, reported that 'the Sherif and his scallywag Arabs take up more time than most of the other theatres of war'.[99] Hopes for a definitive resolution were raised on December 7, 1916, when Lloyd George replaced Asquith as Prime Minister, but as Maurice wrote of the new Cabinet, '[t]heir first action was to return to the charge over Rabegh'.[100] Not until January 8, 1917, did the new War Cabinet decide that British troops would not be sent to Arabia, unless Hussein requested them in writing and issued a proclamation in which he took responsibility for the presence of Christian troops in the Hijaz. By this time, though, the Turkish threat had abated. Hussein never made the request and the Rabegh crisis, at long last, subsided. Robertson, Murray and Clayton had prevailed.

The Turkish withdrawal to Medina meant that, at least for the present, the revolt had survived. There was little cause for optimism though. With more than a hint of criticism, Clayton wrote to Wigram in late November: 'Lack of decision, vagueness and inconsistency, personal jealousy, inability to formulate a definite policy; these are all to be found with the Sherif and his sons, but they are only what one has to expect and after all perhaps they are also to be found elsewhere.'[101] Clayton was doubtless suggesting that the same description could have been applied, and with equal force, to British management of the revolt during its first four months.

On a personal level, Clayton had arrived at a low point as 1916 drew to a close. In late December Wingate was on his way to Cairo to take over for McMahon and Clayton was aware that his own time in the Egyptian capital might very well be coming to an end. The Rabegh crisis had been only the latest and most obvious of several disagreements between the Sirdar and his Sudan Agent. Their differences over the strategic direction of the Arab movement ran deep and Wingate could also point to a substantial and more general list of complaints he had with Clayton's work during the last two years. Clayton had tried, with diminishing success, to serve three masters and the inevitable result was that he had been caught in the cross-fire between Cairo, Khartoum and Ismailia. Two years of frustration, exhaustion, illness and, ultimately, dismissal were the result. The Residency's Oriental Secretary, Ronald Storrs, who knew the British community in Cairo as well as anyone, and had worked closely with Clayton in the effort to bring the Arab movement to reality, described his colleague in a letter of late November. Clayton's 'shares', he wrote, have 'been forced down to almost zero'.[102] It was no exaggeration.

16

Between Upper and the Nether Millstone: The End of Intrusive, 1916

The solitary cyclist pedalling across Cairo's Bulaq Bridge on a warm morning in April 1916 excited no comment from nearby pedestrians and street vendors. Even though he wore the uniform of a British general and was one of the half-dozen most influential men in Egypt, perhaps in the Middle East, Gilbert Clayton was a familiar sight. He had made the daily two and a half mile commute from Gezira – the island squeezed into the Nile where the river pushed through the west side of Cairo – for a year now. Nearly every morning, shortly after eight, the general proceeded down the eastern edge of Gezira, past the fashionable homes of Cairo's European diplomatic community, before turning east on to the bridge, just north of the Gezira Palace Hotel.

Once across, he continued along the Shari' Bulaq, the broad avenue that separated Cairo's Taufiqiya district on the north from the Ismailia district just to the south. Shortly before the Shari' Bulaq terminated at the Ezbekiya Gardens, he turned south into the Shari' Imad el Din, coming to a halt in front of the old headquarters building of the British Army of Occupation, a few yards north of the roundabout known as the Midan Suares. In December 1915, Clayton's commute had been extended by a few minutes as General Maxwell expanded his headquarters and moved them into the city's famous Savoy Hotel, located 600 yards southwest of the Midan Suares. Here too, in the spring of 1916, the Arab Bureau would occupy three rooms in the Military Intelligence offices.

In April 1915, with the help of a loan from his Uncle Charlie of Ventnor, Isle of Wight, Clayton had rented a small house on the river near the northern tip of Gezira, next to the Dutch Consul Van Lenneps, for 'as moderate a rent as possible in this place where they are so exorbitant'. Enid had arrived in Cairo in November 1914, and Clayton was so busy during the following spring that 'the whole burden of the move' to Gezira had fallen on her; she 'had to do everything', he informed Wingate. Although small, the Claytons' new home was 'in an open, cool situation', and even when the *khamsin* – the hot, dry wind from the south – blew in every April and May, Bertie and Enid experienced some relief, as the wind picked up just a little coolness from the river. The daily bicycle ride to his office was a 'longish' one, he said, but at least 'that ensures one getting some exercise'.[1]

Clayton's daily bike ride to work was, in fact, the only exercise he could get. His new home was located a little more than a mile north of the 150-acre Gezira Sporting Club, a nearly all-British enclave that featured tennis and squash courts, hockey, football and cricket pitches, race and steeplechase courses, an eighteen-hole golf course and four polo grounds. But Clayton had no time for any of these activities. Nor did he have time to stop by that most popular of all British watering-holes in Cairo, the Turf Club. He was overwhelmed by work, and had been since the start of the Middle Eastern war. As early as November 1914, well before he took on his many duties additional to those of the Sudan Agent and Director of Intelligence, he admitted to Wingate that he was feeling 'fagged and dispirited'. Three months later, in the aftermath of the Turkish attack on the Canal, he noted that he had his 'nose down to it pretty hard', working 'till about midnight', every day. Intrusive, he added, had become a '"sink" into which everyone casts the questions which they don't know how to deal with'. In April 1915, his work increased again as Aubrey Herbert and George Lloyd left Intrusive for the Dardanelles and Leonard Woolley went to Port Said to supervise the agent drops into Syria and Palestine. And, when Colonel E. S. Herbert, Wingate's Military Secretary and liaison with the Egyptian Sultan, also decamped for Gallipoli, the Sirdar appointed Clayton to replace him, knowing full well this would 'throw a good deal of extra work on you'.[2]

In August 1915, in the wake of the second attempt on the Sultan's life, and at the Sultan's request, Wingate was able to secure the return of Herbert from the Dardanelles. But Clayton was afforded only a brief respite, for in February 1916, the Sirdar again asked Clayton to meet with Hussein Kamil concerning the 'purely political' aspects of the Darfur campaign. Soon Clayton was meeting regularly with the Sultan – every week or ten days, he reported – and on matters unrelated to Darfur. The Sultan, Clatyon said, 'likes a talk with an Englishman'. McMahon's talks with His Highness were 'few and very far between' and, it was reported, he 'mistrusted and hated' Storrs, who often turned up unannounced at the Sultan's Abdin Palace. So, it fell to Clayton to be the Sultan's 'Englishman' and he regularly discussed with Hussein Kamil affairs in the Western Desert, Darfur and later, in 1916, the Hijaz.[3] In August 1915, Clayton described his workload to Wingate: 'If I make an occasional slip I hope you will condone it, as really sometimes I have as much as I can get through. My normal hours are 8.30–2 p.m., 3.30–8 p.m. and generally a couple hours or more after dinner, and a ceaseless flow of questions of all sorts and visitors have to be dealt with – most of them at once. I haven't had a proper day off since 19 Aug last [1914] and sometimes one gets very tired.'[4] Often Enid would discover Bertie the next morning, slumped in his chair and asleep, papers on his lap and strewn about him on the floor.

Some of Clayton's overwork, it must be said, was of his own making. True, Wingate had made him Sudan Agent and Director of Egyptian Army Intelligence, as well as his intermediary with McMahon and the Sultan. And McMahon and Murray had charged him with administering martial law in Egypt and appointed him liaison between GHQ and the Residency. But Clayton himself had volunteered to take over all Intelligence work for the Force in Egypt and to take the lead in Anglo-Sanusi and Anglo-Arab relations, and it was he who took responsibility for the Army's relations with the European Consuls in Egypt when Murray's headquarters moved from Cairo to Ismailia in January 1916. He explained his attitude in a letter to the Sirdar: '[A]ll one can do – and all any true Englishman can do in these times of terrible crisis – is to do one's very best and take on any job which comes one's way – putting aside every personal consideration & with the sole object of furthering our cause'.[5]

Still his work continued and increased. Still he lost men – Newcombe to the Dardanelles, and later to the Western Front, in September 1915, and then Parker, in October, to the War Office to work on the Arab question with his uncle, Lord Kitchener. 'First Newcombe and now Parker and I am left only with civilians', he complained to Wingate.[6] A week later, shortly after his interviews with Faruqi and McMahon's fateful pledge to Hussein was drafted, he was suffering 'from a great deal more work' and worrying about his difficulty in finding 'any time to think'. Clayton asked Maxwell for help, but the GOC's appeal to the War Office 'was not very successful [as] . . . evidently they are very short of officers of experience'.[7] Maxwell then approached Wingate, noting that Clayton 'very nearly broke down with overwork a few days ago' and would therefore 'have to shed Sudan affairs'.[8] But Wingate thought that Maxwell should insist on Clayton having more help, 'or, better still', relieve him 'of the purely Military Intelligence work', and would not agree that Clayton should relinquish his Sudan duties. So, Clayton instead proposed a reorganization of the Sudan Agency that would remove much of the detail work from his shoulders and, to this, the Sirdar agreed.[9]

As a result of Clayton's reorganization, much of the routine work that came to the Agency fell to A. P. Bolland, a ten year veteran of the Sudan service who worked as Commercial Secretary in Cairo. In December 1915, Clayton obtained another man to help Bolland and had a 'private telephone' installed at GHQ that connected him with the Sudan Agency.[10] But, by March 1916, Bolland was himself overworked and near to breakdown. As for Clayton, he was averaging '12 to 14 hours actually hard at it in the office, which is especially trying', he reported, 'as warmer weather is approaching'.[11] His work increased again in the spring of 1916. Just as McMahon and Murray agreed that Clayton should take on the work of administering martial law, the Arab Bureau 'suddenly materialized' in Cairo and Clayton had to attend to its staffing, organization and assignments. With some understatement, he described the additional work given him by Murray at the same time: 'I have rather an increase of work just now as Sir A. Murray has decided to remain at Ismailia and has appointed me his staff officer for all matters concerning the civil government of the country and of martial law and for purposes of liaison between himself and the High Commissioner'. Murray's decision to remain at Ismailia was particularly irksome to Clayton because it required him to travel every week to the Canal by train – two hours each way – to meet with the commander and, more importantly, to act as Murray's representative in the capital. 'As I am the only person left here who is known personally', he explained to Wingate, 'I am being bombarded with all the letters, petitions, etc. which formerly went to the G.O.C. and am pretty well flooded out'.[12]

On top of all this, Clayton's Intelligence duties had increased in December 1915, when Maxwell established his new GHQ in the Savoy and Clayton was made GSO1. In addition to being 'two officers short' at GHQ, he had to send another of his men to Mersa Matruh to take over Intelligence work for the Western Frontier Force, then engaged with the Sanusi. And, as GSO1, he was required to spend one night every week at headquarters, 'as telegrams and messages come in at all times and sometimes have to be dealt with at once'.[13] A few months later, Wingate advanced a proposal that would have further increased Clayton's already stupendous workload. With the defeat of the Sanusi, the Sirdar envisioned the creation of a new administrative district – a 'Western Governorate' – to be placed under Clayton's Egyptian Army Intelligence in Cairo. That, of course, would have extended Wingate's authority to the region. Clayton must have been dismayed by the suggestion, but confined his opposition to practical problems he saw with the idea. An increase of staff would be necessary, he responded, 'and I think one would have to start a separate section as, of course, it entails dealing with administrative matters which are not really part of the work of an Intelligence Department'.[14] He likely breathed a great sigh of relief when Wingate did not pursue the matter.

The Sirdar was certainly aware of Clayton's crushing workload. As early as January 1915, he was referring to the 'too heavy burden thrown upon' him, and Wingate's 1915 letters to his Sudan Agent contain many expressions of sympathy. 'I'm afraid you have been having a very hard and busy time ever since the war began', he wrote in April, 'and I hope you will not over-work'. Again, in September, he acknowledged that Clayton's numerous responsibilities in Cairo, though critically important, were bound to lead to a dangerous situation: 'I hear that your advice and help is sought on all sides & altho there is some personal satisfaction in this, it leads to greatly increased work & it is most important that you should run no risk of breakdown. I know how absolutely indispensable you have made yourself to both the G.O.C. & H.C. I also know how appreciative they are of all you have done – as well they might be.'[15]

Although Wingate was aware of Clayton's overwork, and offered sympathy, he did not offer help. Seven times, between February 1915 and May 1916, Wingate refused Clayton's requests to send someone from the Sudan to relieve him of at least part of his burden of work.[16] It was not that the Sirdar disbelieved Clayton's need for assistance; to the contrary, Lee Stack, on a visit to Cairo in the spring of 1916 'confirmed' to Wingate the Sirdar's 'impressions' that Clayton was 'absolutely overworked and have far more on your hands than you can well get through'.[17] In some measure, Wingate's refusals to help relieve Clayton of work sprang from his belief that the Sudan Government and the Egyptian Army units stationed there were dangerously under-staffed and that he could not afford to send another man out of the country. In May 1915, the Sirdar claimed he had allowed forty British officers to leave the Sudan for Gallipoli and, when added to those lent for various purposes in Egypt and France, the Egyptian Army was 'not far off 100 under establishment'. By January 1916, Wingate recorded that he had lost 86 soldiers and 31 civilians from the Sudan.[18] Yet, the Sirdar was able to find sufficient men to carry through the spring 1916 campaign in Darfur. Perhaps he felt that since Clayton's great load of additional work was not taken on at his request, and did not concern the Sudan, it was not his responsibility to relieve him of that burden.

Regardless whether Wingate was justified in his refusals of assistance, Clayton suffered badly from the strain of overwork. Just as the Turks attacked the Canal in early February 1915, he came down with an 'influenza cold' and was still struggling with it six weeks later.[19] On April 26, after completing their move to Gezira, Enid left for England for the summer to be with the children – Patience, not yet two, and Jane, born on September 30, 1914. By August, Clayton was again weakened by a 'nasty chill and fever' and was sorely missing Enid, and not just her companionship. 'I am beginning to want her to look after me', he wrote, 'as one gets into bad habits of missing meals, etc. when one is busy & has no one to keep one in order'.[20]

Clayton's exhaustion, lack of proper diet, and perhaps the lingering effect of the influenza contracted earlier, soon caught up with him. At the beginning of September 1915, he collapsed. A Sudan colleague visiting Cairo found him in bed looking 'thoroughly run down'. He was moved to the Anglo-American hospital on Gezira where doctors diagnosed bronchitis and forbade any further work. But Clayton still had Cornwallis and Parker come to the hospital so that he could 'settle any conundrums which they cannot dispose of'. Wingate attributed Clayton's illness to his 'high sense of duty' which resulted in overwork: '[I]n your anxiety to do all you possibly could for your various "Masters" you have brought about your unfortunate collapse'. A month later Clayton was still suffering from 'bronchial trouble' and decided to work at home in the afternoons and evenings to avoid the damp night air and the 'large number of visitors' who descended on his office every day. His spirits were buoyed by the return of Enid, along with Patience and Jane, in early October and he was delighted that he would be 'properly looked after now'. Yet, three weeks later, Stack reported that Clayton was continuing to suffer from bronchitis, though 'not sufficient to deter him from doing a pretty long day's work'. The doctors advised a prolonged stay in Europe, but Clayton declined. October 1915, it will be recalled, was the very month in which Cairo concluded that the Arab question had reached a crisis point and while Clayton was, according to Stack, 'having a very heavy time of it', he would not consider leaving Egypt.[21] In mid-November, just as Clayton was finally shaking off his bronchitis, he again had to go on the 'sick list', and was again ordered to bed, this time with a 'very sharp attack of fever'. Wingate was sympathetic. '[T]here is no blinking the fact that you must be suffering badly from over-work. I would give anything to be able to help you but, as you know, I am down to bed-rock'.[22] Clayton's bronchitis would reappear in 1916, and 'fevers' would recur for the remainder of his life.

The effects of Clayton's exhaustion and resulting illnesses were compounded by deteriorating relations with Wingate. The first two years of the war were decidedly unhappy ones for the Sirdar. As described earlier, neither Cheetham nor McMahon had sought his advice concerning Arab affairs and McMahon (or perhaps Clayton) declined to adopt his suggestions for the correspondence with Hussein. Nor had he been consulted concerning Egypt's position on the outbreak of war. The November 1914 debate with London over the issue of the country's status – whether it should be annexed or made a protectorate – was handled by the Cairo 'triumvirate' of Cheetham, Graham and Cecil, none of whom could be described as friends of the Sirdar. McMahon ignored most of his letters and yet Wingate was continually being asked by the commanders in Egypt to supply men and, more so, transport camels, from the Sudan to the fighting fronts. And, he was exasperated when informed by London that the Sudan's annual requirements for arms and ammunition could not be met. '[I]t might almost be imagined', he wrote, 'that the Sudan was a foreign country altogether and had little or nothing to do with the British Empire'. Wingate was even criticized by Sir Ian Hamilton, the commander at Gallipoli, who accused the Sirdar of sending his Sudan men to the Dardanelles for a few weeks at a time 'so that they may afterwards wear cheaply earned medals'. By early 1916, Wingate was near the end of his rope. '[A]t times my patience is strained to the utmost . . . times without number I have had to put my pride into my pocket & take a back seat & to make my officers do the same . . . I cannot leave the Sudan . . . and I have therefore to look to you [Clayton] & Herbert in the first instance to do what you can to prevent the strain reaching [the] breaking point it has now approached 2 or 3 times'.[23]

Wingate was right to refer to his decision not to leave the Sudan. This was undoubtedly one of the reasons he had been marginalized by Cairo and perhaps by London. Despite numerous requests from Clayton, McMahon, even Murray, the Sirdar would not come to Egypt. Wingate may have been justified in his refusal to leave the Sudan, but others who were in a position to know did not think so. Lee Stack, who had served in the Sudan since 1899, who had worked as Civil Secretary – the number two man in the Sudan Government – since 1914, and who would succeed Wingate as Sirdar and Governor-General in January 1917, wrote to Clayton that he would be visiting Cairo in September 1917, 'as I have not the same notion that my absence from the Sudan for a short period will necessarily mean a general "bust up"'.[24] Wingate had known Maxwell for years, but had never met McMahon or Murray and the lack of personal contact likely affected his relations with both. The Sirdar would never complain of his problems directly to the High Commissioner or to the GOC, so it fell to Clayton to be the unfortunate recipient of Wingate's unhappiness. And that unhappiness was often manifested in the form of complaints directed at Clayton and his work.

Some of Wingate's complaints were minor, even petty, as when he complained of mistakes appearing in Clayton's telegrams, or of his failure to advise the Sirdar when the Viceroy Hardinge would be passing through Egypt on his way home, or of his failure to keep the Egyptian War Minister current on affairs in Darfur. Others were more serious. In November 1914, Wingate arranged for several Sudanese nota-bles to telegraph statements of their loyalty to Britain on the outbreak of war, and asked Clayton to obtain a formal government acknowledgment of the telegrams. Instead, Cheetham wired that Wingate could give any public acknowledgment he wished on behalf of the government. At the same time, Clayton provided copies of the Sudanese telegrams to *The Times* correspondent in Cairo, instead of ensuring that they were publicized by the Foreign Office in London. Wingate accused Clayton of misleading Cheetham into an 'appalling omission', and insisted that the Foreign Office issue a public recognition of Sudanese loyalty. 'In the end', Clayton responded, 'I had to draft a telegram' for Cheetham to send home and that produced the expected Foreign Office acknowledgment. The Sirdar's complaints were directed not only to Clayton, but also to Kitchener, the Secretary of State for War: 'Poor little C's efforts to please everyone at the expense of his actual chief (myself) is I fear at the bottom of most of the trouble in Cairo – I am very much disappointed with him, but must make the best of things.'[25]

Again, in the spring of 1916, Wingate was upset by Clayton's attempts to mollify the French concerning the Sirdar's planned assault on Darfur. In early April, it will be recalled, Clayton assured the French Minister in Cairo that an immediate advance on El Fasher was not then contemplated. Wingate was annoyed, doubtless because he did then plan an attack on 'Ali Dinar's capital. Clayton replied that the only statement he had made to the French was that contained in Wingate's own telegram, 'which I gave <u>verbatim</u>'. That the French 'put a very liberal interpretation on your telegram was not my fault', he added, and asked that the Sirdar withdraw his 'very kindly worded reproof'.[26] Clayton's disagreements with Wingate over the strategy that should be pursued for the Arab revolt have already been described. That Clayton, his own subordinate, should have disagreed with the Sirdar concerning the revolt – particularly over the Rabegh question that dominated discussion during the first six months of the rising – must have been particularly annoying to Wingate.

The Sirdar's many complaints may also have stemmed from his uneasiness with Clayton's increasing influence and independence in Cairo, an influence that seemed to grow as Wingate's diminished. That his Sudan Agent had developed a 'personal individuality', that his advice was sought 'on all sides', and his 'personal views' were 'often asked by the G.O.C. and the High Commissioner on various subjects' was perhaps not what Wingate wished to hear from his subordinate. He stressed that Clayton's views should not diverge from his own. And, above all, the Sirdar urged Clayton to be very careful always 'to appreciate the Sudan Government point of view' and, 'in communicating Sudan affairs to [the] Agency to differentiate between purely Intelligence matters and administrative affairs'.[27] This was certainly a fair admonition and Clayton continually reassured his chief: 'I am afraid that you think that I am inclined to lose sight of the interests of the Sudan on account of the various other things which have been thrown at me. I can assure you that this is not the case.' In reality, the Sudan was rarely in the spotlight during the war years, save for the 1916 subjugation of Darfur, and both Cheetham, and later McMahon, exhibited a 'lack of interest in and sympathy for the Sudan aspect of affairs'.[28]

Wingate's attitude towards the Cairo Residency was, in fact, ambivalent. On the one hand, he was offended that neither Cheetham nor McMahon solicited his views; on the other, he welcomed their indifference to the Sudan. He had chafed under the authority of Cromer, Gorst and Kitchener over Sudan affairs and was therefore content to instruct Clayton 'to keep the Sudan in the background' when dealing with the Residency. Clayton assured him he was 'quite "au fait" with the policy you wished followed . . . Leave well alone, but work when possible towards a still greater freedom from a financial point of view . . . I propose not to raise unnecessary questions, but if I am asked my views, I think I know what your wishes would be on most subjects & of course I shall refer to you by wire'.[29] Yet, Clayton repeatedly had to assure the Sirdar that he did not report to the High Commissioner without specific instructions from Khartoum. Again, in May 1915, he emphasized to Wingate that 'I do not discuss Sudan affairs with people here, especially with Graham and Cecil who have nothing to do with the Sudan . . . As regards the High Commissioner & the Residency, I have made it a practice . . . not to tell them anything but mere general news unless I get instructions from you to do so'. McMahon, he later added, has 'always kept the direction of the Sudan entirely in your hands without even asking me any questions about it'.[30]

Still, Wingate continued to worry and to admonish Clayton that he should attend to his Sudan work. And, most important, 'whatever military responsibilities you may have, you should never allow the idea to get about that you are in any way severing your connection with the Sudan'.[31] In 1916, the Sirdar's complaints arrived in Cairo with even greater frequency, as he accused his Agent of inadequately supervising Sudan work, of allowing it to get into 'inexperienced hands'. By this time, Wingate's constant carping was beginning to wear thin on Clayton:

> The Sudan work is done entirely by Bolland and myself so that when you say that you feel sure that the work has been getting into "inexperienced" hands, I am afraid that you should have written "incompetent" for "inexperienced", as neither of us can plead inexperience. What we can plead with some justice, though, is shorthandedness . . . and in addition I have very serious & responsible duties to carry out elsewhere. When I tell you that for well over a year I have been working ten or eleven hours a day in the office, and up to 1 and 2 in the morning after dinner at least four days a week, without one single day, or even afternoon off, it will show you that I can do no more. Moreover, the work is <u>really hard</u> all the time & a continual slave & rush to get through. In all my work, except the Sudan work, I have been able to delegate very largely, but the Sudan work I have kept under my close supervision.[32]

Three months later, he again felt compelled to defend himself against the Sirdar's unremitting complaints: 'As regards your general criticism that I do not sufficiently look after the interests of the Sudan, I can only repeat what I have said before that I have done my best and, though I may have failed in some respects, I venture to think that . . . I have done more than I could have had I been only Sudan Agent & so outside things more . . . [I]n spite of all my other duties I have carried on the work with no one to help me except Bolland most of the time.'[33]

Despite his exhaustion, frequent illnesses and deteriorating relations with Wingate, the story of Clayton's first two years of war was not a tale of unmitigated misery. Enid and the children were with him for most of the war and he was delighted that Enid was expecting the couple's third child, due in late September 1916. He also enjoyed a reunion with his brothers, Iltyd and Jack, whom he had not seen since 1910, and who visited him in early 1916 in Cairo. Iltyd, like Bertie, had started his career in the Artillery, and had been posted to Aden, Karachi and, briefly, to Hong Kong. The outbreak of war in 1914, found him in the quiet backwater of Mauritius. But he longed to see action and tried to 'pull strings' with Bertie and Walter Hunter Blair to secure reassignment to a fighting front. In September 1915, he at last received orders to proceed with his battery to the Canal and, after a brief stint there, moved on to Minya and then Asyut in Upper Egypt and, eventually, to the Kharga Oasis, from where his unit kept a close eye on the movements of the Sanusiyya. In May 1916, Bertie was able to secure his appointment to Intrusive, where he handled Western Desert Intelligence. Iltyd lived with Bertie and Enid in Gezira and, while working at the Savoy, met the 'remarkable staff' Bertie had assembled for the Arab Bureau, including Hogarth, Cornwallis, Philip and Robert Graves and Lawrence, with whom he shared an office for a time. A quarter of a century later, now, like his elder brother, a brigadier-general, Iltyd would return to Cairo where he again worked in the Intelligence, as Director of the Military Intelligence Centre. One day, in 1941, he came across a batch of papers captured from the Italians – now enemies of the Allies – and was surprised to find among them a 'Western Desert Intelligence Summary' written in English. Turning a page, he was astonished to see that the Summary bore a date of 1916, and must have been written by himself. In his memoirs, Iltyd noted that in 1916 'the Italians were our allies and I presume that this copy had been passed to them in the ordinary course of liaison, put away in the Italian War Office archives, and when the 2nd world war broke out and Italy came in against us, was dug out and sent over with other Intelligence material to the Italian forces in the field'. In 1916, though, Iltyd still longed for a fighting unit and, after just three months in Cairo, received orders in early September to join a battery at Salonica.[34]

Like Iltyd, Bertie's youngest brother Jack had also experienced a peripatetic lifestyle during the pre-war years. But Jack had joined the Royal Navy, and when he had last seen Bertie in 1910, was on his way to the China Station. By late 1915, he was serving as navigator on H.M.S. *Cornwallis*, as it covered the evacuation of Entente troops from Gallipoli. Jack had seen plenty of action. He was badly burned when the cruiser H.M.S. *Amphion* hit a mine and sank in the North Sea on August 6, 1914, just hours after the outbreak of war. Later, on January 9, 1917, the *Cornwallis* was torpedoed by the German submarine *U-32*, and went down in the Eastern Mediterranean, although this time Jack survived without injury. Jack would later rise to rear-admiral and serve as Director of Navigation at the Admiralty, coming out of retirement during the Second World War to head the Admiralty's Operational Intelligence Centre.[35]

While Clayton's reunion with his brothers was one of the few bright spots in an otherwise gloomy period, his difficulties were also leavened by official recognition of his efforts. Maxwell had secured his promotion to temporary lieutenant-colonel and Director of Intelligence in the autumn of 1914, and later his appointment as GSO1, and Kitchener had placed him on the War Office list for the CMG in the following June. But Wingate was responsible for his Egyptian Army promotions to *miralai* (colonel, January 1915) and later, in April 1916, to *lewa* (brigadier or major general). The promotion to the temporary rank of *lewa* appears to have been prompted by the announcement of Clayton's promotion to local brigadier-general a week earlier. Murray also twice mentioned Clayton in 1916 despatches, and in June of that year, he was promoted to brevet-major in the Reserve of Officers. The French even honoured him with a decoration, the *Officier de la Légion d'Honneur*, in April 1916.[36] Clayton was also held in high regard by the civil authorities in Egypt. When Ronald Graham was recalled to London in October 1916, to look after Egyptian affairs at the Foreign Office, he recommended that Clayton succeed him as Adviser to the Egyptian Ministry of the Interior. Clayton would come to occupy that position three years later and would have accepted it in 1916, had he been chosen, 'as the rise in pay & position . . . would have been impossible to refuse', but the position went to Lord Edward Cecil's nominee.[37] Clayton was pleased that his efforts had been officially recognized, but he appears never to have sought either promotion or honours. And, on at least one occasion, he turned down promotion. In May 1915, when Wingate first asked him to act as his liaison with the Sultan, the Sirdar also offered Clayton the temporary rank of *lewa*, but he declined: 'I can carry on all right with the Sultan without the temporary rank you so kindly offered me, and I do not anticipate any trouble.'[38]

Clayton also got on well with two of his three chiefs. McMahon was slow to warm to him – as indeed he was slow to warm to anyone – but by mid-1915, he had come to rely heavily, perhaps exclusively, on Clayton's advice concerning Anglo-Sanusi and Anglo-Arab relations. McMahon left Egypt in December 1916 with high praise for Clayton who, he reported to the Foreign Office, 'played a very prominent part in all matters connected with the Arab movement, and the institution and superintendence of the Arab Bureau. I cannot speak too highly of his great ability and energy. His talent for organisation and quick perception combined with the thoroughness of his work, have rendered him of very special assistance to me'. This description warrants comparison with Wingate's own despatch to the War Office in which he noted Clayton's 'valuable' work for the GOC and the discharge of his Sudan work in an 'entirely efficient manner'.[39]

Clayton also got on well with Maxwell and, after the general left Cairo in the spring of 1916, the two corresponded. But Maxwell's successor as GOC, Sir Archibald Murray, was a general of a different stripe. He was neither liked nor respected in Egypt. Nearly fifty-six when he succeeded Maxwell in March 1916, Murray had served in the Intelligence during the Boer War and later as chief of staff to the commander there. When the European war broke out in August 1914, he crossed to France as chief of staff under Sir John French. But, in August 1914, during the retreat from Mons, Murray broke down, appearing to suffer from a series of fainting fits. Described as 'petulant by nature' and difficult to work with, Murray was disliked by his subordinates in France. One brigadier found him 'incompetent, cantankerous, timid & quite useless'. He went on the sick list in January 1915, and, before he could return, French secured his resignation.[40] Despite Murray's poor showing on the Western Front, he was made Deputy Chief of the Imperial General Staff and then, in September 1915, CIGS, serving three months in the post until succeeded by Robertson in December.

Once in Egypt, Murray was soon at odds with Maxwell over the division of military responsibility in the country, a dispute in which Murray prevailed in March 1916, with his appointment as commander of the newly-formed EEF. As described, he promptly moved his headquarters to Ismailia on the Canal, at least in part, to escape the social and political duties accompanying his command, duties in which the affable Maxwell had excelled. General Guy Dawnay, who served under Murray, found him difficult, unclear in his orders, and a man who 'keeps himself very much to himself' and was seldom seen.[41] Ronald Graham provided a civilian perspective: 'M is not easy to get on with . . . One cannot pretend that he is popular with any section of the civilian or military and his last ukase stating that it is not "congruous" for officers to attend races, play cricket or polo or dance has raised a storm, which is none the less violent for being suppressed'.[42] Opinions of Murray's military capacity were similarly negative. One officer observed that he never had the confidence of his men. And A. P. Wavell, then a lieutenant-colonel, but later commander of British forces in North Africa during the Second World War who would rise to the rank of Field Marshal, concluded that Murray's talents were limited to organizational matters: 'I had no great opinion of him as a General . . . though he deserves full credit for his organisation of the advance across Sinai . . . It was his pernickety way of wasting time over trifles that annoyed many people, and his order about people wearing breeches and boots in an office during the hot weather is a typical example.'[43]

Murray's chief of staff, Major-General Arthur Lynden-Bell had also served in South Africa and, later, in the War Office's Intelligence Department. And, like Murray, he served on the general staff in France in 1914–1915. Lynden-Bell, or 'Belinda', as he was referred to – apparently without the slightest trace of affection – was said to have had everyone's confidence and respect when he arrived in Egypt, but not a single word of regret was heard when he left in 1917. Perhaps the British community in Egypt sensed something of the mean-spiritedness in him that is so evident in his war-time letters to the DMO, General Frederick Maurice. Yet, Lynden-Bell seems to have had such influence with his chief, Murray, that one insider concluded that Belinda and the head of Intelligence at Ismailia, Major Godfrey Holdich, were 'the powers behind the throne at G.H.Q.'.[44]

Clayton experienced problems with Murray and his staff from the outset. He was naturally associated with his chief, Maxwell, and Murray and Maxwell were at loggerheads from January to March 1916, during that period of unworkable dual control in Egypt when each maneuvered for the top command. Maxwell and Clayton were career Egyptian Army officers, 'bow and arrow men', as Lynden-Bell contemptuously described them, and were held in low esteem by the Ismailia staff. Murray shared the sentiment: 'One of my difficulties out here,' he reported to the CIGS, 'is that I have little or no faith in the judgment on a military question of any officer who has spent the best part of his life in this country. Men like Wilson and Parker are good Arabic scholars, but their recommendations as to military action are often futile and impossible of execution'.[45] As described earlier, Lynden-Bell was also dismissive of the product of Clayton's Intelligence Department, regarding it as so much 'harem gossip' (see Chapter 9).

Clayton also had the misfortune of being appointed liaison between GHQ and the Residency shortly after Murray took over sole command in Egypt in March 1916. McMahon did not get on well with the military to begin with. Even while Maxwell was still in charge in Cairo, Wingate's Military Secretary, E. S. Herbert reported that there was 'no love lost between the Residency & the Savoy Hotel; scarcely an "armed neutrality"'.[46] If McMahon could not get on with the genial Maxwell, the likelihood of good relations with Murray was much less. Predictably, they were soon at odds and their disagreements increased, in number, frequency and severity, after the start of the Arab revolt in June. Murray's angry opposition to the revolt, described above, was most apparent at the conference held at Ismailia in September. Shortly after the conference, Mervyn Herbert at the Residency saw that 'a really bad situation' had developed between McMahon and Murray. Even Wingate, in distant Khartoum, became convinced that there was 'considerable friction' between the two, and attributed the problem to Murray's fear of another enquiry, like those following the Dardanelles and Mesopotamian failures, should he become involved in the revolt that McMahon had encouraged.[47] And, of course, Clayton's strong advocacy of the Anglo-Hashemite alliance and the revolt was no secret to anyone at Ismailia.

Clayton was well aware that his own position with Murray, and more so his staff, was being compromised by his association with McMahon and his support of the revolt. He also believed – incorrectly – that Murray was unhappy with his administration of martial law in Egypt. In fact, both Murray and Lynden-Bell thought Clayton was doing well in the job, and, as described, Murray was in full agreement with the June 1, 1916 round-up of undesirables in Egypt.[48] The real problem for Clayton in his relations with GHQ lay not his administration of martial law or even his sponsorship of the Arab revolt, but in his supervision of the Arab Bureau. Even before Arbur received formal Cabinet approval in early 1916, Clayton began staffing the new bureau. Since he was also Director of Intelligence, Clayton naturally looked to his department for support and most of the men performing Bureau assignments in the spring of 1916 – Graves, Lloyd, Herbert, Parker, Deedes and Lawrence – were formally members of the Intelligence. Before the revolt began in June, this arrangement was not questioned; it was, rather, encouraged. Hogarth, Arbur's director, noted that three rooms had been assigned to the new organization in GHQ's Intelligence section at the Savoy, that Arbur was 'an integral part' of that section, and that 'the Bureau will do its best service by remaining in its present close connection with the Military Intelligence'.[49]

But the 'pernickety' Murray was not likely to sustain this un-military arrangement and Hogarth was soon singing a different tune: 'The anomaly of the Bureau's situation in a Military Intelligence Section, while deriving its sanction from the

Foreign Office and the High Commissioner, and directed by a naval officer [Hogarth], not formally appointed to the directorship by anyone, has evoked constant question of late from the military authorities in Egypt.'[50] It will be recalled that, in June, Murray's offer to assume supervision of the revolt had been turned down by Robertson. Yet, Clayton's 'Cairo branch' of Murray's Intelligence now appeared to be running the show in the Hijaz, or at least providing logistical support for the revolt, a situation that Ismailia Intelligence found unacceptable:

> Great confusion arises over the Sherif of Mecca's rebellion. It is in no way under Egypforce [EEF] – yet demands for material are made on us by High Commissioner & Sirdar independently. It is complicated by fact that Arab Bureau is under High Commissioner and that Clayton is Sudan Agent . . . and is further liaison between Egypforce & Govt of Egypt and therefore under us. The Arab Bureau works in same office as Clayton in his dual regime at Cairo and it is difficult therefore for Egypforce to know where it stands.[51]

This Intelligence Summary, likley written by Holdich of EEF Intelligence, reflected a sentiment more forcefully expressed by his chief, Lynden-Bell: 'One of the principal stumbling blocks to the smooth working up to now has been an infernal thing called the Arab Bureau. It is run by civilians and is totally unbusinesslike and unmilitary. All demands from the Sherif have, up to a few days ago, been collected in the office of the Arab Bureau, and delay and chaos has been the result.'[52]

It was no coincidence that the very day Clayton left Egypt for England – June 19, 1916 – Murray wrote to McMahon informing him of his order that Cairo Intelligence was 'not to touch the question of operations in the Hejaz'. On the same day Murray asked Wingate to send all communications concerning the revolt that previously had gone to Clayton, or to Intrusive, directly to GHQ, Ismailia. Although McMahon protested that Cairo Intelligence was 'not being used for operations', Lynden-Bell followed with a July 2 order that 'no officer in the Cairo branch of G.H.Q. Intelligence shall attempt to deal . . . with any communications from the Sherif'. They should instead be sent directly to Hogarth at the Arab Bureau.[53]

Murray's isolation of the Bureau was effective. When Clayton returned from England he learned of the order precluding Intelligence officers from working in Arbur and that the Bureau had been reduced to Hogarth, Cornwallis and one clerk. Murray softened the order somewhat by allowing certain officers to 'give their advice when required' and the advice of some of them, especially Lawrence, was sought so often 'as to make them to all intents & purposes workers in the Bureau'. But Cornwallis, a full-time Arbur member, was stripped of his Army commission by the EEF.[54] And, when Hogarth returned to England in early August 1916, Cornwallis was left 'entirely alone' at Arbur. Clayton tried to get another man to help him, 'but it is like drawing a tooth to get an officer for political work'.[55]

Clayton might well have complained to London about GHQ's attitude towards his Bureau, but he surely understood that any officer complaining of his commander was embarking on a perilous course. And, Murray's position, extreme though it may have seemed, could be justified on the ground that Robertson had, after all, rejected the suggested Army supervision of the revolt back in June 1916, when Murray had offered to take charge (*see* Chapter 15). In fact, Clayton did complain, if in a rather oblique fashion, to Blinker Hall, Director of the Admiralty's Intelligence Division, in September. After noting that the Bureau was down to Cornwallis, he expressed the hope that Lawrence would be transferred to Arbur, though he was sure GHQ would object. 'There is no one else,' he added, 'as E.E.F. has drained the place of all local talent'.[56]

Meanwhile, GHQ's obstructionism continued. Holdich refused to keep Clayton's Cairo branch informed of Intelligence obtained at Ismailia. And when the Sirdar was discovered to have corresponded with Cairo concerning reconnaissance for a possible landing at Akaba, Murray informed Wingate that 'Clayton's office is not dealing with the subject as it has been entirely dealt with by G.H.Q. at Ismailia'.[57] Clayton's best course – his only course – was to confront Murray or Lynden-Bell directly. This he did in November 1916:

> [T]here is some jealousy and a tendency to "crab" the Arab Bureau (a child I fear of one or two in G.H.Q. Intelligence who envy Arbur's superior knowledge.) I was a little annoyed at this injustice and went and had it out with the C.G.S. [Lynden-Bell]. I showed him the White Paper of the proceedings of the very strong Govt. committee (including DMI & DMO) which founded the Bureau & laid down its functions, and I think he was rather surprised. I then pointed out that Arbur had no wish to interfere in military matters, for which it was not equipped & which militated against the performance of the functions laid down for the Bureau, but it had been called into the breach at a time when there was no other organization available and when G.H.Q. had refused to touch Hejaz affairs. I thought therefore that – far from being abused – Arbur deserved great praise for what they had done under very serious handicaps & that the number of tons of stuff which had been sent down the Red Sea by a staff of, at most two, and sometimes one, was not too bad. I am very glad I spoke, as the C.G.S. at once came round most handsomely & everything is quite all right now (at the top anyhow).[58]

Clayton was right to refer to 'one or two at G.H.Q. Intelligence' as the author of Arbur's troubles and there was little doubt to whom he was referring – the head of Ismailia Intelligence, Major Godfrey Holdich. Historians have disagreed about the nature and extent of Holdich's malign influence on Clayton's Cairo branch.[59] But Holdich, it seems, was a man with a grudge. He had come out to Egypt with Maxwell, but when the general left Cairo in March 1916, for unknown reasons, he failed to mention Holdich in his despatch, a fact of which Holdich complained in a talk with E. S. Herbert in July 1916. When Cyril Wilson, in Jeddah, learned of Clayton's troubles with GHQ, he observed that 'Holditch [*sic*] will now get his heart's desire and be made a Brigadier General'. Another colleague remarked that Clayton 'feels his treatment by G.H.Q. has not been very considerate to say the least.

He built up the whole very excellent Intelligence organization and now finds himself supplanted by young Holdich and relegated to the position of 'Political Adviser' . . . Holdich is clever . . . but cannot possibly have the knowledge – general and specific – to do much constructive work'. And Storrs, who had his thumb on the pulse of Anglo-Egyptian society, noted in November 1916, that Clayton's 'shares having been forced down to almost zero by the intrigues of Holdich (a madly ambitious faux bon-homme, as yet too young for that elderly role) have now risen again together with those of the Arab Bureau'.[60]

While it seems clear that Holdich and Lynden-Bell, and to a lesser degree, Murray, all wanted to remove Clayton from Intelligence work by the summer of 1916, Wingate, too, was coming to the same conclusion. The Sirdar had never been happy with Clayton's Intelligence role. As early as November 1915, it will be recalled, he expressed the view that it would be best if his Sudan Agent were relieved of his 'purely Military Intelligence work'. And, in February 1916, he agreed that Clayton was right to turn over his Syrian Intelligence system to Ismailia. In fact, since Murray had already taken over his Sinai Intelligence work in January, by the spring of 1916, Clayton had almost no involvement in tactical Intelligence at all. As Deedes observed in March, the Cairo branch was left 'mainly with political, Interior and Arab questions'.[61]

Meanwhile, Wingate's criticisms of Clayton's Sudan work continued. And, rather unfairly, in view of the failure of McMahon, Murray and Wingate to resolve the issue of supervision of the revolt, the Sirdar complained of his management of the Arab Bureau. He was annoyed by 'the general muddle as between the High Commissioner, Sir A. Murray, 'Intrusive', Clayton, Bolland and all sorts of Dicks, Toms and Harries, none of whom know or understand much about what they are dealing with'. Clayton was now exasperated that he was getting 'the kicks and blame for any muddles from all concerned'. To his former chief Maxwell, Clayton remarked that, with complaints coming from all quarters, he now found himself ground 'between the upper and the nether millstone'.[62]

On August 14, 1916, after receiving yet another disapproving letter in which the Sirdar expressed the wonder 'whether I was wise to hand you over so completely to Sir John Maxwell', Clayton reacted angrily: '[Y]our letters lately have discouraged me & I [have] to get something off my chest, as I seem to get the kicks from three quarters now. I daresay you didn't mean what you said in the way I have taken it and only meant to "ginger" me up a bit, but honestly I don't feel that I want "gingering" just now as I am honestly going at full pressure.' Wingate was unsympathetic, replying that Clayton's position in Cairo would have been stronger had he consistently represented himself as Wingate's Agent rather than as a headquarters staff officer and liaison with McMahon.[63] Shortly after sending this reply, Wingate received Murray's letter informing him that all correspondence regarding planning for an Akaba landing should be directed to Ismailia and not to Clayton. Wingate took this as a clear indication that Clayton was 'evidently not wanted' by Murray.[64] In fact, Wingate had already made up his mind. On August 26, the Sirdar informed Wilson in Jeddah that the 'best plan' would be for Clayton 'to revert to the position he had originally and drop G.H.Q. work, confining himself principally to the Arab Bureau and Sudan Agency'.[65] The next day Wingate made the same suggestion to Clayton, adding that he was 'personally rather in favour' of Clayton's dropping the Intelligence, but would 'of course do nothing until I know your wishes'.[66]

But the Sirdar did not wait to learn Clayton's wishes. On August 31, he wrote to the CIGS, Robertson, stating that Clayton's departure from the Intelligence 'would more nearly meet the present requirements of the situation'. He praised Clayton's loyalty and noted that he had carried out 'his various duties in a most efficient and capable manner', but added his belief that Clayton 'had too much to do', and, in any event, changes introduced by Murray had 'somewhat reduced Clayton's general staff activities'. Two days later – again without having yet received Clayton's response to his August 27 letter – Wingate wrote to Murray: 'My own view is (and always has been) that Clayton – with all his G.H.Q. work in addition to the supervision of the Arab Bureau and the Sudan Agency, has far too much to do . . . My fear that his legitimate work would suffer by the Maxwell arrangement has not proved groundless . . . Whatever may be your wishes in the matter, you may be sure I shall readily acquiesce in them'.[67] The suggestion that Clayton's Sudan Agency work was his 'legitimate work', in contrast to his duties as Director of Intelligence in the war against the Turco-German drive for supremacy in the Middle East, reveals the scope of Wingate's loss of perspective.

The next day, September 3, Clayton replied by telegram to the Sirdar's letter of August 27: Having thought the matter over carefully, he would not relinquish his Intelligence duties. In a follow-up letter of September 4, Clayton explained that 'at the present critical juncture' he would not 'be doing right to ask for any change . . . it would be bound to lead to temporary dislocation [and] . . . it would be very wrong to make any move just now'.[68] When Wingate received Clayton's cable of September 3, he responded immediately that he had already written to Murray (he did not mention his letter to Robertson) and gave the GOC 'no very definite' statement concerning him, but rather 'threw it on to' Murray to do what he thought best. 'I did not disguise from him', Wingate added, 'the fact that I thought you had too much to do – after all, if he wants to make changes on his own staff, it is not for me to prevent him'.[69]

In truth, Wingate did not attribute Clayton's troubles with GHQ to overwork. In a long letter of September 13, the Sirdar reviewed for Clayton the history of the ill-defined relationship between the Agent/High Commissioner and the military commander in Egypt since the days of Cromer. Unlike Cromer and Kitchener, McMahon was too weak to establish his primacy in the country and, in consequence, Clayton had become 'the unfortunate shuttlecock in this game of battledore' between the Residency and GHQ. But Clayton's problems, he concluded, were attributable only to Clayton himself: 'Had you in your various memoranda brought in my name in support of your arguments, I think they would have carried more weight – but I have observed from the beginning a tendency to conceal the fact that, in accepting your G.S.O. appointment, you still remained my staff officer and & Sudan Agent as well as D[irector of] of I[ntelligence] . . . Had you frankly admitted that you were in constant touch with me & were representing my views I think you would have found that, with this backing behind you, more attention would have been paid to your appeals & views which – after all – emanate in the main from myself'.[70]

This startling indictment was as malicious as it was unjust. Wingate had not set foot in Egypt for two years and could not possibly have known how Clayton represented his views in Cairo. Moreover, the Sirdar well knew he had been largely ignored by Cairo and London; he had complained of it for two years. And this was far more a result of his own refusal to present his views in person than of any action or inaction by Clayton. So, even had Clayton always represented his own views as those of the Sirdar, they would not have carried additional weight, and might well have carried less. Even a cursory review of Wingate's letter discloses what really rankled him: Clayton's influence had grown significantly since 1914, while the Sirdar's had waned and his Agent often expressed opinions independent of, and inconsistent with, Wingate's. For a man of Wingate's personality, that was intolerable. Clayton was rightly offended by the Sirdar's letter and would not let the charge go unchallenged:

> [Y]ou seem to think that I have not put forward your views as conveyed to me in your letters. This is not so, in fact I have always done so continually & consistently and both the H.C. and the C-in-C have had the full benefit of them. How far they convey them further of course I cannot say. Similarly as regards keeping my position as Sudan Agent in the background – this is also not the case as I have never done so and my positionas such is perfectly well-known & recognized by all.[71]

However unjust Wingate's accusations, Clayton now realized that without support from any quarter his days in the Intelligence were numbered. 'There is nothing I should like better than to chuck all the Military side,' he wrote to Wingate in mid-September; 'I am sick of it and disheartened under the present regime . . . G.H.Q. is I believe coming up here permanently in about a month & when it does I think I shall be able gradually to retire gracefully'.[72]

Murray moved his headquarters back to Cairo on October 23, and, it appears, at about the same time, Clayton's Intelligence duties ended. It is not clear whether Murray removed him, or he was able to 'retire gracefully', but, in either event, he felt he had been sorely used by GHQ. On November 10, he wrote two letters to the War Office. In the first, he informed Colonel Basil Buckley, head of that Office's Near Eastern Intelligence section, that he had 'turned over entirely to Holdich now, so "Intrusive" exists no longer. I am sorry,' he added, 'as "Intrusive" was largely my own child, and I should have liked it to outlive the war'. He also hinted that the elimination of Intrusive was perhaps not the best course to be followed. 'It was . . . rather a patchwork show, but it had the advantage of elasticity. It had many irons in the fire and was perhaps better able to co-ordinate and use all available sources of information than a more regular organization could have done'. In his second letter,

Clayton advised the DMI, Macdonogh, that Holdich had taken over the Intelligence and that his own duties now were 'merely Adviser, when required, on local and especially Moslem questions, general supervision . . . of the Arab Bureau and Sudan Agent'. Again, he suggested that the destruction of Intrusive was inadvisable. It was 'in some ways rather unorthodox, but as you know, I had to start it from nothing and build it up as best I could to meet increasing needs. It had, however, this advantage, that it co-ordinated all sources of information such as R's organization, Arab Bureau and the local civil departments in a way which may not be possible now'.[73]

War Office Intelligence did not, in fact, agree with the decision to remove Clayton. Colonel French, the head of MI1(c), informed Murray that, having dealt with Clayton in the past, 'it would be best to continue so dealing in the future' and that Deedes should be used to ensure liaison between Clayton's Cairo Intelligence and the EEF. In early December, Macdonogh also suggested to the Foreign Office that a Political Intelligence Department, incorporating the Arab Bureau, should be formed at Cairo under Clayton. But Murray's decision concerning his own command could not be overturned and neither proposal was adopted. Clayton was out.[74]

Just as he was coming round to the realization that he was finished as Director of Intelligence, Clayton's worries increased when Enid began experiencing problems, as she had prior to the birth of Patience in 1913. In late September, as the baby was expected, she began sleeping every night in the Anglo-American hospital and both Enid and Bertie were greatly relieved when she gave birth on September 28 to a boy, which they named Thomas Falkingham. However, a fortnight later, the baby fell ill from infection, perhaps from a mosquito bite, and at 6 p.m. on October 24, 1916, Thomas died, probably within a day or two of Clayton's removal from the Intelligence. Worn down by professional and personal strain, Clayton himself fell ill a week later, again with bronchitis, and was again ordered to bed. Thomas' death was a sad blow to them both, but they were 'deeply touched' to receive a message 'about our little son' from King George and Queen Mary, conveyed by Clive Wigram. 'I had never realized,' he wrote to Wigram in reply, 'what hopes one builds as to the future of one's first son.' As he wrote these words, Clayton may also have pondered his own future. Wingate would soon be on his way to Cairo as the new High Commissioner and, in view of their strained relations, he had no reason to be optimistic.[75]

17

Chief of Staff, Hijaz Operations, 1917

By mid-November 1916, Clayton was frankly worried. Wingate had been given political and military control of the Arab revolt in October and, in early November, the news broke that the Sirdar would be succeeding McMahon as High Commissioner for Egypt. Since Clayton's connection with EEF Intelligence ended in late October, his responsibilities were now limited chiefly to Arab Bureau work. After he had confronted Lynden-Bell in early November, and 'had it out with him' concerning GHQ's 'crabbing attitude' towards Arbur, Clayton believed the Bureau's problems were over. But, on November 16, he reported to Wingate that GHQ 'still wish to get their knife into the Bureau'.[1] With Arbur in disfavour and his Intelligence duties terminated, Clayton understood that his future depended largely on the Sirdar's plans for him and, in view of their many disagreements, he was not at all confident that Wingate would employ him in any capacity.

Clayton asked George Lloyd, whom he sent to the Hijaz in early November, to travel via Khartoum and Port Sudan and, while in the Sudan, to sound out Wingate on his plans. But Lloyd reported that while the Sirdar fully appreciated that Clayton had been 'the central point' in Cairo concerning the Arab movement, 'he said nothing as to what he proposed for you'.[2] At the same time, Clayton sent Wingate an uncharacteristically obsequious letter in which he expressed the hope that London, having appointed Wingate High Commissioner, would also make him commander-in-chief in Egypt. He believed – or so he wrote – that the Home authorities should place the whole of the Middle East, from North Africa to Mesopotamia, under Wingate's authority and, he informed the Sirdar, he had even made such a suggestion 'in very general, vague terms' to Lord Curzon and the Foreign Office when he was in London in July. 'They <u>want</u> a big man to take over the Near East & run it for them', he added, 'and no one knows as well as you how to coordinate Military & Civil interests & make the two pull together for the common good'. As for his own role, Clayton could not 'conceive a more enthralling task than working under you towards the realization of such an idea'. Three days later Clayton again wrote to the Sirdar, stressing that he was 'anxious . . . to write today and ask you to ask for me back', but McMahon was strongly against any changes being made in Cairo until Wingate arrived.[3] Clayton's worries increased when he learned that Wingate intended to bring several of his

Sudan staff to Cairo, staff, Clayton thought, that might take over his remaining duties. His concerns were not lessened when, in response to his direct enquiry as to how the Sirdar would 'use me when you come down here', Wingate replied only that he would wait until he arrived in Cairo to decide.[4]

Those who knew Clayton well were convinced that the Sirdar would not dispense with his services. Storrs held that his 'uneasiness will, I am sure, vanish after a week for he is far too valuable to be neglected'. Clayton's long-standing friend Lee Stack, who would succeed Wingate as 'Acting' Sirdar and Governor-General of the Sudan, thought that Wingate would find him 'so useful' that his work would actually increase. And, if Wingate did not use Clayton, Stack offered to take him on as Civil Secretary in Khartoum, effectively the number two position in the Sudan Government.[5]

Clayton's concerns were unfounded. Wingate fully intended that he would continue his work in Arab affairs and some indication of his intent appeared as early as October 1916, shortly after Wingate was given supervisory authority over the Arab revolt. The Sirdar then proposed that his management of the revolt be run through the Arab Bureau. McMahon objected; because the Bureau was 'directly under' the High Commissioner's authority, it could not take on 'discretionary powers' independent of him. However, he proposed that Wingate delegate such powers to Clayton individually who would then exercise them through Arbur. Wingate thought this an 'excellent suggestion' and concluded that 'Clayton's close contact with yourself and [the] C-in-C should help him to exercise them judiciously'. Pleased with his continued involvement in the revolt, Clayton assured the Sirdar that he would exercise his authority in 'minor matters' only and would refer all issues of importance, or 'matters of principle' to Wingate directly. The arrangement did not persist, though, for on November 4, the day after Murray learned that McMahon was to be replaced by Wingate, GHQ ordered that the Bureau was to have no further involvement in the revolt.[6]

Wingate arrived in Cairo on December 26, 1916. Within three days, and with the concurrence of Murray, he appointed Clayton Chief of Staff for Hijaz operations and placed the Arab Bureau under his 'immediate direction'. Clayton described his duties to Lloyd: 'The High Commissioner has . . . made me as it were C.G.S. Hejaz and head of the Arab Bureau. This is satisfactory as it gives me a certain status and I know where I am. I still remain adviser to Murray on local and political affairs.'[7] Stack wrote immediately to Clayton, happy to learn that 'Master has fixed you up . . . I was sure that when he got down he would find he could not do without you'. He attributed Clayton's problems with the Sirdar to the lack of personal contact between them for more than two years, and was confident that all would be well 'as soon as personal touch was re-established between you and Master'.[8] Even before Wingate arrived in Cairo, the Arab Bureau's position had improved. In November, it had 'on one or two occasions proved its utility in a marked manner' and Clayton had wisely discussed the Bureau with Murray personally – thus avoiding the malign influence of Holdich and Lynden-Bell – and the commander expressed himself 'entirely sympathetic'.[9]

In many ways, Clayton's work was unchanged after Wingate's arrival in Cairo. He was still closely involved with the supply and strategic direction of the Arab revolt. He continued to supervise the work of Arbur. And he still advised Murray on 'local and political affairs'.[10] Yet, in one, important respect Clayton's position had changed significantly. As Director of Intelligence, he had reported to Maxwell and then Murray, and often directly to the DMI in London. And, as de facto head of the Arab Bureau, he had answered to McMahon (who, as seen, relied heavily on Clayton) and, through him, to the Foreign Office. But now, with Wingate as High Commissioner and General Officer Commanding, Hijaz operations, Clayton would report only to him as Chief of Staff and as Arab Bureau Director. His ability to devise and implement policy was thus circumscribed by his obligations to his new chief, and he regretted the loss of independence. 'I am bound to carry out the policy of my Chief when he has definitely decided on one', he wrote to Lloyd, 'but I should like to have just five minutes on the War Committee or even five minutes with Mark [Sykes] and leave him to do the rest'.[11]

Despite the new reality of his subordination to Wingate, Clayton could still exert a strong influence on the course of the revolt and, as 1917 began, he turned his attention to the immediate problem of strategy. The Turkish threat to Mecca had eased by mid-January and, even if it had not, London would not dispatch troops to Rabegh without a written request from Hussein, a request that was not now likely to issue. Medina, however, remained a problem and the presence of a strong Turkish force there rankled with the Sherif. Not only was Medina the second city of Islam, Turkish occupation of the place prevented an unqualified Arab victory in the Hijaz and seemed to symbolize the failure, or at least the weakness, of Hussein's rising. The Arabs had neither the manpower nor the equipment to take it. Nor could they isolate the city by permanently cutting the Hijaz railway, Medina's supply line from the north. They could, and did, take up the rails in places and later, from February 1917, Anglo-Arab demolition parties could destroy sections of the line as well as trains moving along it, but the Turks quickly repaired it, for there was a store of spare rails and sleepers in Medina, placed there before the war in anticipation of the extension of the line to Mecca and Jeddah.

Clayton was aware of the advantages of taking Medina, but he also saw that its capture by the Arabs might be a 'mixed blessing'. If the Turks could not send a force from the north to relieve the beleaguered garrison, then 'there is no great urgency for the capture of it by the Sherif, and if they do send troops they would probably recapture it from him even if he had taken it; his loss of prestige therefore, would be far greater if Medina were retaken from him after he had advertised his capture of it than if it were only relieved by the Turks'.[12] By November 1916, he had come to the view that '[t]he Turkish force at Medina can stay there as long as it likes, provided it is rendered incapable of a serious offensive and when eventually the railway is cut permanently, as a result of our activities further North, the Medina Division is lost'.[13]

If the capture of Medina was neither feasible nor clearly desirable, Clayton understood that some measures still had to be taken to sustain the revolt, lest it die of inertia. He thought it 'absolutely vital that we should assist the Arabs to prosecute an offensive as soon as possible . . . [I]n view of the Arab nature, as time goes by we are running an increasing danger of finding that the Arabs get sick of the show and begin to melt away. It is only by an offensive that they can be kept in the field'.[14] Since the Arabs had no regular army and were, in any event, ill-suited to the prosecution of a conventional military campaign, the only viable means of confronting the Turks was through guerrilla warfare. And, from the very beginning of the revolt, Clayton held that the only significant objective of a guerrilla campaign was the Hijaz railway, the Turkish life-line from the north. Throughout the second half of 1916, he argued that the line was 'the key of the whole problem' and that it was 'the permanent cutting of that railway, or at least the dislocating of its running, which is the most important point to aim at'. By 1917, his views had not changed: 'There is only one key to the success of the Arab revolt and that is the cutting of the Hejaz railway.'[15] If the line could be severed permanently, the Turks in the Hijaz would be isolated, cut off from their compatriots and supplies in the north.

How could the railway best be attacked? At most points, the line was one hundred miles or more from the Red Sea coast and, in any event, British troops were precluded for religious reasons from entering the Muslim holy land. That much had become clear during the 1916 debate over a landing at Rabegh. At one point, however, far to the north of the Holy Places, the line approached to within sixty miles of the coast at Akaba. The idea of a landing at Akaba, followed by attacks from that port on the railway, had been under consideration for months by the time Clayton became chief of staff for the Hijaz campaign in January 1917. Clayton himself had assessed the possibility seven months before the revolt began; in a December 1915 Note, he advised against a landing at Akaba, as he then thought it would likely 'offend Moslem sentiment'.[16] But, six months later, the revolt now a reality, his religious concerns had evaporated. During his July 1916 visit to London, Clayton urged the War Office to analyse the merits of an Akaba landing and on July 6 the War Committee instructed Murray and the naval commander in the Red Sea, Admiral Wemyss, to draw up plans for an amphibious landing.[17]

A landing at Akaba had several points to recommend it, points which Clayton made repeatedly during the summer and fall of 1916. First, it would 'directly threaten the railway' at a point where it came closest to the coast. Second, an assault on Akaba was 'a logical part of operations for the reoccupation of . . . Sinai'; a British force there would endanger the Turkish eastern flank in the peninsula. So the British could thus fairly characterize the occupation of Akaba as integral to the defence of Egypt. Third, Akaba was 460 miles north of Medina and 640 miles north of Mecca; so a landing at the port could not be 'construed by hostile propagandists . . . [as] a veiled attempt on our part to occupy Arabia and gain an undue influence over the Holy Places'. Fourth – and this was a point calculated to win over Murray to the plan – an Akaba landing was, for Clayton, a 'nett proposition'; it need not drag the British into larger operations in the interior if things went wrong.[18] Clayton also argued that the capture of Akaba would bring to the Sherif those tribes between Akaba and Yanbu, to the south, who had either supported the Turks or remained neutral. These tribes, if won over, could then be used to conduct raids on the railway. Moreover, if the British took the place, the Turks would need to move a sizeable force to Ma'an, the town on the railway located nearest to Akaba. A Turkish concentration at Ma'an might require a concomitant reduction of the garrison at Medina which would, in turn, relieve pressure on Arab forces in the South. Finally, 'the effect on the morale of the Sherif and his tribes would be the greatest of all the advantages'.[19]

These were all good points and both Wingate and McMahon agreed that plans for a landing at Akaba should be prepared. The Admiralty, too, saw merit in the proposal.[20] For his part, Murray was sceptical, though, in conjunction with the Navy, he did begin 'working out plans and details' for a landing.[21] Murray was fully alive to the strategic and political arguments advanced by Clayton for an Akaba landing. Indeed, Clayton was doing his 'utmost to push it through' at GHQ. But Murray also had to be concerned with the tactical aspects of the scheme, a subject not fully considered by Clayton. The EEF commander was rightly worried about the number and disposition of Turkish troops in the area, about the topography around and to the east of Akaba and about the attitude of the local tribes.[22] Clayton sent Parker to the Hijaz in early August 1916 to obtain answers to these questions, but the Navy could not provide a ship to take him north of Jeddah and then, when he was about to leave Suez for another attempt at reconnaissance, Wilson wired Arbur, asking them to hold Parker in Egypt, as the Sherif did not wish him to undertake the mission.[23] On top of this, Lawrence, who knew something of the topography round about Akaba, reported that the plan was not feasible. A force could be landed easily enough, but any attempt to proceed inland, he reasoned, would meet with the greatest difficulty; the only passage east, through the narrow defiles of the Wadi Itm, was surrounded by towering hills from which the Turks could bring down a withering fire on any invading force.[24] Nor was the timing right for an Akaba landing. In early August 1916, the Turks had some 12,000 men entrenched opposite the British position in Sinai, just east of Katia. Murray could not safely divert troops from that front and redeploy them at Akaba.[25]

By mid-August Murray had reports of aerial reconnaissance of Akaba in hand and reported to Robertson that 'even the initial operations present great difficulties'. At the same time, Lynden-Bell informed the DMO that 'a landing at Akaba will be one of very great difficulty and you may find that it is not worth the candle'. Robertson, who, as seen, was 'stubborn as a donkey' in resisting a British landing at Rabegh, assured Murray that he had 'no intention of pressing you to undertake operations which do not present a reasonable prospect of success and which do not also promise a reasonable return on expenditure . . . [W]e cannot go to Akaba merely for the sake of helping the Sherif. . . .' On August 31, Lynden-Bell was 'greatly relieved' to receive a similar message from the DMO, General Maurice. 'I don't want to be bounced into this operation by the Sherif or anybody else', he replied, 'without knowing what we are in for more or less'.[26] Reassured by Robertson that he would not be pressed to undertake operations at Akaba, Murray was now fully opposed to the plan. As Lynden-Bell explained, Murray now foresaw that as soon as troops were landed at Akaba, 'we shall be called upon to operate towards Maan or some other point on the railway, which will of course involve lines of communications, more troops and, in fact, land us into a very big business'. Nor did GHQ think that an Akaba landing would help Hussein. 'I think we can help him and the general situation much more,' Lynden-Bell added, 'by a vigorous action in Sinai'.[27]

Although Clayton continued to push the Akaba plan, by early September 1916, the scheme was dead.[28] 'First Alexandretta and then Akaba', he wrote to George Lloyd at year's end; 'these two names will be engraved on my heart'.[29] No less disappointed than Clayton was the Sherif himself. He complained bitterly of the British failure to attack the railway in the north, claiming that such an attack was 'one of our decisions' embodied in the earlier correspondence with McMahon. To Wilson, in Jeddah, Hussein protested that an action to 'break' the railway was 'decided in the content of our agreement'. Wingate was taken in by the complaint, arguing to Murray that 'the cutting of the railway was definitely promised' to the Sherif.[30] In fact, no such promise had been made to the Sherif and his September 1916 complaint would represent the first of his many mischaracterizations of the McMahon correspondence.

During the first six months of the revolt Clayton began to realize that Hussein and his four sons were less than ideal allies. The Sherif was already beginning to exhibit something of the capricious and arbitrary conduct that would characterize his post-war rule and that would ultimately result in his ouster from the Hijaz. A deeply suspicious man, Hussein was afraid to delegate responsibility and attempted to control every detail of the revolt. He 'interferes in everything', Lawrence reported from the Hijaz in October 1916. His sons were afraid of him and he regarded them as 'boys not quite fit to act independently'.[31] From the outset of the rising, Hussein demanded equipment for an army of 40,000 men – howitzers, machine guns, artillery, armoured cars, airplanes and wireless sets. These demands were rightly regarded by Clayton as extravagant because, even if the Sherif could assemble such an army, he had no 'skilled and trained personnel to work' the weapons and equipment.[32] Hussein was also receiving very large sums from the British – £125,000 per month from July 1916, and, later, £250,000. By mid-August he had been paid more than £400,000. Yet, the Sherif was 'frightfully jealous of his purse-strings' and little of this money appears to have been turned over to the tribes upon whose support the revolt largely depended. Faisal was reported to be furious with his father for not sending him the funds necessary to bring over the tribes in his area of operations.

Hussein also presented political problems for the British. On October 29, 1916, Wilson, at Jeddah, received a telegram from Abdullah informing him that the Sherif had been proclaimed 'King of the Arab Nation'. This was absurdly presumptuous; there was no 'Arab Nation' and, even had there been, there was not the slightest indication that Arabs outside the Hijaz would accord Hussein such a title. Clayton thought the proclamation 'a great nuisance' that would likely 'injure . . . [Hussein's] own cause outside the Hejaz, as his position is not sufficiently strong to take such a step and he runs the risk of holding his whole movement up to ridicule'.[33] After consultation with the French, it was decided that Hussein would be acknowledged only as 'King of the Hejaz'.

Hussein's four sons were no more promising as war leaders. The Arab forces had been organized into four basic units, each under the command of one of the King's sons, and it soon became apparent that they were ill-suited to the commander's role. Ali (b. 1879), the eldest, was 'short and slim, looking a little old already, though only thirty-seven'. Although 'learned in law and religion', Ali was given to fits of obstinacy and was seen as 'without force of character, nervous and rather tired'. Abdullah (b. 1882) was thought to be made of more promising material. The only son with military experience, he had accompanied Turkish forces in 1911–12 during punitive campaigns against the Idrisi of 'Asir. Perhaps because of his pre-war approaches to Kitchener and Storrs (*see* Chapter 10), Abdullah was also regarded by the Arabs as an 'astute politician and far-seeing statesman'.[34] But, in April 1917, Lawrence spent several days in Abdullah's camp and his subsequent report was damning. He observed that Abdullah understood almost nothing about military operations and took 'little interest in the war in the Hedjaz'. He exercised 'little or no supervision' over his men and spent most of his time 'in reading the Arabic newspapers, in eating and sleeping' and playing practical jokes on members of his retinue. Lawrence concluded that Abdullah was 'incapable as a military commander and unfit to be trusted alone'.[35]

Hussein's youngest son, Zaid, then only twenty, was viewed as equally unsuitable for military command. He was described as 'fond of riding about and playing tricks', a 'young ass', according to Wilson.[36] Storrs, who met Zaid in June 1916, just as the revolt was starting, thought him weak, 'by no means intelligent . . . soft in his ways and vague in his ideas'.[37] As a commander, the young Zaid appeared dangerously inept. In early December 1916, he left unguarded a road in the Wadi Safra, south of Yanbu, and the Turks poured through and moved to within a few miles of the coast. Zaid's force disintegrated and Zaid 'himself fled at top pace' to Yanbu.[38]

Perhaps by process of elimination, the British soon fixed on Hussein's third son, Faisal (b. 1886), as the best of the brothers. Lawrence came to that conclusion as early as October 1916, as he saw that Faisal was 'far more imposing personally than any of his brothers, knows it and trades on it . . . He is hot tempered, proud and impatient, and runs off easily at tangents. [He] possesses far more personal magnetism and life than his brothers, but less prudence. Obviously very clever, perhaps not over scrupulous, [he is] rather narrow minded and rash when he acts on impulse but usually with enough strength to reflect, and then [is] exact in judgment . . . A popular idol, and ambitious; full of dreams and the capacity to realise them, with keen personal insight, and a very efficient man of business.'[39] These impressions were written during Lawrence's first trip to the Hijaz in October 1916, after he had been in the country only ten days. But both Wingate and Clayton took Lawrence's assessment as good. Clayton especially regarded Faisal as 'the only one of the brothers really capable of effective military action and the one on whom we have to depend'.[40] Many years later Lawrence confided to one of his biographers a different view: 'Faisal was a timid man, hated running into danger, yet would do anything for Arab freedom – his one passion, purely unselfish . . . At original attack on Medina he had nerved himself to put on a bold front, and the effort had shaken him, so that he never courted danger in battle again'.[41] But that assessment was provided in 1933; during the war, it was Faisal to whom the British would look for success.

In view of the inadequacies of Hashemite leadership, and especially because of the absence of technical expertise among the Arabs, it was decided in October 1916 to send a British Military Mission to the Hijaz. Hussein did not object to a few British technical experts in the country; they would be confined largely to the coastal towns and were, in any event, essential if the Arabs were to learn to use the weapons and equipment required for the campaign. Clayton was keen on the idea and, in early October, asked McMahon to wire London a request that Newcombe be sent back from the Western Front to head the Mission.[42] By the time Newcombe arrived in January 1917, a handful of British advisers was already in the country. Major Pierce Joyce and Captain W. A. Davenport were Arabic-speaking regular army officers, as was Major Herbert Garland, an engineer skilled in the use of explosives, who would be the first officer to demolish a train on the railway in February 1917. Captain Norman Bray, an Indian Army officer also appeared briefly in the autumn of 1916 and would return in December, gathering Intelligence for Wilson at Jeddah. And Newcombe would be joined by two artillery officers, Vickery and Cox, and a medical officer, Marshall.

T. E. Lawrence was not a member of the Military Mission, but from the time Clayton first sent him to the Hijaz in October 1916, he was the most highly regarded of the British advisers in the country. It will be recalled that Clayton first met Lawrence in December 1914, when he arrived in Cairo with the group of officers sent by the War Office to staff Clayton's newly-formed Intelligence Department. Lawrence was then assigned the task of preparing maps of the region, but in the informal atmosphere of Clayton's Intelligence, he was soon involved in all aspects of the Department's work. As Newcombe later recalled, 'he was in fact as much in the picture as any of us'.[43] Although only twenty-six, Lawrence was not shy about advocating policy. As described earlier, he was a proponent of the plan for a landing at Alexandretta and he shared Clayton's views on the merits of bringing the Arabs into the Entente camp. By early 1915, Lawrence was writing papers on Arab politics and suggesting lines of British policy.[44] No evidence exists disclosing his involvement in the McMahon–Hussein correspondence of 1915–16, but, in view of the close-knit nature of Cairo Intelligence, it seems probable that he was. D. G. Hogarth later wrote that Lawrence had been a 'moving spirit in the negotiations leading to the Arab revolt'.[45]

There can be no doubt that Clayton held Lawrence in high regard. In February 1916, he sent Lawrence's memo, 'The Politics of Mecca' to Blinker Hall, director of the Admiralty's Intelligence Division, noting that 'Lawrence is quite excellent on this and many other subjects, and you may take his stuff as being good'. Two months later, while Lawrence and Aubrey Herbert were in Mesopotamia attempting to negotiate the release of the British force encircled by the Turks at Kut, Clayton suggested to the British Intelligence director there that Lawrence would 'be of the greatest assistance, as his knowledge of Syria and Arabia is almost unrivalled. Moreover, he is full of common sense and practical in all his suggestions'. Again, in October 1916, Clayton advised Wilson, at Jeddah, that he expected that Lawrence 'was of considerable assistance to you as he has a clear head and a great knowledge of the Arabs and their affairs in general'. And, in defending the Arab Bureau against GHQ in the fall of 1916, Clayton wrote that 'in men like Hogarth & Lawrence & in Miss Gertrude Bell . . . [Arbur] possesses the brains of perhaps the three greatest experts on those regions'.[46]

While Clayton thought highly of Lawrence and had a close working relationship with him in Cairo for nearly two years before first sending him to the Hijaz, it also appears that they enjoyed good personal relations. Many years later, Clayton's eldest daughter Patience recalled Lawrence's occasional visits to his chief's house in Gezira:

> My only personal recollection of T.E. Lawrence is when he occasionally came to my parent's house in Cairo, round about tea time, when my sister Jane & I would come down to the Drawing Room to be with my mother . . . This was a happy time for us. Lawrence would sometimes arrive quite unexpectedly and join in the games, much to our delight. If anyone else came to call while he was with us, he would make some excuse and depart, in spite of my mother's protestations. Looking back on it, I have realised that he must have been very fond of children & indeed my mother has since told me that this is so. He was especially taken with my sister Jane, who was a delightful and winsome child . . . I gather that my parents were both very fond of Lawrence and admired his scholarship & other qualities, but considered his occasional anti-authority exclusiveness rather a mischievous nonsense. My mother sometimes told him so in no uncertain terms. He took this in good part with a kind of boyish acceptance of reprimand![47]

Patience's reference to Lawrence's 'anti-authority exclusiveness' is particularly interesting because by the fall of 1916, Lawrence had adopted an insolent attitude towards GHQ, as he tried to break away from Intelligence and join Clayton's Arab Bureau. His provocative attitude may have contributed to Clayton's poor relations with Murray's staff. As Lawrence later recalled, a direct request for transfer was refused; 'so I took to stratagems. I became, on the telephone (G.H.Q. were at Ismailia, and I in Cairo), quite intolerable to the staff on the Canal. I took every opportunity to rub into them their comparative ignorance and inefficiency (not difficult!) and irritated them further by literary airs, correcting Shavian split infinitives and tautologies in their reports'.[48]

Lawrence's impudence did not pay dividends; by late November he was on his way back to the Hijaz on his second mission to the country. He was not keen to go and Clayton would have preferred that he remain in Cairo, working for Arbur. But Wingate wanted Lawrence at Yanbu, at least until Newcombe arrived, so Clayton issued orders to Lawrence 'to go ashore' there 'and do what seemed best'. Clayton's orders were typically vague, but as Lawrence acknowledged 'it would be hard to be more definite'.[49] By late 1916, though, Clayton had sufficient confidence in Lawrence's knowledge, judgment and abilities, that he obviously felt specific instructions were neither necessary nor desirable. In fact, the views of Lawrence and his chief were substantially similar. Both believed it essential that the revolt should be encouraged and adequately supplied by the British. Both held that direct Arab confrontation with the enemy should be avoided and that guerrilla tactics were the only viable means of attacking the Turks. Both considered that interruption of the railway was central to Arab success. And, both appreciated the importance of taking Akaba, for the reasons advanced by Clayton in 1916, although, as will be seen, they would differ about how best to do it. No less important, Clayton and Lawrence had similar views concerning the nature and extent of British involvement in the revolt. Clayton believed that the British could, and should, advise the Arabs concerning the general strategic direction of the revolt, but that matters of detail and tactics should be left to them alone. He was convinced that such matters as the disposition of supplies and armaments, the use of Syrian officers by the Hijazi forces, the employment of Turkish POWs by the Sherif and the question of which tribes should be approached by the King and 'the role to be allotted to such tribes when they do come in', should all be left entirely to Hussein and his sons. '[T]he less we interfere, the better', he wrote to Jeddah in March 1917. Lawrence's philosophy was quite similar, as expressed in a January 1917 letter to Newcombe: 'May I suggest that by effacing yourself for the first part, and making friends with the head men before you start pulling them about, you will find your way very much easier? They tried the forceful game at Rabegh – and have spoiled all the show. After all, it's an Arab war, and we are only contributing materials – and the Arabs have the right to go their own way and run things as they please. We are only guests.'[50]

This was sage advice and it distinguished Lawrence from other British officers in the Hijaz. Lawrence was much better suited to an advisory role than his colleagues. He had a good knowledge – much better than his fellow officers – of the Arabs, their tribes and the lands in which they lived. He was also committed to the Arab programme and this, in turn, enabled him to better tolerate Arab inefficiency and indiscipline, matters of great annoyance to his British colleagues. Nor was Lawrence burdened by the strictures of a regular army background, correctly seeing these as impediments to effective dealings with the bedouins. Finally, Lawrence possessed a sense of 'touch', of intuition, about how to interact with the Arabs that was unrivalled among his compatriots.[51]

While Lawrence was in the Hijaz in late 1916 and early 1917, Clayton pressed GHQ to reconsider the Akaba plan, advancing essentially the same arguments he had made during the fall.[52] British successes in Sinai seemed to warrant reconsideration of the scheme. In August, the EEF had routed two Ottoman brigades at Romani. And, in November, the Turks retreated to the line Gaza-Beersheba, leaving only small outposts to the south. Then, on December 21, 1916, British forces occupied El Arish – only thirty miles south of the Turco-Egyptian frontier at Rafa – without opposition. Most recently, on January 9, the EEF moved up to the frontier and were now positioned only twenty-five miles from Gaza. At the same time, the

War Office informed Murray that a further advance could not be contemplated until the fall of 1917. In view of these victories, Murray's argument that he could not spare any men for a landing at Akaba now seemed to have disappeared. But Lynden-Bell, having learned of support for the plan by Wingate and his 'myrmidons', emphasized to the DMO that 'we shall oppose to our utmost any detachments of this kind'.[53]

Undeterred, Clayton now proposed that the Sherifian forces move north along the coast from Yanbu: 'I am now trying to pull all the weight in from Yanbu north', he informed Sykes. 'Continual harrying of the railway from the coastal towns will hamper its running, and – more important still – will encourage the pro-Sherif tribes to the North . . . to go in and take a shot'.[54] The idea that the Arab forces should move north along the coast was not new; Clayton had argued in November that the Arab base should be moved from Rabegh north to Yanbu. But Wingate and Wilson both then opposed the plan and, because of the renewed Turkish threat to Rabegh and Yanbu in December 1916, no such proposals could be acted upon even if they had supported it.[55]

Meanwhile, Faisal, Ali and Abdullah were discussing a similar plan. They proposed to move the Arab front even further north, to Wejh, a coastal town 180 miles north of Yanbu. This would remove Turkish pressure on Rabegh and Mecca because, from Wejh, Faisal could attack the railway at El Ula, 200 miles north of Medina. This would force the Turks to deploy troops along the railway far to the north of the city, forces that could no longer be used to assault Rabegh and, by extension, Mecca. The Turkish advance on Yanbu in early December delayed further consideration of the scheme, but on December 28, 1916, Faisal met with Wilson, Lawrence and Bray and they agreed on a detailed programme for the advance. The plan called for H.M.S. *Hardinge* to transport 550 Arabs from Yanbu to Wejh where they would be landed for an attack timed to coincide with the arrival from the south of some 8,300 Arabs under Faisal's command. Abdullah would guard Faisal's rear from the Wadi Ais. The *Hardinge* promptly landed its Arab force on January 23, and they soon overwhelmed the 200 Turk defenders. However, Faisal's army did not arrive until the 25th, delayed by a celebration prompted by a small success by Abdullah's force as it moved to Wadi Ais. The specific plan had failed, but the goal had been attained. Faisal was now 240 miles south of Akaba.[56]

For the next three months after the capture of Wejh, little progress was made. Faisal lacked sufficient camel transport to continue his campaign in the north. And, he was fully absorbed in consolidating his position at Wejh. This meant bringing the tribes of the northern Hijaz into the Hashemite camp; the Huwaytat, Bani Atiyah, Billi and Juhayna tribes, among others, all had to be persuaded that it was now in their interest to take active measures against the Turks, and this process took time.[57] As for Faisal's brothers, Abdullah was content to sit in his camp at Wadi Ais and Ali and Zaid were reported to be 'somewhat inert'.[58] The only activity during the period came in the form of demolition raids on the railway, led by Lawrence, Newcombe and Garland. Daring and exciting though these raids were – 'Buffalo-Billy' performances, as Lawrence described them – Garland later admitted that 'our efforts were but little worry to the Turks'. Not only did they have 'an inexhaustible stock of spare rails', the Turks 'showed thoroughly good organisation in repairing our destructions and each time the line was interrupted, they had it working again with but little delay'.[59]

The spring of 1917 also saw a significant change in strategy in the region. On March 5, Intelligence was received 'from an absolutely reliable source' – meaning a wireless intercept – that the Turkish forces in the Hijaz had been ordered 'to evacuate Medina, and the Hedjaz, and to retire by stages to Palestine'.[60] The planned Turkish evacuation of the Hijaz was prompted by a change in British strategy in Sinai. With the British now in possession of Rafa on the frontier, the railway and water pipeline from Egypt – essential to any further advance – had been extended to El Arish during the first two months of 1917. Although the War Office had then ordered a halt to the EEF's further advance, it was decided at an Anglo-French conference in late February that Entente forces on several fronts, including Palestine, should go on the offensive. Murray immediately began planning for an advance into southern Palestine. For their part, the Turco-German forces across the border were ordered to defend Gaza 'to the last man'.[61] A show-down at Gaza now appeared imminent.

If Murray's attack on Gaza was to succeed, it was important that the 12,000 Turkish soldiers in the Hijaz be prevented from joining their comrades in southern Palestine. The demolition raids led by Newcombe, Garland and Lawrence, primarily in the area of El Ula, 200 miles north of Medina, were calculated to achieve this objective – to keep the Turks from augmenting their force in Palestine, to keep them *in* the Hijaz. '[I]t is rather an encouraging change', Clayton wrote, 'to find oneself trying to keep the enemy troops in the Hejaz instead of struggling to save Mecca'.[62] These efforts were largely successful and Clayton was able to report to the DMI in April that 'no considerable withdrawals to the Palestine front have been carried out'.[63]

On March 26, 1917, a British force of 23,000 men launched their attack on Gaza and by early evening, the city was surrounded, save for a small sector to the southwest of the town. Yet, the British field commanders did not realize the extent of their success and, concerned with supply problems and reports of the dispatch of Turkish reinforcements, they decided to withdraw if Gaza was not taken by nightfall. The German commander at Gaza, convinced that the battle had been lost, ordered the destruction of his wireless. But the British withdrew, unaware that the Turks were ready to capitulate. The final mistake was made by Murray himself who failed even to mention Gaza in his March 28 report to the War Office and falsely represented the battle as a qualified British victory.[64] While London and Cairo pondered the next move, the Turco-German defenders dug in and when the second battle of Gaza was initiated by the British on April 19, they were ready. If nothing else, Gallipoli should have taught the Entente armies that an assault on Turkish troops in prepared positions was a very difficult proposition. Although the British attack at Second Gaza, as it was called, was supported by poison gas and even tanks, the EEF made little progress in their frontal assault on the city and the battle was over by the end of the day.

Military historians have pointed to all manner of logistical and tactical mistakes made by the British field commanders at the first and second battles of Gaza, but the ultimate problem lay with Murray and it was not long before the Cabinet came to the conclusion that he must be replaced. Lloyd George, who had just come in as Prime Minister in December, and who had no great liking for generals anyway, later wrote that in 'Palestine and Mesopotamia nothing and nobody could have saved the Turks from complete collapse . . . except our General Staff'.[65] On June 11, Murray was relieved of his command, replaced by General Sir Edmund Allenby. In September, Lynden-Bell was sent packing. Clayton's personality exhibited no hint of *schadenfreude*, so one could forgive him if just the faintest trace of a smile crossed his lips when he heard the news.

While the fight for southern Palestine was raging in the spring of 1917, plans were being drawn up in London which, if adopted, would have altered the course of Clayton's career. On April 1, Lord Hardinge advised Wingate of a Foreign Office plan to take over from the India Office the administration of the Basrah and Baghdad *vilayets* in Mesopotamia. The plan was only in an embryonic stage because British forces in the country had just taken Baghdad on March 11, eleven months after the disaster at Kut. On March 16, the Cabinet established a Mesopotamia Administration Committee, on which Hardinge occupied a seat, and planning for the civil administration of the country was among the first items on the agenda. The Foreign Office envisioned the appointment of a High Commissioner for the country, with the current Chief Political Officer, Sir Percy Cox, holding the post. Because the work-load would be substantial during the early stages of the administration, it was thought that a deputy high commissioner should be appointed to assist Cox and that 'General Clayton, if he could be spared, would be eminently qualified for such a post'.[66]

Although he cautioned Hardinge that Clayton was 'rather tired' due to the 'long strain and hard work occasioned by the war', Wingate agreed that Clayton would be a 'very suitable selection' for the post.[67] In early May, Storrs, who was then visiting Mesopotamia, learned that Clayton's appointment would be welcomed by Cox and others in the country. But Storrs did not inform either London or Cairo of a more fundamental problem: Cox was about to resign. Having quarrelled badly with the commander in Baghdad, General Stanley Maude, Cox confided to Storrs 'that it would be better for himself as well as for the country, to resign now and let Clayton begin with a clean sheet'. On May 23, Cox had 'a big knock up with Maude' and typed up his resignation, which Storrs prevented him from sending home.[68] Had Clayton accepted the deputy high commissionership, and Cox resigned, Clayton might have come to occupy the top civil position in Mesopotamia in 1917, a post he would, in fact, take up twelve years later.

Clayton was unaware of Cox's problems with Maude and did not learn of them until Storrs returned to Cairo in July. Had he known in May of Sir Percy's intent to resign, Clayton may well have accepted the post, as he later confided to Mark Sykes. But, in June, Clayton declined the appointment. Storrs thought Clayton did so because he was 'really lying low & sitting tight' for the post of British Adviser to the Egyptian Ministry of the Interior, a position, it will be recalled, for which he had been proposed by the incumbent, Ronald Graham, in 1916.[69] But Clayton had other, more practical reasons, for rejecting the assignment. He understood that the immediate need in Baghdad was to establish 'a sound and workable system of administration'. In contrast, Clayton's 'whole experience' in Cairo had embraced 'the larger political issues rather than the detail[ed] matters of administration'. He saw that issues associated with Sykes–Picot were likely to arise, and soon, if the British or Arabs moved north. Palestine was also sure to 'present new problems' and the 'crux of the whole question is the establishment of a common line of action between ourselves and the French'. These problems, he argued, could not be managed 'by anyone stationed in Mesopotamia, where the outlook is bound to be local'.[70]

When Clayton wrote those words, he had already learned that he would soon be taking up one of the most important political positions in the region; he was about to replace Mark Sykes as British representative on the Anglo-French Mission to the Middle East. The genesis of the Mission could be traced to an Anglo-French conference held in London on December 28, 1916, during which it was decided that when British forces entered Palestine 'a French Moslem detachment' would be incorporated into the EEF, and a French political officer attached to the British force. Two months later, Sykes learned that he had been appointed Chief Political Officer (CPO) to the EEF, and would act as the counter-part of the French representative.[71] At the same time, Robertson advised Murray, then still EEF commander, of the Cabinet's decision to attach a political officer to his staff 'to advise you as to the political situation in your theatre of operations beyond the Eastern frontier of Egypt and to cooperate with a French Commissioner'. To the north of a line drawn between Akaba and Ma'an, (and including those places), the CPO would act through the EEF commander; south of that line, he would work through Wingate, the GOC, Hijaz operations.[72]

On April 3, 1917, Lloyd George and Lord Curzon met with Sykes and carefully reviewed his instructions, as drafted by the Foreign and War Offices.[73] Because Clayton would soon take over for Sykes, they warrant some detailed consideration. It was first made clear that the Sykes–Picot Agreement would 'be regarded as governing the policy of' the British government towards both the French member of the Mission and 'the native elements' beyond the Egyptian frontier. The EEF commander was to use his CPO, Sykes, and the French member of the Mission – who Paris decided was to be Picot – 'as his joint representatives in any negotiations between representatives of the native elements in areas 'A' and 'B' [delineated as areas of French and British influence in Sykes–Picot] and himself'. Picot would act alone 'and on his own responsibility' in talks with any native elements in the Blue area depicted in the Agreement – the area comprising the Lebanon and western Syria, which was to come under direct French control – unless that area came within the EEF's theatre of operations, in which event the British and French political officers would 'act jointly'. With regard to the Brown area of Sykes–Picot (Palestine), there were to be no talks with any native elements until Palestine was actually occupied.[74] Both the Prime Minister and Lord Curzon, perhaps worried that the mercurial Sykes would leave the rails as soon as he arrived in the East, 'laid great stress on the importance of not committing the British Government to any agreement with the tribes that would be prejudicial to British interests'. They also impressed upon him 'the difficulty of our relations with the French in the region', and Lloyd George added that, while there could be no talks concerning Palestine 'until it was actually occupied', it was important, if possible, to secure 'the addition of Palestine to the British area'. In no event was Sykes to 'enter into any political pledges to the Arabs, and particularly none in regard to Palestine'.[75] With these instructions in mind, Sykes left London for Egypt, arriving there on April 22.

While Sykes was preparing for his visit to the East, Clayton was alerted by Wilson that the Sherif, who had been advised of the Mission, believed that Sykes and Picot were coming to discuss the future status of Syria. Clayton anticipated that problems were likely to ensue. He was, of course, no enthusiast of the Sykes–Picot Agreement; a year earlier he and Hogarth had both criticized the pact when they first learned of its terms. And, knowing that the Arabs were sure to scream duplicity if its provisions were made public, Clayton had urged then that the Agreement be kept secret. But by late March 1917, he was reasonably certain that Hussein was already aware of it, or at least its basic provisions: 'The Sherif has never been officially told of the terms of the Sykes–Picot Agreement, but it appears extremely probable that he is now to some extent aware of those terms and of the fact that those particular districts [Damascus, Hama, Homs and Aleppo] have been admitted by H.M.G. to be within the sphere of French influence'. Three weeks later, he advised Wilson that Hussein knew 'that some arrangement has been made with the French'.[76] How did Hussein learn of Sykes–Picot? There is no direct evidence to support the conclusion, but it is very likely that it was Lawrence who informed Faisal of the secret treaty in mid-February 1917.[77] Since Clayton thought it 'extremely probable' that Hussein knew of the Agreement, it seems equally plausible that Lawrence advised his chief that he had informed Faisal of its basic terms.

As explained earlier, Clayton believed the Sykes–Picot Agreement could be reconciled with the McMahon–Hussein correspondence and, indeed, the Agreement had been crafted by the British with the correspondence in mind. Clayton had not been involved in the Anglo-French negotiations of early 1916, but his involvement in the McMahon correspondence was clear; as noted earlier, he had drafted some of the letters, perhaps even McMahon's crucial letter of October 24, 1915. Because of the intentionally ambiguous character of that letter, he fully expected later controversies to arise. In fact, in April 1916 he had directed the Arab Bureau to begin preparing a 'general resume' of the Arab question 'showing exactly what pledges have been given and how we stand today'. Drafted primarily by William Ormsby-Gore of Arbur, the 'resume' would eventually balloon to some two hundred pages – covering the period October 1914 to November 1916 – and was intended by Clayton to be a comprehensive record, prepared 'entirely on uncontroversial lines', of the 'various letters and telegrams of importance which have conveyed the decisions of the Government, the views of the Indian Government and the recommendations of the High Commissioner on such issues as the pledges made to the Arabs, 'whether the Sherif has ever been encouraged to call himself "King", or what H.M.G. has said with regard to the Khalifate'.[78]

Clayton likely referred to Arbur's massive 'resume' when he received Wilson's March letter alerting him to the Sherif's belief that Sykes and Picot were coming to Jeddah to discuss Syria. In a memorandum of April 3, 1917, Clayton reproduced in full McMahon's letter of October 24, 1915, and correctly emphasized that, while recognizing 'the districts of Damascus, Hama, Homs and Aleppo' as Arab territory, Britain's assurances 'could only hold good' concerning those lands where 'Britain was free to act without detriment to the interests of her ally, France'. Yet, until Cairo was authorized to tell Hussein about Sykes–Picot, Clayton concluded, it was not easy to explain to the King that the Syrian districts 'are outside our sphere and that it is to the French that he will have to look'. Clayton also set forth in his memo some hard truths regarding the McMahon pledge, truths of which the King and his sons would have to be reminded repeatedly during the next few years: 'no mention is made of the form which Arab independence should take, or of the nature of autonomous government which should be set up; more especially, there is no pledge whatever that all those territories should come under the dominion of the Sherif . . . .' Yes, the British had negotiated exclusively with Hussein, but that was because he 'was the only prominent Arab with whom the Arab question could be dealt with . . . [T]his will no doubt be taken by him to imply that we regard him as the future ruler of all the Arab races, but Great Britain has never pledged herself to anything of the sort and has always treated the Sherif rather as the "Champion" (or spokesman) of the Arab races rather than as their rightful and future ruler'. A satisfactory solution of the problem of Syria might well involve various elements of the Syrian population 'selecting Emir Faisal or Emir Abdulla as their ruler', he concluded, 'but it is not for us to force upon the Arab races any ruler'.[79]

Clayton was certainly correct in making these points and they sprang not only from a fair reading of the McMahon letters, but also from a recognition that the Arab movement, as embodied by the Hashemite revolt, had engendered little enthusiasm in the Arab world outside the Hijaz. 'The Arab movement as represented by . . . [Hussein] cuts no ice whatever in Mesopotamia', he advised Wilson in April. The Mesopotamian Arabs were 'obviously indifferent and those in Syria will not welcome a government which they think will be reactionary and non-progressive'. For this reason, Clayton held that 'it is one of the Sherif's sons who we must try to push for Syria'; a 'nominal overlordship on the part of the Sherif would secure the necessary . . . prestige for him'. To Graham, at the Foreign Office, Clayton expressed the conviction that 'Mesopotamia would be no means welcome a Sherifian Govt. The people there appear to have little sympathy or connection with the Arabs of the Hejaz . . . As regards Syria, I notice a certain anxiety on the subject as a somewhat medieval and reactionary government such as Mecca would be most distasteful'.[80]

When Sykes and Picot met with Hussein in May, they duly explained to him the general outline of Sykes–Picot. They did not, however, provide Hussein with a copy of the agreement and, inevitably, misunderstanding arose. Newcombe, Wilson and Lloyd, who were all in Jeddah at the time Sykes and Picot met with the King, reported to Clayton that Hussein came away from the meeting with the belief that France would be 'on the same footing in Syria as England is in Baghdad' and his 'idea of our future status in Baghdad probably differs considerably from that of both . . . Sykes and . . . Picot'. Although Sykes later assured Clayton that he had made it perfectly clear to the King that a 'large measure of control and also British military occupation would be necessary for Iraq for some considerable time to come', Hussein persisted in his belief that he had extracted a major concession from the French.[81]

But Picot had made no concession. Neither he nor his government was privy to the McMahon–Hussein correspondence of 1915–16, and, even had they been, it will be recalled that no understanding had been reached between McMahon and Hussein with respect to the Mesopotamian *vialyets* of Basra and Baghdad. McMahon had specified that both would be subject to 'special measures of [British] administrative control'. Even if it could be said that Hussein had agreed to these 'special measures', he had done so only in the belief that Britain would pay an annual subsidy in return for British occupation of the *vilayets*, and McMahon certainly had given no such agreement. With some irritation, Clayton informed Sykes that the King 'has not at all understood the situation, as explained to him by you and Picot, regarding the future of Syria and Iraq. He seems under the fixed impression that both will fall to him unconditionally and has given this out publicly'. But the fault lay not so much with Sykes as with Hussein, who appeared to be 'pinning his faith' on a letter from McMahon which, he stated, gave him 'all the assurances he wants'. That letter could only have been McMahon's of October 24, 1915, which, Clayton believed, had 'either been badly translated' or misconstrued by the King. In either event, Clayton saw that 'a new element has been introduced . . . by making the French position in Syria dependent upon our position in Baghdad'. That, Clayton reasoned, would make 'the King and the Arabs very much more attentive to what they may consider their rights and interests in Baghdad than would have ever been the case before and . . . may easily be a source of considerable embarrassment to us in Mesopotamia'.[82]

When Sykes returned to Cairo after his meeting with Hussein, he prepared a detailed set of recommendations, including an elaborate administrative structure for the French and British areas depicted on the Sykes–Picot map. Clayton quickly dismissed them: '[T]he whole document appears somewhat vague and ignores the practical difficulties which exist. The situation at present is so undefined that even a general outline of policy on any questions treated is premature and might well tie our hands in the future'. But Sykes also prepared a two-page set of 'Observations on Arabian Policy', and this made Clayton sit up and take notice, for in it, Sykes proposed a revision of his agreement with Picot. It will be recalled that the 1916 Agreement, in addition to describing areas of direct French and British control, designated respectively as the Blue and Red Zones, also delineated areas of French and British influence. The French Zone 'A', as noted, encompassed the four Syrian towns and ran to the east, south of Mosul, and up to the Persian frontier. The British Zone 'B' was a vaguely defined area to the south of Zone 'A', but stopped short of

Arabia, which was to be independent. Sykes proposed that, in this vast area to the south of Zone 'B' Britain should at least 'obtain from the French recognition of our predominant commercial and financial position in the Hejaz'.[83]

For Clayton, Sykes' proposal did not go far enough: 'Recognition of <u>political</u> predominance is essential – commercial and financial predominance are not sufficient'. He later explained that '[i]t is essential that the [Sykes–Picot] agreement should be amended to eliminate the present Southern Boundary of Area B . . . thus ensuring that, for purposes of the agreement between Great Britain and France, the provisions which apply to Area B should also apply to the whole of Arabia South of that area. Anything less than this jeopardizes our whole position in the East'. To Sykes he emphasized that 'our predominance throughout Arabia is vital. Any doubt as to our position on the flanks of the roads Port Said – Bombay and Port Said – Basra would constitute, in my opinion, a grave danger to our whole Near-Eastern scheme'. Again, in July, Clayton wrote to Wigram stating that the Sykes–Picot visit to Hussein 'served to disclose the fact that the terms of their agreement did not . . . sufficiently secure our position in Arabia . . . It is to my mind quite essential that our position in Arabia and the Persian Gulf should be made unassailable'.[84]

There was nothing novel about Clayton's boldly imperial views concerning British control of Arabia; Wingate, Lloyd, Hogarth and many others in London and the East expressed similar ideas.[85] But Clayton's opinion that the French would be amenable to a revision of Sykes–Picot was plainly wrong. He assumed the agreement was 'moribund' and that there was 'a very fair chance of its dying of inanition', as he wrote to Lawrence in September. 'The S-P agreement was made nearly two years ago. The world has moved at so vastly increased a pace since then that it is now as old and out of date as the battle of Waterloo or the death of Queen Anne. It is in fact dead and, if we wait quietly, this fact will soon be realized.'[86] As Clayton would soon discover, the French held very different views.

On June 4, 1917, just prior to his departure for England, Sykes met with Wingate in Cairo and informed him – apparently without any authority from London – that there 'would be no difficulty in Clayton carrying on for him' as CPO after he left. That arrangement required the agreement of the Foreign Office and of GHQ, but Murray was relieved of his command a week later and no objection came from London. Of course, Clayton's new duties brought to an end all consideration of moving him to Baghdad to assist, or replace, Cox. 'With the departure of Sykes and the improbability of his return', Wingate wrote to Graham at the Foreign Office, 'I am sure Lord Hardinge will have realized that it would have been impossible to spare Clayton for Mesopotamia . . . there can be no doubt Clayton would be more useful where he is and replacing Sykes. . . .'[87]

Back in London, Sykes assured Clayton that 'I will get you established as C.P.O. as soon as I can'. Although the Foreign Office briefly resisted, Arthur Balfour, who succeeded Grey as Foreign Secretary in the Lloyd George Cabinet of December 1916, acknowledged Clayton as 'Acting Chief Political Officer' on July 26, 1917. That was enough for Clayton, who regarded Balfour's telegram as 'regularising my own position' as CPO. The Foreign Office confirmed the appointment on August 3.[88] As was usually the case with Clayton though, his appointment to a new position, now Acting CPO, did not result in the elimination of his other jobs. He continued as Wingate's chief of staff, Hijaz operations, as adviser to the EEF commander on local and political matters, as de facto Arab Bureau director and even as Sudan Agent, although in the last role, he now had the pleasure of working with his good friend Lee Stack who had succeeded Wingate in Khartoum.

While the battles were raging in southern Palestine and Clayton's future was being debated in London and Cairo during the spring of 1917, Faisal remained at Wejh, meeting with tribal leaders and pondering his next move. The Amir was considering various schemes, but they all involved an Arab advance to the north, into Syria. 'Emir Feisal's ambitions are undoubtedly concentrated on the North', Clayton advised the DMI, 'and he is inclined to attach minor importance to the capture of Medina, which he regards as a foregone conclusion and leaves to Emirs Ali and Abdulla'.[89] Clayton much preferred that Faisal concentrate on the railway north of Medina, at El Ula and Medain Salih, before undertaking a risky campaign north of Ma'an, and he had sound reasons for advocating this more cautious approach. Most important, the British, having failed in southern Palestine, could not support an Arab expedition deep into Turkish-held territory north of Ma'an. Second, in order to sustain such an extended drive north, depots of supplies, arms and ammunition had to be established along the 230 mile stretch of territory between Ma'an and Damascus. It was unlikely that such depots could be created and, even if they could, the Turks would probably discover them. Third, the Arab lines of communication would be very long and could be easily severed by the enemy, leaving the Sherifian contingent stranded in the north and the entire revolt discredited. And, to the extent Faisal would be able to bring over the Syrians to his revolt, they would be exposed to Turkish reprisals which the British, far to the south, were in no position to stop. Finally, an Arab drive to the north would, according to Faisal, require the occupation of Akaba, and this, too, presented problems. Clayton had argued ceaselessly for the occupation of Akaba by a British force, but an *Arab* assault on the port posed very different concerns. The place could be taken without difficulty, as it was lightly defended, but he doubted the Arabs could hold it in the face of a Turkish counter-attack from Ma'an. And, even if the Arabs could maintain their grip on the port, Clayton argued that 'after the war Akaba may be of considerable importance to the future defence scheme of Egypt. It is thus essential that Akaba should remain in British hands after the war'.[90]

The difficulties attending an Arab northern campaign were pressed on Faisal throughout the spring of 1917, but the Amir would not be dissuaded. And George Lloyd reported from Jeddah that the King supported his son's ambitious plan.[91] Faisal was well aware that his northern strategy posed grave risks, but he was prepared to take them because he knew that the French had designs on Syria and he was determined to pre-empt their claims by moving the revolt north and establishing an Arab priority to the country. As described above, Lawrence had very likely advised him of French designs on Syria, as reflected in Sykes–Picot, and, in April, he was alarmed by a rumour that the French were about to land 60,000 men in Syria.

The rumour was baseless, but Faisal's concerns about France's ultimate designs on Syria were, of course, fully justified.

Lawrence was certainly aware of Clayton's opposition to an Arab move on Akaba, but from mid-April he and Faisal began detailed planning for an attack on the port. Faisal had been intent on taking Akaba for some time and had earlier requested that British ships transport his men for an amphibious landing. How the plan for a land-based assault on Akaba developed is a matter of dispute among historians and biographers. Some argue that the scheme was devised by Lawrence, others that Faisal, or the Huwaytat chief, Auda Abu Tayyi, conceived the plan. However it came about, the plan was put into operation on May 9, 1917, when a small party of fewer than forty bedouins left Wejh under the command of Nasir ibn Ali and accompanied by Auda and Lawrence.

The small party travelled far into the desert to the north-east of Wejh and then turned north into the Wadi Sirhan. From there, they proceeded further north, deep into enemy-held territory, eventually reaching Tadmor and Ras Baalbek, fifty miles north of Damascus. During their 300 mile journey in the north Nasir, Auda and Lawrence met with the local tribes, reconnoitred the area and undertook demolition work on the railway. At one point, Lawrence even approached within three miles of Damascus where he met the Syrian nationalist leader Ali Rida Pasha Rikabi. Returning south in late June, the party, now swollen to some 2,000 tribesman, engaged the Turkish outposts west of Ma'an and then moved into the Wadi Itm. On July 6, they reached Akaba, which was taken without opposition.[92] During the fighting for Akaba, 700 Turks were killed and 650 taken prisoner; Arab losses were four dead and five wounded.

The capture of Akaba had several important consequences. First, and perhaps most important, it transformed what had been seen by many as a rather parochial affair – a local Hijazi insurrection – into an Arab national movement with implications for the Arabs of Palestine, Syria, even Mesopotamia. Second, it persuaded many tribes in the north that the Arab movement was viable, that the revolt might very well succeed. Third, it marked the end of the Hijaz campaign; desultory fighting and periodic railway raids would still occur south of Akaba – Ma'an, but significant Arab activity would now be directed to the north of that line. Fourth, after Akaba, the Arab forces effectively passed from the direction and control of Hussein to the EEF and its new commander, General Allenby. From this time, the Arabs were seen as an adjunct to the EEF, a mobile force on the British right flank that could be employed to harry the enemy and disrupt his lines of communication as Imperial troops moved into Palestine. Finally, whether justified or not, Akaba catapulted Lawrence to the forefront of Britain's advisers on the spot. Sykes thought he should be knighted for the effort. Wingate recommended the Victoria Cross. And Clayton held that Lawrence's northern journey ranked as one of the 'really gallant deeds of the war'.[93] Lawrence was promoted temporary Major and awarded the CB. At the same time Clayton, too, received a CB, for 'valuable services rendered in connection with Military Operations in the field'.[94]

Important though it was, the taking of Akaba did not alter Clayton's views on the strategic direction of the revolt. This can be seen from two memoranda he prepared, one dated July 10, and written before news of Akaba reached Cairo, and the other July 15, drafted after Clayton had debriefed Lawrence and digested the latter's report of July 10, describing his exploits in the north and the capture of the port. In his July 10 memo Clayton listed seven advantages that could be realized from 'a general revolt of the tribes in the Syrian hinterland'. But, he concluded, a Syrian revolt could be initiated by Faisal only 'if a safe line of communication to the base of Arab operations in the Syrian hinterland can be ensured'. On July 15, with Lawrence's report on his northern journey now in hand, Clayton observed that the conclusions reflected in his July 10 memo 'are not modified by the information obtained by Capt. Lawrence in his recent reconnaissance'. He again assessed various proposed operations north of Akaba and again regarded many of them promising. Still, he concluded that the operations 'are entirely contingent on a decision to undertake major operations in Palestine which with the movement of the Arabs must synchronise . . . Unless operations of such magnitude as to occupy the whole of the Turkish Army in Palestine were undertaken, the proposed Arab operations must be abandoned. As complete coordination as possible of the Arab movement with the plans of the Egyptian Expeditionary Force is essential'.[95] Clayton's view would prevail; as 1917 progressed, the Arabs became a contingent of the EEF and no Syrian insurrection was instigated.

Three weeks after Akaba, Clayton received Foreign Secretary Balfour's confirmation that he would be acting as CPO in place of Sykes. He would continue his work related to the revolt, but throughout the second half of 1917, Clayton's time would be increasingly taken up with the political issues associated with the Arab movement and, indeed, with the larger issues confronting Britain's Middle Eastern policy-makers. And, as Faisal began moving his base of operations from Wejh to Akaba in July 1917, preliminary to what he hoped would be a drive to the north, it was apparent to Clayton that large problems were looming on the horizon, not so much with the Turks, but with Britain's Entente partner, France.

18

A Very Deep Game: Anglo-French Rivalry in the Levant

Fashoda-ism. It was an odd word, but one with a clear meaning to British foreign policy-makers during the Great War. It was at Fashoda, in September 1898, just after the battle of Omdurman, that Kitchener had confronted the Frenchman Marchand, a confrontation that came to symbolize Anglo-French rivalry for supremacy in Africa and, more generally, throughout the undeveloped world. Although the Entente Cordiale of 1904 had served to minimize, if not eliminate, many colonial disputes between Paris and London, the Middle Eastern war demonstrated that the spirit of Fashoda was far from dead. The authorities in Cairo were widely regarded as proponents of Fashoda-ism, as advocates of short-sighted policies calculated to undermine French aspirations in the region. McMahon, Murray, Wingate and a great many men on the spot in the East were seen as French antagonists. Not least among them was T.E. Lawrence who, as early as March 1915, had written to his Oxford mentor D. G. Hogarth of his hope that Britain would 'rush right up to Damascus and biff the French out of all hope of Syria'.[1] Hogarth himself was 'credited with a "Fashoda mind"'. 'Only you,' Hogarth wrote to Clayton in 1917, 'are uncontaminated in Cairo'.[2]

Hogarth was correct. In January 1915, Clayton had urged the Foreign Office to reach an understanding with France concerning Syria, and from at least April of that year he acknowledged that Britain had effectively conceded Syria to France. His involvement in McMahon's correspondence with Hussein also reflected his certain belief that Britain could make no pledges to the Arabs concerning Palestine or Syria that were inconsistent with French claims. Clayton appreciated that the Sykes–Picot Agreement, even though a likely source of future trouble among the British, French and Arabs, could be reconciled with the McMahon pledge. Still, he was intent on avoiding such trouble and he made considerable, and successful, efforts through McMahon to dissuade Hussein and Faisal from instigating an Arab revolt in Syria (*see* Chapter 15). His attitude remained unchanged in 1917. 'You need not be afraid of any Fashoda-ism on my part', he assured Sykes. 'The indissoluble Entente is everything'.[3]

Unlike his Cairo colleagues, Clayton did not believe that the French should be excluded from assisting the revolt. While in London in July 1916, he submitted a paper in which he observed that 'Moslem opinion in Syria and Arabia' was 'distinctly unfavourable to French penetration', and suggested several ways in which Arab antipathy to France could be 'overcome'. He proposed that the French send a congratulatory message to Hussein, along with 'an offer of assistance with material, funds and possibly French Moslem personnel'. Even the appointment of 'an experienced French officer to study the whole question locally in Egypt' was unobjectionable.[4] Five weeks later McMahon was approached by Defrance, the French Minister in Cairo, who told him of the plan to send a small mission of Muslims from French North Africa to congratulate the Sherif on his revolt. The High Commissioner did not see how Britain could oppose the idea – formally, Britain occupied no more special position in the Hijaz than France – but was concerned that it reflected the desire of the French 'to establish direct relations with the Sherif and perhaps have a say in Hedjaz affairs'. That, he argued, should be 'discouraged from the outset on the part of France or any other power'.[5]

Clayton was unconcerned and when the French mission, under Colonel Edouard Brémond, duly arrived in Cairo in early September 1916, he set down his views in a letter to Wingate:

> The H[igh] C[ommissioner] seems to view this mission with disfavour & to be afraid that the French want to get their oar [in]. I do not share his apprehensions as the Arabs do not like the French and never will . . . On the other hand, we have made over all interests in Syria to the French, and if they ever go there they will be next door to the Sherif, so unless they are on friendly terms we shall have the same situation over again that we had with Italy and the Senussi.

No less significant, in light of British unwillingness, or inability, to aid Hussein beyond the provision of money and supplies, French support might even help sustain the Arab effort:

> [M]ost important of all, the Sherif wants all the support – moral and material – which he can get and if we are going to be so supine ourselves as we have hitherto, for heaven's sake let us get the French to help and possibly stir our folk up to emulation.[6]

On September 5, 1916, Brémond met with Murray and others at British headquarters and explained the purpose of his mission. Politically, the French would merely acknowledge the Sherif's independence and help him 'lighten the expense of the haj'. In military terms, they would introduce four Muslim Arab officers whose job it was to learn what was needed in the way of arms 'to prevent the Turks [from] recapturing Mecca'. Brémond stressed that 'all action . . . would be undertaken in the name of the Allies conjointly and they would be actuated by the motive of assistance to the Sherif simply and solely'. Clayton thought Brémond 'an exceedingly nice man' and encouraged his efforts: 'I must say I welcome the arrival of this

Mission. It may lead to a certain amount of difficulty later (though I am not apprehensive of this), but Colonel Brémond is a strong, keen, practical man and will I hope introduce a spirit of emulation and an element of "ginger" which is sadly lacking.' Another reason Clayton backed the French mission was that Brémond confided to him his view that the capture of Akaba was of central importance to the success of the revolt, an idea that Clayton had, of course, pushed vigorously throughout the summer and fall of 1916. Brémond spent an entire morning reviewing British maps and plans and, without prompting from Clayton, pronounced that 'Akaba was the key to the whole situation both strategically and politically'.[7]

In mid-September the Foreign Office advised McMahon that the French would be supplying Hussein with personnel and equipment for field and mountain batteries and eight machine guns, as well as engineers, officers and men to enable the Sherif to organize two infantry battalions and four squadrons of cavalry, all Muslim. Grey invited the French government to proceed with the plan based on official assurances that Brémond had been sent strict instructions 'to act in complete accordance with British authorities in Cairo . . . and not to interfere in [the] internal administration of [the] new Arab State nor in any question affecting [the] political status of territories on [the] Red Sea littoral'.[8] Wingate also supported the French Mission. Britain might avoid future trouble if the French offer were rejected, he advised Murray, but the importance of preventing Hussein's collapse in the fall of 1916, 'transcends all other considerations and if this cannot be achieved without French intervention, then we must accept it'.[9]

What London and Cairo did not know, however, was that Brémond had a secret agenda; it had been suggested to him in Paris that he should impede the revolt, not assist it. Oddly, less than three weeks after his arrival at Jeddah, Brémond confided to Wilson, Storrs and the Francophobic Lawrence that the French Mission saw the revolt 'in a different light' than the British. 'They say', Lawrence later reported of the French, '"Above all things the Arabs must not take Medina. This can be assured if an Allied force lands at Rabegh. The tribal contingents will go home, and we will be the sole bulwark of the Sherif in Mecca. At the end of the war we will give him Medina as his reward".' On the same day, Brémond cabled Defrance in Cairo that if the Arabs took Medina 'they would immediately try to go into Syria. It is therefore in our interests that Medina does not fall into the hands of the Sherif . . . before the end of the war'.[10] Why Brémond chose to inform the British of his real views on the revolt is unclear. He may well have thought that the British shared his imperial ideas and recognized that British objectives in the region would also be compromised by a successful Arab revolt. '[T]he partisans of a great Arab kingdom', Brémond added, 'seek afterwards to act in Syria, and in Iraq, from where we – French and English – must then expel them'.[11]

In November, Parker reported that the French commander in the Hijaz, Colonel Kadi, had hoisted the French flag when he landed at Rabegh on the 19th, and informed him that he had no intention of trying to train any of the Arab troops. 'I am certain', Murray advised Robertson, 'that the French are not the least desirous of affording us cordial support in the Hedjaz but have sent their troops to secure political advantages . . . The French fear that if the Sherif is successful in turning the Turks out of the Hedjaz they will find that the Arabs propose to operate in Syria. This would not suit them'.[12] On February 11, 1917, Murray again warned the CIGS of French duplicity. 'I think you must carefully watch what the French are doing or wish to do out here. They are playing a very deep game.' Not only were Brémond and his colleagues bent on foiling the revolt, they were displeased with Murray's recent successes in Sinai, 'and they know further that the Syrians prefer the English to them'.[13] Murray could have added the Hashemites to the Syrians in describing Arab dislike of the French. On March 4, Wilson met with Faisal who was 'very agitated' about the French presence in the Hijaz. He wanted Wilson 'to tell the French they were not wanted', and if Wilson did not tell them, the Amir added, 'he would'. 'Damn Brémond and his nasty ways', Wilson reported to Clayton; 'he creates more beastly situations for me than one would have thought possible'.[14]

Murray, Wilson and Lawrence were likely correct in their descriptions of French scheming. As if to underscore the point, Brémond met with Faisal in late January 1917, and urged on the Amir the merits of his plan for the capture of Akaba – not by the Arabs, but by a British brigade supplemented by French colonial troops. But Faisal would not be drawn; he would welcome British support, but wanted no French assistance in taking the port. It was probably Brémond's overture to Faisal that prompted Lawrence to disclose the terms of the Sykes–Picot Agreement to the Amir in early February. Eventually, even the Francophilic Mark Sykes had enough of Brémond's 'deliberately perverse attitude' and the anti-Arab 'dissension and intrigue' of the French contingent in the Hijaz.[15] In May 1917, the Foreign Office asked Paris to withdraw the mission and, after some foot-dragging, they agreed. Brémond left the Hijaz in the autumn, his obstructionist agenda having achieved nothing except a further deterioration in Anglo-French relations.

Cairo was able to convince London of the malign influence of the French mission to the Hijaz, but the irrepressible Sykes was soon busy concocting another plan to foster Anglo-French cooperation. Shortly after arriving in Cairo in May 1917, Sykes proposed the creation of a small force of regular Arab troops that would 'form and consolidate a national spirit' among the Arabs and, since it was to be formed, trained and funded equally by France and Britain, would 'dispel distrust and illustrate French and British cooperation'. The new Arab Legion, as it was called, would be comprised of Arab POWs from Egypt, Aden, Mesopotamia and India and be led by Arab officers, with Britain and France providing 'advisory officers' only. Once readied for fighting, the Legion would be used 'to bolster the Sherifian forces' or perhaps as 'an adjunct to the British forces'.[16]

Sykes discussed his idea at length with Clayton and Picot and both agreed to the proposal, as did GHQ, who assented not because they thought anything would come of the project, but because they 'wanted to give scope to the energies of the Sykes–Picot Mission'.[17] Although Clayton, Hogarth and Lloyd approved the Legion, they were not enthusiastic about its joint funding by France and Britain. With the problems of the French mission fresh in his mind, Clayton saw that joint funding 'may cause complications should it be found necessary in the future to use the Legion in the Hejaz itself'. That would serve only to maintain a French presence in the country, a notion sure to be objectionable both to Hussein and to his British supporters. The Foreign Office agreed, having recently 'asked for the withdrawal of Colonel Brémond and the French Military Mission'.[18] Clayton must also have entertained doubts about the plan to man the Legion with Arab prisoners of war; less than a year earlier, a similar attempt to use POWs to fight in the Hijaz had failed miserably. Moreover, an Arab regular force was already being formed and trained at Wejh under Ja'far al-'Askari, the Mesopotamian commander formerly employed by the Turks in Libya who had been captured in February 1916, and then come over to the Hashemite camp.

Sykes's plan also met with considerable resistance from Lord Curzon, chairman of the Middle East Committee, a new inter-departmental group that was evolving in London in July 1917 out of the Mesopotamian Administration Committee. Curzon, reported Sykes, 'took an unreasoning hatred of the Arab Legion and delayed and delayed'. But Sykes 'pushed and heaved and got it through'. On July 26, 1917, Balfour at last approved the Legion and directed that Clayton, 'as Acting Chief Political Officer, should be entrusted with British supervision . . . in forming [the] Legion'.[19] Clayton confided to Sykes that he did not think the Legion was 'going to be such a great factor in the situation', but, despite his reservations, he promptly began work on the project. Since Picot, like Sykes, had left the region shortly after their May meeting with King Hussein, Clayton thought it best that he 'should not be the actual person in close contact with' the Legion as it might be thought that Britain was trying, in Picot's absence, to exercise a 'preponderant influence' through Clayton, the new CPO. So, he secured the services of an old Sudan colleague, Lt. Colonel Hugh Pearson, to act as British adviser to the Legion.[20]

Clayton's scepticism concerning the new force soon proved justified. Already, in August, he informed Sykes that the Arab POWs in Egypt could not be used, as they were 'in a nasty frame of mind'.[21] Efforts to recruit Arabs from Aden were equally disappointing; by mid-September only inety-two men had been shipped from there to the Legion's training camp at Ismailia on the Canal.[22] More troubling still were the men sent from India. In September a steamer arrived at Aden carrying 543 Arab officers and men from Bombay. Pearson went to Aden to meet them and found the ship in near-mutiny. The Arab officers exercised no authority and the men 'seemed more fitted for a pensionnaire hospital than anything else'. The rag-tag contingent included Bedouin – who would obey no orders – Christians and even thirty-five Jews. Many refused to wear military uniforms and all claimed to have been 'lured on board ship by false pretences' in that they had been assured they would fight for the Sherif and him alone. Now, it appeared, they might be required to fight outside the Hijaz.[23]

Once in camp at Ismailia, the motley collection of POWs was visited by Clayton on September 29. He saw at once that the recruits were unenthusiastic and the offi-cers were 'undisciplined, unskilled' and showed 'little real keenness'.[24] It was just possible, he thought, that the men could be trained sufficiently to be of help to the Arab campaign, but Sykes' political objectives in forming the Legion were unattainable. 'The Arab Legion is progressing well', Clayton informed Wigram, 'but will never be the political instrument which Mark Sykes and Picot hope for. It will be a moderately useful fighting force, provided it is employed <u>with Arabs in Arab areas</u>, but to use it elsewhere will lead to trouble'.[25] Despite his scepticism, Clayton persisted in trying to instil in the Legionnaires some sense of Arab unity. He arranged for one of Hussein's representatives, Fuad al-Khatib, and Nuri al-Sa'id, an Arab officer working at Wejh with Ja'far al-'Askari, to come to Ismailia and deliver a message from the King. It had an 'excellent effect', Clayton reported, but he declined to deliver a message to the Legion from Sykes which, perhaps because of its risible, overly formal style, might have had a 'disturbing effect' on the men.[26]

By October, Clayton was convinced that the Legion should be deployed exclusively in Arab areas. Faisal was pressing for the immediate dispatch of the force to Akaba and Clayton agreed that it should be sent there to augment the Arab irregulars. And, if the Amir was eventually successful in moving into Syria, 'the presence of a regular force such as the Legion under its own flag, would have an excellent effect in impressing on the Syrians the fact that the Arab is really fighting in earnest for his freedom and independence'. Clayton's French counterpart, M. Maugras, who was acting for Picot as Clayton was acting for Sykes, was more pessimistic. He candidly told Clayton that the Legion was 'a failure from a political point of view and will not do what we thought in promoting Arab unity'. But Clayton, or so he informed Sykes, was 'not entirely of this opinion . . . [T]he general tendency now is to consider [the Legion] as an outward sign of Arab nationality'. Maugras also objected to the Legion 'being sent off until it is fully trained and ready for the field'. Hardened by the experience of the Brémond mission, Clayton was now suspicious of French motives. 'They may have the hope' that the Legion 'will eventually be employed in their own area and under their own auspices', he cautioned.[27] On the same day Clayton advised Sykes that the Legion was being considered as a sign of Arab nationality, he conveyed a different view to his man at Akaba, Colonel Joyce. After assuring Joyce that he intended to ship the force to Akaba as soon as possible, he disclosed his real opinion of the political purpose behind the Legion: 'The Arab Legion has been made a good deal of in London and Paris as a political card and all sorts of nonsense is talked about this being the visible sign of Arab independence, Etc. Etc.'[28]

On November 2, Clayton requested authorization to send the Legion to Akaba, acknowledging that the force was 'not yet fully trained', but was 'quite a serviceable and well equipped unit'. The Foreign Office assented and on November 20, nearly the entire force, some 385 men, embarked for Akaba.[29] The day before they left, Pearson submitted a detailed report on the force which began with the sentence, 'The experiment with the Arab Legion we have had here for the last 8 weeks it must be confessed, has been a failure'. After describing the lack of discipline, and the 'discontent and dissatisfaction' among officers and men alike, Pearson concluded that he could not recommend that any further effort be expended on the Legion. He attributed the failure to misstatements made in India of the conditions of service and of British intentions concerning how and where the force would be employed.

In addition, 'men of all creeds and ages' had been recruited, regardless of their suitability for service and an undisciplined rabble was the result. Moreover, 'unauthorized promises' had been made to the men concerning retention of the rank they previously held in the Turkish Army. This produced a surplus of non-commissioned officers who could not retain their rank in the Legion and thus bore grievances. Finally, the Arab officers proved to be 'devoid of all real patriotism or power of command, incapable of acquiring the respect of their men, and occupied in scheming only for their personal ambition'.[30]

Soon after Joyce received the Legion contingent at Akaba he wrote to Clayton, wondering what he really thought of the force and expressing the hope that the lot would 'be induced to leave for the front shortly! These people really do try one's patience at times almost beyond the limits of endurance'.[31] By December, Clayton had come to the same conclusion as Pearson and Joyce, as he informed Sykes:

I must honestly confess that, viewed as a symbol of Arab nationalism, the Legion has been a failure. It has not been received with any enthusiasm by local Arabs, in spite of much propaganda, and it was viewed as long as it remained here with grave suspicion by the Sherif and by Faisal, who disliked the procedure and wished to get the men direct. I cannot say that it is worth either the money or the time of skilled officers which has been expended on it. The material is not particularly good, consisting practically entirely of Prisoners of War, and the officers . . . busy themselves entirely with politics and disturb the equilibrium of the men. If I thought it were likely to achieve the object for which it was started, I would say go on with it, but I certainly do not think so, and I recommend closing it down.[32]

Clayton might have added that, viewed as a symbol of Anglo-French cooperation, the Legion had done nothing to dispel the suspicion and distrust that continued to impair Entente relations in the region. The Legion was eventually absorbed by Faisal's force and the British made no further attempt to create an Arab regular army.

While Clayton was wrestling with the problem of the Arab Legion, the situation at Akaba during the autumn of 1917 remained static. Faisal continued to meet with leaders of the northern tribes, but he lacked the money and supplies to raise the standard of revolt in the north and was beginning to lose faith in his British allies for failing to provide them. Joyce, now in charge of British advisers in the country, met almost daily with the Amir and struggled to bolster his flagging spirits. Faisal thought it 'absolutely essential that he take the offensive north of Maan forthwith', yet neither his family nor his allies appeared to be doing anything to further his plans. Clayton visited Akaba on September 1, to assure him of British support, but could do nothing about Faisal's family. 'Faisal still considers that his Father and brothers are taking no interest in the Syrian movement and it takes a lot of talk to prevent him getting very depressed on the subject. He is mad keen himself and the indications of an early rising are so promising that all these delays in bringing it about are particularly annoying.' Ten days later Joyce was still struggling with the

Amir, as he reported to Clayton: 'I had a very difficult time with Faisal for a few days. He is not a very strong character and much swayed by his surroundings. However, your messages and information did much to reassure him and we got him over the bad days.'[33]

If Faisal was frustrated and depressed by his inability to move north, his British advisers were not in a much better frame of mind. Joyce, perhaps burdened by his regular army background, had been discouraged for months. '[T]he Arabs . . . are doubtful allies and putting up the rottenest fight', he complained in December 1916; 'we will either have more British officers or we will quit. Either the Arabs must play up or we must have control'. His attitude had not improved much after the move to Akaba. In a draft letter to Clayton – which he apparently decided not to send – his frustration bubbled to the surface. '[H]onestly I am tired of this hand to mouth existence & if nothing is going to be done here, you had better let us quit for we are only wasting our time and yours'.[34]

Joyce persisted, but Newcombe was not proving to be the man Clayton had hoped for when he secured his transfer from France to head the military mission to the Hijaz in late 1916. In October 1917, Clayton had him re-assigned to the EEF, exasperated that he kept 'darting off at a tangent and sending wild suggestions for a practically single-handed onslaught on the Turkish left flank!'[35] George Lloyd provided a different reason for Newcombe's problems in the Hijaz and, at the same time, explained why Lawrence was able to get on so well with the Arabs:

> Anyone who can hold up a train and enable the Arabs to sack it commands temporarily their allegiance . . . it is the mainspring of influence at this game. It is really (by no means only) but a great part of the secret of Lawrence's success, and he will admit this privately with a smile. Newcombe it is true had not Lawrence's gifts . . . His game was merely cutting the line. Would the Arabs help him? Not they – and he dubbed them as cowards. Lawrence conceived the necessity of giving them instant reward and looted and stopped trains, catering at once to their love of sport and of loot. The moment he did this the Arabs showed reckless courage. To them he is Lawrence the arch looter, the super-raider, real leader of the right and only kind of ghazzu [Arab raid] – and he never forgets that this is a large part of his claim to sovereignty over them.[36]

Lawrence had, in fact, carried out daring and successful raids on Turkish trains in September and October and it seems that by this time his reputation had even registered with the enemy, as a wireless message intercepted from the Turkish garrison at Ma'an disclosed: 'An Englishman – "Destroyer of Engines" is with Auda Abu Tayyi; his name is Orens'.[37] Clayton fully appreciated Lawrence's influence with the Arabs, and he believed that the position of the 'Destroyer of Engines' was unique. 'Lawrence is the only man (either British or French) whom they will accept', he advised Wigram in October. 'It is almost impossible to give him any real assistance as it is the personality and influence of the individual which is counting for everything'.[38] Joyce, too, understood Lawrence's influence, but he also saw this as a problem for Clayton. 'The great weakness of your position . . . is having no one except Lawrence with a thorough martial and theoretical knowledge of the situation. We can all help a bit having gained some knowledge but it is his intimate and extensive knowledge of the history and the tribes and the language that really counts'.[39]

Clayton admitted in his October letter to Wigram that the problem with relying on Lawrence was that he was 'difficult to control'. If not clearly disobeying a direct order from his chief, Lawrence had knowingly acted contrary to Clayton's strategy in taking Akaba with an Arab force in July.[40] And now Lawrence was encouraging Faisal's plan to move north and bring the revolt to Syria. For Clayton, that was a very dangerous strategy. But, typical of his style, he did not issue direct orders to Lawrence precluding the northern scheme. In a letter of September 20, 1917, Clayton encouraged Lawrence to continue Bedouin raiding on the railway, even in the north, 'as soon as possible and on as large a scale as possible'. The Bedouin raiding parties were not only small and highly mobile, but could disappear into the desert after an attack with little fear of capture or reprisal. Instigating a revolt in the north was another matter. Yet, he appeared to defer to Lawrence even on this: 'It is up to you and Faisal to decide how far we are justified in urging a revolt in Syria.' But then, Clayton added some sobering thoughts:

> Faisal may take a large slice of Syria by means of a general revolt of the inhabitants, but can he keep it with the British Army tied by the leg far to the South and in [the] face of a strong Turkish concentration in the North? If he cannot keep it, what is the result? You and Faisal know far better than I the situation in Syria and its possibilities and have doubtless weighed the pros and cons fully, but I want to ensure that no action is taken without full appreciation of the situation and that nothing is done which will bring down upon Syria a storm which we cannot avert and for which we shall inevitably have to bear the blame.[41]

Clayton was more direct with others involved in the campaign. He advised GHQ that if it was 'intended to undertake a serious offensive with a view to the defeat and destruction of the Turkish Army in Palestine, then we are justified in raising the Arab tribes of the North. If not, we cannot urge them into a position where they will be open to severe reprisals and Arab operations must be confined to the Maan area'.[42] He delivered essentially the same message to Wingate and to Sykes.[43] And to Joyce, who met regularly with Faisal at Akaba, Clayton repeatedly urged caution. 'We are not justified in encouraging any general revolt until we are certain that it has a reasonable chance of success and will not lead to severe reprisals on the part of the enemy.'[44] For Clayton, the cautionary letters sent to Joyce were particularly important because he believed Faisal was 'rather apt to over rate the power of irregular Arabs and rebels against properly organized troops'. And he was convinced that Faisal and 'also Lawrence to a slight extent' were inclined 'to underrate the enemy'. 'The Turk in Syria', he added, 'with all the appliances of modern war and under

German leadership is by no means the same man as the Turk in the Hejaz, scattered along a long line and tied to the railway by lack of transport'.[45] Clayton's strategy prevailed. Faisal remained at Akaba. The railway raids continued. And Lawrence, although undertaking a daring expedition into Syria in the fall of 1917, did not attempt to bring the revolt to Syria. The Arab movement now depended on the EEF and its new commander, Allenby.

General Sir Edmund Allenby was cut from a different cloth than his predecessor, Murray. Born in 1861 into an 'old-established country family of good repute and comfortable circumstances, but of no particular eminence', Allenby was educated at Haileybury and then the Royal Military College at Sandhurst, which he entered in 1881, having twice failed the exam for the Indian Civil Service.[46] He was the first cavalry officer to qualify for the General Staff College (1896–7), and his early years of service were spent in South Africa, where he achieved some notoriety in the Boer War, during which he commanded a squadron, then a regiment and eventually a column (equivalent to a brigade). From the end of the South African war until the start of the Great War, Allenby's service was limited to England. He rose rapidly in the Army hierarchy, to brigadier (1905), major-general (1909), and the following year to Inspector-General of the cavalry.

Allenby's service on the Western Front – during which he commanded a division, a Corps and then an Army – produced mixed results, an assessment that was a good deal more laudatory than that which could be accorded many of his fellow generals. Field Marshal Wavell, who wrote a biography of Allenby during the Second World War and who knew him well in Palestine where he acted as liaison between Robertson and Allenby, thought his record 'as least as good as that of any other British commander'. Adding in Allenby's work in Palestine as commander of the EEF, Wavell concluded that he could 'be regarded as the best British general of the Great War' – high praise indeed from one of the best of the next war.[47] Wavell also knew Clayton well, later describing him as 'a very fine character' and just 'about the shrewdest head on the spot' in the Middle East.[48]

Allenby was not particularly well-liked by his subordinates. He could be brusque and petulant and '[t]here was an aloofness about him, a suggestion of mental superiority, that kept him from the hearts of his officers and men. . . .' Above all, he was known for an explosive, volcanic temper which could erupt from his six foot four inch frame at any time. And he did not discriminate; anyone from a private to a lieutenant-general might leave an interview with him in tears. Major-General Lynden-Bell, sent home in September 1917, was likely a victim of one of Allenby's rages.[49] Well before the war Allenby had earned the sobriquet, 'the Bull' and in Palestine a signal officer at GHQ routinely broadcast a two-letter coded warning whenever the chief left camp: 'B.L.', which meant 'Bull loose!'[50]

Despite his difficult personality, Allenby was always respected and many officers actually thought him easy to work for, as he rarely interfered in details. General Arthur Money, who would succeed Clayton as the Administrator of Occupied Enemy Territory in April 1918, thought Allenby 'the easiest chief to work with I have ever met. He knew his own mind & once you had gained his confidence, he trusted you right through, left you to do your own job in your own way'.[51] Clayton gained his chief's confidence early on, a fact illustrated by an anecdote recounted by Wavell in his biography of Allenby. The EEF commander, it seems, took great pride in avoiding the destruction of Palestine's historic sites during the campaign. One day Allenby discovered a small ruin with a stone arch which he identified as the remains of a structure erected during the Crusades. Some time later he took a visitor to the site only to discover that the arch – in fact, the entire ruin – had disappeared. After some enquiry, Allenby learned that a young lieutenant of the Engineers had been ordered to construct a store house nearby and had used the stones from the ruin to build it. Allenby exploded; not only had an architectural relic been destroyed, his orders concerning the preservation of historic monuments had been disobeyed. The quaking subaltern was ordered back to Egypt in disgrace and the efforts of more senior officers on his behalf served only to produce further seismic disturbances from the chief. Wavell continued the story:

> Finally, Bertie Clayton, Allenby's political adviser, agreed to approach him after making careful enquiries about the arch. At first, Allenby would hear no further word on the subject; but Bertie Clayton was never afraid of him, and Allenby had learned that Clayton never spoke without reason. When he agreed to listen Clayton told him that the 'Crusader' arch had been constructed less than fifty years before as part of a local wine shop. When Allenby recovered from the shock to the antiquarian knowledge on which he prided himself he took it very well and remitted all penalties on the zealous subaltern.[52]

Allenby had not been pleased with his reassignment from the Western Front; he regarded it as a demotion. But he had been selected by Robertson and by the Prime Minister who told him that the Cabinet expected Jerusalem to be taken before Christmas. For his part, Lloyd George promised to do his best to provide Allenby with the men and equipment necessary for the task.[53] Allenby took over from Murray on June 29, 1917, and immediately got to work. Reinforcements poured into northern Sinai, eventually forming into seven infantry divisions, three mounted divisions and seven heavy artillery brigades. Additional aircraft were flown in, so that by September the EEF had sixty planes available, including several new Bristol fighters, which gave the British an air superiority that they maintained for the remainder of the Middle Eastern war. The rail and water lines were doubled and extended. Allenby did not receive all the artillery he requested, but by October he had some ninety guns at his disposal.

The number of Turkish troops opposing the EEF is uncertain. The *Official History* put the number at 33,000 rifles; modern analyses have revised the Turkish strength to a lower estimate of only 20,000. But, overall, the EEF 'possessed twice the infantry, nine times the cavalry and three guns for every two Turkish guns . . . throughout the battle line'. These disparities, however, would prove even greater because Allenby rejected the single frontal assault on Gaza that had failed so badly in the April battle for the town. Instead, the plan called for a massive four day naval and land-based bombardment of Gaza, during which the bulk of the EEF's infantry and mounted divisions would move secretly to Beersheba, 25 miles to the southeast, where they would have an overwhelming eight to one superiority over the 5,000 Turkish defenders.[54] Once Beersheba and its precious water wells was taken, the EEF would move to the north and west, cutting off the bulk of the Turk force in Gaza. Beersheba was taken on October 31, but the plan did not work to perfection. The Turks were able to pull much of their beleaguered force from Gaza before the city was taken on November 7. But, the outmanned and out-gunned defenders, despite mounting a series of rear-guard actions and even fierce counter-attacks, could not stem the EEF tide. Jerusalem fell on December 9, bringing to an end four hundred years of Ottoman rule. Allenby had delivered the city by Christmas.

The capture of Jerusalem by no means marked the end of the Middle Eastern war; fighting would continue for another eleven months. But the liberation of the holy city was an event heavy with political significance. The Entente was now poised to liberate all Arab lands from the Turkish yoke and, inevitably, this would bring the political settlement of the region to the forefront. It was now time to consider whether, and how, the pledges to the Arabs could be reconciled with the imperial *realpolitik* of Sykes–Picot. The French were not slow to assert their claims. Already, on November 25, Picot appeared in Cairo, intent on participating in Allenby's anticipated entry into Jerusalem and equally determined to assert the French claim to a joint administration of Palestine with Britain. 'The recent success in Palestine has caused the plot to thicken', Clayton advised Gertrude Bell. 'P[icot] has arrived and as M[ark] S[ykes] has not come I am left to face the music of other people's composition – not easy task'.[55] Wingate and Allenby objected to Picot's participation in the official entry into Jerusalem and Wingate requested that Clayton, too, be debarred from the ceremony. Since Clayton was Britain's representative to the Anglo-French Mission, Picot could hardly complain of his own exclusion if his British counterpart was also omitted. But the Foreign Office promptly resolved the issue; Clayton and Picot would proceed together, ten paces behind Allenby, who would enter Jerusalem on foot, symbolizing the Entente's arrival not as conquerors, but as liberators of the holy city.[56]

Picot lost no time in asserting French claims. At a luncheon following the entry, the Frenchman turned to Allenby: 'And tomorrow, my dear General, I will take the necessary steps to set up civil government in this town.' Lawrence, who had participated in the ceremony as Clayton's 'staff officer for the day', described what followed: 'It was the bravest word on record; a silence followed, as when they opened the seventh seal in heaven. Salad, chicken mayonnaise and foie gras sandwiches hung in our wet mouths unmunched, while we turned to Allenby and gaped. Even he seemed for the moment at a loss. We began to fear that the idol might betray a frailty. But his face grew red: he swallowed, his chin coming forward (in the way we loved) whilst he said, grimly, "In the military zone the only authority is that of the Commander-in-Chief — myself." "But Sir Grey, Sir Edward Grey" . . . stammered M. Picot. He was cut short. "Sir Edward Grey referred to the civil government which will be established when I judge that the military situation permits".'[57]

Allenby's definitive assertion of a military administration was no surprise to Clayton. Six months earlier he had 'urged strongly' that Palestine 'should have a purely military administration which would be entirely under the C. in C. and work generally on the lines of the Laws and Usages of War . . . This was done and Colonel Parker was appointed Military Administrator of Occupied Enemy Territory . . . P[icot] was thus faced with a "fait accompli".' This, Clayton saw, would avoid, at least 'for the present . . . all possible commitments both political and administrative'.[58] With the guns still booming just north of Jerusalem, the need for a military administration of Palestine provided an easy answer to the French. But Syria posed a different problem. It was unconquered and the terms of Sykes–Picot had been publicized by the Bolsheviks in the wake of their autumn 1917 revolution. Clayton already saw that 'distrust and uneasiness' was rising in Arab quarters and he proposed to the Foreign Office that the French Government now be asked 'to make a definitive pronouncement disclaiming any idea of annexation in Syria (including the blue area).' Sykes agreed.[59] The French did not.

The capture of Jerusalem had cast in sharp relief the difficult problems suffusing Anglo-Arab–French relations. Those problems, Clayton thought, were not insoluble; with good will and a spirit of compromise, satisfactory solutions could be found for all concerned. But five weeks before Allenby's triumphal march into the holy city, the British government added yet another piece to the complex puzzle of the Middle East. On November 2, 1917, Foreign Secretary Balfour issued his famous declaration promising British support for a national home for the Jewish people in Palestine. After three exhausting years of war, Clayton's problems were just beginning.

PART THREE

DIPLOMACY

19

Jacob and Esau: Arabs and Jews in Palestine, 1918–1919

His Majesty's Government view with favour the establishment in Palestine of a national home for the Jewish people and will use their best endeavours to facilitate the achievement of this object, it being clearly understood that nothing shall be done which may prejudice the civil and religious rights of existing non-Jewish communities in Palestine, or the rights and political status enjoyed by Jews in any other country.[1]

So wrote British Foreign Secretary Arthur Balfour in a November 2, 1917 letter to a leading British Zionist, Lord Rothschild. The origins of the Balfour Declaration, as it was called, were complex and controversial. There was no unanimity behind its promulgation and, indeed, many Jews had opposed the idea of Zionism, of a Jewish national homeland in Palestine. Herbert Samuel, the first Jew to occupy a Cabinet seat (in the Asquith Government) was an ardent proponent of the idea; his cousin, Edwin Montagu – as Secretary of State for India, the only Jew in the Cabinet when the Declaration issued – was just as zealous an opponent. Montagu argued that his family, and those of many other British Jews, had struggled for generations to gain acceptance in England and, whether by talent, hard work or wealth, had succeeded and been effectively assimilated into British society. Now, the Government was advocating the creation of a Jewish homeland to which, it might be argued, Jews of all nations could be relegated. For Montagu, the Balfour Declaration was a profoundly *anti*-Semitic measure, as he contended in a Cabinet memorandum entitled 'The Anti-Semitism of the Present Government'. The last clause of the Declaration was crafted to meet the objections of Montagu and his fellow 'assimilationists', but did little to mitigate their concerns.[2] Other Jews were less concerned with the social and political implications of Zionism, but absorbed by more profound issues, questions that penetrated to the very heart of Judaism. Their views were crystallized in a statement issued by England's Chief Rabbi before the war: The Jews, he proclaimed, were a religious community, not a nation.[3]

Among non-Jews, more practical considerations predominated. The vast majority of Palestine's inhabitants were Arabs – by most accounts, they comprised ninety percent of the population in 1917 – and Lord Curzon posed an uncomfortable question to his colleagues who supported the idea of a Jewish national homeland: 'What is to become of the people of the country?' The Arabs, he warned, 'will not be content either to be expropriated for Jewish immigrants, or to act merely as hewers of wood and drawers of water to the latter'.[4] But, by mid-1917, Curzon found himself in a minority among British policymakers, and in the War Cabinet itself, the Zionists had won over its two most influential members, Foreign Secretary Arthur Balfour and Prime Minister David Lloyd George. Balfour, it was said, had been moved to tears by the impassioned pleas of a Zionist leader.[5] If true, that was a great accomplishment, for the Foreign Secretary was rarely moved by anything. Renowned for his detachment and an almost Olympian indifference to practical politics, he was more comfortable within the confines of abstruse philosophical debate. The aloof Balfour considered most political movements with icy disdain, with a smile that 'was like moonlight on a tombstone'. Nor was he known for translating ideas into action. 'If you wanted nothing done', Churchill once observed, 'A. J. B. was undoubtedly the best man for the task'.[6] Why then Balfour had come to back the Zionist ambition is something of a mystery.

The Prime Minister's support was, in part, tinctured by his youthful interest in the history of the Jews as set down in the Bible; perhaps he felt that these epic stories foretold a great Jewish destiny in the Middle East. Still, it is a little difficult to suppose that the shrewd and calculating Prime Minister was motivated by this essentially emotional appeal. Doubtless both Balfour and Lloyd George were in some measure moved by a vague and rather sentimental identification with Zionist goals, but it is also apparent that more practical considerations lay behind their support. First, Sykes–Picot had consigned Syria to the French. A friendly regime in Palestine, operating under British tutelage, would interpose a buffer between the French in the north and Egypt, and the vital passage of the Suez Canal, to the south. Although the strategic consideration of a buffer State between Syria and Egypt may have had some merit in an age when the spirit of Fashoda was still very much alive, it was not apparent why the buffering State should be Jewish; a friendly Arab State in Palestine would have served the same purpose and, at the same time, avoided the discord within the country that was likely to flow from application of the Jewish national home policy. Second, most members of the government ascribed to the view that Jewish influence in America and Russia was so great that British backing of the Zionist programme would ensure continued support for the Entente in those countries. That idea would later be discounted by historians who observed that the extent of Jewish influence in those countries was absurdly overrated by the British and that it incorrectly presupposed that American and Russian Jews were united in their support of Zionism when, in fact, they were not. Finally, many thought that the Germans themselves were contemplating a declaration in support of the Zionist plan and, if such a declaration issued, world Jewry might align itself with the Central Powers. This rationale, too, has been rejected by many historians who argue that Germany was in no position to impose on its Ottoman ally a Jewish State in Palestine. Yet, the Zionist leaders were clever enough to exploit this misconception and lost no time in warning the British that Germany was attempting to co-opt the

Zionist movement.[7] It was a ploy oddly reminiscent of that used by al-Faruqi in October 1915, when he spoke to Clayton of German efforts to suborn the Arab nationalist movement. Neither Arab nor Zionist claims about German strategy were well-founded, but, in their own way, both were effective.

Whether based on fundamental misconceptions concerning imperial strategy or German intentions or Jewish influence abroad, all these factors were in play in the run-up to the decision to issue the Declaration. Still, it is probable that none of them, singly or collectively, would have won the day for the Zionists without the insistent pressure applied by their leading light, Dr. Chaim Weizmann. Born in Russia in 1874, Weizmann was educated there, in Germany and in Switzerland, where he earned a doctorate in chemistry. He became interested in the Zionist ideal at an early age and later said that he had only two passions in life, Zionism and chemistry. He excelled at both. Moving to England in 1904, Weizmann secured an appointment at the University of Manchester where he taught and conducted research. But every moment of his spare time he spent in promoting the idea of a Jewish national home in Palestine. Early in the war Weizmann developed a formula for the mass production of acetone, an essential ingredient in the manufacture of cordite for use in explosives. He promptly turned his discovery over to the Admiralty, without charge; the only compensation he sought was British support for the Zionist programme.[8] That support was slow in coming but by early 1917, Weizmann had met nearly every prominent figure in British government and brought to bear on them his extraordinary persuasive powers. At the same time, he worked tirelessly to consolidate, or eliminate, the various, sometimes discordant, voices of the Zionist movement in England and abroad and to defeat the forces of assimilation of which Montagu was only one of many prominent adherents.

The struggle for Zionism that Weizmann and his colleagues was conducting in the homes of England's Jewish leaders and in the corridors of Whitehall had scarcely registered in the Middle East before 1917. Before the war some 85,000 Jews resided in Palestine, but the war and Turkish repression had reduced their numbers to about 55,000. Perhaps half that number would have identified themselves as Zionists.[9] Until Allenby's capture of Jerusalem, none of them was in a position to say anything about their aspirations for the country. Among British officials in the East, fully absorbed with the war, Zionism was little more than a word. Clayton's papers contain no mention of Zionists or, indeed, of Jews, until August 1916, after he returned from London. While there, he had been impressed with the 'widespread influence of the Jews', as he explained to Wingate:

> It is everywhere and always on the "moderation" tack. The Jews do not want to see anyone "downed". There are English Jews, French Jews, American Jews, German Jews, Austrian Jews and Salonica Jews – but all are JEWS, and moreover practically all are anti-Russian. You hear peace talk and generally somewhere behind is the Jew. You hear pro-Turk talk and desire for a separate peace with Turkey – again the Jew (the mainspring of the C.U.P.). I do not mean that the Jews are disloyal in any way, but it seems to me that the ties

which bind the Jew to his fellow Jews all over the world must induce in him an attitude of sort of semi-neutrality. On the other hand of course they are an increasing power as the war becomes more and more a question of who has the deepest pocket and the longest credit.[10]

Clayton's letter reflected the widely-held view that the Jews exercised a pervasive and vaguely insidious influence in Britain and elsewhere. This was, in fact, one of the motivations that lay behind the Cabinet's decision to issue the Balfour Declaration fifteen months later. More troubling for Clayton, though, was the notion that the Jews, moved by self-interest, exhibited a commonality of purpose that transcended allegiance to the various countries in which they lived. Thus, French and British Jews might be united in their abhorrence of the Czarist regime in Russia – still a key component of the Entente – and, at the same time, support a separate peace with Turkey.

Clayton was incorrect in suggesting that Jewish opinion was monolithic and 'supra-national'; even British Jews disagreed often, and vehemently, about the correct course that should be pursued in the Middle East. It was true that some Jews favoured a separate peace with Turkey, but so too did some non-Jewish Englishmen. By 1916, Weizmann was firmly opposed to a separate Turkish peace, but he did not speak for all Jews, or for all Zionists, and even as late as July 1917, some of his colleagues still entertained the notion that Turkey could, and should, be dislodged from the German alliance by means of a compromise settlement.[11] It was a view that was by no means unique to Jews; unknown to Clayton and to most in Whitehall, throughout 1916 and 1917, the British government was secretly and tentatively exploring the possibility of a separate Turkish peace, primarily through the medium of dissident Turks living in Switzerland. Clayton was adamantly opposed to any consideration of a separate peace. In June 1917, when he learned of an unofficial peace mission to the Middle East led by the former American ambassador to Turkey, Henry Morgenthau – a mission that included three American Zionists – he recorded his strong opposition.[12] So did Weizmann. The Morgenthau mission foundered on the rock of Gibraltar where it was intercepted by Weizmann who persuaded the Americans that a separate peace was antithetical to Zionist interests.

In Egypt Clayton had few contacts with Jews of any stripe prior to 1917. In August 1915, Cairo Intelligence had been approached by Alexander Aaronsohn, a Jew resident in Palestine, where his brother Aaron headed a Jewish spy-ring, later known as 'Nili'. But Aaronsohn had been turned away, not because of anti-Semitism, but due to a suspicion of 'volunteerism', a legitimate concern that men who arrived from enemy territory, offering their services as spies, were inherently suspect.[13] However, a subsequent overture by the Nili ring was accepted in November 1915, and, while communications with the group proved impossible throughout 1916, contact was renewed in February 1917. Valuable tactical Intelligence was obtained from Nili until the Turks uncovered and smashed the ring in October, with tragic consequences for its members.[14]

There is no evidence that Clayton was aware of the efforts of Weizmann and his colleagues in 1916–17 to secure British sponsorship of a Jewish national home in Palestine. Nor does he appear to have had any notion of the debate going on in Whitehall concerning the Zionist programme. But Aaron Aaronsohn had popped up in Cairo in December 1916, eager to pursue 'schemes which he had started on [in England] under Sir Mark Sykes' instructions' for sending agents to Russia and appealing to Jewish labour parties in Russia and America.[15] Clayton was interested in Aaronsohn's proposals, but had no idea whether they should be encouraged. 'We are in ignorance of the policy which H.M.G. is adopting in regard to the Jewish question and Palestine', he informed the Cairo Residency in July 1917. Our 'complete ignorance . . . is handicapping us considerably in dealing with the local Jewish community'.[16]

In August, the Cairo censors held up publication of a pamphlet that had appeared in Egypt containing excerpts from a speech delivered by Weizmann in London on May 20. In his speech the Zionist leader boldly asserted that 'Palestine will be protected by Great Britain' and that, under such protection, 'the Jews will be able to develop and create an administrative organization which, while safeguarding the interests of the non-Jewish population, will permit us to realise the aims of Zionism. I am authorized to declare . . . that H.M.G. are ready to support this plan'.[17] This appears to have been Clayton's first intimation that London was about to announce support for the Zionist programme. He quickly wrote to Sykes urging that he be informed of the government's position on 'the Jewish question', as Aaronsohn and other Jews in Egypt were 'becoming restive and impatient'. 'I am not sure', he added, 'that it is not as well to refrain from any definite pronouncement just at present. It will not help matters if the Arabs – already somewhat distracted between pro-Sherifians and those who fear Meccan domination, as also between pro-French and anti-French – are given yet another bone of contention in the shape of Zionism in Palestine as against the interests of the Moslems resident there. The more politics can be kept in the background, the more likely are the Arabs to concentrate on the expulsion of the Turks from Syria . . . .'[18]

Clayton's concerns were legitimate. Wingate and he were running an Arab revolt predicated on the notion that the Arabs were fighting to liberate Arab territory from the Turks. If Palestine was now to be turned over to the Zionists, he ought to be so informed. And, having sponsored the Arab movement for more than a year, London ought to consider what effect the Zionist programme would have on that movement. Lawrence, on the front lines with the Sherifian forces, was equally concerned. In a letter to Sykes (which he sent to Clayton for transmittal to London), he asked: 'What have you promised the Zionists and what is their programme?' Lawrence added that he had recently seen Aaronsohn in Cairo who 'said at once the Jews intended to acquire the land-rights of all Palestine from Gaza to Haifa & have practical autonomy therein. Is this acquisition to be by fair purchase or by forced sale & expropriation? . . . Do the Jews propose the complete expulsion of the Arab peasantry or their reduction to a day-labourer class?'[19] These questions were a little too pointed for Clayton and he declined to forward Lawrence's letter on to Sykes. Having dealt with Sykes now for two years, and rejected or modified nearly every scheme concocted by him that had come across his desk, he was not anxious to spur him to further activity. As Clayton explained to Lawrence, he had been advised that Sykes had 'rather dropped the Near East just now . . . and I am somewhat apprehensive lest your letter to Mark raise him to activity'.[20]

Clayton was wrong about Sykes; he had not dropped the Near East. Moreover, he had been busy promoting the Zionist programme since the spring of 1916. And, soon after the Balfour Declaration was published in November of the following year, he was hard at work promoting a plan to bring it to fruition, a plan that involved not only the Jews, but also the Arabs and Armenians. Sykes's idea was that these three great repressed nationalities of the Ottoman Empire could combine forces and press for the freedom of Arabia, Syria, Palestine and Mesopotamia. The united voice of these communities, he argued, would represent a formidable force at an eventual peace conference. Already in November, Sykes had obtained the consent of Weizmann, on behalf of the Zionists, and James Malcolm, a London business man prominent in the Armenian community there. He now needed only Arab concurrence.[21] Like many of Sykes' ideas, the plan seemed sound in principle, but broke down under close inspection. Clayton agreed to promote the scheme, but confessed to the Foreign Office that he did not 'expect much success', for 'in spite of all arguments, Mecca dislikes Jews and Armenians and wishes to have nothing to do with them . . . In any case an Arab–Jewish–Armenian combination is so foreign to any previous experience and to existing sentiment that we must proceed with great caution'.[22] To Gertrude Bell in Mesopotamia, Clayton emphasized that the Arabs would see Sykes's proposed combination as nothing more than an attempt to advance Zionist aspirations at their expense: 'M.S. talks eloquently of a Jewish-Armenian–Arab combine, but the Arab of Syria and Palestine sees the Jew with a free hand and the backing of H.M.G. and interprets it as meaning the eventual loss of his heritage. Jacob and Esau once more. The Arab is right and no amount of specious oratory will humbug him in a matter which affects him so vitally.'[23]

Wingate agreed that the idea was impracticable, informing Allenby that Sykes had been 'carried away with the exuberance of his own verbosity in regard to Zionism'. However, he informed the chief, Clayton had 'written him an excellent letter which I hope may have an anodyne effect'.[24] Clayton did pour cold water on Sykes's plan. 'We will try it', he wrote, 'but it must be done very cautiously and, honestly, I see no possible [here, Clayton struck through 'possible' and inserted 'great'] chance of any real success. It is an attempt to change in a few weeks the traditional sentiments of centuries. The Arab cares nothing whatsoever about the Armenian one way or another – as regards the Jew, the Bedouin despises him and will never do anything else, while the sedentary Arab hates the Jew, and fears his superior commercial and economic ability'.[25]

By the end of 1917, Sykes' combination scheme was among the least of Clayton's concerns. The disclosure of Sykes–Picot and the publication of the Balfour Declaration, both in November, had shaken the Anglo-Arab alliance. And the Syrians – or at least those in Cairo with whom Clayton was in frequent contact – were very uneasy about the progress of the Arab revolt. Of course, they looked forward eagerly to their liberation from Turkish rule, but most had no desire to see a Hashemite regime installed in Damascus. And they were deeply concerned about the Balfour Declaration. Clayton informed Sykes that the Declaration had 'made a profound impression on both Christians and Moslems who view with little short of dismay the prospect of seeing Palestine and even eventually Syria in the hands of the Jews whose superior intelligence and commercial abilities are feared by all alike'. Further, the terms of Sykes–Picot were causing suspicion, distrust and uneasiness, particularly since no 'definite pronouncement against annexation' of Syria by the French had issued from Paris. Finally, with Sherifian forces ready to move north on the EEF's right flank, there was 'a very real fear among Syrians of finding themselves under a government in which the patriarchalism of Mecca is predominant'.[26]

Clayton submitted three suggestions to address these concerns. First, the British should 'avoid any impression that we intend to force King Hussein or any Sherifian form of government on peoples who are unwilling to accept them'. Second, the French Government should 'make a definite pronouncement disclaiming any idea of annexation in Syria (including the blue area) and emphasizing their intention of assuring the liberty of all Syrian communities and helping them along the path towards independence and government by the people. This is particularly urgent'. Finally, Clayton suggested that 'the announcement already made to the Jews should suffice for the present and further concessions should be made with the utmost caution. It will be especially dangerous to permit any general measure of Jewish repatriation or colonization of Palestine just now. In any case, the military situation precludes it to-day and will probably continue to do so for some time to come'.[27]

The French did not issue any statement regarding their intentions for Syria and would not do so until the capture of Damascus ten months later. Nor were the Syrians mollified by suggestions that a Hashemite regime would not be imposed in Damascus. As for the Zionist programme, Clayton could do little more than urge caution. He did bring Arab and Jewish leaders together in Cairo and reported that the Arabs were impressed by the Zionist arguments, but they were 'still nervous and feel that [the] Zionist movement is progressing at a pace which threatens their interest'. He urged Jewish leaders to 'be careful not to frighten [the] Arabs by going too fast'.[28] On December 11, the Foreign Office informed Clayton that the government intended to authorize the dispatch of a Zionist commission to Palestine, as soon as the military situation permitted, to 'assist the military authorities in dealing with the position of the Jewish settlements in Palestine'. The commission was to work under Clayton's guidance.[29] The Foreign Office telegram again prompted Clayton to send Sykes a private letter urging caution:

I am not fully aware of the weight which Zionists carry, especially in America and Russia, and of the consequent necessity of giving them every-thing for which they ask, but I must point out that, by pushing them as hard as we appear to be doing, we are risking the possibility of Arab unity becoming an accomplished fact and being ranged against us. Whatever protestations Jews like Sokolow and Weizmann may make and whatever

Arabs may say, the fact remains that an Arab–Jewish entente can only be brought about by very gradual and cautious action. The Arab does not believe that the Jew with whom he has to do will act up to the high flown sentiments which may be expressed . . . In practice he finds that the Jew with whom he comes in contact is a far better business man than himself and prone to extract his pound of flesh. This is a root fact which no amount of public declarations can get over. We have therefore to consider whether the situation demands out and out support of Zionism at the risk of alienating the Arabs at a critical moment. There is also to be considered the mass of sentiment which is bound to be called forth in every Christian country by the fall of Jerusalem into Christian hands, and which might easily be offended by a wholesale pro-Zionist policy.[30]

At the same time, Clayton cabled the Foreign Office, insisting that the 'military situation at present demands that no one be allowed to proceed to Palestine' and 'the longer that the prohibition is maintained the simpler the political situation will remain'. Clayton intended to apply this prohibition on travel to Palestine not only to the Zionists, but also to the Arab community in Cairo whose request to send emissaries to Palestine was turned down by Clayton in January 1918.[31]

Clayton's insistence on maintaining a purely military administration in Palestine was driven by both military and political considerations. North of Jerusalem, Palestine was still a war zone and the establishment of civil government in the country was obviously premature. At the same time, insistence on a military administration enabled political issues to be deferred, allowing time for careful reflection on how Palestine would be governed and how the Balfour Declaration could be implemented without alienating the Arab population. Clayton had foreseen that Palestine was likely to become a political hotbed as territory was liberated from the Turks and even before the EEF assault on Beersheba at the end of October 1917, he had convinced Allenby to establish a military administration with Parker at its head. Conditions would be governed by the Laws and Usages of War as set down in the *Manual of Military Law* and the principles set forth in the *Manual* were based on strict maintenance of the *status quo ante bellum*, until conditions allowed for the establishment of a civil administration. Clayton also prepared a series of proclamations 'of an entirely military nature with no political colour of any kind at all', underscoring that all administrative actions would be taken 'to meet purely military exigencies'.[32] He would be only partially successful in keeping politics out of Palestine for the next eighteen months; Zionist and Arab politics could not be eliminated, but the competing claims of European diplomatic and religious figures were kept to a minimum.

Much of Clayton's difficulty in trying to mitigate Arab displeasure over the Balfour Declaration arose from a very fundamental point: He did not know what was meant by a 'national home for the Jewish people in Palestine'. Many had the same problem. William Yale, a young American formerly employed by the Standard Oil Company in the region and now reporting to the U.S. State

Department from the American Diplomatic Agency in Cairo, was equally perplexed. Shortly after Clayton's December 1917 meeting with the Arab Committee in Cairo, Yale reported that he had learned from one of Clayton's Arab Bureau subordinates, Lieutenant Fielding, that neither he nor Clayton 'understood what the British Foreign Office meant by the creation of a National Home for the Jews in Palestine'. Fielding added that 'the Arab Bureau were in the dark' as to whether the 'establishment of a Jewish State with a Jewish Government was intended, or whether it only meant that the Jews would have the right to emigrate to Palestine and to colonize there. . . .'[33] Yale thought that Clayton had told the Arabs that Britain did not intend to establish a Jewish State in Palestine.[34] But Yale was not present when Clayton addressed the Arab Committee. And it is most unlikely that Clayton, who had been extremely careful and noncommittal in his talks with the Arabs since early 1915, and who did not know what the national home policy meant, informed them that there was no intention to create a Jewish State. For their part, the Arabs relied on a letter from Sykes, read to them by Clayton, from which they were able to 'deduce' that 'all that the Zionists demand is liberty for the Jews to settle in our country and enjoy full civil rights sharing with the native inhabitants their rights as well as their obligations'.[35]

Clayton could not obtain any explanation from the Foreign Office. Nor was any likely to come, for the phrase 'national home' had been carefully chosen; it was intentionally ambiguous, designed to deflect concerns that the Zionists intended to establish a Jewish State in Palestine. True, the second clause of the Declaration made clear that nothing would be done to 'prejudice the civil and religious rights of existing non-Jewish communities in Palestine'. But if the Zionists intended a Jewish State, how could that intent be reconciled with the civil rights of the non-Jewish communities in the country – the great majority of Palestinians – who had no desire to see a Jewish State? When the Foreign Office did get round to sending Clayton a 'general outline of policy' on January 24, 1918, they provided no help. Clayton was given nine very general points, the seventh of which instructed him to secure the 'maintenance of Zionism on right lines', leaving it to him 'to fill in [the] details'. On right lines? What Clayton thought of that question-begging instruction is not recorded, but he confined himself to a reply that the 'policy pursued hitherto has followed similar lines'.[36]

Without definite instructions from London, Clayton was left to his own devices in applying the British policy on the spot. The Zionist programme – whatever it entailed – had to be applied in some fashion, so Clayton continued to encourage discussions between Arab and Jewish leaders in Cairo and he promoted, no doubt reluctantly, Sykes' fanciful scheme for an Arab–Jewish–Armenian combination. Concerned about the Hashemite reaction to the Declaration, he also 'urged Lawrence to impress on Faisal the necessity of an entente with the Jews'. Faisal, he noted, was 'inclined the other way, and there are people in Cairo who lose no chance of putting him against them. I have explained that it is [Faisal's] only chance of doing really big things and bringing the Arab movement to fruition'.[37] In early January 1918, Hogarth was sent to Jeddah to deliver to King Hussein a Foreign

Office message (drafted by Sykes and Hardinge) reaffirming British support for the Arabs in the wake of the Balfour Declaration. The Hogarth Message, as it was later called, reasserted Britain's determination that 'the Arab race shall be given full opportunity of once again forming a nation in the world'. So far as Palestine was concerned, Britain was 'determined that no people shall be subject to another'. Yet, in view of the religious significance of the country, Hogarth informed the King that a 'special regime' must be established there. The aspirations of the Jews to return to Palestine were noted, as was the policy of the British government, which was 'determined that in so far as compatible with the freedom of the existing population, both economic and political, no obstacles should be put in the way of [the] realisation' of Jewish goals.[38] Hogarth's message did not parallel the Balfour Declaration, which purported to guarantee only 'the civil and religious rights' of the non-Jewish population of Palestine; that was not quite the same as reaffirming 'the freedom . . . both economic and political' of the non-Jewish population there, for if 'political freedom' meant anything like self-determination, the Arabs, Christian and Muslim alike, would surely reject any policy supporting the creation of a Jewish State in Palestine.[39]

The Hogarth Message was thought to be generally consistent with recent Entente proclamations concerning the territories being liberated from Ottoman rule. Even as Hogarth was on his way to Jeddah, on January 5, 1918, Lloyd George, in an address to the Trades Unions on British war aims, stated that Mesopotamia, Syria and Palestine were 'entitled to a recognition of their separate national conditions'. Three days later President Woodrow Wilson promulgated his famous Fourteen Points, the twelfth of which held that nationalities under Turkish rule should be allowed 'an absolutely unmolested opportunity of autonomous development'. But these high-flown statements, significant though they were as general descriptions of Entente views, were of no help to the men on the spot in the Middle East. And, while Clayton persisted in his efforts to bring Arabs and Jews together, nearly all his reports to London contained descriptions of Arab suspicion, distrust and antipathy towards the Zionist programme. A despatch sent to Balfour on March 16, provided a typical example: 'The Arab population is unable to believe that the ultimate ambition of Zionism can be anything but the recovery of the Holy City [and] the establishment of a self-governing Jewish State in Palestine. . . .'[40] Clayton delivered the same message to General Jan Smuts, a Cabinet member sent out to report on the Middle Eastern situation in February 1918. Smuts and his assistant, Leo Amery, who eventually drafted the mission's report, spoke at length with Clayton, Wingate and Allenby. According to Amery, Clayton's 'two important points' were 'not to make too much of a splash locally with Zionism until the Arabs have got a slice of the cake themselves, i.e., Damascus, and to get the French to come out clearly with a declaration disavowing any ideas of colonial annexation and emphasizing their adherence to the idea of Arab autonomy'.[41]

Clayton's policy of caution, of gradualism, in implementing the Zionist programme has been interpreted by some historians of the period as evidence of his opposition to Zionism, or even of anti-Semitism. But Weizmann, who came to know

Clayton well, did not thinks so; he regarded the CPO as 'well disposed towards us'. As he wrote to the American Zionist and U.S. Supreme Court Justice, Louis Brandeis, '[t]he Chief Political Officer here General Clayton and his Assistant Colonel Deedes, know the movement, sympathise with it, and consider a Jewish Palestine as the only worthy aim and possible ultimate solution'.[42] Other Zionists, like the Russian firebrand Vladimir Jabotinsky, considered Clayton sympathetic to Zionism.[43] A review of Clayton's correspondence confirms these views. 'Apart from the fact that support of Zionism is the declared policy of His Majesty's Government', he wrote to Sykes, 'I am personally in favour of it and am convinced that it is one of our strongest cards, but your knowledge of all that has taken place in the past in this area will I know lead you to agree with me in the necessity of caution if we are to bring that policy to a successful conclusion'.[44]

Of course, in examining historic correspondence, the historian must always be mindful of the recipient of letters. Clayton was aware that in writing to Sykes he was addressing not only a Member of Parliament and of the Committee of Imperial Defence, and, now in 1918, an important voice in the Foreign Office, but also an avid supporter of Zionism. The same could not be said, however, of Clive Wigram, King George's assistant private secretary. To Wigram, Clayton confided that he was 'personally entirely in favour of the Zionist policy. From the Imperial point of view, it will, if properly developed, create a strong pro-British buffer to the North of Egypt and the Suez Canal'.[45] When he learned that the Zionist Commission would be sent to Palestine in the spring of 1918, Clayton advised Wingate that 'it would cause a stir in both Jewish and other circles, but if they are reasonable and really make advances to the Arabs on moderate lines, it may do good'.[46]

In writing to Gertrude Bell, the Arab Bureau correspondent in Mesopotamia, Clayton knew he was addressing an opponent of Zionism and would readily find a sympathetic ear if he stated his own opposition. In January 1918, Bell confided that she viewed the Balfour Declaration 'with deepest mistrust . . . Palestine for the Jews has always seemed to me to be an impossible proposition. I don't believe it can be carried out – personally I don't want it to be carried out & I've said so on every possible occasion. . . .' In response, Clayton admitted that it was 'not very easy to co-ordinate the Zionist policy of the Government with the Arab policy which we have been pursuing so long. Still, I do not think that on the broader lines the two policies are necessarily incompatible . . . .' He added that 'Jewish expansion in Palestine . . . will greatly improve the condition of the local peasantry provided it is on [the] moderate and liberal lines sketched out by Dr. Weizmann'. Clayton had 'little doubt that the Zionist policy has been of very considerable assistance to us already and may help us a great deal more not only during the war, but afterwards'. Here, he was thinking of Imperial strategy, as previously described in his letter to Wigram: 'A Palestine in which Jewish interest is established and which is under the aegis of Great Britain will be a strong outpost to Egypt'.[47]

While Clayton was struggling to come to grips with the new Zionist policy, his own position in the Middle East was being debated in London. During the last quarter of 1917, Clayton's work had changed significantly, although without official approval, as he spent less time on the Arab revolt and more on political issues. In early December, he decided that the military operations of the revolt would be managed by Lt.-Colonel Alan Dawnay. It was a logical choice because Dawnay's brother, Guy, was serving as Allenby's operations chief for the EEF campaign in Palestine.[48] At about the same time, Allenby put Clayton 'in charge at G.H.Q. of the whole administration of occupied enemy territory' – the Occupied Enemy Territory Administration, or OETA, as it was called. He was now running Palestine from 'a couple of tents and a table or two' at GHQ, at Bir Salem, twenty-five miles west of Jerusalem.[49] Since he was still CPO to the EEF, director of the Arab Bureau and British representative on the Anglo-French Mission, Clayton had, as Hogarth observed, 'taken on (not for the first time) too much at once'.[50]

But it was not Clayton's workload that prompted the Cabinet to reassess his position in early 1918. Sykes had visited Paris in December and reported that the French were displeased with the political situation in Palestine due to a lack of 'defined control' in the country. According to Sykes, French unhappiness had arisen as a result of a recent visit by Wingate to Jerusalem which suggested to them that the Egyptian administration might be extended to Palestine. That would cause 'serious trouble' with the French, Sykes added, because it was 'well known there existed among the British officers in Egypt, a spirit distinctly hostile to the French'.[51] Hardinge agreed that there should be a 'clear cut' between Egypt and Palestine, that Clayton should be 'made entirely independent' of Wingate, placed in charge of all political matters in both Palestine and the Hijaz, and designated as Civil Commissioner in the latter country, with Wingate being retained as 'an admirable figure-head'.[52] Curzon agreed with the solution, but not the title and the Cabinet's Middle East Committee decided on January 12, that Clayton would be made Chief Political Officer for both Palestine and the Hijaz. In an effort to mollify Britain's Entente partners, it had also been suggested to Allenby that he appoint French and Italian officers to important posts in Palestine. But the general responded that he 'could not see his way to carry out this request, though he was willing to appoint two Frenchmen and two Italians as Sanitary Officers'.[53]

Both Wingate and Allenby objected to the new arrangement; if Clayton was to be both CPO and head of OETA, he could not possibly take on political responsibility for the Hijaz.[54] At the same time, Wingate wrote privately to Graham at the Foreign Office, suggesting that Clayton be relieved of his work on the Anglo-French Mission. He thought Clayton's work as CPO far more important, particularly since he could 'see how much the C-in-C relies on him'.[55] On January 19, with the objections of Wingate and Allenby in hand, the Middle East Committee again considered Clayton's position. By this time, Sykes and Hardinge had concluded that Clayton should be 'freed of administrative responsibilities'.[56] The Committee agreed, deciding that Clayton should relinquish his OETA work and that a 'new and separate branch of the Arab Bureau should be established in Palestine' under his direction. The Committee also concluded that the Foreign Office would 'instruct General Clayton direct on all questions affecting policy in Palestine'. He had been reporting weekly to the Foreign Office, through Wingate, since December, but the new arrangement effectively removed Clayton from the High Commissioner's authority. Having worked directly for 'Master' for ten years, Clayton was now free of his control.[57]

In February 1918, Allenby agreed that Clayton 'should not do administrative work' and, in April, a new man, Major General Sir Arthur Money, was put in charge of OETA. Clayton was relieved, acknowledging that he could not possibly do justice to both the CPO and OETA jobs.[58] But he had mixed feelings about his new role. He enjoyed political work and was pleased to be relieved of the heavy burden imposed by his administrative duties at OETA. But it was now necessary for him to be permanently stationed at EEF headquarters in Palestine and this meant leaving Cairo where Enid, Patience and Jane, as well as the couple's new son, Samuel, born on January 8, 1918, were living. And, shortly after his birth, Samuel fell seriously ill. 'We have had a terribly anxious time over our little son who has been desperately ill for some three weeks', he wrote to Lloyd in early March. 'He is, I trust, on the mend now, but it has been very hard on my wife, especially coming so soon after our loss of eighteen months ago and with me permanently away from her'.[59]

Despite the uneasiness he felt in leaving Enid and the children in Cairo, Clayton left for Palestine determined to work towards some sort of understanding between the Zionists and the Arabs. In March 1918, the Zionist Commission arrived in Egypt and Clayton came down to meet Weizmann and his colleagues. After several long talks with the Zionist leader, Clayton came away greatly impressed. 'We are all struck with his intelligence and openness', he informed Sykes, and Allenby, too, had 'formed a high opinion of him'. Clayton was convinced that once Weizmann appeared in Palestine 'the mutual distrust and suspicion between Arabs and Jews' would disappear. He also got from Weizmann 'an inkling of his real policy' which Clayton suspected, but was 'never really aware of until his arrival'.[60] The 'real' Zionist policy, he learned, was to establish a Jewish State in Palestine, though when such a State could be established was unclear. 'I was not under the impression that the Zionist programme included the immediate establishment of a Jewish State after the war', Clayton wrote two weeks later, 'though I imagined it to be the ultimate aim'.[61] Zionist intentions were no secret to British authorities in London, but, until late March 1918, there is no indication that this knowledge was imparted to Clayton or to anyone else in the East until Weizmann himself informed them of the Zionist programme.[62]

Having learned the objectives of the Zionists, Clayton was now more than ever convinced that caution and a gradual development of their programme was required. '[I]t is very necessary to proceed with caution', he advised Balfour; 'precipitate action will only injure the prospects of a project which, given careful handling, should give great results . . . Arab opinion both in Palestine and elsewhere is in no condition to support an overdose of Zionism just now'.[63] On a personal level, Clayton got on well with Weizmann, 'a very sensible fellow and excellent to work with'. But he was most reluctant to be pushed by either the Zionists or the Foreign Office into a position of overt support for the Zionist policy:

It is all very well for people at home to give vent to high-sounding sentiments but we are up against the practical difficulties. I have impressed all this upon Weizmann and I think he sees that undue haste and precipitate action will wreck his own policy as well as embarrass us. I have written to the F.O. officially in this strain . . . I am very anxious that they should leave the execution of the policy to us here – in so far as regards Palestine itself and not rush us. Indeed, as far as I personally am concerned, I do not propose to be rushed and would rather chuck it and let them choose someone else. I cannot conscientiously carry out any line of policy which will go against our pledges to the Arabs, and I can always return to Egypt if they don't want me, and should in many ways prefer it, as I have no axe to grind here.[64]

Of course, Clayton thought he could – and later he would – reconcile the pledges to the Arabs with the Zionist policy because McMahon's pledge to support Arab independence had been qualified by the proviso that British support for the Arabs could extend only to those areas where Britain was free to act without detriment to the interests of her ally, France. And France *had* laid claim to Palestine and was still doing so, as Picot would make clear to Clayton in 1918.

Weizmann certainly understood Clayton's policy of gradualism, but from the Zionist perspective, he had good reasons for pushing his programme. Having just recorded a major and hard-fought victory with issuance of the Balfour Declaration, it was important to maintain the momentum. And Weizmann and his colleagues were under pressure from Zionists in Palestine and abroad to achieve some practical manifestation of the principle laid down in the Declaration. All Clayton could do in that regard was to encourage an understanding between the Arabs and the Zionists. Already, in late March, while the Commission was still in Egypt, he had arranged for some of its members to meet with Arab leaders. And when the mission arrived in Palestine in early April, meetings were promptly set up with Muslim and Christian Arab notables in the country.[65]

At the same time, Clayton closely monitored the Zionist Commission's activities. He reviewed, and occasionally censored, correspondence and reports emanating from its members and, when Weizmann delivered an important speech at an official dinner in Jerusalem on April 27, he carefully reviewed the Zionist leader's text before it was delivered to the assembled Arab and Christian notables of the city. While assuring the assembly that the Zionists desired only to 'create conditions' enabling the 'moral and national development' of the Jewish people in Palestine, Weizmann emphasized the second clause of the Balfour Declaration, stressing that such 'development will and must not be to the detriment of the great communities already established in the country'. And then he delivered what must be regarded as a masterpiece of equivocation; he cautioned the notables that 'they were not to believe those who insinuate that the Jews intend to take the supreme political power of Palestine into their hands at the end of the war'. The concluding phrase, 'at the end of the war', must have given many of the assembled dignitaries pause because it evaded the question of ultimate Zionist intent; if not at the end of the war, did the Zionists nevertheless intend to take 'supreme political power' in ten years, or twenty, or thirty?[66]

By May 1918, Weizmann had become frustrated with the Palestinian Arabs. He was unable to convince them that the Zionist movement was anything other than the menace they assumed it was. He complained to Balfour not only of the 'treacherous nature of the Arab', but also about the British military administration, which he considered pro-Arab and hostile to Zionism.[67] In making these claims, Weizmann had the avid support of the British political officer assigned to the Zionist Commission, William Ormsby-Gore, a Member of Parliament and former Arab Bureau analyst and now assistant secretary to the Cabinet. Formally, Ormsby-Gore was attached to Clayton's political staff, but he communicated directly with Sykes at the Foreign Office and held very strong pro-Zionist views. 'It is my firm conviction', he wrote to Sykes, 'that the Zionists are the only sound, pro-British constructive element in the whole show'. And he, like Weizmann, complained of the attitude of British officers in OETA; they were 'all Sudan or Gippy [Egyptian] Army men' who exhibited an 'ineradicable tendency . . . to favour quite unconsciously the Moslem both against Christian and Jew'.[68] General Money, the new OETA chief, observed that Ormsby-Gore 'although not a Jew himself' was 'rather more Zionist than the members of the Commission'.[69]

Clayton brought to a halt direct communication between Sykes and Ormsby-Gore and stated that the criticisms of OETA officers were 'unjustified', adding that 'every effort has been made to deal fairly with all communities in Palestine'.[70] Unrepentant, Ormsby-Gore submitted a lengthy report to Clayton which he intended to forward to Balfour. In his paper, Ormsby-Gore claimed that 'maintenance of the status quo in OET[A] according to the Manual of Military Law operates entirely in favour of the Arab Moslem and against the development of Zionism'. That imbalance had to be addressed, he argued, for Zionism was 'a power that is infinitely greater than any Arab majority in Palestine or even of Islam'. 'There is no stopping the Zionist movement now', he added, for 'sooner or later we shall see a Zionist Palestine of this I am convinced'. As for the Palestinian Arab, Ormsby-Gore thought him 'parasitic, treacherous, self-seeking and lacking in ideals, even of patriotism let alone moral ideals'.[71] The young MP was not critical of his chief; to the contrary, he thought the Zionist Commission could 'still perform useful services under the guidance of General Clayton'. But Clayton would not allow Ormsby-Gore's angry diatribe to be sent; across the front of the paper he wrote 'Cancelled' in large letters. And, he drafted a list of ten items, each evidencing favourable treatment rendered by the OETA to Jews in the country. Ormsby-Gore had also attached to his report a letter from Weizmann providing several examples of incidents which, although the Zionist leader admitted he had not verified, demonstrated unfair treatment of the Jews. Clayton's annotations on Weizmann's letter reflected his doubts about the Zionist claims: 'no dates'; 'vague'; 'requires substantiation'; 'unsupported'; 'unfair'; 'a misunderstanding'; 'nor are Arabs allowed', etc.[72]

Although Clayton was justified in quashing Ormsby-Gore's partisan and polemical report, the young MP did make two points that may have given the CPO pause.

Most of the OETA officials were veterans of the Egyptian civil service or the Egyptian Army, and they were, in sentiment, if not in action, favourably predisposed to the Arabs. Money had assembled a staff of thirty officers and, eventually, twelve military governors and they were 'on the whole' recruited from Egypt.[73] But these men had not been employed in Palestine because of any anti-Zionist inclinations. Ninety percent of Palestine was Arabic-speaking, including many Jews who had been living in the country since the 1880s. Obviously, Arabic-speaking officers were required to administer Palestine and the only readily available source was Egypt and the Sudan.[74] They arrived in Palestine with something of a pro-Arab bias, as Clayton admitted to Balfour: 'The British Officials of the Military Administration have been fully informed of the Zionist programme and of the intentions of His Majesty's Government regarding it. It is inevitable, however, that they should experience some difficulties in consequence of the fact that up to date our policy has been directed towards securing Arab sympathy in view of our Arab commitments. It is not easy therefore, to switch over to Zionism all at once in the face of a considerable degree of Arab distrust and suspicion . . . [In] the interests of Zionism itself, it is very necessary to proceed with caution'.[75] This was no answer for the Zionists, however, and for the next two years – until a civil government was set up in July 1920 – they complained loudly of any OETA officer they thought unsympathetic to Zionism. And, so great was the Zionist influence in Whitehall, that they had several OETA men removed from their posts. As early as May 1918, William Yale reported to Washington that 'even among the British there are rumours and complaints that the Zionists are in such favour in London that they are able to keep in direct communication with the British Government, and if measures or officials in Palestine do not please them, they have only to take the matter up with London and their requests are acceded to'.[76]

Fifty years later, R. F. P. Monckton, a young officer posted to Jerusalem in 1918, explained the attitude of many of his fellow OETA officers:

> The Balfour Declaration was vaguely thought to be workable, but nobody understood how it could work . . . British officers in O.E.T.A. were quite prepared to be friends with and work with both Jewish and Arab colleagues, and no difficulties ever arose from this score, but they tended to be anti-Jewish partly because they thought that immigration of Jews was bad luck on the Arabs, and that they were getting a raw deal; and partly because they found the Jews already in Palestine uncongenial to them, as they had little in common; whilst the Jews coming in were difficult, as in other countries they had always been 'agin the government . . . As far as British officers went they were by and large inclined to be anti-Jewish: but I never knew this to be reflected in their work, . . .[77]

The views described by Monckton were shared by many in OETA, including the chief administrator, General Money. He was suspicious of the Zionist Commission, convinced that its 'real programme is undoubtedly Palestine for the Jews, or at any rate, the chief power in Palestine for the Jews'. And, like Clayton, he understood that many men in OETA were finding it difficult to affirmatively assist the Zionists when 'we've been busy the last three years in creating and fostering an Arab movement with [the] King of the Hedjaz, who is still fighting in alliance with us'.[78] After working in Palestine for a year, Money admitted in 1919 that 'speaking personally and <u>privately</u>, I must confess my own inclination is on the side of the Arabs, though in my position I have to be absolutely impartial, and am if anything impelled by orders from home to assist the Zionists. I don't mean however, to be impelled very far in that direction, as it will mean practically a revolution, irrespective of the merits of the case, and if I am pressed further than I consider legitimate or judicious I shall resign'.[79] Money's attitude might have presented problems for Clayton, as the line between administrative and political questions was often very thin and occasionally imperceptible; they often found that they were working on the same problems. But they experienced no difficulties. Money regarded the CPO as a 'level headed fellow' and soon discovered that they worked well together:

> He's a very sound little gunner by name Clayton and we get on capitally. As an administrator he was hopeless, and he got my show into an awful mess whilst he was trying to do both jobs; but in his own line he is excellent, and relieves me of a lot of bother. For instance, if I want to get something done by the F.O. I just tell him and he relieves me of all further bother and gets it settled. He's rather weak in dealing with the Zionist Commission who are always trying to claim exceptional privileges for their Jews, but I recognise his difficulties and the fact that they have a very strong backing from Mr. Balfour and others and [I] turn down his requests on their behalf as politely as possible. As far as the administration is concerned, we treat all classes and creeds alike.[80]

This entry in Money's diary was written on the very day that Clayton prepared a memorandum in which he recognized that equal treatment of 'all classes and creeds' in accordance with the *Manual of Military Law* was 'incompatible with any development of the Zionist Policy as announced by Mr. Balfour'. Because of the demographic disparity, with Jews representing only ten percent of the population, equal treatment of Jew and Arab could only mean that Britain was not using its 'best endeavours' to promote the national home policy laid down in Balfour's Declaration. Clayton thus saw only two choices: defer development of the Zionist policy until a civil government was established in Palestine, or observe the status quo principles of the *Manual of Military Law* 'only so far as they do not preclude gradual and reasonable development of the ideas which lie behind Mr. Balfour's declaration'. If Britain did not actively support Zionism, Clayton believed that Weizmann would withdraw from his leadership of 'pro-British Zionism' and the Commission would leave Palestine. This, he reasoned, 'would be a severe blow to British diplomacy' and 'the result might well be to throw Zionism into the arms of America or even at worst on to Germany. Thus, the death-blow would be dealt to pro-British Zionism'.[81]

Having come to the conclusion that it was necessary to accord the Zionists disparate treatment in order to advance their programme, Clayton was now left with the problem of how best to achieve that end without further antagonizing the Palestinian Arabs. One way, of course, was to continue his efforts to engineer some sort of understanding between Arab and Jew. In May 1918, he arranged for Weizmann to meet with Faisal. The 'sympathetic attitude of the King of the Hejaz and of Faisal', he thought, would 'go far towards a co-ordination of Zionist and Arab policies'.[82] On June 4, Weizmann and Faisal met near Akaba. The Zionist leader gave the Amir his standard message that the Jews did not propose setting up a Jewish government, but would work under British protection to colonize and develop the country without encroaching on Arab interests. And, he suggested that the development of a Jewish Palestine would be helpful to the establishment of an Arab kingdom which would receive Jewish support. Faisal was noncommittal. He could not speak on behalf of an Arab government – only his father could do so, he said – and even if he publicly discussed the possibility of Jewish colonization of Palestine, Turco-German propagandists would use anything he said to undermine the Arab movement. Joyce, who was present during the meeting and kept the only record of the conversation, reported that 'Sherif Faisal personally accepted the possibility of future Jewish claims to territory in Palestine', but could say no more.[83]

Weizmann's suggestion to Faisal that the Zionists would support the Arab nationalist movement was a clever manoeuvre. If he could obtain Hashemite acquiescence to Zionism, he could limit Arab opposition to his programme to Palestine. As he explained to Balfour, with the support of the Arab movement '[t]he so-called Arab question in Palestine would . . . assume only a purely local character. . . .'[84] The strategy made good sense to Clayton, as he believed that the Palestinian Arab had little interest in the Arab movement anyway. 'I have detected but few signs of real patriotism amongst the population of Palestine', he reported to Balfour. 'The Palestinian Arab is not greatly interested in events outside his own country and regards the Sherifian movement with comparative indifference'.[85] He elaborated in a letter to Gertrude Bell:

Palestine itself is to my mind outside the real Arab policy except in so far as discontent and disturbance here might react across the Dead Sea and Jordan as well as in Syria. The so-called Arabs of Palestine are not to be compared with the real Arab of the Desert or even of other civilised districts in Syria and Mesopotamia. He is purely local and takes little or no interest in matters outside his immediate surroundings. The Sherifian movement leaves him absolutely cold as far as taking any active part in it is concerned. The more or less educated class is composed of small traders, land-owners and would-be or ex-Government employees. This class is of course against anything which spells progress or development as they are shiftless and corrupt by inclination and are not anxious for a state of affairs in which it will be necessary for them to compete with more energetic and enterprising elements . . .

In contrast to the Palestinian Arab, was the 'Sherifian Arab':

> [T]here is little doubt that the main ambition of the Sherifian Arab (at any rate of Sherif Faisal) lies in Syria. His eyes are fixed on Damascus and Aleppo and nothing else seems to matter to him in comparison with this. It is this that leads him to welcome Jewish cooperation as he is quite prepared to leave Palestine alone provided he can secure what he wants in Syria.[86]

Clayton's distinction between the 'shiftless and corrupt' Palestinian Arab and the 'real Arab of the desert' appears peculiar at the distance of a century, but it was a commonly held view at the time.[87] The distinction may have been fanciful, but for Clayton it offered one of the few rays of hope in an increasingly gloomy scene. Already, by July 1918, he saw that the Arab merchants, small landowners and 'would-be or ex-government employees' of Palestine were implacably opposed to Zionism. 'There seems no hope of conciliating this section of the population of Palestine', he admitted.[88] The only hope, then, lay with the Hashemites who might be persuaded to support the Zionist programme in some fashion in return for tangible Jewish assistance. But, by November 1918, Weizmann had dropped his plan to limit Arab opposition to Palestine by co-opting Faisal with financial support. After his return to London in September, Weizmann had discussed the proposal with 'the Authorities' and it was decided that the Zionists could not advance any money to help Faisal. 'If we lend money to Feysal', Weizmann explained to Clayton, 'we lay ourselves open to a reproach that we are attempting to put him and his friends under an obligation'. The Zionists might supply 'advisers, both technical and financial', but nothing more.[89]

Throughout the summer and fall of 1918, Clayton continued to struggle with the practical difficulties of implementing the government's Zionist policy. He continued to impress on London the importance of a gradual implementation of the policy; he emphasized the need for 'tact and discretion'; he cautioned that any 'striking development of Zionist policy' was dangerous; he urged that any further declarations concerning that policy should be deferred 'until the future of Palestine has been definitely settled'; and, he specifically requested that if any further statements concerning Zionism were contemplated, they should 'be submitted here for observations before publication'.[90]

Clayton's policy of gradualism did not require that all Zionist proposals be rejected or deferred; he had, after all, acknowledged in May that the Zionists would have to be accorded preferential treatment if the policy of the Balfour Declaration was to have any chance of success. So, he considered every proposal concerning the Zionists on its merits, rejecting some and accepting others as the circumstances allowed. He objected to the release of all 'enemy' Jews interned in Egypt, but agreed that those not of German origin or avowedly anti-Entente should be set free. He acceded to Weizmann's request that a Zionist colleague, Leonard Stein, be allowed to come to Palestine, even though the Foreign Office objected. He supported the Zionist plan to build a Hebrew University in Jerusalem. He censored anti-Zionist articles appearing in Arabic newspapers. He agreed that Hebrew could be recognized as 'the language of the Jewish people in Palestine', although he cautioned that the 'official language' of the administration was 'English only' and that there were many Jews in Palestine who did not speak Hebrew. He allowed a 'Syrian Arab Delegation' to come to Palestine from Egypt, as he thought it would help 'allay the apprehension of the Arab population regarding Zionist aspirations', and he was pleased that the Delegation had a 'tranquilizing effect' on the Christian and Muslim populations in the country.[91]

Other proposals that were too controversial, and likely to incite strong Arab opposition, Clayton did not hesitate to oppose. One such proposal was the Zionist plan to acquire the Wailing Wall in Jerusalem. Clayton knew the plan was sure to 'raise a storm of protest' from the Arabs, for not only was the Wall in the 'immediate vicinity' of the Mosque of Omar, the property in front of the Wall was owned by a Moroccan wakf (charitable foundation). For a time, Clayton tolerated private negotiations initiated by the Zionists to purchase the property, but when a September offer was made public he reported that 'something approaching a panic set in' and he suspended all further talks on the subject.[92] He also opposed a Zionist plan to form a National Bank of Palestine 'from the nucleus of the existing Anglo-Palestine Company'. That company, he knew, was the 'instrument of the Zionist Organisation' and Clayton held that establishment of the bank would convince the Arabs that 'the real intention' of the government 'was to set up a Jewish State in Palestine'.[93] He also opposed a Zionist scheme to fund the development of 250,000 acres of uncultivated land in the country. On practical grounds, the plan had 'everything to recommend it', but from a political point of view, he saw that it would only 'stimulate the apprehensions of the local population'. He proposed that the scheme be allowed to proceed only under the aegis of OETA and with the participation 'not only of the Zionists but also of members of other communities'.[94]

For the most part, the Foreign Office supported Clayton's policy of gradualism. With the very real menace of the Turco-German force still in northern Palestine, London could always 'quote that blessed phrase "military exigencies",' and thereby defer resolution of the persistent political problems posed by application of the Zionist policy. No doubt, Clayton's cautionary approach helped to keep Arab–Jewish tensions from bubbling to the surface in 1918. But Arab-Zionist relations represented only one aspect of the problem of Palestine. Inevitably, as the Turks were pushed north into Syria other issues arose, issues associated with Britain's Entente partners and, for Clayton, they seemed no less formidable than the disagreements between Arab and Jew.

20

A Nest of Intrigue: Allied Disputes in the Levant

On the evening of December 18, 1917, Clayton boarded the 6.15 train at Cairo's main station bound for Kantara on the Canal and then Palestine. He had been in Cairo only a few days following Allenby's triumphal entry into Jerusalem and was now returning to the Holy Land to resume his duties as CPO and OETA Chief Administrator. He was accompanied by his Assistant Political Officer, Edward Cadogan, and by Ronald Storrs, still Oriental Secretary at the Cairo Residency. For a time Clayton regaled his companions with stories of Intelligence tradecraft, including, as Storrs recorded in his diary, descriptions of some sixty-five kinds of invisible ink, many of which, like saliva, revealed their secrets by the mere application of heat. But, as the evening wore on, the conversation flagged and Clayton leaned back into a corner of the compartment where, straining under the 'feeble flickering gas light', he soon became absorbed in a recent issue of the *Grand Magazine*.[1]

Storrs would assume an important position in the administration of Palestine; in ten days he would take up the post of Military Governor of Jerusalem. Alternately assailed by both Arabs and Zionists as biased, Storrs would nevertheless prove a success as Jerusalem's governor, lasting nine years in the post. And Clayton, as CPO and OETA chief, was already the most important non-military figure in the country. He held no executive functions, but on all 'civil, administrative, political, religious and diplomatic issues' Clayton was 'the sole adviser of the chief'; and, as Allenby had neither the time nor the inclination to involve himself in such matters, the CPO's word was generally final.[2]

While Storrs and Clayton were both able to navigate round the treacherous shoals of Palestinian politics, it would have been difficult to find two more different personalities in the country. Storrs, a university man, a dilettante and self-styled aesthete, prided himself on a deep understanding of things Oriental and revelled in the arcana of the ecclesiastical disputes that he would so often confront as Governor of Jerusalem. Most people were divided in their assessments of Storrs. One acquaintance was fascinated by his 'clever conversation', but 'rather repelled by his appalling bumption [*sic*] and pushing personality'. Another colleague thought him 'thoroughly selfish and slightly orientalized', a man of doubtful morals who was 'widely read, very musical' with a 'pretty taste in carpets and curios' and who 'talks well and takes pains with people who matter'. Yet, the same man concluded that it was 'a stroke of genius to make Storrs Governor of Jerusalem', for 'no one else can or will understand the mind and character of the oriental ecclesiastic as he does'.[3]

Sitting across from Clayton on the night train to Kantara, Storrs studied the face of his polar opposite, a man schooled not at Cambridge but at the Atbara and Omdurman, at Wau and Khartoum. Clayton was a man with both feet on the ground, not a scholar, but a practitioner, a problem-solver. Yet, the two men had worked well with one another for three years, drawn together by a shared conviction that the Arab movement could be utilized to split the solidarity of Islam and defeat the Turks. Storrs thought Clayton 'outside & apart from his work, at which he is unimaginatively first class, a commonplace personality, rich in common sense & common knowledge of common objects, but in little else. Rightly self-satisfied, ambitious, hopeful but uncertain of his future, [he] would like (& do well in) the [Egyptian Ministry of the] Interior. . . .'[4] But Storrs, like Lawrence, admired Clayton's management style and admitted the CPO's pervasive influence: Under Clayton's 'unruffled equanimity and sympathy no problem seemed insoluble', Storrs later wrote. 'As Chief Political Officer to the Force he was far too busy (even if he had desired) to interfere in detail. He expected but never inflicted proposals. He was never in the way and never out of the way'.[5] That two such vastly different person-alities would get on so well may have surprised colleagues who knew them both; but in managing the numerous and complex religious and political disputes that emerged in Palestine following the Turkish defeat, both brought to bear their partic-ular strengths.

For centuries Palestine had been a special home to several of the world's great religions. While the emerging conflict between Zionist and Palestinian Arab occu-pied centre stage, their dispute was essentially political, not religious. The same could not be said, however, of the 'constant and deplorable altercations' that arose between and among the various Christian denominations in Palestine.[6] General Money, Clayton's successor as OETA chief, was appalled by the intra-Christian strife: 'They certainly presented to the Moslem world an unedifying exhibition of Christian love and charity! Three creeds – Orthodox Greek, Latin Franciscans, and Armenians – all contest (and literally) for the guardianship of these [holy] places, all have churches or chapels as near to them as they can get, each tries to encroach on the other sects' "pitch" and constant fights, often resulting fatally, occur between their followers actually on and around these sacred places.'[7] The three 'creeds' to which Money referred were then each represented in the country by their great Patriarchs. Nominally supreme as the head of the Roman Catholic Church in Palestine, the Latin Patriarch gave way in practice to the *Custode* – the guardian – of the Franciscans, which had been the predominant Catholic order in Palestine since the thirteenth century. The Franciscans, who quarrelled incessantly with the Orthodox and Armenian communities, were themselves riven by an internal dispute between those inclined to follow their Italian sponsors and those sympathetic to France which, after all, had been recognized for nearly four hundred years as exercising a 'protectorate' over all Latin Christians in the Holy Land. Nor did the Franciscans get on well with their co-religionists. The Salesians were often at odds with them, and objected to an attempt to compel them to preach in Italian. Only the Dominicans – according to Storrs, the 'intellectual aristocracy of Christian Palestine' – remained 'entirely detached from the scrimmage of the communities'.[8]

The Greek Orthodox community in Palestine had their own set of problems. Not only were they involved in frequent skirmishes with the Franciscans, they often came to blows with the Armenians, as when the Greek Epiphany unhappily fell on the same day as the Armenian Christmas. And, like the Franciscans, the Orthodox community was also divided internally. The vast majority of their adherents in Palestine was Arab; the leadership of the Church was entirely Greek. Internecine dispute inevitably ensued and the troubles were compounded by the Orthodox patriarch Damianos who had been deported to Syria by the Turks after running up an unholy debt of some £600,000. The obligation would have been of no particular interest to Storrs or Clayton had it not been secured by land located in and around Jerusalem. It was reported that the debt was being bought up *sub rosa* by the Jews with the intent of foreclosing on the security and taking possession of the land. Clayton refused to tolerate this brazen departure from the status quo required by the Laws and Usages of War and all executions on judgments of foreclosure were brought to an abrupt halt.[9]

Even minor Christian sects contributed to the religious turmoil of war-time Palestine. The Coptic Church, whose Patriarch resided in Cairo, maintained a convent in Jerusalem and even owned a tiny chapel adjoining the Church of the Holy Sepulchre. Since the chapel could accommodate only one person – the priest – those attending the Coptic Mass were obliged to assemble outside, in a right-of-way owned by the Franciscans. Inevitably, the Latins marched through the Coptic congregation and the ensuing melee generated howls of protest from both sides. Not to be outdone, the Copts emptied their slops from the upper windows of their convent, conveniently located just above the Ninth Station of the Cross along the Via Dolorosa. The Franciscans' Friday procession along that famous way again prompted angry recriminations.[10] The tiny Syriac Church of St. Luke, whose adherents spoke the ancient language of Christ, Aramaic, presented a problem of a different type. They owned only one minor holy place – the grave of Joseph of Arimathea – but were in constant conflict with the church's superiors in Antioch and Damascus. Reluctantly, Storrs intervened and twice resolved disputes within the community.[11]

The greatest challenge Storrs and Clayton confronted occurred every spring with the annual confluence of the Christian Easter, Jewish Passover and the Muslim feast of Nabi Musa, the celebration of the 'prophet' Moses. For generations, Storrs later recalled, the spring season in Palestine had meant the 'sharpening of daggers and the trebling of garrisons'.[12] In 1918, Storrs met the challenge and even imported the Greek Patriarch of Sinai, Porphyrios, in replacement of the still exiled Damianos, to lead the highly inflammable Easter eve ceremony of the Holy Fire. Storrs personally joined the cordon assembled to protect the Patriarch as he marched in solemn procession to initiate the ceremony, earning for the effort both the blows of assembled protestors and the praise of Foreign Secretary Balfour.[13] Storrs was less successful in the spring of 1920, when violence and rioting broke out in Jerusalem.

For the most part, Clayton was content to leave these religious fracas to Storrs, confident in the Governor's ability to delve into the details of historic precedent and religious ritual to resolve even the most difficult controversies. But, occasionally, the CPO could not avoid being drawn in, as when an angry disagreement arose between 'two Christian communities' over the right to clean the dirty windows of the Church of the Nativity at Bethlehem. Called in to resolve the dispute, Clayton asked how long it was since the windows were last cleaned. 'Forty years', he was told. 'Well then', he replied, 'let it remain another year'. The dispute was never heard of again.[14]

The case of the dirty windows posed a purely religious question, but underlying many such disputes were political issues and, for these, responsibility lay almost entirely with Clayton. Nearly all the Christian communities in Palestine had European sponsors and, as religious disagreements blew up in the East, angry French, Italian, Greek and Spanish diplomats descended on the Foreign Office in London. One such disagreement occurred in January 1918, when the French and Italians quarrelled over the right to post military guards over the Mosque of Omar and the churches of the Holy Sepulchre and the Nativity. Clayton applied the common sense which Storrs regarded as his defining characteristic. Considering that the French had only 2,000 soldiers in Palestine and the Italians fewer than 1,000, Clayton ordered that the British would guard these holy places four days per week, the French two days and the Italians one.[15] The dispute ended.

Clayton's solution to the problem of European guards over the holy places by no means resolved the differences between the Italians and the French. Picot, it will be recalled, had been peremptorily shut down by Allenby when he had tried to assert French rights to jointly administer Palestine after the fall of Jerusalem. But the mischievous Frenchman was soon planning another means of establishing French interests in the country. As the senior French representative in Palestine, he emphasized France's historic right of exercising a protectorate over all Latin Christians residing there. In practical terms this meant that Picot should be accorded certain honours at Roman Catholic religious ceremonies in Palestine. The Franciscans did not agree and informed Picot that, as the Turks had left, the Order no longer recognized France's status as protector of the Latin communities. Picot promptly objected to Clayton, but the CPO would not be drawn into the dispute; it should be resolved by the French government and the Franciscan authorities in Europe. At the same time, the Italians complained bitterly that while all diplomatic representatives had been excluded from Palestine during the military administration, Picot had been accorded some special status that enabled him to assert French interests in the country.[16] The Italians, it appears, were unaware that Picot held no consular or diplomatic status in Palestine, but was there as the French representative to the Anglo-French Mission established a year earlier.

The competing parties appealed to the Foreign Office. It was an all too common problem. 'We are pestered day and night', Graham wrote from the Office, 'by demands from foreign representatives here to be allowed to send agents or consuls' to Jerusalem.[17] At the same time, the Italians were engaged in their own scheming. Colonel D'Agostino, commander of the small Italian contingent in Palestine, was reported by Clayton to be 'busying himself in a lot of political matters'. As D'Agostino was under Allenby's direct command, Clayton had no authority to halt his intrigues. But when the general gave the Italian 'a hint' – one can only imagine how it was delivered – that 'his place was with his unit', the colonel promptly left Jerusalem. Meanwhile, Rome was pressing for Italy's pre-war consul, Count Senni, to be allowed to return to Jerusalem. Sykes informed Clayton that the Italian ambassador was coming to the Foreign Office 'daily with great clamours' urging restoration of the Count's position in the Holy Land. Clayton would not agree; Senni could not be 'divested of his consular status in the eyes of the general public [and] his coming now would certainly lead to trouble and would incense the French community who are already greatly irritated by the attacks made by Italian Franciscans against the French Protectorate of Latin Christians'. The Foreign Office reluctantly agreed and Rome was informed that Senni would not be allowed to return in either a public or a private capacity.[18]

Clayton's position on the prohibition of foreign diplomatic representation in Palestine was supported by a Foreign Office determination, made in February 1918, that the military administration could not 'admit any claims based on Consular status during the Turkish regime; all consular rights of all countries, including those of Great Britain, must remain in abeyance pending a final settlement of the territories in Military occupation'. As for Picot, any honours he was accorded by the ecclesiastical authorities were not to be regarded as giving him the right to exercise any 'executive authority' or as entitling him to make representations to the military authority on behalf of any 'supra-national religious body'.[19] The French and Italians took their dispute regarding the Latin Protectorate to the Vatican and in March the Holy See decided that the long-standing French Protectorate over the Holy Places must be recognized.[20] The Vatican's decision resolved the religious dispute between France and Italy, but it did not, and could not, accord France any superior political position in Palestine, as Picot had hoped. He was informed by Clayton that Britain did not consider him as holding any consular or diplomatic position in the country.[21]

Despite Clayton's clear statements concerning foreign representation in Palestine, neither the French nor the Italians were convinced that the British were applying the prohibition fairly. They both pointed to the case of the Spanish Consul, Count Ballobar, who resided in Jerusalem and was clearly acting in a diplomatic capacity. However, Clayton was able to distinguish the Spaniard's position from that of his international colleagues. Ballobar had represented Spain before the war and had remained in Jerusalem for the duration, during which he had represented not only Spain, but also neutral countries and even the interests of the Entente Powers in Palestine. He was in Jerusalem when the EEF arrived in December 1917, and he was still there, now overseeing the interests of Spain and the Central Powers in the country. His case was therefore unique. But when Clayton recommended that Ballobar be allowed to make a short visit to Egypt for health reasons, the Foreign Office objected, noting that even his temporary departure from Palestine would put him in the same position as diplomats from other countries and he would not be allowed to return until the ban on diplomatic agents was lifted.[22]

The religious and diplomatic squabbles that arose in Jerusalem after the EEF's 1917 victory had turned the city, Clayton wrote, into 'a nest of political and ecclesiastical intrigue of the class in which our Latin Allies are prone to delight'. But for the CPO, these were all 'minor questions' and presented nothing that could not be 'tackled quite easily' as long as he was 'backed up from home'.[23] And Clayton was backed up; there were very few instances when the Foreign Office did not follow the advice of their man on the spot. The same could not be said, however, of the looming problems of Anglo-French relations that were sure to arise as the EEF moved north in its campaign against the Turks. Of these, the greatest problem remained that posed by the Sykes–Picot Agreement.

Clayton had been consistent in his opposition to Sykes–Picot since he first learned of its terms in April 1916. Once the Agreement was made public in November 1917, he renewed his objections and urged that efforts be made to secure French repudiation of any idea of their annexation of Syria and the Lebanon. He made the same point to Leo Amery when the Smuts Mission appeared in Cairo in February 1918.[24] Everyone seemed to agree. Even Sykes began urging modification of the Agreement as early as August 1917. He did not then propose any departure from the 'agreed geographical boundaries', but supported a change in 'attitude' whereby France and Britain would 'agree not to annex but to administer . . . in consonance with the ascertained wishes of the people'. Any 'ideas of annexation', Sykes argued, 'really must be dismissed [as they are] contrary to the spirit of the time'.[25] By the end of 1917, Sykes had gone even further, now asserting that the pact was 'completely worn out' and 'should be scrapped'. He encouraged Clayton to discuss the Agreement with Picot who, he believed, did not realize 'how far things have gone' and suggested that the Frenchman should now 'take a bold line of Syria for the Syrians and a constitutional government'.[26] Clayton was quite willing to take up the matter with Picot. Despite the problems caused by the Frenchman in Palestine, Clayton's personal relations with him were 'admirable' and he and Picot were 'excellent friends'.[27] Still, neither he nor Picot had the power to abrogate the Agreement – only their respective governments could do that – and, in any case, he was well aware that Picot regarded the pact as 'his bible'. But Clayton advised Sykes that he would give the Frenchman his 'own personal opinion' that Sykes–Picot was 'out of date, reactionary, and only fit for the scrap heap'.[28]

Meanwhile, Sykes began looking for ways to undermine the Agreement that he had co-authored. One such opportunity appeared in April 1918, when seven Syrians resident in Cairo presented a 'memorial' to Wingate that posed a number of questions regarding Britain's intent for the future of Arab lands liberated from the Turks. In essence, the Syrians sought an assurance that the Arabs would be accorded complete independence. Sykes drafted a declaration in response to the Syrians that was sent to

Cairo in mid-June. The declaration reflected a division of the region into four areas. In those areas of Arabia that were 'free and independent' before the war, as well as in those regions emancipated from Turkish control 'by the actions of the Arabs themselves', Britain would recognize 'the complete and sovereign independence of the Arabs'. In a third area – that 'formerly under Ottoman dominion, but occupied by the Allied forces' during the war – Britain desired that any future government would 'be based on the principle of the consent of the governed'. In a fourth area, that comprising regions 'still under Turkish control', Britain expressed the 'wish and desire' that the Arabs would obtain their 'freedom and independence'.[29]

This document, called the Declaration to the Seven, was given to the Syrians on June 16, and, according to one Arab historian, produced a 'wave of jubilation [that] swept the Arab world'.[30] Had it been widely disseminated, the Declaration might well have prompted jubilation, for it was clearly inconsistent with both the Sykes–Picot Agreement and the Balfour Declaration. The EEF, not the Arabs, had liberated Palestine to a point just north of Jerusalem and, in a few months, would drive the Turks from the remainder of the country and from Syria. If then, the future governments of Palestine and Syria were to be based on 'the principle of the consent of the governed', the Syrians would surely reject French involvement in their country and, just as clearly, the Palestinians – ninety percent Arab – would not tolerate a Jewish national home there. Of these points there was no doubt. In other respects, the Declaration reflected formulae just as ambiguous as the Balfour Declaration and the McMahon–Hussein correspondence. What areas were 'free and independent' before the war? Nominally at least, none were; the Turks held sovereignty over all Arab areas in 1914. And, what regions had been liberated 'by the actions of the Arabs themselves'? Arguably, none; the Arabs would not even have liberated the Hijaz without the substantial military, financial and material support provided by Britain. Finally, the Declaration was a unilateral statement; the consent of France had neither been obtained nor sought. So, however much the Declaration represented British intentions for the future, the lack of French acquiescence rendered it only so much paper if Paris could not be persuaded to depart from Sykes–Picot.

Before condemning Sykes for adding yet another layer of mud to the quagmire of Middle Eastern politics, two points must be made. First, although Sykes drafted the Declaration to the Seven and the Sykes–Picot Agreement, both had issued with the imprimatur of the Foreign Office. They thus represented British policy. Second, if the formulae of the Declaration were ambiguous and in obvious conflict with Britain's prior undertakings, the reasons behind them were sound enough. As noted earlier, as the Sherifian army moved north, the Syrians were becoming increasingly concerned about the possibility of being subjected to the medieval and reactionary government of King Hussein. The Declaration was calculated, in part, to dispel those fears, for if the Syrians did not consent to a Hashemite government, they would not be compelled to, at least not by Britain. It was also true that the Syrians, and the Arabs generally, were very apprehensive of the future effect of Sykes–Picot and the Balfour Declaration, both made public only seven months earlier, and both the subject of Turco-German anti-Entente propaganda. To the extent that the

Declaration to the Seven could dissipate those fears and persuade the Arabs that Britain would not agree to hand over Syria to the French and Palestine to the Zionists, it might have some salutary effect. If the Arabs were wavering, it might even help keep them on the Entente side in the war.[31]

This last rationale for the Declaration was particularly important, for less than three months earlier disturbing news concerning Faisal had arrived in Cairo. Wingate reported that he had learned 'secretly' that the Amir had written to the commander of the Turkish Fourth Army, Jemal Pasha, proposing that if the Turks would agree in principle to Arab independence, then he was willing to enter into secret negotiations with a view to a Turco-Arab *rapprochement*. The High Commissioner thought that, if true, Faisal's approach reflected serious doubts about Britain's plans for Palestine and Syria and he was 'putting out feelers' to learn the Turks' views.[32] Wingate's cable set off alarms at the Foreign Office. Lord Curzon concluded that the matter should be taken up immediately by the Cabinet's Eastern Committee. Sykes and Graham feared that the Turks might have told the Arabs of Britain's secret discussions with Turkish representatives in Switzerland, talks undertaken with a view to concluding a separate peace with the Ottoman Empire. Sykes also objected to Wingate's failure to solicit Clayton's views concerning Faisal's apparent duplicity. 'General Clayton reports on Faisal', Sykes complained, and his 'personal views are essential to enable us to come to a correct conclusion'.[33] Wingate certainly had no friend in Sykes. Three weeks earlier Sykes had complained of the High Commissioner's intrusion into an issue involving Syria and suggested that Clayton alone should advise the Foreign Office on all matters involving Syria and Palestine: 'Sir R. Wingate has not General Clayton's knowledge and his staff is comprised of either purely Hijaz specialists or not the best men. All Syrian affairs should be in General Clayton's hands.'[34]

Hardinge and Graham were not inclined to preclude Wingate from advising the Foreign Office on Arab issues, but they readily agreed that Clayton should be consulted.[35] The CPO responded on April 2: 'Shereef Faisal does not necessarily mean disloyalty to us or any intention of making terms prematurely with the enemy. He has already expressed to Major Lawrence the opinion that as soon as the Arabs have secured [their] aim in Arab territories it will be necessary for them to make terms with the Turks. A hostile Turkey immediately north of Arab territory would be a perpetual menace to Arab independence and a source of anxiety to us to whom the Arabs would naturally turn for protection. It does not follow therefore that Faisal is doing more than attempting to ascertain the attitude of Turkey towards an eventual rapprochement.' Clayton also suggested that any overtures Faisal had made to the Turks might have been prompted by a 'deep rooted suspicion of French policy in Syria', by 'distrust of Zionist aims', or even by the Amir's religious beliefs which might have led him to view the destruction of Turkey as a 'great Moslem power' with something less than 'complete equanimity'. Whatever Faisal's motives, Clayton reasoned, the risk of losing Arab support was serious enough that it was 'desirable to cement the Arab Alliance with Great Britain by all possible means'. Clayton's advice was taken seriously in Whitehall and this might very well explain why, when the memorial of the Syrians was submitted only three weeks later, it was thought necessary to provide the assurances reflected in the Declaration to the Seven. But Clayton also provided more immediate and practical suggestions. Faisal should be invited to meet with Allenby and presented by the chief with the K.C.B. The Amir should also meet with Weizmann and be 'reassured with regard to the scope of the Zionist movement' (a meeting later arranged by Clayton, as described above). Picot should be instructed by Paris to give an authoritative statement to Faisal disclaiming any idea of French annexation of Syria. And, finally, the Amir's authority should be recognized 'in all territories east of [the] Jordan'.[36]

Despite the hand-wringing in Whitehall, Faisal had not in fact made any overtures to the Turks. Jemal Pasha had written to *him* on November 26, 1917 – just as the terms of Sykes–Picot were released publicly – suggesting peace talks. Upon receiving the letter, Faisal sent it on to Hussein at Mecca. The King instructed him to respond to Jemal that the time for Turkish offers had passed. But the Turks were not about to give up. In February 1918, another peace overture was made, this by Jemal Pasha the Younger, another Ottoman general in Syria. Hussein passed this correspondence on to Wingate and it was this letter, it seems, which prompted Wingate's March cable to the Foreign Office.[37] The Turkish approach was again rejected but, as Faisal's recent biographer has concluded, the Amir 'was not completely willing to abandon the possibility of a separate peace deal with the Turks'.[38] Indeed, Faisal wrote to the Turks in June 1918, setting forth conditions, the satisfaction of which by the Turks could result in peace with the Arabs. Not until August would the contacts cease. Lawrence had been aware of the earlier correspondence but made no attempt to stop it, perhaps because he thought it inevitable and believed he could control it. But Faisal never told Lawrence about the summer 1918 correspondence and, having secretly obtained a copy of the Amir's June letter, Lawrence later said he became convinced that Faisal was definitely 'selling us'.[39]

Sykes remained concerned. He found Clayton's April 2 cable 'hardly satisfactory', for it was clear that the General was 'unaware of two very important factors in the case'. The first, according to Sykes, was that the Germans had been 'strenuously working' to engineer a Turco-Arab *rapprochement*. The second factor was the very secret talks that had been going on intermittently for months in Switzerland between British and Turkish representatives. Although Sykes proposed that Clayton be informed of the Anglo-Turkish peace talks, the information was not conveyed to Clayton. Indeed, so secret were the talks that they had not even been discussed in the Eastern Committee which included top-level officials, some of whom were Cabinet Ministers. So, the CPO was advised only that the Turco-Arab correspondence had been inspired by the Germans – a claim for which there was no specific evidence – and that Clayton should 'consistently discourage' any Arab compromise with the Turks.[40] Clayton rightly doubted that the Germans were behind the Turkish overtures to Faisal and asked to see the evidence supporting the claim. He also noted that recent Arab operations in the Ma'an area showed 'energy and determination on the part of Faisal' against the Turks and this confirmed to Clayton that British 'influence is counteracting German and Turkish propaganda successfully'.

Finally, he emphasized that his April 2 telegram had 'made it clear' that he would discourage any attempt by Faisal to compromise with Turkey.[41]

One important aspect of the correspondence concerning Faisal's contacts with the Turks in 1918, was the question of Trans-Jordan, to which Clayton had referred in his April 2 wire. 'Trans-Jordan' then referred to the undefined region east of the River Jordan. On the Sykes–Picot map it was delineated as bounded on the west by the River, the territory to the east being largely included in Area 'B', part of the independent Arab State subject to British advice and 'priority of right of enterprise'. Yet, from at least June 1918, it was clear that the Zionists would lay claim to the area.[42] And, in November 1918, the Zionist Organisation in London submitted proposals to the Foreign Office concerning Palestine for the upcoming Peace Conference in which they made clear that the country should be bounded in the East by 'a line close to and west of the Hedjaz Railway'.[43] The Foreign Office was not persuaded; there were no Jewish agricultural colonies east of the Jordan and, in any event, 'the inhabitants have clearly manifested their desire to join the Syrian Arab State'.[44] Clayton would consistently back the Arab claim to Trans-Jordan, not only because he thought it consistent with the McMahon–Hussein correspondence, but because development of the region by the Arabs 'would allow of considerable emigration from Palestine thereby making room for Jewish expansion' within Palestine itself.[45]

Clayton was fully absorbed by the problems of Palestine – the Zionists and Arabs, the diplomatic and religious disputes entirely occupied his time. But, in September 1918, his responsibilities were again revised. And, as always seemed the case with Clayton, they were expanded. On September 2, Allenby wrote to Wingate suggesting that, due to recent changes in EEF Intelligence, 'a reorganization on parallel lines in regard to political questions, particularly those which affect the Arab movement' was needed. The commander proposed that Clayton be made CPO for the Hijaz as well as for Palestine and that the Arab Bureau should be restored to his 'general direction'. All 'questions of policy' concerning Arab areas from the Yemen to Syria should be placed under Clayton's authority.[46] The expansion of the CPO's duties was consistent with that proposed by the Middle East Committee of the Cabinet in January 1918, described earlier. Both Wingate and Allenby had then objected. But now, the High Commissioner agreed with Allenby's proposal, asking only that Clayton consult him on 'questions affecting general "Islamic" policy'.[47] Allenby's suggestion that the reorganization of EEF Intelligence warranted the extension of Clayton's political work to the Hijaz is not altogether convincing. In three weeks he would launch his great assault on Damascus and the focus of Anglo-Arab relations was definitely now in the North. Yet, problems were arising far to the South, in the undefined border region between Najd and the Hijaz, and these problems, Clayton thought, could have wide ramifications for the entire Arab movement. Hussein was threatening to 'resign' as King and, if he did, that action 'would involve disastrous effects on our Arab policy'.[48]

The source of the King's unhappiness was his neighbour to the East, Abdul Aziz Ibn Saud, Amir of Najd, and an opponent of the Hashemites for years. Ibn Saud was not hostile to Britain; he had been in treaty relations with the British since December 1915, a treaty inspired by the Government of India, which became the Amir's primary British sponsor. Ibn Saud took no action in support of the British war effort in Arabia. But he was of no help to the Turks either, and it was enough for India that the Amir was a bitter opponent of the Turkish-sponsored Ibn Rashid of Ha'il in north central Arabia. The Saudi–Hashemite differences, however, had nothing to do with the war. They were deep-rooted and the two sides had begun skirmishing since 1910, when Hashemite forces captured Ibn Saud's brother and the Amir had been compelled, however briefly, to acknowledge Hussein's ascendancy. The personal enmity caused by this event was compounded by profound religious differences. Ibn Saud was an adherent of Wahhabism, an Islamic reform movement dating back to the 1740s, that espoused a return to the purity and essence of the Qu'ran and the Sunna (practice or example) of the Prophet. In some ways, Wahhabism paralleled the Islamic reformism of Sudanese Mahdism and the Sanusiyya movement of Cyrenaica, both of which, it will be recalled, Clayton had confronted during earlier periods of his career. Wahhabism also exhibited the aggressive militancy of those African Islamic movements; for Ibn Saud and his Wahhabi adherents, the Hashemites were infidels, who should be crushed by their fierce Ikhwan warriors.

By December 1917, the Wahhabi Ikhwan were moving on the tribes in eastern Hijaz and, during the following May, Hussein learned that certain tribes only one hundred miles east of Mecca had joined Ibn Saud. The King was very worried and threatened to resign unless Britain took steps to compel Ibn Saud to withdraw into Najd. The British now found themselves in the curious position of having one of their Arabian protégés, Ibn Saud, sponsored by India, in direct conflict with another, Hussein, sponsored by Cairo and the Foreign Office. Less than a week after Allenby had proposed Clayton as CPO Hijaz, and well before he received official confirmation of his appointment from London, Clayton prepared a major policy paper on the course Britain should pursue in view of Hussein's threatened resignation. And, since Allenby likely knew little or nothing of the dispute emerging in Arabia, 800 miles south of Jerusalem, it may well be that Clayton's new appointment originated not with the EEF commander, but with Clayton himself.

Clayton saw two options available. First, Britain could do nothing. But, in that event, he argued, 'we risk the resignation of King Hussein who is the only commanding figure in the Arab Revolt, which must then either collapse entirely or at best relapse into spasmodic tribal action against the Turks. In any case much of the military and the bulk of the political value of the movement must be lost'. The CPO favoured a second option, a choice demanded in part by 'the moral obligation imposed on us by [Hussein's] initiation of the Arab Revolt and his unswerving loyalty to Great Britain'. Under this option, Britain would provide a verbal assurance to Hussein stating that the Government favoured the 'freedom and independence of all ruling chiefs in Central and Southern Arabia within their own dominions'. Further, Britain 'would welcome the union of all these independent states . . . in an Arab Alliance as head of which they would welcome King Hussein with a suitable title to be decided on' later, and would use its 'influence to achieve this policy in so far as is possible without the employment of coercive measures against any friendly Arab Chief'. It was for Hussein 'to prove to all Arab Chiefs concerned his fitness for the position of Head of an Arab Alliance in Central and Southern Arabia'. Inevitably, there was a quid pro quo; Britain would insist that Hussein 'follow the advice of H.M.G. on all matters of external policy and in [his] dealings with other independent Arab rulers and States'. Mesopotamia and Syria were excluded from Clayton's proposal; the fate of those countries, he added, must await the Peace Conference.[49] Clayton described his proposal as the 'suzerain policy', but since he stated that the preferred suzerain in southern and central Arabia was Hussein, London often referred to the same notion as the 'Hussein policy'. However described, the British would adhere to their programme of supporting the King until 1924. And, during that period, Hussein would become so intractable and would threaten to resign so often that London became inured, and eventually amenable, to his resignation.[50] But, in 1918, and throughout the early post-war years, British policy-makers in London and the men on the spot in Cairo and Jeddah made extraordinary efforts to maintain Hussein's position in the Hijaz and to support his sons in Syria, Trans-Jordan and Iraq.

While Clayton was wrestling with the problems posed by the Saudi–Hashemite dispute, Allenby was preparing for his great assault in the North. The EEF's further advance after the fall of Jerusalem had been delayed for a number of reasons. During the early months of 1918, poor weather had rendered an offensive impossible. Then, on March 21, the Germans launched a major attack on Allied positions in Europe, on the Western Front. Immediate demands for men and materiel were made on the EEF, demands which negated any plan for an imminent move north. In April, Allenby lost two British divisions, hurriedly dispatched to France to meet the German onslaught. Throughout April and May, other elements of the EEF, regiments, battalions and artillery batteries, were also moved to France. Although most of these units were replaced by Indian soldiers, the substitutions took time to complete and many of the new units were untested in battle and, in some cases, insufficiently trained. Any major offensive that relied on them would certainly be risky.

Still, Allenby did not sit on his hands. In late March and again in late April, the EEF made significant forays across the Jordan, taking Es Salt and, briefly, Amman. But both incursions were beaten back by the Turks and the EEF retreated back across the Jordan. The Trans-Jordan expeditions were launched for two reasons. First, the Arab forces in the South had made little progress. They had succeeded in taking Tafileh, south-east of the Dead Sea, but a Turkish counter-attack regained the village in March. If Allenby succeeded in taking Amman, the Turkish forces at Tafileh in the south might be cut off or, at least, recalled to the north. But a far more important and strategic reason lay behind the EEF commander's spring 1918 incursions across the Jordan. Allenby had decided early on that his next great assault would occur not in the East, on his right flank, but along the Mediterranean coastal route. So, if the Turks could be persuaded that the EEF intended to move in the East, they might redeploy much of their available force there and thus leave the coastal plain weakly defended. Indeed, the Turks did move significant forces to Trans-Jordan. In broad outline, Allenby's plan was the Gaza-Beersheba offensive of a year earlier, in reverse. Then, the EEF had initiated their attack with a crushing bombardment of Gaza, while the bulk of their attacking force moved secretly to the East for a concentrated assault on Beersheba. Now, the Jordanian forays in the East laid the groundwork for a massive and concentrated attack along the Mediterranean coastal plain in the West.

Overall, the EEF had a two-to-one superiority over the Turks in front-line troops and, although the disparity in artillery was less dramatic, the British still had in place 140 more guns. But, as was the case at Beersheba a year earlier, British superiority at the point of attack was far greater. On a short, fifteen mile front near the coast Allenby concentrated 44,000 troops and 383 guns. And, as at Beersheba, he put in place an elaborate scheme of deceptions, all calculated to mask British intentions. By this time, too, the RAF had established near complete mastery of the skies. By the middle of September the EEF was ready. At 4.30 on the morning of September 19, 1918, the British guns along the coast opened up, delivering more than 1,000 shells per minute on the stunned Turkish lines. EEF infantry and cavalry units quickly poured through the pulverized lines. RAF bombing completely disrupted enemy communications and the Turco-German command was rendered ineffectual as a result. The German commander, Liman von Sanders, was so surprised at Nazareth, it was reported, that he was only just able to escape by fleeing in his pyjamas. Within thirty-six hours, the EEF cavalry had looped behind the retreating Turks, capturing the major towns of northern Palestine and cutting off the Turkish retreat to the North. In the East, Amman was taken on the 25th. In little more than a week of fighting the Turks south of Damascus were finished. At 9 p.m. on September 30, the last Turkish troop train left Damascus for the North.[51]

Just as the Turks were departing, elements of the EEF's Australian Mounted Division entered the city, but almost immediately passed through. Early the next morning, October 1, Lawrence and a few Arabs of the Sherifian army entered Damascus and took possession. Why had the EEF allowed the Arabs priority of conquest? Answers to the question would later be the subject of some dispute, but there are several plausible explanations. By the terms of the Declaration to the Seven, in areas 'emancipated from Turkish control by the actions of the Arabs themselves', Britain would 'recognise the complete and sovereign independence of the Arabs'. Perhaps by allowing for an Arab 'capture' of the city, the British sought to confirm their intent that Damascus, and territories to the East of it, were in the area of Arab independence. That notion was also consistent with the McMahon correspondence of 1915, which had excluded from Arab independence – owing to French interests – those regions to the *west* of the 'districts' of Damascus, Homs, Hama and Aleppo. And, as described earlier, Clayton for months had consistently pressed the Foreign Office to secure a French statement disclaiming any intent to annex Syria. The French had never issued any such statement and were not likely to. So, Faisal was justly apprehensive of French intentions. By allowing the Arabs to enter Damascus first, Britain might be able to calm Arab fears. This last idea was certainly uppermost in Clayton's mind at the time. 'Our permitting the occupation of Damascus by the Shereefians', he cabled London on October 8, 'has allayed some of the suspicion of French intentions'.[52]

Whatever the reasons for allowing the Arabs first entry into Damascus, Clayton still foresaw 'great difficulties in front of us' and an 'extremely delicate situation' developing in Syria. He correctly assumed that Faisal would soon take charge in Damascus. 'He will undoubtedly require assistance in advice and probably funds, but I am very doubtful whether he will accept either from the French. He will probably refuse and turn to us, in which case we will find ourselves in the unpleasant position of having to refuse him if we are going to act up to the undertakings given the French Government. If he continues to refuse, his administration will probably result in chaos and we shall be blamed for leaving him in the lurch.'[53] Of course, the British 'undertakings' given the French were embodied in Sykes–Picot and, under that Agreement, everything to the west of the four Syrian cities was in the blue area, the area of direct French control, while those cities and all areas to the east of them were in Zone A, the region in which the right to advise and 'priority of right of interest' lay with France.

On October 1, Clayton and Allenby travelled by train to Damascus, arriving there on the 3rd. Clayton had already secured the services of Kinahan Cornwallis, the Arab Bureau director, to act as British liaison officer with the Arab administration. He immediately prepared a set of instructions for Cornwallis and shared them with his French counterpart. While both officers were to 'work entirely together and not separate their duties in accordance with the A or B zones as regards their dealings with the Arab administration', Clayton stressed that 'all questions affecting the A area should be referred to the French liaison officer and the policy should be based on the principle that [the] Arab administration must look for advice and assistance in the A area to the French Government'.[54]

Upon arriving in Damascus, Clayton found the chaos he anticipated. Faisal, who arrived the same day, was reported to be 'desperately afraid of French intentions' and, as again predicted, the fledgling Arab administration was turning to the British 'for everything'. But the policy pursued by the CPO was 'to refer the Arab administration to the French for all advice and assistance'.[55] He was acting in the only way he could – in strict accordance with the Sykes–Picot Agreement. Yet, the Arabs, none of whom appeared to have administrative experience, could not obtain French assistance, even had they desired it, for, as Clayton reported, there was no 'French representative of high standing to be found'. He promptly cabled London with a request that Picot, 'or any high French official', be sent out immediately.[56] The Arabs needed everything – food, water, electricity, medical services and, most of all, money. William Yale, the American diplomatic agent in Cairo, soon appeared in Damascus and was appalled by what he saw at the Turkish hospital, where hundreds of unattended Turkish soldiers lay dead or dying. His unpublished memoir contains a description of a confrontation with the CPO concerning the plight of the Turks:

I sought an interview with General Clayton . . . Greatly unstrung by the horrible misery I had seen, and blazing with indignation, I told Clayton that something must be done at once to feed and care for those poor devils in the hospital. I said it was ghastly hypocrisy to talk about German atrocities in Belgium while allowing eight hundred Turks sick and wounded to starve to death. Clayton was a cold, hard, self-controlled man upon whom my emotionalism had no effect. Quite indifferently he told me, "Yale you are not a military man" and seeing my eyes blaze with anger, he continued: "You need not be offended, I am not a soldier either, you do not understand that after such a rapid advance we are in a critical situation and hardly have enough food to feed our own men." The Australian quartermaster had volunteered only that morning the information to me that he had the food. I couldn't betray his confidence. The coolness and indifference of Clayton, following hard on the heels of the ghastly sights I had just seen made me lose my head completely and I stupidly replied hotly, "Well General, you may say you are not a soldier, but you cannot say I am not for I am the military representative of the American Army." I left him and went back to the hospital to check upon the situation there before cabling Washington.[57]

Decades later, Yale reconsidered this account, acknowledging that Clayton's 'statement to me I think was an honest one about the shortage of supplies. It did not seem reasonable to me at the time because of what the Australian had told me. It was hardly his affair and there were complications . . . between [the] civil power of control of Damascus and the British military command'.[58]

Meanwhile, Faisal, in what was now becoming a Hashemite hallmark, was threatening to resign. Relying on the Declaration to the Seven, the Amir had appointed governors in the coastal towns of the Lebanon in an attempt to establish Arab priority there. At the same time, Allenby appointed Frenchmen to administer the towns and, in some places, like Beirut, the Arabs refused to stand aside without orders from Faisal. No incident better illustrated the conflict between the Sykes–Picot Agreement and the Declaration to the Seven, for the Lebanon was clearly within the area of direct French control under the former, while the Arab governors placed in these town by Faisal could form the basis of a claim to Arab independence under the latter. Faisal insisted that if he issued orders for his men to stand down in the Lebanon, he would suffer a loss of prestige. However, Clayton reported that the Amir would withdraw his men if he received an assurance from Allenby that 'whatever arrangements may now be made for the districts in the coastal area, [they] are of a military nature and without prejudice to the eventual settlement, which will be decided . . . at the Peace Conference'.[59] Allenby provided Faisal with his requested assurance on October 17, informing him that his appointments were 'purely provisional' and subject to ultimate resolution at the Peace Conference. And, the commander reminded Faisal that the Allies 'were in honour bound to endeavour to reach a settlement in accordance with the wishes of the people concerned'.[60] The Allenby Assurance, as the commander's statement to Faisal has been called, was enough to persuade the Amir to climb down and withdraw all the Arab representatives he had sent to the coastal towns.[61] It also added yet another layer of complexity and contradiction to the Middle Eastern situation, for it was inconsistent with Sykes–Picot and even the McMahon correspondence. Under the former, France was in no way constrained by the 'wishes of the people' – at least in the blue area, which included the Lebanon – and, under the latter, all areas to the west of the four Syrian cities were subject to French interests, again, quite regardless of the wishes of the inhabitants.

While the problem of the Lebanon was maturing, Clayton continued to urge the Foreign Office, as he had for months, to exert pressure on the French to issue an official statement disclaiming any intent to annex any portion of Syria. It is 'essential that a definite announcement of French policy of a nature to allay [Arab] suspicions be made as soon as possible'.[62] So important was this to the CPO that he made his request for a French statement in telegrams to the Foreign Office of October 12, 14, 15, 18 and 19.[63] What Clayton did not know – because the Foreign Office never troubled to inform him – was that a *joint* Anglo-French declaration was being prepared in Europe. In fact, the two governments had tentatively agreed on September 30, that a declaration would be prepared 'defining their attitude towards the Arab territories liberated from Turkish rule'. The declaration was to disavow any intent to annex any part of the Arab territories and to 'recognise and uphold an independent Arab State' in 'accordance with the provisions of the Anglo-French Agreement of 1916'.[64] Exactly how the idea of Arab independence could be reconciled with Sykes–Picot was a matter that apparently would be left to the sophistry of the draftsmen.

Even before the diplomats in Paris and London began working out the language of their proposed declaration, Allenby's forces continued their drive north of Damascus. Some 19,000 Turkish troops – of the 100,000 that had been available prior to the EEF's September offensive – had been able to escape to the north of Damascus. But they had no artillery, no transport and had been so decimated by the EEF onslaught that no more than 4,000 were able to continue fighting. They had no chance. Tripoli was taken on October 13. Homs fell three days later. Hama, twenty-seven miles further north, was found to have been evacuated. Finally, on October 26, Aleppo was taken. On the same day, a Turkish delegation arrived at Lemnos on the Aegean island of Mudros to negotiate an armistice. It was signed on October 30, 1918. The war in the Middle East was over. The armistice with Germany was signed twelve days later, bringing the Great War to a close.

No evidence of Clayton's reaction to these momentous events could be found. No doubt he was greatly relieved by the end of four years of such unmitigated misery. But the war's conclusion altered neither the nature nor the extent of Clayton's work. He was still consumed with the political problems of Syria and Palestine and would be for the next six months. Indeed, the end of fighting actually resulted in an increase in tension in both countries, for now there was no military impediment to a resolution of the political problems which had bedevilled the region. Clayton's efforts in Syria were certainly appreciated in London. Balfour wired to express his 'appreciation of the zealous and tactful way' in which he had 'handled the situation' in the country.[65]

The Foreign Secretary's acknowledgment of the CPO's good work was doubtless gratefully received, but it was nothing compared to the dazzling array of honours and promotions bestowed on Clayton during and after the war for services rendered during the conflict. When the war began, he was a relatively unknown captain in the Egyptian Army, an employee in the Sudan service. But he had been rapidly promoted to lieutenant-colonel (1914), GSO1 (general staff officer, 1st grade, 1915), brigadier general (1916) and *lewa* (General, Egyptian Army, temporary 1916, permanent, 1919). As described earlier, he had received the CMG (1915; bestowed by King George, July 1916), and the French Legion of Honour (1916). Further honours followed, as the Russians bestowed on Clayton the Order of Saint Stanislaus, and the Italians the Order of Saints Maurice and Lazarus (both 1917). In the same year, he was made a Companion of the Order of the Bath (CB). And, in 1919, he would receive from the Greeks the Order of King George I, and the Order of the Nile from the Sultan of Egypt (3rd class, 1919, Grand Cordon, 1920). In 1920, King Hussein awarded him the Order of al-Nahda (the 'awakening' or 'renaissance'). He was mentioned in despatches no less than five times by Generals Maxwell, Murray, Wingate and Allenby. Finally, in June 1919, he was appointed by King George Knight Commander of the Order of the British Empire (KBE); he was, from that time, Sir Gilbert Clayton. It was an impressive list for a man not called upon to fire a single shot in anger during the conflict.[66]

The much anticipated Anglo-French Declaration was published in the Middle East on November 9. It was, in the words of a later historian of the period 'a piece of humbug as sickening as it was false'.[67] 'The object of France and Great Britain', it began, was 'the establishment of national governments and administrations deriving their authority from the initiative and free choice of the indigenous populations . . . France and Great Britain are at one in encouraging and assisting the establishment of indigenous Governments and administrations in Syria and Mesopotamia . . . Far from wishing to impose on the populations of these regions any particular institutions, they are only concerned to ensure by their support and adequate assistance the regular workings of Governments freely chosen by the populations themselves'.[68] Certainly, neither France nor Britain had the slightest intention of establishing 'national governments' in Syria and Mesopotamia based on the 'free choice of the indigenous populations' of those regions; both intended to control those countries regardless of the wishes of their inhabitants.

Clayton reported that the Declaration was received with jubilation by the Syrians and Palestinians, who apparently chose to focus on the Allies' apparent adherence to the principle of self-determination, while ignoring the caveat that the Europeans would provide 'support' and 'adequate assistance' in those countries. But this was the hook, subtle and oblique, that would enable continued Anglo-French rule in the region. The Declaration, false as it was, obviously ran counter to the Sykes–Picot Agreement. And, Palestine was not referred to at all in the document. Yet, Clayton reported that the 'general impression appears to be that [the] declaration will apply to Palestine and Moslems and Christians are relieved at what they consider a check to extravagant Zionist aspirations'.[69] The British military governors in Palestine 'sent repeated requests' to Clayton asking whether Palestine was meant to be included in the Declaration and the CPO made the same request of the Foreign Office.[70] If that was the intent, then the Anglo-French pronouncement was equally in conflict with the Balfour Declaration, for any 'freely chosen' government there would unquestionably reject the Zionist national home policy. And, if it was not intended that the Declaration apply to Palestine, then it contradicted the Hogarth Message, the Declaration to the Seven and, arguably, the McMahon correspondence. But Clayton was advised by London that the omission of Palestine from the Declaration was quite intentional. If the national home policy was to be effectuated, there could be no hint of self-determination in Palestine.

For the British, the motive behind the Declaration was the same as that underlying the Declaration to the Seven and the Allenby Assurance – to vitiate Sykes–Picot. But Lord Curzon was incorrect when he gave the Eastern Committee his view that the Declaration did 'to a large extent supersede Sykes–Picot'. That was certainly its object, as Lord Robert Cecil, the primary British draftsman, confirmed.[71] But Cecil well knew the French opinion, given both before and after the Declaration's issuance, that it would in no way nullify Sykes–Picot. On October 22, Paul Cambon, the French Ambassador in London, advised the Foreign Office that France considered Sykes–Picot 'as remaining sound and valid until the creation of a new order'. Again, on November 18, after the Declaration was published, he confirmed that 'at no point' does France 'accept any reduction in its rights under the agreement of 1916'. And, for good measure, Cambon added that 'Palestine does not lie outside our agreements of 1916, which specify on the contrary that France has in Palestine . . . rights exactly equal to those of England'.[72] Small wonder that Cecil observed to his colleagues on the Eastern Committee that 'France would rather give up anything in the world than give up that claim to Syria; they are mad about it, and Cambon himself is quite insane if you suggest it.'[73] Compounding the confusion was the Syrian view that Palestine and Syria were part and parcel of the same country. These Syrians, Clayton reported to the Foreign Office, 'deprecate any separation of Palestine from Syria . . . Their programme envisages an autonomous Syria, including Palestine'.[74]

It must have come as a great relief to Clayton to be granted at least a temporary reprieve from the incessant claims of the Arabs, Jews and French under the competing and conflicting statements generated during the last four years. On the afternoon of December 21, 1918, he boarded a ship at Port Said, bound for Marseilles. He had not been home on leave for nearly four and a half years. Clayton kept no diary during the period, so what thoughts occupied his mind during the journey home must be left to conjecture. But one could well imagine that he ruminated on the incredible political muddle that Britain had created in the Middle East during the war. Nearly a year earlier, shortly after the Balfour Declaration was published, he had come to the uncomfortable realization that Britain had now 'backed three horses in the same race . . . the French, the Arabs and the Jews. The three policies are very hard to bring together', he concluded with considerable understatement, 'and we shall find it a hard task to fulfil our pledges to all three'.[75] And now, at the end of 1918, a new problem was looming on the Middle Eastern horizon, for very serious trouble was brewing in a place few people expected: Egypt was about to flare into violent rebellion.

21

The Shadow and the Substance: The Egyptian Revolution, 1919

There was nothing remarkable about the career of Alexander Pope Bey. He had been in Egyptian service for thirty years and, like most of the nearly 1,700 other foreigners in the employ of the Egyptian government – more than ninety percent of them British – he had laboured away anonymously over the years in several Egyptian departments. He was now an inspector of government prisons. At 6.50 on the morning of March 18, 1919, Pope and his Egyptian assistant, Rifaat Hafiz, boarded the northbound train from Luxor at Asyut station, some 240 miles south of Cairo. Already aboard were two British officers and five 'other ranks', returning from a brief holiday in Luxor. All were unarmed.

Two stations further along the line, Pope's train squealed to a halt just as another pulled in from the North. It was overflowing with Egyptians. Armed with knives, picks, clubs, even stones, they swarmed over the roofs and sides of the carriages, shouting 'down with the English' and, when their train stopped, they quickly clambered over the rails to Pope's northbound train. He and the British soldiers, now aware that they were in serious trouble, just as quickly retreated to the first class carriage. Hafiz offered Pope his fez and a black cloak in a feeble attempt at disguise, but the inspector declined both. He then ran back down the train to address his frenzied countrymen, assuring them that there were no English aboard. But the crowd could not be calmed and surged forward through the carriages as the train slowly pulled away from the station, the Englishmen now barricaded in the first class. At the next stop, Deirut station, more Egyptians boarded the train and were easily able to break through the weak British barricade. Apart from a few 'soda water bottles and bits of luggage', Pope and his compatriots were defenceless. Hafiz bravely stood in front of the door to Pope's compartment, insisting to his compatriots that only his own wife was inside. But he was beaten to the floor as Pope was dragged from the compartment and thrown out onto the rails. A witness later reported hearing the Englishman cry out, 'I have served you thirty years. I am an Egyptian official!' Although beaten and stoned by the rampaging mob, Pope somehow managed to regain the carriage, but was again clubbed and thrown out the other side. Someone picked him up and carried him to the brake van, but he was probably already dead. The soldiers fared no better. One officer was killed outright. Three men bolted from the train. One was shot dead. A second was stabbed in the stomach. The third tripped over the rails, fell and was bludgeoned to death on the spot. One of the dying men had dirt stuffed into his mouth, as he was found to be just still breathing. All the Englishmen were now dead, but the mayhem continued. An Egyptian was seen cutting the legs off one of the dead men at the knees and carrying them away. Another drank blood from the breast of a dead soldier.[1]

The horror of Deirut was the worst episode of that terrible Egyptian spring of 1919, but it was not the first violent incident and would not be the last. Rioting had broken out eight days earlier in Cairo where student mobs had rushed into the streets from al-Azhar, the great Muslim university and centre of religious learning, and then from the law school and the technical colleges. On March 11, government offices and the law courts ceased to function. Rioting then spread to the Nile Delta, north of Cairo, where most major cities flared into revolt. British army units turned their machine guns on the rampaging crowds, killing thirty in one city, fifteen in another, fourteen at Alexandria and thirteen in Cairo. In the provinces, trains were wrecked, stations burned, rails torn up and telephone and telegraph lines cut. By March 15, Cairo was effectively cut off from the outside world. Upper (southern) Egypt was also soon isolated and, in order to rescue the beleaguered European communities there, the Nile waters stored behind the Aswan Dam had to be released so that the river could be raised and troop ships dispatched to the south.[2] When the violence finally subsided, the grim statistics disclosed that over 800 Egyptians had been killed and thirty-six British and Indian troops as well as four British civilians, among them the hapless Alexander Pope, had died. In the ensuing trials, 102 were sentenced to death. More than half those sentences were commuted, but forty-seven Egyptians were eventually executed, thirty-four of whom had been involved in the savagery at Deirut.[3]

Terrifying though it was, political violence was not a new phenomenon of Egyptian life in 1919. Nine years earlier, the Egyptian Prime Minister, Boutros Ghali, had been assassinated and, as described earlier, in 1915, two attempts had been made on the life of the Sultan, Hussein Kamil. And there had been occasional attacks on British soldiers and citizens in the years preceding the war, although few of these appear to have been politically motivated. In fact, there had always been opposition to the British presence in Egypt; nationalist parties had been a feature of Egyptian politics since 1879, even before the British occupation.[4] But the events of spring 1919 were different. Now, the whole country seemed to have risen. Even the normally placid *fellahin*, the Egyptian peasantry, had been roused to violence. The Christian Copts, usually shunned by their Muslim countrymen, were reported to be preaching in mosques, vehemently denouncing British rule. And, on March 16, for the first time in modern Middle Eastern history, Egyptian women took to the streets, waving banners and crying out for independence as they marched through Cairo.[5]

The immediate impetus for the Egyptian revolt was provided by the arrest and deportation of the nationalist leader Sa'd Zaghlul and three of his colleagues of the recently formed Wafd (delegation) Party. But Zaghlul's banishment was no more the cause of the 1919 rising than was the June 1914 assassination of Archduke

Franz Ferdinand the cause of the Great War; both events merely provided the spark to an already highly flammable situation. There can be no doubt the British were caught by surprise. While everyone knew of Egyptian opposition to the British presence, no one had anticipated the 1919 rebellion, for Britain had always exercised her rule over Egypt with a light hand and had little reason to expect such an upheaval. The great British pro-consul and arch-defender of Empire, Lord Alfred Milner, who had worked in Egypt under Cromer and later wrote a book about the country, *England in Egypt* (1894), characterized British rule as a 'veiled protectorate'. Veiled it may have been – to Europeans – but to Egyptians, the reality of British rule was all too apparent.

In December 1914, it will be recalled, the veil was dropped. British rule became overt when a protectorate over Egypt was formally declared, primarily for the purpose of bringing Turkish suzerainty to an end, and as a step preliminary to the deposition of the pro-Turkish khedive Abbas Hilmi and placement of the country on a war footing. Martial law had been imposed earlier by General Maxwell. The Egyptian Legislative Assembly was prorogued and would not sit again until after the war. At the same time, though, as if to assure the Egyptians that these measures did not reflect an attempt to turn the country into a British colony, Maxwell emphasized that they would not be called upon to actively participate in the war effort; Britain would carry the entire burden of defending Egypt. The protectorate declaration also stated that it was Britain's intention 'to associate the governed in the task of Government' and that the new arrangement, in more clearly defining the British position in the country, would 'accelerate progress towards self-government'. In the words of the official British commission later appointed to investigate the causes of the 1919 insurrection, 'the Egyptians were certainly given to understand that efforts would be made at the end of the war to satisfy their national aspirations'.[6]

Scarcely was the ink dry on the lofty statements of 1914, than they were violated. Egyptian Army artillery units were sent to the Canal in January 1915 to help repulse the Turkish attack of the following month. Then, in the spring of 1915, as Imperial forces were landing at Gallipoli, an Egyptian Labour Corps was created. The Egyptians of the Labour Corps were not used in combat roles, but for entrenching work and, later, in Sinai and Palestine, for railway and pipeline construction. By 1918, more than 125,000 Egyptians were working on term contracts, not only in Palestine, but also in Salonica, Mesopotamia and even in France.[7] The men of the Corps were well paid, but as the war dragged on, it became increasingly difficult to obtain new men and 'recruitment' was entrusted to Egyptian village headmen (*omdahs*) who drew many unwilling workers into the system, unless, that is, they could buy their way out. As a result, the labourers and their families came to bear heavy grievances against the British. By 1917, some 21,000 Egyptians were also working in the Camel Transport Corps. Operating closer to the front lines than their compatriots in the Labour Corps, by war's end the Egyptian camel-men had suffered 220 killed and 14,000 wounded. Another 4,000 died of wounds or disease in hospital.[8] The *fellahin* had still more grievances. Great numbers of their animals, mostly camels and donkeys, were requisitioned during the war for use by the army.

Compensation was paid, but payment was often delayed and, it seems, the village *omdahs* who obtained the animals, often did so at below-market rates, realizing hefty profits on re-sale to the army. Even if the system had been fairly applied, the *fellahin* still would have suffered because the animals were essential to their livelihood and could not be replaced.[9]

In addition to the legitimate complaints of the *fellahin*, other war-time measures adversely impacted the Egyptian economy. In late 1914, restrictions were imposed which limited the amount of land that could be cultivated for cotton, Egypt's most profitable crop, so that more land could be devoted to the production of cereals to meet the growing demands of the British army. Meanwhile, the price of cotton rose dramatically, from $12 per *kantar* (about 99 pounds) in 1914, to $39 a *kantar* in 1917. The large Egyptian landowners protested, the restrictions were removed, and a shortage of foodstuffs soon resulted. A family of four, it was later reported, 'could not, at the beginning of 1919, obtain a sufficiency of food except at a cost which considerably exceeded the ordinary rate of wages'.[10] Compounding these economic problems, in 1918, a voluntary collection campaign was begun in Egypt for Red Cross funds, an appeal unfortunately sponsored by the High Commissioner's wife, Lady Wingate. While the sultan and many Egyptian notables contributed generously to the fund, the *mudirs* (provincial governors) were also encouraged to raise money and they, in turn, leaned on the *omdahs*, who promptly turned what was intended to be voluntary giving into a compulsory exaction, an assessment that was once again borne by the unfortunate *fellahin*.[11] If the Egyptian lower classes had good cause to complain of these war measures, the 'official class' – that comprised of literate Egyptians who held, or aspired to hold, government posts – were equally unhappy. Overall, by 1919, Egyptians held 86 percent of government posts and drew 71 percent of the salaries. But these figures were misleading, for in the higher government posts, the percentage of Egyptians had actually declined from 28 percent in 1905 to only 23 percent in the post-war period, while the British share of such posts increased from 42 percent to 59 percent during the same time-frame.[12] Yet, despite these many grounds for discontent, there was little evidence of Egyptian unrest during the war. Not only did Egypt cooperate in the British war effort, the government actually contributed more than £E3,000,000 to the Entente cause in the form of forgiven debt, decreased import taxes and lower railway rates. Clayton put the amount at £E4,000,000, and stated that the Egyptian contribution was made without any British pressure being applied.[13]

This was the situation, then, on November 13, 1918, when High Commissioner Wingate received Sa'd Zaghlul and two of his colleagues at the Cairo Residency. Zaghlul pointed out, with considerable accuracy, that 'Egypt had shown a spirit of great loyalty during the War' and that England should now acknowledge that loyalty by making good on her pledge of Egyptian self-government. The phrase used by the Wafd Party leader was one that would be uttered repeatedly, that would become a constant refrain of Egyptians, during the ensuing months: *istiqlal tamm* – complete independence. Not only was this warranted by the spirit of the age, as reflected in President Wilson's principle of self-determination, Zaghlul argued, it was also consistent with declarations made by the British themselves to people who were far less capable of independent government than the Egyptians. Here, he was referring to the Anglo-French Declaration, made less than a week earlier, to the Arabs, Syrians and Mesopotamians, who had been promised 'national governments . . . deriving their authority from the initiative and free choice of the indigenous populations'. If these 'under-developed' peoples were to be accorded independence, the Wafdists asserted, then why not the more sophisticated Egyptians? Zaghlul closed his interview with Wingate by requesting that he and his colleagues be allowed to travel to London to present their case for independence to the British government. On the same day as his interview with Zaghlul, Wingate met with Prime Minister Hussein Rushdi and another influential Minister, Adli Yakan. They, too, sought to present the Egyptian claim to independence in London and it soon became apparent to Wingate that Zaghlul and Rushdi and perhaps even the Egyptian sultan Fu'ad – who had succeeded to the sultanate on the death of his brother in October1917 – were working together to advance the Egyptian claim.

Sa'd Zaghlul had been well-known in British circles for years. Born in the Delta in the late 1850s, he came from *fellahin* stock, though his father was a village *omdah* and quite prosperous. He was educated at al-Azhar, and first worked as a journalist and then as a lawyer and judge. In 1892, Zaghlul was appointed a judge in the court of appeals and, in his late 30s, he began studying law at the French law school in Cairo, earning a Paris LLB in 1897. A year earlier, Zaghlul had married the daughter of the pro-British Prime Minister Mustafa Fahmy and no doubt profited from the connection, for in 1906 he was appointed Minister of Education. Politically active even before his appointment as Education Minister, Zaghlul and others soon formed a new political party, *Hizb al Ummah* (the People's Party). Moderate and secular in its proposals, the party espoused parliamentary government and the attainment of Egyptian independence through gradual reform in cooperation with the British. Admired for his moderation and good judgment, Zaghlul could list among his British supporters none other than Lord Cromer, who thought him honest and capable – a man, he said, 'who should go far'. In 1910, Zaghlul was made Minister of Justice and, three years later, was elected to, and named vice-president of, the new Legislative Assembly, a position he obtained because of his great oratorical skills, a 'natural gift', it was said, 'of popular eloquence'.[14]

After Zaghlul's November 13 meeting with Wingate, the High Commissioner recommended to London that both Zaghlul and current members of the Egyptian government, Rushdi and Adli, be allowed to come to England to plead their case before the British government. But neither Balfour nor Curzon would consider the proposal; 'no useful purpose would be served', they wired Cairo, 'by allowing Nationalist leaders to come to London to advance immoderate demands'. At the same time, Wingate was accused of not having previously supplied London with any 'indication of such Native aspirations'. And, on December 2, 1918, the Foreign Office informed him that his reception of 'extremist leaders' at the Residency was 'unfortunate'.[15] Wingate promptly offered to resign as High Commissioner and he was right to have done so, for Balfour's statements were not only unwarranted, but dangerous. For a year or more, Wingate had repeatedly advised the Foreign Office that the war's end would see a recrudescence of Egyptian nationalism. In December 1917, he had warned Hardinge that 'we must expect a very frank exposé of national aspirations when the war is over'.[16] Also, Wingate's reception of the Wafdists on November 13 was fully in line with the British tradition, dating to the days of Cromer, of listening to all shades of Egyptian opinion, no matter how unsavoury they might appear. In any case, it was not Wingate's reception of the nationalists that ignited the ensuing trouble, but rather the failure of the Foreign Office to allow them to air their grievances. On December 31, the Foreign Office modified their position somewhat, informing Wingate that the Egyptian Ministers could come to London in February, but not the Wafdist leaders, and, in no event, were any Egyptians to be allowed to stop in Paris to make their complaints at the Peace Conference, which was to open in three weeks. But it was now too late; Rushdi and Adli realized that the political momentum had shifted to Zaghlul and his supporters and they refused to leave Egypt unless accompanied by the Wafd. As for Wingate, he was called to London for consultation and left Egypt on January 21, 1919. He would never return.

By 1919, Wingate had, in fact, lost all support in the Foreign Office. Graham had been a critic since November. Eyre Crowe, who would succeed Hardinge as Permanent Under-Secretary, thought the High Commissioner 'deplorably weak'. And, most damaging of all, on January 4, Lord Robert Cecil, Assistant Secretary of State and now in charge of Middle Eastern affairs in the Office, informed his cousin, Foreign Secretary Balfour, 'that everyone to whom I have spoken about Wingate is confident he is not up to the job'. No doubt, Lord Robert had held a poor opinion of Wingate for some time, for his brother, Lord Edward Cecil, former Adviser to the Egyptian Ministry of Finance, despised Wingate and had been at odds with him for years. And, as the political situation in Egypt worsened during February, it seems that not only Lord Robert, but also Curzon – acting Foreign Secretary while Balfour was in Paris – and even Prime Minister Lloyd George, were coming round to the view that Wingate should be replaced by General Allenby. Lord Robert had suggested as much to Lloyd George on January 4, and reported that he agreed wholeheartedly.[17] An even earlier suggestion came from an unexpected source, as described on January 1, by Leo Amery, now Parliamentary Under-Secretary to Lord Milner at the Colonial Office: 'General Clayton came round . . . and we had a long talk about Palestine and Syria and about the situation in Egypt which is evidently drifting into a bad mess from the sheer absence of a really big man at the Egyptian end and anybody capable of giving any decision at this end. I asked Clayton whether making Allenby High Commissioner wouldn't improve matters and his answer was that the whole trouble would shut up like a book. I put these points to Lord M[ilner] afterwards.'[18]

Wingate was replaced by Allenby on March 20, 1919. Initially, the general was designated 'Special High Commissioner', but in October, his permanent succession to Wingate was confirmed. Deeply embittered by his removal, Wingate spent much of 1919 immersed in the preparation of elaborate memoranda, supported by thick piles of documents, all calculated to justify his Egyptian policy and to show that he had been wrongly treated by the government. Nobody cared. But of some significance here is Wingate's attribution of his dismissal, in part, to disloyalty among his staff in Cairo. Among the many at whom Wingate pointed a finger was Clayton: '[F]inally there was B. C. [Bertie Clayton] who by that time had seen the possibility of bettering himself if R. W. [Reginald Wingate] was replaced by E. A. [Edmund Allenby] . . . E. A., the Palestine campaign being over, was looking about for future employment – why should he not become H. C. [High Commissioner] & combine in one hand the supreme civil & military authority? It is probable that B. C. who knew R. W.'s views as to the future of N. A. [North Africa?] suggested this plan to E. A'.[19] No evidence could be found that Clayton suggested to Allenby that he should seek the position of High Commissioner of Egypt. But, in view of the evidence described above, in Chapter 16, it is plausible that Clayton thought he would, in future, be better off working for Allenby than Wingate. And, based on his January 1 discussion with Amery, it appears likely Clayton concluded that, in view of the impending political problems in Egypt, Britain would be better served by Allenby as High Commissioner.

Between Wingate's departure from Egypt on January 21, and the arrival of Allenby on March 25, Milne Cheetham acted as High Commissioner in Cairo. Just as in the autumn of 1914, he had been thrust into the position in a time of crisis. He again found himself in a difficult spot. Rushdi and Adli, who had tendered their resignations in December in the face of British intransigence, made them final and public on March 1. Egypt was now without a government. A few days later, Zaghlul delivered an insolent and threatening message to the Sultan, on the heels of which Cheetham requested Foreign Office authorization to arrest and deport the nationalist leader. It was given on the 7th and Zaghlul and three of his Wafd colleagues were sent to Malta on March 9, prompting the demonstrations of March 10 and the ensuing violence.[20] By chance, Clayton arrived in Cairo the very day that Zaghlul was deported. He had returned from England in late January and, on March 2, he and Enid left the Egyptian capital for a week-long holiday in Palestine, returning to Cairo on the 9th.[21] Although his responsibilities did not then encompass Egypt, Clayton was soon drawn into the crisis. On March 16, he and General Watson, the senior commander in Cairo, met with a group of nationalists. Although the Egyptians wanted to discuss the merits of their independence programme, Clayton refused. 'I cannot go into the rights or wrongs', he told them, 'the Delegation confess themselves leaders and cannot absolve themselves from their responsibility'. They must 'use their influence', he concluded, 'to stop the present movement'.[22] The next day Clayton drafted a two-page memorandum on the Egyptian situation, a document that embodied a startling conclusion:

> The present movement is national in the fullest sense of the word. It has the sympathy of practically all classes from the highest to the lowest throughout the country . . . The Copts have shown their sympathy as have many elements among the foreign community. Our policy is condemned by all as entirely

contrary to the spirit of the times and the principles of the League of Nations. Forcible measures may succeed in restoring control but it would be a grave error to minimize the depth of feeling aroused throughout the country and to imagine that it is possible to stamp it out. Force can only mean considerable bloodshed and the creation of lasting bitterness. The movement must be met by a generous recognition of legitimate Egyptian aspirations and a readiness to consider reasonable requests.[23]

Clayton made five specific recommendations in his memo. He was aware that some would interpret them 'as a sign of weakness', but he dismissed the idea, for 'no reasonable Egyptian imagines that Great Britain . . . is unable to crush Egypt if she so desires'. He proposed first that a statement be issued from Paris that 'the Peace Conference recognizes the British Protectorate over Egypt', or that the Conference has entrusted Britain with a Mandate for Egypt. Second, he suggested that London issue a statement that future relations between Egypt and Britain 'as the protecting (or mandatory) Power . . . shall be the subject of immediate consideration'. He also recommended that the government announce that a Royal Commission 'is being sent at once to Egypt' to examine the situation. Clayton thought that sending such a commission might 'render superfluous' the dispatch of an Egyptian delegation to Europe, 'but if suitable Egyptian delegates still wish to go. . . [the] Government will offer no objection, and those individuals . . . who were recently deported will not be prevented from accompanying the delegation – if so desired'. Finally, he thought it imperative that 'a responsible Egyptian Ministry be formed at once' to restore order in the country and to punish those responsible for the violence. The Wafd, he concluded, 'must openly recognize and actively support this Ministry'.[24] As will be seen, the Wafd leaders were released and allowed to go to Paris, the Peace Conference did acknowledge the British Protectorate over Egypt, Britain did send a commission to Egypt to examine the causes of the revolt and to make suggestions regarding Egypt's future status, and a new Egyptian Ministry was formed at the end of March. It would be an overstatement to attribute these developments solely to Clayton; the decisions approving these measures involved several people, many of them senior to Clayton. But, it may be said that he was the first man on the spot to propose them and that he influenced Allenby's decision to alter British policy along the very lines suggested in Clayton's March 17 paper.

Although Clayton's memorandum proposed nothing less than a complete reversal of Britain's Egyptian policy, Cheetham adopted it without hesitation. On the evening of the day Clayton wrote the memo, Cheetham sent a cable to London 'embodying the sense of [Clayton's] appreciation + recommendations'.[25] As Clayton had begun his memo, so did Cheetham begin his telegram: The Egyptian movement, Cheetham wired, 'is national in the full sense of the word'; it had 'apparently the sympathy of all classes and creeds, including the Copts'.[26] The Acting High Commissioner's adoption of Clayton's policy was oddly reminiscent of the situation more than four years earlier when, during a different crisis, Cheetham, then Acting British Agent, sent to London, over his own name, Clayton's telegrams proposing

British support of the Arab movement (*see* Chapter 10). Although some historians would later accuse Cheetham of exhibiting a complete failure of nerve in 1919, of panicking in the face of crisis, that charge, if true, must also be applied to Clayton and to General Bulfin, acting commander-in-chief while Allenby was in Paris and who, on arrival in Cairo on March 17, stated his agreement with Clayton's memorandum.[27] And, it must also be applied to Allenby himself who, within a week of his arrival in Cairo, adopted Clayton's proposals, even down to the point of urging the release of Zaghlul and allowing him and his Wafdist colleagues to travel to Paris.

While Clayton recommended a comprehensive change in Britain's Egyptian policy, he did not suggest that those responsible for the violence of March 1919 be treated leniently. The 'rioting and destruction of life and property . . . must . . . be dealt with by the sternest repressive measures no matter what political settlement may eventually be arrived at. A bitter lesson is necessary, especially now that British officers and civilians have been murdered'. But after order was restored and 'severe punishment . . . dealt out', the government should promptly declare a policy 'showing that H.M.G. intend to deal with Egypt on wide and generous lines in accordance with the principles which they have always supported at the Peace Conference'.[28] To Wingate, Clayton made the same point. 'The principles of Nationalism and desire for independence', he wrote, 'have bitten deep into all classes, and I am convinced that our policy in Egypt must be very carefully reconsidered on lines of increased sympathy with national aspirations in so far as they keep within legitimate limits'.[29]

On March 25, Allenby arrived in Cairo. He had been selected by Balfour and Lloyd George in Paris where they were attending the Peace Conference. If anyone could restore order in Egypt, most agreed that the 'Bull' was the man for the job. Yet, in almost every other way, the selection of Allenby was questionable. No one doubted his strength or will, but as Curzon correctly observed, the EEF commander had 'no experience of Egypt or its political and administrative problems'.[30] The opinion of Dorothea Russell, wife of Cairo's Commandant of Police, Thomas Russell, was probably typical of the Anglo-Egyptian view: 'Allenby of course is a strong man – honest to a fault, fearless and straight as a die – and of course a fine soldier. But he has no knowledge of the East nor of that most intricate of all Eastern subjects – Egypt. Nor can one see how he can know much of either politics or administration . . . We all sigh for a Cromer who . . . [knew] the country as well as being a very able man and a great personality'.[31]

Allenby seemed to confirm these opinions when, less than a week after his arrival in Egypt, he dropped a bombshell on London. He had just met with Rushdi and Adli, he wired on March 31, who asked him to remove all travel restrictions on the Egyptians, including Zaghlul and his companions, now interned at Malta. Allenby strongly recommended adoption of the proposal; not only would it restore tranquillity, it would enable the formation of a new Egyptian Ministry, a critical step since Egypt had been without a government since the resignation of Rushdi a month earlier. The second point was particularly important because British rule in Egypt had always been consensual; neither the High Commissioner nor the British advisers to the Egyptian Ministries nor the British in government service had any executive powers. The British could only advise the Egyptians and, while that advice was invariably followed, the government could actually function only through the Egyptians themselves. Still, Ronald Graham informed Cheetham that Allenby's decision 'came as a great surprise to us' at the Foreign Office. Curzon too, was 'much startled' and approached Andrew Bonar Law, acting as Prime Minister while Lloyd George was in Paris, to persuade him of the error in Allenby's judgment. But Bonar Law, 'on the face of it' was 'inclined to agree with Allenby'. So too were Balfour and the Prime Minister. Having appointed Allenby just ten days earlier, the government would look ridiculous if they disavowed his very first decision; it was critical, they thought, to 'avoid any appearance of mistrusting his policy'. At the same time as they grudgingly approved Allenby's proposal regarding the Egyptians, Lloyd George and Balfour suggested appointment of a commission, led by Colonial Secretary Lord Milner, to come to Egypt and investigate and report on the causes of the rebellion.[32] That, too, had been recommended by Clayton on March 17.

To what extent was Allenby influenced by Clayton at the end of March 1919, or, indeed, during the next three years, while the two served together in Egypt? There is very little in the way of direct evidence that suggests an answer. Neither the Allenby papers nor the Clayton papers shed much light on the subject. Years later, Lady Clayton explained why she had been able to find only one letter of substance between her late husband and Allenby: 'I suppose that all through the Palestine campaign there was no correspondence between them. I know they used to see each other every morning, so that everything was verbal, of which there is no record.'[33] The one letter Enid did find was written by Allenby and dated August 27, 1920. At that time, Foreign Secretary Curzon proposed that Clayton be appointed to head a new Middle Eastern department that Curzon intended to form in the Foreign Office. Although the appointment did not materialize (because the new department was formed in the Colonial Office), Allenby learned of the proposal and wrote to Clayton: 'They spoke to me the other day at the F.O. about you being put into the proposed Near East Department & I told them that they could not have a better man. Though sorry to lose you, I hope you will take it.'[34] Since Allenby thought highly of Clayton, it is fair to assume that the chief relied heavily on his CPO in treating the political issues that arose in Palestine and Syria during the campaign. That was certainly Wingate's impression; by 1918, he could see 'how much the C in C relies on' Clayton.[35] And, as the General knew little of Egypt and its problems, it is equally plausible that he would have relied on his CPO during the political crisis that emerged there in the spring of 1919. After all, Clayton had worked in Egypt and the Sudan for more than twenty years.

The question must also be examined from Allenby's perspective. He appears to have known no one upon whom he could rely when he arrived in Egypt in March 1919. Wingate had left two months earlier, and there is no evidence that he had even met Cheetham or any of the Residency staff prior to his March arrival. Nor did Allenby know any of the British Advisers to the Egyptian Ministries. And, when he did come to know them, he promptly fired three of the five – the Advisers to the Interior, Justice and Education. He clearly had no confidence in them.[36] Of course, Allenby knew well his number two, General Bulfin. But Bulfin had been in Egypt only eight days before Allenby arrived and, in any case, he had already expressed his agreement with Clayton's policy on March 17. If this were not enough, Allenby made clear his reliance on Clayton when, on June 7, GHQ in Cairo wired the War Office to inform them that 'Palestine and Egypt will be dealt with direct' by the CPO, then still Clayton. Then, two weeks later, without even seeking Foreign Office approval – with whom authority for the appointment of British Advisers in Egypt resided – the chief offered the job of Adviser to the Egyptian Ministry of the Interior to Clayton. And, in August 1919, Allenby decided that the 'Ministry of the Interior, on the return of Brig-General Clayton [from leave] will take over the organisation and control of Political Officers in Egypt and will deal with Political questions in Egypt under an arrangement to be made on the return of . . . Clayton [with the Brigadier General Intelligence]'. Clayton was also given martial law powers in Egypt while Allenby was absent from the country and he was put in direct contact with the Secret Intelligence Service, (MI1(c)), office in Italy, as the SIS then had no men in Egypt.[37] Based on all this evidence, it is perhaps safe to conclude that no one guided Allenby in his Egyptian policy more than Gilbert Clayton. Indeed, one scholar, who made a detailed study of those tumultuous years in Egypt between 1919 and 1922, concluded that 'Allenby acted not under the influence of the Foreign Office, but of Sir Gilbert Clayton, who as chief political officer . . . was very close to him.'[38]

On April 7, Allenby announced the release of Zaghlul and his colleagues. As seen, Clayton had made the proposal for their release three weeks earlier. He thought it 'a necessary measure as the deportations had been a mistake and it was better to cut our loss than to persist in the error'.[39] Clayton interviewed those members of the Wafd party who had not been sent to Malta just before they left Egypt for Paris. After listening to their long list of grievances, as described above, he thought 'the case they made was a very strong one . . . [W]hile it was possible to pick holes in the details of the argument, substantially it held good'. He also rejected the Foreign Office view that Zaghlul and the Wafd 'were not representative of the country'. Clayton thought that nonsense; not only had Zaghlul been vice president of the Legislative Assembly, which was 'chosen by an elected body, several others were members of the Assembly, and all had held high official posts of one kind or another'.[40] He was correct; of the fourteen original Wafd members, seven had held seats in the 1913–14 Legislative Assembly.[41]

Regardless of the merits of the Egyptian nationalist position, the release of Zaghlul and the lifting of travel restrictions, coming so soon after the violence of March, was seen by most Britons resident in Egypt as abject capitulation, as knuckling under in the face of crisis. Allenby was vilified by the Anglo-Egyptian community.[42] And, as Clayton's views were equally well known, he, too, must have been the subject of local complaint. When he was named by Allenby as Adviser to the Egyptian Interior Ministry in June, one Foreign Office expert opined that even though Clayton 'was the best man available', his 'appointment will not be popular among [British] Egyptian civil servants'.[43] Many of those who levelled criticisms at Allenby, and perhaps Clayton, may have sighed, like Dorothea Russell, for the days of Lord Cromer. But the easy, contented lifestyle of the Cromerian era was fast disappearing. Those comfortable days when the British official could complete his four-hour work day and then repair to the Turf Club or the Gezira Sporting club to sip his gin and tonic and gossip over the day's events, oblivious to the millions living round him, would soon be a memory. The Great War had changed the world. Nationalism was no longer merely the programme of a few discontented members of the native intelligentsia; it was a mass movement that could not safely be ignored. Clayton's view that nationalism and the desire for independence had 'bitten deep into all classes' was echoed by Allenby when he wrote in early May that 'there lurks below the crust great animosity to us; . . the nationalist movement has its roots very deep'.[44]

Of course, Britain could crush the Egyptian national movement, but at what cost and for how long? The CIGS, Sir Henry Wilson observed that 'unless Egypt is kept quiet we shall be called on for more troops' and that, he added, would present 'a matter of extreme difficulty'.[45] It was beyond difficult; in the spring of 1919, Allenby was demobilizing the 320,000 Imperial troops still in the Middle East at the rate of 20,000 men a month. He had to act quickly; Britain, already up to her ears in debt, could not afford them – $4.7 billion was owed the United States alone. What Churchill would later say, in 1921, was equally applicable in 1919: 'Everything that happens in the Middle East is secondary to the reduction of expense.'[46] The Clayton–Allenby policy of conciliation, then, was not just sound on its merits, it was the only viable policy available.

While it was apparent to Clayton that major concessions would have to be made to the Egyptians, he fully appreciated that Britain had significant interests and obligations in the country – strategic, economic, even moral – that must be maintained. The challenge was to determine what was essential to Britain and what could be relinquished. By the summer of 1919, Clayton's views began to coalesce. He confided to Gertrude Bell in September, that Britain should 'guard (a) Imperial necessities in Egypt, (b) international interests for which we have made ourselves responsible, and let all the rest go. We must maintain control of the Suez Canal, the Nile water (leaving the details of irrigation in native hands with a general British supervision) the army and the police'. He also thought that all British Advisers to the Egyptian Ministries should be withdrawn, leaving the High Commissioner with his own advisers in each department, but without executive powers.[47] Clayton described his notion of the proper course to follow in Egypt, as well as his emerging ideas on the British Empire in the post-war world, in a September 1919 letter to his father:

> The political situation still remains very difficult and will do so, in my opinion, as long as we hold to the hated word "Protectorate". Egypt has always been a national entity and they cannot bear the idea of losing their individuality and being merged as a small factor in the great British Empire. They

fully realize (or at least all but the most extreme and violent do) that England must stay here and must have a large measure of control, but they want the arrangement to be something in the nature of an alliance between the "big brother and the small brother" rather than the relationship of the "master to the slave." I . . . well realize that they [the British government] only have to give a sop to Egyptian "amour propre" in order to get all that (and more than) they want. I fear greatly that they will cling on to the shadow and therefore lose much of the substance, whereas if they give all the shadow to the Egyptians they will get every atom of substance. The time has passed when developing peoples can be ruled by force and England cannot afford to dissipate her strength in trying to do it. It is by sympathetic alliance and community of interest that we must maintain our control over subject nations whom we have educated out of childhood into adolescence. We need a loyal and contented Egypt as the centre of Moslem interest in the Near East where the horizon looks none too clear. Turkey is in the melting pot, France is in Syria, the Zionists are about to swallow Palestine. Islam is disturbed and apprehensive. We cannot afford to allow Egypt to become a second Ireland.[48]

The essential idea in this letter concerning Egypt's status would be repeated by Clayton, not only to his father, but also to members of the Milner Mission, sent out by the government in December 1919 to examine the causes of the revolt. The view that Britain could, and should, dispense with the protectorate (the shadow), while maintaining her grip on key strategic and economic interests (the substance) would later find expression in statements made by members of the Mission.

The 1919 rebellion had caused a complete revision of Clayton's thinking on the subject. When the European war broke out in 1914, it will be remembered, Clayton had expressed the hope that Britain would annex Egypt (Chapter 9). Annexation was rejected in 1914, largely at the insistence of the Cairo triumvirate of Cheetham, Cecil and Graham, who argued that a protectorate would be more palatable to the Egyptians. But the question arose again in 1917, as a result of Britain's increasing control over Egypt's war-time economy and the deteriorating health of Sultan Hussein Kamil, whose death, it was thought, would provide an opportunity to reconsider Egypt's status.[49] London then solicited the opinion of Wingate, who turned to Clayton for a memorandum on the subject. In 'The Future Political Status of Egypt', Clayton came down squarely in favour of annexation. His reasons were largely imperial and based on the assumption that Turkey would still be able to exercise influence in the post-war Middle East. Above all, Clayton reasoned, Britain must have 'complete and absolute predominance' in Egypt in order to protect 'the vital cord of our Empire', the Suez Canal. He also thought annexation essential to the future prosperity of Egypt and maintained that the 'vast proportion of Egyptians' would accept the 'fait accompli' of annexation 'and swallow their principles rather than lose their salaries'. Curiously, and without explanation, he concluded that if Egypt were annexed then, in 1917, 'it will be possible eventually . . . to grant a far larger measure of self-government than can ever be given with safety under the' protectorate. The only argument against annexation that Clayton saw in 1917 – and it was a good one – was that 'to abolish the Protectorate would be a breach of faith. If this is so, the Protectorate must stand'.[50]

It is possible that Clayton's 1917 paper was written to order for Wingate, who adhered strongly to the annexationist view. But it is more likely that the views expressed in his memorandum were his own and that it took the momentous events of March 1919 to alter his thinking.[51] Now, in the summer of 1919, he had come to the striking realization that the protectorate status of Egypt really meant nothing for Britain; provided vital strategic interests were protected, the word, and the status, could be discarded. And, dispensing with the protectorate would have the added advantage of mollifying many Egyptians who found the word deeply offensive. It 'stinks in the nostrils of the Egyptians', he told Gertrude Bell. Clayton's friend at GHQ, Colonel A. P. Wavell, agreed: 'It's only the <u>word</u> Protectorate that is tickling the gizzards of the majority', he wrote in November. 'I think if one could <u>call</u> it independence they would swallow as much British control with it as we like'.[52] That was overstatement, but it was true that the Arabic word for 'protectorate' – *himaya* – carried connotations of subordination, even subservience, that offended many Egyptians.[53] The irony was that, for the British, the word carried no clear definition at all, a point demonstrated in the following exchange between Balfour and his cousin, Lord Robert Cecil, at an Eastern Committee meeting in December 1918:

MR. BALFOUR: . . . We use the word "Protectorate" as if we understood it. There may be persons here more fortunate than myself, but frankly I do not understand it. It is one of the loosest words you can possibly conceive. Had we a Protectorate over Egypt before the war?

LORD ROBERT CECIL: No, certainly not.

MR. BALFOUR: What had we?

LORD ROBERT CECIL: No one knows, but we had not a Protectorate.

MR. BALFOUR: Have we a Protectorate over anything?

LORD ROBERT CECIL: Over Egypt now.

MR. BALFOUR: That is enough for me to go on with my questions. A Protectorate over Egypt amounts really, for all practical purposes, to absolute sovereignty.

LORD ROBERT CECIL: No. It did before, but I do not think there is a very great deal of difference between the amount of our power in Egypt now and the amount of our power before the war.

MR. BALFOUR: I do not care which you choose. I will take either.

LORD ROBERT CECIL: A Protectorate is really a formal matter. You declare a Protectorate. It is what you say you have got, and you bring in any amount of influence. There is this difference . . . that thereupon the protected Power cannot have any relations with any other Power; it ceases to have any foreign policy . . . It is quite simple. When we say we will not have a Protectorate, we mean exactly what we say, and that is a perfectly well-defined expression in diplomatic language. It means that we will not declare a Protectorate . . . and it does not mean anything else.[54]

If this colloquy disclosed anything, it was that Clayton's conclusion was correct; the Protectorate was little more than a name, a 'shadow', that could be dispensed with, provided Britain's essential interests, the 'substance', were secured. The Milner Mission would reach that same conclusion by early 1920, and the next two years would be absorbed by debate and negotiation concerning what Britain's essential interests were and the form in which they should be maintained. As Lord Robert had suggested, control of Egypt's foreign relations would present a stumbling block, but not an insuperable barrier, to the eventual solution.

While Clayton was grappling with the problem of reconciling Britain's imperial interests with the reality of Egyptian nationalism, the Wafd were in Paris, pushing their agenda at the Peace Conference. They made no progress. On April 20, 1919, the Americans recognized the British protectorate over Egypt, a severe blow to the nationalists, who now realized that Wilsonian self-determination was only as viable as circumstances would allow. Then, in June, the Peace Conference 'recognized' the protectorate, as Clayton had hoped it would in his March memo. Recognition came in a backhanded way, as Germany was compelled to acknowledge the protectorate in Article 147 of the Treaty of Versailles, the implication being that what was forced on the losers must be palatable to the victors.[55]

As the Wafd were failing in Paris, conditions again appeared to be deteriorating in Egypt. Most of the violence had subsided by April, but a general strike was called in the same month and Cairo again ground to a halt. Allenby and Clayton met with Prime Minister Rushdi, who had resumed office on April 9, and informed him that he should immediately publish an announcement that any government employee who did not return to work at once would lose his pay and pension. And, Allenby warned, if Rushdi did not make the announcement promptly, he, Allenby, would. Rushdi complied and the strike ended.[56] Short-lived though it was, the April strike demonstrated that Clayton had been wide of the mark when he advised Amery on January 1, that the trouble in Egypt would 'shut up like a book' when Allenby was appointed High Commissioner. Still, the violence had largely subsided and this may, in part, be attributed to the presence of Allenby and to his adoption of Clayton's programme of conciliation.

In mid-June 1919, just before he was about to return to England on leave, Clayton accepted Allenby's offer of the post of Adviser to the Egyptian Ministry of the Interior. He had been considered for the post in the fall of 1916, on the recommendation of the incumbent Ronald Graham, and would have accepted it then (*see* Chapter 16). But the position went to James Haines, the nominee of Lord Edward Cecil, and Haines was still occupying it in 1919. An arrogant man, Haines had been unable to establish a rapport with the Egyptians, a critical shortcoming in a post 'which involved the most frequent contact with Egyptians'.[57] Allenby thought little of Haines, later accusing him of a lack of judgment, and, although the Adviser was about to retire in 1919, the rumour circulating in Cairo was that Haines was 'invited' by the Bull to 'expedite his resignation'. Curzon was annoyed that Allenby had not consulted him about Clayton's appointment beforehand, but the CPO was well known to the acting Foreign Secretary and, as he wrote in early July, Allenby had 'only anticipated the strong hint I was about to give him' concerning the appointment.[58] Clayton had spent nearly all of March, April and May in Cairo, conducting his Palestine and Syria work by telephone and telegraph.[59] So, his new appointment could have come as no surprise to those in Egypt. But the timing was opportune, for no sooner did he return to London in early July than Clayton learned of a new and disturbing development – the Zionists, it seems, now had their knife into him.

22

Peace and Empire: The Middle Eastern Settlement

'What do you mean by a Jewish National Home?' The questioner was U.S. Secretary of State Robert Lansing; the date, February 27, 1919; the place, Paris; the occasion, a meeting of the Supreme Council of the Peace Conference. The responder was Chaim Weizmann, who promptly defined the National Home to mean an administration which would arise in Palestine and – while safeguarding the interests of non-Jews – would allow for such Jewish immigration that 'Palestine would ultimately become as Jewish as England is English'.[1] This statement would be fixed upon by Palestinian Arabs as evidence of the real intent of the Zionists. To them, it confirmed that the Jews were now going far beyond the parameters of the Balfour Declaration with the specific intention of turning Palestine into a Jewish State.

Clayton was troubled about the effects the Zionist leader's statement might have in Palestine. Weizmann's definition of the national home seemed to signal a change in Zionist policy that Clayton had begun to detect some months earlier. Throughout the winter of 1918–19, he repeatedly warned the Foreign Office that the Zionists in Palestine were being 'over-zealous', that they were making 'exaggerated demands', which were causing 'distrust and apprehension' among the Arabs. He asked the Foreign Office to urge the Zionist authorities in London to restrain the 'more impatient elements of Zionism' in Palestine. Because of his concern that intemperate statements by the Zionists might lead to violence, Clayton specifically requested, in three separate telegrams sent during the last months of 1918, that any further statements concerning Zionist policy be submitted to him 'for observations' before publication.[2] Clayton was not alone. J. W. A. Young, a political officer in Jerusalem, observed that immigrant Jews were arriving in Palestine declaring that 'the country belonged to them' and exhibiting a 'boastful and proprietary attitude' that 'shocked conservative Moslems as well as Christians and put them on the defensive'.[3] OETA Administrator Arthur Money also noted that 'feeling at present is very bitter against the Jews, owing to rumours that have arrived from the Peace Conference that they are going to be given special privileges out here . . . I warned both the Foreign Office and the War Office many times as to what would follow if they encouraged Zionist pretensions too far'.[4]

By March 1919, Clayton was reporting that feeling was 'now running very high among Christians and Moslems', feelings which 'were increased by the actions and words of the Jews themselves and by the pronouncements which appear by leading Zionists in [the] Press in England, America and elsewhere'.[5] On March 28, he forwarded a telegram from the 'Christian Moslem Society of Jerusalem' to the British Government, in which the Society professed to be 'deeply wounded' by Zionist appeals to the Peace Conference which would place 'Palestine under a system of misrule and false pretences'. The Society flatly rejected the Zionists' historical claim to Palestine, predicated on the Jewish presence in the country 2,000 years ago: 'If Jewish claims be admitted', they argued, 'by analogy, [the] Arabs should claim re-occupation of Spain and other one-time possessions'. Protesting that the rights of ninety percent of the Palestine population were being ignored, the Society asked for 'recognition of our rights, rejection of Zionist claims and prevention of Jewish emigration [*sic*]'. The Arabs, they concluded, 'will if need be defend the country by every means in their power until [the] last drop of blood and as long as there is life in them'.[6]

There was some basis for attributing increasing Christian and Moslem discontent in Palestine to changes in the Zionist programme that had recently come to light. In early December 1918, Clayton received a copy of a telegram from Weizmann to David Eder, now heading the Zionist Commission in Palestine, in which Weizmann stated that Palestine should be placed under 'British trusteeship' and 'all opportunities should be afforded for ultimate development of [a] Jewish Commonwealth'.[7] The Balfour Declaration had said nothing of a British trusteeship over Palestine or of a Jewish Commonwealth. A few weeks later, Lord Curzon, chairman of the Cabinet's Eastern Committee, came upon another telegram from Weizmann to Eder reflecting the same proposal and he immediately focused on the change in the Zionist programme: 'Now what is a Commonwealth? I turn to my dictionaries and find it thus defined: "A State." "A body politic." "An independent community." "A Republic." . . . What is the good of shutting our eyes to the fact that this is what the Zionists are after, and that the British trusteeship is a mere screen behind which to work for this end?'[8] On the same day, Curzon wrote to Balfour. 'I feel tolerably sure, therefore, that while Weizmann may say one thing to you, or while you may mean one thing by a National Home, he is out for something quite different. He contemplates a Jewish State, a Jewish nation, a subordinate population of Arabs, etc. ruled by Jews; the Jews in possession of the fat of the land, and directing the Administration. He is trying to effect this behind the screen and under the shelter of British trusteeship.'[9] In so addressing Balfour, Curzon was wasting ink, for the Foreign Secretary was irrevocably committed to Zionism, regardless of any prejudice the Arabs might experience. 'Zionism, be it right or wrong, good or bad,' he wrote in August 1919, 'is rooted in age-long traditions, in present needs, in future hopes, of far profounder import than the desires and prejudices of the 700,000 Arabs who now inhabit that ancient land'.[10] Still, in the spring of 1919, even Balfour was concerned that the Zionists were being too aggressive in promoting their programme. He warned Weizmann that the Zionists in Palestine were 'behaving in a way which is alienating the sympathies of the other elements of the population'. And, repeating Clayton, the Foreign Secretary emphasized that local discontent had increased as a result of the 'press pronouncements of leading Zionists in England, America and elsewhere and by the rash actions and words of the Jews in Palestine themselves'.[11]

Although Weizmann may have been unaware of the development, his idea of a British trusteeship over Palestine was already beginning to take shape in December 1918. Early in that month Lloyd George met with French Prime Minister Georges Clemenceau who, during an informal discussion, asked his British counterpart what he wanted from the French. As Lloyd George later described the exchange, 'I instantly replied that I wanted Mosul attached to Irak and Palestine under British control. Without any hesitation, he agreed.'[12] Of course, both concessions represented significant departures from the Sykes–Picot Agreement; Mosul had been located in the French Zone 'A' and Palestine was destined for international administration under the 1916 Agreement. Lloyd George did not record what Clemenceau demanded, or received, in return for the French concessions; perhaps it was British acquiescence to the balance of French claims under Sykes–Picot – the Lebanon and Syria – or a share of expected oil reserves in the Mosul region, or maybe even a guarantee of British support for France on the Rhine in the event of a future German attack.[13]

Whatever the quid pro quo, in the same month Lloyd George and Clemenceau met, ideas were emerging about the proper method of disposing of the overseas possessions of the defeated Powers. Jan Smuts, the South African Prime Minister and a member of the Imperial War Cabinet and Eastern Committee, was the first to suggest the idea of Mandates, a notion similar to Weizmann's concept of trusteeship. The Mandate system was predicated on the conclusion that Germany and the Ottoman Empire would not be permitted to retain their foreign possessions in the post-war world. At the same time, everyone recognized that the German and Turkish pre-war colonial empires could not be dissolved instantaneously, for few, if any, of the indigenous populations of these territories were capable of immediate self-rule. Some form of guidance or assistance would need to be provided to the inhabitants of these recently liberated lands. Under Smuts' Mandate scheme, some former colonies, designated 'C' Mandates, were so small, undeveloped, or remote (Germany's Pacific colonies and German South-West Africa, for example) that they were best administered as 'integral portions' of a Mandatory power – in effect, that is, as a colony of one of the countries that had emerged victorious from the war. Other German colonies, primarily those in Central and East Africa, were to be administered as 'B' Mandates, 'under conditions which will guarantee freedom of conscience and religion, subject only to the maintenance of public order and morals'. Again, the Mandatory would be one of the victorious Powers. Finally, 'A' Mandates were to encompass territories formerly part of the Ottoman Empire. Communities in these regions, it was declared, 'have reached a stage of development where their existence as independent nations can be provisionally recognized subject to the rendering of administrative advice and assistance by a Mandatory until such time as they are able to stand alone. The wishes of these communities must be a principal consideration in the selection of the Mandatory'.[14] The Mandate system was approved by the Peace Conference in April as Article 22 of the Covenant of the League of Nations and incorporated into the Treaty of Versailles, signed on June 28, 1919.

To the cynical observer, the Mandate scheme represented nothing more than a reallocation of colonies among the victorious Powers, a division of the spoils of war. In one sense this was certainly correct for, in April 1920, at San Remo, Italy, the Mandates for Mesopotamia and Palestine were awarded to Britain, and that for Syria and the Lebanon to France. The Mandate system was thus substantially consistent with, and seemed to propagate, the old-fashioned imperialism of Sykes–Picot. And nothing in the Covenant or in the subsequent Mandate documents specified the nature or degree of control to be exercised by the Mandatory Power in the regions assigned to it; if they chose, France and Britain could run their Mandates as virtual colonies. However, provision was made for at least a semblance of international control that distinguished the Mandates from pre-war colonial rule; a Permanent Mandates Commission was established under the aegis of the League of Nations to which the Mandatory was required to report. And, in theory at least, recalcitrant or abusive Mandatories could be sanctioned by the League.

Even though the Mandate concept was adopted in April 1919, no decisions had yet been reached on the disposition of the Arab territories of the Ottoman Empire. During the previous winter Lord Curzon's Eastern Committee had met several times to develop a consensus position concerning Arab lands that Britain could advance at Paris. Lawrence appeared before the Committee three times during this period, arguing strongly for a 'Sherifian solution' in the Middle East, a solution under which three of Sherif Hussein's sons would occupy ruling positions in the region. Lawrence proposed that Faisal be supported as the ruler of an independent Syria. At the same time, he suggested that Abdullah be appointed ruler in Baghdad and Lower Mesopotamia and that Zaid, Hussein's youngest son, occupy a similar position in the north of the country, perhaps centred at Mosul.[15] Although he enjoyed the support of the Foreign Office, Lawrence's plan was not particularly well received by the Eastern Committee. Opposition to the Syrian plan came primarily from the India Office and its senior representative on the Committee, Sir Arthur Hirtzel. He contrasted 'the purely parochial importance of the Arab question' with the 'ecumenical importance of the maintenance of cordial relations with France'. Hirtzel's logic was unassailable: 'If we support the Arabs in this matter, we incur the ill-will of France and we have to live and work with France all over the world. We have no interests of our own in Syria at all commensurate with those in Mesopotamia; and, if we had, and could eliminate the French in our own favour, could we possibly undertake the control of Syrian politics and administration in addition to our responsibilities in Mesopotamia and the Arabian peninsula?' As for Mesopotamia, Hirtzel argued that Lawrence had 'practically no first-hand knowledge of the country', that his plan 'had nothing to recommend it', and that the claims of 'Hussein and his scheming sons' should be rejected.[16]

The Eastern Committee were convinced of the desirability of cancelling that 'deplorable agreement' Sykes–Picot, if possible, by adhering to the principle of self-determination and thereby enlisting American support. But Balfour and Cecil were equally firm in their conviction that the French ought not to be given 'the impression that we are trying to get out of our bargains with them'. So, the Committee decided that in Syria, Britain should 'back Faisal and the Arabs as far as we can, up to the point of not alienating the French'. As for Palestine, the idea of an international administration as laid down in Sykes–Picot – already nullified by Lloyd George's handshake deal with Clemenceau – was rejected. For strategic reasons, and in order to ensure the viability of the Jewish national home, a single Power should assume responsibility for administering the country and that Power should be Britain or the United States, a decision that should be based on the wishes of the Zionists and the Palestinian Arabs. In Mesopotamia, there should be no annexation and one or more Arab governments should be established in accordance with Arab wishes. However, 'whether a single Arab State or a number of Arab States be set up . . . the support of a Great European Power will be . . . indispensable'. Of course, 'the security of the Indian Empire' required that the responsibility should be assumed by Britain. Mesopotamian opinion would have to be sounded before any proposals regarding an Arab ruler, or rulers, could be considered. Finally, Arabia was not to be subject to the authority of any foreign Power. And, contrary to the suggestion made two months earlier by Clayton (*see* Chapter 20), the foreign relations of the Hijaz should not be controlled by Britain or any other country. Still, the Committee proposed that efforts should be made to secure from the French and the Italians a recognition of Britain's 'special political position in the [Arabian] peninsula'.[17]

The Eastern Committee's conclusions did not reflect final British policy; they were merely recommendations which the British delegation at Paris might advance at the Peace Conference, or not, as they saw fit. Others made different proposals. Clayton's were reflected in a memorandum of March 11, 1919, that must have been seriously considered, for it found its way into the hands of the Prime Minister.[18] In his paper, Clayton confined himself to an analysis of the problems posed by Palestine and Syria, where, he concluded, Britain had committed to three distinct policies that 'are incompatible one with the other' and under which 'no compromise is possible' that would be satisfactory to the French, Arabs and Zionists. 'We are forced, therefore, to break or modify at least one of our agreements'. He was referring, of course, to the McMahon pledge, the Sykes–Picot Agreement and the Balfour Declaration. For Clayton, there could be no question of departing from the principle of the Jewish national home in Palestine. Even though 'the initial outlines of the Zionist programme have been greatly exceeded by the proposals now laid before the Peace Congress', Britain was 'still committed to a large measure of support' for Zionism.

The problem for Clayton, then, reduced itself to Syria and to the obvious objection of the Arabs to a French presence there. He correctly predicted that 'the French will certainly meet with great obstruction and possibly armed resistance from the Arabs'. In that event, British influence with the Arabs would be 'greatly impaired' for, having already compromised her position with the Arabs by support of the 'unpopular Zionist programme', Britain would now be seen as having 'sold Syria to the French'. With a discontented Arab population in Syria and Palestine, Britain would need to maintain 'a considerable Army of Occupation in Palestine' to ensure order. So, he concluded, if 'France must have Syria it would be preferable that America, or some Power other than Great Britain or France, be given the Mandate for Palestine'. That suggestion was no doubt immediately rejected by the Prime Minister, for he had extracted from Clemenceau only three months earlier the French concession of Palestine to Britain. But the only alternative Clayton saw was to offer France some 'inducement as will lead her to renounce her claims in Syria, and . . . to give to some other Power the mandate for both Syria and Palestine'. If Britain could secure the Mandate for both territories, that 'would entail grave responsibilities and would mean undertaking a difficult and possibly thankless task', but it would also secure distinct advantages for the British Empire: 'it would put the seal on British predominance throughout the Arab countries; would render Great Britain paramount in Islam; and would safeguard the Eastern Mediterranean and the routes to Mesopotamia and India by securing control of the Aleppo-Mosul line'.

Clayton's suggestions suffered from two basic misconceptions, both of which arose from his lack of exposure to the wider political context of the Middle Eastern problem. First, he did not fully appreciate the depth and strength of the French determination to secure Syria. Unlike the Eastern Committee, he was unaware that the French became 'quite insane' if anyone even suggested they relinquish their claim to the country. But then, neither was Lloyd George fully aware of the French attitude. Nine days after Clayton's March 11 memo, he met with Clemenceau and President Wilson and, in effect, tried to talk the French out of Syria. But the French were adamant and when the Prime Minister tried again on May 21–22, both he and Clemenceau 'lost their temper(s) entirely' and the meeting degenerated into a 'first class dog-fight'.[19] Second, although Clayton recognized there was substantial doubt whether the Americans would consider taking a Middle Eastern Mandate, he did not appreciate the depth of American isolationism. Few did in March 1919. It was not until July that Lawrence informed the Prime Minister's private secretary that he had received a letter from Henry Cabot Lodge, Republican leader in the Senate, who wrote that 'under no circumstances would America accept a Mandate in Turkey or its late territories and that he had a majority in the Senate with him on the point'.[20] Lodge did have the support of his Senate colleagues; they not only rejected the idea of taking any Middle Eastern Mandates, but also the Versailles Treaty and American membership in the League of Nations.

Because Clayton was insufficiently informed about the strength of American isolationism and French imperialism, the solution he suggested to the problem of Syria had little chance of being adopted. He proposed that France relinquish her claim to Syria and, in return, be given control of Constantinople from where she would undertake the 'reorganization and reconstruction of the future Turkish State'. America, he added, would undertake the 'resuscitation of Armenia as an autonomous State', acting as a buffer between France in the north and Britain to the south. Finally, Britain would take a Mandate 'for the eventual establishment of autonomous Government in Syria and Palestine, with due regard for Arab aspirations and Zionist aims'. Whether Lloyd George was influenced by Clayton's thinking is unknown, but he, like Clayton, probably had imperial and strategic considerations in mind when he confronted Clemenceau in March and May of 1919. In any event, the Prime Minister failed completely and acknowledged that failure in September by ordering the withdrawal of all British troops from Syria. By year's end, the country was completely in French hands.

The Arab position on the future of the Middle East was presented to the Peace Conference by Faisal, who appeared before the Supreme Council on February 6. His basic proposal was straightforward – independence for the Arabs in all lands south of a line drawn from Alexandretta east to the Persian frontier.[21] But the Amir's plan was not quite that simple. Earlier, with the assistance of Lawrence, he had prepared a memorandum for the Council that reflected his recognition of the reality that some of the recently liberated Arab territories were not yet capable of operating fully independent governments and, more subtly, that the imperial designs of the victorious Powers would have to be acknowledged in some degree. Syria, however, was not among them, for it was 'sufficiently advanced politically', he argued, 'to manage her own internal affairs'. To the extent foreign technical advice was required, the Syrians would pay for it in cash, 'for we cannot sacrifice any part of the freedom we have just won for ourselves by force of arms'. Mesopotamia, he admitted, would 'have to be buttressed by the men and resources of a great foreign Power. We ask, however, that the Government be Arab in principle and spirit'. The Hijaz, by contrast, was a 'tribal area . . . suited to patriarchal conditions'. It should retain its complete independence. Palestine presented a special case. Faisal emphasized the 'enormous majority' of the Arabs in the country while, at the same time, he asserted that there was 'no conflict of character' between the Arab and the Jew. Still, he cautioned, the Arabs could not assume sole responsibility for harmonizing the races and religions of Palestine; for that, the 'super-position of a great trustee' was required, working in conjunction with a 'representative local administration'. In effect, then, Faisal accepted the Mandate concept for Mesopotamia and Palestine, but rejected it for Syria. He was aware that Britain would assert its position as trustee, or Mandatory, in Mesopotamia and France in Syria, but did not mention either Power in his paper. Nor did he state that his own family, the Hashemites, should rule in any of the regions mentioned, though he did describe his father, King Hussein, as occupying 'a privileged place among Arabs, as their successful leader, and as head of their greatest family, and as Sherif of Mecca'.[22]

Faisal may also have suggested during his February 6 appearance before the Supreme Council that an international commission be sent to the Middle East to ascertain the views of the inhabitants concerning the future governance of Arab lands.[23] Whoever first made the suggestion, it was adopted by President Wilson during the course of his meeting with Lloyd George and Clemenceau on March 20.[24] Shrewdly, Clemenceau agreed to the commission, provided that its remit included an investigation of opinion in Palestine and Mesopotamia. As the Frenchman doubtless expected, his statement effectively foreclosed British participation in such a commission. Clearly, neither Britain nor France wished to send an objective commission of fact-finders to the region, for the results might undermine their imperial goals if they disclosed that the Syrians did not want the French and the Mesopotamians and Palestinians did not desire a British Mandate. When the Council met again on May 21–22, Clemenceau announced that France would not participate in any commission of enquiry until the British agreed to withdraw their troops from Syria. Lloyd George was equally adamant that Britain would not be party to the commission unless France was, and would not withdraw British troops until France ceded territory in Syria that would allow for a British railway from northern Mesopotamia to Palestine, a line that must pass through the French Zone 'A'.

The commission that was eventually sent to the Middle East in June 1919 comprised only two representatives, Americans Charles Crane, a Chicago toilet manufacturer, and Henry King, president of a small Ohio college. While the two knew next to nothing about the Middle East, they at least had the advantage of objectivity, particularly so since the U.S. did not desire any position in the region and thus had no stake in the outcome of the investigation. Clayton suspected that the King–Crane Commission was a sham. A week before it arrived, Picot informed him that Syria would be disposed of without regard to the Commission's findings, that the Commission was 'only coming out to keep Faisal in the dark'. The CPO thought that, if true, this was 'a dangerous game to play', for if the Amir discovered that 'the fate of Syria has been decided without his knowledge and before [the] Commission has made its report, he will undoubtedly take hostile action'. Clayton was angry; if the Commission was really a sham, he cabled to Curzon, 'I would suggest that I ought to have been informed by you'.[25] If the CPO had any complaint, though, it was not against Curzon, but rather Balfour and Lloyd George, who made no effort to keep either Clayton or the Foreign Office informed of the true state of affairs. 'One can understand Gen. Clayton's irritation', minuted a Foreign Office analyst, and 'one is sorely tempted to tell [him] . . . that we have been kept in just as complete ignorance as he himself has'.[26] On June 8, Clayton again warned Curzon that 'if any idea gets abroad that the Commission is not an authoritative one whose recommendations will be considered seriously by the Peace Conference, or that the decision has already been reached in principle and that the . . . Commission is merely a matter of form, there is little doubt that a grave situation will arise'. In that event, he concluded, the Arabs would see the Commission's enquiry as a 'complete negation' of Article 22 of the Covenant, the principle of self-determination and the Anglo-French Declaration of November 1918.[27]

Despite entertaining profound doubts about its legitimacy, Clayton met with the King–Crane Commission on June 12, two days after it arrived at Jaffa. He was greeted by William Yale, now acting as secretary to the Commission. Clayton advised Yale to exercise caution in the way interviews would be conducted by the Commission as conditions were such that there might be bloodshed if any partiality were shown. But Yale rebuffed Clayton, insisting that since the Commission was comprised only of Americans, 'we will carry on our own affairs'.[28] Clayton retreated, leaving King and Crane to proceed as they saw fit, and contented himself with a final warning to the Foreign Office that 'no decision regarding the future status of

Syria and Palestine should be published until [the] Commission has made its report'.[29] The King–Crane Commission spent two weeks in Palestine and ten days in Syria. It never did reach Mesopotamia. And, when the Commission's report was produced in August 1919, it contained no surprises. The Syrians were strongly opposed to the French, the Palestinians emphatically against the Zionist programme. The United States was the desired Mandatory, with Britain the second choice. These results, while expected, were certainly not what Britain or France wished to see. Although the findings were generally known, they were ignored by the Peace Conference. The Commission's report disappeared into the files of the State Department and was not published until 1922, two years after the Middle Eastern Mandates were awarded to France and Britain at San Remo. So much for Wilsonian self-determination.

For the men on the spot in the Middle East, it hardly seemed necessary to dispatch a commission to the region to ascertain the wishes of the Palestinian Arabs; Clayton and OETA chief Arthur Money were convinced that the Arabs were unalterably opposed to the Zionist plan and, if Britain was to sponsor that plan, they were equally opposed to a British Mandate in Palestine. On May 2, 1919, Clayton forwarded to the Foreign Office a report by Money which underscored these points.

> The Palestinians desire their country for themselves and will resist any general immigration of Jews, however gradual, by every means in their power including active hostilities. The people of Palestine think that Great Britain is more systematically committed to the Zionist programme than either the United States or France . . . If a mandate for Great Britain is desired by His Majesty's Government it will be necessary to make an authoritative announcement that the Zionist programme will not be enforced in opposition to the wishes of the majority . . . [T]he idea that Great Britain is the main upholder of the Zionist programme will preclude any local request for a British mandate and no mandatory Power can carry through [the] Zionist programme except by force and in express [? opposition to] the wishes of the large majority of the people of Palestine.[30]

In forwarding Money's report to the Foreign Office, Clayton added his own observations: 'I consider [the] above a true appreciation of the situation. Fear and distrust of Zionist aims grow daily and no amount of persuasion and propaganda will dispel it.' If the government intended to take a Mandate for Palestine 'on the lines of the Zionist programme', he added, that would 'mean the indefinite retention in the country of a military force considerably greater than that now in Palestine'.[31] One Foreign Office analyst thought Clayton's conclusions 'particularly sound'. Graham took the view, though, that Britain was 'committed to the Mandate for Palestine & will have to make the best of it'. Curzon, unaware that the Commission that was about to be sent to the Middle East was nothing more than a sham, wondered what would happen if the Commissioners reported against a British Mandate for Palestine.[32] In the War Office, the views of Money and Clayton were severely criticized by MI2, the section responsible for the Middle East. The men on the spot did not appear to realize the strategic importance of a 'strong Palestine under a British Mandate', MI2 noted. Nor did they realize the advantages which 'will accrue from the general stabilizing of the world if the Jews are permitted to establish their national home in Palestine'. To that remarkable view MI2 added that 'our officers in Palestine do not view this subject . . . from a world-wide or imperial point of view'. So, they concluded, 'new blood should be introduced into our political administration' in the Middle East. It was suggested that Colonel Richard Meinertzhagen, a self-confessed 'ardent Zionist', be sent to Palestine to assist the CPO.[33]

Balfour responded to the views of Money and Clayton on May 18. First, the Foreign Secretary declared, there could be no question of announcing that the Zionist programme would not be enforced in opposition to the majority of the Palestinians. '[I]t might be well to recall to General Clayton', Balfour added, 'that both the French, United States and Italian Governments have approved the policy set forth in my letter to Lord Rothschild of November 2nd 1917'. He also agreed with the War Office view that 'a further adviser on Zionist matters' – specifically, Colonel Meinertzhagen – should be sent to Palestine 'to assist General Clayton'. But, both Allenby and Clayton should be consulted before dispatching Meinertzhagen to the region. Finally, Balfour suggested that the Foreign Office might consult with the Zionists in London concerning any proposals they might have 'as to how the present hostility to Zionism in Palestine can best be allayed'.[34] For Clayton, Balfour's admonition demonstrated that the Foreign Secretary had completely missed the point of his May 2 telegram. 'I was aware when I despatched my telegrams regarding the situation in Palestine and Syria', Clayton responded, that the French, U.S. and Italian Governments had approved the Jewish national home policy. And, he added, this unity of Allied opinion on Zionism has been 'emphasized in responsible quarters in Palestine'. But, 'unity of opinion among the Allied Governments on the subject of Palestine . . . is not a factor which tends to alleviate the dislike of non-Jewish Palestinians to the Zionist policy'.[35]

It has been argued that Balfour's response to Clayton's May 2, cable and his suggestion that Meinertzhagen be sent out to assist Clayton, 'amounted to an announcement of a loss of confidence in Clayton'.[36] It may well have, but Balfour did not force Meinertzhagen on Clayton; the option was left open for the CPO to reject him if he so decided. In the event, Clayton welcomed Meinertzhagen; 'he will be useful to me', he responded on June 9.[37] But Allenby declined to accept the colonel, though he did agree that Meinertzhagen could replace Clayton as CPO after the Foreign Office confirmed Clayton's appointment as Adviser to the Egyptian Ministry of the Interior.[38] It was also true that Weizmann and his colleagues objected far more to Storrs as Governor of Jerusalem than they did to Clayton, and Storrs was not removed from his post. So, it is unlikely that, having declined to dismiss Storrs, Balfour would have removed the less objectionable Clayton. And, Balfour continued to solicit Clayton's views, as, for example, when he informed the CPO that Weizmann and the American Zionist Louis Brandeis were soon coming out to

Palestine and wondered if there were any 'questions which could be quietly taken up and pushed forward a little with the British authorities on the spot'.[39]

From the Zionist perspective, the real problem in Palestine was not so much Clayton, as it was the entire military administration of OETA. On May 31, as directed by Balfour, the Foreign Office solicited the views of Herbert Samuel, chairman of a Zionist planning committee, as to how the current hostility to Zionism in Palestine might best be allayed.[40] In response, Samuel went on the offensive. Ignoring the claim that conduct on the part of the Zionists, in Palestine or elsewhere, was responsible for anti-Zionist hostility, he attributed problems in the country to the British authorities there and asserted that their attitude was not in harmony with British policy, that they did not conduct their relations with the Arabs on the basis that the Balfour Declaration represented settled British policy, and that they thus encouraged the Arabs to think that, by agitation or threats, they could cause Britain to abandon the national home policy. Samuel added that the government 'should send definite instructions to the local administration' that British policy contemplates concession of the Palestine Mandate to Britain and that the Balfour Declaration would be incorporated into the terms of the Mandate. Finally, Samuel suggested that an officer 'personally in sympathy' with the Zionist programme be sent to Palestine to convey to the local administration 'the views of the Government'.[41]

Curzon was angered by Samuel's peremptory tone. 'I cannot see why policy should be suggested or dictated to us by Mr. Herbert Samuel who is not a member of H.M.G. Neither do I see why we should lay down policy in anticipation of the decision of the Peace Conference (a) that we are going to receive the Mandate [and] (b) what its terms are going to be'. Here, Curzon was correct; Samuel and the Zionists were attempting to dictate policy based on decisions not yet made. But, as Acting Foreign Secretary, Curzon could do no more than complain that if Balfour decided that Samuel's letter did reflect British policy, 'I have nothing more to say'.[42] For their part, the Zionists were not content with sending letters of complaint to the Foreign Office. On June 11, 1919, Samuel Landman of the Zionist Bureau came to the Foreign Office to complain in person of OETA who were, he said, 'showing increasing signs of anti-Zionist feeling'. However, when pressed for examples, Landman could cite only two weak instances, one where British officers had remained seated during the playing of the Zionist national anthem and another where Zionists had been forbidden to attend a property sale in Jerusalem. Still, the Foreign Office were now convinced that the Zionists had OETA in their cross-hairs and that they particularly had 'their knife into' Ronald Storrs, Governor of Jerusalem.[43]

Landman's Foreign Office appearance was followed by Samuel and Weizmann who arrived separately on July 2. Samuel complained to Graham that OETA officials 'took every opportunity of injuring Zionist interests' in Palestine, again pointed a finger at Storrs, and asked that the Government make changes in the administration of Palestine by appointing new officers sympathetic to the Zionist programme. Soon after Samuel left, Weizmann arrived and complained 'in far more violent terms' of the 'marked hostility to the Jews' of OETA officers who 'lost no opportunity of not only injuring . . . [Zionist] interests but of humiliating them'. Weizmann added that 'every encouragement was given to the Arabs as against the Jews' and that the Jews in Palestine were now 'in a far worse position than they had been under the Turkish regime'. The Zionist leader even took on Allenby who, he said, was 'too much occupied with Egyptian and Syrian questions to take an interest in Palestine'. Weizmann also denounced Storrs 'with great bitterness' and then rounded on Clayton. According to Graham, Weizmann complained that the CPO 'showed no strength in handling the situation'.[44] In his zeal to promote the Zionist programme, Weizmann could act with duplicity. Storrs visited the Foreign Office shortly after Weizmann's appearance there and was surprised when 'Lord Curzon came in and told me of a fierce attack made on me on the 2nd . . . by Weizmann, who stated openly that I ran an anti-Jewish campaign . . . At the same time he continues to send me friendly and encouraging messages and asks me to lunch and dinner once or twice a week, so that it is a little difficult to know where one stands'.[45] Clayton, too, must have entertained doubts about Weizmann's tactics. A few months earlier the Zionist leader had written to him, stating that he found 'it difficult to thank you in words for all the kind help you have given, for all the kindness you have shown and above all for your guidance'.[46] Now, to the Foreign Office, Weizmann was denouncing Clayton for his weakness.

Clayton arrived in England on leave shortly after the July 2 appearances of Samuel and Weizmann at the Foreign Office and was immediately deputed to meet the Zionists at their London headquarters. Graham was to have joined him, but then found he 'could not be present'. So, on July 8, Clayton went unaccompanied to meet with Weizmann, Rothschild and thirteen other leading Zionists. The meeting must have been an uncomfortable one for Clayton. He was aware of Weizmann's complaints about him made to Graham on July 2, and now had to listen, without any support from the Foreign Office, to a litany of Zionist grievances. But the CPO was unflappable and unimpressed. As he reported that afternoon to the Foreign Office, the 'general criticisms' of the Zionists 'were not illustrated by specific instances, except in the case of one or two incidents of minor importance'. Clayton responded to them by observing that the present British administration in Palestine was 'temporary and provisional and was not therefore justified in pushing a Zionist policy at a time when the future status of Palestine had not been decided by the Peace Conference. However confident that the Zionists might be that the eventual decision would be in their favour, it would be incorrect for the occupying Power to prejudice that decision by acting as though the Mandate had already been given to Great Britain'. And, he informed them, 'precipitate action would only provoke increased opposition'.[47]

By the time of his July 8 meeting with the Zionists, Clayton had already accepted Allenby's offer of the position of Adviser to the Egyptian Ministry of the Interior. Whether the Zionists would have requested, or, more accurately, demanded, his removal as CPO is therefore uncertain. What is clear, however, is that they were delighted the 'ardent Zionist' Meinertzhagen was chosen to replace Clayton as CPO. 'The Zionists are triumphant about this', a Foreign Office analyst later reported, and

'Mr. Landman could not conceal his satisfaction at Gen. Clayton's departure'.[48] General Money also resigned his position as OETA chief in July, although he had planned to retire as early as November 1918, and his departure does not appear to have been prompted by the Zionists.[49] Balfour instructed the Foreign Office to appoint as replacements whoever Weizmann wished.[50] Clayton was perhaps pleased to leave the problems of Palestine and Syria behind him. But, as was typical of Clayton's career, he was leaving one set of problems only to confront another. And, in Egypt, the difficulties he was about to encounter were to prove no less formidable than those of Palestine.

23

A Witch's Cauldron: Egypt, 1920–1922

Unpleasant though his July 1919 meeting with the Zionists must have been, Clayton's summer leave did have its bright moments. On July 16, he attended a Royal garden party at Buckingham Palace at which Enid was presented to the King. Ten days later Clayton returned to the Palace to receive the KBE from King George, just as the King had personally presented him with the CMG three years earlier. And, on August 15, now as Sir Gilbert, he returned for an audience with His Majesty, who wished to hear of his experiences in Palestine and, presumably, Egypt.[1] But Clayton's leave was cut short. Allenby was now in Cairo without a single adviser to assist him and he telegraphed for Clayton's prompt return.[2] Five days after his audience with the King, Clayton left for Egypt to take up his new duties as Adviser to the Egyptian Ministry of the Interior.

Second only to his British counterpart at the Finance Ministry, the Adviser to the Ministry of the Interior occupied the most important position held by a foreigner in the Egyptian government. Certainly, no other senior official came into more frequent contact with the Egyptians than the Adviser to the Interior, for, as Clayton wrote, '[t]he Ministry of the Interior is, more than any other, the actual machine of government in the country'.[3] When Clayton took up his duties on September 1, 1919, the Ministry was comprised of seven departments: public security, public health, personnel & equipment, municipalities, administration, prisons and lunacy. Of those seven, six were headed by Englishmen and Clayton was fixed on a course of reform that would alter this arrangement – he was determined to bring more Egyptians into the business of running the country. In his view, the work of administering Egypt should devolve upon the Egyptians. This notion was developed by Clayton even before he was formally offered the job of Adviser by Allenby in mid-June. 'I am all for that Devolution policy in Egypt', Hogarth had written to him in May, 'and I hope you'll stick firmly to it and get your way'.[4] Of course, Clayton's 'devolution policy' was not one likely to be endorsed by the Anglo-Egyptian community, many of whom would lose not only their prospects, but also their jobs as a result. And it was recognized in the Foreign Office that Clayton's policy 'abandons the solicitude we have displayed for 40 years for the orderly conduct of Egyptian domestic affairs'.[5]

Clayton was aware of these arguments; he knew that turning over control of domestic affairs to the Egyptians ran counter to the British policy of forty years and, inevitably, would result in mistakes, inefficiencies and even abuses, but he held that in view of the events of March 1919, devolution, at least in the area of domestic affairs, was essential:

> The lesson of 40 years in Egypt stares us in the face. I feel that we should start slowly and let the people come to us for help and guidance in their difficulties, rather than impose Western efficiency too suddenly on Orientals to whom it has been unknown for centuries. I fear that catch word "British efficiency". Our charter for the rule of decadent Oriental peoples is not primarily "efficiency", but "honesty & sympathy" . . . The "white man's burden" requires never failing patience and understanding with but little hope of visible individual achievement – the ruined civilizations of the East cannot be revived in a generation.[6]

Clayton sought to put these ideas into effect first by changing the way in which British officials interacted with the Egyptians. Ever since the days of Cromer, officials had appeared, much like 'the Lord' himself, as rather remote figures, determining policy and making decisions in consultation with other authorities and perhaps with Egyptian Ministers, but rarely in contact with the Egyptian people. Clayton disagreed with this attitude and offered the Residency suggestions about how British officials in Egypt should conduct themselves. 'It is by personal contact and conversation . . . that the British official can best make his influence felt', he enjoined the Residency. Public speeches by government officials, he added, should rarely, if ever, be made. Public pronouncements were invariably 'distorted by expert Egyptian "intellectuals" in such a manner as to destroy completely their meaning to the limited comprehension of the masses and thus . . . render them harmful rather than beneficial'. Above all, religion was a subject which it was 'wise to leave alone in a predominantly Moslem country' like Egypt.[7]

Soon after he became Adviser to the Interior, Clayton put these principles into practice. As he advised the Residency, 'nothing has so great an effect as the visible appearance in the provinces of high British officials. I have endeavoured to carry out this policy by visiting nearly every Mudiria [province] and Markaz [provincial subdivision] and I cannot but think that . . . the result has been good'.[8] In early March 1920, Clayton began an eighteen day inspection tour of Upper Egypt. He and Enid – an unusual step, in itself, for an Adviser to take along his wife – travelled by train to Aswan where they joined the British Inspector in the region, John Young. The trio then journeyed downriver on Young's steamer 'visiting all the Mudiria and Markaz towns along the way'. As Young later described the tour, '[e]very day was fully occupied in business and hospitalities. Mudirs and Mamurs were entertained at lunch and dinner on the steamer and omdahs and notables made constant calls. At Fashn, when we visited the Arab omdah, Lamlum Pasha, just before the Claytons came to the house, a goat was slaughtered across the threshold and in order to enter they had to step over the flowing blood. A mark of honour! Sir Gilbert Clayton was always charming to Egyptians and altogether the tour was a complete success'.[9] Even while in his office in Cairo, Clayton kept his mornings open for meetings with Egyptians, high and low, reserving his paperwork for afternoons and evenings.[10]

Another example of Clayton's interest in engaging Egyptians at all levels, was provided years later by his sister, Ellinor, who recounted the visit of a small contingent of British Members of Parliament to Egypt in September 1921. One day, while Clayton was escorting the party by car through Cairo, they stopped at a railway crossing to wait for a passing train. Suddenly, an old man who kept a peanut stall by the roadside, came forward to exchange pleasantries with Clayton and ask about his family. Stunned by the exchange, one of the MPs asked, 'But do you <u>know</u> that old man?' 'Yes', Clayton replied, 'known him for years.' 'But do you know many like him?' the MP persisted. 'Yes, I should think some hundreds', Clayton answered.[11] Unusually for the time, Clayton also promoted better relations between the wives of British officials and Egyptian women. Major E. E. Waley of GHQ Intelligence noted in a letter to the Foreign Office that 'hardly any visiting by English ladies' with Egyptian women occurred in the country. 'A great deal of good could be done', he added, 'by careful and friendly communication and association between the ladies of the English Colony and local Moslem women, and I think Clayton is going to see what can be done about it'.[12] He did do something about it, and Enid was a willing participant. Clayton's desk diary for 1920, contains several references to 'harem tea parties' organized by Enid, most of which appear to have been held at the Claytons' house on Gezira. On February 11, 1920, Enid even dined with Madame Zaghlul, wife of the Nationalist leader who had been deported in March 1919, and herself an ardent Nationalist.[13]

While Clayton took practical steps to bring the British community into closer touch with the Egyptians, his immediate concerns were with the Ministry of the Interior and, more specifically, its Public Security Department. He was well aware that the British had been taken by surprise by the events of March 1919, and that the failure lay in large measure with Public Security which had provided no warning of the revolt. Soon after his arrival in Egypt in early September he asked his friend from war-time Intelligence and Palestine, Wyndham Deedes, to come out to assist in reorganizing the Department. The matter is one of 'extreme urgency' he wired Deedes, 'as without an efficient system of control and Intelligence, we are practically helpless against subversive elements which are working in Egypt and from abroad'. Deedes agreed at once. At the same time, Clayton requested that another acquaintance, Harold MacMichael of the Sudan Service, come to Cairo to help and both Lee Stack, Governor-General of the Sudan, and MacMichael agreed.[14] The Adviser also asked GHQ Intelligence 'to establish for him an M.I.5', which would enable him to exchange information with the C-in-C and the Residency.[15]

Clayton could reorganize and revitalize the Interior on his own initiative, but in order to put in place his policy of devolution, in order to eliminate or reduce British positions in the Ministry, he would require the support of the High Commissioner and even the Foreign Office. In the winter of 1919–20, he was provided a medium through which he could advocate his policy – the Milner Mission. As described earlier, Clayton had proposed the dispatch of a Royal Commission to Egypt in March 1919. The idea was not novel; Wingate had made a similar proposal in December 1918. Still, it was not until April 1919, on the heels of the uprising, that Curzon came to advocate sending such a commission to Egypt.[16] But the Mission was delayed. The Colonial Secretary, Lord Milner, who was to head it, prevaricated. Allenby changed his mind, at first suggesting it be delayed and then agreeing that it should be sent, and still later asking again that it be deferred. Then, in August, it became apparent that the Wafd would resist the Mission, demanding that it be boycotted by the Egyptians.[17] Clayton himself now came to doubt the wisdom of sending a commission as he realized that 'most of the important . . . [Egyptians] would refuse to give evidence, while the waverers would [be] terrorized into withholding it and those who persisted would earn popular denunciation for having given it'. The findings of the Mission would thus 'be discredited from the first as having been based on insufficient data'.[18]

Despite these reservations, the Milner Mission was eventually assembled and arrived in Egypt on December 7, 1919. Milner knew his task was a large one. 'A witch's cauldron', he wrote to Curzon, has 'been brewing' in Egypt since the days of Cromer and change would not be easy to achieve.[19] The Colonial Secretary was accompanied by five others, two of whom, like himself, had significant Egyptian experience. Sir Rennell Rodd, British ambassador to Italy, had worked for several years in Egypt under Cromer. And General Sir John Maxwell, Clayton's old chief from the early war years, had nearly twenty years experience in the country. The Mission also included Cecil Hurst, the Foreign Office's legal adviser, J. A. Spender, a prominent Liberal and former editor of the *Westminster Gazette*, and General Sir Owen Thomas, a Labour MP. Milner, Spender and Hurst appear to have taken the most active role in the work and subsequent conclusions of the Mission.[20] By the time the Mission arrived, the Egyptian boycott was in full force. And it was effective; as Clayton predicted, no Egyptians appeared formally before the Mission, although informally, and often clandestinely, Milner and his colleagues met with several current and former Ministers of the Egyptian government. But there was little doubt that the Mission had been effectively stymied by the boycott. The Arabic press was unanimous in its denunciation of the Mission and had been for two months before Milner arrived. As Clayton observed, so thoroughly was the press in the control of the 'extremist party' that any opposition 'on the part of any particular journal results in such a drop in sales as to threaten bankruptcy'.[21] Without Egyptian participation, it seemed most unlikely that the Mission could carry out its brief of ascertaining the causes of the insurrection, or reporting on the existing situation, or suggesting a form of Constitution which would enable Egypt 'under the Protectorate' to advance towards self-governing institutions.[22]

Without evidence from the Egyptians, the work of the Mission was largely reduced to taking testimony from British officials in the country. Clayton appeared three times before Milner and his colleagues, on December 18, 19 and 23. Although he proposed a reorganization of the Interior Ministry, and especially the

Public Security Department, Clayton's devolution policy permeated nearly all his suggestions. The Public Security, he testified, 'must be a local Egyptian Department, i.e., largely staffed by Egyptians'. And, the pay of all the directors in the Department 'should be [the] same . . . whether English or Egyptian'. His plan was that in the two most important sections of the Public Security, Political and Crimes, there should be two directors, one English and one Egyptian, which would allow for a period of tutelage until the Egyptian director would be able to run his section unaided by his British counterpart. Clayton also proposed a complete over-haul of the Inspectorate, the system in place since the early days of Cromer, whereby British inspectors resided in the provinces and, in essence, controlled the local administration. Clayton intended to remove all the inspectors from the provinces and bring them into the Interior Ministry in Cairo, leaving the Mudirs in sole con-trol. The only function of the reformed Inspectorate would be to tour the provinces and report to the Interior. Again, the pay of British and Egyptian inspector would be equal and the British would be phased out gradually over time. Most surprising of all, Clayton anticipated the removal of the Adviser himself: 'The Inspectorate would be directly under the [Egyptian] Minister and the Adviser would draw back. If it was decided later to make the Interior over to the natives, the British Adviser would go and British Inspectors would gradually retire.'[23]

Even before he presented the Milner Mission with these remarkable proposals, Clayton had begun to put his ideas into practice. One inspector wrote to the Foreign Office on November 11, 1919, that 'Clayton's policy [was] to withdraw inspectors from the provinces. But in order to make [the] Mudirs take undivided responsibility and not because they [the Inspectors] were in any kind of danger'.[24] However, there was some risk in Clayton's reform of the Inspectorate, for now there was no overt official British presence in the provinces. As the same inspector noted in a subsequent letter, '[p]ractically no Inspectors are out now, with the result that the Europeans are very nervous'.[25] Clayton also recommended to the Mission that the current system for selecting British inspectors be discontinued. For years, young university graduates had appeared before the Egyptian and Sudan Selection Board every summer as candidates for such positions. Clayton himself had sat on the Selection Board before the war (see Chapter 7). But, in his view, the disadvan-tage of the process was 'that young men with no knowledge of natives are put into positions of considerable importance and it is impossible to predict whether they will be a success or not'. So, he proposed that until the British inspectors were phased out, 'Englishmen from the Sudan who have had 3 or 4 years experience under a British Mudir' be used in Egypt. As he had explained earlier to Gertrude Bell, 'Egypt can no longer be regarded as a nursery for the training of young men in administration'. Bell summarized Clayton's view: 'the Egyptian Civil Service is, in fact, dead'.[26]

Recognizing that his proposals were dramatic and believing they were unlikely to appeal to the Mission if he urged immediate adoption, Clayton suggested a gradual implementation of his reforms. He would not, he said, feel justified in immediately reducing the number of British officials in the Interior 'in view of the absolute necessity of safeguarding British and Foreign interests' in the country. '[W]e must not withdraw all English officials and then let the natives fail in their task of running things unaided.' His idea, then, was 'to put an Egyptian to work side by side with an Englishman and then if the Englishman is withdrawn the native can carry on'.[27] In fact, Clayton's concerns were unfounded; Milner and his colleagues agreed fully with his devolution policy. As stated in their eventual report, 'as regards . . . domestic affairs, Egypt would be completely self-governing except in respect of the privileges of foreigners'.[28] The 'privileges of foreigners' referred to the Capitulatory rights, then held by thirteen countries in Egypt, rights by which specified countries enjoyed exemptions from taxation and from the process of Egyptian courts.[29] But Clayton's devolution policy was accepted and gradually put into effect. The 1926 report of the Interior Ministry noted that 'for some time prior to 1922 the policy of the then Adviser [Clayton] would appear to have tended more and more in the direction of transferring authority from English to Egyptian hands'. That same report reflected that, by 1926, 'the Inspectors have gone' and the number of foreign officials in the Interior had been reduced by eighty percent.[30]

In addition to his formal testimony before the Milner Mission, Clayton met several times with the Mission, and its individual members, informally. Milner, especially, was impressed by Clayton. They met on December 16, when Milner recorded that he 'found himself in very general agreement with his views'. On the 18th, Clayton lunched with the Mission and gave 'a further expression of his views – on the broader political issue'. 'They seem to me very good', Milner recorded. The next day, after Clayton again testified for two hours, the Colonial Secretary added that '[w]e all continue, I think, to be very favourably impressed by Clayton'. Again, after his testimony on the 23rd, Milner found his evidence 'once more of great interest'. On December 28, Milner met with Clayton and Allenby and the Adviser persuaded the High Commissioner to adopt Milner's recommendation that certain political prisoners should be released, after Clayton consulted with the Egyptian Prime Minister, Yusuf Wahba.[31] Clayton also met with Maxwell on December 13 and 19.[32]

What were the views Clayton gave to the Milner Mission on December 18, on 'the broader political issue' in Egypt? It will be recalled that two months earlier Clayton had written to his father of the importance of Britain maintaining control of her vital interests in Egypt – the 'substance' – while relinquishing control of the unimportant features of British rule, like the Protectorate designation – the 'shadow'. It was a message he repeated to his father a month after his luncheon with the Mission. 'It is the shadow which these people chiefly want', he wrote on January 17, 'and if we give it to them we can get the substance; whereas if we try and keep the shadow we shall inevitably lose much, if not all, of the substance.'[33] Clayton likely repeated his idea of the 'shadow' and the 'substance' to Milner, for ten days after his lunch with Clayton the Colonial Secretary repeated the notion in a letter to Lloyd George, in which he informed the Prime Minister that Egyptian moderates were more concerned with the 'appearance' than the 'substance' of any agreement that might address the political problems of Egypt.[34]

Just before leaving Egypt in March 1920, the Mission prepared an abbreviated version of its eventual report, in which the 'General Conclusions' of Milner and his colleagues were summarized. Clayton met privately with Milner four days before the General Conclusions were finalized and, unsurprisingly, the Missions' summary reflected many of Clayton's ideas.[35] Alluding to the Egyptians' 'love of forms and phrases', the Mission stated that Britain should 'seek to give to the future status of Egypt the greatest appearance of independence compatible with the maintenance of the absolutely indispensable minimum of British control' – an idea very close to Clayton's 'shadow' and 'substance'. Like Clayton, they advocated elimination of the post of Adviser to the Interior; indeed, they went further and proposed the removal of *all* British Advisers, except for those in Finance and Justice, the two Ministries most closely associated with the Egyptian debt and the rights of foreigners in Egypt under the Capitulations. They agreed with Clayton's conclusion that there were too many British officials in Egypt and that those who remained should receive no greater salary than their Egyptian counterparts. They also agreed with him that provincial authority should devolve upon those Egyptians manning the provincial councils, the municipalities and local commissions. And, they concurred in his view that 'the British Administration in Egypt should make a far greater effort to establish contact with the Egyptian people'.[36]

While Clayton's imprint on the Milner Mission's General Conclusions and its subsequent report is unmistakable, his influence on the Mission must not be overstated. Other officials testified before the Mission and some of the opinions propounded by Clayton were held by others in the Anglo-Egyptian community. Moreover, some members of the Mission may have been predisposed in favour of a policy of devolution in Egypt. Hurst, for example, held that Britain should make 'spontaneous concessions' to the Egyptians, relinquishing control over all aspects of the administration not 'vital' to British interests. Still, Hurst's paper advocating this policy was written two months after Clayton's testimony and informal discussions with the Mission.[37] Similarly, in an undated memo, Spender proposed that Britain give up 'formal control' over the Egyptian administration.[38] It should be noted, though, that when Clayton was on leave in England in the summer of 1920, his diary reflects meetings with both Milner and Spender. He may also have met with Hurst during his leave – though there is no direct evidence to support it – because Clayton worked in the Foreign Office, where Hurst was employed, for nearly the entire months of September and October 1920.[39]

After the Milner Mission left Egypt in March, Clayton continued his work at the Interior and made another trip to the provinces. It appears that he was also deeply engaged in Egyptian politics, making efforts to work with the 'moderates' in Egypt, those who, unlike the more extreme nationalists, might be persuaded to reach an accommodation with Britain. The moderate leaders were all 'well known to and nursed by Clayton' according to one official in a report to the Foreign Office.[40] He also maintained important connections with former acquaintances from Palestine and Arabia. On April 14, he met with Weizmann, who was then passing through Cairo. If Clayton harboured any ill feelings toward the Zionist leader, they were not reflected in his diary notation of the meeting. He also met three times with Amir Abdullah, King Hussein's second son, who visited Cairo in late April and early May 1920. And, most enjoyably, Clayton's brother Iltyd arrived in April and spent a few weeks with Bertie and Enid before leaving in May to join the British administration in Iraq, as Mesopotamia was now coming to be called.[41] At his brother's request, Iltyd had been assigned to political duties after the war and, for most of 1919, had worked as a political officer in Damascus, where he reported to his brother of his struggles to maintain relations, now deteriorating, between Faisal and the French.[42]

On June 13, 1920, Clayton's work at the Interior came to an abrupt and tragic halt. On that day, the Claytons' second child, Jane, then just three months short of her sixth birthday, fell seriously ill. At the direction of the Public Health Department, Bertie, Enid and Jane left that same evening for Port Said in the company of a doctor. But nothing could be done and, at 5 a.m. on Monday, June 14, Clayton sadly recorded in his diary that 'our darling Janey died'.[43] Bertie and Enid returned that same night to Cairo, where Jane was buried the next morning. Within twenty-four hours, the Claytons' eldest child, Patience, not yet seven, also fell ill and, in Enid's words, 'was at death's door until Friday night [June 18] when she pulled through a . . . crisis'. At the same time, two servants and a nurse attending the Clayton children were also sent to hospital 'with high fever & glands'. Bertie and Enid and their only 'well' servant were quarantined in tents on the beach at Port Said and put 'under observation' by orders of the Public Health. Enid explained what had happened in a letter to Bertie's mother: 'we had an epidemic of <u>bubonic plague</u>. Darling Jane had the most virulent form which killed her before symptoms appeared: Pacey [Patience] of course caught it & the 2 servants & we naturally have had to be isolated. It must have been in the house. They caught 90 rats in the gardens & 1 in the house, but not a <u>single one</u> had the plague'.[44] Shocking though Jane's death must have been, the plague was not uncommon in Egypt; in 1918 more than 1,600 people had succumbed to the disease.[45] Still, the incidence of plague must have been much lower amongst the European community in the country.

Desperate to get the children out of Egypt, Bertie and Enid put their two year old, Sam, and a nurse aboard a ship for England on the 27th and, shortly after Patience was released from hospital, she, Bertie and Enid sailed for home on July 5.[46] The Claytons had now lost two children to disease in Egypt. Thomas had lived less than a month before succumbing to infection in the autumn of 1916. But the loss of Thomas, painful though it must have been, was not nearly so devastating as the death of Jane who, at nearly six, had emerged as a delightful and winsome personality. One could easily understand Enid's feelings when she confided to Bertie's mother, 'Oh how we long & ache to be at home & out of this country.'[47] Clayton, too, must have been badly shaken by Jane's death, for a week later he advised a colleague that he doubted he would remain much longer in Egypt. And, in early September, in describing the 'grim experience' of Jane's death to Wingate, he added that 'it has rather upset our views of the future, as I cannot ask my wife to return to Egypt again – at least for some time, nor am I keen on staying much longer myself. I am not sorry, therefore, that the march of events looks as though the services of an Adviser to the Interior would no longer be required'.[48]

Clayton was right about the future of the Adviser. By the time he arrived in London on July 27, 1920, the removal of all British Advisers from Egypt, save for those to Finance and Justice, had been conceded during talks that had been ongoing between Milner and Zaghlul for nearly two months. Milner had invited the Wafd leader to London for the purpose of working out the terms of an Anglo-Egyptian treaty along the lines of the Mission's General Conclusions prepared in early March. Milner was convinced that, in view of the major concessions he was prepared to make, such a treaty was attainable. Echoing Clayton, the Colonial Secretary believed that the nationalists 'stick only at "Protectorate", but under the guise of a "Treaty" are prepared to give us almost everything'.[49] Clayton's influence on the Milner–Zaghlul negotiations, if any, is impossible to detect on the existing record. He arrived in London only two weeks before the talks concluded. It is possible, though, that Clayton's discussions with Spender and Milner at the end of July influenced the joint 'Memorandum' that resulted from the negotiations two weeks later.

This Memorandum, often described as the 'Milner–Zaghlul Agreement' – incorrectly, as it was not an agreement, but only a joint expression of intent – disclosed that both Milner and Clayton were overly optimistic about the willingness of the Egyptians to concede major points allowing for Britain's continued presence in Egypt, if the Protectorate was dissolved. The Memorandum contemplated a treaty under which Britain would 'recognise the independence of Egypt as a constitutional monarchy with representative institutions', in return for which Egypt would 'confer upon . . . Britain such rights as are necessary to safeguard her special interests' in the country. In a major departure from the Mission's prior position, Britain would concede Egypt's 'right to representation in foreign countries', provided that the Egyptians did not enter into any agreement with a foreign Power 'prejudicial to British interests'. The Egyptians were to allow Britain to maintain 'a military force on Egyptian soil for the protection of Imperial communications' and would agree to the continued presence of British Financial and Judicial Advisers, who would ensure that the Egyptian debt was properly administered and that the rights of foreigners in the country were adequately protected. What Milner envisioned was that Britain would conclude agreements with the twelve countries still holding Capitulatory rights in Egypt whereby those rights were, in effect, assigned to Britain who would, in turn, ensure that citizens of the countries holding those rights would not be subjected to arbitrary or unfair applications of Egyptian law. The Memorandum also provided that the British High Commissioner would 'be accorded an exceptional position in Egypt and will be entitled to precedence over all other representatives'. Finally, Egypt would be allowed to remove all foreign officials in Egyptian service within two years of the effective date of a treaty embodying the Memorandum's terms, provided all rights to pensions and compensation were protected.[50]

The Milner–Zaghlul Memorandum closely paralleled the ideas Clayton had conveyed to Gertrude Bell and the Milner Mission in 1919: the Protectorate was discarded; Britain's imperial communications were protected, and a British force would remain to ensure that they were; the rights of foreigners in Egypt would be protected via British Advisers to Finance and Justice; and, in domestic affairs, all responsibility would devolve upon the Egyptians, unless they wished to retain the services of foreign officials. Still, Milner made two fundamental mistakes in reducing his understanding with Zaghlul to paper. First, he did not ensure that the Wafd leader explicitly agreed to the terms of the Memorandum. Zaghlul would need to consult his constituents, he said – the Egyptian people – on its terms, and he dispatched four of his colleagues to Egypt to do just that. Inevitably, the terms of the Memorandum would become widely known; they would become public. And, once they were, Britain could not retreat from concessions already made, concessions that were sure to form the starting point of any subsequent negotiations between the parties. This point was immediately recognized by three Cabinet opponents of the Milner–Zaghlul Memorandum, Churchill, Montagu and Curzon, who were also annoyed that Milner had made such sweeping concessions without consulting the Cabinet.[51] Clayton agreed that there could be no retreat from the points conceded in the Memorandum. As he advised Wingate, 'I understand that the Govt. do not consider themselves bound by Lord M[ilner's] pronouncements, but in my humble opinion they are so bound, in that if they attempt to go back in any way on them, they will incur an irredeemable reputation for bad faith and will have the fat in the fire worse than ever.'[52] No less important than Milner's mistaken negotiation tactic, was his failure to understand fully Zaghlul and the Wafd. Their power, and Zaghlul's immense popularity among the Egyptians, sprang from one source – defiance of the British. Theirs was the politics of opposition. Indeed, in its early years, the Wafd had no social, economic or agricultural programmes.[53] So, by agreeing to anything short of complete independence – *istiqlal tamm* – the Wafd would lose its very *raison d'être*. Unsurprisingly, no agreement resulted from the summer 1920 negotiations. And, when talks were resumed the following year, the Egyptians would not retreat from the concessions made by Milner in 1920.

Shortly after the Milner–Zaghlul Memorandum was presented to the Cabinet, Clayton began a two-month period of work at the Foreign Office where he was asked to advise on issues dealing with Palestine and Arabia.[54] He may have accepted the assignment, in part, to occupy his mind following his daughter's death, but he also saw that the temporary work might lead to a permanent position in the Office. For some months, discussions had been taking place in Whitehall concerning the creation of a new Middle Eastern Department, perhaps as an independent office of State, but more likely, as a section within one of the existing departments, such as the Foreign or Colonial Office.[55] During the preceding October, Curzon had succeeded Balfour as Foreign Secretary and was now strongly lobbying for placement of the new department in the Foreign Office. 'I am in a position', he advised the Cabinet in August 1920, 'to recommend as head of this . . .[department] an officer who has an almost unique experience of the Middle East'.[56] There was no doubt to whom he was referring. After Allenby visited the Foreign Office in mid-August, he wrote to a colleague that 'Clayton will probably be given the control of the proposed Near East Department of the F.O. when and if it is formed'.[57]

During his time at the Foreign Office, Clayton was involved in a wide variety of issues. He probably watched with some disappointment as the fortunes of his war-time protégés, the Hashemites, began to crumble in 1920. In July, as Clayton had predicted, the Arabs and the French came to blows in Syria. The French easily prevailed and Faisal was promptly turned out of Damascus. The Amir pleaded for support, but the British book on Syria was closed. As Clayton informed Faisal's representative in London, 'any risk of a quarrel with France over this question was unthinkable'.[58] That did not mean, however, that Faisal was finished as an Arab leader, for no sooner was he ejected from Syria, than the Amir came under consideration as the future ruler of Iraq, the Mandate for which had been assigned to Britain in April 1920.[59] And, despite the angry protests of the French, and the hurt feelings of his brother Abdullah, Faisal was 'elected' as the first King of Iraq in 1921.

While Faisal's prospects appeared grim in the summer of 1920, those of his father were little better. The King was being subjected to persistent pressure by his rival to the East, Ibn Saud and, while the Foreign Office generally favoured supporting Hussein against his Arabian rival, the King was already becoming a 'pampered and querulous nuisance' to his British sponsors.[60] He refused to sign the Versailles Treaty – because it would have reflected his acquiescence to the French Mandate in Syria and the Jewish national home in Palestine – and he persisted in mischaracterizing his 1915–16 correspondence with McMahon, arguing that the British were in breach of their 'agreement' with him. It fell to Clayton to remind Hussein's emissaries in London of McMahon's reservation regarding French interests. 'In any case', he informed them, 'no assurance had ever been given or implied that the Arab territories would be formed into a single State under one ruler', such as Hussein.[61]

While at the Foreign Office, Clayton also attended several meetings of an Inter-Departmental Conference on Eastern Affairs (IDCE), a lower-level successor to the Eastern Committee of 1918. During the summer of 1920, the IDCE was absorbed with revising the draft Mandates for Palestine and Iraq. While the Mandates had been assigned in April, the actual enabling document that would define the parameters of the Mandates, and would be submitted to the League of Nations for approval, had not yet been finalized. Clayton had little to say about the Mandates, with one, important exception – Transjordan. The Zionists were intent on bringing the undefined region to the East of the River Jordan under the Palestine Mandate and thus subjecting it to the national home policy. Curzon was 'very concerned' about the region, as he saw that Herbert Samuel, the first High Commissioner of Palestine and a confirmed Zionist, wanted Transjordan 'as an annex of Palestine and an outlet for the Jews'. 'Here I am against him', the Foreign Secretary added.[62] Clayton agreed, and thought that the territory should be reserved for the Arabs. '[T]here is much to be said in favour of carrying out the spirit of the Sykes–Picot Agreement in our sphere by gradually establishing a small Arab State in Trans-Jordania which would eventually gravitate towards Mesopotamia, Palestine or the Hejaz'.[63] And, as he argued before the IDCE, drawing the Palestine boundary east of the Jordan – as the Zionists intended – would 'deprive any future State that . . . might . . . be set up in the territory east of Palestine of almost its only source of natural wealth, and would exclude it from an outlet on the Gulf of Akaba'.[64] He advised that the Foreign Office should 'warn Sir H. Samuel again against undertaking any administrative responsibilities' in Transjordan.[65] The area east of the Jordan was eventually made a part of the Palestine Mandate, but it was expressly provided that the Jewish national home policy would not be applied there. As will be seen, Clayton would have more to do with Transjordan in the mid-1920s.

On October 25, 1920, Clayton left for Egypt – alone. As he had related to Wingate, he could not ask Enid to accompany him. She and the children remained at Ryde, on the Isle of Wight, where Clayton had rented a comfortable house on the water. When the couple's fifth and last child, John, was born there on February 13, 1921, Clayton was in Egypt. Yet, until early 1921, he fully expected to be called back to England as the new chief of a Middle Eastern Department in the Foreign Office. That was Curzon's intent and it was the hope of those working on Middle Eastern affairs in the Office. And it was certainly Clayton's hope.[66] But, on the last day of 1920, in a close vote, the Cabinet decided to create the new Middle Eastern Department in the Colonial Office. It was only a qualified defeat for Curzon; the Colonial Office's Middle Eastern responsibilities would be confined to the Mandated territories of Palestine and Iraq. Milner would not, however, be in charge of the new department. The Colonial Secretary, now aged sixty-six, was played out. In February 1921, he turned over the Office to the new Colonial Secretary, Winston Churchill. Before leaving office, Milner was asked how the new Middle Eastern Department should be staffed. 'Clayton – the Egyptian man', he said, should be the 'Arabic expert'.[67] But the new Colonial Secretary had other ideas. Throughout the early months of 1921, he was advised on Middle Eastern affairs by Arthur Hirtzel of the India Office and Hirtzel recommended as head of the new department his own man, John Shuckburgh, a proposal promptly accepted by Churchill.

Although Clayton continued his work of reform and devolution in the Interior Ministry, his attention was now, more than ever, focused on the political situation in Egypt. Shortly after his arrival in Cairo, at Allenby's request, he produced a memorandum reflecting his views on the situation which the High Commissioner promptly forwarded to London. Clayton was convinced that even though Zaghlul and the Wafd had no official status, they were 'by far the most powerful force in Egyptian politics . . . and are able to exert a widespread influence throughout the country . . . [T]here is no doubt that they command the sympathy and support of the majority of articulate opinion in the country'. Although there was opposition to Zaghlul, his firm stand on abolition of the Protectorate and his rejection of the Milner proposals of 1920 had strengthened his hand and caused his opponents to 'crumble'. Clayton also pointed to Egypt's deteriorating economic condition – a 'heavy fall in the price of cotton', strikes, exorbitant prices – to conclude that 'the soil . . . is prepared for the seed the agitator'. He was not writing 'in any alarmist spirit', he concluded, but the Government would be incurring a 'grave risk' if its military policy was 'framed on the basis of a "peaceful Egypt"'.[68] He plainly warned Allenby, and the Foreign Office, that if British policy was 'definitely unfavourable to Egyptian aspirations', a renewal of disturbances was certain.

At the same time Clayton was preparing his warning to London, he was working with Egyptian moderates to form a new government, one that would appoint a delegation to negotiate an Anglo-Egyptian treaty on the basis of the final report of the Milner Mission, only just submitted to the Cabinet in December 1920. The current Egyptian government, under Prime Minister Taufiq Nasim Pasha, had been able to maintain order and comparative calm in Egypt since the previous May, but Taufiq himself admitted that a stronger Ministry would be required to negotiate a treaty that would be acceptable to the Egyptian people.[69] The attentions of Allenby and Clayton focused on Adli Yakan, a moderate who had participated in the Milner–Zaghlul negotiations of 1920. Milner thought that Adli would 'gladly accept "half a loaf" rather than let a settlement . . . fall to the ground altogether'.[70] In his talks with Taufiq and Adli, Allenby was assisted by three men upon whom, more than any others, the High Commissioner would rely during the next, critical year – Clayton, Maurice Amos, Adviser to the Ministry of Justice, and Walford Selby, First Secretary in the Cairo Residency.

The negotiations with Adli were made considerably easier by an official statement from London, delivered to Sultan Fu'ad on February 21, 1921. The British had concluded, it said, that 'the status of protectorate is not a satisfactory relation in which Egypt should continue to stand to Great Britain'. The statement also requested the formation of a delegation which would negotiate a relationship in substitution of the Protectorate that would secure the 'special interests of Great Britain' while still meeting the 'legitimate aspirations of . . . the Egyptian people'.[71] Despite this encouraging statement, the Sultan was not keen on the proposed Ministry. He disliked Adli and it took meetings with Clayton on March 7 and Allenby on the 12th – perhaps involving some arm-twisting – before Fu'ad agreed to the Adli government.[72] The essential problem with the Adli Ministry, though, lay not in the displeasure of Fu'ad, but in its failure to include any 'Zaghlulists'. If Clayton was correct that Zaghlul and the Wafd formed the 'most powerful force in Egyptian politics', then any arrangement Adli reached with the British would need to receive Zaghlul's support. It was not likely to materialize. Soon after Adli took over on March 16, Zaghlul announced from Paris his opposition to the new government, unless he was appointed to lead any future British negotiations. Then, on April 5, after a two year absence, the Wafd leader returned to Egypt, making a triumphal progress from Alexandria to Cairo. Four hundred thousand Egyptians, it was said, thronged the short distance from the Cairo railway station to Zaghlul's house. To the Egyptian masses, Clayton later concluded, Zaghlul was 'almost a deity'.[73] Watching the huge crowd celebrate the return of their hero, Thomas Russell, Commandant of the Cairo Police, wrote that Zaghlul 'is going to cause us a lot of trouble. He is an absolute extremist'.[74]

Russell's opinion was reinforced by Harry Boyle, Oriental Secretary for many years under Cromer. He came out in April, probably at the request of the Foreign Office, to report on the political situation. Boyle had known Zaghlul well during his years in Cairo and met with the Wafd leader several times during May 1921. He concluded that Zaghlul was living 'in a fool's paradise . . , intoxicated with the atmosphere of excitement, adulation and apparent enthusiasm' of his surroundings. He appeared to Boyle as 'utterly uncompromising and deaf to argument of any kind'. Any opposition or even slight disagreement 'evokes an outbreak of irritation on his part'. Above all, his rivalry with Adli had become 'almost a monomania' with Zaghlul.[75] Ernest Scott, who acted as High Commissioner while Allenby was on leave from August to November 1921, agreed with Boyle, and went further. He thought Zaghlul 'unbalanced mentally' and 'suffering from acute and increasing megalomania'. Scott was convinced that Zaghlul would not accept any settlement with the British 'not achieved by himself'. 'It is Sir Gilbert Clayton's opinion', Scott added, 'that it would be impossible ever to work with a man of his mentality'.[76]

These were particularly discouraging assessments because, in July 1921, Adli arrived in London to again attempt what he and Zaghlul had failed to achieve in 1920 – a negotiated settlement with the British. Any agreement Adli might reach in London, however, was certain to be opposed by Zaghlul and Adli's recognition of this reality likely made him more intransigent than he otherwise might have been. Although Curzon met with Adli six times during the summer of 1921, little progress was made in the talks. Eventually, the Foreign Secretary conceded Egyptian diplomatic representation abroad, but Adli balked over the issue of British troops and proposals concerning the protection of foreigners in Egypt. Frustrated, the Foreign Secretary turned the negotiations over to Ronald Lindsay, an under-secretary in the Foreign Office who had Egyptian experience. But Lindsay could do little. On the critical issue of Britain's obligation to protect foreigners in Egypt, he wired to Cairo to solicit Clayton's advice. Clayton thought it essential that that the British police commandants be maintained in Egypt's three largest cities, Cairo, Alexandria and Port Said. Maintaining British commandants in the cities was all the more important for Clayton because only three months earlier serious riots had occurred in Alexandria (May 20–21) in which several foreigners had been killed. But that was not sufficient; important though they were, the commandants could not ensure the security of foreigners outside the cities, so Clayton also proposed that a British Director – or, at least, a British Assistant Director – of Public Security be maintained in the Ministry of the Interior.[77] But these proposals also proved unacceptable to Adli and, by November 1921, it was apparent that the negotiations had failed.

The failure of the 1921 talks did have one important effect: it transferred the initiative from London to Cairo. From the autumn of 1921, Allenby and the Advisers would take the lead in achieving a resolution of the Egyptian problem.[78] Signs of this began to appear as early as June when Sir William Hayter, legal adviser to the Residency and to the Egyptian Finance Ministry submitted a paper in which he stated definitively that '[n]o Egyptian Minister can fairly be asked to sign a treaty fixing the permanent status of Egypt at anything short of complete independence'. Hayter proposed not a treaty, but an interim accord – a *modus vivendi* for a ten year period – in which Britain would grant immediate independence to Egypt, reserving British rights to protect foreigners, safeguard Imperial communications and maintain a force for defence of the country. If the Egyptians refused to accede to such an arrangement, Hayter proposed that it be 'put into force by proclamation' from London.[79]

Clayton, who was away from Egypt on leave from 18 March to 12 July, 1921, did not see Hayter's paper until he returned to Cairo. But after reviewing it, he stated his 'complete agreement': 'no Egyptian negotiators can hope to secure popular acceptance of an agreement which is based on anything less than the independence of Egypt'.[80] Indeed, in the words of acting High Commissioner Scott, Clayton went 'even further' than Hayter in his proposals.[81] Clayton believed that the principal sticking point for the Egyptians was the maintenance of a British military force in the country; even for the moderate Adli, that meant British 'occupation pure and simple'.[82] In Clayton's view, the British force in Egypt served three purposes: the protection of the country from 'external foes', the securing of Imperial communications and the protection of foreigners in the country. But, if either Egypt or the Suez Canal was attacked by a foreign Power, that 'would presumably mean that Great Britain was at war with that Power', and the full military resources of Britain would be brought to bear on the aggressor. So, the only real function of the British force in Egypt was to protect foreigners living there. The British Army, however, was not necessary for that; it could be removed to the Canal, or even to Sinai, to protect the Canal itself. To protect foreigners in Egypt, Clayton proposed the creation of a specially trained 'corps of British constables under British officers'. However, since he envisioned that the corps 'would be under the control and direction of the Egyptian Government' and paid for by Egypt, the objection to a British Army of occupation would be eliminated and foreigners would be afforded all the protection they required.[83] It was a clever plan, and Allenby endorsed it, but the Foreign Office was critical – concluding the Egyptians would object to the cost – and the idea was not further pursued.[84]

While Clayton and his fellow Advisers were now exerting pressure for a unilateral British declaration of Egyptian independence, Zaghlul busied himself with efforts to undermine his rival Adli and his London negotiations. In early September Clayton learned of plans by a group of Four British Labour Party MPs to visit Egypt. The MPs had been invited by Zaghlul and, it appeared, 'the entire visit was being paid for from Zaghlul's party funds'.[85] Clayton immediately conferred with Scott – still acting for Allenby who was on leave – and they proposed that the Foreign Office refuse passports for the MPs to travel to Egypt.[86] Curzon would not withhold their passports, but the Foreign Office did inform them that they would be held responsible for any 'disturbances' that resulted during their visit.[87] Soon after their arrival it became apparent that the MPs were acting under Zaghlul's direction. They made no effort to confer with any Egyptians outside the Wafd and had 'no intention of arriving at [an] impartial judgment of [the] situation'.[88] One of the MPs was interviewed by an Egyptian inspector and candidly told him that 'he did not care a penny about Egyptians or their politics. All he wanted was to serve the interests of Labour at home and to save the taxpayer from paying money for a country in which he had no interest'. When the Inspector referred to Prime Minister Adli during the course of the discussion, the MP asked him 'who Adly was'.[89]

Clayton was well aware that the MPs were being used by Zaghlul and that their visit was motivated by Labour politics in England. But his primary concern was the effect their conduct might have in Egypt. When he learned that they and Zaghlul intended to travel to Tanta – a hotbed of anti-British sentiment – Clayton and General Walter Congreve, the British commander in Egypt, called the MPs to a meeting at Shepheard's Hotel in Cairo. Clayton advised them of the risk of disturbances occurring and politely asked them to call off their visit. When asked whether he was making a request or issuing an order that the visit be cancelled, he made clear that the trip would not be allowed.[90] Curzon was sufficiently concerned with the activities of the MPs that he gave Scott the authority to arrest and deport them if such measures were necessary to maintain order.[91] But the MPs backed down and, having achieved nothing, left Egypt on October 7. The Reuter's correspondent in Cairo later concluded that Clayton had 'handled a difficult situation skilfully and fairly'.[92]

Foiled in his attempts to undermine the Adli government and British rule through the Labour MPs, Zaghlul soon launched another scheme. In October 1921, he began a tour of Upper Egypt by steamer, a tour, he said, that was calculated 'to break the present government'.[93] However, all of Upper Egypt was not in the Zaghlul camp; many in the south were adherents of the Adli government. Incidents occurred at two places along the Nile and several were wounded in skirmishes between Zaghlul's followers and those of Adli. Alarmed by the Wafd leader's progress, the Mudirs of three provinces, Qena, Minia and Fayum, telegraphed the Interior Ministry asking that Zaghlul's tour be stopped.[94] Clayton met with Scott on October 19, and suggested that the tour be halted under martial law. Scott agreed and on the next day, Zaghlul was ordered to cancel the remainder of his journey.[95]

The failure of the Adli negotiations and the events in Egypt during the autumn of 1921, now convinced Clayton and his fellow Advisers that dramatic steps had to be taken to end the impasse and prevent further violence. On November 17, Clayton, Hayter and two other Advisers, Sir Reginald Patterson, Adviser to the Ministry of Education, and Ernest Dowson, acting Adviser to Finance – and a former classmate of Clayton at the Isle of Wight College – joined in a memorandum that effectively threw down the gauntlet:

[A] decision which does not admit [the] principle of Egyptian independence and which maintains the protectorate must entail serious risk of revolution throughout the country and, in any case, result in complete administrative chaos, rendering Government impossible. It must be realized that the whole structure of Government is Egyptian and that British officials are, almost exclusively, either in advisory, inspecting or technical capacities. It is therefore impossible to exercise any British control without full Egyptian cooperation in all branches of administration . . . Unless His Majesty's Government are prepared to give substantial satisfaction to [the] expectations which Egyptians have legitimately formed . . . it will be impossible to form any Ministry. This will sooner or later lead to strikes or organized obstruction among Government officials and in such an event [the] police and probably the army would side with the majority.

The Advisers were so convinced of this that they followed with a not too thinly veiled threat:

> The Advisers have been carrying on over two years in the belief that a policy of liberal concessions would be adopted and have undoubtedly given this impression to various Ministers and others with whom they have been in contact. They feel bound therefore to point out that if a contrary policy is adopted they cannot expect to retain the confidence of Egyptian Ministers or be able to render useful service in the future.[96]

Allenby had returned to Egypt on November 11, and there can be no doubt that he concurred in the statement of the Advisers and it soon became apparent that they were acting in concert. On December 6, after stating that he had the full support of the Advisers, Allenby proposed a unilateral abolition of the Protectorate by the British Government. He repeated the proposal on December 11, emphasizing that the idea of resolving the Egyptian problem by a negotiated treaty should be 'definitely' abandoned.[97] On December 5, Adli returned from England and resigned as Prime Minister six days later. Egypt was once again without a government. But London could not be moved and Curzon, though sympathetic to Allenby's proposal, pointed out that the Prime Minister had stated in the House of Commons in October that the status of Egypt would not be modified until Parliament had been afforded an opportunity of discussing the question.[98]

While Allenby was sparring with the home government, Clayton was pondering what to do next. He had been living at Walford Selby's house in Cairo and was joined there by Enid, who returned to Egypt in late November – without the children. It was at Selby's house, on December 20, 1921, that Clayton met with Russell, the Cairo police commandant. Russell was alarmed; he had just learned that Zaghlul was planning a large meeting of nationalists for the 23rd. If the meeting was allowed to take place, Russell warned Clayton, he could not be responsible for maintaining order in the city. Clayton and Selby left immediately to inform Allenby. Once at the Residency, Clayton 'exposed the problem' and, echoing Russell, delivered 'his <u>strong</u> advice' that he could not maintain order if the meeting were allowed.[99] The High Commissioner did not hesitate: Clayton was directed to stop the meeting. Selby then asked what Allenby would do if Zaghlul defied the order. 'I will order him to the country', he replied. What would he do if the Wafd leader defied *that* order, Selby persisted. 'Well', Allenby answered, 'I am ready for deportation'. Selby pointed out that there was sure to be trouble in the event Zaghlul was again deported, and Upper Egypt, where there were no British troops, would be defenceless, as it had been in March 1919. At this point, 'the Bull' lost his patience: 'Stop your buts ifs and ands; I have given the order to stop the meeting and I do not care if the whole place goes up in smoke. He turned to Bertie Clayton: "Stop the meeting and hand Cairo over to Congreve".'[100] Acting on Allenby's instructions, Clayton delivered an order to Zaghlul, directing him to stop all political activity and retire to his home in the country. As expected, the Wafd leader defied the order and was promptly arrested and deported on December 23.[101]

With Zaghlul now removed, Allenby continued his efforts to form a new Egyptian government under another moderate, Abd al-Khaliq Thawrat Pasha. Assisted by Clayton, Amos and Selby, the High Commissioner succeeded by mid-January 1922, in assembling a new Ministry, a government that even included a member of the Wafd, elements of which were beginning to split from Zaghlul's imperious rule.[102] Allenby now thought the time was right for Britain to show 'a striking act of conciliation' by unilaterally abolishing the Protectorate and declaring the independence of Egypt. This proposal, he emphasized, has 'the solid and whole-hearted support of my advisers without the least divergence'.[103] At the same time, the High Commissioner submitted to the Foreign Office a letter he proposed to hand to the Sultan. 'Without waiting for conclusion of a treaty', it said, Britain would abolish the Protectorate and recognize Egypt 'as an independent sovereign State'. Only *after* such recognition would Egypt and Britain negotiate on four points which remained critical to Britain: Imperial communications, the defence of Egypt against foreign aggression, the protection of foreigners in the country and – a subject as yet little discussed – the Sudan.[104] The timing of Allenby's proposal seemed especially propitious because the next day Clayton and Selby met with two dissentient members of the Wafd and persuaded them that British policy could be reconciled with their aims. Two days later, the Cairo newspapers announced that a split had occurred in the Wafd, led by the two members Clayton and Selby had met on the 13th.[105]

Despite these promising signs, the Cabinet rejected Allenby's proposal on January 18, 1922, and suggested that he send Clayton and Amos to London to further discuss the matter. Allenby flatly refused; the Advisers, he wrote, 'completely agree with me and have nothing to add to the views they have already expressed'. More ominously, he added, 'this is my final considered opinion which I have formed after prolonged discussion with those best fitted to offer advice'.[106] In fact, Allenby had now lost all patience with London. On January 20, and again, on the 25th, he offered to resign if the Cabinet did not accept his proposal. The Advisers, including Clayton, having already threatened resignation by their memorandum of November 17, made clear they would do the same.[107] Curzon's support of the High Commissioner in the Cabinet was not enough; the Prime Minister, and more so Churchill, would not agree to abolish the Protectorate and grant Egyptian independence except in the context of a fully negotiated treaty. On January 28, the Cabinet requested that Allenby himself come to London. It was beginning to appear as if Allenby would go the way of McMahon and Wingate. But Allenby agreed and, on February 3, he, Clayton and Amos left for England for what promised to be nothing less than a showdown with His Majesty's Government.[108]

The dispute that had now matured between Cairo and London was largely a function of the scope of their respective concerns. Allenby, Clayton and the Advisers were on the spot, struggling daily with Egyptian dissent, truculence and, occasionally, violence. They had assembled, and then watched crumble, a succession of ineffectual Egyptian governments, each thwarted by failed negotiation and the intransigence of Zaghlul and his coadjutors. They had vainly tried to run an Egyptian administration frustrated by strikes, discord and non-cooperation. And, they had watched helplessly as two years of talks and negotiations seemed only to deepen the divide between Egypt and Britain. Lloyd George and his fellow Cabinet Ministers, though, had wider concerns. If Britain appeased the Egyptians, what effect would such a policy have throughout the Empire? Would Indian nationalism be encouraged? How would concessions to the Egyptians be regarded in the newly Mandated territories of Palestine – where Arab discontent had flared into riot in 1920 – or Iraq, itself the site of a violent uprising in 1920, that cost millions to suppress? And, most pressing, would capitulation to Egyptian demands upset the current, uneasy truce in Ireland or derail implementation of the Prime Minister's hard-won Irish treaty? Indeed, if Egyptian independence resonated in all, or any, of these places, the Lloyd George Government might itself fall in the face of angry Conservative opposition in the House of Commons.

All these imponderables were in play when Allenby, Clayton and Amos arrived in London on February 8. Two days later Allenby met with Curzon. The Foreign Secretary, now desperate to avoid the High Commissioner's resignation, summoned all his best arguments, but 'the Bull' was inflexible; if his terms were not agreed to, he would resign. Frustrated, Curzon fixed on the Advisers, concluding in a 'bitter diatribe', that they were the source of the Field Marshal's stubborn resolve.[109] Almost in tears, the Foreign Secretary saw that he could get nowhere with Allenby.[110] The next day, having sufficiently regained his composure, Curzon called Clayton to a meeting. He proposed 'some form of assurance' which might be agreeable to Allenby, while at the same time avoiding the unilateral declaration of Egyptian independence the High Commissioner demanded. But Clayton proved as unmovable as Allenby. 'I find it difficult . . . to suggest', he wrote to Curzon the next day, 'any formula which would serve your purpose and at the same time preserve intact the spirit of Lord Allenby's proposals, of which the essence is an unilateral declaration by His Majesty's Government, as opposed to a bargain'.[111]

At 11.00 a.m. on February 15, 1922, Allenby, accompanied by Clayton and Amos, met with Lloyd George and Curzon at 10 Downing Street. Allenby made his position clear at the outset – a unilateral declaration of Egyptian independence was essential. A treaty was impossible without such a preliminary concession and, he said, he had personally promised Tharwat that he would recommend to the British government that the Protectorate be lifted now. His views, he added, 'were perfectly well known in Egypt' and if the Cabinet did not concur in them, he would resign immediately. Lloyd George was equally inflexible: the 'Government did not intend to give up Egypt'. 'No British Government', he repeated, 'would be willing to give up British control of Egypt'.[112] Clayton said nothing during the meeting and it was a wise decision, for when Amos intervened in an effort to explain Allenby's simple, straightforward position, Lloyd George turned on him and demanded that he put the position in writing. It appeared that the Prime Minister was attempting to create a written record which he could use against Allenby to justify a Cabinet decision to accept his resignation – a subtle, but still clear attempt to intimidate the High Commissioner. Lloyd George then suggested that the group reconvene later that afternoon to consider Allenby's statement.

In fact, Lloyd George's position was not as strong as he suggested. With one exception, the ultra-conservative *Morning Post*, all the leading British newspapers opposed the Government's Egyptian policy. Those papers owned by the influential Lord Northcliffe – *The Times*, *Daily Mail* and *Evening News* – specifically supported Allenby's proposal to unilaterally grant Egyptian independence, a fact recognized by Curzon and repeated to the Cabinet.[113] Nor was the Cabinet entirely behind Lloyd George. Churchill, it was true, was determined 'to fight to the end', but the entire Cabinet was evenly divided.[114] When Allenby, his Advisers and Lloyd George met again, at 6.00 p.m. on the 15th, it appeared that cracks were showing in the foundations of the Prime Minister's position, so inflexibly laid down that same morning. Both sides were now comparing drafts of the declaration of independence Allenby had cabled to London on January 12. The Prime Minister still attempted modifications; twice Allenby rejected them; twice he reiterated his offer of resignation. Now, 'the Bull' was losing his patience: 'I have waited five weeks for a decision, and I can't wait any longer. I shall tell Lady Allenby to come home [from Egypt]. With this, Lloyd George rose and put his hand on Allenby's arm. 'You have waited five weeks, Lord Allenby', he said; 'wait five more minutes'.[115] Agreement was reached and the next day, the Cabinet concurred. After more than two years of unremitting effort, Allenby, and no less Clayton, had prevailed.

The final language of the British declaration was drafted by a committee comprised of Clayton, Amos, John Murray of the Foreign Office and Sir Edward Grigg, the Prime Minister's private secretary.[116] It was presented to the Sultan in a letter of February 28, 1922: 'The British protectorate over Egypt is terminated and Egypt is declared to be an independent sovereign State'.[117] The declaration was still subject to the four reserved questions – Imperial communications, the defence of Egypt, the protection of foreigners and the Sudan – and could not therefore be said to be a grant of complete independence. And, unquestionably, Britain still was, and would remain for decades, the preeminent foreign Power in Egypt. But as much had been gained as Clayton hoped or expected. The hated designation 'Protectorate' was gone; control of Egypt's domestic affairs was now in Egyptian hands; and Egypt could control her own foreign affairs, provided they did not run afoul of Britain's own international policies. Still, Clayton's essential idea, developed nearly two years earlier, had prevailed – Britain had relinquished the 'shadow' and yet retained the 'substance' of what was important in Egypt.

Clayton knew that the 1922 Declaration would not eliminate all Egyptian dissent, but he recognized that his own work in Egypt was finished. 'We had a strenuous but very interesting week', he wrote to Wingate on February 26, but 'finally H.M.G. decided to adopt a policy which I hope will at last put us firm ground, even if it does not lead to any rapid solution to the Egyptian question . . . I hope to come back shortly for my leave and it is probable that I shall retire from Egyptian service altogether. I have had enough of it and would much prefer to seek my chances elsewhere'.[118] Even before the London meetings of February, Clayton had begun to put his personal plan into operation. On January 1, he had prepared a memorandum noting that the post of Adviser to the Interior had 'not proved entirely satisfactory' and should be abolished, a proposal he had advanced more than two years earlier to the Milner Mission. He now suggested that only a British under-secretary be maintained in the Ministry, a man who would 'be entirely and solely concerned with public security'. These proposals, he wrote, could be carried out immediately, 'without any loss of control or efficiency'.[119] On April 13, 1922, he re-submitted his memorandum to the Residency and, a month later, tendered his resignation from Egyptian service to Tharwat.[120]

On the evening of May 12, 1922, a banquet was held in Clayton's honour at the Continental Hotel in Cairo:

> [O]ver 250 were present, including the Prime Minister and all the members of the Cabinet, the ex-Premiers, Adli Pasha Yeghen and Mohammed Pasha Tewfik Nessim . . . all the Provincial Governors and Notables from every province of Egypt. Representing the Committee of Notables, Mohammed Pasha Sherei spoke in expression of gratitude for all that Sir Gilbert Clayton had done for Egypt. The Prime Minister spoke of the exceptional personal appreciation in which all classes of native Egyptians held the retiring Adviser, whose action had been a fine example of self-denial, for, in helping to lay the foundations of the new regime, he did so, well knowing that it must lead to his own retirement . . . Mohammed Pasha Tewfik Nessim (representing the King [as the Sultan became after the Declaration of independence]), the Prime Minister and ex-Ministers, and a large number of Egyptian and European officials and notables, were at Cairo station to bid farewell to the retiring Adviser when he left for Port Said and England on Saturday morning May 15th. Mohammed Pasha Sherei and a deputation of Egyptian notables accompanied Sir Gilbert as far as Port Said.[121]

That Clayton left behind a grateful nation cannot be doubted. Yet, gratifying though his Egyptian send-off must have been for Clayton, he had risked a great deal by taking such a firm and provocative stance against the British Government's position. His opposition was particularly well known to those two Ministers who controlled any future he still had in government service, Foreign Secretary Curzon and Colonial Secretary Churchill. Now that Clayton was out of a job, his future was, to say the least, uncertain.

24

Palestine Revisited: Chief Secretary in the Mandate, 1923–1925

In August 1924, Abdullah ibn Hussein, Amir of Transjordan, made one of his frequent visits to Jerusalem, a short forty-five miles from his capital at Amman. On this occasion, the Amir was appearing as the house guest of the Officer Administering the Government of Palestine, General Sir Gilbert Clayton. Sir Gilbert's official position was Chief Secretary of the Palestine Mandate, the number two man in the Mandatory government. But, while the High Commissioner, Sir Herbert Samuel, was away from the country during his long summer leaves, Clayton assumed the top position. As Abdullah walked down a corridor in Clayton's house, two young boys, Sam, then six, and his brother John, three years younger, darted into the hallway at the opposite end. The Clayton boys pulled up short and their eyes grew wide when they saw the Amir, a vision in traditional Arab dress, with a menacing curved dagger displayed prominently on his waist. Renowned equally for his affability and his generosity, Abdullah was delighted with the impression he had made on the boys and, the next day, a box arrived at the Clayton household containing a present for them – two, beautiful, hand-crafted daggers.[1]

Abdullah and Clayton were no strangers; they had known each other since the war years. But neither would have predicted then that they would meet years later in Palestine. Abdullah's path to Amman had indeed been a tortuous one. Unlike his brother Faisal, the Amir was held in low regard by the British at war's end. He had done very little in the way of fighting Turks and, although thought to be the cleverest of Hussein's sons, was regarded as a 'sensualist, idle and very lazy'.[2] Still, in late 1918, largely on the recommendation of Lawrence, the Cabinet's Eastern Committee considered Abdullah as the future ruler of Mesopotamia and a group of Mesopotamians, assembled at Damascus in March 1920, had even proclaimed him king of the country. But none of the Allied Powers recognized the Damascus proclamation and, when Faisal was turned out of Syria by the French in July 1920, attention immediately shifted to Abdullah's younger brother for rule in Baghdad. Abdullah was bitterly disappointed, fell out with Faisal over what he regarded as his brother's rank opportunism in pursuing the Iraqi throne, and was not reconciled with him until 1923. While the British thought little of Abdullah, his position in the Hijaz was no more promising. In May 1919, the Amir had suffered a crushing defeat at the hands of Ibn Saud's Wahhabis at Turaba near the eastern border of the Hijaz. Furious, Hussein stripped his son of the position of Hijaz Foreign Minister and effectively exiled him to Ta'if.[3] Then, in the autumn of 1920, Hussein sent Abdullah north, to Ma'an, in the undefined border region between the Hijaz and Transjordan. The King's stated intention was that Abdullah would raise an army there for the purpose of moving north, where they would engage the French and drive them from Syria. Nobody – including probably Abdullah – really believed such a fantastic plan possible. 'I know Abdullah', Lawrence wrote at the time, 'you won't have a shot fired'.[4]

Whatever Abdullah's real intention, he soon moved north to Amman. Meanwhile, the experts in London were considering what should be done about Transjordan. Nominally at least, while Faisal ruled in Damascus, the territory was under his authority as part of OETA East. But when Faisal was ousted during the previous July there was some concern that the French would now move into the area. A handful of British officers was dispatched to the region to forestall that possibility and to maintain order as best they could but, due to the pressing need to cut expenditure in the Middle East, no one favoured a formal British presence in Transjordan. Ideally, the area would be placed under an Arab ruler amenable to the British, but at no cost to the British taxpayer. Arab rule was thought appropriate because, with the exception of the Zionists, few thought Transjordan should be subject to the Jewish national home policy embodied in the Balfour Declaration and, later, in the Palestine Mandate. As described earlier, Clayton argued that the territory should be formed into an Arab State and that such a proposal was consistent with Sykes–Picot and the McMahon pledge of 1915. Under the strained Foreign Office interpretation of that pledge, Palestine could be excluded from the area of Arab independence because it lay to the west of the 'districts of Damascus, Homs, Hama and Aleppo'. But, even under this interpretation, if a line were drawn through those four cities and extended southwards, Transjordan lay to the *east* of those 'districts' and should logically be included in the Arab independent area. That was Clayton's view and so the question arose as to who should assume responsibility for the territory. Various proposals were advanced during the autumn of 1920, but Abdullah's arrival at Amman during the next spring presented the experts with something of a *fait accompli*. He was there. The notion of a 'Sherifian solution' thus developed in Whitehall in early 1921. This idea, primarily advanced by the new Colonial Secretary Winston Churchill, and his principal adviser, T. E. Lawrence, had at least a superficial appeal: With the Sherif – King Hussein – in the Hijaz, one son, Abdullah, in Transjordan, and another, Faisal, in Iraq, Britain would be able to exert widespread influence in the Middle East through their wartime protégés.[5]

As time passed, serious flaws would be exposed in Britain's 'Sherifian solution' for the Middle East. But when Churchill, Lawrence and a host of British experts assembled at Cairo in March 1921 to develop a comprehensive policy for the Mandated territories, they quickly endorsed the plan to sponsor Abdullah as Amir of Transjordan. Churchill travelled to Jerusalem in late March to present the proposal to the Amir. He was less than enthusiastic. However, after four meetings with the Colonial Secretary, Abdullah reluctantly agreed to remain in Transjordan for six months, during which time he would keep order in the territory and maintain stability along the Syrian and Palestinian borders. In support, Britain would provide a small grant-in-aid (£180,000), much of which would be used to subsidize a small contingent of native troops. As added inducement, Churchill may also have suggested – rather dishonestly, since he knew it to be untrue – that if the Amir did his part, there was a possibility that he could regain Syria for the Hashemites.[6]

If Abdullah had followed a winding and uncertain road to Amman, Clayton's path to Jerusalem was hardly more direct. When he relinquished his position as Adviser to the Egyptian Interior Ministry and arrived in London in May 1922, his prospects were dim. Four months earlier, Allenby, acting on a rumour of the incumbent's departure, proposed Clayton as adviser on Egyptian affairs at the Foreign Office. The Field Marshal would have liked nothing better than that the author of his Egyptian policy should advise the authorities in London. But the current occupant stayed on.[7] Then, in March, Clayton learned that the Colonial Office were 'most anxious' for him to take up a position in Iraq as 'Counsellor and second in command' to the High Commissioner, Sir Percy Cox. However, Clayton turned down the offer, just as he had declined the same post in 1917.[8] When he left Egypt in May 1922, then, Clayton had no job and no prospects.

Ten days after his arrival in London Clayton met with Herbert Samuel, the High Commissioner of Palestine, who promptly offered him the post of Chief Secretary in the Mandate. Clayton declined. He was, he said, concerned about the 'vagueness' of the government's Palestine policy. It was a legitimate concern, for no definitive policy statement had issued from the Lloyd George government since the Balfour Declaration was published in November 1917. No less important, Clayton was 'apprehensive of possible personal embarrassment in view of [his] intimate political connection with Palestine and with the Arabs during the war and during the earlier phases of the Military Administration'.[9] These were good reasons, so it must have come as a surprise to Samuel and to the Colonial Office when, only a month later, Clayton reversed course and accepted Samuel's offer on July 4. Churchill was 'delighted' that Clayton had changed his mind and Hubert Young of the Office's Middle Eastern Department, agreed. 'Nothing could be better for the prospect of success in Palestine', he wrote. Clayton 'is universally beloved by the Arabs and his appointment will do more than anything to reassure them'. Samuel was particularly pleased, not just because he regarded Clayton 'as much the best man in view',[10] but perhaps more so because he knew that the Palestinians were convinced that they could not possibly receive fair treatment when the two top men in the Mandate government were ardent Zionists. Indeed, Churchill had so described Samuel in a House of Commons speech of June 14, 1921, as the Arabs were well aware.[11] As for the current Chief Secretary, Wyndham Deedes – the man Clayton was to succeed – he had made his views clear two years earlier in a letter to Weizmann: 'from now on the whole of such abilities and strength as God has given me will be devoted unreservedly to the realisation of your ideal'.[12] There seems little doubt, then, that Samuel offered Clayton the post of Chief Secretary, in some measure, to disarm Arab opposition to the Zionist policy.[13]

Why had Clayton accepted the position, having rejected the offer for cogent reasons only a month earlier? He told Samuel he changed his mind because a definite government policy concerning Palestine had been enunciated and the situation had now been 'made clear'. Clayton was referring to the June 1922 White Paper, written in part by Samuel, and just published on July 3. On the one hand, the White Paper 'made clear' that the government were re-affirming the Balfour Declaration. The Jewish people, it was stated, were in Palestine 'as of right and not on sufferance'. But the Paper also rejected the notion that Britain intended to promote a Jewish State in Palestine; it rejected the statement attributed to Weizmann, and described earlier, that 'Palestine would become as Jewish as England is English'. Nor was the 'disappearance or subordination of the Arab population, language or culture' contemplated. And, to the dismay of the Zionists, the White Paper underscored that the special position accorded to the Zionist Commission in Palestine – now called the Palestine Zionist Executive – did not entitle it to share 'in any degree' in the government of the country. In order to address Arab fears concerning the influx of Jews into Palestine, it was stated also that immigration would not be allowed to exceed the 'economic capacity of the country at the time to absorb new arrivals'. Finally, the White Paper set forth the government's plan for a Legislative Council, a critical step, it was said, in the 'development of self-governing institutions' in Palestine.[14] But for the Arabs, the promise of a Legislative Council was an empty one, for it was structured in such a way that, despite the clear Arab numerical superiority in Palestine, the Arabs on the Council could never vote to stop Jewish immigration or to reverse the national home policy.

The June 1922 White Paper may have clarified Britain's Palestine policy to an extent sufficient to remove Clayton's reservations regarding Samuel's offer, but it also appears that his acceptance was motivated by financial concerns. His small savings had been consumed during his service in Egypt and by his move back to England. And, as he explained to Deedes, 'I have no private means beyond my pension from Egypt and a very small one from the War Office'.[15] The amounts *were* relatively small – £1200 per year from Egypt and a mere £150 from the War Office. Upon leaving his position at the Interior Ministry, his gross income was, he said, reduced to 'considerably less than half'.[16] Clayton struggled to augment his finances. From September 1922, he engaged in a long correspondence, spanning more than two years, with the Egyptian authorities in pursuit of additional compensation to account for the premature termination of his position at the Interior Ministry. But, despite approaches to Allenby, the Financial Adviser and even to his old chief, former Prime Minster Taufiq Nasim Pasha, no further compensation was provided. Taufiq was 'sympathetic', though, about the pension rights of Clayton's heirs and eventually the Egyptian government responded generously, ensuring that after Clayton's death, his family received funds sufficient to pay for the university education of Patience, Sam and John.[17]

By accepting the Palestine offer Clayton could meet his immediate financial needs; with salary and allowances, his compensation amounted to £E2000 per annum. But, in those days, high-ranking Colonial officials were expected to meet additional expenses from their own resources. When Clayton learned that he would require a further £1100 to ship his effects to Palestine, furnish a home there and purchase a car, the Colonial Office were not inclined to meet his request for an additional allowance. Less than half that amount was offered and even then only if he committed to three years service in Palestine. The balance would be advanced, subject to repayment through monthly deductions from his salary. Clayton accepted with reluctance. He had served twenty-seven years abroad, he explained to Deedes, and did not wish to commit to foreign service 'for the remainder of my working life'. Nor did he wish to tie himself to service in Palestine 'or anywhere else under the CO'. On the strength of the Colonial Office's offer, Clayton gave up his house in the spring of 1923, only to learn a few days later that the Treasury had revised the terms of his allowance, and now required him to repay the entire sum advanced through periodic deductions from his salary. Justifiably upset, he asked the Colonial Secretary to appeal to the Treasury. Although he agreed to proceed to Jerusalem, he informed the Colonial Office that he would leave his family in England 'and refrain from establishing myself permanently' there until his case was reconsidered.[18] It was a bad way to start a new job.

Despite his financial concerns, Clayton enjoyed a welcome respite from the troubles of the Middle East during the remainder of 1922. He leased a house, Winkfield Cottage, at Hayward's Heath some forty miles south of London where he, Enid and the children enjoyed a leisurely summer visiting with family and friends. Clayton's younger brother Jack was now stationed with the Royal Navy at Portsmouth and the two met often. A few months earlier Jack had married Florence Schuster, a daughter of the renowned physicist, Sir Arthur Schuster, and Bertie had been able to act as best man at the ceremony, which occurred a week after the showdown with the Lloyd George Cabinet over the Egyptian question.[19] Clayton also found time to attend meetings of the British (later, Royal) Institute of International Affairs and the Central Asian Society. And, in August, at the request of Lawrence, he agreed to sit for a portrait by the well-known painter William Nicholson to be used in a book Lawrence had written 'about that dog-fight of ours in Arabia' called *Seven Pillars of Wisdom*. Clayton sat twice for Nicholson who produced a wood-cut, the print from which appears in illustrated editions of the book. Nicholson's wood-cut resulted in one of the best portraits in *Seven Pillars*. While not producing a literal likeness, he succeeded in capturing something of his subject's personality, depicting a quiet, self-possessed figure whose eyes suggest a wisdom transcending Clayton's forty-seven years.[20] Lawrence was pleased with the result and equally glad that Clayton had agreed to go to Palestine. 'If any person of any race or creed anywhere in that country trusted one single person in government for two minutes', he wrote Clayton, 'things there would be more stable. You'll do more than that!'[21]

Clayton was not scheduled to take up his post as Chief Secretary until April 1923, and, whether through boredom or a desire to supplement his small pension income, he wrote to the Colonial Office asking if there was any temporary work he could take on before leaving for Palestine. Young saw an immediate opportunity. Abdullah was scheduled to visit London in October for talks concerning Transjordan and his own position in the Mandate and Young thought that Clayton, 'a personal friend of Abdullah', should conduct the negotiations. Churchill agreed and, on October 16, Clayton met with Abdullah and his chief minister, Ali Rida al-Rikabi.[22]

By all accounts, Abdullah's eighteen month rule in Transjordan had not been a success. He took no interest in the country and, as he informed the British representative at Amman, he could not be bothered with the details of administration. As a result, the country had been poorly run, taxes were not collected and disorder prevailed in the northern and southern regions. To the extent it was administered at all, Transjordan was run by the Amir's *majlis* – his council – comprised largely of Syrian expatriates who were members of *hizb al-istiqlal*, the independence party. Their programme called for the unification of 'Greater Syria', by which they meant the Lebanon, Syria, Palestine and Transjordan. More interested in promoting their political agenda than in running the country, the Syrians were widely regarded as troublemakers and were disliked by the local population. Abduallah was not particularly fond of them either. But he could not avoid using them, for there were very few native Transjordanians who had government experience and the Syrians, for all their noisy militancy, were for the most part, experienced and capable.

In June 1921, the French High Commissioner in Syria, General Henri Gouraud, was ambushed while touring in the south of the country near the Transjordan border. The French claimed the attack had been inspired by Abdullah and the Syrian malcontents in his council. No proof could be obtained linking Abdullah to the incident, but he did offer safe harbour to a few men who were most likely involved. The Gouraud attack was the last straw for Samuel and Deedes; in July 1921 they recommended that Abdullah's rule should not be extended beyond the six month provisional period agreed to by Churchill and Abdullah in March. And most in the Colonial Office's Middle East Department agreed. One who did not, though, was Churchill's Arab adviser, T.E. Lawrence. Dispatched to Amman in October to investigate, Lawrence soon produced a surprising report that assigned blame for the poor state of affairs in Transjordan as much to British indifference as to Arab incompetence. Churchill, who followed Lawrence's advice on nearly all Middle Eastern issues, concurred. The Amir would stay on at Amman.[23]

Abdullah was not particularly enthused about remaining in Transjordan, but he had no other prospects. He had no realistic hope for Syria, particularly after the Gouraud attack; his brother Faisal was now King of Iraq; and, he acknowledged that he 'would look ridiculous' if he returned to the Hijaz.[24] Still, Abdullah had no reason to be happy about his future east of the Jordan. His own position there had not been officially recognized in any way by the British and, indeed, the position of Transjordan itself was uncertain. In September 1922, the League of Nations finally confirmed that the country would not be subject to the Jewish national home policy, but Transjordan was still undeniably part of the Palestine Mandate.[25] Yet, as early as July 1920, the Foreign Office had agreed that the administrative authority of the

Palestine government should not be extended east of the Jordan.[26] So, the conclusion that Transjordan would not be subject to the Zionist policy or administered by Palestine, yet still be included in the Mandate for that country presented a situation that certainly called for clarification.

When he met with Clayton on October 16, Abdullah made his intentions clear immediately. He desired 'complete independence' – *istiqlal tamm*, a phrase all too familiar to Clayton from his Egyptian days – and a treaty relationship with Britain. Of course, in a literal sense, complete independence was impossible. As Abdullah well knew, Britain would not detach Transjordan from the Mandate and he had earlier acknowledged the fact.[27] In addition, a treaty between Transjordan and Britain implied Transjordanian sovereignty, a concept inconsistent with the country's position as part of the Mandate. Clayton adroitly side-stepped the conceptual difficulty; the High Commissioner would sign any treaty, not as head of the Palestine government, but in his 'imperial capacity' as representative of the Mandatory Power.[28] The problem of Abdullah's position was clarified more easily, for the Colonial Office had decided before the talks began that 'the provisional policy of the Cairo Conference has justified itself and everything tends to the direction of establishing Abdullah firmly on his throne'.[29]

On the day of Clayton's first meeting with Abdullah, Churchill fell ill with appendicitis and, three days later, Lloyd George's coalition government fell. In the succeeding Conservative government established under Andrew Bonar Law, the Ninth Duke of Devonshire replaced Churchill as Colonial Secretary. Described as a 'sleepy but pleasant' man 'with little energy or drive', the Duke knew little about the Middle East and took no particular interest in the region.[30] Admittedly out of his depth when confronted with the complexities of the Middle East, Devonshire was content to follow the advice of his subordinates in the Middle East Department. Young was happy to take the lead. Acting promptly upon receiving Clayton's report of his first meeting with Abdullah, he drafted an 'Assurance' which, when published, would confirm British recognition of Abdullah's rule in Transjordan. Subject to approval by the League, it stated that Britain would recognise an 'independent government in Trans Jordan' under Abdullah, provided the government was constitutional and Britain could fulfil its international obligations in the country by means of an agreement to be concluded between the two governments.[31] On October 26, only two days after taking up his office, Devonshire agreed that the Assurance could be given orally to Abdullah and Clayton did so two days later. But the statement was not published and no treaty had been negotiated by the time Abdullah left London on November 14. Publication had been delayed by the Foreign Office's concern over possible negative French reaction. Not until the following May was publication approved and the Assurance proclaimed in Amman, where it was accompanied by a celebration of Transjordanian independence, the Amir conveniently ignoring the unfulfilled conditions set forth in the document.

After Abdullah's departure, Clayton continued treaty negotiations with al-Rikabi. But the chief minister had been given definite instructions by the Amir and the differences that emerged soon proved insuperable. Abdullah, it appears, had been influenced by the Anglo-Iraqi treaty, just concluded on October 10. That treaty had provided for eventual Iraqi representation in foreign capitals and for British sponsorship of Iraq's entry into the League of Nations. If his brother could be accorded such rights, Abdullah reasoned, so too should he. Abduallh, and then al-Rikabi, also sought to limit the influence of the Palestine government in Transjordan. They objected to the jurisdiction of the Palestine courts over foreigners in the country and both insisted on a clause reflecting the Amir's ability to ignore any British advice inconsistent with Transjordanian independence. Neither the Colonial Office nor the Foreign Office – which was also reviewing treaty drafts – were prepared to make such concessions. The Foreign Office especially thought the requests grossly 'out of proportion to the size and importance of Transjordan and its present position of financial dependence'.[32] Although Clayton and Rikabi negotiated four drafts of the treaty, by December it was apparent that their differences were so substantial there was no point in prolonging the talks. Al-Rikabi left London on December 19, and, like Abdullah, he departed empty-handed.[33]

Although Clayton's autumn 1922 negotiations were unsuccessful, they did serve to confirm Abdullah's position in Transjordan and to isolate the points about which the Amir was most concerned. For Clayton, the talks provided valuable negotiation experience and also brought him current with the state of affairs in the country. And they confirmed the opinion in London and in Jerusalem that Clayton was the man best-suited to handle Transjordanian issues once he arrived in Palestine. Samuel later acknowledged that he had 'specially charged' Clayton to 'look after Trans Jordan affairs' during his tenure as Chief Secretary.[34]

Clayton arrived in Jerusalem on April 6, 1923. The duties he was undertaking were not defined in any Colonial Office document, but Samuel had outlined his view of the position three years earlier in a letter to Clayton's predecessor, Deedes. The Chief Secretary would exercise 'the general control of political and other business' of the Mandate which fell outside the spheres of the Financial and Legal Secretaries. He was to be the 'second Officer of the Administration' and to act as its head when the High Commissioner was absent.[35] Clayton would soon take advantage of this definition of duties, for three months after his arrival, Samuel departed on his summer leave and Clayton assumed responsibility for the Mandate as the Officer Administering the Government (OAG) of Palestine.

The central problem in Palestine – the problem that informed all others – was Arab–Jewish relations. The Arabs remained adamantly opposed to the Zionist programme and, since Clayton left Palestine in 1919, Arab–Jewish discord had occasionally bubbled to the surface in a violent form. Rioting had occurred in Jerusalem in April 1920, and again in November 1921. But the most serious violence appeared at Jaffa in May 1921, when forty-seven Jews and forty-eight Arabs were killed and more than 200 wounded. Samuel was shaken by the Jaffa riots, but they did not cause him to abandon his goal of trying to reconcile the Arabs to the Zionist policy by bringing them into an active role in the Mandate government. That was, in fact, the idea behind the Legislative Council proposal outlined in the June 1922 White

Paper. But the Arabs effectively boycotted the elections held preliminary to formation of the Council; in all Palestine only 1,397 votes were cast, of which 1,172 were Jewish.[36] There was no choice but to abandon the scheme.

Next, Samuel tried to constitute an Advisory Council from the broken shards of the Legislative Council plan, reviving a similar council he had created in the autumn of 1920. But, as its name suggested, the Council possessed no real power; it could only advise and suggest. Samuel proposed his Advisory Council scheme at the end of May 1923, nominating eight Muslims, two Christian Arabs and two Jews for seats on the Council. But the High Commissioner left Palestine on June 20 for his annual leave and it fell to Clayton to persuade the Arab nominees to take up their seats in the new body. He met with the Arab nominees on July 11, when they put him off with a request that they postpone their acceptance until the end of the month. Although the Arabs appeared amenable, it was clear to Clayton that they did not wish 'to court the accusation of injuring the Arab cause' when it was widely thought that the British Cabinet was again discussing the future policy to be pursued in Palestine.[37]

The Arabs were correct; the Conservative government was then taking a fresh look at the Palestine problem. It was no secret that the Tories were very uncomfortable with the Zionist policy. In June 1922, the Conservative-dominated House of Lords passed a motion by the decisive margin of 60–29, declaring the Palestine Mandate to be 'inacceptable'. But that decision was effectively reversed by the House of Commons, which resoundingly reaffirmed the Balfour Declaration policy a fortnight later by a vote of 292–35. Still, since the 1922 Parliamentary votes, Conservative unhappiness with the Zionist programme had not abated. The Colonial Office acknowledged that the McMahon pledge of 1915 had to be 'somewhat strained' in order to exclude Palestine from the area of pledged Arab independence, a view with which Curzon, Devonshire and Shuckburgh, head of the Middle East Department, all concurred.[38]

Prompted by Devonshire, the new Tory government first reassessed Britain's Palestine policy in February 1923, only to conclude, with some reluctance, that there could be no retreat from British sponsorship of the Zionist programme. It had been accepted at the San Remo conference in April 1920, when the Mandates were assigned; it was embodied in the Turkish Treaty of Sèvres in August 1920; it was reflected in the Mandate for Palestine approved by the League of Nations in July 1922; it was confirmed by Churchill in the House of Commons in June 1921; and, it was reaffirmed in the June 1922 White Paper. When it came to the Jewish national home policy, the Lloyd George government had effectively painted all future British governments into a corner. The Colonial Office found some small solace for the maintenance of a British presence in Palestine not in the merits of Zionism, but in the imperatives of Empire. Shuckburgh advised the Cabinet of Clayton's view that 'the retention of British control in Palestine is essential from the standpoint of Imperial strategy'. Before the war, Clayton observed, the Suez Canal could be defended by maintaining British naval strength in the Eastern Mediterranean and by controlling Egypt. But now, the development of aviation and political devolution in Egypt 'has shifted the key to our Eastern communications by sea and air from Egypt to Palestine'.[39]

On June 27, 1923, the Cabinet again decided to reconsider Britain's Palestine policy, a decision prompted in part by the resignation of Bonar Law, due to ill health, and the succession of Stanley Baldwin as Prime Minister on May 22. The Cabinet appointed a Palestine Committee, comprised entirely of Cabinet Ministers, to once more assess the situation. On the same day, June 27, yet another debate on Palestine occurred in the House of Lords during which the government's policy was again assailed. It was this debate in the Lords that prompted Clayton to send a major despatch to Devonshire challenging the assumptions underlying the government's policy. He may also have been aware of the recent appointment of the Cabinet's Palestine Committee and sought to influence its deliberations. Clayton's despatch was made possible by the departure from Palestine of his chief, Samuel. The Mandate government could communicate officially with the home government only through the High Commissioner, but, as noted, when Samuel was absent from the country, Clayton assumed his responsibilities as the OAG and there was no rule or principle laid down that precluded him from advancing his own views, even if they involved major policy proposals. Just as he had in Egypt a few years earlier, Clayton would take an independent and controversial line.

Clayton viewed the situation in Palestine with 'considerable misgiving' and regarded the views expressed by the few defenders of the Zionist policy in the House of Lords debate as 'too optimistic and based to some extent on false premises'. Contrary to the views expressed 'in some quarters' – and here he was challenging also the views of Samuel – the political situation in Palestine was not 'steadily improving', but was instead approaching a crisis. The notion that opposition to the Zionist policy was 'merely the work of a few agitators' was incorrect, he argued; to the contrary, the opponents of Zionism had 'the sympathy of an overwhelming majority of the Arab population – and that, to a steadily increasing extent'. And, he believed that the Mandate government had lost prestige and the sympathy of the people as a result of its policies. Pointing also to deteriorating economic conditions in Palestine, Clayton anticipated further trouble. Yet, he argued that, unlike the situation he had encountered in Egypt, Arab opposition was not driven by extremists and there was 'little or no trace . . . of anti-British feeling'. Nor, he said

> does there appear to be any deep-rooted objection to the Zionist policy, or even to the Balfour Declaration as defined in the White Paper. The contention of the Arabs is that they are always put off with declarations and formulas but that in actual practice these formulas are not adopted and that the administrative policy of the country is heavily weighted by Zionist influence. They also maintain that the Zionist provisions of the actual text of the Mandate are not consistent with the statement of policy enunciated in the White Paper, and [they] object to certain Articles which imply preferential treatment to the Jews.

Although some historians would later interpret Clayton's despatch as a plea for discarding the Zionist policy, he made clear that he had no such idea in mind:

> There is, I consider, no ground whatever for advocating the abandonment of the Zionist policy or relinquishing the Mandate. The question is how that policy is to be brought to a successful conclusion in the best interests not only of Jew and Arab, but of the British Empire. Is the present state of affairs to be allowed to continue with risk of producing a situation which can only be dealt with by force, entailing serious economic loss to Palestine and probably heavy expense to the British taxpayer? Or can a way be found, by modifying objectionable Articles in the Mandate or, at least, by removing all possible grounds for any charges of partiality or bad faith, to dissipate the present fear and distrust of the Arabs, and thus enable Zionism to develop by its own inherent merits, unhampered by political difficulties and without prejudice to the interests of the population of Palestine?[40]

To Richard Meinertzhagen, a zealous advocate of Zionism who was then employed at the Colonial Office, it appeared that Clayton had gone behind Samuel's back to propose an anti-Zionist policy. 'Clayton never was a friend of the Zionists', he confided to his diary. 'In 1919 when he was Chief Political Officer he openly advocated in a despatch the abandonment of the Zionist policy. Why he was chosen for his present post is a mystery to me. Never was a man less suited to carry out a policy which he detests and will do his best to ruin'. Meinertzhagen thought Clayton was 'trying to force his own private opinion down the Government's throat' and was 'failing to carry out the policy with which he has been entrusted. He is also acting contrary to the best interests of his own country'.[41] Unlike Clayton, Meinertzhagen believed that 'opposition to Zionism [was] largely artificial and that it is by artificial intrigue and to satisfy personal aims that the Arab bogey has been kept alive'.[42] In fact, Clayton had been forthright with Samuel, giving his opinions to the High Commissioner in a private letter before he sent his July 6 despatch. And, as shown by the language of his despatch, Clayton did not advocate abandonment of the Zionist policy. Nor is there any reason to doubt his belief, repeated in a letter to Shuckburgh of July 13, that 'it is not the White Paper policy, or even the Balfour Declaration to which the Arabs object. It is the practical application of the policy which they consider to be not entirely impartial, and their main objection is to the position and influence given under the Mandate to the Zionist Organization'.[43]

Meinertzhagen was alone in his view that Clayton's despatch was anti-Zionist and disloyal. Certainly, Samuel did not agree with all of Clayton's opinions but, as he informed him, 'I by no means take exception to your cautionary despatch . . . It was clearly your duty to inform HMG of the views you had formed'. Still, Samuel did not agree with Clayton's view that a 'crisis is really at hand'.[44] And he prepared a memorandum for the Cabinet in which he challenged some of his Chief Secretary's opinions. With Clayton's basic point that objection to the Zionist policy 'has the support of the great majority of the Arab population', Samuel had no quarrel. And he agreed that the Arabs believed 'that the administrative policy of the country is heavily weighted by Zionist influence'. But the High Commissioner challenged that belief because, he argued, the Arabs could not point to a single 'concrete instance' evidencing Zionist influence in his administration. Nor did he think that Arab opposition was increasing or that the Mandate government had 'lost prestige' or even the 'sympathy of the people'. To the contrary, Arab opposition, he observed, had decreased during the last two years and public security in Palestine was much better than it had been for some time. In short, Samuel thought his Chief Secretary unduly pessimistic.[45]

Taking a short-term view of their competing positions, Samuel had the better argument. There had been no sectarian strife in Palestine since November 1921, and public security was better than it had been two years earlier. But, in the long term, Clayton's prognostications would prove more accurate and they were regarded as more convincing by the Cabinet. Devonshire had directed that the competing papers of Samuel and Clayton be submitted to the Cabinet and when the Palestine Committee submitted its report on July 27, there was no doubt the Committee found Clayton's views more persuasive. Samuel's forecasts for the future of Palestine, they concluded, 'may turn out to be unduly sanguine; already they have to some extent been checked by the less rosy forecast of Sir G. Clayton'. Echoing Clayton's view, the Committee concluded that

> it is not so much the existence of the Mandate, or the Balfour Declaration, or the recognition of the Jewish National Home (in its later and narrower inter-pretation) to which [the Arabs] object, as it is the preferential position which has been accorded to the Zionists in the country, and the universal Arab belief that the scales are weighted against the Arabs in the Administration.[46]

And, unlike Samuel, the Cabinet did see 'concrete instances' of preferential Zionist treatment:

> The appointment of a Jewish High Commissioner, however able and impar-tial (and Sir H. Samuel has been both in no ordinary degree); the existence of a Jewish Agency in Palestine with special access to the High Commissioner; the not inconsiderable (although restricted) immigration of many thousands of Jews since the war; the encouragement, however expedient and cautious, of Jewish enterprise . . . have all fostered this belief that the Jews are being unduly favoured and that the Arabs are being pushed into a background where the spoils of Palestine will be for others, and never for them.[47]

The Committee shared Clayton's pessimism and, indeed, went further in stating that 'it is difficult to blame those who argue . . . that the entire Mandate is built on the fallacy of attempting to reconcile the irreconcilable, and to combine in the same framework the creation of Jewish privileges with the maintenance of Arab rights'. But, like Clayton, the Committee agreed that neither the Zionist policy nor the

Mandate should be abandoned. More accurately, Clayton had argued that they *should* not be abandoned, the Committee that they *could* not: 'it is well-nigh impossible for any Government to extricate itself [from the policy of the Balfour Declaration] without a substantial sacrifice of consistency and self-respect, if not honour'. In searching for a solution, the Cabinet again turned to Clayton's paper, quoting his suggestion that by modifying objectionable Articles in the Mandate, or at least by 'removing all possible grounds for any charges of partiality or bad faith', Arab distrust might be overcome. The Cabinet agreed: 'it is to the terms of the Mandate that we should look for a solution . . . [I]f we can address the alleged preference to the Jews, by offering similar or analogous advantages to the Arabs, we may succeed in removing the sting'.

The Committee decided to address the problem by creating an Arab Agency which would 'occupy a position exactly analogous to that accorded to the Jewish Agency under the terms of the Mandate'. This was regarded as 'a great concession to Arab sentiment', for under Article IV of the Mandate a Jewish Agency had been 'recognised as a public body for the purpose of advising and cooperating with the administration of Palestine in such social, economic and other matters as may affect the Jewish national home and the interests of the Jewish population in Palestine'.[48] Similar rights regarding the non-Jewish populations were now to be accorded to an Arab Agency.

Meanwhile, Clayton was instructed to continue his efforts to form the Advisory Council.[49] On August 1, he reported that six of the ten Arab nominees had agreed to serve. Clayton tried to persuade the remaining four to follow suit, but admitted that strong pressure was being applied to prevent their acceptance. A Palestine Arab delegation was now in London trying to convince the government to abandon the Zionist policy and, as Clayton observed, if the delegation failed in its efforts, the Arabs proposed for seats on the Council believed that they, by appearing to cooperate with the Mandate government, would be held responsible for that failure.[50] In the event, the Palestinian delegation did fail, for the Cabinet Committee refused to meet with them and Devonshire suggested to Clayton that he might now wish to reconsider whether further efforts should be made to form the Council.[51] But the Chief Secretary soldiered on until early September when he reported that three Arab nominees had withdrawn their acceptances and only three of the original ten remained willing to serve. On September 7, he finally conceded defeat, informing Devonshire that the Council could not likely be formed and that he was now 'strongly opposed' to making any further attempt to do so.[52]

Samuel returned to Palestine on September 18, and three weeks later met with Palestinian leaders to present them with the Cabinet's proposal for an Arab Agency. Within minutes the Arab leaders gave their unanimous refusal. Musa Kazem Pasha Husseini, president of the Arab delegation, bluntly informed Samuel that the Arabs had 'never recognised the status of the Jewish Agency' and thus had 'no desire for the establishment of an Arab Agency on the same basis'.[53] The Arabs had now rejected the Legislative Council, the Advisory Council and the Arab Agency. The Colonial Office had had enough; no further 'concessions' would be offered to the

Arabs.[54] But Samuel's optimism was unquenchable. The day after the Arabs rejected the proposal for an Arab Agency, he submitted three new proposals to Shuckburgh, suggesting the appointment of Arab 'sub-governors' in the Palestine districts, the re-establishment of 'elected municipalities' and a revival of the old Turkish system of District Councils – all measures calculated to bring the Arabs into the administration of the Mandate government. The Colonial Office promptly rejected all three proposals without explanation.[55] The High Commissioner also revived his idea of an Arab confederation, a proposal he had first advanced more than three years earlier. Under this scheme, the Arabs of the Hijaz, Syria, Palestine, Transjordan, Iraq, and perhaps even Najd would be encouraged to form a loose confederation to promote a common economic – but not a political – agenda. Thus united, the Arabs' national aspirations would be satisfied and attention would be deflected away from Palestinian opposition to Zionism. Curzon was unenthusiastic. Devonshire thought it likely to be counter-productive.[56] This idea too went nowhere.

All of the schemes proposed or supported by Samuel sprang from his unflagging optimism and his apparently sincere belief that the Arabs could be reconciled to the Zionist policy. 'There is no innate antipathy between Arab and Jew', he confided to Clayton. 'If there were our policy would indeed be doomed to failure'.[57] He could not accept that failure, perhaps because he believed it would signify his own failure as High Commissioner. And so he persisted in floating one improbable plan after another, each calculated to co-opt the Palestinians by giving them the false impression that they had some say in the governance of the country or, at least, signifying by their participation an implicit acquiescence to the Zionist policy. Samuel seemed quite incapable of acknowledging that the Arabs would not accept anything less than what they believed their numerical superiority warranted – real political power – and that they were implacably, unalterably opposed to any proposal that did not accord them such power.

Clayton, however, was coming to the realization by late 1923 that the Arabs could never be induced to cooperate with the Mandate government. Still, there is no reason to question the sincerity of his opinion that neither the Mandate nor the Zionist policy should be abandoned. And, as an officer of the government, he well understood that it was his duty to effectuate the government policy of supporting the Zionist programme. A review of his activities during his two years in Palestine confirms this understanding. In August 1923, for example, Clayton backed a proposed concession to the Jewish Colonial Association whereby the government would transfer some 2.3 million square metres of marshy waste land to the Association which they would then reclaim for cultivation. The Arabs objected, although they held only common rights in, not ownership of, the land. Clayton favoured invoking the government's expropriation power to acquire the Arab common rights and convey the property to the Jewish Association. But the Colonial Office rejected his proposal, as they doubted that acquiring the property rights in this manner for conveyance to the Jews was clearly for the 'public benefit'.[58]

More controversially, Clayton proposed the appointment of a Jew, and avid Zionist, Albert Hyamson, as head of the Palestine government's department of immigration and travel. He knew the Arabs would howl once they learned that a Jew was to be put in control of the immigration of Jews into Palestine, but Clayton countered that Hyamson would not be setting immigration policy, only effectuating it, and, in any event, he thought it would be 'unfair to Hyamson himself', an experienced and capable man, to deny him the post. The Middle East Department was divided on the appointment, but Shuckburgh deferred to Clayton and Devonshire agreed.[59]

Again, in July 1924, the Palestine Attorney General, Norman Bentwich, also a Jew, came under fire from several British newspapers for allegedly exhibiting an anti-Arab bias and from the Middle East Department for the 'unsatisfactory manner in which draft legislation' for Palestine was being prepared. Two members of the Department thought Bentwich should be removed. But Clayton defended the Attorney General and he stayed on.[60]

Clayton also objected to the suspension of immigration, as recommended by the Mandate government's Controller of Labour, at a time when there were 4,000 unemployed in Palestine, 2,500 of whom were Jews. Although he acknowledged that the level of unemployment warranted curtailment of immigration – particularly in view of the White Paper policy that immigration should not exceed the absorptive capacity of the country – Clayton proposed maintaining current levels because Weizmann was then in the United States trying to raise money for the Zionists and the imposition of restrictions on Jewish immigration would undermine his efforts.[61]

In 1924, Clayton wrote to Shuckburgh expressing himself in sympathy with a Zionist plan to construct a jetty at Tel Aviv, despite the Mandate government's official objections and despite his own belief that the project was 'unsound'.[62]

Again, in 1924, Clayton authorized the secret arming of Jewish colonies to protect against possible Arab attacks. Under this plan, a number of armouries were established by the government near remote Jewish colonies and more than 1,000 rifles placed in them in case of emergency. The armouries may also have been established as a means of controlling the illicit traffic in arms sponsored by the *Haganah*, the clandestine Jewish defence force.[63] These examples suggest that if Clayton was intent on doing his best to 'ruin' the government's support of the Zionist policy, as Meinertzhagen thought, his conduct in 1923–24, certainly does not support that view.

While it may have seemed that Clayton was consumed with Arab–Jewish relations during his tenure as Chief Secretary, his work actually encompassed the full range of the Mandate government's business. Next to political stability, the first concern of the government was the Palestine economy and any consequent expense to Britain. Samuel and Clayton came under continual pressure from the Colonial Office to reduce expenditure. For the most part, the cost of civil administration was borne by local revenues, although the Mandate government, in anticipation of a public loan, had incurred a floating debt of about £1,620,000 to the Crown Agents for the Colonies. The cost to the British taxpayer came not from subsidizing the Palestine administration, but in maintaining a British garrison in the country and a 700-man British gendarmerie. To maintain these forces the British taxpayer had to pay £4,000,000 in 1921–22; £2,000,000 in 1922–23; £1,500,000 in 1923–24; and £1,000,000 in 1924–25. By 1924, the garrison was small – dangerously so – having been reduced to two infantry companies and one RAF squadron, along with the gendarmerie.[64] Meanwhile, Clayton continued to look for economies in every direction. While acting as OAG in 1923, he even proposed some 'drastic changes in [the] organization' of Palestine itself by reducing the number of government districts and restructuring the Public Security Department, both measures calculated to reduce expenditure.[65] Clayton's economic policy was, in his own words, 'Cromerian'; that is, he favoured low taxation, strict economy in administration and great caution in 'undertaking capital expenditures'.[66] The Colonial Office was quick to agree and applauded Clayton's view that 'further and drastic retrenchment' was required in Palestine. In July 1923, he proposed expenditure reductions of £230,000 for the revised 1923–24 Estimates, to be achieved through a series of austerity measures which were so detailed they even included an analysis of the question whether the services of a gardener for Government House could be procured for less than £20 per month. Clayton also believed that economies could be achieved in a manner similar to that he had proposed for political reform in Egypt in 1919. '[T]he best results, both administrative and political', he argued, 'are to be achieved by a small, carefully selected, and, above all, contented staff of British officials supervising and controlling a predominantly Palestinian staff'.[67] If devolution could achieve political reform in Egypt, so too could it achieve political and economic reform in Palestine.

In January 1924, a Labour government under Ramsay MacDonald succeeded Baldwin's Conservative government and the demand for economies in the Mandates became, if anything, more strident. The Colonial Office objected angrily when Samuel submitted Estimates for 1924–25 disclosing a £186,000 deficit. '[I]f British responsibility for Palestine is to continue', wrote the new Colonial Secretary, J.H. Thomas, 'it is [an] absolutely necessary first condition that local revenue should cover local expenditure other than defence charges borne temporarily by [the] British Exchequer'.[68] When Clayton took over as OAG in the summer of 1924, he managed to increase revenue and decrease expenditure sufficiently to create a small surplus of £18,350 in the revised Estimates for 1924–25. And, he proposed 'drastic' economies for 1925–26, by reducing the strength of the gendarmerie and suppressing a number of junior administrative posts. But, in true Cromerian fashion, Clayton continued to resist the imposition of tax increases on the Palestinians and, instead, pursued a policy of 'financial devolution', by which he meant 'a system under which expenditure which is now defrayed by the Treasury will be gradually transferred to local funds'. The maintenance of schools, sanitary services and even hospitals were to be transferred to municipalities.[69] In order to reduce the burden on the home government, he also recommended amalgamation of the British and Palestine gendarmeries under a single command and a gradual reduction of the British component until not more than one hundred remained. However, when the Colonial Office pressed for a reduction in the grant for Palestine to £600,000 for 1925–26, Clayton objected strongly, insisting that a grant of less than £750,000 would compromise public security.[70]

Clayton was less successful in the area of legal reform. Since the Turkish defeat, Ottoman codes, both criminal and civil, had continued in use in Palestine. But the laws were badly out of date and both Bentwich and Clayton favoured revision, based primarily on the model of Egyptian law. The Colonial Office disagreed, insisting on the use of English law as a basis for recodification. The disagreement remained unresolved by the time Samuel and Clayton left Palestine in 1925.[71]

The Chief Secretary also continued to wrestle with several problems associated with Palestine's religious communities, some of which persisted from his time as CPO, five years earlier. Chief among them was the debt of the Greek Orthodox Patriarchate, which now stood at a whopping £700,000. A government commission had been established in 1920 to examine the problem and another was set up by ordinance in 1921, which, with the acquiescence of the Orthodox synod, began selling off property owned by the Order to liquidate the debt. In 1923, the Patriarch, Damianos, objected to sales directed by the committee and sought to re-establish his control over the Order's property. Clayton resisted his efforts and a long struggle ensued, with the Chief Secretary eventually prevailing.[72]

The Chief Secretary was less inclined to involve himself in disputes persisting among the Jewish communities in Palestine. Despite his best efforts, Weizmann had failed to win over the ultra-orthodox community in Palestine, whom he referred to as 'Challukkah Jewry'.[73] In the words of Norman Bentwich, the orthodox community were not merely opposed to Zionism, they were 'aggressively anti-Zionist'. They refused to speak Hebrew for any purpose, except in prayer, while the Zionists insisted on its use in all aspects of Jewish life in Palestine. 'Rak Ivrit' – only Hebrew – was a sign prominently displayed in the windows of many Zionist-owned shops in the country, to the great displeasure of the orthodox Jews.[74] So upset were they by what they perceived as the threat to their religious practices that, in 1924, the Council of the Ashkenazic Jewish Community of Palestine appealed directly to the League of Nations, objecting strongly to the government-sponsored Jewish Communities Ordinance which, they said, threatened the very existence of orthodox Jewry. To the Ashkenazic community, the Zionists were 'irreligious Jews', animated by 'secular and national principles alone'.[75]

Clayton opposed the demand of the Orthodox community for official 'recognition of separate Orthodox institutions', as based on political rather than 'conscientious grounds'. After all, he argued, any individual or Jewish congregation could elect not to be subject to the Jewish Communities Ordinance. By legislation, the government had sanctioned only the Rabbinical Courts of the 'recognized Jewish Community'. In such matters as marriage, divorce, alimony and the confirmation of wills, there could be only a 'single recognized judicial authority' in the Jewish community. But again, if anyone objected to that authority, he could have his case referred to the civil courts.[76] Nevertheless, on this sensitive subject the Ashkenazi community were successful in having the Communities Ordinance reconsidered.[77] The differences between the Zionists and the Orthodox Jewish community in Palestine would remain long after Clayton's departure.

Clayton's absorption in the political, economic, administrative and religious problems of Palestine – not to mention the persistent problems of Transjordan, discussed below – had again resulted in overwork. The Middle East Department recognized that the Chief Secretary and his small staff were being 'worked to the bone' in Jerusalem, but the pressure to reduce expenditure in the country precluded any possibility of additional manpower being supplied.[78] Despite the press of work, Clayton did find time to tour the country, both as Chief Secretary and as OAG, just as he had toured Egypt as adviser to the Interior Ministry. Enid came out to join him in May 1923, and, as she had in Egypt, often accompanied him on tour. And, as in Egypt, wherever he went in Palestine, Clayton was well-received. Whether he appeared in Jewish colonies or Arab villages, large and enthusiastic crowds turned out to greet him.[79] Although he had left England on a rather sour note when the government refused his request for an allowance, Clayton did not adhere to his stated intention of leaving his family in England. The British Treasury never did approve the requested allowance, but when Clayton's sister Phyllis arrived in Jerusalem in November 1923, she brought Patience and Sam with her, and when his sister Ellinor appeared during the following April, she was accompanied by the Claytons' youngest child John, then just three.[80] Clayton also enjoyed a visit from Iltyd and his youngest sister Norah, who made the journey from Baghdad to Jerusalem by car.

While the arrival of Clayton's family doubtless eased the stress of his work, 1924 brought no relief from the problems of Palestine. And, rather more ominously, new troubles were brewing across the Jordan, troubles which would threaten to shake the very foundations of Churchill's Sherifian solution for the Middle East.

25

Trouble in Transjordan: Clayton and Abdullah, 1923–1925

Transjordan. It was not a name that evoked much interest among Britons in the 1920s. The country, if such it could be called, contained at most 250,000 people. Amman, its largest 'city', was home to fewer than 5,000. The land itself was unpromising, largely devoid of natural resources. Its southern and eastern boundaries had never been drawn and nobody seemed inclined to make the effort. In 1920, Transjordan produced a total revenue of £E30,000. Even officials in the Colonial Office's Middle East Department saw little to warrant their attention. 'Trans Jordan is a small country', wrote the Department's chief Sir John Shuckburgh, 'and its affairs are of comparative insignificance'. His subordinates agreed. 'We regard Trans-Jordania more as a buffer to Palestine than as a country capable of development in itself', Young added.[1]

With such attitudes prevailing, it was not surprising that the Colonial Office was very reluctant to provide financial support for Abdullah. 'The reason we are spending money in T. J. is . . . to save spending more money in Palestine . . . The British taxpayer will not be a penny . . . better off if the country blossoms like a rose', wrote one official. A colleague in the Office was more blunt: 'There is no real reason why the British taxpayer should pay anything for Transjordan'.[2] Clayton, however, took a slightly broader view and, as was often the case with the Chief Secretary, a view defined by British Imperial interests. As he informed the Duke of Devonshire in 1923, 'British interests may be defined as: (a) the protection of the cultivated and cultivable areas of Trans-Jordan from hostile incursions which would constitute a menace to Palestine; (b) the safety of the Trans-Desert Air Route'.[3] The Air Route was defined by the furrow, scratched out in the desert between Amman and Baghdad, which Clayton would follow six years later on his way to the Iraqi capital to take up his post as High Commissioner. In his view, it was essential that the route travel over British-controlled territory. Neither France, to the North in Syria, nor Ibn Saud, to the south and east, should be allowed to impinge on that vital Imperial link; it was necessary, Clayton concluded, that 'it should lie within Trans-Jordan and Iraq territory'.[4]

Because Clayton regarded the protection of Palestine and the Air Route as important Imperial interests, he believed that Transjordan should be supported financially, if only to maintain the country's small, 750-man Reserve Force. In 1921, Churchill had secured Parliamentary approval of a £180,000 grant for Transjordan for just that purpose. But, in 1922–23, the grant was reduced to £90,000. For the following financial year it was agreed during Clayton's London negotiations with Abdullah that the grant would be raised to £150,000. However, the post-war retrenchment movement was unstoppable and when Treasury parsimony resulted in a proposed reduction of the grant to only £20,000 for 1924–25, Clayton objected and 'urged strongly' that a grant of £80,000 was required. Again, he pointed to the importance of maintaining the desert Air Route. And, he argued, by supporting the Reserve Force – renamed the Arab Legion in 1923 – Britain was actually reducing expenditure in Palestine. Since its inception in 1921, the Transjordanian force had prevented 'serious raids into Palestine' from the East and this, in turn, 'has enabled reductions to be made in the military expenditure in connection with Imperial forces in Palestine'.[5] These arguments carried the force of logic, particularly when one considered the alternatives. Failing the payment of a grant for Transjordan, the Chief Secretary saw only two options: 'to annex Trans-Jordan to Palestine in direct contradiction of the pledges given to the Arabs; or to allow it to slide into administrative and financial bankruptcy'.[6] But none of these arguments persuaded the Treasury; without even consulting the Colonial Office, they eliminated the Transjordan grant altogether for 1924–25.[7]

If the Colonial Office, and more so the Treasury, appeared extraordinarily tight-fisted, Abdullah's fiscal management of Transjordan suggested that their attitude was amply justified. A portion of every annual grant for the country was allocated to the Amir, as a 'civil list', for his personal use. Of the initial 1921–22 grant of £180,000, some £30,000 was earmarked for the purpose. Abdullah blew through two-thirds of that amount in one month. By August 1921, his entire civil list had been consumed and his personal debt was estimated at £22,000. Between September 1921 and April 1922, when the new financial year began, the Amir somehow collected another £29,000 – from his father, King Hussein, from the Hashemite Agent in Cairo, from funds he misappropriated from the Hijazi garrison at Ma'an, even from the meagre revenue collected by the Transjordan government – but still he was deeply in debt. The Colonial Office was sufficiently alarmed that they reduced Abdullah's civil list for 1922–23 to £15,000. Still the Amir spent. Still his debt grew. And, after his declaration of independence in May 1923, he became even more intemperate. During 1923–4, it was reported that the Amir had squandered something like £100,000, and had appropriated for his own use 25 percent of Transjordanian revenue – about £50,000.[8]

Despite Abdullah's prodigality, no one knew how these large amounts were being spent. The Amir himself did not appear to be leading a lavish lifestyle. But he was by nature 'absurdly generous' and Samuel and Clayton believed that he was also subsidizing certain tribes to ensure their loyalty.[9] Philby, the Chief British Representative in the country, disagreed, but the Bani Sakhr were known to be recipients of Abdullah's largesse and some, including Clayton, believed he had good reason to subsidize the tribe. As one of the largest and most powerful tribes in the eastern regions of the country, they were thought to provide a vital bulwark against the ideological and military encroachments of Ibn Saud's Wahhabis. And, since the Wahhabis posed the greatest threat to Transjordan in the early 1920s, any money spent on the Bani Sakhr was money well spent.[10]

In May 1923, a month after arriving in Palestine, Clayton made his first trip to Amman. His first priority was to get Abdullah's spending under control. He informed the Amir that further payment of the Transjordan grant must be contingent on his acceptance of four conditions: he was to make the expenses of the Reserve Force a 'first charge' on the country's revenues; to provide adequate details of local revenue and expenditure to justify the grant; to submit to periodic Colonial Office audits; and to reorganize the system of taxation in the country in order to maximize revenue.[11] Always affable, the Amir readily agreed. But, only two months later, Clayton had to advise Devonshire that the financial outlook in Transjordan was 'not promising'. The Transjordanians had done nothing to place 'their financial system in proper order' and the Amir himself, an 'extremely extravagant' man, had failed 'to recognise that his expenses must be cut down'. Clayton may have been a 'personal friend' of Abdullah, as Young had stated in the fall of 1922, but that did not affect the Chief Secretary's view that the Amir 'must be forced into a proper attitude . . . [H]e must either consent to reduce his expenditure to proper proportions or else to leave Trans-Jordan'. Clayton also recommended, and the Colonial Office agreed, that the grant be removed from Transjordan control and, in future, be disbursed by Britain's representative at Amman, Harry Philby.[12]

By June 1923, Harry St John Bridger Philby had become Abdullah's *bête noire*. Despite the serious reservations of Samuel and many in the Colonial Office, Philby had been appointed Chief British Representative in Transjordan in November 1921, largely on the strength of Lawrence's recommendation. Everyone agreed that Philby was capable and that his excellent command of Arabic would prove a valuable asset, but he was also regarded as a man of decided prejudices whose 'fanatical nature [was] apt to allow his personal bias . . . to outweigh his duty'.[13] Percy Cox had sent him packing from Baghdad in 1921, when Philby refused to support the government's sponsorship of Faisal as King of Iraq, a refusal attributed to his 'pronounced anti-Sherifian tendencies'.[14] By that time he had already acquired a reputation as an opinionated and extraordinarily contentious figure. 'Philby is . . . as cantankerous as ever', wrote one Foreign Office acquaintance. 'I never met such a fellow. Any scheme that anyone else puts up he disagrees with. His great phrase is "I join issue with you" and he spends his life joining issue with someone'.[15]

During his first eighteen months in Amman, Philby got on well with Abdullah due, in large part, to their similar political agendas. Both were keen proponents of Transjordanian independence and both believed that it could best be achieved by 'riding off all attempts of the Palestine Government to encroach' on the Amir's prerogatives. Not surprisingly, Philby antagonized nearly everyone in Jerusalem for, as he later admitted, he 'was almost continuously in a state of conflict with the Palestine authorities'.[16] He also managed to alienate most British officials in Transjordan, including Frederick Peake, commander of the Reserve Force.[17] Only with Clayton did Philby seem to enjoy reasonably good relations; there is no record of any serious dispute between them. But Clayton got on well with everyone and he and Philby agreed on most issues concerning Transjordan. Still, Philby, a strong proponent of Arab independence, thought that Clayton was 'at heart an imperialist, a very benign one . . . What he [Clayton] wanted was an independent Trans-Jordan entirely dependent on Great Britain'.[18]

As Philby had trouble with most of his British colleagues, few thought he would be able to remain on good terms with the lavish and lackadaisical ruler of Transjordan. And, as anticipated, the two fell out in June 1923, when they quarrelled bitterly over the Amir's dismantling of an historic site at Amman. Philby used the incident as an excuse to raise a wide variety of issues with Abdullah, most of them political and nearly all of them unrelated to antiquities. Clayton travelled to Amman in July and partially succeeded in patching up their differences, but reported that Abdullah 'continues to feel considerably aggrieved' and it was doubtful that 'any useful degree of cordial relations' could be restored between the two.[19] Privately, Clayton advised Shuckburgh that Abdullah had told him that either he or Philby must go; if an opportunity arose elsewhere that did not entail a loss of prestige or position for Philby, Clayton suggested that he 'should be moved'.[20] As for Philby, he now turned on the Amir, complaining of his 'megalomaniacal thriftlessness' and his 'reckless despotism'.[21]

Philby was certainly correct in criticizing Abdullah's immoderate spending, but the Amir also had a legitimate grievance against the British representative. As Clayton informed Shuckburgh, Abdullah 'has it firmly in his head – quite without reason – that Philby is the convinced supporter and ally of Ibn Saud'.[22] Here, Clayton was wrong; Philby *was* a supporter of the Najdi sultan. As early as January 1922, he acknowledged to Samuel that his 'personal friendship for and admiration of' Ibn Saud prevented him from 'countenancing, far more from proposing, anything detrimental to his interests'.[23] It was a startling admission and one that certainly did not bode well for Abdullah, for during the early 1920s Ibn Saud and his Wahhabi followers seemed to be expanding in every direction. In November 1921, Ibn Saud captured the north Arabian Rashidi stronghold of Ha'il and now, supreme in central Arabia, he was poised to move either east or west. A May 1922 agreement with Iraq temporarily halted Wahhabi aggression in the East and the Sultan promptly turned his gaze westward, focusing on the small oasis village of Jauf.

Although some strategists thought Jauf had value for an alternative air route or as a possible staging post for a future trans-desert railway or pipeline, few saw any immediate justification for spending money to secure the place. The village was located 270 miles southeast of Amman at the bottom of Wadi Sirhan, a broad valley that ran in a north-westerly direction to a point some forty miles southeast of the Transjordanian capital. Although Jauf was important to the tribes who migrated annually to the Wadi for pasturage, Abdullah's primary interest in the place arose from his study of the map, on which the Wadi Sirhan appeared almost like a broad avenue along which the Wahhabis could march on their way to Amman. And the southern gate to the Wadi was at Jauf.

Probably on the initiative of Lawrence, in February 1922 the Colonial Office rather half-heartedly authorized Samuel 'to extend the political influence of the Transjordanian administration in the Wadi Sirhan . . . to Jauf'.[24] But few liked the idea. Shuckburgh was opposed to 'incurring commitments in these out-of-the-way regions', and Young complained that Jauf was 'a third of the way to Iraq, right in the heart of central Arabia'.[25] For his part, Philby privately admitted that he had no objection to Ibn Saud's occupation of the village.[26] In fact, Jauf was simply too remote to defend and scarcely a murmur was heard in London or Jerusalem when the Wahhabis occupied the village in July 1922. More worrisome, though, was Ibn Saud's action three weeks later when a large Wahhabi force attacked two villages only twelve miles from Amman, leaving thirty-five Transjordanians dead. The Colonial Office directed Percy Cox in Baghdad to deliver a strong protest to Ibn Saud, along with a warning that his relations with Britain would be 'seriously affected' by further encroachments in the Wadi Sirhan. But the threat was an empty one because, at the same time, Samuel was instructed 'to limit military action to that essential for [the] defence of Trans-Jordan itself'.[27] Of course, since no eastern border had been demarcated, no one knew what constituted 'Trans-Jordan itself'.[28] But, whatever it was, Transjordan did not encompass Jauf. Abdullah did not agree. Dismayed by the Wahhabi capture of Jauf, and alarmed by the attack near Amman, he began assembling a Bedouin force for an expedition to re-occupy the village. The Colonial Office promptly quashed the plan, instructing Samuel to 'take no action which involves additional commitments of a military or financial nature'.[29]

By the time Clayton arrived in Palestine in April 1923, attention was focused on the village of Kaf, located in the Wadi Sirhan about half-way between Jauf and Amman. In September 1922, Samuel had authorized Abdullah to occupy the place and 140 men of the Reserve Force, along with 80 bedouin, were now stationed there, uneasily awaiting the next Wahabbi move. Meanwhile, Ibn Saud was planning to take all of the Wadi, right up to Azrak, some thirty miles from Amman. The Wahhabi leader's plan was to move incrementally up the Wadi, pausing with each step to gauge the British reaction. If no reprisals resulted, he would move again. Two motives lay behind his desire to possess the Wadi. First, he regarded the valley as an economic unit, 'indivisble from all practical points of view'.[30] Since he possessed Jauf, he reasoned that he should now have all of the Wadi. Second, Ibn Saud wanted badly to extend Najdi territory to the north, right up to the Syrian border, so that he could drive a wedge between his Hashemite enemies ruling in Iraq and Transjordan.[31]

Clayton was well aware of the Najdi leader's intentions; he had no doubt that the Wahhabis would 'continue their policy of semi-peaceful penetration until they have captured the whole of the Wadi Sirhan'.[32] But the Chief Secretary was not alarmed by Ibn Saud's plans because, he said, 'I cannot imagine Abdullah being able to permanently hold any part of the region, and I should prefer his frontier to be along the line of the [Hijaz] Railway behind the strip of desert lying theoretically within his territory'. Again, Clayton's reasoning was based on Imperial strategy: 'The only real thing we have to preserve is the Air Route to Baghdad on which Ibn Saud should not be allowed to encroach, and it seems necessary that it should lie entirely within Trans-Jordan and Iraq territory.'[33] Contrary to Ibn Saud's plan of driving a wedge between Iraq and Transjordan, Clayton was determined that there would be no separation between the two countries, as the Air Route must pass over British-controlled territory. That issue would become critical in the negotiations that would occur between Clayton and the Wahhabi leader in 1925. However, the Wadi Sirhan terminated south of the Air Route and, as Clayton believed the Wadi's loss inevitable, he was opposed to any British operations or funds being expended to defend it. No British military action should be taken against the Wahhabis, he advised the Colonial Secretary, 'unless it is absolutely necessary for the preservation of Trans-Jordan itself', by which he meant the 'cultivated and cultivable' areas of the country. If Ibn Saud's advance was to be checked at all, it should be by diplomatic pressure or perhaps 'by means of our control over his sea-borne trade on the Persian Gulf'.[34] Clayton was right about Kaf; the Wahhabis attacked the village in June and again in August 1923. No British military assistance was provided, but the small garrison there hung on for another year, until Clayton ordered that it be withdrawn in August 1924.[35]

Meanwhile, relations between Abdullah and Philby continued to deteriorate. At the end of September 1923, the Amir 'declared definitely' that he could no longer work with the British representative. Samuel wrote privately to Shuckburgh giving a half dozen reasons why he could no longer 'place full confidence in Philby's judgment'. The only option was to move Philby out of Transjordan, for, in Samuel's view, there could 'be no question . . . of the Emir Abdullah being removed'. Not only had the government recognized the independence of Transjordan 'under his rule', there would be 'serious complications with King Hussein and King Feisal' if Abdullah were deposed. Nor could Samuel think of any other Arab prince who could 'suitably succeed him'. And, the alternative, that Britain should assume responsibility for directly administering the country, was 'not one that can be contemplated'. The High Commissioner admitted that Abdullah's rule had been far from exemplary, but, on the other hand, he had proved himself 'loyal' to Britain and had 'kept the peace in so far as Palestine is concerned'.[36] Shuckburgh was far less sanguine about Abdullah's rule; he thought that 'the experiment of quasi-independent Arab government' in Transjordan had been a failure. Still, while Britain was in the uncomfortable position of 'conniving at and subsidising a thoroughly inefficient and corrupt form of government', he reluctantly agreed with Samuel that there could be 'no question of removing Abdullah'. Instead, the Colonial Office proposed that Clayton be dispatched to Amman for a month or so, during which time he would complete the treaty negotiations begun in London in 1922, and establish a 'constitutional' regime in Transjordan. At the same time, the Colonial Office would transfer administration of the grant to the Mandate government in Jerusalem and decree that the Chief British Representative, and all his subordinates, would henceforth be officials of the Palestine administration.[37]

Of course, Philby's antipathy towards the Palestine administration was well known and both Shuckburgh and Samuel anticipated that once Philby was informed that he was to become an official of the Mandate government, he would resign.[38] He did. In mid-January 1924, Philby informed Samuel of his decision to leave in April.[39] Clayton doubtless supported the decision; Philby's incorrigible personality had rendered his position in Transjordan untenable. But, in some ways, the Chief Secretary was probably sorry to see Philby go, for he agreed with many of his views. He agreed with him that Saudi occupation of the Wadi Sirhan was inevitable and that Britain had no interest in fighting to prevent it. He was sympathetic, too, with Philby's desire to see a constitutional regime – an elected assembly – established in Transjordan, if only as a means of curbing the Amir's extravagant and arbitrary rule.[40] And he, like Philby, thought that an extension of the Mandate government's administrative authority to Transjordan should be resisted. He acknowledged to Devonshire that Transjordan's 'administrative independence under [the] general control of the Mandatory power' created more work for officials on both sides of the Jordan, but he argued that it was 'inadvisable for political reasons that the High Commissioner should exercise his authority through the normal channels of the Palestine administration'.[41] With that sentiment Philby certainly would have agreed.

By the spring of 1924, Clayton had become thoroughly disillusioned with the situation in Transjordan. He was not interested in resuming treaty negotiations with Abdullah, as the Colonial Office requested, because he thought they would be of no 'practical value as long as the present situation exists'. In a candid letter to Samuel, the Chief Secretary expressed his view that the present policy of the British government was 'based on two complete fallacies': That Transjordan 'can support an Amir and a central government . . . on its own resources' and that 'adequate British administrative or financial control, on British Treasury lines, is compatible with [the] administrative independence of the Trans-Jordan Government'. The budget for 1924–25 disclosed a deficit of £124,000 and yet, he complained, the British Treasury had refused to provide any grant. As a result, the Arab Legion would have to be drastically reduced and since it provided not only security, but also the principal means of tax collection, the country was likely to fall further behind. The new British representative was being instructed to exercise strict political, administrative and financial control over the country but, Clayton argued, 'to enforce this control he has no weapon whatsoever'. The threat of withholding grant money had previously provided leverage, but the grant was now being discontinued. And, he added, 'we cannot threaten the use of military force or the removal of the Amir'.[42] The outlook was, to say the least, bleak.

The new British representative at Amman did not yet share Clayton's pessimism. A veteran of the Sudan service and, most recently, district governor of Nablus in Palestine, lieutenant-colonel Henry Cox was determined to succeed. 'I will make Transjordan', he said, 'or Transjordan will break me'.[43] Shortly after his arrival, Cox drafted a set of detailed financial regulations for the Transjordan government. Abdullah declined to apply them. Indeed, as Cox reported, the Amir resisted 'any form of efficient control . . . because his only interest in the country is to squeeze out of it every piastre he can'. Cox was starting to sound rather like Philby. On June

27, 1924, Abdullah left Amman to attend the pilgrimage at Mecca. Cox used the opportunity to send a stinging indictment of the Amir to Clayton. And, unlike Samuel, Shuckburgh and Clayton himself, Cox was prepared for a drastic remedy. Abdullah, he reported, 'is in fact a blight on the country and should not be allowed to return here from the Hedjaz'. The Amir should 'be got rid of'.[44] Two days later, Cox sent another letter, again detailing Abdullah's contumacy and proposing that he – Cox – along with Peake and the Amir's Chief Minister be allowed to 'disregard the Amir and run the country in spite of him'.[45]

When Clayton received Cox's letters he was acting as OAG, as Samuel had just left Palestine on his annual leave. He mulled over Cox's proposals. Clayton agreed that 'the removal of the Amir might become necessary' and that the time had come for 'drastic action', but he balked at the idea of deposing Abdullah. Such action could have wider political ramifications that Cox had not perhaps considered. Not only would Britain's relations with her Hashemite protégés in Iraq and Hijaz 'become strained', Britain's position in the Arab world generally might be cast in a bad light. The first concern, Clayton thought, could be addressed by offering the 'Amir-ship' of Transjordan to Abdullah's younger brother, Zaid. But no one could predict how Britain's apparently high-handed treatment of an 'independent' Arab ruler might be perceived in the Arab world. After carefully considering the situation, Clayton opted for a less drastic course. Abdullah should be given an ultimatum: submit to financial control, in writing, or leave.[46]

Clayton's despatch recommending the ultimatum was reviewed at the Colonial Office by Young, who advised that the proposal be approved. The Colonial Secretary agreed, without comment, and, on August 12, Prime Minister Ramsay MacDonald concurred. If Abdullah did not submit, he would be removed.[47] On August 14, Clayton prepared a letter which Cox was to hand to Abdullah on his return from the Hijaz. Clayton came right to the point. The British government viewed the situation in Transjordan with 'grave displeasure', would not allow the country to become the focus of disorder, and would not permit the 'financial irregularities and unchecked extravagance' to continue. Clayton then set forth six conditions to which the Amir was requested to adhere, in writing, all of which had the effect of tightening British control over the country. The last condition was the most important and conveyed the definitive tone of Clayton's ultimatum: 'Your Highness and your government should accept immediately and without reservation such measures of financial control as HMG considers necessary'. His last sentence made clear the consequences of Abduallh's refusal to submit: 'I trust that Your Highness' definite acceptance of the above conditions will render it unnecessary for HMG to reconsider the whole position in Transjordan'.[48] As a precaution – or perhaps as a dose of intimidation – Clayton dispatched a squadron of British cavalry to Amman shortly before Cox was to deliver the ultimatum.[49]

On the morning of August 20, 1924, Cox handed Clayton's letter to the Amir. Tears welled up in Abdullah's eyes as he read the terms of the ultimatum. It came as 'a great shock to him', he said, and he wondered whether Britain had lost confidence in him. But Abdullah realized he had no alternative. He signed the paper reflecting his agreement and, in Cox's words, 'unconditionally surrendered'.[50] The crisis was over. Although Clayton was quick to credit Cox for his 'tact and firmness' in dealing with a 'difficult and delicate situation', an historian later analysing the events of the summer of 1924, described Clayton as 'the master-mind of the operation'.[51] Clayton would continue to oversee Transjordan for another eight months, but there were no further crises during his tenure.

Resolution of the summer 1924 crisis in Transjordan enabled Clayton to re-focus on the problems of Palestine. Concerning the essential problem of reconciling the Arabs to the Zionist policy, Clayton saw no solution. The Arabs had rejected every plan advanced by Samuel or the Colonial Office to bring them into an active role in the Mandate government and no attempt was made to revise those clauses of the Mandate the Arabs found objectionable. The Colonial Office had effectively given up. By the end of 1923, Clayton, too, had lost heart. In December, during a visit to Amman, he had a long talk with Philby and told him 'that he had made up his mind to give up his thankless task in April'. According to Philby, Clayton said 'he was not "disposed to acquiesce in the forcible application" of what he regarded as our wrong-headed Zionist policy'.[52] In January 1924, Clayton again visited Amman and, again according to Philby, stated that he 'had been induced' – by whom Philby did not record – to defer the date of his departure from Palestine in order to act as OAG while Samuel was on leave. 'He told me, however, that if things had not changed for the better by then, he would certainly go'.[53] During yet another visit to Transjordan in February, Clayton appeared to Philby to be 'thoroughly disgruntled'. 'He obviously disagreed with the official policy', Philby later wrote, 'while at the same time he was far from being in agreement with me'.[54]

Philby's descriptions of Clayton's attitude were confirmed by Humphrey Bowman, head of the Palestine Education Department, and a long-standing friend of the Chief Secretary. In early February 1924, Bowman recorded in his diary that Clayton 'was pretty sick of the whole thing . . . I doubt if he will stay long. He hates the atmosphere and is out of sympathy with [Samuel] and his eternal optimism'.[55] Clayton's views were shared by others in the British community in Palestine, including Bowman and Ernest Richmond, head of the political section of the Mandate administration. Richmond had arrived in Palestine in 1918, and, in October 1920, was appointed Assistant Civil Secretary under Deedes. Known to be in sympathy with the Arabs, he soon became a sort of connecting link between the Mandate government and the Arab politicians, a link that could not be established by either Samuel or the pro-Zionist Deedes. The Zionists suspected the worst of Richmond and sought to have him removed, believing that he had played an active role in torpedoing the Legislative Council elections and the Advisory Council scheme.[56]

Paradoxically, Richmond was supported by Samuel, at least until September 1923, when the High Commissioner came across a memo by Richmond in which he appeared to advocate abandoning the national home policy.[57] But even as late as March 1924, Samuel tried to persuade Richmond to stay on. The High Commissioner's thinking and Richmond's reaction were explained by Bowman: Richmond 'feels that he is being exploited, as many of us do, as being a kind of set-off to the pro-Jewish proclivities of the H[igh] C[ommissioner] & Bentwich. The H. C. actually told him he wanted him to stay, as he thought the people of Pal. relied on him to see that the second part of the Balfour Declaration (that relating to Arab rights being safe-guarded) was carried out, as he – the H. C. – and Bentwich were Jews and inclined to Zionism; and, [as] the H. C. felt that he might be regarded as a partisan, it was his duty to have someone to make the balance even!'[58] Bowman ascribed these same feelings to Clayton and perhaps the Chief Secretary did feel he was being exploited by Samuel. But, unlike Clayton, Richmond did not possess the tolerance and diplomatic skill required to enable him to continue under such circumstances. In March 1924, Richmond resigned, inform-ing Samuel of his conviction that the Zionist Commission, the Middle East Department and Samuel's administration were 'dominated and inspired by a spirit which I can only regard as evil'.[59]

Clayton's own views were set down in an unusually revealing letter written to his friend from Egyptian days, Walford Selby:

I will open my heart to you and tell you something of how I feel about things in my part of the world, as we know each others views and have been through times together. Egypt I felt I could compete with, but Palestine under the present regime and with the present methods of carrying out the policy beats me. There is an intangible "something" behind everything, an unseen influ-ence – which has to be felt to be realized. Frankly, unless the place is to be run by Englishmen on British lines, I am off and that within a few months. To you in confidence I will say that this Palestine policy – difficult and contra-dictory as it is – has only one chance of success which is that it be implemented by pure-bred Britishers whose justice and impartiality cannot be questioned. If I were to say that this is so openly, I should not unnaturally be accused of wanting the job, but you know that has nothing to do with it – indeed I should envy no man the task – but the long and short of it is that you cannot have Jews – however upright and honourable – in control and hope to convince the Arabs that they are going to get a fair run. In general, a year in Palestine has made me regard the whole adventure with apprehension. We are pushing an alien and detested element into the very core of Islam, and the day may well come when we shall be faced with the alternatives of holding it there by the sword or abandoning it to its fate! The Arabs are under-dog for the moment but will bide their time and wait.

Clayton's pessimism extended even to his view of the future of the Empire:

I feel sometimes that the time will come – perhaps soon – when England will have to go for a "White" Empire policy – the Dominions & Great Britain and leave all idea of dominating "brown" peoples ("blacks" are still behind and may be ruled with safety & benefit to all concerned for some time yet). Ocean routes, open seas and no commitments in confined spaces like the

Mediterranean. That is freedom in war and the ability to take the initiative from the very outset. In peace, the same chance for all everywhere and the most energetic man of business gets the trade and economic power. Think of the freedom if we could say that, if war were to come again, we did not care a d__n for [the] Mediterranean or Suez Canal. A strong Home Fleet, Gibraltar blocked, and the Red Sea stopped from the East, and the Mediterranean stews in its own juice with Dago pulling Dago's tail to their heart's content.[60]

The views of Clayton and Bowman concerning the Palestine administration under Samuel were expressed privately. But Richmond made no attempt to keep his feelings to himself and as for Philby – refractory as ever – he vented his opinions in an angry diatribe sent to the Colonial Secretary shortly after his departure from Transjordan. Samuel, he wrote, had exhibited an attitude that has 'convinced me that it is quite impossible for a Jewish High Commissioner with Zionist enthusiasms to hold the scales even between Arab and Jew, where their interests and aspirations clash'.[61]

On June 13, 1924, Clayton wrote to Shuckburgh informing him of his decision to leave Palestine the following April. He had undoubtedly made his plans clear to Samuel earlier, perhaps even in late 1923. He would have preferred to leave sooner, in the fall of 1924, he advised Shuckburgh, but Samuel wanted him to stay on until a time near to the expiration of his own five-year term as High Commissioner in July 1925. And, Clayton noted, there had been a 'certain amount of talk recently regarding the resignations of Philby, Richmond, and others' and he had 'no desire to become an additional subject of public gossip and rumour'.[62] During his remaining ten months in Palestine, Clayton continued to work on the problems confronting the Mandate government, but he made no further effort to 'reconcile the irreconcilable' – to persuade the Arabs to accept the Zionist policy. Still, there was plenty to do. In September 1924, he and Enid made a two week trip to Syria where they toured the country and visited with the French High Commissioner, General Weygand. It was the first leave Clayton had taken since his arrival in Palestine in April 1923.

Two months later, the Claytons visited Cairo as the guest of Allenby, then still High Commissioner for Egypt. They arrived in Cairo on the morning of November 19, and immediately drove to the Residency where they joined Lord and Lady Allenby for lunch. Also in attendance was the former Prime Minister Herbert Asquith. Shortly after sitting down to lunch, the party heard a commotion in the street just outside the Residency. Suddenly, the Residency doors were thrown open and three Englishmen, covered in blood, entered. One of them had to be carried in; he was Sir Lee Stack, Sirdar and Governor-General of the Sudan. While driving through the streets of Cairo, Stack, his aide and driver had been attacked by Egyptian extremists. A bomb was thrown at the car. It did not explode, but several shots followed and Stack was hit in the hand, foot and, more seriously, in the stomach. The Governor-General was soon taken to the Anglo-American hospital where an operation was performed and a blood transfusion given. He regained consciousness on the 20th, but shortly before midnight, he died.[63] Stack's assassination came as a terrible blow to Clayton. He had followed in Stack's footsteps as Wingate's private secretary and then as Sudan Agent in Cairo. Stack had been his confidant and greatest friend in the East for a quarter century.

In London, the Cabinet went into emergency session. In Cairo, an outraged Allenby decreed a series of reprisals so severe that they caused the Foreign Office to question his judgment and precipitated a series of steps that led to the High Commissioner's resignation in 1925. In Jerusalem, Samuel wrote immediately to the Colonial Office suggesting that Clayton be appointed to succeed Stack. If Sir Herbert harboured any ill will as a result of Clayton's decision to leave Palestine, it was not reflected in his letter to Shuckburgh. 'My intimate knowledge of him during the last eighteen months,' he wrote, 'has led me to form a very high opinion of his capacity. He has the combination of caution, firmness and sound judgment which is needed in that post'. The Colonial Secretary, Leo Amery, while admitting that the Sudan appointment was 'outside the province' of his office, promptly forwarded Samuel's letter to Foreign Secretary Austen Chamberlain, the man responsible for the decision.[64] But Stack was a general and so too was Clayton. And, although neither had acted in a military capacity for several years, Chamberlain wanted a civilian to serve as the next Governor-General of the Sudan. The Cabinet agreed and, on November 24, Sir Geoffrey Archer, Governor of the Uganda Protectorate, was appointed to the top post in Khartoum.[65] Shortly before leaving Cairo, Bertie and Enid went to the British cemetery in the city to 'visit our graves', where two of their children, and now Clayton's best friend, lay buried.[66]

On December 3, Clayton returned to Jerusalem only to learn, five days later, that his mother had died on December 7. On the 14th, he and his sister Ellinor, who was then visiting Palestine, left for home, leaving Enid and the children behind in Palestine.[67] Maria Martha was 74, and had been 'somewhat of an invalid for a long time before her death'. But, as Clayton wrote to an acquaintance, 'the pain which comes from the breaking of so close a tie is none the less for that'.[68]

Clayton arrived in England on December 20, and remained for a month. On December 30 and 31, he visited the Colonial Office where he discussed the situation in Palestine with Shuckburgh, head of the Middle East Department. On one of those days, Shuckburgh – who must have been acting with the approval of Amery – asked Clayton whether he would accept the High Commissionership of Palestine if it was offered to him.[69] Almost certainly, Shuckburgh's suggestion came as no surprise to Clayton. Rumours had been afloat for some time that Samuel might resign, or even be removed. Indeed, in December 1923, the Arab Press in Palestine had come out in support of Clayton as Samuel's successor.[70] The High Commissioner had, in fact, fallen out of favour with London and even with a great many Zionists. As early as 1921, several Zionist leaders, including Weizmann, had become thoroughly disenchanted with Samuel. They thought that in making efforts to conciliate the Arabs, he had actually undermined the Zionist programme.[71] And, by the summer of 1923, the Colonial Office, and even some members of the Cabinet, had soured on Samuel, although for reasons very different from those given by the Zionists. According to

Humphrey Bowman, Shuckburgh had confided to him that Samuel's appointment had been a mistake, that the High Commissioner seemed 'to be ignorant of the real state of feeling in Palestine', and that the Arabs, while always abhorring the policy he represented, had 'now lost respect for him as a man, as they think he has been bluffing them'.[72]

If the displeasure of the Colonial Office and Cabinet sprang from Samuel's perceived ignorance of the real state of feeling in Palestine, that displeasure must be attributed in some measure to Clayton. It was Clayton's despatch, submitted to the Cabinet's Palestine Committee in July 1923, that took issue with Samuel's optimism and, at least implicitly, suggested that the High Commissioner was out of touch with Palestinian feeling. Still, Samuel persisted and both official London and the Zionists came round to the view that he should serve out his term, which was to end in July 1925. In February 1924, Weizmann – who had actively sought a replacement for Samuel in the summer of 1921 – expressed the hope that the High Commissioner would stay on for another year and, possibly, 'for another term of office'.[73] But, by the fall of 1924, it was clear that Samuel would not stay on beyond his July 1925 term-end. Who would succeed him? According to Bowman, Weizmann confided to Clayton at a dinner party in Jerusalem in October 1924, that he was going to support Clayton as the next High Commissioner. Bowman, who was apparently repeating Clayton's description of his talk with the Zionist leader, recorded Weizmann as saying 'We want an English High Commissioner, for he is the only man who can make Zionism succeed. Sir Herbert's appointment was a bad political blunder.'[74] Weizmann may have spoken those words, but no record could be found in the Colonial Office files, or in any correspondence, reflecting Weizmann's official support of Clayton as the next High Commissioner of Palestine. Certainly, Bowman and many others in the British community in Palestine, favoured Clayton's appointment: 'I can see no better choice than that of Bertie Clayton, who is deservedly popular with everyone – British, Arab and Jew. He is straight and honest . . . full of common sense and is an English gentleman'.[75]

While one might have expected Clayton's friends to support him, the most impressive endorsement came from Samuel himself, reflected in a letter to the Colonial Secretary: 'Failing a public man of exceptional position and qualities, . . no better appointment could be made than that of Sir Gilbert Clayton . . . I have the most complete confidence in his character and judgment. If he were in control here, the Secretary of State could feel easy that things would not go wrong in Palestine through any blundering or neglect . . . He has a close knowledge of people and tendencies . . . he also has an intimate knowledge of Egypt and Transjordania and a personal acquaintance with Syria. He speaks Arabic and – very necessary here – French.'[76] Leo Amery had known Clayton since early 1918, when he appeared in Egypt as a member of the Smuts Mission (Chapter 19). But the Colonial Secretary was 'not quite sure that the time has come for the good promoted official. If I were to select one of that class', he responded, 'I should, I think, agree with you in selecting Clayton, whom I have a very high opinion of and who I think is very much designated for the post after the next man, if he does not get it now'. The man Amery had in mind was Lord Plumer, the sixty-eight year old Field Marshal and veteran of the Western Front. Plumer knew little about Palestine or the Middle East, but was undoubtedly a commanding figure and Amery, in suggesting him, was 'really going . . . on my great belief in his personality'.[77] Samuel did not press the issue. He agreed that Plumer was an 'interesting' choice and that he had 'position' and 'prestige'. True, he was a little old and, until recently, his experience had been 'purely military', but he had no objection to the suggestion.[78]

Despite his suggestion of Plumer, it seems the Colonial Secretary was still considering Clayton as late as March 1925, for on the 19th of that month, he offered Plumer the Governor-Generalship of Australia. By that time, Clayton had the support of the Middle East Department, Weizmann, Samuel, the Zionists and the Arabs – a stunning consensus for such a conflicted country as Palestine.[79] But Plumer turned down Australia; he could not afford it, he said. So, in late March or early April, Amery offered Palestine to the Field Marshal and he accepted. If Clayton was disappointed, there is no indication of it in his papers. It seems, though, that had he been offered the position, he would have accepted.[80] Amery had acted alone in appointing Plumer; neither his own Middle East Department nor the Zionists were consulted.[81] Clayton, it appears, 'learned that he would not be appointed just 12 hours before Plumer's appointment was announced in *The Times*'.[82] Samuel was disappointed for Clayton and wrote to Amery asking that he speak to him soon after Clayton's return to England. '[H]is non-appointment as High Commissioner will be a distress to him, perhaps following on his not being chosen for the Sudan'.[83] On April 16, 1925, a farewell dinner was held for Clayton in Jerusalem and three days later he boarded a train for Egypt and the boat home to England. Perhaps he was disappointed in being passed over for the top spots in Khartoum and Jerusalem. But if he had any such feelings, they did not persist, for he would soon be immersed in new problems far to the south, in the deserts of Arabia.

26

Desert Diplomat: The Arabian Treaties, 1925–1926

Most people thought the old man was mad. And, if King Hussein's actions in the early 1920s were any indication, there was plenty of evidence to support that view. His rule in the Hijaz was so arbitrary, so capricious and unreasonable, that by 1919 many Hijazis were longing for a return of Turkish rule. The British could do nothing with the incorrigible old King and when his British subsidy was terminated in February 1920, they relinquished whatever leverage they had over him. True, the Foreign Office had gamely supported him in the immediate post-war years and, indeed, had gone to considerable lengths to forestall Ibn Saud's encroachments in the eastern Hijaz in 1919. But before long, Lord Curzon began to lose patience with Hussein. The Foreign Secretary was highly annoyed by his persistent mischaracterizations of McMahon's 1915 pledge; ignoring the qualifications and provisos in the correspondence, the King insisted on describing the pledge as a 'treaty' in which he had been promised the complete independence of the entire Arabian peninsula. And, quite apart from the McMahon correspondence, if the British did not meet Hussein on every point or issue he raised, his response was to threaten to 'resign' as King.[1] His threats became so regular and insistent that the exasperated Curzon soon began to hope for the King's departure from the scene. 'If only that dreadful old man really would abdicate', he scribbled at the bottom of a Foreign Office paper in 1922.[2]

Clayton, too, deplored Hussein's 'lamentable . . . mal-administration' in the Hijaz, but he also understood that the King could not be simply discarded. The reasons were provided by Clayton's former Arab Bureau colleague Kinahan Cornwallis: '[I]t must not be forgotten that he is the man whom we chose to open the Arab Revolt . . . Hussein as a personality is nothing; as a symbol of the Arab Revolt he stands for a good deal in Moslem minds & his disappearance by our agency would not only be a confession of the failure of our whole Arab policy, but it would be eagerly seized upon by our ill wishers as proof of our cynicism'.[3] Cornwallis might have added that, as guardian of the Muslim holy places of Mecca and Medina, Hussein was also responsible for the *hajj*, the annual pilgrimage to those cities. If the King was thought to have been removed from this role by the British, there might be serious repercussions throughout the Muslim world. But Hussein himself eliminated any such concerns, for his management of the *hajj* was so bad in the early 1920s, that most *hajjis* would have regarded his removal with relief. He mulcted the pilgrims of their very last piastre by imposing a staggering array of taxes, dues, charges and fees; he mismanaged the quarantine through which every *hajji* was required to pass before entering the country; and security was so bad that, in 1923, the Medina pilgrimage degenerated into chaos, as pilgrims were robbed, kidnapped and even murdered by the Bedouin. Hussein compounded these problems by mistreating the Indian *hajjis*, stopping the pilgrimage from Najd for two years (perhaps with good reason in view of the possibility of an influx of Wahhabis) and disrupting the Egyptian pilgrimage to Mecca. Naturally, he was vilified in the Muslim press in Egypt and India.[4]

In view of the many problems associated with Hussein's rule, some were perhaps surprised to learn in 1921, that the British proposed to conclude a treaty with the Hijaz. But those who were surprised by the proposal failed to understand the motive behind it. The Anglo-Hijazi treaty was not designed to secure Hussein's rule in the country. Although the British proposed to offer diplomatic assistance in the event of aggression against the Hijaz, no one wanted to promise armed assistance in the face of a Wahhabi invasion. The impetus behind the treaty was not to confirm or support Hashemite rule in the country, but rather to legitimize British rule in the Mandates. Every version of the proposed treaty contained a clause reflecting the King's acknowledgment of the Mandates. If King Hussein, descendant of the Prophet, guardian of the holy places and father of the Arab national movement, could be induced to sign a treaty reflecting his acquiescence to the Mandates, then Arab nationalists – particularly those opposed to the Palestine Mandate and its embodiment of the Jewish national home policy – might just be mollified. But the King was sane enough to understand the British purpose and would not agree. And he was consistent. He refused to ratify the Versailles Treaty or to sign the Treaty of Sèvres – the Turkish treaty – both of which incorporated the Mandate concept, and he formally protested the San Remo decisions of 1920, by which the Middle Eastern Mandates were assigned to France and Britain. Lawrence was despatched to Jeddah in July 1921 to negotiate the agreement, but Hussein proved inflexible and talks were suspended in September. Although negotiations continued intermittently until September 1924, it was clear that Hussein would never agree to the one point which provided London its only reason for the treaty – the Mandates.[5]

While Hussein's position was steadily deteriorating during the early 1920s, Ibn Saud's stock was on the rise. By 1922, he had consolidated his rule in central and eastern Arabia and his relations with Britain were generally good. His treaty relations with Britain dated back to December 1915, when he signed an agreement under which the British recognized his independent rule in Najd and certain adjacent principalities and even agreed to come to his aid in the event of aggression by a foreign Power. A small subsidy and a promise of arms were provided as added inducement. In return, Ibn Saud consented to follow British advice, to refrain from entering into agreements with, or ceding any of his territories to, any foreign Power, and to keep open the pilgrimage routes through his territories. At the same time, he agreed not to interfere in those territories on the western littoral of the Persian Gulf with whom Britain was in treaty relationship, including Kuwait, Bahrain, Qatar and the Oman coast. He did not, however, agree to take up arms against the Turks and, for the duration of the war, the Najdi ruler did nothing to aid the British war effort.[6]

By the early 1920s, London was slowly coming round to the view that the future of Arabia lay with Ibn Saud and not with his Hashemite adversary, King Hussein. It was Ibn Saud who appeared as the moderate in the ongoing dispute with Hussein over villages in the undefined region between Najd and the Hijaz. When it came to the contested villages of Khurma and Turaba, Hussein was obdurate, insisting on his right to the towns, while the Wahhabi leader appeared conciliatory and willing to negotiate. The British were sufficiently pleased with Ibn Saud that in 1920 he was awarded a British honour and officially recognized as the 'Sultan of Najd and its Dependencies'.[7] Still, the Sultan presented problems for his British overlords. He had embarked on a programme of territorial expansion in the 1920s and those tribes in the border regions of Iraq and Transjordan – some of whom were not fully under his control – often raided into territory the British regarded as subject to their Mandates. The Wahhabi raids into the Wadi Sirhan, described earlier, provided recent and palpable examples of Saudi aggrandizement. An attempt was made in May 1922 to solve the problem in the East by treaty, when Iraqi and Najdi representatives met at Muhammara at the top of the Persian Gulf. Although agreement was reached, Ibn Saud refused to ratify the treaty, asserting that his agents had exceeded their authority.[8] In fact, the Sultan was uncomfortable with the very notion of borders. For the Bedouin of Arabia, allegiance was owed to their tribe, not to any 'State', and they moved about the desert, as they had for centuries, and just as they wished. The concept of a nation-state, demarcated by fixed boundaries which could not be crossed, was a Western innovation, altogether foreign to them. But Britain had international obligations imposed by the Mandates and quite naturally insisted on drawing lines in the sand. So, in November 1922, the parties reconvened at Uqair on the Arabian shore of the Persian Gulf. The British representative was Iraq High Commissioner Sir Percy Cox, an imposing figure and a veteran of more than twenty years in the region. Before long, he lost patience with the 'childish attitude' of Ibn Saud and unilaterally defined the Iraq, Kuwait and Najd borders, reducing the Sultan to tears in the process.[9]

Although the Uqair Protocols, as they were called, defined the boundaries of Najd in the northeast, they did not bring to an end tribal raiding in the border regions of Iraq. Nor did they resolve Najd's western boundaries, those separating the Sultanate from Transjordan and the Hijaz. Those issues were addressed at yet another conference, convened at Kuwait in December 1923. Faisal and Abdullah were quick to send agents to Kuwait. But Hussein was very reluctant to send a representative to treat with the delegates of Ibn Saud and, when he did agree, he deputed his youngest son, Zaid, then still in his twenties, for the purpose. And the King effectively undermined the negotiations before they began by giving Zaid strict instructions not to negotiate unless the Najdis acknowledged his pre-1914 boundaries, which included Khurma and Turaba in the Hijaz. For his part, Ibn Saud had little incentive to negotiate with his Hashemite neighbours at all. He already possessed much of the Wadi Sirhan as well as the disputed villages. So, the Sultan conceded nothing and no one was surprised when the conference was dissolved in April 1924, without agreement.[10]

By the spring of 1924, and in the wake of the failed Kuwait Conference, Hussein had lost all support among his former British sponsors. And to many Arabs still loyal to the King, it must have seemed as if Hussein was fixed on a course of self-destruction. No better proof was available than that provided by the events of March 1924. On March 3, while Hussein was visiting Abdullah in Amman, the Turks announced the abolition of the Caliphate. Four days later, the Amir proclaimed that his father had assumed the office, in response to 'numberless telegrams of allegiance'.[11] Abduallh, it seems, was behind his father's *contretemps* and, although some Arab historians would later assert that the Amir had conceived the idea only after the Turkish announcement, and that he had to persuade a reluctant Hussein to accept the office, many recognized that a Hashemite Caliphate had been the goal of Abdullah and his father since the early years of the War.[12] A few Arabs in Syria and the Lebanon, and even some Indian Muslim leaders, recognized Hussein as the new Caliph, but most regarded his move as presumptuous, even offensive. In Jeddah, British Agent Reader Bullard, a man known more for his wit than his diplomacy, reported that the Hijazis received the news 'in dead silence', since they would 'as readily have proposed that relativity or bimetallism should become the State religion' as they would that Hussein should become Caliph.[13]

With Hussein's fortunes now at a low ebb, Ibn Saud saw his opportunity. On September 4, 1924, the Wahhabis attacked and occupied Ta'if, only 70 miles from Mecca. So far had Hussein's fortunes fallen by this point, that in London news of the Wahhabi advance was met with indifference. The Colonial Office proposed only that Ibn Saud be advised that the pilgrimage routes should be kept open and safe for British Muslim subjects, for whom the Sultan would be held responsible 'if and when Mecca was taken'.[14] The government's official position issued on October 1, when Prime Minister Ramsay MacDonald announced in Parliament that Britain would not interfere in events in the Hijaz, events which were characterized as 'religious matters'.[15] Three days later, in response to the pleas of a group of Arab notables assembled at Jeddah, Hussein, at long last, abdicated and left by ship for Akaba. On October 6, the King's eldest son, Ali, assumed the throne. But there was nothing the hapless Ali could do to stem the Wahhabi tide, which swept into Mecca in mid-October. Ibn Saud arrived in the holy city in December, where he paused and waited for the reaction of the British and, no less important, of the Muslim world.

By the time Clayton returned to England from Palestine in May 1925, Ibn Saud had swallowed up most of the Hijaz. Only Medina, Jeddah and Yanbu remained under Hashemite control and Hussein, still at Akaba, could do nothing except supply Ali with money for his beleaguered forces. Clayton, meanwhile, was in much the same position he had been after his return from Egypt three years earlier; he was without a job and no prospects appeared on the horizon. He visited the Colonial

Office in May and June and met with Amery in July, but the Colonial Secretary informed Clayton that he 'could find no post for him'.[16] He even applied for the lieutenant-governorship of Malta, but Amery had already selected a man for the post.[17] Still, Clayton kept busy, meeting with family and friends and renewing acquaintances from the East. In July, two weeks after his 50th birthday, he purchased his first automobile, a 1924 Morris Cowley 'chummy' car, and immediately took driving lessons to learn how to operate it.[18]

Although Clayton was probably unaware of the fact, in late June his name was raised in connection with another Eastern assignment. On May 28, the Cabinet's attention was drawn to an impending crisis in Arabia where 'ex-King Hussein had indulged in acts of an un-neutral character against Ibn Saud', and the men on the spot believed that the Sultan was preparing to attack Hussein at Akaba. Of course, Britain had already declared its neutrality in the Saudi–Hashemite fight, but Akaba was considered to be within the Palestine Mandate and, situated at the top of the Gulf of Akaba, it was Transjordan's only outlet to the sea. Aggression on the port could not be allowed. Although the Cabinet was prepared to negotiate with Ibn Saud for the purpose of delimiting the Najd–Transjordan boundary and settling 'all outstanding questions between himself and Transjordan and Iraq', the decision to initiate talks was delayed until the responsible government departments could further study and report on the situation.[19] A week later, a sub-committee, comprised of officials from the Colonial, Foreign and War Offices, as well as the Admiralty and Air Ministry, concluded that Hussein should be 'induced' to leave Akaba by mid-June – a step that would likely prevent a Wahhabi attack on the town – and that the local authorities should take 'any steps necessary to include Maan and Akaba' in the Palestine Mandate. These recommendations were approved by the Committee of Imperial Defence on June 22, with the additional suggestion that Amery should arrange a conference between Ibn Saud and a British emissary 'to settle all questions in dispute and particularly those connected with boundaries'. By the time the Cabinet approved those recommendations on July 1, Hussein had been persuaded to leave Akaba for Cyprus, thus removing the immediate problem.[20] But talks with Ibn Saud were still considered desirable, particularly in view of the undefined border between Najd and Transjordan.

Hubert Young of the Colonial Office, who had sat on the CID sub-committee in June, was quick to recommend Clayton as the British emissary to Arabia, just as he had proposed him for the 1922 London negotiations with Abdullah.[21] Amery readily agreed and, on July 31, 1925, Young invited Clayton to undertake the mission, noting that the Colonial Secretary wanted a man 'whose name is well known to the Arab world' to conduct the negotiations.[22] Clayton accepted the next day, adding only that he wished to be accompanied on his mission by George Antonius of the Palestine Education Department. Antonius was to prove a great asset to Clayton, joining him on five diplomatic missions to Arabia and the Yemen during the next three years and later acquiring some notoriety as the author of the first English language account by an Arab of the Arab Revolt and its aftermath, *The Arab Awakening* (1938). Born of Greek Orthodox parents in the Lebanon in 1891,

Antonius was educated at Victoria College, Alexandria and King's College, Cambridge. In 1925, he was the number two man in the Education Department, behind the director, Clayton's friend, Humphrey Bowman. In Clayton's estimation, Antonius possessed unique talents, combining 'a perfect knowledge of English and Arabic with extreme tact and trustworthiness'.[23]

In serving as 'Commissioner and Plenipotentiary', Clayton was to be paid his out-of-pocket expenses, a £30 outfit allowance and ten guineas a day for every day he was away from England on his mission – not perhaps a very generous compensation considering the rigours of late-summer negotiations in the Arabian desert, but Clayton had no quarrel with the terms.[24] In August and September he paid several visits to the Colonial Office to work out the formal instructions that would guide him in the negotiations. He also met with Foreign Office officials and, since Iraq would be a subject of negotiation, he met twice with King Faisal who was then visiting London.[25] Clayton's instructions used the failed Kuwait Conference negotiations of 1923–1924 as a template. The Kuwait talks had been concerned not only with Iraq and Transjordan, but also the Hijaz. Since the time of Kuwait, the issue of the Hijaz–Najd border had been rendered irrelevant by Ibn Saud's actions of the previous autumn; he now controlled nearly the entire country. Indeed, Clayton was officially instructed to avoid any discussion concerning the fight; Ibn Saud had declined a British offer to mediate the dispute, so Britain would stand aside and maintain an attitude of 'strict neutrality'. But Clayton was authorized to negotiate an agreement to prevent 'trans-frontier raiding between the tribes of Irak and Najd' – an issue left unresolved at Kuwait – and to settle 'claims arising from past raids'.

The main object of the talks, however, concerned the Transjordan-Najd boundary. A border had been proposed at Kuwait that conceded most of the Wadi Sirhan to Ibn Saud. But, after the Kuwait talks, British military advisers had concluded, for strategic reasons, that the village of Kaf should now be included in Transjordan; only as a 'last resort' was Clayton to concede the place to Ibn Saud. Regardless of any such concession, though, Clayton was instructed that in no event was he to assent to an extension of Najdi territory to the north, such that Transjordan would be separated from Iraq. Clayton himself probably insisted on this instruction since, as noted earlier, he was determined that the Desert Air Route must fly over British-controlled territory. Nor was he authorized to negotiate a boundary between Transjordan and the Hijaz. That would be inappropriate while the fight for the Hijaz was still underway; so, he was instructed to treat the issue as if it had already been decided – a 'chose jugée'. Britain would regard that border as already fixed, extending along a line from a point just south of Akaba, straight to the east, where it crossed the Hijaz railway.[26]

Clayton left London on September 24, and arrived at Port Said six days later. In Egypt, he met the rest of his small party – Antonius, a 'stenographer' seconded by the Palestine government for clerical work, and Taufiq Bey al-Suwaidi, an Iraqi sent from Baghdad to assist Clayton in his talks concerning the Najd and Iraq tribes. Technically, Clayton could not sign any treaty with Ibn Saud that bound Iraq; by law, all treaties had to be approved by Faisal and the Iraqi Parliament. But Clayton was assured by Faisal and by the Iraq government that he had 'full authority' and that any settlement he reached would likely be approved.[27] No Transjordanian was sent to assist Clayton, as no one could be found who would be anything more than a 'figurehead', and might even be an 'embarrassment'. In any case, Antonius was well-prepared, having made two trips to Transjordan before leaving for Egypt, during which he met with Abdullah, Henry Cox, Peake and the principal sheikhs of the Ruwalla, Bani Sakhr and Huwaytat, those tribes in eastern Transjordan most likely to be affected by any settlement involving the Wadi Sirhan.[28]

Clayton was to have travelled by ship from Suez to Jeddah, but the Admiralty declined to spend the £300 required for his transport. So, the party journeyed by train and Nile steamer from Cairo to Atbara in the Sudan where they changed for Port Sudan and the fifteen hour voyage across the Red Sea to Jeddah. Along the last stretch of rail to Atbara, Clayton passed Darmali and his mind ranged back to 1898, when he saw the 'little mud hut in which we had our mess still standing' and recalled that suffocatingly hot summer when he and his fellows in the Artillery waited for their advance on Omdurman to begin.[29] The party arrived in Jeddah on October 9, and, on the same day, Clayton had two formal and rather uncomfortable interviews with a disconsolate King Ali. With the Wahhabis poised only two miles outside Jeddah and Clayton explaining that his mission was 'in no way concerned with the Hejaz-Najd struggle', Ali certainly knew that his days in the Hijaz were numbered.

Passing through to the Wahhabi lines the next morning, the party was conveyed in the Sultan's cars to Bahra, a ruined village mid-way between Mecca and Jeddah. About two miles from Bahra, Ibn Saud had erected a large tent camp, where the talks were to be held. Clayton was provided a spacious tent, carpeted with rugs and 'containing a good writing table, several cane-bottomed armchairs and a camp bed'. Nearby, a reception tent had been put up, 'quite a gorgeous affair, highly decorated and equipped with a large table and a number of gilt armchairs upholstered in red satin'. Soon after their arrival, the Clayton party was visited by the 'Shaikh ash-Shuyukh', the 'sheikh of sheikhs', 'Abdul al-'Aziz al Rahman al Sa'ud, known generally as Ibn Saud. Clayton found the Sultan a 'striking and commanding figure'. 'Well over six feet' and 'strongly built', he had a 'clean-cut handsome face, with a sallow, but not dark, complexion', which was 'in repose rather sad, even at times sulky'. But his face 'lit up attractively' when he smiled.[30]

Formal negotiations opened on October 11, and Clayton raised the most difficult issue first – Transjordan. It 'proved a tough nut to crack'. Unlike the negotiations at Uqair three years earlier, when the Sultan had capitulated in the face of Percy Cox's temper, Ibn Saud was now 'somewhat exalted and very much more difficult to deal with' as a result of his recent successes in the Hijaz. He appeared to Clayton 'obstinate and self-willed', and it soon became apparent that Kaf, the small village in the Wadi Sirhan, was the critical point for Ibn Saud. He was inflexible; Kaf must be included in his domains. And, he wanted territory to the west of Wadi Sirhan, including four east-west running wadis that debouched into the larger valley of the Wadi Sirhan. Although his instructions stated that he was to concede the village only as a 'last resort', Clayton himself regarded the place as insignificant. When acting as Chief Secretary in 1923–24, it will be recalled, he had downplayed its significance and even ordered the withdrawal of the Kaf garrison in 1924. Still, he recognized that it was 'practically the only card' he had 'up his sleeve' and he had to be very careful how he used it.[31] As for Ibn Saud's desire to drive a wedge of Najdi territory to the north, between Transjordan and Iraq, and right up to the Syrian frontier, Clayton informed the Sultan during their first meeting that his instructions left him no discretion: there would be no separation between the British Mandated territories.[32]

Much of the difficulty in the initial talks came in the form of the Sultan's two advisers, Sheikhs Hafiz Wahba and Yusuf Yasin. For Clayton, these men represented 'the familiar type of "pinch-beck" oriental politician whose methods consist in arguing every small point, employing a certain amount of low-cunning, and resorting at all times to a policy of consistent obstruction'. Both men were deeply distrustful of British intentions. Wahba, an Egyptian, had succeeded during the last decade in being deported by the British from Egypt, then India, and, finally, from Bahrain, before landing in Riyadh. Yasin was a Syrian nationalist, equally suspicious of the British envoy. Clayton partly solved the problem of the obstructionist sheikhs by deputing Antonius to meet with them daily, during which they argued details, while he and the Sultan discussed matters of principle in a generally more amicable atmosphere.

By October 14, it was apparent that no progress was being made on the Transjordanian front, so Clayton abruptly dropped the subject and turned the discussions to Iraq. The negotiations concerning Iraq should have proved much less difficult than those posed by the Transjordan border. Percy Cox had, after all, drawn the Iraq–Najd boundary in 1922. And the failed Kuwait discussions of 1923–24 had resulted in preliminary agreement regarding the persistent issue of cross-border raiding; it was established at Kuwait that tribes raiding the territory of another government must be punished and that the armed forces of one country should not pursue refugees across the Najd–Iraq frontier into the other, except by mutual agreement. Yet, at Bahra, the negotiators soon reached an impasse over the issue of tribal extradition. Ibn Saud was adamant that any tribe that raided in either Najd or Iraq, and then crossed the border to seek refuge in the other country, must be extradited. Clayton was equally insistent that Iraq would not abandon the principle of political asylum; only in the case of 'common criminals' would he concede the right of extradition.[33] Clayton's typical negotiating style reflected a combination of 'firmness and spirit-breaking patience', but on the extradition issue he 'had to come down pretty heavily with both feet'. He candidly told the Sultan that his position was 'exceedingly unreasonable' and that he could not see why Ibn Saud 'should obstinately maintain his attitude and refuse to consider anything that did not give him everything he wanted'. He bluntly gave the Wahhabi leader a 'choice between an abatement of his demands and a rupture' in the negotiations, adding that he would prepare a draft agreement rejecting the concept of tribal extradition which Ibn Saud could accept or reject as he chose. This approach was successful and the Sultan gave way during the third day of talks on Iraq on October 21.[34]

The Iraq–Najd treaty, known as the Bahra Agreement, was signed on November 2, 1925. The Agreement reaffirmed the Muhammara Convention and the Uqair Protocols of 1922, and regulated the movement and activities of the border tribes. Tribal cross-border movements were allowed only after permits had been secured; raiding was to be severely punished by the government in whose jurisdiction the offending tribe resided; and a special tribunal was to be established for the resolution of any claims arising from raids. And, as tentatively agreed at Kuwait, the parties affirmed that the forces of Iraq and Najd would not be allowed to cross the frontier in pursuit of offenders, except with the consent of the other government. This last clause would prove to be a source of dispute during Clayton's 1928 negotiations with Ibn Saud. Regarding extradition, the parties agreed to 'initiate friendly discussions' in the future, but only 'in accordance with the usage prevailing among friendly States', a clause intended by Clayton to preclude the wholesale extradition of tribes seeking asylum in either Iraq or Najd, as Ibn Saud had previously insisted.[35] One issue described in Clayton's instructions that the parties could not resolve concerned the restoration of loot and the payment of compensation as damages for past cross-border raids. Clayton and Ibn Saud could only exchange letters 'laying down the principles and the procedure' for resolving compensation and restoration issues because, much to Clayton's surprise and annoyance, al-Suwaidi did not possess the detailed information required to reach agreement on the issue.[36]

By the time agreement was reached on Iraq, Clayton had been at the Bahra camp for eleven days and the conditions were beginning to wear on him. It was 'villainously hot', with mid-day temperatures consistently around 112° F, and reaching 115° on some days. And soon the flies appeared, in swarms, and increased 'day by day' as the camp got 'more fouled'. Ibn Saud also insisted that the party 'should be his guests as regards food', so Clayton ate only Arab fare, which he found 'somewhat disturbing to the internal economy of the average European'. And, as the Bahra camp was isolated and there was nowhere to go and nothing to do outside the business at hand, the daily routine soon developed into a 'monotonous regularity'. Clayton rose at 5:00, well before dawn, when a servant brought him a bowl of fresh camel's milk. At the first glimmer of light, the *muezzin's* plaintive call to prayer echoed throughout the camp and, at 6:15, he took a cup of tea and a biscuit as he read or wrote for a bit before shaving, bathing and dressing. At 8:00 breakfast appeared – 'three diminutive Hejaz eggs, lightly boiled', served with bread, cheese and a 'preserved apple from Taif'. From 9 until 11, Clayton met with Ibn Saud and often with his two advisers, Wahba and Yasin, whom Clayton and Antonius had now begun to describe as 'the Vultures'. Then, at noon, Clayton performed 'an important ceremony' consisting of a 'split gin and tonic water' downed in the seclusion of his tent. As alcohol and tobacco were strictly forbidden by the Wahhabis, cigarettes, the noon-time gin and tonic and an evening whiskey and soda all had to be consumed in Clayton's tent, making him 'feel rather like a schoolboy who is breaking the rules'. At 12:30, the party enjoyed a lunch which, when the cook learned what Clayton liked, soon became a fixed menu – soup, chicken, a *bamiya* (a kind of gumbo thickened with unripe okra pods) with small pieces of meat in it, onions and gherkins, rice, a sweet, bananas and pomegranates and unsweetened Arab coffee. After lunch, the party worked, read or even napped – if sleep was possible in the stifling heat – until 3:30, when Antonius went off to spar with the Vultures for a couple of hours. At 5:30 every day Antonius and Clayton took their daily walk, escorted by a fully armed Arab slave. After his evening whiskey and soda – 'The Bahra Cocktail' – Clayton bathed and changed and then had a 'private and informal talk' with the Sultan for an hour or so, which was followed by dinner, 'a repetition of lunch', and then, 'at a decent interval', by bed and sleep'.[37]

Clayton's monotonous routine was broken only by Ibn Saud's occasional visits to Mecca, some twenty miles from Bahra, and by an unfortunate run-in with two Arabs on October 25. On that day, Clayton and Antonius were taking their usual afternoon stroll, when they passed between two Arab tents about 100 yards apart. '[I]mmediately out came two fanatical looking Arabs who began gesticulating and obviously cursing us roundly as dogs of Christians'. Clayton's escort was able to calm the irate Wahhabis, but the incident was reported to Ibn Saud who, despite Clayton's intervention on behalf of the Arabs, was furious that his guests had been insulted and that the famous Arab hospitality had been breached. The offenders 'were each given thirty lashes in the Sultan's presence and then sent straight off to prison in Mecca that very night'.[38]

On the evening of October 21, Clayton turned the discussions back to Transjordan and the boundary issue. He began by putting Ibn Saud on the defensive, complaining to the Sultan that 'every point of importance which I had raised had been hotly debated, and I had noticed a tendency to introduce into our discussions an atmosphere of contention and bargaining on every point'.[39] Undeterred, Ibn Saud returned to his earlier arguments, insisting that all of the Wadi Sirhan, as well as the four east-west running wadis, be included in his domains. And, even more frustrating, he persisted in his claim to an extension of Najdi territory up to the Syrian border, a point which Clayton had told him earlier, and definitively, was not open for discussion. Clayton's diary during this period discloses his growing frustration with the Sultan, as his entries are peppered with such adjectives as 'obstinate', 'uncompromising', 'obdurate' and 'stubborn'.

By October 24, Clayton had become convinced that 'no form of persuasion would induce Ibn Sa'ud to voluntarily give up Kaf'. He had been given discretion to concede the village to the Sultan and he now decided to exercise that discretion in the form of a draft agreement which he gave to Ibn Saud the following day. Clayton understood that he might well have been able to arbitrarily dictate the boundary, much as Percy Cox had done at Uqair in 1922, for Iraq. But he was not inclined to take such an approach because he believed that 'even if successful in securing the desired object, [this] would leave a sore which must neutralize to a great extent the benefits to accrue from the agreement which it was my mission to conclude'.[40] So, he conceded Kaf, and the Wadi Sirhan south of the village, to Ibn Saud in return for a Wahhabi guarantee of non-agression and a concession that the four east-west running wadis would remain in Transjordan. Although the Sultan continued to argue strongly for a northern corridor to Syria on the 26th and 27th, Clayton repeated that there would be no such concession and, on both days, he threatened to break off negotiations if Ibn Saud did not relent. The best that Clayton could offer was that Najdi trading caravans could be given 'certain restricted facilities of transit into and from Syrian territory'. That proved to be enough and, after two more days of squabbling over details between Antonius and the Vultures, agreement was reached on October 29, and the Transjordan treaty, called the Hadda Agreement, was signed on November 2.[41] The frontier delimited in the Hadda Agreement, which shows the large indentation in Transjordan's eastern boundary is the same as that which, with minor alterations, defines the Jordan-Saudi Arabia border today. And, as Clayton had insisted, Jordan and Iraq still maintain a common border.

Their negotiations now concluded, on November 1, Ibn Saud entertained the Clayton party at a great banquet at which Clayton recorded, 'we ate with our fingers in true Bedouin style'.[42] Before leaving Bahra on November 3, Clayton was also given several presents by the Sultan, including rugs, Bedouin clothing, an Arabian mare – which he had no idea what to do with – 'two daggers and two beautiful Arab swords, richly mounted in gold'.[43] The next day, Clayton returned to Jeddah where he wired the basic terms of his two treaties to the Colonial Office. Both Amery and Foreign Secretary Austen Chamberlain were pleased with the results and cabled Clayton their warm congratulations on the successful completion of his mission.[44] For his part, Clayton was quick to credit others with his success; in his official report, he observed that 'the results achieved by my Mission are due in a large measure to the tact and firmness' displayed by Antonius in his talks with the Sultan's advisers.[45]

On his return journey, Clayton again travelled via the Sudan, making only a short two day diversion to Khartoum where, he noted in his dairy, he renewed many old acquaintances from his Sudan days and 'the ghosts of Sir Reginald and Lady Wingate confronted me at every turn'.[46] By November 15, he was back in Cairo, writing up the detailed report of his mission. And, he found time during his week in Egypt to meet with the Egyptian Prime Minister, Ziwar Pasha, and with King Fu'ad, whom he found 'coquetting with the idea of becoming Caliph', a notion that Clayton thought was likely to land the King 'in serious trouble'. He also met with the Financial Adviser in his continuing, and ultimately successful, effort to secure 'pension terms for my widow'.[47]

Clayton's plan on leaving Egypt was to travel to Jerusalem, where he would explain the Hadda Agreement to Plumer, and to Abdullah at Amman, and then to Baghdad to secure approval of the Bahra Agreement by Faisal and the Iraqi government. These plans were sanctioned by London on November 18, in a telegram which also included an unexpected request: Would Clayton be willing to undertake 'another negotiation' while still in the Middle East? The subject was the Yemen, the territory just north of the Aden Protectorate in the southwest corner of the Arabian peninsula. The country's ruler, Imam Yahya, had been causing trouble for the British for years and was now 'actively, if not openly, encouraging his followers to encroach upon the Aden Protectorate' to the south. The British had been trying unsuccessfully for the last three years to conclude a treaty with the Imam who had recently requested that a British envoy be sent to his capital, Sanaa, to, in Amery's words, 'clear up the few outstanding points' preliminary to a formal treaty. Clayton replied on November 20 that he was 'ready to undertake mission to Yemen'. He would have preferred, he added, to discuss the Yemen situation and his instructions in London, but he was willing to proceed direct to Aden after his visit to Baghdad. And he again requested that Antonius, who 'was largely instrumental in [the] successful result with Ibn Saud', accompany him to Sanaa.[48]

Clayton left Cairo on November 22, but not before driving to the British cemetery to visit 'our little graves', where his children Thomas and Jane lay buried. The next day he arrived in Jerusalem where he met 'countless friends' and enjoyed the 'wonderfully home-like atmosphere'. He was particularly pleased by the many enquiries made by his Arab friends about Enid, Sabria (Patience), Sami (Samuel) and Yahya (John). That evening he attended the opening night of the opera, where he was the subject of a 'gratifying although somewhat embarrassing' incident. At the end of the second act, someone saw him, shouted his name, 'and the whole house rose and cheered and clapped', a fitting tribute perhaps for a man whose honesty, impartiality and sense of fair play transcended political division.[49] Having explained his treaties to the Palestine authorities and secured the services of Antonius for the Yemen mission, Clayton was off to Amman on November 28. There he met Abdullah who was 'very friendly and cordial as usual', but was 'not pleased with the terms' of the Hadda Agreement, which did not meet 'his very extravagant aspirations'. However, Clayton added, 'he took it all in good spirit'.

The next morning Clayton motored twelve miles south to Ziza where he and Antonius boarded a Vickers Vernon aircraft for the seven hour flight to Baghdad. It was Clayton's first flight over the Desert Air Route, which he had secured for Britain during his recent negotiations. Owing to a leaking radiator, they were forced down after 'six hours of continuous flying' at Landing Ground No. 1, twenty miles short of Ramadi on the Euphrates, but managed to reach Baghdad the next morning. As in Palestine, Clayton was welcomed by many old acquaintances, British and Arab alike. Iltyd was still training the Iraqi army and Bertie was pleased to join his brother at a dinner attended by several old friends, among them, Kinahan Cornwallis, now advising King Faisal, Colonel Pierce Joyce, his liaison with the Arabs during the 1916–18 Revolt, and Gertrude Bell, whom Clayton had sent to Basra in 1916 as his Arab Bureau correspondent in Mesopotamia. Bell was quite taken with 'Bertie the Peacemaker', as she described him in a letter to her father. He 'is one of the cleverest of men', 'quite enchanting . . . one of the nicest people I have ever met'.[50] Unlike his brother Abdullah, King Faisal was 'well pleased' with the results of Clayton's treaty-making. And the Prime Minister, Abd al-Muhsin al-Sa'dun, and War Minister, Nuri Pasha al-Said – Clayton's 'old friend' from the Arab Revolt – were equally satisfied with the Bahra Agreement. On December 3, Clayton formally presented the treaty to the Iraqi Council of Ministers, which promptly passed a resolution thanking him for his services.[51]

Having agreed to take on the Yemen negotiations, Clayton decided to travel from Baghdad to Bombay where he would review the Government of India's records concerning the Yemen and the Aden Protectorate and hopefully secure the 'sympathy and assistance' of the Indian authorities.[52] He and Antonius left Baghdad on December 4, and arrived in Bombay eight days later. Although he was able to review some files concerning the Yemen at Bombay, most of the documents relating to prior negotiations with the Imam were kept at Aden, as the Political Resident there, General Sir John Stewart, advised Clayton by cable that he dealt with 'all political matters in [the] Aden sphere directly under orders of the Colonial Office'. At the same time, Stewart informed him that, contrary to the Colonial Office view, he feared the negotiations would be 'far from an easy task'. Clayton was also annoyed to learn that the dates for his talks with the Imam had not yet been fixed. He was 'certainly not going to hang about Aden awaiting the Imam's convenience. It would be most undignified'. So, he delayed his departure from India for a week. Meanwhile, the cables he was receiving from Aden were beginning to make Clayton feel uneasy about his new assignment, as he confided to his diary: 'I don't feel very happy about this mission. I am afraid that the Colonial Office have rather rushed into it, and that the actual situation may be the reverse of favourable. If that is the case, I shall inform the Colonial Office and urge that negotiations be postponed indefinitely rather than court undignified failure'.[53]

With an extra week at their disposal, Antonius and Clayton decided to spend their time in Delhi, which they reached by train on December 17. Although he met with Sir Denys Bray, Foreign Secretary of the Government of India, and had 'a long talk with the Military Intelligence people', most of Clayton's time in Delhi was spent sightseeing. He also found time to make a short trip to Agra, where he visited 'the glorious Taj Mahal'.[54] But he was back in Bombay on December 24 and, two days later, sailed for Aden, regretting only that he had missed spending Christmas with Enid and the children. On December 30, Clayton, Antonius and an Indian stenographer fluent in Arabic, arrived at Aden.

When he put in at Aden at the end of 1925, Clayton was arriving at a port with more than 300 hundred years of British history. An East India Company ship had first dropped anchor in Aden harbour in 1609. And for the next two hundred years Company merchants made handsome profits in the Mocha coffee trade, as British trade expanded into the Yemeni hinterland above Aden. By the nineteenth century, though, the coffee trade was in decline and Aden would have become little more than a footnote in Imperial history if not for the introduction of the steamship and the consequent need to develop coaling stations along the route to India and the East. In 1839, the Indian Navy took over the port and, when the Suez Canal opened in 1869, Aden quickly gained added importance as a critical link in Imperial communications. The Red Sea, now book-ended by strong installations at Suez in the North and Aden in the South, was effectively transformed into a British lake.

The Turks, of course, had their own interests in southwest Arabia and, from the 1860s, had been engaged in a programme calculated to subjugate the Yemeni tribes to the Sultan's control. Inevitably, British and Ottoman interests collided and, largely in order to forestall a Turkish advance to the south towards Aden, in 1839, Britain began entering into a series of treaties with the tribes in the regions to the north of Aden – some two dozen of them by 1904 – all designed to ensure loyalty to the Crown in return for protection against foreign, that is, Ottoman, incursions. Whatever wisdom lay behind these treaties, they did not lessen the likelihood of conflict between Britain and the Ottoman Empire; to the contrary, they increased it. And so, it was with some relief that an Anglo-Turkish commission was able to work out a boundary between the Aden Protectorate and the Yemen in 1904–5. One man who did not recognize the border of the Aden Protectorate, however, was the Imam, Yahya Muhammad Hamid al-Din, leader of the Zaydis, a Shiite sect that controlled the highlands of the interior. The Zaydis had exercised authority in this territory for centuries and, indeed, had been fighting the Turks, off and on, since the 1860s. The region had proved so troublesome for the Ottomans that Yemen soon became known as 'the graveyard of the Turks'.[55]

Eventually, the Turks were able to sign an agreement with the Imam in 1911, which, if nothing else, ensured that during the War he would not be brought over to the British side, as had his neighbour to the North, the Idrisi of 'Asir. Yahya did not actively assist the Turks during the War, but neither did he hinder them when they moved some 14,000 troops south across the Aden Protectorate frontier in 1915. Eventually, the Turks captured Lahej, only twenty miles from Aden, and had moved even further south before they were repulsed by British Indian forces. After the 1918 Armistice, the Turks withdrew from the Yemen but the Turkish void was filled by the Imam who sent government officials and elements of his own forces into the Protectorate, into areas which he considered the Zaydis had historic rights. The British were naturally disturbed by Yahya's action, not so much because he posed an immediate threat to Aden, but because the tribes under British protection had been brought unwillingly under the Imam's control and he refused to acknowledge the 1904 Convention defining the Protectorate boundary. The expense of a military expedition to such a remote corner of the world could not even be considered with Britain groaning under the burden of a staggering war debt. And the cheaper alternative of aerial bombardment, employed most recently in 1925, had yielded only temporary and unsatisfactory results. Thus, a negotiated approach to the problem posed by the Imam seemed the only viable solution. Correspondence was exchanged. Draft treaties were sent, most recently by the British in August 1924. But no agreement had been reached and none appeared likely without a personal meeting with the Imam himself. Such was the situation when Clayton arrived at Aden at the end of 1925.

If Clayton was uneasy about his mission, the Colonial Office's instructions, received at Aden shortly before his arrival, did nothing to alleviate his concerns. In a one page telegram, he was instructed to secure the Imam's agreement to the August 1924 draft treaty and to make 'quite clear' to the Yemeni leader that Britain had 'no intention of making any concession with regard to [the] Aden Protectorate boundary'. Withdrawal of the Imam's troops from the Protectorate would not be a prerequisite to signature, but was stated to be a 'necessary corollary' of the treaty.[56] Clayton saw two fundamental problems with London's instructions. First, the Imam was not party to the 1904 Anglo-Turkish convention demarcating the Protectorate boundary. He did not recognize it. Nor did he or his predecessors recognize Britain's treaties with those tribes located within the Protectorate. From Yahya's point of view, the Imamate had exercised suzerainty over those tribes for centuries and the British had been infringing on *his* authority. Therefore, in order to induce the Imam to relinquish his historic claim to these lands and the tribes that inhabited them, Britain would have to offer something in return, a quid pro quo. This presented the second problem with the instructions – Britain had nothing to offer. The 1924 draft treaty was predicated on the notion that Yahya would be offered the port of Hudaydah, an important outlet to the Red Sea, then held by the Imam's enemy, the Idrisi of 'Asir. If Britain could induce the Idrisi to relinquish the port, the Imam might, in turn, accept Hudaydah as a quid pro quo for his withdrawal from the Protectorate and his acknowledgment of the boundary. The proposal might have been sound had not the Imam himself taken the port in 1925.[57] Nor could Clayton purchase Yahya's agreement, for the British Cabinet had had enough of paying Arab rulers and eliminated all Arabian subsidies in 1924. Further, any threat Clayton might make of military action against the Yemen was sure to be seen as an empty one because the Imam had been in possession of Protectorate territory since 1919 and, apart from an occasional dropped bomb, no such action had been taken by Britain.

With all these points in mind, Clayton had come to the conclusion even before he left for Sanaa that his task 'involved considerably more than the mere "clearing up of a few outstanding points" [as] envisaged' in the Colonial Office telegram inviting him to undertake the negotiations.[58] In view of his unrealistic instructions, and the current reality of Yahya's position, Clayton found himself 'in the position . . . of having to face the Imam with what amounts to an ultimatum in regard to the question of the Protectorate boundary without being able to offer any compensating advantage'.[59] Perhaps Clayton should have suggested a postponement of the talks and a reconsideration of his instructions, as he had considered doing earlier. Yet, despite his serious reservations, he did not. He spent the next twelve days at Aden carefully preparing for the negotiations, reviewing documents and compiling detailed lists of the Aden Protectorate's tribes and the territories occupied by the Imam.

On January 12, 1926, Clayton left Aden by ship, sailing round the southwest corner of the Arabian peninsula and north into the Red Sea. After putting in at Perim and Kamaran Island, the party arrived at Hudaydah on January 17, and left the next morning for Sanaa. Travel by car was possible for only two hours to the village of Bajil, where the party met their forty-four man Yemeni escort and the mules and camels that would convey them on their 170 mile journey east to Sanaa. The Yemen presented a very different landscape from that confronted by Clayton in the Hijaz. The territory was mountainous – at one point the party traversed a pass at 9,400 feet – and the lower elevations were cultivated, the hills having been terraced to support the coffee, wheat and barley crops grown in the region. The nights were bitterly cold and Clayton and his companions often had to sleep in the open in the sparsely populated region between the coast and the high plateau on which Sanaa was situated. In some places the terrain was so difficult they all had to dismount and walk their animals. But, after a week of vigorous trekking, the party at last reached the Imam's capital at Sanaa, arriving on January 24.[60] Two days later, Clayton met the Imam, a man 'of middle height and rather inclined to stoutness, rather dark in complexion, with a small beard trimmed in the usual Arab style'. 'He speaks a little thickly', Clayton added, 'as if his tongue was slightly too large for his mouth. His face is rather full, but not fat, and he has, as is usual with Arabs, a nice smile which lights up his face and gives it a very pleasant expression'. Yet, 'in spite of his pleasant manner', Yahya gave 'the impression of being very obstinate and tenacious'.[61]

Clayton's initial impression of the Imam was correct. 'He came straight to the point and put his case frankly', and Yahya's case was that he did not recognize either the Anglo-Turkish convention defining the Aden Protectorate boundary or Britain's treaties with the tribes in the Aden hinterland. So, he would not evacuate those regions within the Protectorate that he occupied and would not relinquish his sovereignty over the tribes within them. During the next twenty-four days Clayton employed every technique he had used with Ibn Saud five months earlier in an attempt to move the Imam. He used Antonius to meet with Yahya's subordinates concerning details of the proposed treaty; he deferred discussion on critical points in the hope of resolving differences on minor ones; he presented treaty drafts for the purpose of isolating points of difference; he made oblique threats of military action and stressed the isolated position of the Yemen, surrounded by the British in the south and west and a hostile Ibn Saud and Idrisi in the north and east; he presented the Yemenis with an ultimatum – agree or risk Britain's displeasure. Nothing worked.

By February 9, Clayton had come to the conclusion that he now faced an uncomfortable choice: He could insist on the Imam's agreement to the August 1924 draft treaty, as the Colonial Office had instructed, 'thereby closing the door on further discussion', or he could exceed his instructions 'by modifying the draft to suit the existing circumstances'. The second option was dangerous, for even if Clayton succeeded, at best, London might repudiate any agreement reached that was inconsistent with his instructions and, at worst, his own future in government service might be imperilled by what could be regarded as rank insubordination. Yet, in his subsequent report on the mission, Clayton boldly admitted that he 'had no hesitation in taking the responsibility' for departing from his instructions.[62] The next day he produced a draft which stated that the Imam would recognize Britain's treaties with the tribes, prevent armed incursion across the frontier laid down in 1904, and refrain from interfering with the tribes residing on the Aden side of that boundary. In return – and this represented the departure from his instructions – Britain would defer ultimate settlement of the Imam's claims to lands lying within the present boundary of the Protectorate which would form the subject of later, 'friendly negotiation' between the parties.[63] Still, even this approach was unsuccessful; four days later the Imam produced a counter-draft that 'was entirely unacceptable in almost every way and leaves us further from a settlement than when we began'.[64]

Adding to the frustration of the negotiations was the deteriorating condition of the mission. The Indian clerk fell ill with malaria and Antonius went down with fever for a full week. Clayton, too, was feeling poorly, troubled by lumbago which, at one point, was so painful that he could scarcely walk and which confined him to bed for two days. He also admitted to feeling uneasy at Sanaa, a 'place which seems so peculiarly remote and unreal and gives one the impression of living in a rather unpleasant dream'. His movements were not so restricted as they had been at Bahra; he was able to walk about the city, including the Jewish quarter, which had existed at Sanaa since pre-Islamic times, but his unease could not be dispelled. More out of boredom than as a panacea for his back pain, Clayton even sampled *qat*, a leaf commonly chewed in the Yemen that produced a mildly narcotic effect on the consumer. But it had 'no sort of effect' on him, apart from producing a bad taste in his mouth for the remainder of the day.[65]

By February 17, Clayton was convinced that no agreement with the Imam was possible. Yahya refused to recognize the Protectorate boundary or to evacuate any district within the Protectorate he now occupied. Clayton believed that the Imam desired a treaty with Britain, but was constrained by a 'considerable and powerful public opinion in his country' that held a 'deeply ingrained belief . . . that the Aden Protectorate was an integral part of the Yemen'.[66] There was some evidence to support this opinion, for Clayton learned secretly that a 'large meeting of notables' was held on the 17th and that 'the majority were against having any treaty at all'. Still, he was 'not sorry on the whole' that the negotiations had failed, 'as a definite break is better than an unsatisfactory agreement'.[67] Clayton had tried his best. 'I strained my instructions to the limit', he explained in his report, 'indeed, I may perhaps be held to have gone too far'. But, he added, 'bearing in mind the change which has taken place in the situation since the Draft Treaty of August 1924, was drawn up, it was impossible to negotiate any treaty strictly on those lines'.[68]

Clayton had little to offer in the way of recommendations for dealing with Yahya now that negotiations had failed. He believed that the Imam 'would not offer very obstinate resistance to measures for his forcible expulsion' from Protectorate territory, 'provided he was convinced that His Majesty's Government were determined to carry the matter through and had provided the means . . . to do so'. But he also understood that the British Government would likely find it 'impossible to undertake military operations on the scale which would be required'. He could suggest only as a 'not very satisfactory' alternative that Aden be supplied with additional aircraft to repel any further encroachment by the Imam's forces on the Protectorate. This was, in fact, the policy followed in Aden until Saudi forces began pushing into Yemen from the north in the early 1930s and the Imam, facing opponents north and south, finally concluded a pact with the British, the Treaty of Sanaa, in February 1934.[69]

On February 21, 1926, Clayton and his party finally left Sanaa. Travelling south through the mountains to Ibb, Ta'izz and Lahej, the party again spent several nights in the open and Clayton soon developed 'a rousing catarrh', fever, and a 'slight touch of pleurisy' which he attributed to the dust and the cold night air. Arriving in Aden on March 3, Clayton spent a week at the port during which he recovered and began writing up his report of the mission. It was with considerable relief when he, at last, boarded ship for home on March 10. Arriving in England ten days later, he was 'glad-dened by the sight of dear Enid on the platform' of London's Victoria Station. But, by this time he was so sick with another 'go of malaria' that Enid took him straight to a London hospital, where he 'tumbled gratefully into a clean, comfortable bed'. His 'very interesting and rather arduous trip' to the East had lasted just three days short of six months.[70]

27

Rome and Jeddah: Eastern Diplomacy, 1927–1928

Thirty years of Eastern service had taken a toll on Clayton. Less than two months after his 'go of malaria' he was back in hospital with bronchitis, this time for a fortnight, during which he endured an operation on his nose intended to remedy his chronic bronchial problems. In July 1926, he was again suffering from catarrh, for which he was subjected to a series of inoculations. And, throughout 1926–27, he paid many visits to a London physician for his painful lumbago.[1] Perhaps because of his health problems, by the spring of 1926, Clayton may have been contemplating an end to his Middle Eastern career. In April, he bought a small house, 'Apple Porch', at Peaslake, near Guildford, for £1,200, and took possession in early June. 'It's quite a nice little cottage', his sister-in-law Florence recorded in her diary, 'but I shouldn't like to live in [such] tiny rooms'.[2] All the Clayton children were enrolled in schools now, as John, not yet six, had begun receiving instruction at a local vicarage, and perhaps Bertie and Enid were also reluctant to disrupt their schooling by another foreign posting. And, by this time, Clayton had achieved some public notoriety that might lead to work in England. As a recognized authority on Egypt, Palestine and Arabia, he began delivering lectures on those countries to local associations, the Central Asian Society and the (now Royal) Institute of International Affairs, where, at one meeting, he occupied the chair for a discussion on 'the present position in Egypt'.[3]

Although no full-time position in the East would be offered to him for the next two years, Clayton was certainly held in high regard by those concerned with Middle Eastern affairs and his past services were well-recognized. In April 1926, he was honoured to receive an invitation to spend a night at Windsor Castle where he had 'half an hours interview with the King before dinner' and afterwards sat next to the Queen at a 'cinema show'.[4] Two months later, the Colonial Office delivered a letter to the King's Private Secretary, Lord Stamfordham, containing the request of Amery, who was 'very anxious' to recommend Clayton for another honour, the KCMG, Knight Commander of the Order of St Michael and St George. This knighthood, bestowed for distinguished service overseas, or in connection with foreign affairs, was intended, in Clayton's case, to recognize his recent work in Arabia and the Yemen. However, Amery made the recommendation at a time very near to the date on which the King's Birthday Honours List was to be published; the Colonial and Foreign Offices, it seems, had been unable to decide until the last moment which office should recommend Clayton for the honour – a curious example of the divided control over Middle East decision-making that still prevailed in Whitehall. The King's official approval could not be secured in time, but Stanfordham took it upon himself to telephone the Colonial Office, telling them he was 'sure the King will grant informal approval of the proposed honour to Sir Gilbert Clayton, especially as I know His Majesty thinks well of Sir Gilbert'.[5] The next day, the King did approve and, on July 12, 1926, Sir Gilbert was invested by His Majesty with the KCMG at Buckingham Palace.

Although Clayton now held no official position in government service, anyone working at the Colonial or Foreign Offices might have thought otherwise, so often did he appear in Whitehall in 1926. Two issues had been raised by his 1925–26 negotiations at Bahra and Sanaa and both engaged the Eastern Department of the Foreign Office and the Colonial Office's Middle East Department. The first had been broached by Ibn Saud during a discussion with Clayton at Bahra on November 1, 1925. The Sultan was anxious for a new treaty with Britain; the terms of the 1915 agreement were out-of-date, he argued, in view of the events of the last decade. Clayton had declined to discuss a new treaty at Bahra. That would be inappropriate, he said, and inconsistent with Britain's declaration of 'strict neutrality' during the ongoing fight for supremacy in the Hijaz.[6] But, since the time of the 1925 negotiations, Ibn Saud had taken all of the Hijaz. Jeddah had surrendered on December 22, 1925, and King Ali abdicated and left the country the next day. On January 10, 1926, the Sultan was formally proclaimed King of the Hijaz.[7] The Colonial Office, however, was not particularly enthused about a new Saudi treaty, as it was thought there was little to gain from the new King: '[S]o long as he does not interfere with our pilgrims and refrains from encroaching upon areas for which we are responsible, or embarrassing us in the discharge of our mandatory duties, we want nothing from him'.[8] Still, they were prepared to consider a revised treaty after consulting with Clayton on its advisability and terms.[9]

More pressing than a new Saudi treaty was the problem posed by recent Italian intrigues in the Red Sea. Italian activity in the region was certainly not a new phenomenon. Italian merchants had appeared in the southern Red Sea as early as the 1860s. And, with the establishment of Italian colonies in Somaliland and, more especially, in Eritrea, on the African coast across from 'Asir and the Yemen – both in the 1880s – Italian merchants began travelling regularly to southwest Arabia. During the War, London was so concerned about Italy's activities in the southern Red Sea that, despite Rome's entry into the War on the Allied side, British troops were landed on Kamaran Island, off the Yemeni coast, not to counter the Turks, but 'to forestall the Italians'.[10] In 1916, Rome also began expressing interest in another Red Sea island group, the Farsan Islands, located to the north of Kamaran. Both had strategic, and perhaps, economic importance. Kamaran featured what was said to be the third largest natural harbour in the world, both Kamaran and the Farsan Islands could support air fields, and the latter group was thought to contain oil deposits.

Rome's claims were persistent enough that, at the Paris peace conferences, Lord Milner became convinced that the Italians had designs on the islands and 'some undefined ambition to have a finger in the Arabian pie'.[11] Throughout the early 1920s, Italy increased her presence in the southern Red Sea. From London's perspective, Italian activities in the region were puzzling. Everyone recognized that Italy had a legitimate interest in increasing trade between her east African colonies and southwest Arabia, but few believed that Rome's actions in supplying arms to Arab rulers in the region furthered those interests. Indeed, in 1925, Italy was reported to be shipping arms to *both* the Imam and his rival, the Idrisi.[12] And, the governor of Eritrea, Jacopo Gasparini, did nothing to dispel British concerns. An intriguer and something of an Anglophobe, Gasparini had resisted Anglo-Italian cooperation in Abyssinia and was now thought to be concocting schemes to undermine British influence in the Red Sea region.

By early 1926, Foreign Secretary Austen Chamberlain was becoming concerned about Italian aspirations in the East. Since Benito Mussolini's rise to power in 1922, Italy seemed to have embarked on a new programme of Eastern expansion. Many of Il Duce's public statements could be discounted as so much Fascist bombast, but Italian muscle had actually been flexed in Abyssinia and Albania.[13] And now, in 1926, the Fascist leader appeared to have fixed his gaze on the Farsan Islands. Whether this was for strategic reasons, or because of the Islands' potential oil deposits, or simply to exhibit defiance to the British Empire, no one knew. But, ominously, in April, it was reported that an Italian ship had put in at Hudaydah with aeroplanes and military equipment destined for the Imam.[14] 'If we, in the same way, were to arm the Idrisi', Chamberlain informed the Cabinet in July, 'the two tribes would in effect be at war, with the support of Great Britain and Italy respectively'.[15] The prospect of a southwest Arabian war being waged by British and Italian proxies was unacceptable to the Foreign Secretary, wholly inconsistent with his broader policy of keeping on good terms with Rome: '[I]t is essential that we should keep Italy, a growing power, in sympathy with our policy and in co-operation with us. This may be vital in the future either to maintain peace in Europe or to restrain or guide Italy outside Europe.'[16] Still, British concern increased when it was learned that Gasparini had engineered a treaty of 'amity and commerce' with the Imam in August 1926, an unfortunate ramification, some said, of Clayton's failure to reach agreement with Yahya six months earlier.

In the same month that the Italo-Yemeni treaty was concluded, an inter-departmental conference convened in London to assess the situation. Clayton attended and provided some unsettling opinions. Nothing could be done with the Imam, he concluded; it was useless to resume negotiations with him concerning the Aden Protectorate boundary and an expedition to eject him from the Protectorate would require a military campaign on 'a considerable scale', a scale that would be prohibitively expensive. Moreover, current British policy was unsatisfactory and possibly dangerous, for, while the Italians were supplying war material to the Imam, Britain was now covertly arming the Idrisi through a British syndicate to which he had recently granted an oil concession in the Farsan Islands.[17] The proxy war feared by

Chamberlain seemed to have materialized. The Foreign Secretary was sufficiently concerned that, at the end of September, and with the Cabinet's approval, he travelled to Italy to meet with Mussolini and explain to him the nature of Britain's strategic interests in the Red Sea. The Italian leader assured him that Italy's interests in the region were purely commercial and suggested that British and Italian experts should meet to discuss the developing situation in the Red Sea, a proposal readily agreed to by Chamberlain.[18]

Meanwhile, back in London, a Committee of Imperial Defence sub-committee consisting of the Chiefs of Staff met to define precisely Britain's interests in the region and to suggest how they might be secured. Clayton was again present and his proposal that the RAF contingent at Aden should be increased to prevent further encroachments by the Imam on Protectorate territory was readily accepted by the military chiefs. On the larger, strategic issue the Chiefs were quite clear: 'We consider it of vital importance that no European Power should be permitted to gain a foothold on the Arabian shores of the Red Sea, and more particularly on Kamaran or the Farsan Islands.'[19] Even before the Chiefs of Staff met on November 8, Chamberlain had decided that Clayton would represent Britain in the talks with the Italians.[20] The Foreign Secretary confirmed this at a meeting of the CID on November 25, during which the Committee also accepted Clayton's proposal for increasing the RAF's strength at Aden, as endorsed by the Chiefs of Staff. Chamberlain was anxious that Clayton should leave for Rome as soon as possible, for it was now clear to him that 'Italy and Great Britain were waging war with each other under the flags of the Imam and the Idrisi'. The Cabinet promptly approved the CID recommendations on December 1, adding that Clayton's instructions should be based on the Chiefs of Staff earlier report which had made clear that Britain would not tolerate the presence of any European Power on the Arabian shores of the Red Sea.[21]

Chamberlain's instructions to Clayton were simple and straightforward. The 'cardinal interest' of Britain in the Red Sea was the 'maintenance of the safety of Aden and of Imperial communications with the East'. That interest would be threatened by the establishment 'by any European Power of a base on the Arabian shores of the Red Sea or at Kamaran or the Farsan Islands'. Nor could any 'unfriendly Arab ruler' – and this was certainly a reference to the Imam – be permitted to occupy either place. Clayton was instructed to secure explicit Italian acknowledgment of these points. Apart from these bedrock principles, Chamberlain added, Britain had 'no political ambitions' in the Red Sea and, indeed, was 'in favour of equality of commercial opportunity' throughout the region. This latter point was important, for if Mussolini had been honest in describing Italian interests as purely commercial, then there should be no conflict with Britain's strategic requirements. Clayton was to be guided in his talks by the advice of the British ambassador to Italy, an old friend from his war-time service in Egypt, Sir Ronald Graham. There was to be 'no question of negotiation' by Clayton and Graham with the Italians and no formal agreement with them was required. Clayton was merely to act 'as the mouthpiece' of the British government and to 'promote general political co-operation' by a 'frank exchange of explanations and views' which, it was hoped, would lead to 'an agreed summary of results'.[22]

Clayton undertook his new assignment with a healthy dose of scepticism; he had a long experience with the Italians in the East and it had not been positive. Nearly twenty years earlier, as Wingate's private secretary, he had seen evidence of Italian designs in eastern Sudan, and his 1909 expedition to Somaliland with the Sirdar to confront the Mad Mullah had yielded no good results, due in part, it was thought, to Italian scheming (Chapter 7). Then, in 1915, Rome had attempted to draw Britain into Italy's fight with the Senussi at a time when Clayton believed it was not in Britain's interest to engage in a campaign in Egypt's western desert (Chapter 14). And, when he learned in December 1926, that Gasparini was to be one of the Italian representatives in the talks that were about to begin in Rome, his suspicions of Italian motives were certainly not lessened.[23] To the contrary, they seemed to be confirmed when the Foreign Office received a telegram from George Lloyd, now High Commissioner in Egypt, who had learned that Gasparini had recently sent several sheikhs into 'Asir with instructions to foment anti-British feeling in the hope of securing a withdrawal of the Idrisi's concession given to a Shell Oil joint venture in the Farsan Islands.[24]

It was with some misgiving, then, that, on January 11, 1927, Clayton and Graham appeared at the Palazzo Chigi, home of the Italian Foreign Ministry, for their first meeting with Gasparini and a senior Ministry official, Raffaele Guariglia.[25] Clayton began by setting forth the British position concerning the Red Sea, following precisely the language set forth in his instructions, including the admission that, so far as commercial and economic matters were concerned, Britain favoured 'equality of opportunity' in the region. Although there had been some concern that Gasparini might be pursuing his own agenda during the talks, Guariglia immediately acknowledged that Britain's 'predominantly political' interests in the Red Sea would not conflict with Italy's 'purely commercial' concerns which were connected only with the 'economic expansion of . . . Eritrea'.[26]

During their second meeting, held the next day, the Italians 'showed their hand'. They were concerned about two, developing problems. The first was the Farsan Islands. They objected to any foreign naval base in the Islands and also to the Idrisi's exercise of sovereignty over them. Instead, they supported the rival claim of the Imam to the Islands. Despite these essentially political points, though, it soon became clear that what the Italians were really concerned about was the Idrisi's grant of an oil concession to a British firm. Graham responded by complaining of Gasparini's recent attempts to incite opposition to the concession by the local sheikhs and both Graham and Clayton 'made it perfectly clear that in no circumstances would we accept control of the Islands passing into the hands of either the Italians or the Imam'. Guariglia would not concede that the British oil concession was valid, but eased the increasing tension by asking whether, even if it were so regarded, there might not also be room for Italian participation on some basis. By the end of their second meeting with the Italians, then, Clayton and Graham were convinced that 'unless we let the Italians in on some footing or other as regards participation in oil interests, they will do all they can to render the situation as diffi-cult as possible'. The admission of Italy into some role in oil exploitation in the Islands, however, raised an issue that had not been addressed in Clayton's instruc-tions, so reference would have to be made to London before he could respond.[27]

The second issue that the Italians were 'much exercised over' also lay outside the scope of Clayton's instructions. During their first meeting on January 11, Gasparini advised the Englishmen that Rome had just learned of an agreement concluded between Ibn Saud and the Idrisi whereby the latter, while retaining internal autonomy in 'Asir, had ceded complete control of his country's foreign affairs and defence to the Sultan. This agreement, signed on October 21, 1926, appears to have come as a complete surprise to the British in Rome and in London. They knew nothing of it. Even though Ibn Saud had been in negotiation with the British Agent in the Hijaz in December, the Sultan never mentioned his treaty with the Idrisi. But now, with the powerful Ibn Saud poised on the northern flank of the Yemen, the Italians' own treaty partner, the Imam, was directly threatened. Gasparini and Guariglia were, therefore, most anxious that Britain should refrain from recognizing the Ibn Saud–Idrisi treaty.[28] Indeed, Gasparini warned Clayton at a private meeting on January 15, that if Britain recognized the treaty, that would 'definitely alienate' the Imam from Great Britain and 'throw him into the arms of various influences that were hostile to British policy'. Clayton was unimpressed; the Imam was no friend to the British and the only influences hostile to British policy into whose arms he could be thrown were, arguably, the Italians themselves.[29] Still, he said nothing in response to Gasparini's warning, for his instructions did not address an Ibn Saud–Idrisi treaty and, on this issue too, he would require further instruction from London.

One potential issue that did not materialize during the initial talks was Kamaran Island. In the course of their third meeting with Clayton and Graham, the Italians argued that Kamaran should be regarded as belonging to the Imam, as it lay just off the coast, adjacent to territory then held by Yahya. And, Guariglia attempted to assert an Italian interest in the Island based on the presence of a quarantine station there, used by pilgrims coming into Arabia by sea from Africa and the East. Clayton cut the Italians off, though, by asking what percentage of the total number of pilgrims passing through Kamaran came from Italian colonies, knowing full well that the number was insignificant. Guariglia was content to let the matter rest; it was unnecessary, he said, to 'press for any change of status in regard to Kamaran'.[30]

After his third meeting at the Palazzo Chigi on January 14, Clayton set down his impressions of Italian strategy in a private note. Contrary to the Italians' state-ments, he was convinced that Rome wanted to establish a 'strong political influence in southern Arabia' and that they intended to do so through the medium of the Imam, over whom they intended to assert a 'predominant influence'. That, Clayton reasoned, was why the Italians objected so strongly to the Idrisi's treaty with Ibn Saud who, they recognized, was stronger than Yahya, could foil the Imam's plans, and thus, by extension, thwart Italian objectives. For this reason, Clayton did not favour a British disavowal of the treaty, for, even if London did not expressly recog-nize the agreement, its very existence would make the Imam more amenable on the issue of the Aden frontier. If Yahya was exposed to a Saudi threat in the north, he would be far less likely to engage in aggressive action in the south, in the direction of Aden. As for Gasparini, Clayton believed he was pursuing his own agenda as Governor of Eritrea. Yet, this was no great concern to Clayton because he thought – perhaps too optimistically – that Mussolini would look at the issue of Italy's position in the Red Sea 'from a much broader point of view' and would therefore resist any arguments calculated to put the parties at odds in the region.[31]

No doubt Clayton considered that his personal views on Italian objectives could best be presented to Chamberlain verbally. And, since he had no instructions on either the Farsan Islands oil concession or the Ibn Saud–Idrisi treaty, he decided to return to London to discuss these points with Chamberlain before continuing the Rome talks.[32] After dining with Mussolini and others at the British embassy on January 17, Clayton left for London the next day. During the next ten days he met at least twice with Chamberlain and a revised set of instructions was prepared that covered the new points raised by the Italians. The Foreign Secretary was 'entirely satisfied with the results so far achieved', but instructed Clayton to return to Rome to draw up an 'agreed record' of the discussions. He was, first, to obtain an 'unqualified acceptance' of Britain's strategic interests in the Red Sea as laid down in his initial instructions. Regarding the Farsan oil concession, Britain would be 'favourably disposed' towards Italian involvement and any suggestion as to how they proposed to participate would be 'gladly and sympathetically considered'. While this might have been regarded as a major concession to the Italians, it was fully consistent with the principle of 'equality of commercial opportunity' set forth in Clayton's initial instructions. And Chamberlain's position coincided with the Colonial Office view that 'no active encouragement' was to be given to British commercial enterprises in the Red Sea, for the British had 'no intention of shaping our policy in these regions to serve the needs of commerce'.[33]

The issue of Ibn Saud's treaty with the Idrisi was more complex. If Clayton was correct about Italian political aspirations in the Red Sea, and about Rome's intent to use the Imam to advance them, then the treaty should be recognized by Britain. But, in an effort to at least partially meet the Italians, London could agree not to 'volunteer' recognition of the agreement and, since Ibn Saud was likely to press for British acknowledgment of his new status in 'Asir, to defer recognition for as long as possible. Further, the British would inform the Sultan that they did not recognize any 'territorial provisions' of the Idrisi treaty. Concerning Kamaran, because of uncertainty surrounding the legality of Britain's occupation of the island, Clayton was to do his utmost to prevent the question of its 'juridical status' being discussed. If the number of Italian pilgrims warranted the presence of an Italian representative there in the future, Britain would favourably consider the possibility.[34] His revised instructions having been completed, Chamberlain was anxious that Clayton return to Rome as soon as possible. His concern was that Gasparini was about to return to Eritrea and, if Mussolini 'issue[d] his fiat' and approved an agreed record of the talks before the governor left Rome, then he would be compelled to 'dance to Mussolini's tune' and would be less likely to be carried away by his 'local enthusiasms'.[35]

On January 28, 1927, Clayton left for Rome, this time accompanied by Enid. Although Graham and Clayton would meet with their Italian counterparts six times during the next week, the work was neither arduous nor time consuming, and Bertie and Enid were able to spend a good deal of time visiting Rome's historic and religious sites. As for business, Clayton laid out the British position on the Ibn Saud–Idrisi treaty and the Farsan oil concession during his first meeting with the Italians on January 31. Gasparini and Guariglia were satisfied with the British statements on both issues and the remaining meetings were confined to resolving differences regarding the agreed record of the talks. One new area of Italian concern, though, was raised at the meeting on the 31st. By this time, the RAF contingent at Aden had been increased to squadron strength and the Italians were worried that Britain was now planning an attack on their protégé, the Imam. Clayton assured them that there was 'no question of instituting an offensive' against Yahya, 'at any rate, at present'. However, he made clear that 'any further encroachment on the Aden Protectorate or any attack on the Farsan Islands would render him liable to retaliatory measures'.[36]

By February 7, the parties had worked out an agreed record of their talks, based largely on an Italian draft which was much shorter and more general in its terms than the longer, detailed record prepared by Clayton and Graham. In seven short paragraphs the parties agreed to use their influence in pursuit of a policy of pacification in the region, to refrain from intervening in any conflict that might break out between or among the Arab chiefs and to 'maintain close touch with each other in all questions affecting the Red Sea and Southern Arabia'. Italy recognized Britain's 'vital Imperial interest' in the region and *both* parties agreed that no European Power should establish itself on the Arabian shore of the Red Sea or on Kamaran or the Farsan Islands. The mutuality of this latter provision might have been regarded as something of a victory for the Italians, as it precluded a British base in the islands, but, since Britain had no plans for a base in the region additional to that at Aden, London was content with the provision. Regarding the oil concession issue, it was stated only, and generally, that 'there should be economic and commercial freedom' on the Arabian coast and the Red Sea islands. Finally, although the Italians did not relinquish their claim to an Italian presence at the quarantine on Kamaran, the British agreed to reconsider the question should the number of pilgrims originating in Italian possessions warrant an Italian representative there.[37]

Chamberlain was pleased with the results of the Rome talks, expressing his 'great appreciation of the tact and ability' exhibited by Clayton in the performance of his duties and congratulating him on the 'unqualified success' of his mission. A potentially dangerous situation had been averted and the Foreign Secretary's broader policy of maintaining good relations with the Italians had been preserved. His diplomatic work now complete, Clayton had one remaining meeting in Rome, an interview with Mussolini on the evening of February 7, 1927. Typically, the Italian dictator's meetings with foreign diplomats were designed to intimidate and Clayton's was no exception. He had to walk the length of a very large room at the Chigi Palace, at the end of which Mussolini remained seated behind an enormous desk.[38] No doubt Clayton's meeting with Il Duce involved little more than an exchange of pleasantries, masking perhaps the deep suspicions harboured by both men. But, with few minor exceptions, the events of the following years would demonstrate Italian and British adherence to the letter and the spirit of the 1927 accord. Disagreements would emerge between the two countries during the ensuing decade, but none of them would originate in the Red Sea or Arabia.

Less than a month after his return from Rome, Clayton was called upon to undertake yet another diplomatic mission for the Foreign Office. Negotiations with Ibn Saud for a new treaty with Britain had been suspended three months earlier when the acting British Agent and Consul at Jeddah, S. R. Jordan, had failed to reach agreement with the new king. Clayton was well familiar with the issues, having attended four inter-departmental conferences in 1926, during which the terms of the proposed agreement with Ibn Saud were debated by the departments involved. But, as usual when it came to Arab affairs, there were too many cooks in the kitchen. The Government of India first opposed the treaty altogether and then insisted on a clause reflecting Ibn Saud's acknowledgment of 'the freedom of religious observances and rites' of 'Moslem British Nationals' in the Hijaz and another repeating his 1915 agreement to refrain from aggression on, or interference in, British-protected territories along the Persian Gulf. The India Office departed from India's demands concerning religious observances and rites, as it was thought that such a provision would be regarded as interference in Muslim religious matters.[39] The Mandate governments in Palestine and Iraq also made proposals regarding the contents of the treaty and the Foreign and Colonial Offices, of course, had their own, occasionally divergent, views on the treaty. Even the Air Ministry attended the four inter-departmental meetings convened to debate the terms of the proposed agreement.

Clayton's ideas comported with those of the Foreign Office; 'the new treaty', he wrote, 'should contain as little detail as possible'. And he concurred in Hubert Young's opinion that 'the really important thing was to conclude a treaty with Ibn Saud . . . what was put in and what left out of that treaty was of less importance'.[40] As always, Clayton's eyes were focused on Imperial strategy: 'the existence of an Arabian policy at all is . . . chiefly due to the necessity of safe-guarding Imperial communications with the East, as represented by the Suez Canal and the Red Sea from Port Said to Perim'. Ibn Saud, he added, 'will ask for something from H.M.G. and the more moderate British requests are, the better the position will be from which to reject extravagant or impossible demands on his part'. Still, he saw advantages for Britain in a new Arabian treaty. First, it would pre-empt 'other Powers [who] may enter the field'. Here, Clayton was thinking of Italy, and perhaps even Russia, both of which might want to treat with Ibn Saud and thus, however remotely, compromise Britain's paramount position in the Red Sea and the Persian Gulf. Second, the very fact of a British treaty with the strongest Arab ruler in the region would make the Imam 'more amenable' in the Yemen. Third, the 1915 treaty with Ibn Saud had obligated Britain to defend him against 'foreign aggression'; the new agreement, Clayton thought, could, and should, eliminate that obligation. Apart from these fundamental points, Clayton held that the new treaty should contain little of substance. There was no immediate need to address such points as commercial preferences, or the Hijaz–Transjordan boundary, or even Ibn Saud's recognition of Britain's status as Mandatory in Palestine and Iraq. Such points could all be addressed at a later date, if necessary.[41]

Clayton was the obvious choice to negotiate the new treaty with Ibn Saud. Indeed, George Antonius, who had accompanied Clayton to Bahra in 1925, thought 'it would be folly on the part of H.M.G. to entrust the work to anyone else'. But, whether because of Clayton's poor health or the belief that the negotiations would be less difficult than those of 1925, the Foreign Office assigned the responsibility to Jordan, the British Agent at Jeddah. Clayton did not disagree with the choice, but strongly recommended that Antonius – whose native Arabic and familiarity with the King's advisers he thought invaluable – should accompany Jordan. However, Antonius was very reluctant to participate in the talks unless Clayton headed the mission. He was aware of the 'impression' Clayton had made on the Najdi ruler in 1925, and of 'the great importance in Arab countries of the personal factor'.[42]

Despite his reservations, Antonius did accompany Jordan to Hamra Namleh, some fourteen miles southwest of Medina, where the negotiations for the new treaty were to take place. Still, he was frankly pessimistic. The problems he would be confronting, he thought, were not as difficult as those he and Clayton had faced at Bahra, and yet he did not 'contemplate success'. True, Jordan was *persona grata* with Ibn Saud, but, in Antonius' opinion, he was 'not the man for the job'. Not only was the Agent inexperienced, he made 'the fatal mistake of relying too much on his "influence" with Ibn Saud and of mistaking compliments and protestations of good will for omens of certain success'. His concerns increased when Sheikh Yusuf Yasin, his negotiating adversary at Bahra, called on him shortly before the mission left Jeddah for the interior and, as Antonius wrote to Clayton, 'told me that Ibn Saud had been expecting you and wanted to know whether you were coming later to see this thing through'.[43]

Within a week of his arrival at Hamra Namleh on November 24, Antonius' concerns proved justified. Jordan was not confined by the language of a draft treaty, as Clayton had been at Sanaa in 1926. Instead, Clayton had seen to it that the Agent was given a draft of the proposed treaty along with a set of instructions that allowed him room to depart from the draft as the talks developed.[44] But, even with this flexibility, Jordan had neither the strength to confront Ibn Saud's strong objections to certain terms nor the confidence to depart from provisions of the treaty draft and still meet the essential points of his instructions. And the Sultan-King had many objections. He would not recognize Britain's 'special position' in the Mandates, as specified in the draft treaty. He demanded an express surrender of Britain's capitulatory rights in his domains. And he refused a provision calling for his suppression of the slave trade and his recognition of the British Agent's power to manumit slaves. This power, which allowed a British consular officer to release from servitude a slave seeking refuge at the British Agency and repatriate him to his country of origin, was important to the Foreign Office, for not only was public opinion in England strongly opposed to slavery, Britain was a party to the League of Nations

Anti-Slavery Convention of 1926, which committed all signatories to bringing about 'the complete abolition of slavery in all its forms'. And, in the Hijaz, manumission was a power actively and frequently invoked; during the preceding year, ninety-seven slaves had been freed and repatriated by the Agent at Jeddah.[45] In addition to these points, Ibn Saud refused to agree to the Hijaz–Transjordan frontier along the line insisted upon by Clayton at Bahra and now set forth in a protocol accompanying the treaty. Nor would he agree to refrain from aggression on or interference in the Gulf sheikhdoms with whom Britain was in a treaty relationship, as he had agreed in 1915. In the face of these insuperable difficulties, the talks were suspended in mid-December.

Contrary to the advice of Clayton and Young, the London departments had attempted too much by their initial treaty draft. Consistent with his view that the treaty should contain as little detail as possible, Clayton had anticipated that Ibn Saud would not recognize Britain's 'special position' in the Mandates, that he would resist any present attempt to define the Hijaz–Transjordan boundary and that he would not explicitly agree to refrain from aggression on, or interference in, the British-protected Gulf sheikhdoms.[46] But provisions embodying all these points had been included in the draft treaty and, predictably, Ibn Saud had objected. In a series of four meetings held during January–February 1927, the London departments reassessed the situation. Because of his involvement in the Rome negotiations, Clayton was not present. However, Antonius, having returned from Arabia, was well aware of Sir Gilbert's views and did not hesitate to state them. When the India and Colonial Offices suggested terminating the treaty negotiations altogether, Antonius advanced good reasons – reasons that Clayton likely would have propounded – for continuing the effort to reach agreement with the King: Ibn Saud was 'destined to become an increasing force and friendly relations with him [were] . . . of great importance in view of his position on the confines of the Middle Eastern territories and in the neighbourhood of the Red Sea', Antonius argued. No less important, a treaty with him would also 'counter-balance the activities of the Italians in South West Arabia'.[47] The Foreign Office agreed and the departments ultimately decided to resume negotiations. In order to give them a fair chance of success, though, many of the provisions to which Ibn Saud had objected were either dropped or substantially modified.

On February 18, with the Rome talks now complete, the Foreign Office formally asked Clayton to take over the Arabian negotiations. Although he was again ill, and confined to bed, Sir Gilbert accepted immediately.[48] A review of his instructions for the renewed negotiations discloses that Clayton's task had been made considerably easier than that presented to Jordan in the autumn of 1926. A draft treaty was again prepared and, while it embodied 'the limit of the concessions' the British were prepared to make, Clayton would not be bound by its 'exact terms'. The concessions, however, were significant. There was no express relinquishment of capitulatory rights, but it was stated that British citizens and British-protected persons in the Hijaz and Najd would be subject to the jurisdiction of local courts, an implicit abandonment of those rights within Ibn Saud's territories. At the insistence of India,

Clayton was also instructed to press for the King's agreement to refrain from aggression on, or interference in, the Persian Gulf territories in treaty relationship with Britain, but 'as a last resort', he could agree to a clause simply requiring Ibn Saud to maintain 'peaceful and friendly relations' with those territories. Nor would Britain insist on the King-Sultan's agreement to the Hijaz–Transjordan frontier as laid down by Clayton at Bahra, provided that, pending final settlement of that frontier, he agreed to maintain the status quo, under which the Ma'an-Akaba district was administered by Transjordan. Only on the right of manumission were the British inflexible; it would not be abandoned. However, if the King would not acknowledge that right in the text of the treaty, Clayton was empowered to exchange notes with Ibn Saud, to be published with the treaty, in which he acquiesced in the British Agent's power of manumission.[49]

Clayton left London on April 15, 1927, and arrived in Jeddah, with Jordan and Antonius, on May 2. The negotiations began at Jeddah on May 10, and lasted ten days, during which the parties held nine formal meetings. Despite the concessions made by the British, by the close of the sixth meeting on May 16, 'agreement was not yet in sight'. By this time, Clayton had made further concessions, as allowed by his instructions, and was becoming annoyed with the King's intransigence. Ibn Saud would not agree to sign the treaty protocol defining the Hijaz–Transjordan boundary and would not admit the right of the British Agent to manumit slaves in the Hijaz. In response, Sir Gilbert ticked off for the King the major concessions made by Britain: The 'somewhat onerous' 1915 treaty was being cancelled; Britain was recognizing the King's complete independence and sovereignty in the Hijaz and Najd; the clause requiring him to acknowledge Britain's 'special position' in the Mandates had been withdrawn; Britain now recognized fully the jurisdiction of the Hijazi and Najdi courts over British citizens in Ibn Saud's domains; Clayton had modified the British position concerning the Persian Gulf sheikhdoms, requiring only the King's maintenance of 'friendly and peaceful relations' with those territories; and he had agreed to omit the manumission clause from the text of the treaty and reflect the principle in an accompanying note. 'Against all this', Sir Gilbert asked only that Ibn Saud agree to the Transjordan boundary and admit, in a note or letter, the British Agent's right to manumit slaves.[50]

Rather chastened by Clayton's admonition, Ibn Saud asked for a personal interview with him on May 16. Clayton later described the meeting: 'Somewhat to my surprise, he said that he had now come to me, as a trusted friend, to ask my frank and impartial opinion as to his best course of action, and was prepared to accept and act upon my advice'. Clayton was adamant; unless the manumission right and the Transjordan frontier 'were adequately safeguarded, no treaty was possible'. The King promptly conceded the right of manumission; he would agree in the treaty to cooperate in the suppression of the slave trade and would acquiesce to manumission in a separate, published note. The boundary issue proved more difficult. If he were to sign the protocol now, Ibn Saud argued, he would 'expose himself to violent criticism not only by his enemies, but also by his friends'. Clayton described his thinking concerning the King's purported dilemma:

I could, perhaps, have induced Ibn Saud at that stage to sign the protocol [defining the Hijaz–Transjordan boundary] and I felt it was very desirable to reach a definite settlement without delay. On the other hand, his arguments against this course were cogent, and it was obviously undesirable to force him into a really difficult position; moreover, I was convinced that it would be better, in the interests of future co-operation and good relations, to ensure that the treaty should be signed in a spirit of real amity and confidence than to leave behind me a feeling that it had been concluded in an atmosphere of coercion as opposed to one of mutual agreement.[51]

Clayton drafted the notes on both the manumission issue and the Transjordan frontier and, as he had agreed, Ibn Saud signed both. The King agreed to maintain the status quo in the Ma'an-Akaba district and promised not to interfere in the administration of that district by Transjordan until circumstances permitted a final settlement. The notes signed on the manumission right were less satisfactory. After Clayton fully elaborated the British position in his note, Ibn Saud responded only that he was confident that the British Agent would always act 'in accordance with the spirit in which our agreement was arrived at, and that he will not permit any confusion as this might have undesirable effects on the administration and economic aspects of the question'. That language did not reflect the King's clear acquiescence to the right of manumission as Clayton's instructions had specified. In the words of one historian, it was the only aspect of the Treaty of Jeddah that was 'felt to tarnish Clayton's otherwise considerable diplomatic achievement'.[52]

With the slavery and manumission issues now resolved, it appeared that the road to signature was now clear. However, on May 18, the King's advisers raised 'a number of new points', the most important of which was a demand for an express relinquishment of Britain's capitulatory rights. The King asserted that 'the question was one of life and death to him' and a rupture in the talks now 'appeared almost inevitable'. Clayton was baffled and angered. Article 6 of the British draft treaty stated that 'all questions' arising within Hijazi or Najdi territory between the subjects of Ibn Saud and British or British-protected citizens would be settled in the Hijazi and Najdi courts – an implicit, but nonetheless very clear waiver of Britain's capitulatory rights. But, perversely, the King's advisers considered this specific concession as a disguised attempt to retain 'the principle of the Capitulations'.[53] It was now time for Clayton to speak 'with some sharpness'. If the King would not agree to the treaty in its current form, Clayton demanded a written explanation from him which he would then take back to London. After some discussion, it was agreed that Article 6 would be withdrawn altogether and an innocuous sentence added to the end of Article 5 stating that 'the principles of international law between independent governments shall be respected' – a provision less favourable to the King than the deleted Article 6.

During the negotiators' ninth meeting, held on May 20, agreement on all points was finally reached and the Treaty of Jeddah and the accompanying notes were signed. That night the King hosted a great banquet, as he had at Bahra nearly two years earlier, at which the diplomats again dined in true 'Bedouin style'. Gifts were exchanged, Clayton receiving, among other items, two Arabian stallions, which he shipped to England, and Ibn Saud a set of Hornby toy railway trains for his children.[54]

Not everyone in Whitehall was entirely satisfied with the Treaty of Jeddah. Some expressed disappointment concerning Ibn Saud's vague and equivocal recognition of the British Agent's manumission power, and the India Office were unhappy that Clayton had not secured greater protection for the Persian Gulf sheikhdoms,[55] although, it must be said, the language of this treaty provision was fully consistent with the 'last resort' concession allowed by his instructions. However, Foreign Secretary Chamberlain had nothing but praise for Clayton's efforts, considering 'the treaty and notes entirely satisfactory' and congratulating him on his 'tact and ability' as well as his 'patience and diplomatic skill'.[56] Typically, Clayton praised others – Jordan for his invaluable help, local knowledge and experience, and, of course, Antonius to whom he attributed 'in no small measure' the results achieved. He even recommended Antonius for an honorary CMG. The Foreign Office declined, but did recommend him for a CBE, which he duly received in August 1927.[57]

The Treaty of Jeddah would endure; it was renewed, with insignificant changes, in 1936 and 1943, and formed the basis of Anglo-Saudi relations for years to come. The southern Transjordan border with Saudi Arabia – as Ibn Saud's kingdom would be called from 1932 – would not be formally demarcated until 1965 (when Akaba and Ma'an were included in Jordan) and, most likely, the King did try to respect the status quo as reflected in the boundary described in Clayton's May 1927 note. But Ibn Saud's statement that he would have been assailed by friends and enemies alike had he agreed to the boundary in 1927, may very well have been accurate, for the ink of the Treaty of Jeddah would not be dry for six months before events further East, on the Iraqi border, would demonstrate the tenuous and uncertain nature of his rule in Arabia. And those events would once again draw Clayton into the thicket of Anglo-Arab relations.

28

The Attack of the Ikhwan: The Arabian Threat to Iraq, 1928

They swept silently out of the desert in the dead of night. The attackers were forty Ikhwan warriors of the Mutayr tribe and their objective on that chilly night of November 5, 1927, was the small Iraqi police post at Busaya, some seventy miles north of the border with Najd. Within minutes it was over; twenty Iraqis lay dead in the desert sand as the Ikhwan turned south, melting again into the desert gloom on their return to Najd. During the following months more attacks from Najd followed, the deadliest led by the Mutayr chief, Faisal al-Dawish. By March 1928, the Ikhwan had made no less than eight raids into Iraq and neighbouring British-protected Kuwait, killing 163 and making off with more than 31,000 sheep, donkeys and camels.[1] Bedouin raiding had been a feature of desert life for centuries but, unlike the traditional raid, the *ghazzu*, these attacks were made not just for plunder and sport, but with a deadly purpose. And, since Ibn Saud had agreed to Iraq's border with Najd five years before the attack on Busaya, the raids posed very serious political issues.

The big question, of course, was whether Ibn Saud had inspired or condoned the raids of 1927–28. If he had, then the Sultan was in clear violation of his earlier treaties executed with Percy Cox (Uqair, 1922), and Clayton (Bahra, 1925; Jeddah, 1927). And, if Ibn Saud had not sponsored the raids, then the problem was perhaps even greater, for that suggested that the Najdi leader had lost control of the Ikhwan and that Najd, with its long borders with British Mandated territory in Transjordan and Iraq, might be in a state of civil war. Sir Henry Dobbs, Britain's High Commissioner for Iraq, held that the raids were likely authorized by Ibn Saud, and the Iraqi King, Faisal, was convinced that the Najdi leader was encouraging if not actually planning the Ikhwan incursions.[2] However, Faisal's opinions were discounted by the Colonial Office, for the King was a confirmed enemy of Ibn Saud and could not be regarded as objective. After all, it was Ibn Saud who had brought Hashemite rule in the Hijaz to an ignominious end; Faisal's brother, Abdullah, been routed by the Ikhwan at Turaba in 1919, his father had been forced to abdicate as King of the Hijaz after the Wahhabi leader's occupation of Mecca in 1924, and his elder brother, Ali, had done likewise in December 1925, as the Ikhwan took over the whole of the Hijaz from Akaba to 'Asir.

In fact, Ibn Saud had lost his grip on the Ikhwan by 1927, and the attack on Busaya most likely occurred without his approval.[3] The Sultan's relations with the Ikhwan (the brethren, or brotherhood) could be traced to early 1913, when they were formed from the Bedouin of several Arabian tribes who began gathering at that time in settled agricultural colonies in central Najd called *hijra* (pl. *hujar*). Whether Ibn Saud was instrumental in forming these colonies is unclear, but he certainly encouraged and supported them, both spiritually and economically, after they were created. The Ikhwan were held together not only by strong economic and communal ties, but also by a singular devotion to the fundamental doctrines of Wahhabism, principles with which Ibn Saud's family had been associated since the inception of the movement under Muhammad ibn Abd al-Wahhab (1703–92) in the mid-eighteenth century.

The Wahhabis espoused a return to the purity of Islam, based solely on the Qur'an and the example of the Prophet, Muhammad. They resolutely rejected contemporary Islamic practices, such as the veneration of saints and the erection of shrines on their tombs, and roundly denounced any Muslim sect that did not adhere to their views.[4] Some Muslims, like the Shi'i of Persia, southern Iraq and eastern Arabia, they regarded as infidels, not Muslims at all. During the 1926 *hajj*, a group of Egyptian pilgrims, accompanied by a band of musicians, were set upon by the Ikhwan who objected to any form of music or singing near the Islamic Holy Places; in the ensuing melee, twenty-five people were killed.[5] When coming into contact with Christian infidels, the Ikhwan would cover their faces with their hands and turn away. Modern innovations, like motor cars, airplanes and the telegraph, even wrist-watches, were considered to be the work of the devil. They were only partially reconciled to two such instruments of modern life when passages from the Qur'an were read over the telephone and then broadcast on the radio.[6]

The Ikhwan were imbued with such intolerance by a special cadre of religious men known as *mutawwa'a*. These *mutawwa'a* were educated in the rudiments of Islamic ritual and jurisprudence by the *'ulama* (religious scholars), most of whom resided in Ibn Saud's capital at Riyadh. Dispatched by the *'ulama* to the various Ikhwan settlements, the *mutawwa'a* instructed the brethren with remarkable severity. Failure to attend daily prayers, the display of personal ornamentation, or departures from strict proscriptions governing personal appearance, even the type and length of clothing that could be worn, rendered one subject to punishment.

By 1927, there were more than twenty Ikhwan settlements in Najd, populated by some 150,000 devoted adherents.[7] They provided a ready and willing source for Ibn Saud's military ventures and, from the early 1920s, the Ikhwan formed the bulk of Ibn Saud's military force. United by religious fervour, hardened by the privations of desert life and skilled in mobile warfare, they represented a formidable opponent for any sedentary population. They were particularly feared for their savagery in battle; men, women and children were killed indiscriminately by the Ikhwan, as the residents of Ta'if learned when that Hijazi city was overrun by the Ikhwan in 1924. When the Hijaz was conquered by Ibn Saud in 1924–5, his attacking forces were comprised entirely of Ikhwan.[8]

For Ibn Saud, though, the sword of the Ikhwan was double-edged. The Sultan was certainly a devout Wahhabi and he valued and benefited from the military prowess and success of the Ikhwan. But their uncompromising severity also posed problems. After the conquest of the Hijaz, Ibn Saud became responsible for the holy cities of Mecca and Medina and for the *hajj*. And the pilgrimage was attended by Muslims from throughout the Islamic world, the vast majority of whom did not ascribe to the fundamentalist tenets of the Wahhabis and were appalled by the ruthlessness of the Ikhwan. If Ibn Saud was to legitimize his rule in the Hijaz in the eyes of world Islam, he must exhibit tolerance to all shades of Muslim belief and practice, an attitude the intolerant Ikhwan were not likely to endorse. The Sultan also understood that if he was to persevere in the modern world, he must have motor cars, telephones, the telegraph, even airplanes – all the appliances of modern civilization that would enable him to succeed in a country surrounded in the west, north and east by western-controlled regimes. It was the 1925 conquest of the Hijaz, then, that brought the differences between Ibn Saud and his Ikhwan warriors to the fore.

By 1926, Ikhwan opposition to Ibn Saud began to coalesce around the principal sheikhs of three of the most powerful tribes in Najd, the 'Ajman, the 'Ataiba and the Mutayr. Although Ikhwan displeasure with the Sultan was usually couched in terms of his purported failure to adhere to the strict tenets of Wahhabism, it was also apparent that the dissident sheikhs had been angered by frustrated political ambition. Faisal al-Dawish of the Mutayr had hoped to be appointed governor of Medina and the leading sheikh of the 'Ataiba aspired to the governorship of Ta'if. Neither appointment materialized and, by early 1927, the Ikhwan sheikhs were in open opposition to Ibn Saud. But the Sultan was in no position to oppose the Ikhwan in battle; he had relied on them for years and had no forces with which to confront them. So, he adopted a temporizing policy. He met with the Ikhwan leaders, professed sympathy with their views and, at the same time, began fostering divisions among the sheikhs. In part, the Ikhwan raids into southern Iraq in the winter of 1927–28, represented the sincere objection of the Najdi tribes to Iraq's erection of police posts in the border region. But just as clearly, they reflected a challenge to Ibn Saud's authority to treat with the infidel British and to agree to a boundary that interfered with the traditional migratory movements of the Najdi Bedouin. Faced with this dilemma, the Sultan played both sides. He informed the British that the Ikhwan raids were contrary to his orders, but that Iraq's erection of police posts in the border region violated his 1922 treaty made with Cox at Uqair. At the same time, he agreed with the Ikhwan that they could continue their raiding in southern Iraq and Kuwait.[9] The British had no alternative; in December 1927, the RAF was authorized to respond to the raids with armoured cars and aerial bombing. During the following January, RAF bombing runs crossed the border into Najd. Iraq and Najd were on the brink of all-out war.

While the situation was deteriorating in Najd and along the border with Iraq, Clayton was enjoying a peaceful summer and autumn in England. He had returned to London on June 4, 1927, after his successful negotiations with Ibn Saud that resulted in the Treaty of Jeddah. Although his diary entries for the period contain a few references to meetings at the Foreign and Colonial Offices, most of his time was consumed by social engagements and frequent appearances at meetings of the Central Asian Society and the Royal Institute of International Affairs. On September 4, 1927, Clayton's father, William, died at Harpenden, the family home on the Isle of Wight, and he and Enid attended the funeral at Sandown three days later. It was a sad time, for William Clayton's death, at the age of 82, brought to an end the long association of Clayton's immediate family with the Isle of Wight, as Harpenden was sold the following year.[10]

In early February 1928, Sir Gilbert and Lady Clayton left England for a month-long holiday in Gibraltar and Spain. While in Gibraltar, Clayton enjoyed visiting with his brother Jack, then an officer on H.M.S. *Nelson*, and, with Enid, he toured the Spanish cities of Seville, Cordova and Granada. But within forty-eight hours of his return to England on March 7, he was called to the Foreign Office where he learned that 'the Cabinet want me to go out & try & settle up difficulties with Ibn Saud'. The 'situation', he added in his diary, 'is serious'.[11] Even before Clayton left England on his Spanish holiday, his name had been brought up in connection with the Iraq–Najd dispute. Clayton's former Arab Bureau colleague, George Lloyd, now High Commissioner for Egypt, recommended three times that Clayton be sent to Arabia without delay and he reported that Ibn Saud also wanted Sir Gilbert to come out. Dobbs, in Baghdad, agreed, as did the British Resident in the Persian Gulf who had initially been selected to meet with Ibn Saud, but had been rejected by the Sultan.[12]

On March 7, the day Clayton arrived in England, the Cabinet decided that he should 'be placed in touch with Ibn Saud at the earliest possible moment'.[13] Clayton agreed two days later, but, as will be seen, he did so with some reservation. During the next six weeks he met often with the departments involved and, as usual when it came to Arab affairs, there were several and their views did not coincide. The Colonial Office, responsible for the administration of the Iraqi Mandate, was inflexible; Iraq should not dismantle its desert posts, as demanded by Ibn Saud, and the Ikhwan raiders should be met with an aggressive military response. These views were supported fully by Sir Samuel Hoare, the Secretary of State for Air, and by his Chief of Air Staff, General Sir Hugh Trenchard. The RAF had been responsible for Iraq's defence since 1922, and Trenchard was convinced that the RAF bombing sorties of January–February 1928 had 'considerably shakened' the morale of the Ikhwan. And, he argued, for full effect, air action 'must be used to attack the enemy in his own country'.[14] In making that argument, the Air Chief appears to have been unaware of, or indifferent to, the 1925 Bahra Agreement, under which Iraq and Najd had agreed that the forces of one country could not pursue raiders retreating into the territory of the other without permission (*see* Chapter 26).

The Air Ministry and the Colonial Office were opposed by the Foreign Office, the Government of India and the India Office. India was particularly concerned that attacks on Ibn Saud would rouse Indian Muslim opinion against Britain and might also interfere with the *hajj*, for which Ibn Saud was now responsible. No less important, the security of Britain's position in the Persian Gulf, and the western approaches to India, might be undermined by a hostile Arabia. The Foreign Office view, supported by George Lloyd from Cairo, was even broader. Not only might Britain's position in the Persian Gulf be compromised, Foreign Secretary Chamberlain was concerned about the effect military action against Najd would have in Egypt, the Sudan, the Yemen, and even Persia, whose current nationalist government was not particularly well-disposed towards Britain.[15] The Colonial Office policy prevailed, as reflected in the instructions prepared for the upcoming talks, but Foreign Secretary Austen Chamberlain was so concerned he advised Amery that if Clayton reported that the only obstacle to agreement was an Iraqi refusal to demolish the fort at Busaya, he 'reserve[d] the right to appeal to the Cabinet' to have the post removed.[16]

Although Clayton had agreed to undertake the negotiations with Ibn Saud, an issue arose in March 1928, that very nearly prevented his participation in the talks. During the May 1927 negotiations for the Treaty of Jeddah, Ibn Saud requested that he be allowed to purchase arms and ammunition from British manufacturers. The sale of war materiel to Arabia had been embargoed by Britain, but this did not preclude the Sultan from purchasing such materiel from other countries. The consensus in London was that if Ibn Saud was intent on purchasing arms, it was preferable he do so from British suppliers. So, Clayton was authorized to append a letter to the Treaty of Jeddah in which he formally advised Ibn Saud that 'the embargo on the export of war materiel to Arabia has been removed'.[17] The Sultan promptly placed orders with British suppliers. However, the events of 1927–28 had altered the British position. The Cabinet now concluded that if the Sultan was behind the Ikhwan raids into Iraq, 'it would be monstrous that British airmen should be shot at by arms supplied from this country'. Clayton shared the concern, but informed the Foreign Office on March 9, that 'he would hesitate to undertake . . . negotiations [with Ibn Saud] if an embargo were placed' on the recently ordered materiel. The Cabinet approached Clayton again on the issue, but he maintained that it would be 'well nigh disastrous to stop the despatch of arms' and 'adhered to the opinion previously expressed that his utility as a negotiator would be seriously prejudiced by a decision to hold up . . . the munitions already ordered' by the Sultan. Clayton argued that Ibn Saud would surely regard this as a breach of the 1927 treaty, and he might believe that the arms he had ordered would now be used by Britain against him. Chamberlain supported Sir Gilbert's position. Amery opposed it. The Cabinet compromised; the arms would be allowed to leave England, but would be held up at Port Sudan, pending receipt of Clayton's report from the Hijaz. Finally, on May 9, while Clayton was in Jeddah, the Cabinet gave him complete discretion to decide whether the arms should be released.[18]

Yet another disagreement arose in connection with Clayton's authority. On whose behalf was Sir Gilbert negotiating, and what powers did he possess? The Foreign Office decided initially that he should represent Britain, not Iraq, in the talks, but later concluded that he should receive 'full power' from Faisal to bind the Iraqi government. The Colonial Office agreed that Sir Gilbert should represent Iraq, but insisted that any resolution reached must be ratified by the Iraqis:

Clayton must negotiate a settlement with Ibn Saud and then, as he had at Bahra three years earlier, persuade the Iraqis to ratify the agreement. The Colonial Office position was adopted. As for Clayton's authority, all agreed that he would be the 'sole plenipotentiary' and that any others joining the mission would act in an advisory capacity only.[19]

With these disagreements resolved, Clayton left London on April 19 and arrived in Jeddah on May 2, the same day he had landed at the port a year earlier to negotiate the Treaty of Jeddah. At his own request, he was again accompanied by Antonius. Joining them was Kinahan Cornwallis, Sir Gilbert's former Arab Bureau colleague who was now Adviser to the Iraqi Interior Ministry, Captain John Bagot Glubb, an expert on the border tribes who had been working in the southern Iraqi desert to repel the Ikhwan raids, and a young RAF officer, Guy Moore, who had served in Iraq and knew Arabic. Ibn Saud arrived on May 7, and talks began the following day. Although Clayton was 'able to rub in [his] point of view', within a week he was convinced that there was 'no chance of a settlement'.[20] The Sultan made two demands. First, Iraq must demolish the desert posts, including Busaya. Second, she must agree to the surrender of fugitives, that is, the extradition of Najdi individuals or tribes seeking refuge in Iraq. This second demand, it will be recalled, had been rejected by Clayton at Bahra in 1925; Iraq would not abandon the right to grant asylum to political refugees seeking safe harbour in Iraq (*see* Chapter 26).

The real stumbling-block, though, was the desert posts. There was no question that the fort at Busaya was seventy miles inside Iraq, or, indeed, that the half-dozen other Iraqi frontier posts were well inside the country. But the Sultan insisted that the posts violated article 3 of the December 1922 Protocol he had signed with Cox at Uqair. That provision stated that 'the two Governments mutually agree not to use the watering places and wells situated in the vicinity of the border for any military purpose, such as building forts on them, and not to concentrate troops in their vicinity'. The Sultan now insisted that this clause prevented the 'erection of any fortified posts at any of the water points in the desert area' and that he was unable to accept a 'restricted interpretation' of article 3 or to agree to the maintenance of the posts 'without losing [the] complete confidence of his tribesmen and consequently his ability to control them'.[21] Clayton could not agree to the Sultan's interpretation of the Uqair Protocol; Britain, he said, must maintain the principle that either government – Iraq or Najd – could take 'whatever measures it may consider necessary for proper control and defence of the desert within its own territory'. He certainly could not admit 'so wide an interpretation of article 3' as the Sultan demanded.[22] The fort at Busaya was not 'in the vicinity of the border'; it was 70 miles inside Iraq! Sir Gilbert 'used every means of persuasion and pressure at [his] disposal' but could not move the Najdi leader. '[N]ot only was Ibn Saud unwilling on grounds of general policy to give way on the question of the posts', Clayton was convinced that 'he was precluded from doing so by the attitude of his people'.[23]

While Clayton was engaged in discussions with Ibn Saud on the central issue of the desert posts, Cornwallis, Glubb and Moore met with the Sultan's advisers to work on subsidiary issues, including a draft extradition treaty. But they made no more progress than Clayton. As at Bahra three years earlier, Ibn Saud was advised by 'the Vultures', Hafiz Wahba and Yusuf Yasin, and they were joined by Fuad Hamza, a former journalist and Palestinian schoolmaster, and Dr. Abdullah Damluji, an Iraqi and now the Sultan's Minister of Foreign Affairs. None of them appeared the least amenable to reaching agreement and none seemed to know the first thing about the Bedouin. Glubb was amused 'on more than one occasion' to find himself 'explaining to them the Bedouin way of life'.[24]

Glubb also attended some of the meetings with Ibn Saud, at one of which the Sultan complained bitterly to Clayton that Cox had assured him at Uqair that no forts would be built in the desert; yet now Clayton was telling him that the language of the Uqair Protocol allowed for the construction of such forts. 'How do I know?' the Sultan angrily protested; 'I am a Bedouin and that was what Cokus [Cox] told me and I trusted him'. Glubb was disappointed with Sir Gilbert's rejoinder; 'it was pathetic to hear Clayton in return making vague, polite assurances of friendship'.[25] He was also critical of Clayton's negotiating style, accusing him of naïvely believing that 'oriental diplomacy required flowery compliments and a circuitous and courtly approach' when, in fact, he would have done better tackling the Sultan directly and talking to him 'man to man'.[26] Still, Glubb 'liked and admired' Sir Gilbert; he was 'one of the most charming chiefs' under whom he had worked, was 'always kind, considerate and interested' and 'patiently allowed' Glubb to advance his own views concerning how the problem of the desert posts should be resolved.[27] But he realized that even his proposal would not likely lead to agreement because 'a solution was in reality impossible, as long as the Ikhwan were out of control'. He was convinced that the Ikhwan 'were really in revolt against' Ibn Saud and that in order to maintain his dwindling support in Najd, the Sultan had been forced to adopt an uncompromising stance: The Iraqi posts must be demolished or there would be no agreement.[28]

In the face of Ibn Saud's intransigence, Clayton had no difficulty in deciding to break off the talks. Indeed, his instructions were clear in stating that Britain would not concede that Iraq was in violation of any treaty in erecting the desert posts and would not agree to demolish any of them. Not only would this have reflected an infringement of Iraqi sovereignty, the desert posts were designed to protect a future pipe-line and railway from Haifa to Baghdad. Thus, 'imperial as well as local issues' were implicated. Clayton understood that an impasse had been reached, but he was unwilling to give Ibn Saud 'a final refusal', for 'a definite rupture in the present state of things would be ill-timed and possibly dangerous'. He suggested instead a suspension of the talks. London agreed and on May 21, 1928, Clayton and Ibn Saud signed a document agreeing to resume talks at a later date and, during the period of suspension, to refrain from 'offensive action' and 'acts of aggression'.[29] So preoccupied were Ibn Saud and Clayton with the issue of the posts, the Sultan never did raise the issue of his British arms purchases.

Although Clayton had tried his best, it appears that he did not expect to succeed with Ibn Saud. As he advised Dobbs, 'I never anticipated . . . that more would be gained than a certain period of calm in which angry passions might subside and the atmosphere become more favourable'.[30] He assumed, correctly, that the Sultan was in a difficult position with the Ikhwan and could not afford to agree with Britain on the desert posts without further estranging the dissident sheikhs and compromising his position in Najd. And, he believed that the RAF, by crossing the border into Najd, had given Ibn Saud an additional argument against acquiescing to the Iraqi posts. The Air Force's bombing in Najd, the Sultan argued – correctly – represented a violation of the Bahra Agreement,[31] and had so infuriated the Najdi Bedouin that he could not possibly agree to the maintenance of the posts. If that were not enough, while Clayton was in Jeddah, several Transjordanian tribes launched raids into Najdi territory.[32] True, the raids had been made in retaliation for a February raid by a Najdi tribe into Transjordan in which 162 persons had been killed, but this fact undercut the strength of Clayton's protest of the Ikhwan raids in Iraq.[33]

Meanwhile, in London, the impasse reached at Jeddah was fully engaging the Committee of Imperial Defence and the Cabinet. On May 22, the CID convened to consider the situation and agreed that there would be no concession on the principle involved; 'the only possible conclusion was to refuse to dismantle the [Iraqi] posts'. At the same time, Amery acknowledged that Ibn Saud lacked sufficient control of the Ikhwan to stop the raids and that Clayton 'should be put in a position' when the talks were resumed 'to make an offer which will convince Ibn Saud that we are doing our best to meet him in the matter'. The Air Ministry was directed to re-examine 'the whole question of frontier posts' and determine 'which were essential and which could be dispensed with'.[34]

And then Amery made a surprising announcement. He informed the CID that he had been in consultation with Chamberlain and they had decided to appoint Sir Gilbert Clayton to succeed Dobbs as High Commissioner for Iraq. The Colonial and Foreign Secretaries certainly regarded Clayton as suitable for the position, but the timing of the appointment was important. Dobbs was not due to retire from Iraq until June 1929, but if Sir Gilbert, 'who was a friend of Ibn Saud', was authorized to tell Ibn Saud now that he 'was shortly to be High Commissioner of Iraq, it would do more to reassure him than anything else we could say, short of a definite and concrete concession'. The next day the Cabinet endorsed all the CID recommendations, including the proposal to appoint Clayton High Commissioner.[35]

Chamberlain had Clayton in mind for Iraq at least as early as April 1928.[36] And he certainly agreed with Amery on the appointment before the CID meeting of May 22. The Foreign Secretary considered it 'incontestable that Ibn Saud has a great personal regard or even friendship for Clayton' and, once he was told Sir Gilbert would be in charge in Baghdad, the Sultan would be 'far less suspicious regarding the future'.[37] Amery agreed, and favoured the appointment for another reason. Dobbs had not got on well with Faisal and some in the Colonial Office were convinced that 'half the trouble [in Iraq] was due to Feisal and Dobbs not hitting it off at Baghdad'. Faisal's modern biographer states that by early 1928, Dobbs and the King could 'barely tolerate being together'.[38] Dobbs himself was reluctant to remain in Iraq beyond 1928 and suggested that either Cornwallis or Clayton should succeed him.[39] Chamberlain wanted Sir Gilbert 'in the saddle at the earliest possible date', preferably in late 1928, but Amery would agree only that Clayton should take up his duties in early 1929.[40] The King's approval was required for the appointment and was sought in June, with the additional request that Clayton also be permitted to inform Faisal of his appointment 'as he and Sir Gilbert are old friends'. On June 26, His Majesty approved the appointment and agreed that Ibn Saud and Faisal could be advised of the decision.[41]

Clayton arrived in London on June 9, and met immediately with officials at the Foreign and Colonial Offices and the Air Ministry, including Amery and Trenchard. Amery promptly prepared a memorandum on the 'Akhwan Situation' and five days later the Cabinet established a special sub-committee of the CID to consider Clayton's failed negotiations and the basis, if any, for renewing them. The composition of the sub-committee suggests the importance the Cabinet assigned to the matter. Chaired by Prime Minister Stanley Baldwin, its members included Amery, Chamberlain and the Secretaries of State for India, War and Air, the CIGS and the Chief of the Air Staff, Trenchard. After considering Amery's memo, a Note from the Air Staff, an interim report from Clayton and cables from Dobbs in Baghdad, Sir Gilbert was called before the sub-committee on June 26.[42]

In both his interim report and in his testimony, Clayton was clear: the desert posts were essential and 'it should be made quite clear to Ibn Saud that His Majesty's Government insisted now, and for all time, on the principle that they could brook no interference with what was done on the Iraq side of the frontier'. Still, because he was convinced that Ibn Saud was in a difficult situation with the Ikhwan, Clayton proposed that the number of posts might be reduced or that Britain might agree that they be constructed no closer than a fixed distance from the frontier. He added that Ibn Saud had 'some slight justification' for interpreting the phrase 'in the vicinity of the border', as set for the in the Uqair Protocol, in the way he had, as there was a 'divergence between the Arabic and the English texts'. At Bahra (1925), and again at Jeddah (1927), Clayton had insisted the treaties provide that in the event of a disagreement on language, the English version of the treaty would control over the Arabic. But Cox had not done this at Uqair. Nor had he kept minutes of his discussions with the Sultan or provided a detailed report describing them. So, it was necessary for the CID to consider the meaning of the Arabic words used at Uqair for 'in the vicinity of the border'.

The Arabic phrase used was '*ala atraf al-hudud*', a phrase, Clayton observed, that could be translated as 'on both sides of the border', rather than 'in the vicinity of the border'. So, when article 3 of Uqair precluded the parties from establishing forts in the vicinity of the border, the Arabic phrase used might have suggested to Ibn Saud a wider area than that intended by the British. Clayton's suggestion was challenged by Hoare, and Amery regarded the Sultan's claim of a treaty violation based on the text of Uqair 'as little more than a pretext'. The India Office did not accept the argument either, though they acknowledged that more precise Arabic words could have been used for the English equivalent of 'in the vicinity of the border'.[43] The Arabic phrase used may be accurately rendered as 'on the sides of the border', but Clayton's suggestion that the Arabic words might allow for Ibn Saud's expansive interpretation was weak, for if the phrase had any meaning at all, it must imply a distance limitation. Baghdad was on the Iraqi side of the border, as was Riyadh on the Najdi side; but no one could seriously claim that the language used precluded the construction of forts at either place. Later, Cox was consulted. He reported that the words meant to him – and he was sure they meant to Ibn Saud – 'within rifle shot' or 'within sight of' tribes using watering holes on the frontier. He regarded '10 or 15 miles from the frontier as a most liberal estimate'.[44]

In their report of July 10, the CID disregarded these interpretive arguments and accepted the basic proposals of Amery and Clayton. There would be no concession on the principle: the frontier posts were essential and, as if to underscore the point, the right of Iraq to administer its own territory and to construct posts within its territory was said to be 'essentially a British interest'. As for the number of posts, and their distance from the frontier, Britain would take 'as conciliatory a line as possible'. The Air Staff agreed that the number of posts could be reduced from eight to six. The CID also agreed that the Bahra Agreement's prohibition against either country crossing the frontier in pursuit of raiders would be applied not only to Iraq, but also to British forces, such as the RAF. Only in the case of an 'organised attack on a township or post' – as opposed to a mere tribal raid – or in the event of a series of raids with which Ibn Saud was unable or unwilling to contend, would cross-border pursuits be allowed. Finally, all agreed that Clayton should return to Arabia to resume talks with the Sultan 'as an act of courtesy and on account of Sir Gilbert's friendly relations with him'.[45] On July 11, the Cabinet adopted the recommendations of the CID sub-committee, adding only that Clayton was authorized to spend up to £500 on a gift of his own choosing for Ibn Saud.[46]

Although Clayton was committed to the principle that Iraq could do whatever it wished in the way of defence on the Iraqi side of the frontier, he confessed in a letter to Trenchard that he did 'not much care for the idea of fortified posts thrown out at wide intervals far into the desert'. He doubted their efficacy. And, he strongly disagreed with the Air Staff's position that 'air operations have produced situations favourable to the conduct of peace negotiations'. To the contrary, the RAF bombing campaign in Najd in January and February 1928 served only to 'exasperate the Akhwan rather than intimidate them'. Also, the RAF's bombs, at times, had landed on tribes who had nothing to do with the raids into Iraq, and had thus 'hardened the [Najdi] northern tribes in their attitude of opposition to the posts'. At the same time, the bombing had given Ibn Saud a 'useful argument' against the forts. Had the bombing not been extended to Najd, Clayton argued, he might have reached agreement with the Sultan, or, 'in any event, he would have had a poor case'.[47] Relying on his experience of the 'big raid' by the Ikhwan near Amman in 1923, which had been met by 'terrible punishment by aeroplanes and armoured cars without any necessity for crossing the frontier', Clayton maintained that the Najdi attacks should be met in Iraq 'with concentrated forces' and hit hard. Such a strategy would be 'efficacious and economical' and open to no criticism from Ibn Saud. Clayton also offered the Air Chief some general advice concerning the use of air power. He understood the important role the RAF played in the defence of Iraq and in the protection of Imperial communications, but he suggested that aircraft 'should be used . . . with extreme caution and even reluctance in aid of the normal civil administration'. His work in Egypt during the 1919 uprising had convinced him that 'every time the civil administration calls in the military force, their prestige and authority are seriously damaged, and every time they succeed in dealing with a crisis themselves, they are proportionately enhanced'.[48]

By July 19, the conclusions of the CID and the Cabinet had been embodied in a set of instructions that would guide Clayton in his renewed talks with Ibn Saud. He was authorized to offer a reduction in the number of posts from eight to six and to propose that none would be situated within 25 miles of the Najdi border. But there was to be no concession on the general principle advocated by Clayton and accepted by the CID and the Cabinet – Iraq could do as it wished in its own territory.[49]

While the British were prepared to make some concessions in matters of detail regarding the desert posts, the Iraqis were, in several ways, even more amenable. Of course, they would not concede that any existing treaties had been infringed 'in any way' by Iraq, but they were prepared to compromise in order to bring the raids to an end. As early as March 1928, the Iraqis agreed that the dispute concerning the meaning of article 3 of the Uqair Protocol could be submitted to arbitration at The Hague.[50] They agreed to Ibn Saud's erection of posts on the Najdi side of the border and to the erection of a joint, Iraqi-Najdi post in the neutral zone, a large rectangular area sitting astride the frontier that had been created by Cox in 1922.[51] Further, Iraq would agree to a proposal that enumerated the watering places in the southern desert and specified those where no posts could be erected. If that proved unacceptable to the Sultan, Iraq would concede that no Iraqi post would be maintained within 25 miles of the Najd border.[52] The Iraqis were even prepared to make important general concessions to the Sultan as inducements to settling the dispute. If agreement was reached on the posts, Faisal would allow amendment of the Bahra Agreement to provide for the extradition of Najdi tribes entering Iraq without permission, an issue that had nearly prevented Clayton from reaching agreement with Ibn Saud in 1925 (see Chapter 26).[53] Iraq would even go so far as to accord recognition of Ibn Saud's rule in Najd and the Hijaz – no doubt a bitter pill for Faisal to swallow – and to exchange diplomatic representatives with Najd.[54]

With all these concessions in hand, Clayton collected his instructions at the Colonial Office on July 19, and he and Antonius – who was accompanying Sir Gilbert on his fifth diplomatic mission – purchased a sporting rifle and an astronomical telescope as gifts for the Sultan. They left London the next morning and arrived in Jeddah on July 30. Three days later he had his first meeting with Ibn Saud. Clayton 'explained everything' to the Sultan and 'used all [his] arguments, but he remained firm on the question of the posts'.[55] Ibn Saud exhibited no 'sign of hostility or unfriendliness' and Clayton was 'convinced that he [was] anxious to avoid any serious trouble on [the] frontier and will do his utmost to prevent it'. But, 'the main consideration which is influencing him' was 'obviously the attitude of his people and he hopes doubtless that his refusal to come to terms will be of assistance to him in consolidating his authority and preventing any serious outbreak'.[56]

On the evening of August 2, after his first meeting with Ibn Saud, Clayton began to feel 'very unwell'. Despite still feeling 'very seedy', he met again with the Sultan the following day, and asked Ibn Saud to think 'very deeply' about his position on the posts. Not only would he be relinquishing the possibility of the extradition treaty that he had sought since 1925, as well as Iraqi recognition of his kingdom of the Hijaz, he 'might even endanger his relations with the British Empire'.[57] Clayton was sure the Sultan realized the important concessions he was 'throwing away', but there was 'nothing doing'.[58] By the end of the second day, the talks were finished; no agreement on the posts was possible and Clayton therefore declined to discuss any subsidiary agreements, such as those concerning extradition, recognition, and the exchange of representatives.[59]

On Saturday, August 4, Clayton was confined to his bed; he was down with fever, as he had been so many times before. But this illness was different; he complained of 'faintness and shortness of breath' and he was extremely restless, unable to sleep. Ibn Saud sent his doctors and the Italian Consul in Jeddah, a physician, came to see him in the evening. The Italian 'found a certain dilatation of the heart' and gave Sir Gilbert digitalis. He had a very bad night and felt no better the following day, when Ibn Saud came to see him. On the 6th, though, he began to feel better. His heart was now 'quite all right' and his restlessness had gone. The next day he was still weak and unable to eat solid food, but was able to sleep in his 'very hot and airless' quarters. On August 8, he had a final 'business interview' with Ibn Saud and decided to leave Jeddah the next day. Clayton was no doubt disappointed in the results of his mission but, as he admitted in a letter to Dobbs, he 'did not expect that very tangible results would come of it'. Still, he was glad that he had come out again to communicate the decisions of the government personally to the Sultan. He detected 'a considerable improvement' in Ibn Saud's attitude and was convinced that Ibn Saud was 'sincerely anxious to avoid real trouble'.[60]

Clayton was correct in thinking that Ibn Saud could not afford to back down on the issue of the desert posts without compromising his position in Najd. Even as Sir Gilbert was negotiating at Jeddah, the principal Ikhwan sheikhs were concocting plans to overthrow Ibn Saud and divide up Arabia among the Mutayr, 'Ajman and 'Ataiba leaders.[61] In December 1928, the Sultan convened a great assembly at Riyadh and offered to abdicate if the *'ulama* and the Ikhwan leaders were dissatisfied with his rule. This dramatic gesture stunned the assembly and had the effect of bringing the majority of the Najdi tribal leaders back into the Sultan's camp and isolating the rebel Ikhwan chiefs. Ibn Saud would soon be ready to contend with them. In late March 1929, the Ikhwan leaders were confronted by the Sultan's forces in central Arabia and suffered a crushing defeat. Although the rebel threat would not subside completely until January 1930, the revolt of the Ikhwan was finished.

29

Final Posting: High Commissioner for Iraq, 1929

During the last four months of 1928, Clayton was preoccupied with preparations for his new post as High Commissioner for Iraq.[1] He was supplied by the Colonial Office with piles of documents concerning the country – treaties, annual reports, departmental memoranda and Intelligence reports. He dined with the Sultan of Muscat, met with Sir John Cadman, chairman of the Anglo-Persian Oil Company, and had lunch with Ja'far al-'Askari, the Iraqi officer who had been captured in Egypt's western desert in 1916, joined Hussein's Arab Revolt and, during the 1920s, had held several high offices in the Iraqi government, including Defence Minister and Prime Minister.

He visited with Trenchard and met Air Vice Marshal Sir Robert Brooke-Popham, who would soon take up the responsibility for Iraq's defence as the RAF's Air Officer Commanding in Baghdad. On October 8, Sir Gilbert's appointment as High Commissioner was announced publicly and he spent several days answering the many congratulatory messages he received. One such letter arrived from T. E. Lawrence who wrote to his former chief of his delight that Clayton was 'back in the saddle again' and 'how very lucky' Iraq was to have him appointed to the top post in the country, for Baghdad, he wrote, 'requires the diplomatic so much more than the administrative understanding'. Lawrence concluded with a request that the new High Commissioner give his old friend Faisal his best regards and with the advice that Sir Gilbert should 'guard [his] own head against him [Faisal] & everybody'.[2]

Although he appears to have had no recurrence of the heart problem he experienced at Jeddah in August, Clayton's health was still not good. In September, he received a series of inoculations 'against catarrh' and, throughout October, suffered from another bout of lumbago for which the doctors prescribed 'antiphlygostine', x-ray treatments and 'blisters'. On November 7, in preparation for his departure, he saw his doctor and had a 'thorough over-haul'. If the examination disclosed any problems, he did not record them in his diary. In October, Clayton put Apple Porch, his home at Peaslake, up for sale. It did not sell, but he signed a short-term lease on a house in Woking, called Crosslea, where the family would spend the holidays. On December 21, the entire Clayton family – Sir Gilbert's three sisters and two brothers

– gathered at Crosslea and 'Bertie supplied the champagne for the great meeting, the first time in 18 years they had all been together'.[3]

Clayton also continued his public speaking and, as he had for years, attended meetings of the Central Asian Society and the Royal Institute of International Affairs. On December 4, he delivered a speech at the Institute, entitled 'Arabia and the Arabs', which he described, correctly, as 'entirely innocuous – even to the point of dullness'.[4] The speech was printed in the January 1929 *Journal* of the Institute, the only work he ever published. At only one point in his presentation did Clayton refer to his own policies in the East:

> I am satisfied that our Arab war-policy was, as a whole, more than justified by the result achieved, and I am content to await the verdict of history with an easy mind. I have heard the opinion expressed that we backed the wrong horse, Husain instead of Ibn Sa'ud. To this criticism I would reply that, although the two horses ran at the same meeting, they did not run in the same race. We put our money on both and in neither case did we lose it. Ibn Sa'ud could not have influenced the course of operations in Palestine any more than Husain could have helped us in Mesopotamia. It is beside the point that the two horses subsequently ran in the same race, when Ibn Sa'ud proved to be the better horse at the distance. We did not bet on that occasion.[5]

By mid-January 1929, Clayton was ready to leave for Iraq. On the 24th, he met with the Prince of Wales, and received final briefings from Amery and Chamberlain. Five days later he made out his last will and testament at Lloyd's Bank and the next day left London for the Continent, accompanied by Enid, a maid and his brother-in-law, Commander Arthur Thorowgood, who would serve as Sir Gilbert's private secretary in Baghdad. His plan was to travel overland, through France, Switzerland, Italy, Yugoslavia, Bulgaria, Turkey, Syria, Palestine and Transjordan. From Amman, he was to 'follow the furrow' by air and arrive in Baghdad on February 16.[6] But on February 2, while travelling through Thrace, his train was held up by a blizzard and the party were snow-bound for eight days. Coal was brought in from a local factory to keep the engine from freezing, and all the passengers were moved into a single coach, bundled up against the frigid temperatures. Nearly three years later another traveller, the mystery writer Agatha Christie, was held up on the same line by another winter storm, an event which inspired her book *Murder on the Orient Express* (1934). The Clayton party experienced no murders, but the journey was 'becoming a regular nightmare' for them and they did not reach Constantinople until February 10.[7] The next day Clayton and Sir George Clerk, the British Ambassador to Turkey, travelled by train to Angora (Ankara), where Sir Gilbert met with the Turkish Prime Minister and Minister for Foreign Affairs. Clayton made an 'excellent impression' on the Turks as they discussed issues of common interest to Iraq and Turkey during a meeting that a Foreign Office analyst noted had 'done more than many months of correspondence and negotiation'.[8]

Clayton's plane finally touched down in Baghdad on the afternoon of March 2, 1929, and, as so often was the case in his career, he arrived in the middle of a crisis. The government of Prime Minister 'Abd al-Muhsin al-Sa'dun had resigned in January and the country was in political turmoil. Ministerial crises were nothing new in Iraq; there had been several during the decade following the end of the war and there was little evidence from the period to suggest the development of stable government in the country. For nearly three years after the Turkish armistice of October 1918, Iraq was governed by a British administration, staffed largely by British civil servants from India, in conjunction with an Iraqi Council of Ministers. Their rule was unpopular and shortly after it was announced at San Remo in April 1920 that the Mandate for Iraq had been assigned to Britain, the country exploded in revolt. Although opposition to British rule provided a focal point for the revolt, it could not fairly be described as a 'national' rising, similar to that which had occurred in Egypt in 1919. There was certainly displeasure over the prospect of a prolonged period of British rule, but the tribesmen of the mid-Euphrates region who were the first to rise in June 1920 were perhaps more concerned with local issues – land tenure, taxation and the loss of local autonomy – that could not be attributed solely to the British administration.[9] There was then, and there is now, no unanimity concerning the causes of the revolt, but there was no disagreement about the cost. It was high; there were 'over 2,000 British casualties, missing or prisoners, and 8,450 Iraqis'.[10] And, to the dismay of the Lloyd George government, and to a British public squeezed by post-war stringencies, the cost to suppress the insurrection came in at a whopping £32,000,000.

In the wake of the 1920 revolt, many at home would have preferred that Britain relinquish all responsibility for the country, that London adopt a policy of 'scuttle'. But others understood that important British interests were at stake. Some were strategic. Britain could not allow another Power to dominate the head of the Persian Gulf. Nor could she abandon the desert air route, just established in 1921, and a key link in Imperial communications with India. Other interests were economic. Oil was not yet being produced in Iraq but, by 1919, speculators had already focused on northern Iraq as a potential source of vast deposits. And even if they were proved incorrect, Britain had a significant interest in Persian oil, which had been produced for years, and refined at the large facility at Abadan near the top of the Gulf since 1909. Others, less concerned about oil, observed that Britain had fought the Turks in Iraq for four years, at a staggering cost in blood and treasure. To them, it was unthinkable that Britain should now throw away that hard-earned victory, only to see the Turks re-occupy the country without opposition. And the Turks were ready to do just that; by mid-1922, Turkish officials had re-established themselves in three districts in the northeast of the country,[11] and it was no secret that Turkey was intent on taking over the entire Mosul *vilayet*. Finally, Britain had just accepted the Mandate for Iraq in April 1920. If she were to cut and run now, the loss of British prestige in the Middle East, not to mention Europe, would be incalculable.

With all these considerations in mind, London decided to stay the course. But, in an attempt to make British rule more palatable, the notion soon arose that, unlike

Palestine, where the Mandate was unilaterally imposed and embodied in a formal Mandate, British trusteeship in Iraq would be reflected in a treaty, more or less negotiated with the Iraqis, which would then be presented to the League of Nations for approval. Meanwhile, in March 1921, the new Colonial Secretary, Winston Churchill, proposed that a constitutional monarchy should be established in Iraq under the Amir Faisal who, it will be recalled, had been turned out of Syria by the French only eight months earlier. At the same time, Churchill suggested a daring cost-saving measure; Anglo-Indian troops would be withdrawn from Iraq over time and the RAF would assume responsibility for the defence of the country, assisted only by a battalion or two of locally raised Assyrian 'Levies'. The Cabinet agreed to both proposals. In August 1921, Faisal was duly 'elected' as the first King of Iraq and treaty negotiations began the following February. The talks did not go easy. Faisal, eager for real power and worried that he would be perceived as a British puppet if he did not get it, resisted provisions in the treaty vesting control in the British High Commissioner. The nationalist parties in the country contested the very notion of a Mandate. After considerable arm-twisting, the treaty was finally signed in October 1922, but ratification was not secured from the newly created Iraqi constituent assembly until June 1924.[12]

The 1922 treaty defined Iraq's relationship with Britain and quite clearly reflected Iraq's subordinate status. The king agreed to be 'guided' by the advice of the High Commissioner 'on all important matters affecting the international and financial obligations and interests of' Britain. And, British predominance was confirmed in a series of detailed and complex 'Subsidiary Agreements' accompanying the treaty and dealing with military, financial and judicial matters, as well as Iraq's employment of British officials who, along with Iraqi nationals, were the only officials allowed to serve in the country without the 'concurrence' of the British. Provision was also made for an 'Organic Law' – a constitution – that would be approved by an elected constituent assembly and would ensure freedom of conscience, the free exercise of 'all forms of worship' and the absence of discrimination in Iraq based on 'race, religion or language'. The term of the treaty was twenty years and Britain agreed to 'secure the admission of Irak to membership in the League of Nations as soon as possible'.[13]

The agreement to secure Iraq's admission to the League was critical, for, once admitted, Iraq's status as a Mandated country would terminate; the country would then become an independent nation. But the qualifying phrase, that Britain would seek Iraq's admission 'as soon as possible' was, of course, intentionally vague; it did not operate to terminate the treaty – and thus, British control – and it left to Britain to decide when it was 'possible' for Iraq to be admitted. The next seven years would be characterized by increasing tension – persistent pressure from Faisal and the Iraqis for a definite agreement by Britain to support Iraq's admission to the League by a date certain was met by British refusals to commit to admission until, in their absolute discretion, admission was warranted. In April 1923, a Protocol to the treaty was signed providing for the termination of the 1922 treaty upon Iraq's admission and 'in any case not later than four years after the ratification of peace with Turkey'.[14]

But again, this was a vague formulation. A Turkish peace treaty had been signed in August 1920, the Treaty of Sèvres, but events in the region quickly rendered many of its provisions meaningless. The treaty had to be entirely renegotiated, and a new pact with the Turks was not signed until July 1923, at Lausanne, and not ratified by all parties until August 1924.

One problem the negotiators at Lausanne could not resolve was that posed by the former Turkish *vilayet* of Mosul. The Turks wanted it. So, too, did Iraq, not only because the province was thought to be rich in oil, but also because, without its largely Sunni population, the Shi'i would be preponderant in a truncated Iraq. Faisal was Sunni, and the various Iraqi ministries appointed since his election were dominated by Sunnis. A predominately Shi'i country ruled by Sunnis would not augur well for the future. Because of the impasse reached at Lausanne, the League appointed a commission to study the contested province and in July 1925 it decided that the Mosul *vilayet* should be included in Iraq. The League approved the decision in December 1925, but with an important qualification: Britain and Iraq must sign a new treaty 'ensuring the continuance for twenty-five years of the mandatory regime defined by' the 1922 treaty, unless Iraq was admitted to the League before the expiration of that 25 year period.

So, in January 1926, a new Anglo-Iraqi treaty was signed providing that the Mandate would remain in force for 25 years, but that, in 1928, and at subsequent four-year intervals, the British would actively consider whether conditions were such that Britain could 'press for admission' of Iraq to the League. The Subsidiary Agreements signed in conjunction with the 1922 treaty would remain in effect until the Mandate was terminated.[15] The 1926 treaty may have represented the price the Iraqis were prepared to pay for inclusion of the Mosul *vilayet* in Iraq, but it did not dampen the desire of Faisal and his compatriots for an early termination of the Mandate. They soon began pressing for Iraq's admission to the League at the earliest date contemplated by the 1923 Protocol – the fourth anniversary of the ratified Treaty of Lausanne, August 1928.

The Iraqi position was not unanimously rejected by the British. Indeed, as early as March 1927, High Commissioner Henry Dobbs began urging a 1928 admission. Dobbs argued that the basic preconditions to independence laid down by Churchill in 1922 – the establishment of settled frontiers and a stable government set up in accordance with an Organic Law – had now been satisfied and that 'any apparent disqualifications for membership of the League from which Iraq suffers are common to other countries which are already members'. Therefore, he concluded, 'the good faith of Great Britain and the best interests of Great Britain and 'Iraq' required an application for League membership in 1928.[16] Colonial Secretary Amery disagreed. First, France would resist Iraq's membership, for if it were allowed, the Syrians would surely argue that they, a more 'advanced' country than Iraq, should also be accorded admission and the French had no interest in terminating their Syrian Mandate. Second, the Council of the League would itself reject such an application. Amery noted that the League's decision to include the Mosul *vilayet* in Iraq 'clearly contemplated that a much longer interval should elapse before Iraq was released from mandatory control'. And, if the British pressed for Iraq's admission in 1928, they would likely be accused of 'sharp practice', laying them open to a charge that they had 'secured a favourable frontier award by undertaking obligations [a 25 year Mandate] we had no real intention of discharging'. In June, Amery cabled that the most to which he could agree was that 'if all goes well in Iraq in the interval', Britain would support Iraq's admission in 1932.[17]

With this policy now set, a new round of negotiations began with Faisal in the autumn of 1927. By November the parties were deadlocked. Faisal insisted on treaty recognition of Iraq's complete independence – 'istiqlal tamm', a phrase Clayton and others had encountered so often before – and abrogation of the right of the High Commissioner to tender advice to Iraq 'on all important matters'.[18] But, on November 28, after meeting with Foreign Secretary Chamberlain, Faisal agreed to abandon his claim for complete independence,[19] and, with this stumbling-block removed, a new treaty was signed on December 14, 1927. Faisal's objection to the right to give advice was solved by the insertion of watered-down language: the king would place the High Commissioner 'in a position to give information' to the British government and, for his part, the High Commissioner would 'bring to the notice' of the king any matter that Britain considered 'might prejudicially affect the well-being of Iraq'. Most important, the 1927 treaty incorporated the proviso laid down by Amery in June. '[I]f the present rate of progress in Iraq is maintained and all goes well in the interval', Britain would support Iraq's admission to the League in 1932. The treaty was not to be ratified until the 1924 military and financial agreements were revised.[20]

Although the 1927 treaty appeared to have resolved the nagging problem of Iraq's admission to the League by providing a specific date, it instead ushered in 'a period of renewed and more intense disagreement' between the two governments.[21] The problem, of course, lay in the provisional character of the British pledge; Iraqi politicians were convinced that even if Iraq continued to make progress, and even if all went well 'in the interval', the British would still conjure up some excuse to justify a refusal to support Iraq's admission in 1932. Throughout 1928, Dobbs became increasingly disheartened and disillusioned.[22] No progress was being made in negotiations to revise the financial and military agreements, and so, the 1927 treaty remained unratified. He was at loggerheads with Faisal and the king was quarrelling with Prime Minister al-Sa'dun who was seeking some way out of the impasse. In September, Dobbs confessed to Amery that he was 'feeling depressed . . . as to whether we are really drawing nearer to our goal of an independent Iraq bound to us by ties of gratitude and self-interest'.[23] In December 1928, al-Sa'dun, equally disheartened, offered his resignation and Dobbs himself was now more than ready to leave, regretting only that 'Clayton's beginnings should be disturbed'.[24]

In London, the Conservative government of Prime Minister Stanley Baldwin remained inflexible; there would be no retreat from the proviso laid down by Amery in June 1927. At the Foreign Office, attention turned to Clayton and the faint hope was expressed that 'Sir Gilbert . . . will be able to rescue us from this dilemma'.[25] The new High Commissioner was certainly willing to try. A week after his arrival, he began talks with Faisal and the leading Iraqi politicians. Al- Sa'dun had resigned in January 1929, but, with some reluctance, he and his cabinet colleagues agreed to stay on as mere 'caretakers', pending the result of discussions with Clayton. Twelve days after taking up his post, Sir Gilbert reported that 'the root of the difficulty lies in suspicion and lack of confidence'. '[E]ven the moderate men', he added, 'are inclined to believe that His Majesty's Government will find some excuse for not recommending Iraq for admission when 1932 draws near'. The problem was that the proviso in the 1927 treaty was 'vaguely worded'; a 'more definite assurance' would, Clayton believed, have 'a great effect'. Faisal made five proposals to Sir Gilbert, two of which went to the heart of the dispute. First, he suggested that the 1927 treaty be dropped altogether and that Britain and Iraq simply carry on under the 1926 treaty and prolong the terms of the 1924 military and financial agreements. Second, the king proposed that the British inform the League 'at the first opportunity' that they would recommend admission 'on a specified date'.[26]

Clayton saw no disadvantage in dropping the 1927 treaty and carrying on under the existing agreements. But he did not agree with the king's proposal concerning League admission; it was 'too far-reaching' and would not only bind the British to bring the question officially before the League, 'but also to recommend admission on a specified date, whatever new factors may have arisen in the meantime'. He recommended 'holding to 1932' and advising the Iraqis that they may apply for admission 'as soon as they like'. The British would forward their application to the League but, at the same time, advise the Council that while they could not, 'in view of various important internal and external questions which are still under settlement, recommend immediate admission', they wished the application to be placed on the League's agenda for consideration in 1932.[27]

Amery remained firm. He could agree to drop the 1927 treaty, but Faisal's proposal regarding League admission was 'impracticable'. The League's Council would not 'accept notice of [a] question to be considered three years hence when existing circumstances might have changed completely'. And, the alternative suggestion made by Clayton was open to the same objection. The Colonial Secretary would only agree to inform the League that the 1927 treaty was being dropped and that Britain would recommend Iraq's admission in June 1932, 'unless in the meantime any serious check in the political or economic progress of the country has occurred'.[28] This, of course, was essentially the same proviso he had laid down in June 1927, and repeated in the December 1927 treaty. The Cabinet approved Amery's position on April 17, 1929, at a meeting during which Chamberlain stated his concurrence with the policy. With the Colonial and Foreign Offices in agreement, there was no chance that removal of the proviso burdening Iraq's admission would be approved.[29] In response to the British position, al-Sa'dun promptly handed in his resignation and not until May was a new cabinet formed under Taufiq al-Suwaidi. Clayton knew him well; four years earlier he had joined Sir Gilbert as an Iraqi adviser during the negotiations with Ibn Saud at Bahra. Despite Amery's inflexibility, Clayton continued to urge the Colonial Office to make concessions to the Iraqis and, as he had in Egypt eight years earlier, he stressed that concessions made spontaneously would have a much greater effect than if given at the end of a period of 'acrimonious bargaining'.[30] Amery was unmoved.

But the situation changed significantly when the Conservatives suffered defeat in the May 1929 general election and, on June 5, were replaced by a Labour government, once again led by Ramsay MacDonald. The new Colonial Secretary was the socialist Sidney Webb, raised to the peerage later in June as Lord Passfield. The Foreign Office went to Arthur Henderson, a strong advocate of international cooperation under League auspices. When it came to Imperial policy and foreign affairs, the byword of both was 'conciliation'.[31] Diplomatic relations with the Soviet Union, suspended by the Conservative government in 1927, were restored; India was publicly promised Dominion status; the arch-imperialist George Lloyd, High Commissioner in Egypt, was sent packing. The prospects for Iraq suddenly seemed much better.

Meanwhile, after his proposal was rejected in March 1929, Clayton busied himself with other problems. The Ikhwan threat had not entirely subsided by the time of his arrival, but he was able to report that, during the first three months of 1929, Ikhwan raiders had penetrated into Iraq on only one occasion.[32] Ibn Saud was pleased to learn of Clayton's assumption of the top post in Iraq and on April 24 he wrote to the High Commissioner of the 'fatal blow' he had dealt the Ikhwan rebels at the end of March. As a result of his 'strong and harsh measures', the Sultan added, 'affairs on the frontier have calmed down completely'.[33] For his part, Clayton advised Ibn Saud that although certain of his 'recalcitrant subjects' had sought refuge in Iraq and Kuwait, Iraq would 'spare no effort to turn them back' to Najd.[34] The problem of the desert posts, though, remained unresolved. Despite Clayton's insistence that Iraq had no hostile intentions towards Najd and despite his renewed offer to submit the Uqair Protocol to arbitration, Ibn Saud continued to insist on the demolition of the desert posts, leading the British Agent at Jeddah to conclude that the Sultan's 'deeper object' was 'to secure a revision' of the Najd–Iraq frontier.[35] The issue remained unresolved in 1929.

Clayton also worked on a number of comparatively minor issues. One involved the rectification of the Iraq–Syria boundary. A line had been drawn, rather carelessly, in a Convention of 1920, but it divided 'certain homogeneous sections of the population'. Although Clayton exchanged several letters with the French High Commissioner in Syria, no resolution was reached in the summer of 1929.[36] Sir Gilbert also put the finishing touches on an Anglo-Iraqi extradition treaty, the terms of which were substantially agreed to in September.[37] Far more complex were the issues swirling round the proposed abrogation of the 1924 Judicial Agreement, one of the 'subsidiary agreements' made in conjunction with the 1922 treaty. The Judicial Agreement had been a sore spot with the Iraqis from the time of its signature five years earlier. Under its terms, certain foreign nationals – those formerly enjoying rights under the Ottoman-era Capitulations – were accorded legal rights more favourable than those provided to the Iraqis and to the nationals of other Asian states, including the Persians. Before Clayton's arrival, it had been suggested that the 1924 Agreement should be abrogated and replaced with a new arrangement ensuring equal justice for all. But the proposal was stalled by a number of complicating factors. Abrogation required League approval and the French and Italians objected; only if the number of British judicial officers in the country were increased were they likely to acquiesce. To this, the Iraqis objected. The Shi'i insisted on being tried in courts presided over by Shi'i judges and they linked the issue to a dispute over the Iraq boundary with Persia in the south of the country. Finally, League consideration was delayed by a complaint received from the Bahai sect in Iraq who protested that they had been subjected to a judgment that resulted in an illegal deprivation of property rights. Clayton struggled with these complex issues throughout the spring and summer of 1929, but this problem, too, remained unresolved when political questions returned to the forefront in late July.[38]

Clayton was also keenly interested in Iraq's economic development. Oil production was the most obvious source of foreign investment, but exploration was delayed by uncertainty concerning the status of the Mosul *vilayet*. And, even after the League awarded the province to Iraq, the grant of a concession to the Turkish Petroleum Company (a consortium of British, French, Dutch and American companies) was delayed by acrimonious negotiations concerning the nature and extent of Iraq's interest. Eventually, the concession was approved by the Iraqi Assembly in June 1926, and the first 'gusher' came in near Kirkuk in October 1927. However, production was slowed by world-wide surpluses and it was not until the 1950s that oil revenue began to make a substantial contribution to the Iraqi economy.[39] Since oil would not be an immediate source of revenue, Clayton repeatedly urged the Colonial Office to assist in the economic development of the country. Iraq was politically stable now, he argued with some exaggeration, and if Britain did not assist the Iraqis, others would. And, perhaps more important, the political problems which would confront Britain in an economically struggling Iraq would become 'increasingly difficult'. The Colonial Office agreed that Iraqis required foreign capital for development, but pointed out that the British government could not raise it for them. Capital could only be generated privately and to achieve this, the Iraqis must first get 'their own house in order'. They must be far less suspicious of and more generous towards investors. And they would need to ensure foreign companies that conditions in Iraq were such that concessionaires could be confident their investments were safe.[40] In short, the Conservative government were not prepared to pursue any measures calculated to assist in the economic development of the country.

By July 1929, Clayton was ready to resume his efforts to break the deadlock in Anglo-Iraqi relations. On July 22, he sent off a lengthy despatch to the Colonial Office, its timing almost certainly prompted by the return of the Labour government in June. He began by ticking off Britain's Imperial interests in Iraq – 'safe and open communications between the Mediterranean and the Persian Gulf'; 'the predominance of British influence in Iraq, or at least protection against any other foreign penetration or interference'; and, the 'preservation of legitimate British interests in the country'. In order to secure these interests, Clayton proposed a new treaty with Iraq, a treaty that could only materialize if the British made three important 'gestures' to the Iraqis. First, and most important, the government 'would be well advised to reconsider their decision' to support Iraq's entry into the League only if Amery's June 1927 proviso remained in place; that is, Britain should advise the Iraqis now that she would support Iraq's admission in 1932, *without* qualification. For Clayton, Amery's proviso – re-asserted as recently as March 25, 1929 – was unnecessary: 'If any check to the political or economic progress of Iraq were to take place in the meantime [*i.e.*, between 1929 and 1932] which would warrant a withdrawal of their promise by His Majesty's Government, it would be of so serious and obvious a nature as to provide full justification'.

Clayton's two additional 'gestures' were of a more minor, yet symbolically significant, character. Colonial Office control of Iraq, he asserted, should be transferred to the Foreign Office, thus removing a sign of 'permanent subservience' in the eyes of the Iraqis. And, the obligation of Iraq to pay a portion of the cost of the High Commissioner's establishment in Baghdad should be terminated. Britain should bear the entire expense. Although the amount was small – the additional expense was only about £50,000 – this was another symbol of subservience, the removal of which would have a great effect on the Iraqis. Sir Gilbert fully appreciated that his proposals ran counter to the prevailing attitude in the Colonial Office; he knew that Iraqi independence would likely 'result in the undoing of much of the work accomplished'. But, he did not believe that maintenance of the 'well-managed State' was essential to Empire. And, as he had argued earlier with regard to Egypt and Transjordan, the Iraqis should be allowed to make their mistakes: 'Iraq has reached a stage at which further progress in self-Government and self-reliance can only be achieved as a result of a system of trial and error. She will only realize and learn to surmount her difficulties by being able to face them herself.'[41] On the same day he sent his official despatch, Clayton wrote privately to Shuckburgh, underscoring his strong feeling 'that it is now essential to decide on a final policy which should be drawn up on wide and liberal lines'.[42]

Having recommended a reversal of the Conservative government's Iraq policy, Clayton could now do little except wait for the reaction of Passfield and his Labour colleagues. Summers in Baghdad were not generally conducive to waiting and the summer of 1929 was worse than most. Temperatures often approached 120° F. and for days on end there was not a breath of wind to relieve the stifling heat. Enid had returned to England in June to spend the summer with the children and, and the Baghdad heat was so debilitating that Sir Gilbert rarely left the Residency before 5 p.m. He was pleased to be joined by his sister Ellinor who came out for a few weeks, but Clayton's only recreation came in the form of polo which he played regularly in the early evenings at the RAF grounds at Hinaidi south of the city.[43] Meanwhile, he continued to keep a close eye on the Iraqi political situation. It was not encouraging. Although Faisal had asked al-Suwaidi to form a government at the end of April, within a few weeks the king was reported to be scheming to undermine the new cabinet. On August 25, he succeeded and al-Suwaidi submitted his resignation. But when al-Sa'dun was approached to form a new government, he refused, unwilling to take responsibility in the uncertain climate of Anglo-Iraqi relations.[44] Iraq was again without a government.

While the political situation was deteriorating in Baghdad, trouble was brewing in the west, in Palestine. Violence broke out between Jews and Arabs in Jerusalem on August 17 and soon spread to the countryside. By the end of the month, 109 Jews, eighty-two Muslims, and four Christians had died and more than 300 were wounded in the rioting. Clayton reported that the events in Palestine 'roused deep interest' in Iraq and that Iraqi sympathy was 'violently pro-Arab'. Although he did not anticipate any serious trouble, inflammatory speeches were being delivered in the Baghdad mosques and attempts were being made to organize demonstrations.[45] On September 1, Sir John Chancellor, the High Commissioner in Palestine issued a proclamation condemning the 'ruthless and bloodthirsty evildoers' and 'the savage murders perpetrated on defenceless members of the Jewish population'.[46] However accurate in laying blame for the violence on the Palestinian Arabs, it was not a statement calculated to have a calming effect. On September 3, Clayton met with Faisal and 'urgently' impressed on the king the need for him to issue a public statement warning the population against any 'popular manifestations' of discontent with events in Palestine. At the same time, he cabled Passfield, warning the Colonial Secretary that any punitive measures taken in Palestine suggesting the Arabs were the 'aggressing and only blameworthy parties' might lead to a dangerous situation in Iraq.[47]

On September 1, Clayton reported that the general situation in Iraq was 'still good but gradually deteriorating', not so much a result of the stir created by events in Palestine, but because of 'doubt and uncertainty as to H. M. Government's real policy'. He continued with a sobering observation. Available ground troops for dealing with urban disturbances consisted of two armoured car sections at Baghdad, three at Basra and one at Mosul, as well as two Assyrian infantry battalions required on the Kurdish frontier – hardly an adequate force. He was not describing the situation 'in any alarmist spirit', he added, but he 'could not ignore the lessons of 1920', an obvious reference to the Iraqi revolt of that year. Clayton thought it essential that a new Iraqi ministry be formed as soon as possible. But in order for this to occur, he 'must have something in . . . hand to offer' the Iraqis. In addition to removing the proviso accompanying Britain's agreement to propose Iraq's admission to the League – already suggested in his July 22 despatch – he now recommended that the date for admission be advanced from June 1932 to September 1931. He concluded with a request that the situation in Iraq 'be treated as a matter of extreme urgency. The moment has come for an immediate decision whether to advance on generous and liberal lines or to remain stationary' with the consequence of having to reinforce British military forces in the country.[48]

By the time he sent his September 1 telegram, Clayton's July despatch had been under consideration at the Colonial Office for a month. No one had been moved to action. But now, the Palestine riots and the resignation of al-Suwaidi added a sense of urgency to the High Commissioner's July proposals. The tone of his telegrams was vaguely reminiscent of those sent in October 1915 when, after his talks with Faruqi, he had convinced London that a crisis was in the offing, that an immediate proposal must be made to Hussein lest the Arabs join the Turco-German alliance

(Chapter 11). The 1929 situation differed only in that there was some real evidence of impending trouble in Iraq. But, in both 1915 and in 1929, Clayton was able to convey a sense of urgency, of crisis, to the decision-makers in London. The analysts at the Colonial Office were certainly convinced. One noted that the situation in Iraq was 'clearly deteriorating' and 'extremely urgent'. 'We have not much time', added another; 'there must be no avoidable delay in taking such action as may . . . strengthen . . . Clayton's hands'.[49] For his part, Passfield reported to the Cabinet that conditions in Iraq were 'critical'. The Iraqis were 'profoundly stirred' and the Palestinian riots 'might well lead to disastrous results', supplying 'the spark which would set the whole country ablaze'.[50]

Any doubts that may have lingered in the Colonial Office concerning Clayton's July proposals were now removed. There was complete agreement that the Amery proviso should be discarded and that Britain should announce support for Iraq's admission to the League in 1932, without qualification:

> Apart from the possibility of serious internal disorders or an interruption of constitutional government, I cannot imagine any occurrence or development in Iraq which would be covered by the wording of the . . . proviso and thus would justify H.M.G. in declining to fulfil their undertaking in 1932. A mere refusal by the Iraq Government to accept any . . . conditions proposed by us concerning, for example, the continued presence of a British Air Force in Iraq, or the position of British officials in that country could not . . . legitimately be described as an interruption in Iraq's progress. We could not, therefore, in the event of such a refusal decently make use of the proviso and threaten Iraq with withholding our support of her candidature for League membership . . . In short, the proviso is of no practical use to us in obtaining the satisfaction of Imperial needs.[51]

While the Colonial Office agreed with Clayton that the Amery proviso should be removed, neither they nor the Foreign Office recommended acceptance of Clayton's proposal that the date of Iraq's admission should be advanced to September 1931. The time available to make the 'necessary arrangements' for Iraq's admission in 1932 was 'already too short'.[52] But Passfield did support another of Sir Gilbert's 'gestures'; he recommended that, with the beginning of the next fiscal year, Britain should bear the entire cost of the High Commissioner and his staff. The suggestion that responsibility for Iraq affairs should be transferred from the Colonial Office to the Foreign Office was not accepted, but Passfield was amenable to the notion that, while his Office should retain responsibility for Iraq, all communications between London and Baghdad should be run through the Foreign Office. There was precedent for such an unusual arrangement; Afghanistan policy was determined in the first instance by the India Office, but, in deference to Afghani concerns, all communications with Kabul were handled by the Foreign Office.[53]

On September 9, Clayton's proposals finally came before the Cabinet. 'In view of the urgency of a decision', the Cabinet quickly agreed that he should be given 'immediate authority' to inform the Iraqis 'without qualification or proviso' that Britain would support Iraq's admission to the League in 1932. It was also decided that the Foreign and Colonial Offices should draft a new treaty to be concluded with Iraq prior to League admission and that Passfield should arrange that, in future, the High Commissioner 'should correspond direct with the Foreign Office'.[54] Foreign Secretary Henderson was not present at the Cabinet meeting of September 9, and his Office promptly objected to the latter decision with the result that Iraq remained under the aegis of the Colonial Office.[55] Decision on the proposal to relieve Iraq of all responsibility for payment of the High Commissioner's establishment was deferred and the Treasury later objected, so that Iraq remained obligated for this small charge. On September 11, officials from the Foreign and Colonial Offices prepared a telegram to Clayton describing the results of the Cabinet meeting of the 9th. Early that evening it was ready for transmission.

On the day the Cabinet adopted his proposal for Iraq, Sir Gilbert wrote a long letter to Enid who was planning to leave England on October 1 to join him for the winter season in Baghdad. It was still very hot in Baghdad and the 'crisis in Palestine' made it impossible for Clayton to leave the city. 'There is a lot of tension', he wrote, 'and the ice is not too thick. What with pro-Arab agitation, no Ministry, shortage of staff and various other things, I am having a very warm summer in every sense of the word'. Still, Sir Gilbert had the company of Ellinor and his brother-in-law, Arthur, and he had been joined at the Residency by the historian Arnold Toynbee, who was stopping in Baghdad for a week on his way to the Far East. And, despite the heat, Clayton was 'getting regular polo' at the RAF grounds south of the city.[56]

Late in the afternoon of Wednesday, September 11, 1929, Clayton was being driven back to the Residency after playing polo at Hinaidi when he was suddenly taken ill. Upon arrival, he was helped into the hall of the Residency and his aide immediately telephoned for the RAF medical officer in Baghdad. He and an assistant, a very junior officer not long qualified as a physician, arrived within minutes and they were soon joined by a civilian doctor. 'They all agreed that it was a case of angina pectoris.' Soon the civilian doctor went off to procure 'some special drug used for such cases' and, just after he left the Residency, Sir Gilbert suffered another attack. As he lay dying, the telegram relaying the Cabinet's decision adopting his Iraq policy left London. It would not arrive until the following morning. At about 7.30, Sir Gilbert looked up and spoke to the young RAF doctor, now distraught that he was unable to help the High Commissioner. 'Don't worry', he said, 'I know that there is nothing that you can do'.[57]

30

Conclusion: Friend of the Arabs

Shortly after 7.30 on the evening of September 11, 1929, Air Vice Marshal Brooke-Popham, now the Acting High Commissioner, wired the news of Clayton's death to the Air Ministry in London. Someone at the Ministry promptly relayed the information to Lawrence, then stationed at an RAF facility near Plymouth. Concerned that Lady Clayton would first learn of her husband's death in the morning newspapers, Lawrence quickly contacted an RAF colleague at Southampton who crossed over to the Isle of Wight in the early morning hours of September 12 to convey the tragic news to Enid, then still with the children at Totland Bay.[1] Captain Jack Clayton was less fortunate; he experienced the 'dreadful shock' of learning of his brother's death in the morning papers.[2]

Sir Gilbert was buried the next day in the British cemetery at Hinaidi, where he had been playing polo less than twenty-four hours earlier. According to the *Baghdad Times*, a 'vast assemblage' thronged the route of the funeral procession: 'From four o'clock onwards there was an endless procession of cars, motor buses, arabanas and cyclists on the road to Hinaidi; never before had we seen such a general exodus from the city. All transport was at a premium and hundreds of people walked the fourteen miles to Hinaidi and back, . . a remarkable spontaneous tribute to the able British administrator whose life's work was consecrated to his friendship for the Arabs and to the amelioration of their lot.'[3]

News of Clayton's death swept across the Middle East. King Faisal, who had not yet learned of London's acceptance of Clayton's recommendation for Iraq's unqualified admission to the League, met Brooke-Popham on September 12 'with a heart full of grief'. 'I am expressing to you my sorrow in which the whole Iraqi nation shares', he added, 'for one . . . who formed the best possible link between the Arabs and the British'.[4] The Baghdad newspaper *al-'Iraq* agreed, describing Sir Gilbert as 'a model to be emulated by British statesmen in the East'.[5] From Riyadh, Ibn Saud wrote of his 'great grief' on learning of the death 'of our dear friend . . . We feel we have lost a very great champion and faithful worker towards the good relations existing between us and the British government'.[6] In Cairo, Faris Nimr, the editor of *al-Muqattam* and a 'friend' of Clayton since 1914, collected newspaper cuttings of articles written by prominent Egyptians, one of whom wrote that Clayton's death 'caused more grief and consternation throughout all Egypt than the death of any foreigner who had ever come to Egypt because he was to them a true and devoted friend and won their confidence and affection from the highest Emir down to the lowest fellah'.[7] Clayton was mourned in Palestine and, in the Lebanon, the Arabic newspaper *al-Ahrar* reported Clayton's death under the headline, 'Gilbert Clayton, the Friend of the Arabs is Dead!'[8]

Were these statements mere examples of eulogistic excess or accurate assessments of Clayton's policies and actions in the Middle East? With qualification, it may be said that the appraisals were justified. For many years, Clayton's conduct had reflected a genuine and sincere friendship for the Arabs. During the war, he was a proponent of Arab independence, at least in so far as the Arab Revolt was a manifestation of that independence. But he did so not because he believed the Arabs could then form a nation, or even because he thought the Revolt would be militarily significant. The evidence is clear that he backed the Arab movement for defensive reasons – to foil the Sultan's call to *jihad* and split the solidarity of Islam, and to remove the possibility of a hostile Arab population ranged along the eastern banks of the Suez Canal and the Red Sea, both vital links in Britain's Imperial connections with the East. And, the documentary record discloses that his support of Arab national aspirations in Syria and the Lebanon was equivocal. As early as 1915, he recognized that Britain had acknowledged French primacy in those countries and, for Clayton, the Anglo-French alliance was of far greater import than Arab nationalism. He discouraged Hashemite plans for an Arab revolt in Syria in 1915 and, after Akaba was taken in July 1917, he warned Lawrence that an extension of the Revolt to Transjordan and Syria was ill-advised, that it would leave the Arab populations in those territories dangerously exposed to Turkish reprisals at a time when Allenby's Palestine offensive had not yet begun and Britain was in no position to protect them. No less important, an extension of the Revolt into Syria would surely antagonize the French, whose claim to Syria had now been confirmed by the Sykes–Picot Agreement.

The Egyptians had better reasons to regard Clayton as a friend. As early as March 1919, he recognized the force of Egyptian nationalism and espoused a policy of devolution and internal autonomy for Egypt. And he did so recognizing full well that his policy would be strongly opposed by the British community in Egypt and by the Lloyd George government at home. He even proposed the elimination of his own position as British adviser to the Egyptian Ministry of the Interior, an act of selflessness that registered deeply with the Egyptians. By early 1919, Clayton had come to recognize that 'the time has passed when developing peoples can be ruled by force', and there is no reason to doubt his honesty in describing to Gertrude Bell his 'fear of that catchword "British efficiency"'. 'Our charter for the rule of . . . Oriental peoples', he added, 'is not primarily "efficiency", but "honesty & sympathy"'.[9] Yet, even in Egypt, Clayton's ideas were tempered by the recognition that while Britain could afford to relinquish matters of form, of 'shadow', such as the British protectorate, control must be maintained over matters of 'substance' – the Sudan, the Nile waters, protection of the foreign population in Egypt, and, most important, the Suez Canal.

In Palestine and Transjordan, too, Clayton was rightly regarded as a friend of the Arabs. He proposed amendment of the Mandate to accord the Arabs greater rights in Palestine. But he did not advocate abandonment of the Jewish national home policy, and it is remarkable that Arab and Jew alike regarded him as a great friend when he left Jerusalem in 1925. Clayton was also a proponent of an Arab State in Transjordan and, from 1918, he rode off Zionist attempts to subject the territory to the national home policy, convinced that both the McMahon-Hussein correspondence and Sykes–Picot warranted the creation of an Arab State across the Jordan. And, while he was quite prepared to overthrow Hashemite rule in Transjordan in 1924, and to concede large tracts of land to the east to Ibn Saud in 1925, at no point did he retreat from his view that Transjordan should be an Arab State. However, in Palestine and Transjordan, as in Egypt, his support of Arab aspirations was always subordinated to his fidelity to Empire. Palestine he regarded as strategically significant, a sort of buffer between the French in the north and the British to the south. And both Palestine and Transjordan were critical to the desert air route, that connecting thread that tied together Britain's Eastern Empire.

Faisal was equally correct in thinking Clayton a friend and he was doubtless sincere when he described Sir Gilbert as 'as the best possible link between the Arabs and the British'. As in Egypt, Clayton was quite content to let the Iraqis run Iraq, even if they made mistakes in the process and 'undid' many of the accomplishments of British administration. Once again though, he was no proponent of *istiqlal tamm* – complete independence – that phrase Clayton had heard so many times during the last fifteen years of his life. In Iraq, as in Egypt, Palestine and Transjordan, Britain must retain, and maintain, important Imperial interests. The desert air route, the planned trans-desert oil pipeline from Iraq to Haifa on the Mediterranean, British predominance in the Persian Gulf – all these demanded that the British presence in Iraq persist. In the Yemen and Arabia, too, Clayton's ideas were dominated by Imperial strategy. He stated many times that the British should not involve themselves in the internal affairs of the Arabian Peninsula. Indeed, he asserted that the only reason that Britain should have an Arabian policy at all was to protect Imperial communications. When Ibn Saud attempted to drive a wedge between Transjordan and Iraq, Clayton was adamant; there would be no separation and the desert air route would traverse only British-controlled territory. And when the Ikhwan penetrated southern Iraq in the late 1920s, Clayton concurred fully in the Colonial Office view that maintenance of the desert posts in Iraq implicated not only Iraqi sovereignty, but British Imperial interests as well. In the southwest of the peninsula, he failed to achieve a negotiated withdrawal of the Imam from the Aden Protectorate, but made clear to Yahya that there would be no lasting agreement with the British until he did retreat. There must be no threat to Aden, perhaps Britain's most important port in the Middle East. And he was quite content to negotiate a 'self-denying ordinance' with the Italians that allowed free economic exploitation in the southern Red Sea, but precluded military installations by either party in the region. Since Britain already controlled the Suez Canal in the north and Aden to the south, the Red Sea would remain a British lake.

In the vast panorama of British Empire history, then, Clayton may be placed among that growing company of men who believed that the Empire could no longer, and should no longer, be maintained by strict control of every aspect of a subject country's affairs. The well-managed colonial State in the Middle East held no appeal for Clayton and he recognized that the force of post-war nationalism would not long allow for it. He was not a theoretician; he was interested in policies that would work. And in the Middle East, Clayton understood that Britain could best maintain her important interests by acknowledging the rights of the Arabs to manage their own affairs – even, within limits, their own foreign policy – and by concluding treaties of friendship and cooperation with them. By the end of the war, Clayton had come round to the view best expressed by Lawrence in a 1919 letter to Lord Curzon. 'My own ambition', Lawrence wrote, 'is that the Arabs should be our first brown dominion and not our last brown colony'.[10] And by 'dominion', Lawrence meant those former British territories that were now essentially autonomous, but loosely bound to Britain by treaties of friendship and motives of mutual self-interest. The idea was neither unique nor original, but it may be said that Clayton was among the first and most effective proponents of it in the post-war Middle East.

It might be argued that, despite his advocacy of devolution, of internal autonomy for the Arab countries, Clayton was still, at bottom, an imperialist, that he still aimed at British dominance in the Middle East and that this aim operated to the detriment of the indigenous populations. True, he did not propose complete independence for any Arab country, with the possible exception of Najd, and he held that Britain should remain preponderant in the region. In this sense, he may be labelled an imperialist. Whether this is a legitimate criticism, though, is questionable, for it is a more appropriate indictment of those living in the second half of the twentieth century, not the first. During Clayton's lifetime, imperialism had yet to be universally equated with notions of demeaning subjugation and crass exploitation. That equation would not be widely drawn for more than a generation after his death, and neither he nor any other historical figure may be fairly judged out of context, taken out of the time in which he lived. It is certainly fair to demand many positive qualities of historical figures – hard work, probity, honesty, good judgment – but prescience is not among them.

That Clayton was able to secure the friendship of the Arabs may be attributed in large measure to the force of his personality or, perhaps more accurately, to the lack of force in it. During his thirty-three years in the Middle East he met a great many people and his frequent tours of the countryside in Egypt, Palestine, and even in Iraq during his short time there, impressed the local populations. He was always engaged, interested, unaffected. And one has the impression that he rarely turned away those seeking interviews with him. Even during the war years, when at times he carried the crushing burden of five jobs, he found time to meet with Arabs, high and low, and he rarely did so for the purpose of ventilating his own views. He was a good listener and he possessed the ability of making others believe he was convinced that what they were saying was important, even if it was not.

Clayton's influence among his British colleagues may be attributed to the unique circumstances of the war. At the remove of a century it is perhaps easy to forget the stupendous, transformative experience of the Great War. Quite apart from the 30 million dead and wounded produced by the fighting, four great empires – the Russian, German, Austro-Hungarian and Ottoman – disappeared virtually overnight and the lives of many more millions were irrevocably altered. And, since it scope and magnitude were unprecedented, the impact of the war was greater than any event in world history. In such circumstances, it is perhaps unsurprising that no comprehensive, over-arching plan emerged for the Middle East during or after the war. The focus was on winning the world's first global conflict and the men directing the effort had neither the time nor the inclination to develop carefully-wrought plans. British Middle East policy was thus responsive, ad hoc, formulated on the fly. London's policy-makers were inclined to defer to their men on the spot, men who, it was thought, possessed thorough local knowledge, acumen and adaptability. And this is the context in which the career of Gilbert Clayton must be considered.

When war broke out in 1914, there was little in Clayton's background to suggest his suitability for the large responsibilities he was about to undertake. He had no experience in Intelligence, almost none in diplomacy. And what abilities he possessed – and they were to prove considerable during the next fifteen years – were often diluted by his willingness to take on more work than he could manage. He occasionally made mistakes of judgment – he overrated the influence of pan-Islam, the scope of Arab nationalism and the threat of an Arab–Turk–German alliance; he underrated French determination to adhere to Sykes–Picot and the amenability of the Egyptians to a British presence if the Protectorate were discarded. But far more often than not, he erred on the side of caution; good examples were provided by his over-estimation of the strength of Turco-German forces in early 1915, his deportation of undesirables from Egypt in 1916, and his determination to form an Anglo-Arab alliance for purely defensive purposes. And he was not afraid to promote unpopular positions, measures that could endanger his own career, as when he disagreed openly with his chief Wingate over a British landing at Rabegh in 1916, or when he advocated a unilateral declaration of Egyptian independence in 1922 – knowing full well that Curzon, Lloyd George and the Anglo-Egyptian community were opposed – or when he exceeded his instructions in 1926 in an effort to secure a treaty in the Yemen, or when he disagreed with Amery in 1929 concerning Iraq's unqualified admission to the League of Nations.

Although Clayton often promoted unpopular or controversial policies, it is remarkable that of the many individuals with whom he worked during his long career and left impressions of him in their papers, there appears almost no personal criticism. Most pointed to character traits that inspired the confidence and admiration of subordinates and superiors alike. King George's private secretary Clive Wigram was impressed by his 'quiet unassuming nature', Keith-Roach by his 'imperturbability', Storrs by his 'equanimity', Lawrence by his calm and his ability to lead by influence and suggestion rather than by directive.[11] Kitchener, Allenby, Chamberlain, Amery, even Curzon, despite their disagreements regarding Egypt, thought highly of him. Nor was Clayton a self-promoter; no instance could be found where he actively sought honours, promotion or position. These qualities did not suggest weakness or indecision. To the contrary, Brooke-Popham confided to Lord

Passfield that 'there's no one I would sooner have worked with in a crisis' than Clayton, and an obituary writer for *The Times* pointed to his 'quiet humour and the power to be pleasantly but definitely final'.[12]

Rather sadly, not so long after his death, the memory of Sir Gilbert Clayton began to fade into the mists of Middle Eastern history, his career eclipsed by the hyperbole surrounding the life of his war-time subordinate T. E. Lawrence. But, if nothing else, the story of Clayton's life may serve to remind some historians and critics of imperialism of a more benevolent side of Empire, a side populated by civil servants who were not animated by notions of cultural superiority or characterized by venality and rank opportunism, but by a desire to do good, to help the people of the countries in which they worked and who sought no reward for their efforts. Lawrence saw such qualities in his former chief and to him the last words on Clayton may appropriately be allowed. On September 14, 1929, he wrote to Lady Clayton of his 'sense of loss' at Sir Gilbert's 'going so suddenly and too soon'. 'His balance and courage and foresight and gentleness and decency were great possessions, which made the Middle East fortunate and rich, and there is nobody alive who can take his place.'[13]

Appendix: Biographies

ABDULLAH ibn Hussein (1882–1951). Second son of Hussein, King of the Hijaz (1916–24), Abdullah was a member of the Ottoman Parliament (1908–14) and commanded the southern Arab army during the Arab Revolt (1916–18). In late 1920, he moved into southern Transjordan and, in March 1921, was offered the Amirate of that country by the British. He ruled as Amir of Transjordan (1921–46) and then as King of Jordan (1946–51). Clayton negotiated with Abdullah in 1922 concerning an Anglo-Transjordanian treaty and issued an ultimatum to the Amir in 1924, requiring him to reform his government or leave the country. Abdullah was assassinated in Jerusalem in July 1951.

ABDULLAHI ibn Muhammad ['the Khalifa'] (c.1846–1899). Educated as a holy man, he became a follower of Muhammad Ahmad (the Mahdi), in 1880 and was named successor in 1881. After the Mahdi's death in 1885, he faced several challenges to his rule (1885–91). The Khalifa's forces were comprehensively defeated by Kitchener's Anglo-Egyptian army at Omdurman (2 September 1898), and the Khalifa himself was run to ground and killed fifteen months later (24 November 1899).

AHMAD Sharif al-Senussi (1873–1933). Grandson of Muhammad ibn Ali al-Senussi, founder of the Senussi religious order in Cyrenaica (Libya). When Muhammad's son, Muhammad al-Mahdi died in 1902, Ahmad was named as successor, as al-Mahdi's son, Muhammad Idris, was then only twelve years old. Resistant to European penetration of North Africa, Ahmad fought the French in Chad (1901) and the Italians in Libya (1911–16). Although Clayton forestalled Senussi hostilities against Egypt throughout 1915, Ahmad was encouraged by the Turks and attacked British positions near Libya in November 1915. He was soundly beaten by March 1916, and effectively conceded leadership of the Senussi to his nephew, Muhammad Idris.

ALI ibn Hussein (1879–1935). Eldest son of Hussein, King of the Hijaz (1916–24), Ali served with the Arab forces during the Arab Revolt (1916–18) and succeeded his father as King of the Hijaz (October 1924–December 1925) after Hussein's abdication. Ali could do nothing to stop the Wahhabi forces of Ibn Saud from overwhelming the Hijaz and ending Hashemite rule there. He resided for the rest of his life in Baghdad, where his brother Faisal was King of Iraq (1921–33).

ALLENBY, Edmund Henry Hynman, Field Marshal, first Viscount Allenby of Megiddo (1861–1936). Commissioned in 1882, after Haileybury and Sandhurst, Allenby served in South Africa in the 1880s, and then completed the Staff College course at Camberley (1896–7). He fought in the Second Boer War (1899–1902), and was named brigadier (1905), major-general (1909) and inspector-general of cavalry (1910). During WW I he commanded the Cavalry Division and the 5th Corps before assuming command of the Third Army (October 1915) in France. Selected by Prime Minister Lloyd George to take command of the EEF, (June 1917), he routed the Turks in the third battle of Gaza and liberated Jerusalem on 9 December 1917. In his final offensive (Megiddo, September-October 1918), he took Damascus and drove the Turks north of Aleppo. He succeeded Wingate as High Commissioner for Egypt (1919–25). Allenby relied heavily on Clayton while the latter was CPO to the EEF (1917–19) and Adviser to the Egyptian Interior Ministry (1919–22).

AMERY, Leopold Charles Maurice Stennett (1873–1955). A product of Harrow and Balliol College, Oxford, Amery reported for *The Times* (1899) and was called to the bar (1902). He served under Milner in South Africa, where he developed his life-long, unwavering commitment to Empire. During the war, he served as an Intelligence officer, until appointed assistant secretary to the War Cabinet. An avid supporter of the Zionist programme, Amery helped draft the language of the Balfour Declaration (1917). In 1919, he was parliamentary under-secretary at the Colonial Office and then at the Admiralty (1921), where he was later named First Lord (1922). As Colonial Secretary (1924–9), he closely monitored Clayton's diplomatic missions to Arabia, Yemen and Iraq.

ANTONIUS, George Habib (1891–1942). Educated at Victoria College, Alexandria, and Trinity College, Cambridge, Antonius was a censor during the war and later rose to the number two position in the Palestine Education Department. He accompanied Clayton on five diplomatic missions (Bahra, 1925; Yemen, 1926; Jeddah, 1927, 1928 (twice)). Clayton was unstinting in his praise of Antonius, insisting that he be awarded a British honour, which he received in 1927 (honorary CBE). Antonius resigned from Palestine service in 1930, and joined the Institute of Current World Affairs in New York. He remained an advocate of the Palestinian Arabs for the rest of his life. His book, *The Arab Awakening* (1938), although later criticized by scholars, was the first English language account by an Arab of the Arab revolt and its aftermath.

al-'ASKARI, Ja'far (1885–1936). Born in Iraq, al-'Askari was educated at military colleges in Baghdad, Constantinople and Germany (1910–12). He fought in the Ottoman Army at Gallipoli and with the Sanusi in Libya (1915–16). He was captured by the British in the spring of 1916, and later joined the Sherifian army in the Hijaz campaign against the Turks. After the war, he served as military governor of Aleppo and, when Faisal became the first king of Iraq (1921), he was appointed defence minister, a post he held several times during the following years. He also served as Iraqi foreign minister and twice as Prime Minister (1923–4, 1926–7). He was murdered in the Bakr Sidqi coup of 1936.

BALFOUR, Arthur James, first Earl of Balfour (1848–1930). After Eton and Trinity College, Cambridge, Balfour was elected to Parliament (1874), and became private secretary (1878) to his uncle, the third Marquess of Salisbury, and future Prime Minister. During a long political career, Balfour held many posts, including Secretary for Scotland (1886–7), Chief Secretary for Ireland (1887–91), First Lord of the Treasury (1891–2, 1895–1905), Prime Minister (1902–5, in succession to Salisbury), leader of the Conservative Party (1902–11), First Lord of the Admiralty (1915–16), and Foreign Secretary (1916–19). In 1919, as Foreign Secretary, Balfour criticized Clayton for what he regarded as the Chief Political Officer's inadequate support of the Zionist programme in Palestine.

BARING, Evelyn, first Earl of Cromer (1841–1917). Grandson of a founder of Barings Bank, he completed the course at the Royal Military Academy, Woolwich, in 1858, and served in Corfu, Malta and Jamaica. He passed out first from the Staff College in 1870, and then served four years in India as private secretary to the Viceroy, his cousin, Lord Northbrook (1872–6). Baring was British representative to the Egyptian debt commission (1876–9), and then one of two controllers-general during the Anglo-French 'dual control' of 1879–82. He was appointed British Agent and Consul-General in Egypt in 1883, and held that post until 1907, during which time he was regarded as the effective ruler of Egypt. Even after his retirement, Cromer was invariably consulted on issues involving Egypt or the Middle East. His *Modern Egypt* (1908) is regarded as a classic in the literature of imperialism.

BELL, Gertrude Margaret Lowthian (1868–1926). Educated at Queen's College, London and Lady Margaret Hall, Oxford, she travelled widely in Europe and the Middle East before the war. In late November 1915, Bell was attached to Clayton's Intelligence department in Cairo, where she soon adopted her chief's views of the merits of an Anglo-Arab alliance. Bell was appointed the Arab Bureau's liaison in Iraq in 1916, and was later named Assistant Political Officer, under Percy Cox, and then Oriental Secretary at the Baghdad Residency (1917–26).

CECIL, Lord Edward Herbert Gascoyne (1867–1918). Fourth son of the third Marquess of Salisbury (1830–1903), he was educated at Eton and commissioned in the Grenadier Guards (1887). Cecil served as aide-de-camp to Kitchener and was present at Omdurman (1898). After service in the Second Boer War, he joined the Egyptian Army and was appointed Sudan Agent and Director of Intelligence for the Sudan Government in Cairo (1903). In 1912, he was named Adviser to the Egyptian Ministry of Finance. Along with Clayton and legal adviser, Sir William Brunyate, Cecil exercised great influence during the High Commissionership of Sir Henry McMahon (1915–16), who had no Egyptian experience. With Wingate's arrival in Cairo as High Commissioner (1917), Cecil was marginalized. His witty, sometimes caustic book, *The Leisure of an Egyptian Official* was published by his widow in 1921.

CHAMBERLAIN, Sir (Joseph) Austen (1863–1937). Son of the great Liberal Unionist politician Joseph Chamberlain and half-brother of Neville Chamberlain (Prime Minister, 1937–40), Austen was educated at Rugby and Trinity College, Cambridge, and in France and Germany. During a long political career (1892–1931), he served as Civil Lord of the Admiralty, Financial Secretary to the Treasury, Postmaster General, Chancellor of the Exchequer (1903–5, 1919–21), Secretary of State for India (1915–17), Lord Privy Seal, First Lord of the Admiralty, Conservative Leader in the Commons, and Foreign Secretary (1924–9). He was awarded the Nobel Peace Prize, largely on the strength of his negotiation of the Locarno Pact (1925). As Foreign Secretary, Chamberlain had high praise for Clayton's work in Arabia (1925, 1927–28) and Rome (1927).

CHEETHAM, Sir Joshua Milne Crompton (1869–1938). Educated at Christ Church, Oxford, Cheetham entered the diplomatic service in 1894 and served in Madrid, Paris, Tokyo, Berlin, Rome and Rio de Janeiro, before arriving in Cairo (1910), where he worked as Counsellor at the British Agency/Residency. He acted as Agent/High Commissioner during two critical periods in Egyptian history (May–December 1914, and January–March 1919) and, on both occasions, relied heavily on Clayton's advice. During the 1920s, Cheetham served as Minister in Peru & Ecuador, France, Switzerland, Greece and Denmark, retiring in 1928.

CLAYTON, Lady Enid Caroline (née Thorowgood) (1886–1973). Wife of Sir Gilbert Clayton, Enid was born in Madras, India, and educated privately in England and Switzerland, where she acquired fluency in French and German. She studied art in Paris and London, became an accomplished painter, and later exhibited her work. Enid met Gilbert in 1911 at Kelburn Castle and the two married in 1912. They had five children, three of whom survived to adulthood: Patience (1913–2009), Samuel (1918–2004) and John (1921–). Active in the Y.W.C.A. and the Girl Guides, Enid accompanied Gilbert to Khartoum, Cairo, Jerusalem and, briefly, to Baghdad. After Sir Gilbert's death in 1929, Lady Clayton lived on the Isle of Wight and, from 1937, at Hampton Court Palace.

CLAYTON, Brigadier-general Sir Gilbert Falkingham (1875–1929). After attending the Isle of Wight College, and the Royal Military Academy, Woolwich, Clayton was commissioned in the Royal Artillery (1895). He served in Kitchener's 1898 campaign against the Dervishes, joined the Egyptian Army (1900) and worked as Inspector for the Sudan Government in the Bahr al-Ghazal (1902–3). He served as Wingate's private secretary (1907–13), and was then appointed Sudan Agent and Director of Intelligence for the Sudan in Cairo (1913–14). During the first two years of the war he was Director of Intelligence for the British forces. In 1917, he was appointed chief of staff, Hijaz operations and, later, Chief Political Officer for the Egyptian Expeditionary Force (1917–19). He then worked for the Egyptian government as Adviser to the Ministry of the Interior (1919–22), Chief Secretary in the Palestine Mandate (1923–25), and as special envoy to Ibn Saud of Arabia (1925, 1927, 1928), during which he negotiated three treaties with the Sultan/King. He died while serving as High Commissioner for Iraq (1929).

CLAYTON, Brigadier-general Sir Iltyd Nicholl (1886–1955). Brother of Gilbert Clayton, Iltyd was educated at Lancing College and the Royal Military Academy, Woolwich, and was commissioned in 1906. He served in Mauritius, Egypt, Salonika and Palestine during the war and was briefly attached to Gilbert's Cairo Intelligence in 1916. He worked as a political officer in Syria (1919), and was assigned to the Iraqi Army (1920–8). After retirement, he was recalled to service in 1939, and became head of the Military Intelligence Centre, Cairo, 1941–3, after which he was Adviser on Arab Affairs, Minister of State (1943–5), special adviser to the head of the British Middle East Office and attached to the British embassy, Cairo, as Minister (1947–8).

CLAYTON, Rear Admiral John (1888–1952). Gilbert's younger brother, John (Jack) was trained for naval service on the *Britannia* (1903) and served during the Great War on two ships that were sunk by the enemy, the *Amphion* (1914) and the *Cornwallis* (1917). Between the wars, John rose steadily in the Royal Navy, commanded several ships, and was appointed Director of Navigation at the Admiralty (1933–5). He retired in 1939, but was recalled to active service on the outbreak of the Second World War, when he was chosen to head the Admiralty's Operational Intelligence Centre.

CORNWALLIS, Sir Kinahan (1883–1959). After Haileybury and University College, Oxford, Cornwallis entered the Sudan Civil Service (1906), and occupied posts at Kassala and Khartoum, where he worked as assistant private secretary to the governor-general (1912–13), under Clayton. He transferred to the Egyptian Ministry of Finance in 1914, and, on the outbreak of the war, Clayton moved him to the Intelligence department and then to the Arab Bureau (1916), where he succeeded Hogarth as director. In 1919, as a political officer, he advised Faisal in Syria and, from 1921, in Iraq. He remained in Baghdad from 1921 until 1935, serving at the Ministry of the Interior and as a trusted personal adviser to King Faisal. He returned to Iraq as British ambassador (1941–5).

COX, Sir Percy Zacariah (1864–1937). Commissioned in 1884, after his schooling at Harrow and Sandhurst, Cox served in British Somaliland (1893), as political agent and consul at Muscat (1899), and as acting resident, and then resident, in the Persian Gulf (1904, 1909). He was named chief political officer of the Indian Expeditionary Force that landed in Mesopotamia in the fall of 1914, and served in that capacity until war's end. After the armistice, Cox was named acting minister in Tehran, where he concluded an Anglo-Persian treaty (1920), and then was appointed first High Commissioner for Iraq under the British Mandate (1920–3).

CURZON, George Nathaniel, Marquess Curzon of Kedleston (1859–1925). Educated at Eton and Balliol College, Oxford, where he was President of the Union, Curzon entered Parliament in 1886, and travelled widely in Asia (1887–95). He served as under-secretary of state for India (1891–2), and for Foreign Affairs (1895–8). He was later Viceroy of India (1899–1905), and Lord Privy Seal (1915–16), leader of the House of Lords (1916–24, 1924–5) and Foreign Secretary (1919–24). In the latter post, he proposed Clayton as the head of a planned Middle Eastern Department in the Foreign Office (1920), but the newly Mandated territories of Palestine and Iraq were assigned to the Colonial Office. He opposed the Allenby-Clayton proposal to unilaterally abolish the Egyptian Protectorate (1922). Although far more knowledgeable of Eastern matters than his Cabinet contemporaries, Curzon was hampered by a bad back and a difficult personality that kept him from Downing Street.

DEEDES, Sir Wyndham Henry (1883–1956). After attending Eton, he joined the Army (1901) and was stationed in South Africa, Bermuda, Ireland and Malta. He learned Turkish and worked before the war in Anatolia and in Libya, where he reformed the gendarmerie. He was later seconded by the Foreign Office to the Turkish Interior Ministry (1913). After the outbreak of war, he served in an Intelligence role during the Gallipoli campaign and was then assigned to Cairo Intelligence where he worked under Clayton. In April 1918, he met Chaim Weizmann and became a strong advocate of Zionism. In 1919, he assisted Clayton in the Egyptian Interior Ministry. Deedes preceded Clayton as Chief Secretary in Palestine (1920–3), and then devoted his life to social work among London's poor.

DOBBS, Sir Henry Robert Conway (1871–1934). Educated at Winchester and Brasenose College, Oxford (no degree), he entered the Indian Civil Service in 1892, and was transferred to the political department in 1899. He worked largely on the northwest frontier and travelled extensively in Baluchistan, Afghanistan and Persia. During the war, he served in the civil administration of Mesopotamia as revenue commissioner (1915–16). In 1919, he was named foreign secretary to the government of India and in 1920–1, negotiated the Anglo-Afghan treaty. He followed Percy Cox as High Commissioner for Iraq in February 1923 and served six years in that role, when he was succeeded by Clayton. Dobbs confronted a variety of complex and difficult issues as High Commissioner and, as early as 1927, advocated Iraq's admission to the League of Nations, although Clayton would posthumously receive much of the credit for the 1929 British decision supporting Iraq's admission in 1932.

FAISAL ibn Hussein (1883–1933). Third son of Hussein, King of the Hijaz (1916–24), Faisal was educated privately in Constantinople. In early June 1916, he inaugurated the Arab Revolt by launching an unsuccessful attack on Medina. More effective as a military leader than his brothers, he moved his force up the Red Sea coast and took the key port of Akaba (July 1917), with T. E. Lawrence. After Akaba, Faisal's force became an adjunct of Allenby's EEF as it moved north into Palestine after the third battle of Gaza (October-November 1917). With the capture of Damascus (October 1918), Faisal struggled to establish an Arab State there but, despite being named King of Syria (March 1920) by an assembly of Arab notables, he was turned out of the country by the French in July 1920. Faisal was then selected by the British as the first King of Iraq (1921–33) under the British Mandate.

FU'AD I (1868–1936). Seventh son of the Khedive Isma'il (r.1863–79), Fu'ad was the younger brother of Hussein Kamil (Sultan, 1914–17). He assumed the title of Sultan on his brother's death and was proclaimed King Fu'ad in March 1922, following the declaration of Egyptian independence.

GRAHAM, Sir Ronald William (1870–1949). Educated at Eton, Graham entered the diplomatic service in 1892, and served in Paris, Tehran and St Petersburg before being sent to Cairo (1907), where he was attached to the British Agency. In 1910, he was appointed adviser to the Egyptian Ministry of the Interior, serving in that position until 1916, when he returned to the Foreign Office as assistant under-secretary of state. From 1921, until his retirement in 1933, he was British ambassador to Italy. In 1927, Graham and Clayton negotiated with the Italians in Rome, resolving Anglo-Italian tensions in the southern Red Sea.

GREY, Edward, first Viscount of Fallodon (1862–1933). After Winchester and Balliol College, Oxford, Grey was elected to Parliament (1885) as a Liberal. He served as under-secretary of state for Foreign Affairs (1892–5) and for eleven years as Foreign Secretary (1905–16). He supported Clayton's plan for an Anglo-Arab alliance. Grey later served as ambassador to the United States (1919–20), leader of the Liberal Party in the House of Lords (1923–4), and Chancellor of the University of Oxford (1928–33).

HARDINGE, Charles, first Baron Hardinge of Penshurst (1858–1944). After Harrow and Trinity College, Cambridge, Hardinge joined the Foreign Office and served in Constantinople (twice), Berlin, Washington, Sofia, Bucharest, Paris, Tehran and St. Petersburg. In 1903, he became an under-secretary at the Foreign Office and, in 1904, returned to St. Petersburg as ambassador. In 1906, Hardinge was appointed permanent under-secretary at the Foreign Office, and, in 1910, was named Viceroy of India and raised to the peerage. He was badly wounded in a terrorist attack in 1912, but stayed on in India until 1916, when he returned to the Foreign Office, again as permanent under-secretary. He was criticized by the commission enquiring into the disaster that befell the Anglo-Indian army in Mesopotamia (Kut, 1916), but his offer to resign was rejected. He ended his career as ambassador to France (1920–2).

HERBERT, Aubrey Nigel Henry Molyneux (1880–1923). Son of the fourth Earl of

Carnarvon, and brother of Mervyn, Herbert was educated at Eton and Balliol College, Oxford. Despite suffering from an eye affliction that rendered him effectively blind, Herbert travelled widely in the East and served as honorary attaché in Tokyo and Constantinople (1904). First elected in 1911, he was an MP for the remainder of his life. Herbert was keenly interested in Balkan politics. A proponent of Albanian nationalism, he was twice offered the throne of that country. During the war, he served in France, where he was wounded and briefly held captive, and then joined Clayton's Intelligence department in December 1914. He also served in Gallipoli (1915). Herbert's adventurous life formed the model for the hero of John Buchan's popular eastern spy thriller, *Greenmantle* (1916).

HERBERT, Mervyn Robert Howard Molyneux (1882–1929). Third son of the fourth Earl of Carnarvon, Mervyn was the full brother of Aubrey and the half-brother of George Herbert, fifth Earl of Carnarvon, who financed Howard Carter's excavations of Tutankhamun's tomb. Educated at Eton and Balliol College, Oxford, Mervyn entered the diplomatic service in 1907, and served in Rome, Lisbon, Madrid and Cairo. While in Cairo, he worked at the Chancery attached to the British Residency and became a critic of High Commissioner Sir Henry McMahon.

HOGARTH, David George (1862–1927). After a brilliant academic career at Winchester and Magdalen College, Oxford, Hogarth travelled widely in the Near East, participating in numerous archaeological excavations throughout the Ottoman Empire. Appointed director of the British School at Athens (1897), and then keeper of the Ashmolean Museum in Oxford (1908), he published many technical studies and several popular accounts of his travels and excavations. On the outbreak of the world war, he served in naval intelligence in London and then, for a time, as director of Clayton's Arab Bureau (1916). Like his protégé, T. E. Lawrence, Hogarth backed Arab aspirations in the Middle East and opposed French ambitions in the region. He returned to the Ashmolean in 1919, sadly disillusioned with the course of Britain's eastern policy. He was named president of the Royal Geographical Society in 1925.

HUSSEIN ibn Ali (*c.*1853–1931). Born in Constantinople, he was educated there and in the Hijaz. Hussein lived in the Ottoman capital from 1893 until 1908, when he was appointed Sherif of Mecca by Sultan Abdulhamid. As Sherif, he resisted the Ottomanization of the Hijaz and declared the Arab Revolt in June 1916. He later proclaimed himself King of the Arab Nation (October 1916), but the Entente Powers recognized him only as King of the Hijaz. An opponent of the Mandates, he refused to ratify the post-war treaties and would not agree to an Anglo-Hijazi treaty (1921–4). He declared himself Caliph in 1924 (perhaps inspired by his son, Abdullah), but abdicated as King of the Hijaz in October 1924, in the face of the Wahhabi onslaught of Ibn Saud. He lived in exile in Cyprus (1925–30) and died in Transjordan.

HUSSEIN Kamil (1853–1917). Son of the Khedive Isma'il, (r.1863–79), Hussein Kamil was declared Sultan of Egypt in December 1914, after the deposition of his pro-Turk nephew Abbas Hilmi II and the establishment of the British Protectorate. Generally regarded as pro-British, a moderate and a man of sound judgment, Hussein met regularly with Clayton (1915–16), who kept him apprised of developments in Arabia and the Sudan. Hussein was succeeded by his brother, Ahmad Fu'ad, who became King Fu'ad shortly after the British recognized Egyptian independence in February 1922.

KITCHENER, Horatio Herbert, Earl Kitchener of Khartoum (1850–1916). Commissioned in the Royal Engineers (1871) after attending Woolwich, Kitchener joined the Egyptian Army in 1883, and was appointed its Sirdar (commander) in 1892. He fought in several actions against the Dervishes in the Sudan until leading the Army in the culminating battles of the Atbara and Omdurman (April, September 1898). After serving as the Sudan's first governor-general (1899), Kitchener was named second-in-command, and then commander (Nov. 1900), of British forces in the Second Boer War. He served as commander-in-chief, India (1902–9), and then as British Agent and consul-general in Egypt (1911–14), before being appointed Secretary of State for War on the outbreak of World War I. He died at sea in June 1916, when the *Hampshire*, conveying him on a diplomatic mission to Russia, struck a mine off the north coast of Scotland.

LAWRENCE, Thomas Edward (1888–1935). A graduate of the Oxford High School and Jesus College, Oxford, Lawrence travelled in Syria and Palestine before the war and participated in several archaeological expeditions (1909–14). With Woolley and Newcombe, he completed a survey of Sinai (1914) and was sent out to join Clayton's Intelligence department in December 1914. From October 1916, he fought with the Arab forces of King Hussein against the Turks. Lawrence attended the Paris Peace Conference (1919), and was employed as Churchill's Arab adviser at the Colonial Office (1921–2). Throughout the immediate post-war years, Lawrence advanced the Hashemite cause in a reordered Middle East. As early as 1919, he achieved notoriety as 'Lawrence of Arabia'. He later published an account of his exploits in the Arab Revolt, *Seven Pillars of Wisdom*.

LLOYD, George Ambrose, first Baron Lloyd (1879–1941). After Eton and Trinity College, Cambridge (no degree), Lloyd served as honorary attaché in Constantinople (1905) with Aubrey Herbert. Entering the House of Commons in 1910, Lloyd joined Clayton's Intelligence department in late 1914, served at Gallipoli and then in the Arab Bureau. He was later Governor of Bombay (1918–24), High Commissioner for Egypt (1925–29), Colonial Secretary (1940–1), and leader of the House of Lords (1940–1). Arch-defender of Empire, Lloyd published a two-volume justification of his tenure in Cairo, *Egypt Since Cromer* (1933–4).

LYNDEN-BELL, Major-General Sir Arthur Lynden (1867–1943). Commissioned in

1885, after attending Sandhurst, he saw service on the northwest frontier of India and in the Second Boer War. In 1914, he was assistant quartermaster general of the British Expeditionary Force in France, and then CGS, Mediterranean (later, Egyptian) Expeditionary Force (1915–17), when he served in Egypt and Palestine. A severe critic of Clayton and the Arab Bureau, he left the EEF shortly after Allenby assumed command in June 1917.

al-MASRI, Aziz Ali (1879–1965). Of Egyptian and Circassian ancestry, al-Masri graduated from the Ottoman Military Academy (1901) and then the Ottoman Army Staff College. Initially a member of the CUP, he fell out with Enver and left the movement. He co-founded two Arab nationalist societies, *al-'Ahd* and *al-Qahtaniyya*, and was eventually arrested and expelled from the Ottoman Empire. He met Clayton in Cairo in the fall of 1914, and tried to persuade him to back his plans for an Arab rising in Mesopotamia. Al-Masri joined the Arab army in 1916, but did not get on well with Hussein or the Sherif's eldest son, Ali. He later directed the Cairo Police Academy (1927–36) and was inspector general of the Egyptian Army (1938).

MAXWELL, General Sir John Grenfell (1859–1929). After schooling at Cheltenham and Sandhurst, Maxwell was commissioned (1879), fought at Tell el-Kebir (1882), and joined the Egyptian Army (1883). He remained in Egypt and the Sudan until 1899, participating in Sudan frontier operations (1885–89) and in Kitchener's Sudan campaign, commanding Egyptian and Sudanese brigades at the Atbara and Omdurman (1898). He commanded a brigade in the Second Boer War (1900–2). After service in Ireland and Malta (1902–8), Maxwell returned to Egypt as commander of British forces (1908–12). After a short period on the western front in 1914, he again returned to Cairo as commander in Egypt (September 1914 – March 1916). His service as commanding officer in Ireland in the aftermath of the Easter rising of April 1916, was the subject of much criticism. Maxwell was a member of the Milner mission to Egypt (1919–20), and retired in 1922.

McMAHON, Sir (Arthur) Henry (1862–1949). After attending Haileybury and Sandhurst, McMahon was commissioned in 1882. He spent nearly his entire career in India, most prominently in the Indian political department (1890–1914). He delineated the boundary between Afghanistan and Baluchistan (1894–6) and later, the line between Tibet and China (1913–14). From 1911–14, he served as foreign secretary to the government of India. Appointed on the advice of Kitchener, he arrived in Cairo in January 1915, as the first High Commissioner for Egypt under the British Protectorate. A retiring man, McMahon proved ill-suited to his position. He knew no Arabic, little of Egypt, and was disliked by his subordinates and by the military commanders. His ambiguous and controversial correspondence with Sherif Hussein of Mecca (1915–16) – almost certainly drafted by Clayton and Storrs – generated decades of ill-will on the part of Arab nationalists, who accused Britain of promising Palestine to the Arabs and then giving it to the Zionists in the 1917

Balfour Declaration. McMahon was recalled in late 1916, and replaced as High Commissioner by Wingate.

MILNER, Alfred, first Viscount Milner (1854–1925). After his schooling in Germany and at Balliol College, Oxford, Milner was called to the bar in 1881, and wrote for the *Pall Mall Gazette* (1882). He served as private secretary in the Treasury (1886), and then spent four years in Egypt under Cromer (1889–92), as director-general of accounts and then under-secretary of finance. In 1897, he was named Governor of the Cape Colony and High Commissioner for South Africa and then Administrator (1901) and later Governor (1902–5), of the Transvaal and the Orange River Colony. He was a member of the War Cabinet (from December 1916), and later served as Secretary of State for War (1918–19) and then Colonial Secretary (1919–21). In 1919–20, he headed a commission of enquiry to Egypt and was influenced by Clayton's ideas for promoting Egyptian internal autonomy.

MONEY, Major-General Sir Arthur Wigram (1866–1951). After joining the Royal Artillery in 1885, Money served in India (1890–1900) and in the Second Boer War (1900–2). He then returned to India and, except for a brief period at the War Office (1910–12), held various positions there until 1915, when he was attached to the Indian Expeditionary Force in Mesopotamia (1915–18). He succeeded Clayton as Chief Administrator in Palestine (1918–19), and retired in 1920.

MUHAMMAD Ahmad ['the Mahdi'] (1844–1885). Born in Dongola Province, Sudan, Muhammad Ahmad became dedicated to a religious life as a young man. He was an adherent of the Samaniyya Sufi sect and early on devoted himself to prayer, devotion and an ascetic lifestyle. In 1870 he moved to Aba Island in the White Nile south of Khartoum. A skilled orator and inspiring teacher, he acquired a large following and, on 29 June 1881, pronounced himself the Mahdi. With his *Ansar* warriors (known in the West as Dervishes) he won several battles against the Egyptian forces sent to quell his movement and, on 26 January 1885, took Khartoum, killing General Gordon in the process. The Mahdi himself died six months later and was succeeded by Abdullahi ibn Muhammad, the Khalifa.

MURRAY, General Sir Archibald James (1860–1945). Gazetted in 1879, upon leaving Sandhurst, Murray served in Hong Kong, Singapore and then South Africa, during the Zulu rising (1888). He served with distinction in the South African War, where he was wounded (1902). Murray held several important staff appointments before the Great War and was made CGS of the British Expeditionary Force in 1914, but appears to have broken down at the end of 1914, when he returned to England. He acted briefly as CIGS, (September–December 1915), when he was replaced by Robertson. By early 1916, Murray was in Egypt as commander of the Mediterranean (later, Egyptian) Expeditionary Force. Although a skilled administrator, Murray failed at the First and Second Battles of Gaza (March-April 1917), and was replaced by Allenby as EEF commander in June 1917. Adamantly opposed to British participation in the Arab campaign, Murray was also a critic of Clayton and the Arab Bureau.

NASIM Pasha, Muhammad Taufiq (1874–1938). Of Turkish descent, Nasim Pasha trained as a lawyer and became a leading Egyptian political figure in the 1920s and 1930s. He served three times as Prime Minister of Egypt (1920–1, 1922–3, and 1934–6), and was Minister of the Interior (November 1919–May 1920), while Clayton served as Adviser to that Ministry. A moderate, Nasim was awarded an honorary GCMG by King George V in 1920.

NEWCOMBE, Lt.-Col. Stewart Francis (1878–1956). Commissioned in the Royal Engineers (1898), after attending the Royal Military Academy, Woolwich, he served in the Second Boer War and in the Egyptian Army (1901–11). He completed the survey of Sinai (1914) with Woolley and Lawrence and served in Clayton's Intelligence department (1914–15), before transferring to Gallipoli (Sept.-Dec. 1915), where he was awarded the DSO. After a time in France, he was appointed chief of the British Military Mission to the Hijaz and conducted demolition raids on the Hijaz railway (1916–17). Newcombe was captured during the third battle of Gaza (November 1917), but later escaped from a Turkish POW camp.

ORMSBY-GORE, William George Arthur, fourth Baron Harlech (1885–1964). Educated at Eton and New College, Oxford, he was elected an MP (1910–38) and served in the Arab Bureau (1916) under Clayton. As British liaison officer to the Zionist mission to Palestine (1918), he was an avid proponent of the Jewish national home policy and critical of the British military administration of the country. He was later parliamentary under-secretary at the Colonial Office (1922–4, 1924–9), Colonial Secretary (1936–8), and High Commissioner for South Africa (1941–4).

PARKER, Colonel Alfred Chevallier (1874–1935). A nephew of Kitchener, Parker was educated at Harrow and Sandhurst and commissioned in 1895. After service on the northwest frontier of India, he arrived in Cairo in 1899, was assigned to the Military Intelligence department in 1901 and made its deputy in 1905. He was appointed Governor of Sinai (1906–12), and later, commandant of the Cairo Police School. On the outbreak of war, he was sent by Clayton to Suez, where he gathered intelligence. He was assigned to the War Office in October 1915, but returned to Cairo in 1916, and made several trips to the Hijaz after the start of the Arab Revolt. He returned to Sinai in late 1916, and served as governor there until 1923.

PHILBY, Harry St John Bridger (1885–1960). Educated at Westminster and Trinity College, Cambridge, Philby entered the Indian Civil Service in 1908, and, from October 1915, served in Mesopotamia under Percy Cox. He was dismissed by Cox in 1921, due to his refusal to support the British choice of Faisal as first king of Iraq. A contentious and contrary man, Philby next served as Chief British Representative in Transjordan (1921–4), but left that post, and government service, because of differences with Abdullah and the Palestine government. A friend and adviser to Ibn Saud, Philby published fifteen books about the Middle East, several of which recounted his various explorations in Arabia. Philby's son, Kim (1912–88), became a spy for the Russians during the Cold War.

RIDA, Muhammad Rashid (1865–1935). Widely regarded as one of the leading Islamic thinkers and reformers of the early twentieth century, Rashid Rida was a proponent of Islamic modernism. In 1898, he launched the influential Arabic periodical *al-Manar* in Cairo. Clayton met frequently with him during the early war years and, while he thought Rashid Rida's ideas for an independent Arab empire to be utopian, Clayton did not discourage him for fear of driving the Arab nationalists into a Turkish, pan-Islamic alliance.

RUSHDI, Hussein (1863–1928). Of Turkish descent, Rushdi served as Egyptian Prime Minister, 1914–19, and was regarded as a strong supporter of the British war effort in the Middle East. An ally of Adli Yakan and an opponent of Zaghlul and the Wafd, Rushdi nevertheless resigned (twice) as Prime Minister during the spring of 1919, as Egypt erupted in revolt. He headed a commission established in 1922 to draft a new Egyptian constitution.

al-SA'DUN, 'Abd al-Muhsin (1879–1929). Of Turkish origin, al-Sa'dun was an aide de-camp to Sultan Abdulhamid II, and served in the Ottoman army during the war. He was four times Prime Minister of Iraq (1922–23, 1925–26, Jan. 1928–April 1929, and Sept.–Nov. 1929). During his 1926 tenure, he secured approval of the Anglo-Iraqi and Turco-Iraqi treaties of 1926. He committed suicide on 13 November 1929.

SAMUEL, Herbert Louis, first Viscount Samuel (1870–1963). Born into a wealthy Jewish banking family, Samuel completed his education at Balliol College, Oxford (1893), and entered Parliament in 1902. He held several minor government posts and twice served as Home Secretary (1916, 1931–2). From November 1914, Samuel was a strong advocate of the Zionist programme and, in 1920, became the first High Commissioner for Palestine under the British Mandate. Clayton served as Chief Secretary (1923–5) and, often, as Officer Administering the Government, during Samuel's tenure in Jerusalem. Unlike Samuel, Clayton did not believe the Palestinian Arabs could be reconciled to the Jewish national home policy without modification of the Mandate in ways more favourable to the Arabs. Despite their differences, Samuel thought highly of Clayton and recommended him as High Commissioner when Samuel's appointment expired (1925).

SHUCKBURGH, Sir John Evelyn (1877–1953). After attending Eton and King's College, Cambridge, Shuckburgh entered the India Office in 1900, and rose to become secretary to the political department. He then transferred to the Colonial Office (1921), as assistant under-secretary of state. As head of the Colonial Office's

Middle Eastern Department, he met frequently with Clayton during the 1920s. With Herbert Samuel, he drafted the 1922 White Paper on Palestine, an attempt to reassure the Palestinian Arabs while, at the same time, affirming the government's national home policy for the Jews. Shuckburgh soon became disillusioned with the government's Palestine policy, but stayed on in the Colonial Office until 1942, when he retired.

STACK, Sir Lee Oliver Fitzmaurice (1868–1924). Stack was educated at Clifton and Sandhurst, receiving his commission in 1888. He joined the Egyptian Army in 1899, and was appointed Wingate's private secretary in 1904, and then, in 1908, Sudan Agent and Director of Intelligence for the Sudan. Clayton succeeded Stack in both posts. In 1914, Stack was appointed civil secretary in the Sudan Government and, after Wingate became High Commissioner for Egypt, Stack was named acting Sirdar and governor-general (permanent, October 1917). A great friend of Clayton, Stack was assassinated in Cairo in November 1924, while Clayton was visiting Allenby at the British Residency.

STORRS, Sir Ronald Henry Amherst (1881–1955). Educated at Charterhouse and Pembroke College, Cambridge, Storrs served in the Egyptian Civil Service (1904–09) until appointed Oriental Secretary at the British Agency/Residency in Cairo (1909–17). Like Clayton, Storrs was a keen proponent of an Anglo-Arab alliance and the two men worked closely in drafting the McMahon–Hussein correspondence (1915–16) that proved instrumental in bringing the Hijazi Arabs into the war against the Ottomans. Despite strong criticism from Zionist leaders, who held that he undermined the Jewish national home policy in Palestine, Storrs enjoyed a long and successful tenure as Military Governor (1917–20) and then Civil Governor (1920–26) of Jerusalem. He later served as Governor of Cyprus (1926–32) and then of Northern Rhodesia (1932–34). His popular and erudite memoir *Orientations* (1937), is still regarded as an important source for historians of the modern Middle East.

al-SUWAIDI, Taufiq (1892–1968). Educated in Constantinople and Paris, al-Suwaidi was a lawyer, who also taught law in Damascus during the war. He served three times as Iraq's Prime Minister (1929, 1946 and 1950) and, in 1932, was Iraq's first representative to the League of Nations (1932). At various times he also served as minister of foreign affairs, minister of justice, controller general and as a member of Iraq's regency council. He was arrested during the 1958 revolution in Iraq, but was pardoned and spent his remaining days in Lebanon.

SYKES, Sir Mark, sixth Baronet (1879–1919). Educated abroad and at St. John's College, Cambridge (no degree), Sykes travelled widely throughout the Middle East before the war and published four books describing his experiences (1904–15). He served in the Second Boer War (1900–2) and as honorary attaché in Constantinople (1905–6). He was an MP from 1911 until his death. Clayton met Sykes in the summer of 1915, and persuaded him of the merits of an Anglo-Arab alliance. The two men also worked together in forming the Arab Bureau (1916), and the Arab Legion (1917) and in promoting – cautiously, on Clayton's part – the Zionist programme in Palestine (1918). Sykes was later much maligned for the Sykes–Picot Agreement (1916), whereby France, Britain and Russia carved up the Middle East along colonial lines in anticipation of an Entente victory in the war.

WIGRAM, Clive, first Baron Wigram (1873–1960). After Winchester and the Royal Military Academy, Woolwich (1891–3), he served in India and then in the Second Boer War. He returned to India as aide-de-camp to the Viceroy, Lord Curzon, and then became assistant private secretary to King George V (1910), under private secretary, Lord Stamfordham. He succeeded Stamfordham as private secretary in 1931. Wigram and Clayton met in July 1916, and corresponded during the war, as the King took an interest in Arab affairs.

WILSON, Colonel Cyril Edward (1873–1938). A contemporary of Clayton at the Isle of Wight College, Wilson later attended Clifton and Sandhurst, after which he was commissioned (1893). He served in Kitchener's Sudan campaign (1898), and in the Second Boer War (1900–2). Wilson was later seconded to the Egyptian Army and worked for the Sudan Government as Governor of the Sudan provinces of Sennar, Khartoum and the Red Sea. After the outbreak of the Arab Revolt in 1916, in the guise of 'Pilgrimage Officer', he was assigned by Wingate as British liaison to King Hussein of the Hijaz (1916–18) and played a central role in planning the course of the Revolt.

WINGATE, General Sir (Francis) Reginald, first Baronet (1861–1953). After attending the Royal Military Academy, Woolwich, he was commissioned in 1880, and served briefly in India and Aden. In 1883, Wingate joined the Egyptian Army and rose steadily until appointed director of military intelligence in 1892. He served in that role during Kitchener's Sudan campaign and was present at Omdurman and Fashoda (1898). In December 1899, Wingate was appointed Sirdar (commander) of the Egyptian Army and governor-general of the Sudan, in succession to Kitchener. He administered the Sudan until 1917, and was largely responsible for restoring order and system to the Sudan in the wake of the *Mahdiyya*. Wingate served as High Commissioner for Egypt from January 1917 to March 1919, when he was replaced by Allenby, in the wake of the Egyptian revolution. Clayton worked for Wingate, in various capacities, from 1907 until 1918.

WOOLLEY, Sir Leonard (1880–1960). After New College, Oxford, Woolley embarked on an archaeological career. He worked with Lawrence in excavating the ancient Hittite city of Carchemish (1912–14) and in completing a survey of Sinai (1914). Assigned to Clayton's Cairo Intelligence in December 1914, Woolley ran agents into Syria until captured by the Turks when his vessel struck a mine off Alexandretta (1916). Author of more than a dozen books on archaeology, Woolley returned to archaeology after the war and became well known for his excavations at Ur, in Iraq.

YAHYA Muhammad Hamid al-Din [Imam Yahya] (1869–1948). Leader of the Zaidi (Shi'ite) sect in southwest Arabia, Yahya ruled in Yemen from 1904 until 1948, when he was assassinated. Although he sided with the Turks during the Great War, Yahya did not actively support the Ottoman advance on Aden. Clayton negotiated unsuccessfully with the Imam in early 1926, in an effort to remove the Imam's forces from the Aden Protectorate. Later that year, Yahya signed a pact with the Italians which, in part, prompted Clayton's 1927 negotiations in Rome concerning Anglo-Italian interests in the southern Red Sea.

YAKAN, Adli (1864–1933). An important Egyptian political figure of the 1920s, Adli served three times as Egyptian Prime Minister (1921, 1926–7, and 1929–30). He was also Foreign Minister and Minister of the Interior. Although an advocate of Egyptian independence, Adli was a moderate and a critic and opponent of Sa'd Zaghlul and the Wafd party. He was present at a dinner given for Clayton on his departure from Egypt (May 1922), when Tharwat spoke of the great appreciation which 'all classes of native Egyptians' had for Clayton, who had helped 'lay the foundations for the new regime'.

YALE, William (1887–1975). A graduate of Yale University, he was employed by the Standard Oil Company of New York in the Middle East (1910–17). In 1917–18, he reported to the U.S. State Department from Cairo. He attended the Paris Peace Conference and was later a member of the King–Crane Commission to the Middle East (1919). After leaving the Middle East, Yale taught history at the University of New Hampshire.

YOUNG, Sir Hubert Winthrop (1885–1950). Educated at Eton and the Royal Military Academy, Woolwich, Young served in the Indian Army before the war, when he was transferred to Mesopotamia and worked in political and administrative roles (1915–18). He also served as GSO2, Hijaz operations, from March 1918. As an adviser in the Eastern Department of the Foreign Office (1919–21) and the Middle East Department of the Colonial Office (1921–6), he was in frequent contact with Clayton. He returned to Iraq as counsellor (1929–32) and then was appointed governor of Nyasaland (1932–4), Northern Rhodesia (1934–8), and Trinidad and Tobago (1938–42).

ZAGHLUL, Sa'd (c.1859–1927). Born in the Nile Delta, Zaghlul attended Al-Azhar University, became a judge, Minister of Education (1906–8), Minister of Justice (1910–12), and vice president of the Egyptian Legislative Assembly (1913). During his early years in public life, Zaghlul was held in high regard as a moderate. But, after the war, he and his Wafd party adopted an uncompromising attitude, demanding complete independence from British rule. Twice exiled by the British,

Zaghlul became a national hero among the Egyptians. He served briefly as Prime Minister of Egypt (1924), but resigned following the November 1924 assassination of Lee Stack.

ZAID ibn Hussein (1898–1970). Fourth son of Hussein, King of the Hijaz (1916–24), Amir Zaid was educated in Constantinople and at Balliol College, Oxford. He served in the Hashemite army during the Arab Revolt (1916–18), and as Iraqi ambassador to Germany and Turkey during the 1930s. He was Iraqi ambassador to Great Britain at the time of the Iraqi coup d'état of 1958, which overthrew the Hashemite monarchy there, and remained in London until his death.

Notes

1 Introduction: Following the Furrow

1 Information concerning Clayton's 1929 flight to Iraq and the furrow comes from: Iraq Command, Monthly Diary, March 1929, AIR 5/1291; RAF Operations, Iraq, 1929–1932, AIR 20/187; Frederick Peake, unpublished autobiography, Frederick Peake Papers, 78/3/2, IWM; McGregor, 'Flying the Furrow', pp. 24–31; Hill, *The Baghdad Air Mail*; and Omissi, *Air Power and Colonial Control*.

2 Vectensian: Youth, 1875–1895

1 Hope Moncrieff, *Isle of Wight*, p. 11.

2 Jones, *Isle of Wight,* p. 121.

3 Hope Moncrieff, *Isle of Wight*, p. 19.

4 'Apley House', pp. 838–9. Kindly provided to the author by Sister Eustochium of St Cecilia's Abbey, Ryde, Isle of Wight.

5 It is unclear why Phoebe Clayton decided to leave her home at Peckham in Surrey for the Isle of Wight. Her eldest daughter, Susan Prestwood Clayton (1796–1859), had married on the Isle of Wight in 1826 (Green Book, p. 25 [unpublished partial family history, see Bibliography]), and very likely lived there in 1830. It is probable, then, that Phoebe, 64 years of age in 1830, simply wished to be near to her eldest daughter.

6 Green Book, p. 284.

7 Green Book, p. 271; Rodger, *Command of the Ocean*, p. 228. Professor Rodger lists Edward Falkingham as 'Controller' of the Royal Navy in February 1755 (p. 634).

8 Green Book, p.7.

9 Sir John Wittewronge's brief family history is reproduced in Green Book, pp. 313–335, and in Clutterbuck, *County of Hertford*, I, p. 411.

10 Green Book, p. 340.

11 Green Book, pp. 32, 38. Phoebe's second son, Edward Walker Clayton (1801–29), died, unmarried, before she moved to Ryde.

12 Green Book, p. 38.

13 In a letter of 21 June 1903, Gilbert F. Clayton, the subject of this book, wrote to his mother from the Sudan: 'I fully expected to see in your later letters that Dad [William] was in bed with a severe attack of epilepsy – His fits must have been of alarming frequency and violence! However I suppose he is getting over it, as you say nothing about his having collapsed.' Collins Papers, SAD 942/7/170. No other mention of William's apparent condition appears in Gilbert Clayton's papers and, since Gilbert was, in other contexts, singularly vague and careless in describing medical conditions, it cannot be stated with confidence that his father, in fact, suffered from epilepsy.

14 Dr. John Pilkington Clayton, C.V.O. to the author, June 2010.

15 Partial memoir of Sir Iltyd Nicholl Clayton, *c.*1938, I.N. Clayton Papers, MECOX, Box

1, File 5. A typescript of the memoir was also kindly provided by Sir Iltyd's daughter, Margaret Gosling and her husband, Professor Justin Gosling.

16 William noted in the Green Book (p. 346) that he and Maria Martha had visited Harpenden, the ancestral home of the Wittewronges, in Hertfordshire on 22 September 1891, and doubtless it was this visit that prompted William to adopt that name for his new house just completed that same autumn in Sandown.

17 Clayton to his mother, 19 February 1903, Collin Papers, SAD 942/7/134.

18 Clayton, *Arabian Diary*, p. 47; and Dr. John P. Clayton, C.V.O. to the author, June 2010.

19 Green Book, p. 72.

20 Teesdale, *Isle of Wight College*. The original manuscript is held by the Carisbrooke Castle Museum; the author thanks Christine Yendall of the Museum for making a copy available.

21 'The Isle of Wight College. Memories of a Notable Education Experiment', by a 'Vectensian', *Isle of Wight County Press*, June 9, 1956. A copy of this article was provided to the author by Sister Eustochium of St. Cecilia's Abbey, Ryde, Isle of Wight. The Abbey now occupies the site of the former College.

22 Sister Eustochium, St. Cecilia's Abbey, Ryde, to the author, 13 July 2011.

23 Undated Prospectus, likely from the 1880s, kindly provided to the author by Mr. R.E. Brinton of Ryde, Isle of Wight.

24 The references are to the Royal Military Academy at Woolwich, where the Army's engineers and artillerymen were trained, the Royal Military College at Sandhurst, which trained men for the cavalry and infantry, the Royal Indian Engineering College at Cooper's Hill, where engineers for the Indian Public Works Department, and foresters for service in India were educated.

25 The 1891 census lists Gilbert F. Clayton at 'Apley College, St. Helens, Isle of Wight', suggesting that, at least in that year, Bertie was living at College, rather than at home in Sandown. Courtesy of David S. Thorne. For Iltyd and John, *see* Iltyd Clayton partial memoir, I.N. Clayton Papers, MECOX, Box 1, File 5, p. 17.

26 Spiers, *Late Victorian Army*, pp. 97, 189.

27 *See, e.g.*, *Hampshire Telegraph and Sussex Chronicle*, 18 June 1887, containing a College advertisement.

28 Teesdale, *Isle of Wight College*, p. 5 (passed 20th); *Isle of Wight Observer*, 23 August 1890 (drawing prize); Dr. John P. Clayton, C.V.O. to the author, June 2010 (contributions of essays and verse to *Vectensian*). The books reflecting Clayton's academic prizes are in the possession of the Clayton family. G .F. Clayton to the author, 23 March 2014.

29 Iltyd Clayton, partial memoir, I.N. Clayton Papers, MECOX, Box 1, File 5, p. 19.

30 Teesdale, *Isle of Wight College*, p. 7.

31 Clayton to his mother, 28 May 1898, Collins Papers, SAD 942/7/46. Many years later, in his short, unpublished history of the College, K. J. M. Teesdale, perhaps the Headmaster's son, listed Gilbert Clayton as one of a dozen distinguished alumni of the College.

32 Spiers, *Late Victorian Army*, pp. 98–9. *See also* Magnan, *Games Ethic and Imperialism*, pp. 44–70.

33 Dr. John P. Clayton, C.V.O., to the author, June 2010.

34 The College regulations were printed on the back of the Prospectus, an example of which from the 1880s was provided to the author by Mr. R.E. Brinton of Ryde, Isle of Wight.

35 From a photograph of the window, kindly provided by Sister Eustochium, St. Cecilia's Abbey, Ryde, Isle of Wight.

36 *Green Book*, p. 72.

37 *Records of the Academy,* pp. 120, 151–2; Farwell, *Kipling's Army*, p. 142.

38 *Records of the Academy*, p. 152.

39 *Green Book*, p. 72.

40 *Records of the Academy*, p. 129.

41 Farwell, *Kipling's Army*, p. 144.

42 Weekes, *Origins of Lexham Gardens*, pp. 26–7.

43 Manchester, *The Last Lion*, p. 181.

44 Churchill, *My Early Life*, p. 28.

45 Civil Service Commission, Table of marks obtained by candidates for admission to the Royal Military Academy, Woolwich, June 1893, CSC 10/996, TNA.

46 Civil Service Commission, Table of marks, competition for admission to the Royal Military College, Sandhurst, June 1893, CSC 10/997, TNA. Churchill scored lower than Clayton on all three of the required subjects and, interestingly, for one of the masters of twentieth-century prose, lower in English composition.

47 Guggisberg, *The Shop*, pp. 1–2.

48 Farwell, *Kipling's Army*, p. 141 (Wellington); Spiers, *Late Victorian Army*, p. 109 (Cambridge). The Duke of Cambridge was likely referring to the Staff College at Camberwell in making his statement, but the comment may be taken to reflect the Duke's views on military education generally.

49 Spiers, *Late Victorian Army*, p. 102.

50 Alfred Wilks Drayson, *The Gentleman Cadet: His Career and Adventures at the Royal Military Academy Woolwich* (London: Griffith & Farran, 1875), p. 136. Drayson claims that bullying at Woolwich was at its height in the 1840s, but was routinely 'winked at by the authorities'.

51 *Records of the Academy*, pp. 122, 147–9.

52 *Ibid.*, p. 131. Bifurcation was abandoned in 1896, as it was discovered that the system deprived cadets of any incentive to study after their first year when their positions were largely fixed.

53 Woolwich Register of Cadets, Sandhurst Collection, WO 149/7.

54 *The Evening Standard*, 12 September 1929, p. 10.

55 Clayton, *Arabian Diary*, p. 48.

56 Clayton to his mother, 1 May 1898, Collins Papers, SAD 942/7/33.

57 Guggisberg, *The Shop*, p. 245.

58 Spiers, *Late Victorian Army*, pp. 63–5; General Walter Kirke, partial memoir, Imperial War Museum, London, Walter Kirke Papers, WK 13, IWM.

3 The Lion and the Sphinx: The British Empire and the Middle East

1 Clayton to his mother, 15 January 1896, Collins Papers, SAD 930/9.

2 Steevens, *Egypt in 1898*, pp. 13–14.

3 Morris, *Pax Britannica*, p. 38.

4 *Ibid.*, p. 422.

5 *Ibid.*, p. 430.

6 Farwell, *Kipling's Army*, p. 21.

7 *Ibid.*, p. 59.

8   Clayton to his mother, 22 May 1898, Collins Papers, SAD 942/7/42; *and see* Clayton, *Arabian Diary*, p. 48.
9   *Alphabetical List of the Officers of the Royal Regiment of Artillery*; Army List, 1897, p. 184.
10 Hedrick, *Tools of Empire*, p. 155.
11 Steevens, *Egypt in 1898*, p. 64.
12 Mostyn, *Egypt's Belle Epoque*, p. 126.
13 Steevens, *Egypt in 1898*, p. 180.
14 Sattin, *Lifting the Veil*, p. 155.
15 Steevens, *Egypt in 1898*, p. 176.
16 Green Book, p. 73.
17 Strachey, *Eminent Victorians*, p. 360.
18 Roberts, *Salisbury*, p. 308.
19 Holt, *Mahdist State*, p. 22.
20 *Ibid.*, pp. 42–50. 'Ansar' means helpers and was the name given to the helpers of the Prophet at Medina.
21 Trench, *Road to Khartoum*, p. 200.
22 *Ibid.*, pp. 202, 207.
23 Holt, *Mahdist State*, p. 83.
24 Roberts, *Salisbury* p. 292.
25 Spiers, *Late Victorian Army*, pp. 183–92.
26 Roberts, *Salisbury*, p. 641.
27 Churchill, *River War*, pp. 112, 108.

4   A Smack at the Khalifa: The Sudan Campaign, 1898

1   Clayton to his mother, 5–7 March 1898, Collins Papers, SAD 942/7/2.
2   *Ibid*. The reference to Lady Churchill's son was to her son Jack, as Winston was then in India. Lady Churchill was then trying to pull every string available to secure for Winston a position in the Anglo-Egyptian Army, a move strongly resisted by the Sirdar.
3   *Ibid.*
4   Clayton to his mother, 9–11 March 1898, Collins Papers, SAD 942/7/6. Philae is now totally submerged as a result of the construction of the new Aswan dam.
5   Clayton to his mother, 13–14 March 1898, Collins Papers, SAD 942/7/10.
6   Clayton to his mother, 27–29 March 1898, Collins Papers, SAD 942/7/12.
7   Clayton reckoned the total force at 'over 15,000 men'. (*Ibid.*). However, Churchill, *River War* (p. 147), put the total force at 14,000, as does Keown-Boyd in *A Good Dusting*, p. 192.
8   Holt, *Mahdist State*, pp. 214–19.
9   Clayton to his mother, 27–29 March 1898, Collins Papers, SAD 942/7/12.
10 Steevens, *With Kitchener to Khartum*, p. 110.
11 Clayton to his mother, 5, 7, 10 April 1898, Collins Papers, SAD 942/7/21.
12 *Ibid.*
13 Spiers, *Late Victorian Army*, p. 245.
14 Keown-Boyd, *A Good Dusting*, p. 200.
15 Clayton to his mother, 5, 7, 10 April 1898, Collins Papers, SAD 942/7/21.
16 *Ibid.*
17 Clayton to his mother, 17 April 1898, Collins Papers, SAD 942/7/27.
18 Clayton to his mother, 23 April 1898, Collins Papers, SAD 942/7/30.

19 Clayton to his mother, 22 May 1898, Collins Papers, SAD 942/7/42.
20 *Ibid.*
21 Clayton to his mother, 19 June 1898, Collins Papers, SAD 942/7/55.
22 Clayton to his mother, 3 July 1898, Collins Papers, SAD 942/7/61.
23 Clayton to his mother, 8, 9 and 10 July 1898, Collins Papers, SAD 942/7/63.
24 Clayton to his mother, 17 April 1898, Collins Papers, SAD 942/7/27.
25 Clayton to his mother, 22 May 1898, Collins Papers, SAD 942/7/42.
26 Clayton to his mother, 17 July 1898, Collins Papers, SAD 942/7/67.
27 Keown-Boyd, *A Good Dusting*, p. 206 (on the incidence of typhoid); Clayton to his mother, 27 July 1898 and 29 July 1898, Collins Papers, SAD 942/7/70, 72.
28 Clayton to his mother, 4 August 1898, Collins Papers, SAD 942/7/75. A cholera belt was a cloth band that was strapped round the waist and was thought to ward off diseases, including cholera, by keeping the abdomen warm.
29 Churchill, *River War*, p. 165; Steevens, *With Kitchener to Khartum*, p. 241; Ziegler, *Omdurman*, p. 66.
30 Clayton to his mother, 7, 12 September 1898 (containing most of Clayton's diary entries for the period 21 August to 12 September 1898), Collins Papers, SAD 942/7/81–88.
31 Hunter to his brother, 14 October 1898, reproduced in Harrington and Sharf, *Omdurman 1898*, p. 154.
32 *Ibid.*
33 Clayton to his mother, 7, 12 September 1898, Collins Papers, SAD 942/7/81–88.
34 *Ibid.*
35 Steevens, *With Kitchner to Khartum*, p. 293.
36 *Ibid.*, p. 264.
37 Clayton to his mother, 7, 12 September 1898, Collins Papers, SAD 942/7/81–88.
38 Clayton diary, 5 September 1898, private collection.

5 Bimbashi: Clayton in the Egyptian Army

1 Warburg, *Sudan Under Wingate*, pp. 79–80; Daly, *Empire on the Nile*, pp. 82–3.
2 Stirling, *Safety Last*, pp. 29–30.
3 Partial memoir of General Sir Walter Kirke, *c.* late 1940s, Kirke Papers, WK 13, IWM; *and see* Spiers, *Late Victorian Army*, p. 64.
4 November 12, 1900 contract, CP, SAD 473/2/1. The currency then used in Egypt and the Sudan was the Egyptian pound (£E). At the time £E 1 was equal to £1.0.6 sterling.
5 Cromer to Lansdowne, 3 June 1902, quoted in Daly, *Empire on the Nile*, p. 107.
6 Clayton to his mother, 5 December 1900, Collins Papers, SAD 930/9.
7 Clayton diary, 9 May 1901, private collection.
8 Clayton to his father, 26 May 1903, Collins Papers, SAD 942/7/167-9.
9 Clayton diary, 19 May 1901, private collection.
10 Clayton diary, 4 June 1901, private collection.
11 Shambe Field Force report, May 1902, quoted in Collins, *Land Beyond the Rivers*, p. 91.
12 ffrench Comyn, *Service and Sport in the Sudan*, pp. 79 – 118.
13 Clayton diary, 30 October 1901, private collection.
14 Clayton diary, 8 November 1901, private collection.
15 Clayton to his mother, 13 December 1901, Collins Papers, SAD 930/9.
16 *Ibid.*
17 Clayton diary, 4–5 April 1902, private collection.

18 The details of Clayton's 1902 leave appear in Clayton diary, 28 March – 11 August 1902, private collection.

19 Clayton diary, 7 October 1902, private collection.

6   It A'int all Violets Here: Inspector in the Southern Sudan, 1902–1903

1   Collins and Tignor, *Egypt and the Sudan*, p. 16.

2   Clayton to his mother, 28 October 1902, Collins Papers, SAD 942/7/88.

3   Daly, *Empire on the Nile*, p. 81.

4   Clayton to his mother, 28 October 1902, Collins Papers, SAD 942/7/88.

5   *Sudan Gazette*, no. 46, April 1903, FO 867/25.

6   Daly, *Empire on the Nile*, p. 115.

7   *Ibid.*

8   Clayton to his mother, 2 November 1902, Collins Papers, SAD 942/7/90.

9   Clayton to his mother, 5 – 7 November 1902, Collins Papers, SAD 942/7/95.

10 Clayton to his mother, 11–13 November 1902, Collins Papers, SAD 942/7/99.

11 *Ibid.*

12 *Ibid.*

13 Collins, *Land Beyond the Rivers*, pp. 20–41.

14 Clayton to his mother, 11–13 November 1902, Collins Papers, SAD 942/7/99.

15 Collins, *Land Beyond the Rivers*, p. 41.

16 Clayton to his mother, 28 November 1902, Collins Papers, SAD 942/7/104.

17 Clayton diary, 28, 30 November 1902, private collection.

18 Clayton to his mother, 28 November 1902, Collins Papers, SAD 942/7/104.

19 See note 22.

20 Clayton diary, 24, 25 December 1902, private collection.

21 Daly, *Empire on the Nile*, pp. 80, 149.

22 Clayton to his mother, 5, 9 January 1903, Collins Papers, SAD 942/7/109.

23 *Ibid.* The Bahr al-Ghazal was not a money-making proposition for the government. The actual figures for revenue and expenditure, respectively were, £E2,518 and £E 11,573 for 1902, and £E2,000 and £E17,781 for 1903. Sikainga, *The Western Bahr al-Ghazal*, p. 31.

24 Clayton to his mother, 18, 21 January 1903, Collins Papers, SAD 942/7/117.

25 Clayton to his mother, 6–9 February 1903, Collins Papers, SAD 942/7/123.

26 Clayton to his mother, 19 February 1903, Collins Papers, SAD 942/7/133.

27 Clayton to his mother, 10, 16, 20, 22 and 25 May 1903, Collins Papers, SAD 942/7/152.

28 *Ibid.*

29 Clayton to his mother, 19 February 1903, Collins Papers, SAD 942/7/133.

30 Clayton to his mother, 10 March 1903, Collins Papers, SAD 942/7/140.

31 Clayton to his mother, 10, 16, 20, 22 and 25 May 1903, SAD 942/7/152.

32 *Ibid.*

33 Clayton to his mother, 20 March 1903, Collins Papers, SAD 942/7/143.

34 Clayton to his mother, 10, 16, 20, 22 and 25 May 1903, Collins Papers, SAD 942/7/152.

35 Clayton to his mother, 20 March and 6–8 April, 1903, Collins Papers, SAD 942/7/143, 147.

36 Clayton to his mother, 6–9 February 1903, Collins Papers, SAD 942/7/123.

37 *Ibid.*

38 Clayton to his mother, 10, 16, 20, 22 and 25 May 1903, Collins Papers, SAD 942/7/152.

39 Clayton to his father, 26 May 1903, Collins Papers, SAD 942/7/166.

7 Master: Private Secretary to Wingate, 1907–1913

1 Iltyd Clayton, partial memoir, *c.*1938, MECOX, I.N. Clayton Papers, Box 1, File 5, p. 26.

2 Green Book, p. 74. Malta fever, also known as undulant fever, Gibraltar fever or Mediterranean fever, and, technically, as brucellosis, is a bacterial disease caused by ingesting unpasteurized milk or by working regularly round livestock. Its symptoms include fever, chills, aches, sweating and depression.

3 G. F. Clayton, 'Note on Service of Captain Clayton', n.d., Collins Papers, SAD 930/9.

4 Clayton Diary, 18 January 1906, private collection.

5 Clayton, 'Note on Service', Collins Papers, SAD 930/9; *Sudan Gazette*, No. 100, 1 September 1906, FO 867/28.

6 Clayton to his mother, 17 May 1906, Collins Papers, SAD 930/9.

7 Clayton to his mother, 12 September 1906, Collins Papers, SAD 930/9.

8 Clayton to his mother, 23 October 1906, Collins Papers, SAD 930/9.

9 *Sudan Gazette*, No. 110, 1 April 1907, FO 867/29 (Clayton re-transferred to army, 16 March 1907). *Sudan Gazette*, No. 128, 1 March 1908, FO 867/30 (Stack appointed Sudan Agent and Director of Intelligence and Clayton appointed private secretary, both 28 February 1908).

10 Daly, *Empire on the Nile*, pp. 66–7.

11 Wingate to Talbot, 25 January 1903, quoted in Daly, *Empire on the Nile*, p. 66.

12 *Ibid.*, p. 67.

13 Warburg, *Sudan Under Wingate*, p. 209.

14 Wingate to Clayton, 4 April 1910, CP, SAD 469/2/40 (good work); Clayton to Wingate, 31 August 1911, WP, SAD 301/2/143 (scarlet fever); Wingate to Clayton, 17 September 1910, WP, SAD 297/3/92 (school for Victoria); Clayton to Wingate, 16 November 1911, WP, SAD 301/5/49 (bridge).

15 Clayton to Wingate, 21 September 1910, WP, SAD 297/3/114, and Wingate to Clayton, 22 September 1910, WP, SAD 297/2/123 (Iltyd); Wingate to Clayton, 6 September 1911, CP, SAD 469/3/45 (Malcolm).

16 Clayton to Wingate, 29 August 1911, WP, SAD 301/2/119.

17 Wingate to Clayton, 11 December 1913, CP, SAD 469/5/64.

18 Daly, *Empire on the Nile*, p. 93.

19 *Ibid.*, p. 101.

20 *Ibid.*, pp 100–4; and Daly, *The Sirdar*, pp. 159–67, 179–180.

21 Clayton to Wingate, 5 August 1911, WP, SAD 301/2/16.

22 Daly, *Empire on the Nile*, p. 96.

23 Quoted in Warburg, *Sudan Under Wingate*, p. 13.

24 Gorst to Wingate, 16 March 1910, CP, SAD 469/2/35.

25 Stack to Clayton, 22 February 1917, CP, SAD 470/6/15.

26 Green Book, p. 85.

27 Daly, *The Sirdar*, pp. 139, 152–4.

28 Clayton to Wingate, 30 June 1915, WP, SAD 195/4/306.

29 Mohrig to Clayton, 10 April 1912, WP, SAD 183/2/17 (citizenship); Clayton to Carr,

5 June 1912, WP, SAD 181/3/10 (cattle trade); Clayton to Bishop Geyer, 6 March 1912, WP, SAD 180/3/7 ('Thrift'); Clayton to Asser, 25 October 1912, WP, SAD 183/1/78 (polo balls); Clayton to Bonham Carter, 18 January 1913, WP, SAD 185/1/68 (skating rink, postal convention).

30 Clayton to Phipps, 6 March 1913, WP, SAD 185/3/41.

31 Mangan, *Games Ethic and Imperialism*, pp. 71–100; Daly, *Empire on the Nile*, pp. 83–9. In 1910 Wingate acknowledged that the Sudan Civil Service was falling into 'disrepute', but attributed the problem to the 'impossibility of disconnecting Egypt and the Sudan'. Wingate to Clayton, 2 July 1910, CP, SAD 469/2/55.

32 Clayton, draft letter to Mrs. G. Barron, 1 November 1912, WP, SAD 183/1/60.

33 Wingate to Clayton, 8 September 1911, CP, SAD 469/3/47.

34 Clayton to Wingate, 15 August 1911, WP, SAD 301/2/60.

35 Wingate to Clayton, 18(?) August 1912, CP, SAD 469/4/25.

36 Wingate Diary, April–June 1909, WP, SAD 125/5 (quoted); *and see* Wingate to Crew, 20 May 1909, WP, SAD 125/3/2.

37 Clayton to his mother, 1 May 1909, Collins Papers, SAD 930/9.

38 Wingate Diary, WP, SAD 125/5.

39 Wingate to Clayton, 6 March 1910, CP, SAD 469/2/22.

40 Daly, *Empire on the Nile*, pp. 219–223.

41 Wingate to Clayton, 6 August 1913, WP, SAD 187/2/53 (sound criticisms); Clayton to Wingate, 8 August 1913, WP, SAD 187/2/83.

8   Sudan Agent: Cairo, 1913–1914

1   Clayton to Civil Secretary, Sudan Government, 15 January 1910, Clayton Family Papers; Extracts from Minutes of the [Sudan] Government Selection Board, signed 30 January 1910, CP, SAD 472/11/3; War Office (London) to Clayton, 9 December 1910, CP, SAD 472/12/5.

2   Wingate to Clayton, 5 January 1912, CP, SAD 469/4/1 (Miralai); Clayton to Wingate, 10 November 1913, CP, SAD 469/5/36 (Medjidieh). The Egyptian Army, like the British Army, used temporary and local ranks for its officers.

3   Interview of Dr. John P. Clayton, C.V.O., 17 August 2010, York, England; 'Biographical Notes' concerning Enid Caroline Thorowgood, n.d., Clayton Family Papers.

4   Wingate to Clayton, 28 July 1912, CP, SAD 469/4/10.

5   Biographical Notes concerning Enid Caroline Thorowgood, n.d., Clayton Family Papers.

6   Clayton to Wingate, 23 September 1912, WP, SAD 182/3/160.

7   Clayton diary, 26 November 1912, private collection.

8   Dr. John P. Clayton, C.V.O., to the author, June 2010.

9   Wingate to Clayton, 8 November 1913, Clayton Family Papers.

10 F. Nason, 'Duties of Sudan Agent, Cairo', 23 February 1903, FO 141/448/8.

11 Daly, *Empire on the Nile*, p. 56.

12 Warburg, *Sudan Under Wingate*, pp. 59–63.

13 Clayton to Wingate, 10 December 1913, CP, SAD 469/5/62 (Italians); Clayton to Wingate, 12 January 1914, CP, SAD 469/6/2 (French).

14 Wingate to Clayton, 21 August 1915, CP, SAD 469/10/35. For the array of designations used by Wingate on his correspondence, see Daly, *Empire on the Nile*, pp. 66–7.

15 Wingate to Clayton, 29 March 1914, CP, SAD 469/6/86; Clayton to Wingate, 4 May 1914, WP, SAD 157/5/6.

16 Clayton to Wingate, 2 February 1914, CP, SAD 469/6/17.

17 Clayton to Wingate, 1 April 1914, CP, SAD 469/6/88.

18 Wingate to Stack, 1 June 1914, WP, SAD 157/6/1.

19 Wingate to Clayton, 29 January 1914, CP, SAD 469/6/12.

20 The original was destined for the British Museum and may be seen there today.

21 Enid did so and the head of Caesar Augustus remains a possession of the Clayton family to this day. Interview of Dr. John P. Clayton, C.V.O., 24 April 2010.

22 Clayton to Wingate, 24 November 1913, CP, SAD 469/5/45

23 Clayton to Wingate, 9 December 1913, WP, SAD 188/3/60; Clayton to Wingate, 11 March 1914, CP, SAD 469/6/66.

24 Clayton to Symes, 15 April 1914, WP, SAD 131/3/11, enclosing Kitchener to FO, at SAD 131/3/25-30, and Clayton Note at 131/3/16-20.

25 Clayton to Wingate, 8 April 1914, CP, SAD 469/6/93.

9 Intrusive: Organizing a Middle Eastern Intelligence, 1914–1915

1 Clayton to Wingate, 31 July 1914, WP, SAD 157/8/22.

2 Storrs, *Orientations*, pp. 128–9.

3 Quoted in Sheffy, *Palestine Intelligence*, p. 8.

4 *Ibid.*, pp. 9–10.

5 *Ibid.*, p. 6; Fergusson, *British Military Intelligence*, p. 238.

6 Gudgin, *Military Intelligence*, p. 22.

7 Occleshaw, *Armour against Fate*, p. 32.

8 Grey to Lowther, 12 January 1909, HD 3/139, TNA in Sheffy, *Palestine Intelligence*, p. 13.

9 *Ibid.*, pp. 16, 19.

10 Clayton, 'Memorandum on the Advisability of Maintaining in Existence After the War Colonel Samson's Secret Service Bureau, and of Affiliating it to the Cairo Intelligence Directorate', *c.*early 1916, CP, SAD 694/3/71, p. 1.

11 Sheffy, *Palestine Intelligence*, p. 33.

12 Wingate to Clayton, 16 September 1914, CP, SAD 469/7/1.

13 Clayton to Jennings-Bramly (Sinai), 21 August 1914, WP, SAD 193/1/75; Clayton to Wingate, same date, WP, SAD 193/1/70 (quoted).

14 Sheffy, *Palestine Intelligence*, pp. 39–40.

15 Mallet (Constantinople) to Grey (FO), 4 telegrams of 12 October 1914, conveying consular reports, FO 371/2140.

16 Clayton to Wingate, 21 October 1914, WP, SAD 192/1/87 ('I think we have been fairly successful in getting information & my arrangement with the consuls in Syria is bearing fruit.')

17 Intelligence Department Note, 'Appreciation of Situation in Arabia', 6 September 1914 (Hussein); Cheetham (Cairo) to Foreign Office, 21 September 1914, (Ibn Saud), both in FO 371/2140.

18 Clayton, Notes, 7 and 9 September 1914, WO 157/687.

19 Sheffy, *Palestine Intelligence*, p. 219. The British also had two, small stations operating in the Persian Gulf.

20 Maxwell to Wingate, 27 September 1914, WP, SAD 191/3/83.

21   Maxwell to Kitchener, 21 October 1914, Maxwell Papers, box 4, folder 5, Princeton University Library.

22   Maxwell to Wingate, 27 September 1914, WP, SAD 191/3/83; Elgood, *Egypt and the Army*, pp. 65–6.

23   Clayton to Wingate, 28 September 1914, WP, SAD 191/3/64. T. E. Lawrence confirmed Clayton's impression of Maxwell, describing him as 'a very queer person: almost weirdly good-natured, very cheerful with a mysterious gift of prophesying what will happen, and a marvelous carelessness about what might happen.' Lawrence to his mother, 12 February 1915, in Brown, ed., *Lawrence Letters*, pp. 69–70.

24   Clayton to Wingate, 21 October 1914, WP, SAD 192/1/87.

25   Grey to Cheetham, 18 October 1914, FO 371/2140.

26   Clayton to Wingate, 21 October 1914, WP, SAD 192/1/87.

27   Clayton to Wingate (letter), 1 November 1914, WP, SAD 193/4/2; Clayton to Wingate (telegram), n.d., but late October 1914, CP, SAD 693/8/7 (quoted).

28   Sheffy, *Palestine Intelligence*, pp. 44–5.

29   Maxwell to Wingate, 15 November 1914, WP, SAD 192/2/91; Clayton to Wingate, 14 November 1914, WP, SAD 193/4/109.

30   Intelligence Report, 'Artillery', 26 December 1914, WO 157/689.

31   Intelligence Report, 'The Proposed Turkish Invasion of Egypt', 31 December 1914, WO 157/689.

32   Clayton to Wingate, 6 January 1915, WP, SAD 194/1/27.

33   Clayton to Wingate, 16 January 1915, WP, SAD 194/1/45.

34   Stirling, *Safety Last*, p. 60.

35   The phrase is attributed to Admiral Rosslyn Wemyss by Gudgin, *Military Intelligence*, p. 10; Clayton to Wingate, 16 January 1915, WP, SAD 194/1/145.

36   Maxwell to Kitchener, 16 March 1915, Maxwell Papers, box 4, folder 5, Princeton University Library; Clayton to Wingate, n.d., but March–April 1915, WP, SAD 134/5/7.

37   Clayton to Wingate, 4 November 1914, WP, SAD 192/2/9.

38   Clayton to Wingate, 9 December 1914, WP, SAD 192/3/53; Sheffy, *Palestine Intelligence*, pp. 49–51.

39   Sheffy, *Palestine Intelligence*, pp. 50–1, 95.

40   MI5, "D" Branch Report, 'The Organisation of the Eastern Mediterranean Special Intelligence Bureau', 1921, p. 65, KV 1/17, TNA.

41   Symes, *Tour of Duty*, p. 23 ('Stuart king'); Clayton to Wingate, 4 November 1914, WP, SAD 192/2/9 ('sedition-mongers').

42   Cheetham to Foreign Office, 10 November 1914, Cheetham Papers, file 4, MECOX.

43   Clayton to Wingate, 23 December 1914, WP, SAD 192/2/93; Maxwell order, 19 December 1914, FO 371/2355.

44   Clayton to Wingate, 23 December 1914, WP, SAD 192/2/193. Not mentioned by Clayton, but part of the group sent from London, were Harry Pirie-Gordon, a journalist who had travelled widely in the Middle East, and J. Hay, about whom almost nothing is known, except that, according to Lawrence, he 'did the Tripoli [western] side of Egypt'. Lawrence to E. T. Leeds, 24 December 1914, in Brown, ed., *Lawrence Letters*, pp. 68–9.

45   Clayton to Wingate, n.d., but December 1914, WP, SAD 192/3/294 (Cornwallis); Philip Graves, 'Report re Turkish Military Preparations and Political Intrigues Having

an Attack on Egypt as their Object', 10 November 1914, WO 157/689; Sheffy, *Palestine Intelligence*, pp. 45–6 (Robert Graves). Philip Graves was the half-brother of the writer, Robert Graves.

46 Diary of Samuel Cockerell, George Lloyd Papers, GLLD 9/1, Churchill College, Cambridge; Charmley, *Lord Lloyd*, pp. 38–42.

47 FitzHerbert, *Biography of Herbert*, pp. 144–5, 151.

48 Lawrence to Hogarth, 2 February 1915, in Garnett, ed., *Letters of Lawrence*, p. 192; Winstone, *Woolley of Ur*, pp. 59–80.

49 Lawrence, *Seven Pillars of Wisdom* (1935 edn.), pp. 58–9.

50 Clayton to Wingate, 30 December 1914, WP, SAD 192/3/256.

51 'Notes on Turkish Forces in Syria up to Dec. 15th 1914', WO 157/689.

52 Note, 'Artillery, 26-12-14', WO 157/689.

53 'The Proposed Turkish Invasion of Egypt, 31.12.14', WO 157/689.

54 Clayton to Wingate, 28 December 1914, WP, SAD 134/8/126.

55 Clayton to Wingate, 30 December 1914, WP, SAD 192/3/256.

56 'Report on the Movement of Turkish Troops', 4 January 1915, WO 157/689.

57 'Further Information as to the Proposed Turkish Invasion of Egypt', 6 January 1915', WO 157/689.

58 Clayton Note, 3 January 1915, CP, SAD 694/3/1; and 'Further Report on the Proposed Turkish Invasion of Egypt', 7 February 1915, WO 157/689.

59 Note, 10 January 1915, WO 157/689.

60 'Turkish Invasion of Egypt, Summary of News since January 7th 1915', 20 January 1915, WO 157/689. In an undated telegram appearing in the Clayton Papers, it was reported that 'we must count on Turkish having 100,000 men available [and] . . . probably 50 to 60 guns'. But from the context it appears that the cable pre-dated the aerial reconnaissance of 17–19 January. WP, SAD 134/9/41.

61 Clayton to Wingate, 14 January 1915, WP, SAD 134/9/45; Clayton to Wingate, 25 January 1915, WP, SAD 134/9/70.

62 Sheffy, *Palestine Intelligence*, p. 54.

63 Clayton to Wingate, n.d., but 11 or 12 February 1915, WP, SAD 134/9/102.

64 Sheffy, *Palestine Intelligence*, pp. 55–6.

65 Maxwell despatch, 16 February 1915, WO 33/796; Falls and MacMunn, *Military Operations, Egypt and Palestine*, I, p. 48; Elgood, *Egypt and the Army*, pp. 20, 136–7 (failure to pursue retreating Turks).

66 Sheffy, *Palestine Intelligence*, pp. 55–6.

67 Clayton to Wingate, 20 January 1915, WP, SAD 194/1/183.

10 Our Friends Across the Water: Origins of the Anglo-Arab Alliance

1 R. E. M. Russell, 'Précis of Conversation with Abd el Aziz El Masri on 16th August 1914', 17 August 1914, FO371/2140.

2 Clayton to Cheetham, 30 October 1914, FO 371/2140.

3 Tauber, *Arab Movements*, pp. 2–3.

4 *Ibid.*, p. 9.

5 Clayton, 'Appreciation of Situation in Arabia', 6 September 1914, and Cheetham to Grey, 7 September 1914, both in FO 371/2140.

6 Storrs, *Orientations*, pp. 148–9.

7 Quoted in Kedourie, *Labyrinth*, p. 15. Kedourie erroneously concludes that Clayton

wrote to Kitchener at this time; in fact, Clayton merely approved Storrs's letter to Kitchener.

8 Clayton to Symes, 13 March 1915, WP, SAD 123/2/38 (Clayton's approval); Cheetham to Grey, 26 (quotes) and 28 October 1914, FO 371/2140.

9 Clayton to Wingate, 4 November 1914, WP, SAD 192/2/9; Abdullah's reply is quoted in Kedourie, *Labyrinth*, p. 17.

10 Grey (for Kitchener) to Cheetham, 31 October 1914, FO 371/2139.

11 Kedourie, *Labyrinth*, pp. 20–1; Clayton to Wingate, 9 December 1914, WP, SAD 192/3/53.

12 Storrs, *Orientations*, pp. 122–3.

13 Cheetham to Grey, 13 November 1914, FO 371/2140; emphasis added. Clayton's draft of the telegram appears in in WP, SAD 193/4/172, with his handwritten note: 'The above was drafted by me and . . . was sent home practically as it stands. I believe the memorandum [of 30 October, describing Clayton's meeting with al-Masri on 26 October] has been sent since by mail or is going'.

14 Grey to Cheetham, 14 November 1914, FO 371/2140.

15 Cheetham to Grey, 16 November 1914, *ibid.*, emphasis added; Clayton's draft of the telegram is in WP, SAD 193/4/171 ('This draft was sent home by the Agency as it stands.')

16 Clayton to Wingate, 14 November 1914, WP, SAD 193/4/109; Storrs to Fitzgerald (Kitchener's private secretary), 10 November 1914, Kitchener Papers, PRO 30/57/45, TNA.

17 Memoranda describing the views of Rashid Rida and a 'leading . . . Syrian Christian' [Dr Nimr] in McMahon to Grey, 15 February 1915, FO 371/2480; *and see* 'Dr Nimr's views', 22 January 1915, WO 157/689.

18 Clayton to Wingate, n.d., *c.* February 1915, WP, SAD 134/2/17.

19 Clayton to Wingate, 14 July 1915, WP, SAD 158/6/16.

20 Clayton to Wingate, n.d., *c.* February 1915, WP, SAD 134/4/39 (Pan-Islamic Party); Clayton to Wingate, 3 March 1915, WP, SAD 134/3/1 ('own good time').

21 Clayton Note, 7 February 1915, CP, SAD 694/3/12.

22 Storrs to Fitzgerald, 2 May 1915, Kitchener Papers, PRO 30/57/47, TNA; Gertrude Bell Diary, 30 September 1919, Newcastle University Library website, http://gertrude-bell.ncl.ac.uk/diary.

23 Quotes from Kedourie, *Labyrinth*, p. 35; *see also* Long, *British Pro-Consuls*, pp. 7–29.

24 Clayton to Wingate, 23 January 1915, WP, SAD 123/2/8.

25 Clayton to Wingate, 21 April 1915, WP, SAD 195/1/187 ('retiring'); Clayton to Wingate, 30 June 1915, WP, SAD 195/4/306 ('oyster'); Stack to Wingate, 24 April 1915, WP, SAD 195/1/252 ('difficult'); Clayton to Wingate, 2 October 1915, WP, SAD 197/1/5 ('extreme caution').

26 Herbert Diary, vol. I, entry for 18 December 1915, Mervyn Herbert Papers, MECOX.

27 *Ibid.*, entry for 11 November 1916.

28 *Ibid.*, entry for 1 June 1916.

29 Clayton Note, 3 January 1915, CP, SAD 694/3/1.

30 Intelligence Department Memorandum, 5 January 1915, CP, SAD 694/3/7. Wilson, in *Lawrence of Arabia*, p. 171, persuasively argues that this memo was written by Lawrence.

31 Cheetham to Grey, 7 January, and McMahon to Grey, 15 February 1915, FO 371/2480.

32 Grey Minute, _ January 1915, FO 371/2480, No. 5189.

33 Callwell to Robertson, 10 February 1915, William Robertson Papers, 7/2/4, LHCMA; Grey to McMahon, 17 February 1915, FO 371/2480.

34 Cromer to Wingate, 11 March 1915, WP, SAD 134/3/90.

35 Kedourie, *Labyrinth*, pp. 40–1.

36 Clayton to Wingate, 11 August 1915, WP, SAD 158/7/38.

37 Cromer to Wingate, 18 May 1915, WP, SAD 134/6/35.

38 Clerk Minute, 25 August 1915, FO 371/2486, no. 118580; Chamberlain to Loraine, 10 November 1925, Austen Chamberlain Papers, AC 52/594, BUL; Report of Committee of Imperial Defence, 'Establishment of an Arab Bureau in Cairo', 10 January 1916, FO 371/2670.

39 India Office to Foreign Office, 11 December 1914, and Grey to McMahon, 18 December 1914, both in FO 371/2140.

40 Clayton to Wingate, 26 February 1915, WP, SAD 123/2/22.

41 Clayton to Wingate, 3 March 1915, WP, SAD 134/3/1.

42 India Office to Foreign Office, 24 June 1915, FO 371/2486.

43 Hardinge to Wingate, 28 March 1915, WP, SAD 194/3/273.

44 Clayton Note, 3 January 1915, CP, SAD 694/3/1.

45 Foreign Office to High Commissioner, Egypt, 12 January ('strongly opposed'), and 15 April 1915, FO 141/587/2.

46 Clayton to Wingate, 25 May 1915, WP, SAD 195/2/146.

47 Hardinge to Wingate, 10 June 1915, Hardinge Papers, vol. 94, no. 27, Cambridge University Library; Hardinge to Chamberlain, 6 August 1915, Austen Chamberlain Papers, AC 62/39, BUL.

48 Clayton Note, 24 July 1915, WP, SAD 135/1/53.

49 Wingate to Hardinge, 9 January 1915, CP, SAD 469/8/6.

50 Wingate to Clayton, 27 February 1915, CP, SAD 469/8/44.

51 Wingate to Clayton, 24 February 1915, CP, SAD 469/8/46 ('embryo'); Wingate to Clayton, 20 March 1915, CP, SAD 469/8/58 ('thick and thin').

52 Wingate to Cromer, 14 May 1915, WP, SAD 134/6/19; Wingate to Hardinge, 26 August 1915, Hardinge Papers, vol. 94, no. 94, CUL; Wingate to Grey, 15 May 1915, WP, SAD 134/6/30.

53 Wingate to Hardinge, 28 December 1918, quoted in Kedourie, *Labyrinth*, pp. 46–7.

11   Clayton and the Pledge: The McMahon–Hussein Correspondence

1 Sa'id, *Al-thawra al-'Arabiyya al-kubra* [The Great Arab Revolt] (Cairo, 1934), I, p. 109 ('King'); Antonius, *Arab Awakening*, pp. 158–9 ('spokesman').

2 Kedourie, *Labyrinth*, pp. 3, 40.

3 Clayton to Samuel, 12 April 1923, Herbert Samuel Papers, SAM H/5, vol. V, fo. 64, 1923, Parliamentary Archives.

4 Parliamentary Papers, 1939, Cmd. 5957. All further quotations from the correspondence are taken from Cmd. 5957.

5 Clayton to Wingate, 21 August 1915; Storrs Note, 19 August 1915, both in WP, SAD 135/2/32, 38.

6 McMahon to Grey, 22 August; India Office to Foreign Office, 24 August (with Nicolson (25 August) and Grey (n.d.) Minutes); Grey to McMahon, 25 August; and McMahon to Grey, 26 August 1915, all in FO 371/2486.

7 Clayton to Wingate, 30 August 1915, WP, SAD 196/3/94; Clayton to Wingate, 29 September 1915, WP, SAD 135/3/32.

8 Wingate to Clayton, 27 August 1915, CP, SAD 469/10/42 ('definite encouragement'); Wingate to Clayton, 1 September 1915, CP, SAD 469/10/45 ('Arab Union'); Clayton to Wingate, 8 September 1915, WP, SAD 196/3/94 ('Frankenstein').

9 Wilson, *Lawrence of Arabia*, p. 198.

10 'Statement of Mulazim Awal (lieutenant) Mohammed Sherif El Farugi', n.d., but October 1915, WP, SAD 134/5/25.

11 Clayton to Wingate, 9 October 1915, WP, SAD 135/4/10; original emphasis.

12 Clayton Memorandum, 11 October 1915, WP, SAD 135/4/19.

13 An 'Intelligence Summary for Period 6th October to 12th October, 1915', WO 157/696, supports this. It was there reported that £300,000, to be followed by a further £500,000' was being sent from Constantinople to Baghdad.

14 Friedman, *Question of Palestine*, p. 70.

15 It was later stated that, in addition to Faruqi's statements, Clayton was relying on information from Aziz al-Masri, from a man named Mukhtar Bey in Athens, 'as well as from the various intelligence sources available to the military authorities in Mudros and in Egypt'. Arab Bureau Summary, 29 November 1916, p. 86, WO 158/624.

16 Tauber, *Arab Movements*, p. 61.

17 Fromkin, *Peace to End All Peace*, p. 177 ('duped'); Karsh, *Empires of the Sand*, p. 217 ('self-delusion'); Friedman, *Question of Palestine*, p. 71 ('faulty intelligence'); Kedourie, *Labyrinth*, p. 77 (influence policy).

18 Clayton to Wingate, 13 October 1915, WP, SAD 158/9/27; Storrs to Fitzgerald, 13 October 1915, Kitchener Papers, PRO 30/57/47, TNA. On October 26, Storrs wrote to his mother: 'I am anxious about the Arabs & only hope that we shall not be too late with them.' Storrs Papers, box II, file 3, Pembroke College, Cambridge.

19 Wingate to Clayton, 23 October 1915, WP, SAD 134/5/64 ('pray'); Wingate to Callwell, 19 October 1915, *ibid.*, 134/5/54.

20 Wingate to Clayton, 20 October 1915, WP, SAD 135/4/58; Wingate to Clayton, 29 October 1915, WP, SAD 197/1/305.

21 Clayton to Wingate, 20 October 1915, WP, SAD 158/9/58 (discussed with Maxwell his telegrams to Kitchener); Maxwell to Kitchener, 12 October 1915, WP, SAD 135/4/17, and second of same date, FO 371/2486 (quoted).

22 McMahon to Grey, 12 October, Maxwell to Kitchener, 16 October, and McMahon to Grey, 18 October 1915, all in FO 371/2486.

23 Clayton to ??, __September 1915, CP, SAD 694/3/56; 'Intelligence Summary for the period 6th October to 12th October, 1915', WO 157/696.

24 Murray to Robertson, 23 October 1915, Robertson Papers, 7/3/2, LHCMA.

25 Intelligence Summary, 8 September 1915, WO 157/695.

26 Wingate to Clayton, 5 October 1915, FO 141/461/1.

27 Cromer to Wingate, 22 October 1915, WP, SAD 197/1/194.

28 Clayton to Storrs, 13 October 1915, WP, SAD 135/4/35 ('definite statement'); Clayton to Wingate, 13 October 1915, WP, SAD 158/9/27.

29 Clayton Note, 8 December 1915, FO 141/734/1.

30 McMahon to Grey, 18 October, and Grey to McMahon, 20 October 1915, FO 371/2486.

31 The suggestion that Storrs was the author is made by Kedourie in *Labyrinth*, p. 98. The draft on Intelligence Department paper is in FO 882/19. Wingate's proposed response is in WP, SAD 135/4/62. Clayton to Wingate, 24 October 1915, WP, SAD 135/4/67 reflects McMahon's decision on the terms of the reply. The Residency Note of 25 October 1915 is in FO 141/461/1.

32 McMahon to Grey, 26 October 1915, no. 131, FO 371/2486.

33 Clayton to Samuel, 12 April 1923, Herbert Samuel Papers, SAM H/5, vol. V, fo. 64, 1923, Parliamentary Archives.

34 'The Arab Question', n.a., n.d., but enclosed in McMahon to Foreign Office, 19 April 1916, FO 141/734/1.

35 Clayton to Wingate, 12 November 1915, WP, SAD 135/5/80; Hardinge to Nicolson, 15 November 1915, Hardinge Papers, vo. 94, no. 136, Cambridge University Library ('fatuous'); Hardinge to Graham, 8 December 1915, *ibid.*, vol. 94, no. 149 ('Arab State'); Hardinge to Chamberlain, 4 November 1915, FO 371/2486 ('revenues'); Chamberlain Memorandum, 8 November 1915, FO 371/2486 ('nonentity').

36 Grey to McMahon, 6 November 1915, FO 371/2486.

37 Clayton to Wingate, 12 November 1915, WP, SAD 135/5/80.

38 Parker, 'Note on Arab Movement', n.d., *c.*November 1915, FO 141/734/1.

39 Clayton to Wingate, 21 December 1915, WP, SAD 135/7/174.

40 Clayton's arguments for the landing are reflected in a Note of 6 November 1915, CP, SAD 694/3/64.

41 Clayton to Wingate, 10 December 1915, WP, SAD 158/11/24.

42 The *vilayet* of Beirut then extended southwards to a point some thirty miles north of Jerusalem.

43 Clayton to Wingate, 28 January 1916, WP, SAD 136/1/183; *and see* Clayton's 24 January notes for the draft reply at WP, SAD 136/1/193.

44 Wingate to Clayton, 21 August 1915, CP, SAD 469/10/26.

45 Note, 'The Arab Question', n.d., enclosed in McMahon to Foreign Office, 19 April 1916, WP, SAD 136/1/204.

46 Clayton to Hall, 2 March 1916, CP, SAD 693/10/17.

12 Like Permeating Oil: Counter-intelligence

1 Stoddard, 'Teşkilat ı Mahsusa', (dissertation), pp. 23–45; McMeekin, *Berlin–Baghdad Express*, pp. 123–37.

2 Clayton memorandum, 'Situation on the Western Frontier of Egypt', 15 March 1915, WP, SAD 131/4/11.

3 Hopkirk, *Like Hidden Fire*, pp. 19, 54–65.

4 McMeekin, *Berlin–Baghdad Express*, pp. 86–99, 141–165.

5 Intelligence Summary, 2 July 1915, WO 157/693.

6 Intelligence Summary, 4 July 1915, WO 157/693. In fact, Oppenheim's mother was Catholic and his father, though born Jewish, had converted to Christianity. McMeekin, *Berlin–Baghdad Express*, p. 17.

7 Intelligence Summaries, 29 and 30 June 1915, WO 157/692; Clayton to Wingate, 30 June 1915, WP, SAD 158/5/47.

8 Intelligence Summaries, 8 September (heckled), and 14–21 September (Jewish manner) 1915, WO 157/695.

9 Note on propaganda on the part of the Germans, n.d., FO 141/465/5, enclosed in

Clayton to Cheetham, 23 October 1915, and McMahon to Grey, 24 October 1915, FO 371/2354.

10 Storrs Note, 12 November 1915, FO 882/12.

11 Intelligence Summary, 4 July 1915, WO 157/693; *Arab Bulletin* No. 33, 4 December 1916, FO 882/25 (*Emden*); Intelligence Summary, 18 September 1915, WO 157/695 (intensely hostile).

12 Clayton to Wingate, 29 February 1916, FO 882/12.

13 McKale, 'Germany and the Arab Question', pp. 236–253; McKale, 'German Policy Toward the Sherif of Mecca', pp. 303– 314.

14 Stoddard, 'Teşkilat-ı Mahsusa', p. 59. The number of 'agents' in Egypt seems inflated, but may refer, more generally, to those who merely supplied information to the Turks, and were not formally agents of the organization.

15 Clayton to Wingate, 11 February 1916, WP, SAD 136/2/45.

16 Clayton to Wingate, 14 April 1915, WP, SAD 195/1/137.

17 Clayton to Wingate, n.d., *c.* June 1916, WP, SAD 137/2/38.

18 Clayton to Wingate, 27 July 1915, WP, SAD 158/6/41.

19 Clayton to Wingate, 3 August 1915, WP, SAD 196/2/3.

20 Clayton to Wingate, 11 February 1916, WP, SAD 136/2/42.

21 Clayton to Wingate, 3 March 1915, WP, SAD 134/3/1.

22 Clayton to Graham, 10 August 1915, WP, SAD 196/2/84.

23 Clayton to Wingate, 4 November 1915, WP, SAD 197/2/49.

24 Steevens, *Egypt in 1898*, p. 66.

25 Clayton to Wingate, 9 April 1915 (WP, SAD 195/1/83), and 24 January 1916 (WP, SAD 199/1/166).

26 Clayton to Lloyd, 30 January 1916, George Lloyd Papers, GLLD 9/2, Churchill College, Cambridge; and Clayton Note, 'Enemy Trading in Egypt', 30 January 1916 (submitting Lloyd's memorandum), Lloyd Papers, GLLD 9/8.

27 Clayton to Wingate, 4 May 1916, WP, SAD 159/5/45 (original emphasis).

28 Clayton to Wingate, 29 May 1916, WP, SAD 136/6/150.

29 Murray to Robertson, 26 May 1916, Archibald Murray Papers, box 79/48/3, IWM; Murray, War Diary, 1916, entries for 25, 27 and 31 May and 1 June, 1916, box 79/48/2, IWM.

30 Lynden-Bell to General Frederick Maurice, DMO, 2 June 1916, Arthur Lynden-Bell Papers, ALB 1/2, IWM.

31 Murray to Robertson, 17 June and 1 July 1916, Murray Papers, box 79/48/3, IWM.

32 Clayton to Wingate, n.d., but early June 1916, WP, SAD 137/2/38.

33 Intelligence Summary, 21 May 1915, WO 157/691.

34 Intelligence Summary, 23 May 1915, WO 157/691.

35 Intelligence Summaries, 19 August (WO 157/694), 6–12 October (WO 157/696), and 10–17 November 1915 (WO 157/697).

36 Clayton to Wingate, 1 December 1915, WP, SAD 135/7/8; Intelligence Summary, 1– 7 December 1915, WO 157/698.

37 Clayton to Wingate, 24 December 1915, WP, SAD 131/6/121; Clayton to Wingate, 6 January 1916, WP, SAD 136/1/36; Clayton to WO, 15 January 1916, FO 371/2668.

38 Intelligence Memorandum, 19 February 1916, WO 157/701.

39 Clayton to Wingate, 21 February 1916, WP, SAD 159/2/169.

40 Intelligence Summary, 14 May 1916, WO 157/704.

41 Intelligence Summary, 7–14 December 1915, WO 157/698 (figures conflicting); Summary, 4–10 January 1916, WO 157/700 (32,000); Summary, 18–24 January 1916, WO 157/700 (26,000; exaggerated).

42 *See* Intelligence Summaries in WO 157/690, 691 and 692, and Clayton to Wingate, 7 July 1915, WP, SAD 196/1/65 *(suqs)*.

43 Clayton to Wingate, 21 January 1916, WP, SAD 199/1/138.

44 Loder to his mother, 3 December 1916, John deVere Loder Papers, box 1, MECOX.

45 Intelligence Summary, 18 September 1915, WO 157/695 (27 subs); Clayton to Wingate, 30 June 1915, WP, SAD 195/4/306; Clayton to Wingate, 21 July 1915, WP, SAD 196/1/169. A review of the War Office, MI5 and Admiralty papers at TNA did not disclose further information regarding Clayton's anti-submarine scheme.

46 Intelligence Summary, 21 May 1915, WO 157/691.

47 Sheffy, *Palestine Intelligence*, pp. 222, 228–9.

48 *Ibid.*, pp. 219–223, 246–256.

49 Lawrence, *Seven Pillars of Wisdom* (1935 edn.), p. 57.

50 Clayton to Wingate, 20 March 1916, WP, SAD 159/3/59 ('bombarded'); Storrs, *Orientations*, p. 129 ('best known').

13   Reorganizing the Intelligence, 1916

1 *Historical Sketch of the Directorate of Military Intelligence During the Great War, 1914–1919*, 6 May 1921, WO 32/10776; Jeffery, *MI6*, pp. 3–50; Gudgin, *Military Intelligence*, pp. 46–51; and Andrew, *Secret Service*, pp. 73–80. Cumming's biographer, Alan Judd, in *The Quest for C*, p. 288, casts doubt on the extent of MI1(c)'s authority over the SIS and suggests that MI1(c)'s control over SIS was nominal only.

2 Sheffy, *Palestine Intelligence,* p. 84.

3 Clayton to 'C', 29 November 1916, CP, SAD 693/10/84; Clayton, 'Memorandum on the Advisability of Maintaining in Existence after the War Colonel Samson's Secret Service Bureau, and of Affiliating it to the Cairo Intelligence Directorate', (hereafter, 'R Organisation Memorandum'), *c.*late January 1916, CP, SAD 694/3/71.

4 Private information.

5 Jeffery, *MI6*, p. 131.

6 Samson to Newcombe, 3 August 1915, WO 158/922 ('dislocation'), quoted in Wilson, *Lawrence of Arabia*, pp. 94 and 1009, notes 97–99. Wilson's belief that Lawrence became Samson's representative in Cairo for a time is questioned in Sheffy, *Palestine Intelligence*, p. 100, note 91, who finds the notion 'unsupported by the documents'.

7 MI5, "D" Branch Report, 'The Organisation of the Eastern Mediterranean Special Intelligence Bureau', 1921, KV1/17, p. 3 (hereafter, 'Organisation of EMSIB').

8 Clayton, R Organisation Memorandum, CP, SAD 694/3/71.

9 Organisation of EMSIB, KV1/17, pp. 7–8, 10–11.

10 Nicolson (FO) to McMahon, 29 February 1916, FO 882/2. Sheffy suggests that Nicolson rejected Clayton's proposals in their entirety (*Palestine Intelligence*, p. 124), but appears not to have had available to him the EMSIB history appearing in KV1/17, which was not made public by MI5 until 1997, and which shows that Clayton's basic proposal of an amalgamated Intelligence bureau, at least in the area of counter-intelligence, was accepted by London.

11 Organisation of EMSIB, Appendix A, KV1/17.

12 Organisation of EMSIB, Appendix B, KV1/17.

13 Private information.

14 Jeffery, *MI6*, p. 68.

15 Clayton to Wingate, 3 August 1915, WP, SAD 196/2/3; Clayton to Symes, 12 August 1915, FO 882/2.

16 Mark Sykes, Appreciation of Arabian Report No. XIV, 15 October 1916, FO 371/2781.

17 Clayton to Wingate, 27 July 1915, WP, SAD 158/6/41 (avail; Aden); Clayton to Wingate, 21 April 1915, WP, SAD 195/1/187 (nothing in return).

18 Clayton to Wingate, 26 November 1915, WP, SAD 135/6/40.

19 Clayton to Parker (WO), 3 December 1915, WP, SAD 135/7/28; Clayton to Sykes, 13 December 1915, FO 882/2.

20 Clayton to Wingate, 3 December 1915, WP, SAD 158/11/13. Wingate agreed, observing that he had 'persistently urged' the creation of such a bureau 'for some time past', and added: 'By all means do what you can to strengthen the Cairo Near East Bureau & if necessary make it the head office, but you will have to be very careful not to hurt Indian susceptibilities'. Wingate to Clayton, 8 December 1915, WO, SAD 158/11/21.

21 Sykes had carried with him to Cairo, Basra and Delhi draft copies of the Report of the deBunsen Committee, an inter-departmental panel on which Sykes sat and which laid down British desiderata for the post-war Middle East. For Clayton's views on the deBunsen proposals, *see* Clayton to Wingate, 14 and 27 July 1915, WP, SAD 158/6/16, 41.

22 Adelson, *Mark Sykes: Portrait of an Amateur*.

23 Clayton to Buckley (WO), 8 February 1916, CP, SAD 693/10/5.

24 McMahon (for Sykes) to Lord Robert Cecil (FO), 26 November 1915, FO 371/2357.

25 Sykes to Clayton, 28 December 1915, FO 882/2, fos. 9–15; Sykes, 'Constitution and Functions of the Arabian Bureau', n.d., *c*. December 1915, FO 371/2357, fos. 315–17; Sykes, 'Organisation: Cairo', n.d., FO 882/2, fos. 7–8.

26 Clayton to Nicolson (FO), 3 January 1916, FO 882/2; Hall (ADM) to Clayton, 20 December 1915, FO 882/2; and McMahon to Grey (FO), 8 January 1916, FO 371/2670.

27 Clayton to Hall, 13 January 1916, FO 882/2.

28 Clayton to Hall, 13 January 1916, FO 882/2 (quoted); and Clayton to Hall, 2 February 1916, CP, SAD 693/10/1 ('It is no use laying down the plan of a very elaborate structure until we see what sort of foundation we have been able to make.')

29 Wingate to Clayton, 10 December 1915, WP, SAD 158/11/21. Wingate probably intended that the liaison office be part of the Intelligence Directorate because, as seen, as of 10 December 1915 the War Office Intelligence sections had not yet been split out from the Operations Directorate.

30 Clayton to Hall, 13 January 1916, FO 882/2; Clayton to Sykes, 14 January 1916, FO 371/2670. In this letter, Clayton also proposed that the bureau should be in close touch with MO6, then – organizationally, at least – the governing authority of the SIS, which was soon to move to the new MI1(c).

31 Clayton to Wingate, 11 February 1916, WP, SAD 136/2/42.

32 CID Report, 'Establishment of an Arab Bureau in Cairo', 10 January 1916, FO 371/2670.

33 FitzGerald to Clayton, 20 January 1916, FO 882/2.

34 Lancelot Oliphant, Minute, 10 January 1916, FO 371/2670, fo. 539.

35 Hirtzel (IO) to Oliphant (FO), 17 January 1916, FO 371/2670, fo. 547; Oliphant Minute, 26 January 1916, FO 371/2670, fo. 541.

36 Chamberlain to Hardinge, 18 January 1916, Austen Chamberlain Papers, AC 62/66, Birmingham University Library.

37 Clayton to Wingate, 11 February 1916, WP, SAD 136/2/42 ('materialized'); Clayton to Hall, 2 February 1916, CP, SAD 693/10/1 ('hoped').

38 Westrate, *Arab Bureau*, pp. 3–9, 39–53.

39 *Ibid.*, pp. 32–33.

40 fforde to Grant (Government of India), 14 July 1916, quoted in Mohs, *Military Intelligence and the Arab Revolt*, p. 181, note 134.

41 Westrate, *Arab Bureau*, p. 43.

42 Wingate to Clayton, 24 February 1916, CP, SAD 470/1/85.

43 Westrate, *Arab Bureau*, p. 36.

44 Sattin, *Lifting the Veil*, p. 212.

45 Sheffy, *Palestine Intelligence*, p. 122; Intelligence Summary, 17 December 1915, WO 157/698.

46 Clayton to Wingate, 30 November 1915, WP, SAD 135/6/81.

47 Maxwell to Wingate, 1 December 1915, WP, SAD 135/7/12; Intelligence Summary, 6 January 1916, WO 157/700 (Medforce Intelligence moves to Cairo).

48 Clayton to Wingate, 27 December 1915, WP, SAD 135/7/85; Clayton to Wingate, 6 January 1916, WP, SAD 136/1/35.

49 Maxwell to Wingate, 22 January 1916, WP, SAD 199/1/46 ('hurt'); Maxwell to FitzGerald, 9 March 1916, Maxwell Papers, box 3, folder 9, Princeton University Library ('absurd'); Maxwell to Robertson, 7 March 1916, Robertson Papers, 4/5/3, LHCMA, ('four Intelligence Departments'; original emphasis).

50 Maxwell to Wingate, 22 January 1916, WP, SAD 199/1/46; Clayton to Wingate, 6 January 1916, WP, SAD 136/1/36.

51 Clayton to Wingate, 17 January 1916, WP, SAD 136/1/101 ('untouched'), and, 21 January 1916, WP, SAD 199/1/138 ('little interference').

52 Intelligence Summary, 12 January 1916, WO 157/700; Clayton to Wingate, 14 January (WP, SAD 136/1/92), and 31 January 1916 (WP, SAD 161/1/24).

53 Clayton to Wingate, 17 January (WP, SAD 136/1/101; 'no conception'), and 14 January 1916 (WP, SAD 136/1/92; 'butting in'); Intelligence Summary, 12 January 1916, WO 157/700.

54 Lynden-Bell to Maurice (DMO, WO), 16 January 1916, Arthur Lynden-Bell Papers, ALB 1/2, IWM.

55 Sheffy, *Palestine Intelligence*, pp. 120–21.

56 Intelligence Summary, 22 January 1916, WO 157/700; Lynden-Bell to Maurice, 24 January 1916, Lynden-Bell Papers, ALB 1/2, IWM.

57 Clayton to Wingate, 21 January 1916, WP, SAD 199/1/138; Deedes to his mother, 8 January and 15–17 January 1916, Wyndham Deedes Papers, box 2, file 9, MECOX.

58 Clayton to Wingate, 18 February 1916, WP, SAD 159/2/30; Lynden-Bell to Maurice, 2 February 1916, Lynden-Bell Papers, ALB 1/2 IWM.

59 Sheffy, *Palestine Intelligence*, pp. 83, 135, 156.

60 Clayton to Wingate, 21 February 1916, WP, SAD 159/2/169.

61 Lynden-Bell to Maurice, 27 March 1916, Lynden-Bell Papers, ALB 1/2, IWM.

62 Clayton to Wingate, 24(?) March 1916, WP, SAD 159/3/59.

63 Sheffy, *Palestine Intelligence*, p. 126.

64 Kitchener to McMahon, 13 March, and McMahon to Kitchener, 15 March 1916, Edward Grey Papers, FO 800/48, TNA, fos. 471, 472; Murray Diary, 14 March 1916, Archibald Murray Papers, box 79/48/2, IWM.

65 Clayton to Wingate, 31 March 1916, WP, SAD 136/3/93.

14 Egypt's Little Wars: the Conflicts in Libya and Darfur

1 Clayton to Wingate, 9 December 1914, WP, SAD 192/3/53.

2 Diary of Bimbashi Hewitt, O.C., Sollum, 4 November 1914, WO 157/688 (3,000 regular troops).

3 McGuirk, *Sanusi's Little War*, pp. 20–24; McMeekin, *Berlin–Baghdad Express*, pp. 259–74; McKale, *War by Revolution*, pp. 145–51.

4 McGuirk, *Sanusi's Little War*, p. 24.

5 Clayton to Wingate, 18 November 1914, WP, SAD 193/4/114.

6 Clayton to Wingate, 4 November (WP, SAD 192/2/9; 'friendly'), and 5 December 1914 (WP, SAD 134/4/18; self-interest).

7 Clayton to Wingate: 4 November 1914 (WP, SAD 192/2/9; Royle); 6 January 1915 (WP, SAD 194/1/27; Australians); 2 June 1915 (WP, SAD 195/4/8; letters from McMahon and Maxwell); 8 June 1915 (WP, SAD 195/4/82; naval cruisers); 4 August 1915 (WP, SAD 158/7/1; talks with Muhammad Idrisi); 22 May 1915 (WP, SAD 195/2/46; McMahon's FO telegram based on Clayton Note of 13 April 1915); and 4 August 1915 (WP, SAD 158/7/1; McMahon cable to FO sent after 'long talks' with Clayton). Muhammad Idrisi should not be confused with Muhammad Idris, the son of the second Grand Sanusi, Muhammad al-Mahdi, and cousin of Ahmad al-Sharif, the Sanusi leader in 1915.

8 Wingate to Clayton, 29 June 1915, WP, SAD 195/4/292.

9 Clayton to Wingate, 9 December 1914, WP, SAD 192/3/53.

10 Clayton to Wingate, 9 March (repeating McMahon to FO of 26 February 1915) and 10 March 1915, WP, SAD 131/4/2 and 4. Clayton's Note of 24 February 1915 was repeated in McMahon to FO of 26 February.

11 Grey to McMahon, 23 February 1915, WP, SAD 131/4/8.

12 Rodd (Rome) to FO, 24 March 1915, WP, SAD 131/4/25.

13 Clayton Memorandum, 'Situation on the Western Frontier of Egypt', 15 March 1915, WP, SAD 131/4/11.

14 Clayton Memorandum, 13 April 1915, WP, SAD 131/4/17, contents repeated in McMahon to FO, 6 May 1915, FO 371/2353. In a 28 March 1915 letter to Wingate (WP, SAD 131/4/14), Clayton noted: 'I cannot help thinking that Italy would like to embroil us with the Senussi. It would give her a claim to our assistance in Tripoli of which our Somaliland experience shows us she would not be slow to take advantage.'

15 Clayton, Note on the Senussi, 26 April 1915, WP, SAD 131/4/31.

16 Clayton to Wingate, 16 June 1915, WP, SAD 195/4/148.

17 Treaty of London, 26 April 1915, reproduced in Hurewitz, ed., *Documentary Record*, vol. II, pp. 21–24.

18 Clayton to Wingate, 29 May 1915, WP, SAD 195/2/195 ('Scylla and Charybdis'); Clayton to Wingate, 22 May 1915, WP, SAD 195/2/146 ('gingered up'; wire to Ahmad).

19   McMahon to FO, 3 June 1915, FO 371/2353.

20   Intelligence Summaries, 16, 18 May 1915, WO 157/691.

21   Grey to McMahon, 26 July 1915, FO 371/2353; Clayton to Wingate, 4 August 1915, WP, SAD 158/7/1 ('catspaw').

22   Maxwell to Callwell (DMO), 28 August 1915, Maxwell Papers, box 2, folder 20, Princeton University Library.

23   Clayton to Wingate, 8 September 1915, WP, SAD 196/3/94.

24   McMahon to Grey, 22 September 1915, FO 371/2354; Clayton to Wingate, 22 September 1915, WP, SAD 196/3/287, demonstrating that McMahon's cable embodied Clayton's 'proposal'.

25   Clayton to Wingate, 21 July (WP, SAD 196/1/169; 'cajolery'); and 4 August 1915 (WP, SAD 158/7/1; 'bullet').

26   Clayton to Wingate, 25 August 1915, WP, SAD 196/2/237 (attack on Sollum; ego); Maxwell to Kitchener, 30 August 1915, WO 33/747 (letters from Ahmad); McKale, *War by Revolution*, pp. 148–9 (sub attack; letters)

27   Maxwell to Kitchener, 1 October 1915, WO 33/747.

28   Clayton to Wingate, 27 August (WP, SAD 158/7/93; no desire for hostilities); and 2 October 1915 (WP, SAD 197/1/5; not formidable).

29   Clayton to Wingate, 13 October 1915, WP, SAD 158/9/27. Muhammad Idrisi's brother, Mustapha, had been employed by Clayton in March 1915 to help conclude the treaty made between Britain and the Idrisi of 'Asir.

30   Maxwell to WO, 18 November 1915, WO 33/747.

31   Western Desert Intelligence Summaries, 23 November and 23–30 November 1915, WO 157/697; Clayton to Wingate, 11 November 1915, WP, SAD 135/5/66 (*Tara*); Maxwell to WO, 21 November 1915, WO 33/747.

32   McGuirk, *Sanusi's Little War*, pp. 157–75.

33   Clayton to Wingate, 20 December (WP, SAD 131/6/104; round-up); and 24 December 1915 (WP, SAD 131/6/119; hostages).

34   Casualty figures from Intelligence Summary, 2 February 1916, WO 157/700; and Clayton to Wingate, 31 December 1915, WP, SAD 131/6/131. On the 25 December battle, see McGuirk, *Sanusi's Little War*, pp. 186–98.

35   Maxwell to FitzGerald, 9 March 1916, Maxwell Papers, box 3, folder 9, Princeton University Library.

36   McMahon to FO, 8 January 1916, FO 371/2669 (4 conditions); Wingate to Clayton, 13 January 1916, CP, SAD 470/1/6 ('concoction').

37   Grey to McMahon, 4 March 1916, FO 371/2669.

38   Maxwell to FitzGerald, 9 March 1916, Maxwell Papers, box 3, folder 9, Princeton University Library ('real Senussi'); McMahon to FO, 13 March ('offensive policy') and 27 March 1916, FO 371/2669; Grey to McMahon, 31 March 1916, FO 371/2669 (FO agrees).

39   Clayton to Maxwell, 2 May 1916, Maxwell Papers, box 2, folder 26, Princeton University Library (Murray adheres to four conditions); Intelligence Summary, 2 April 1916, WO 157/703 (Murray consults Clayton).

40   Daly, *Darfur's Sorrow*, pp. 87–114; Daly, *Empire on the Nile*, pp. 171–91.

41   Wingate to Clayton, 30 September 1914, CP, SAD 469/7/12.

42   Wingate to Clayton, 17 May 1915, CP, SAD 469/9/25 (avoid Darfur expedition);

Clayton to Wingate, 20 May (WP, SAD 131/4/44; Senussist 'programme'); 22 May (WP, SAD 195/2/146; 'material assistance'); and 29 May 1915 (WP, SAD 195/2/195; 'bluff').

43 McMahon to FO, 28 July 1915, FO 371/2353.

44 Clayton to Wingate, 25 December 1915, WP, SAD 131/6/123, describing Intelligence that Nuri wrote to 'Ali Dinar in February 1915; Daly, *Empire on the Nile*, p. 179 (letter takes one year to reach Darfur).

45 McKale, *War by Revolution*, pp. 105, 149.

46 The correspondence between 'Ali Dinar and the Sanusi's agent at Kufra is reproduced in Spaulding and Kapteijns, *'Ali Dinar and the Sanusiyya*, pp. 157–77.

47 Clayton to Wingate, 13 October 1915 (WP, SAD 158/9/27; 'working together'); and 20 October 1915 (WP, SAD 158/9/58; 'play the fool'); Wingate to Clayton, 28 July 1915, CP, SAD 469/10/10 ('Ali Dinar infected with Turco-German propaganda).

48 McMahon to Grey, 31 August 1915, FO 371/2354 ('renunciation'); Clayton to Wingate, 24 and 25 December 1915, WP, SAD 131/6/119, 123 ('rifles').

49 Daly, *Empire on the Nile*, p. 179.

50 *Ibid.*, p. 183.

51 Wingate to Clayton, 27 December 1915, CP, SAD 469/11/45; Wingate to Clayton, 4 February 1916, CP, SAD 470/1/37.

52 Wingate to Clayton, 17 May 1915, CP, SAD 469/9/25.

53 Daly, *Empire on the Nile*, p. 181; Wingate to Clayton, 15 February 1916, CP, SAD 470/1/55.

54 Clayton to Wingate, 16 February (WP, SAD 127/6/20; WO approves reinforcements); 21 February 1916 (WP, SAD 159/2/169; fully explained); and Wingate to Clayton, 17 March 1916 (CP, SAD 470/1/94; keep secret Wingate's approach to Kitchener).

55 Clayton to Maxwell, 2 May 1916, Maxwell Papers, box 2, folder 26, Princeton University Library.

56 Clayton to Wingate, 17 March 1916, WP, SAD 159/3/24 ('biggish request'); Clayton to Wingate, 28 February 1916, WP, SAD 127/6/83 (railway).

57 Clayton to Wingate, 4 April (WP, SAD 128/1/23; 'grave inconvenience'); Wingate to Clayton, 24 April (WP, SAD 159/4/68) and Clayton to Wingate, 4 May (WP, SAD 159/5/45; French objections are political); Clayton to Wingate, 17 April (WP, SAD 128/1/83; keep France & Italy in the war); Clayton to Wingate, 1 May (WP, SAD 159/5/8; 'pitched it mild'); and Clayton to Wingate, 11 April (WP, SAD 128/1/42), and 17 April 1916 (WP, SAD 128/1/83; French satisfied); Intelligence Summary, 24 May 1916, WO 157/704 (French 'demonstration').

58 Wingate to Clayton, 4 June 1916, CP, SAD 470/2/77.

59 Wingate to Cromer, 8 June 1916, WP, SAD 159/6/31.

60 Wingate to Kitchener, 15 March 1916, WP, SAD 199/3/13.

61 Wingate to Clayton, 17 March 1916, CP, SAD 470/1/94.

15 Revolt!: The Arab Rising, 1916

1 On the von Stotzingen mission *see Arab Bulletins*, No. 13 (1 August 1916), and No. 22 (19 September 1916), both in FO 882/25; and McKale, *War by Revolution*, pp. 172–8.

2 Hogarth Memorandum, 10 June 1916, Ronald Storrs Papers, box II, file 4, Pembroke College, Cambridge.

3 Wingate to Clayton, 14 April 1916 (#391), FO 141/461/2 (6–8 weeks); Clayton to Wingate, 17 April 1916, WP, SAD 136/5/26 (5,000 rifles and two million rounds of ammunition).

4 Clayton to: FitzGerald, 13 March (CP, SAD 693/10/15); Macdonogh, 19 April (CP, SAD 693/10/22); Buckley (WO), 19 April (CP, SAD 693/10/23; and Wingate, 7 April (WP, SAD 136/4/8), and 21 April 1916 (CP, SAD 693/10/29).

5 Clayton to DMI, 17 May 1916, enclosed in Clayton to FitzGerald, 17 May 1916, Kitchener Papers, PRO 30/57/48, TNA ('public declaration'); Clayton to Wingate, 8 May and 22 May 1916, WP, SAD 136/6/36 and 103 ('definite declaration'); Clayton to Maxwell, 2 May 1916, John Maxwell Papers, box 2, file 26, Princeton University Library.

6 Clayton to Beach (Mesopotamia), 17 April 1916, CP, SAD 693/10/19; Clayton to Maxwell, 2 May 1916 (note 5, above).

7 Clayton to Wingate, 22 April 1916, WP, SAD 136/5/57.

8 Clayton to Wingate, 21 April (CP, SAD 693/10/26) and 1 May 1916 (WP, SAD 159/5/8).

9 Wingate to Clayton: 14 April (No. 392), FO 141/461/2 (Syrian hinterland); 23 April, WP, SAD 136/5/65 (Khalifate); and 2 May 1916, CP, SAD 470/2/26 (heart set on Syria).

10 Clayton to Wingate, 1 May 1916, WP, SAD 159/5/8; and McMahon to Hussein, 8 May 1916, WO 158/624.

11 McMahon to Hussein, 24 October 1915, Cmd. 5957 (British pledge); Clayton, Note, 3 January 1915, FO 371/2480 (quoted); Cheetham to Grey, 7 January 1915, FO 371/2480, repeating 'views of the Intelligence Department' for 'some definite understanding' with France regarding Syria; and McMahon to Grey, 15 February 1915, FO 371/2480.

12 Clayton to Wingate, 3 April 1915, WP, SAD 195/1/14.

13 Clayton to Cheetham, 27 September 1915, WP, SAD 196/3/47; McMahon to Grey, 9 October 1915, WP, SAD 197/1/74; Grey to Cambon, 30 October 1915, FO 141/654/1.

14 Clayton to Wingate, 4 November 1915, WP, SAD 197/2/49; McMahon to Grey, 2 November 1915, FO 371/2486.

15 *See* FO Minutes accompanying McMahon to Grey, 26 October 1915 (No. 158561), FO 371/2486.

16 Parker (WO) to Clayton, 18 November 1915, FO 141/734/1.

17 Barr, *A Line in the Sand*, p. 23; Eldar, 'French Policy towards Husayn', pp. 329–50.

18 'Results of second meeting of Committee to discuss the Arab question and Syria', 23 November 1915, FO 141/734/1.

19 Clayton, 3 Notes of 8 December 1915, (Note "C"), *ibid.*

20 Parker to Clayton, 25 and 29 November 1915 (attaching 'Note on the Arab Movement' of 29 November), *ibid.*

21 'Results of third meeting of Committee to discuss the Syrian question', 21 December 1915, *ibid.*

22 The correspondence embodying the Sykes–Picot agreement appears in Hurewitz, *Documentary record*, vol. II, pp. 60–4.

23 Antonius, *Arab Awakening*, p. 248 (quotes); Kedourie, *England and the Middle East*, pp. 38, 40–3 (consistent).

24 Clayton to Wingate, 14 January (WP, SAD 136/1/87), and 28 January 1916 (WP, SAD 136/1/183).

25 Intrusive (Deedes), Cairo to DMI, London, 3 May 1916, FO 882/16 ('The present arrangement . . . does not clash with any engagements which have been given to the Sherif'.)

26 FO (for Sykes) to McMahon (for Clayton), 14 April 1916, FO 141/734/1 (sends outline of Sykes–Picot); Clayton to Wingate, 8 May, telegram and letter (quoted), WP, SAD 136/3/31 and 36; Hogarth to Hall (Admiralty), 3 May, and Hogarth to McMahon, 4 May, FO 141/734/1; Clayton to Wingate, 20 July 1916, WP, SAD 160/1/68 (useful guide).

27 Young (Jeddah) to Arbur, 25 September 1916, WP, SAD 140/7/24 (Ta'if).

28 FO to McMahon, 29 May 1916, FO 141/734/1. Two weeks earlier Clayton himself had suggested privately to a War Office colleague that he make a short visit to England 'to exchange ideas with those at home', as 'one is apt to get too local in one's ideas when one stays too long in the same place'. Clayton to Buckley, 15 May 1916, CP, SAD 693/10/33. The timing of Clayton's letter and the French request appear to be coincidental.

29 McMahon to FO, 30 May 1916, FO 141/734/1; FO to McMahon, 13 June 1916, *ibid.* ('urgently necessary').

30 Clayton to Wingate, 15 June 1916, WP, SAD 137/4/7; Wingate to Clayton, 15 June 1916, CP, SAD 470/2/86.

31 Clayton to Wingate, 20 July 1916, WP, SAD 160/1/68. For the Indian telegrams *see* Government of India to IO, 1 July 1916, WP, SAD 138/2/66 ('We are confronted with great difficulty in dealing with this [Arab] movement.'), *and see* the cables from India to the IO, 29 and 30 June and 1, 3 and 6 July 1916, all in CAB 42/16.

32 Clayton to Wingate, 20 July 1916, WP, SAD 160/1/68 (describing London meetings).

33 Hardinge to Sir Valentine Chirol, 3 August 1916, quoted in Mohs, *Military Intelligence and the Arab Revolt*, pp. 57–8.

34 Clayton to French, 27 July 1916, FO 882/2; 'Report regarding the Organisation of the Eastern Mediterranean Special Intelligence Bureau' (1921), KV 1/17, p. 83 (applications to enter Egypt).

35 Précis of Evidence of Lieutenant-Colonel Sir Mark Sykes, 6 July 1916, CAB 42/16.

36 Minutes of War Committee meeting of 11 July 1916, CAB 42/16.

37 War Committee, Draft Conclusions, 10 July 1916; McMahon and Wingate telegrams of 8 and 10 July 1916; and, FO to McMahon, 12 July 1916, CAB 42/16.

38 Diary of King George V, 10 July 1916, RA: GV/PRIV/GVD/1916, Royal Archives, Windsor.

39 Interview, Dr. John P. Clayton, C.V.O., 17 August 2010, York, England.

40 Clayton to Wingate, 20 July 1916, WP, SAD 160/1/68 (King nervous; Stamfordham anti-Sherif); Wigram to Wingate, 31 July 1916, CP, SAD 470/3/20 (quiet, unassuming).

41 Clayton to Wigram, 13 August 1916, King George V Papers, RA: PS/PSO/GV/C/Q, Royal Archives, Windsor (stamps); Clayton to Wigram, 21 October 1916, *ibid.*; Hogarth to Clayton, 17 August 1916, Hogarth Papers, file 1, MECOX (provides Clayton memo to Wigram).

42 Clayton to Wingate, 20 July 1916, WP, SAD 160/1/68 (epoch-making); Clayton to Wingate, 3 August 1916, WP, SAD 139/1/58 (suggestions adopted).

43 Wingate to Robertson, 9 June 1916, WP, SAD 137/1/62.

44   Murray to Robertson, 15 June 1916, and Robertson to Murray, 16 June 1916, both in FO 141/461/3; Maurice to Lynden-Bell, 6 July 1916, Lynden-Bell Papers, ALB 1/3, IWM.

45   Murray to McMahon, 19 June 1916, and McMahon to Murray, 20 June 1916, FO 141/461/3.

46   McMahon to Wingate, 26 and 28 June 1916, WP, SAD 137/6/17 and 23; Wingate to McMahon, 30 June 1916, WP, SAD 137/6/24; and Wingate to McMahon, 3 July 1916, WP, SAD 138/2/42.

47   Lynden-Bell, Note on telephone conversation with Arab Bureau, 2 July 1916, FO 141/461/3.

48   Parker to Wingate, 6 July 1916, WP, SAD 138/3/69.

49   Murray to Wingate, 31 July 1916, WP, SAD 138/16/66; Lynden-Bell to Maurice, 19 September 1916, Lynden-Bell Papers, ALB 1/3, IWM.

50   Wingate to Parker, 8 July 1916, WP, SAD 138/4/55; Wingate to Robertson, 3 August 1916, WP, SAD 139/1/49; Wingate to Murray, 10 August 1916, WP, SAD 139/2/110.

51   Wingate to Robertson, 31 August 1916, WP, SAD 139/7/95.

52   McMahon to Wingate, 10 July 1916, WP, SAD 138/7/16.

53   Parker to Wingate, 10 July 1916 (McMahon afraid); and Parker to Wingate, 20 July 1916, WP, SAD 160/1/21 and 70 (could not convince McMahon).

54   Lynden-Bell to Maurice, 6 October 1916, Lynden-bell Papers, ALB 1/3, IWM.

55   Clayton to Wingate, 7 September 1916, WP, SAD 140/2/72 (want of control); Clayton to Wingate, 31 August 1916, WP, SAD 139/7/103 (system hopeless).

56   Clayton to Wingate, 7 September 1916, WP, SAD 140/2/72.

57   Robertson to Wingate, 8 August 1916, WP, SAD 139/2/113.

58   Clayton to Wingate, 3 August 1916, WP, SAD 139/1/58.

59   Wilson to Wingate, 7 June 1916, WP, SAD 137/1/38 ('holy muddle'); Wilson to Clayton, 7 June 1916, WP, SAD 137/1/34 (nought left off); Boyle (Royal Navy) to Wilson, 16 June 1916, WP, SAD 137/3/107 (Japanese rifles); Wilson to Wingate, 16 August 1916, WP, SAD 139/4/47 (howitzers); Clayton to Wingate, 23 August 1916, WP, SAD 139/5/98 (Hussein refuses al-Masri's services); Wilson to Wingate, 27 October 1916, WP, SAD 141/2/146 (Ali hindering al-Masri); *Arab Bulletins*: no. 18 (5 September), no. 19 (9 September), and no. 20 (n.d.), FO 882/25 (Rabegh sheikh and supplies); Clayton to Wingate, 3 August 1916, WP, SAD 139/1/77 (Parker sent to Hijaz); Arbur to Wilson, 23 August 1916, WP, SAD 139/5/94 (Parker returns); Clayton to Wingate, 24 August 1916, WP, SAD 139/6/91 (Parker stopped from returning to Hijaz); McMahon to Wilson, 21 September 1916, WP, SAD 140/5/33 (WO approves planes to Rabegh); Wingate to Wilson, 16 October 1916, 1916, WP, SAD 141/1/250 (planes ordered to return to Suez); Arbur to Wingate, 18 October 1916, WP, SAD 141/2/34 (Turk planes arrive as British planes depart). The Kunfida incident is described in Busch, *Britain, India and the Arabs*, p. 239.

60   Wingate to Parker, 8 July 1916, WP, SAD 138/4/55.

61   Clayton to Wigram, 29 November 1916, King George V Papers, RA: PS/PSO/GV/C/Q/2521/98, Royal Archives, Windsor.

62   Murray to McMahon, 31 August 1916, WP, SAD 139/7/119; Lynden-Bell to Maurice, 31 August 1916, Lynden-Bell Papers, ALB 1/3, IWM.

63 Wingate to Robertson, 31 August 1916, WP, SAD 139/7/89; Robertson to Wingate, 8 September 1916, WP, SAD 140/2/118; Murray to Robertson, 1 September 1916, Murray Papers, box 79/48/3, folder 6, IWM.

64 Parker to Wingate, 10 July, and Hogarth to Wingate, 13 July 1916, WP, SAD 160/1/21, 31.

65 Clayton to Wingate, 10 August 1916, WP, SAD 201/5/45; Wingate to Hogarth, 4 July 1916, WP, SAD 138/3/51.

66 Wingate to McMahon, 11 June 1916, WP, SAD 137/2/31.

67 Elgood, *Egypt and the Army*, p. 85.

68 McMahon to Wingate, 25 June 1916, WP, SAD 137/5/34 (troops should be disguised); McMahon to Wingate, 2 July 1916, WP, SAD 138/2/21 (Sultan opposed).

69 Clayton to Wingate, 28 July 1916, WP, SAD 138/15/19; Herbert to Wingate, 6 September 1916, WP, SAD 140/2/50.

70 Clayton to Wingate, 13 June 1916, WP, SAD 137/3/43 (request to Government of India); Arbur to Sirdar, 5 July 1916, WP, SAD 138/3/60 (POW plan); Clayton to Wingate, 28 July 1916, WP, SAD 138/15/19 (POWs change their minds); Clayton to Wingate, 31 July 1916, WP, SAD 160/1/115 (Arabs will go); Arbur to Wingate, 2 August 1916, WP, SAD 139/1/30 (delay request to India); Clayton to Wingate, 14 August 1916, WP, SAD 201/5/96 (Arabs refuse to fight, have had enough); Wilson to Arbur, 17 August 1916, WP, SAD 139/4/12 (families 'destroyed').

71 Robertson to Wingate, 27 October 1916, WP, SAD 141/4/107.

72 Lynden-Bell to Maurice, 29 September 1916, Lynden-Bell Papers, ALB 1/3, IWM.

73 Wilson to Arbur, 10 September 1916; Wilson, 'Notes on the Military Situation in the Hedjaz', 11 September 1916, WP, SAD 140/3/28 and 89.

74 Lynden-Bell to Maurice, 11 September 1916, Lynden-Bell Papers, ALB 1/3, IWM; Murray to Robertson, 22 September 1916, Murray Papers, box 79/48/3, folder 6, IWM.

75 Wilson to Wingate, 20 September 1916, WP, SAD 140/5/18. Colonel E.S. Herbert, the Egyptian Army Military Secretary in Cairo wrote to Wingate on 25 September, reporting his view that McMahon and Murray would not last out together, as 'they cannot hit it off at all'. WP, SAD 140/7/47; original emphasis.

76 'Minutes of a Conference held at Ismailia, 12 September 1916, to discuss the Hedjaz Question', FO 882/4; *and see* War Diary, 12 September 1916, WO 157/708.

77 Clayton to Wingate, 14 September 1916, WP, SAD 140/3/105.

78 McMahon to FO, 13 September 1916, repeating his memo to Murray, WP, SAD 140/3/105.

79 Clayton to Wigram, 18 September 1916, King George V Papers, RA: PS/PSO/GV/C/Q/2521/93, Royal Archives, Windsor.

80 McMahon to Wilson, 21 September 1916, WP, SAD 140/5/33 (flight approved); Robertson memo, 'Assistance to the Sherif', 20 September 1916, George Macdonogh Papers, WO 106/1510, TNA; Clayton to Wingate, 21 September 1916, WP, SAD 140/5/67 (volte face).

81 Wilson to Arbur, 27 September 1916, WP, SAD 140/8/2; Parker to Arbur, 30 September 1916, WP, SAD 140/8/33.

82 FO to McMahon, 28 September 1916, WP, SAD 140/8/28; Note by General Clayton, 28 September 1916, FO 141/462/1.

83 Clayton's idea of a 'band' or 'belt' across Arabia also finds expression in Clayton to:

Buckley (WO), 29 September (CP, SAD 693/10/61); Thesiger (Abyssinia), 30 September (CP, SAD 693/10/67); and Maxwell, 30 September 1916 (Maxwell Papers, box 2, file 26, Princeton University Library).

84 Clayton to Wingate, 12 October 1916, CP, SAD 693/10/70. A slightly different version appears in CP, SAD 694/4/36. Murray's argument concerning the time to send the brigade is in Murray to Wingate, 11 October 1916, WP, SAD 141/1/150.

85 Clayton to Wingate, 12 October 1916, CP, SAD 693/10/73.

86 Clayton to Lynden-Bell, 14 October 1916, CP, SAD 693/10/70.

87 FO to McMahon, 4 October, WP, SAD 141/1/57 (military control to Wingate); McMahon to FO, 4 October, WP, SAD 141/1/54 (reconsider); FO to McMahon, 10 October 1916, WP, SAD 141/1/122 (concede political control).

88 Grey to Wingate, 11 October 1916, WP, SAD 160/4/10; Wemyss to Wingate, 19 November 1916, WP, SAD 143/5/50 (decipher yourself).

89 Clayton to Wigram, 21 October 1916, King George V Papers, RA: PS/PSO/GV/C/Q/2521/96, Royal Archives, Windsor.

90 Murray to Wingate, 14 October 1916, WP, SAD 141/1/206 (troops and planes); Murray to Wingate, 18 October 1916, WP, SAD 141/4/24 (2,000 Turks); Murray to Robertson, 12 December 1916, Robertson Papers, 4/4/64, LHCMA (accept risk).

91 A thorough discussion of Lawrence's October-November 1916 mission to the Hijaz appears in Wilson, *Lawrence of Arabia*, pp. 302–32. On the Rabegh crisis, *see* Mohs, *Military Intelligence and the Arab Revolt*, pp. 63–106; and Fisher, 'The Rabegh Crisis', pp. 73–92.

92 Clayton's covering Note and Lawrence's report, both dated 18 November 1916, appear in CP, SAD 694/4/42-5. Lawrence's Note was likely written earlier though, as the gist of it was conveyed to the War Office on the 17th (Murray to Macdonogh, 17 November 1916, Macdonogh Papers, WO 106/1511), and Robertson referred to it in a telegram of the 16th (Robertson to Murray, 16 November 1916, Robertson Papers, 4/4/57, LHCMA).

93 Wingate to Wilson (Jeddah): 6 November, WP, SAD 143/5/4; 12 November, WP, SAD 143/5/18 (influenced); and 23 November 1916, WP, SAD 143/6/52 (visionary; Arab Bureau).

94 Wingate to Murray, 12 October 1916, WP, SAD 141/3/40.

95 Sirdar to WO, 12 November 1916, Macdonogh Papers, WO 106/1511.

96 Robertson to Murray, 16 October 1916, Murray Papers, box 79/48/3, folder 6, IWM.

97 Robertson to Murray, 1 December 1916, *ibid*.

98 Robertson memorandum, 'Despatch of an Expeditionary Force to Rabegh', 13 November 1916 (describing FO meeting of 10 November); C-in-C, Egypt to CIGS, 29 September 1916; GOC, Force "D" (Mesopotamia) to CIGS, 28 September 1916; and Viceroy to IO, 28 September 1916, all in Macdonogh Papers, WO 106/1511.

99 Maurice to Lynden-Bell, 21 November 1916, Lynden-Bell Papers, ALB 1/3, IWM.

100 Maurice to Lynden-Bell, 13 December 1916, *ibid*.

101 Clayton to Wigram, 29 November 1916, King George V Papers, RA: PS/PSO/GV/C/Q/2521/98, Royal Archives, Windsor.

102 Storrs to S. Graham, 27 November 1916, Storrs Papers, box 2, file 4, Pembroke College, Cambridge.

16 **Between the Upper and the Nether Millstone: The End of Intrusive, 1916**

1 Clayton to Wingate, 6 April 1915, WP, SAD 195/1/37. Clayton's house, along with those of 103 other British officials resident in Gezira in 1916, is depicted on a map (n.d., but likely 1916), appearing in the papers of Sir Frederick Rowlatt at MECOX.

2 Clayton to Wingate: 30 November 1914, WP, SAD 192/2/221 (fagged & dispirited); 21 April 1916, WP, SAD 128/2/44 (Turf Club); 26 February 1915, WP, SAD 123/2/22 (nose down, sink); and Wingate to Clayton, 5 May 1915, CP, SAD 469/9/13 (Sultan liaison).

3 Wingate to Clayton: 11 August 1915, CP, SAD 469/10/15 (recalls Herbert); 29 February 1916, CP, SAD 470/1/86 (meet with Sultan re Darfur); Clayton to Wingate: 1 May 1916, WP, SAD 159/5/8 (every 7–10 days); 21 April 1916, WP, SAD 128/2/44 (talks with an Englishman); Kenny to Wingate, 7 July 1916, WP, SAD 160/1/85.

4 Clayton to Wingate, 11 August 1915, WP, SAD 158/7/38.

5 *Ibid.*

6 Clayton to Wingate, 27 October 1915, WP, SAD 135/4/77.

7 Clayton to Wingate, 4 November 1915, WP, SAD 197/2/49.

8 Maxwell to Wingate, 1 December 1915, WP, SAD 135/7/12.

9 Wingate to Clayton: 17 November 1915, CP, SAD 469/11/20 (relief from Military Intelligence); 10 December 1915, CP, SAD 469/11/38 (reorganization); Clayton to Wingate, 10 December 1915, WP, SAD 158/11/24.

10 Clayton to Wingate, 24 December 1915, WP, SAD 131/6/119.

11 Clayton to Wingate, 31 March 1916 (handwritten, 2 pp.), WP, SAD 136/3/92.

12 Clayton to Wingate: 31 March 1916 (typewritten, 4 pp.), WP, SAD 136/3/93 (increase of work); 24 March 1916 (bombarded), WP, SAD 159/3/59.

13 Clayton to Wingate: 20 December 1915, WP, SAD 131/6/104 (2 officers short); 27 December 1915, WP, SAD 135/7/185 (nights at GHQ).

14 Wingate to Clayton, 9 April 1916, CP, SAD 470/2/4; Clayton to Wingate, 21 April 1916, CP, SAD 693/10/26.

15 Wingate to Clayton: 3 January 1915, CP, SAD 469/8/2 (burden); 20 April 1915, CP, SAD 469/9/7 (busy time); 11 September 1915, CP, SAD 469/10/53 (breakdown).

16 Wingate to Clayton: 24 February 1915, CP, SAD 469/8/46; 5 October 1915, CP, SAD 469/11/3; 22 November 1915, CP, SAD 469/11/22; 2 December 1915, CP, SAD 469/11/32; 23 March 1916, CP, SAD 470/1/117; 20 April 1916, CP, SAD 470/2/16; and 22 May 1916, CP, SAD 470/2/51.

17 Wingate to Clayton, 22 May 1916, CP, SAD 470/2/51.

18 Wingate to Clayton: 11 May 1915, CP, SAD 469/9/19; 13 January 1916, CP, SAD 470/1/4.

19 Clayton to Wingate: 3 February 1915, WP, SAD 134/2/12; n.d., but mid-March 1915, WP, SAD 134/5/7.

20 Jane's birth date is recorded in Clayton's bible, in the possession of Dr. John P. Clayton, C.V.O.; Clayton to Wingate: 25 August 1915, WP, SAD 196/2/237 (chill & fever); 27 August 1915, WP, SAD 158/7/93 (missing meals).

21 Pearson to Wingate, 4 September 1915, WP, SAD 196/3/49 (run down); Clayton to Wingate, 8 September 1915, WP, SAD 196/3/94 (conundrums); Wingate to Clayton, 14 September 1915, CP, SAD 469/10/54 (various Masters); Clayton to Wingate, 2 October 1915, WP, SAD 197/1/5 (works at home; return of Enid); Stack to Wingate:

20 October (doctors advise Europe), and 23 October 1915 (heavy time), WP, SAD 197/1/165, and 203.

22 Wingate to Clayton, 17 November 1915, CP, SAD 469/11/20; Clayton to Wingate, 19 November 1915, WP, SAD 197/2/192 (sharp attack of fever); Wingate to Clayton, 25 November 1915, CP, SAD 469/11/25 (bed-rock).

23 Clayton to Wingate, 30 November 1914, WP, SAD 192/2/221 (triumvirate); Wingate to Clayton: 10 July 1915, CP, SAD 469/10/3, and 28 July 1915, CP, SAD 469/10/10 (arms & ammunition); Hamilton to Wingate, 25 June 1915, CP, SAD 469/9/46 (medals); Wingate to Clayton, 11 February 1916, CP, SAD 470/1/47 (breaking point).

24 Stack to Clayton, 22 March 1917, CP, SAD 470/6/24.

25 Clayton to Wingate, 21 November 1914, WP, SAD 192/2/112; Wingate to Clayton, 25 November 1914, CP, SAD 469/7/65; Clayton to Wingate, 9 December 1914, WP, SAD 192/3/53; Wingate to Kitchener, 2 December 1914. WP, SAD 192/3/10.

26 Clayton to Wingate, 4 April 1916, WP, SAD 128/1/23; Wingate to Clayton, 24 April 1916, WP, SAD 159/4/68; Clayton to Wingate, 1 May 1916, WP, SAD 159/5/8.

27 Clayton to Wingate, 11 August 1915, WP, SAD 158/7/38 (personal individuality; personal views); Wingate to Clayton, 3 October 1914, CP, SAD 469/7/16 (Sudan view); Wingate to Clayton, 25 November 1914, WP, SAD 193/4/204 (differentiate).

28 Clayton to Wingate, 30 November 1914, WP, SAD 192/2/21.

29 Wingate to Clayton, 7 January 1915, CP, SAD 469/8/10; Clayton to Wingate, 6 January 1915, WP, SAD 194/1/27.

30 Clayton to Wingate: 29 May 1915, WP, SAD 195/2/195; 8 June 1915, WP, SAD 195/4/82.

31 Wingate to Clayton, 9 April 1916, CP, SAD 470/2/4.

32 Wingate to Clayton, 11 May 1916, CP, SAD 470/2/35; Clayton to Wingate, 22 May 1916, WP, SAD 136/6/103 (original emphasis).

33 Clayton to Wingate, 14 August 1916, WP, SAD 139/3/85.

34 Clayton to Wingate, 3 December 1915, WP, SAD 158/11/13 (Iltyd appears on Canal); Iltyd Clayton, unpublished partial memoir (c. 1940s), Iltyd Clayton Papers, box 1, file 5, MECOX; Clayton to Wingate, 3 August 1916, WP, SAD 139/1/54 (Iltyd to Salonica).

35 Iltyd Clayton, unpublished partial memoir, Iltyd Clayton Papers, box 1, file 5, MECOX. See also Beesly, Very Special Intelligence. Jack's son, Admiral Richard Pilkington Clayton, GCB (1925–1984), served as a midshipman in the Royal Navy during World War II, and eventually rose to be Controller of the Navy, Third Sea Lord and Commander-in-Chief, Naval Home Command.

36 Clayton to Wingate, 16 January 1915, WP, SAD 194/1/45 (miralai); Wingate to Clayton, 20 April 1916, CP, SAD 470/2/16 (lewa); Clayton to Wingate, 14 April 1916, WP, SAD 136/4/49 (brigadier-general); London Gazette, Third Supplement, 20 June 1916, p. 6181, and Fourth Supplement, 22 September 1916, pp. 9338–9 (despatches); London Gazette, Supplement, 3 June 1916, p. 5566 (brevet-major); Clayton notes, n.d., listing mentions in despatches, honours and promotions, CP, SAD 473/2/11 (French medal).

37 E. S. Herbert to Wingate, 14 September 1916, WP, SAD 160/3/75; Graham to Wingate, 5 November 1916, WP, SAD 236/5/70 (proposes Clayton for the Interior); Clayton to Wingate, 24 September 1916, WP, SAD 140/6/56 (would have accepted).

38 Clayton to Wingate, 22 May 1915, WP, SAD 195/2/146.

39 McMahon to FO, 20 December 1916, FO 141/734/1; Wingate to Clayton, 20 August 1916, CP, SAD 470/3/36 (describing his WO despatch).

40 Robbins, *British Generalship on the Western Front*, pp. 116–17.

41 Dawnay to his wife, 6 February 1916, Guy Dawnay Papers, 'Egypt and Palestine, 1916–1917' volume, IWM.

42 Graham to Maxwell, 18 August 1916, Maxwell Papers, box 3, folder 17, Princeton University Library.

43 Russell to Maxwell, 13 October 1917, Maxwell Papers, box 5, folder 11, Princeton University Library (lacks confidence of his men); Wavell to Bartholomew, 2 February 1939, Allenby Papers, 6/8, LHCMA.

44 E. S. Herbert to Wingate, 23 November 1916, WP, SAD 143/6/58.

45 Lynden-Bell to Maurice, 21 December 1916, Lynden-Bell Papers, ALB 1/3, IWM; Murray to Robertson, 14 November 1916, Murray Papers, box 79/48/3, folder 6, IWM.

46 E .S. Herbert to Wingate, 3 March 1916, WP, SAD 159/3/2.

47 Mervyn Herbert diary, volume I, entry for 23 September 1916, MECOX; Wingate to Wilson, 29 September 1916, WP, SAD 140/8/108.

48 Lynden-Bell to Maurice, 21 March 1916, Lynden-Bell Papers, ALB 1/2, IWM ('we shall be able to get on quite well with Clayton'); Murray to Robertson, 4 April 1916, Murray Papers, box 79/48/3, folder 6, IWM ('Colonel Clayton is doing the work very well'). Murray's approval of the June 1 round-up appears in Murray to Robertson: 26 May, 2 June, 17 June and 1 July 1916, Murray Papers *ibid*.

49 Hogarth, 'Arab Bureau, First Report', 1 May 1916, FO 371/2771.

50 'Arab Bureau, Second Report', 30 June 1916, WP, SAD 137/6/98; *and see* Hogarth to Wingate, 29 June 1916, WP, SAD 137/6/84 ('The "Arab Bureau" is simply (in fact if not in theory), an integral part of the Intelligence Section.')

51 EEF Intelligence Diary, 24 June 1916, WO 157/705.

52 Lynden-Bell to Maurice, 10 November 1916, Lynden-Bell Papers, ALB 1/3, IWM.

53 Murray to Wingate, 19 June 1916, WP, SAD 137/3/111; Murray to McMahon, 19 June; McMahon to Murray, 20 June; and Lynden-Bell Note, 30 June 1916, all in FO 141/461/3.

54 Clayton to Wingate: 24 July 1916, WP, SAD 138/4/14; 28 September 1916, WP, SAD 140/8/69 (Lawrence, Cornwallis).

55 Clayton to Wingate, 24 September 1916, WP, SAD 140/6/56.

56 Clayton to Hall, 10 September 1916, CP, SAD 693/10/57.

57 Clayton to Wingate, 7 August 1916, WP, SAD 139/2/45 (GHQ not keeping Cairo informed); Murray to Wingate, 18 August 1916, CP, SAD 470/3/35 (Akaba).

58 Clayton to Wingate, 13 November 1916, WP, SAD 160/5/58.

59 Sheffy, in his *Palestine Intelligence*, pp. 126–33, argues that the claim that GHQ's hostility to Clayton's Cairo branch 'stemmed from Holdich's jealousy' was 'far from the truth'. Wilson, in *Lawrence of Arabia*, p. 291, contends that 'Murray's anger against Clayton was nurtured by Colonel Holdich'. Based on the evidence adduced here – not cited by Sheffy or Wilson – it seems that Wilson's conclusion is nearer the mark.

60 Wingate to E .S. Herbert, 26 July 1916, WP, SAD 201/3/81 (describing Herbert's talk with Holdich and the latter's grudge); Wilson to Wingate, 15 October 1916, WP, SAD 141/3/64 (heart's desire); Russell to Wingate, 1 November 1916, WP, SAD 160/5/1 (supplanted by Holdich); and Storrs to Sybil Graham, 27 November 1916, Storrs Papers, box 2, folder 4, Pembroke College, Cambridge.

61 Wingate to Clayton, 17 November 1915, CP, SAD 469/11/20 (purely Military Intelligence); 24 February 1916, CP, SAD 470/1/81 (Syrian Intell); Clayton to Wingate, 31 January 1916, WP, SAD 161/1/24 (Sinai Intell); Deedes to his mother, 9 [March?] 1916, Deedes Papers, box 2, file 9, MECOX (political, Interior and Arab questions).

62 Wingate to Stack, 29 June 1916, WP, SAD 137/6/82 (Dicks Toms & Harries); Clayton to Wingate, 3 August 1916, WP, SAD 139/1/58; Clayton to Maxwell, 2 May 1916, Maxwell Papers, box 2, file 26, Princeton University Library.

63 Wingate to Clayton, 6 August 1916, CP, SAD 470/3/11; Clayton to Wingate, 14 August 1916, WP, SAD 139/3/85; Wingate to Clayton, 20 August 1916, CP, SAD 470/3/36.

64 Murray to Wingate, 18 August 1916, CP, SAD 470/3/35; Wingate to Clayton, 7 September 1916, CP, SAD 470/3/57.

65 Wingate to Wilson, 26 August 1916, WP, SAD 139/7/1.

66 Wingate to Clayton, 27 August 1916, CP, SAD 470/3/46.

67 Wingate to Robertson, 31 August 1916, WP, SAD 139/7/95; Wingate to Murray, 2 September 1916, WP, SAD 140/1/47.

68 Clayton to Wingate, 3 September 1916 (telegram), WP, SAD 140/1/47; Clayton to Wingate, 4 September 1916, WP, SAD 140/1/110.

69 Wingate to Clayton, 3 September 1916, CP, SAD 470/3/49.

70 Wingate to Clayton, 13 September 1916, CP, SAD 470/3/61.

71 Clayton to Wingate, 24 September 1916, WP, SAD 140/6/56.

72 Clayton to Wingate: 14 September 1916, WP, SAD 140/3/167 (quote); and 28 September 1916, WP, SAD 140/8/69 ('G.H.Q. are . . . coming up here sometime next month, which will . . . probably do away with any necessity for me in a military capacity.')

73 Clayton to Buckley; Clayton to 'General' [Macdonogh], both 10 November 1916, CP, SAD 693/10/78 and 80. That 'General' referred to Macdonogh was made clear in Clayton to Lloyd, 13 November 1916, Lloyd Papers, GLLD 9/8, Churchill College, Cambridge.

74 French to Murray, n.d., but late November-early December 1916, CP, SAD 694/5/5. On the DMI's proposal to establish a Political Intelligence Department in Cairo and India Office objection to it, *see* Mohs, *Military Intelligence and the Arab Revolt*, pp. 73 and 194, n.113.

75 Clayton to Wingate: 24 September 1916, WP, SAD 140/6/56 (Enid sleeping in hospital); 19 October 1916, WP, SAD 141/4/47 (Thomas ill for the last week). Thomas F. Clayton, dates of birth and death, recorded in Clayton's bible, in the possession of Dr. John P. Clayton, C.V.O. Clayton to Wigram, 29 November 1916, King George V Papers, RA: PS/PSO/GV/C/Q/2521/98, Royal Archives, Windsor (message from King and Queen).

17   Chief of Staff, Hijaz Operations, 1917

1 Clayton to Wingate, 16 November 1916, WP, SAD 160/5/74.

2 Lloyd to Clayton, 21 November 1916, George Lloyd Papers, GLLD 9/8, Churchill College, Cambridge.

3 Clayton to Wingate: 13 November (original emphasis) and 16 November 1916, WP, SAD 160/5/58 and 77.

4   Clayton to Wingate, 4 December 1916, WP, SAD 160/6/30; Wingate to Clayton, 10 December 1916, CP, SAD 470/4/51.

5   Storrs to 'Colum', 21 December 1916, Ronald Storrs Papers, box 2, folder 4, Pembroke College, Cambridge; Stack to Clayton: 4 January 1917, CP, SAD 470/6/1 (useful); 18 December 1916, CP, SAD 470/5/8 (Civil Secretary).

6   McMahon to Wingate, 16 October; Wingate to McMahon, 17 October; and McMahon to Wingate, 18 October 1916, all in FO 141/738/1; Clayton to Wingate, 19 October 1916, WP, SAD 141/4/47; Murray Diary, entry for 3 November 1916, Archibald Murray Papers, box 79/48/2, IWM; Lynden-Bell to Maurice, 10 November 1916, Arthur Lynden-Bell Papers, ALB 1/3, IWM (Sirdar to communicate direct with GHQ on 'all matters concerning the Sherif').

7   Wingate, Memorandum, n.d., *c.* 30 December 1916, CP, SAD 694/5/4; Wingate to Murray, 30 December 1916, WP, SAD 144/3/109; Clayton to Lloyd, 28 December 1916, 7 January 1917, Lloyd Papers, GLLD 9/8, Churchill College, Cambridge.

8   Stack to Clayton, 7 January 1917, CP, SAD 470/6/5.

9   Clayton to Wingate: 20 November, WP, SAD 160/5/98; and 27 November 1916, WP, SAD 143/6/88.

10 Clayton to Lloyd, 28 December 1916, 7 January 1917, Lloyd Papers, GLLD 9/8, Churchill College, Cambridge.

11 *Ibid.*

12 Clayton to Gabriel, 28 July 1916, CP, SAD 693/10/39 (quoted); Clayton to Wingate, 24 July 1916, WP, SAD 160/1/84; Clayton, 'Note on the Situation in Regard to the Hejaz and the Arab Movement', 30 July 1916, FO 141/461/3.

13 Clayton to Wingate, 20 November 1916, WP, SAD 143/6/1.

14 *Ibid.*

15 *Ibid.* (dislocating); Clayton to Lloyd, 28 December 1916, 7 January 1917, Lloyd Papers, GLLD 9/8, Churchill College, Cambridge (only one key).

16 Clayton, Note, 8 December 1915, FO 882/2, fo. 170.

17 Parker to Wingate, 10 July 1916, WP, SAD 160/1/21 (Clayton pressing Akaba landing while in London).

18 Clayton to Wingate, 10 and 14 August 1916, WP, SAD 201/5/45 and 96; Clayton to Wigram, 13 August 1916, King George V Papers, RA: PS/PSO/GV/C/Q/2521/92, Royal Archives, Windsor.

19 Clayton, Note (for GHQ) on the occupation of Akaba, n.d., but enclosed in Clayton to Wingate, 7 September 1916, WP, SAD 140/2/72, 75.

20 McMahon to FO, 13 August 1916, WP, SAD 139/3/44; Wingate to Clayton, 20 August 1916, WP, SAD 139/5/4; Jackson (Admiralty) to Wemyss, 14 September 1916, Rosslyn Wemyss Papers, 4/4, Churchill College, Cambridge.

21 Murray to Robertson, 14 July 1916, Murray Papers, box 79/48/3, folder 6, IWM.

22 Murray to McMahon, 29 August 1916, FO 141/461/3.

23 Clayton to Wingate: 17 August, WP, SAD 201/5/107; 24 August, WP, SAD 139/6/9; 4 August, CP, SAD 693/10/49 (Parker sent); 24 August 1916, WP, SAD 139/6/9 (Parker held up).

24 Lawrence, *Seven Pillars of Wisdom, 1922 Text*, Chapter 41; Wilson, *Lawrence of Arabia*, pp. 293–5.

25 Clayton to Wingate: 3 and 4 (telegram) August 1916, CP, SAD 693/10/42, 49.

26 Murray to Robertson, 18 August 1916, Murray Papers, box 79/48/3, folder 6, IWM;

Robertson to Murray, 29 August 1916, *ibid.*; Lynden-Bell to Maurice, 31 August 1916, Lynden-Bell Papers, ALB 1/3, IWM.

27 Lynden-Bell to Maurice, 11 September 1916, Lynden-Bell Papers, ALB 1/3, IWM.

28 McMahon to FO, 30 August 1916, WP, SAD 139/7/74: 'We are not in a position at present to take active operations in the direction of Akaba and Ma'an'; Intelligence Summary, 12 September 1916, WO 157/708.

29 Clayton to Lloyd, 28 December 1916, 7 January 1917, Lloyd Papers, GLLD 9/8, Churchill College, Cambridge.

30 Hussein to McMahon, 25 August 1916, WP, SAD 140/5/61; Hussein to Wilson, 12 September 1916, WP, SAD 140/5/64; Wingate to Murray, 2 September 1916, WP, SAD 140/1/47.

31 Lawrence to Clayton, 18 October 1916, in Brown, ed., *Lawrence Letters*, pp. 88–90.

32 McMahon to FO, 9 July 1916, WP, SAD 138/5/4 (army of 40,000); Faruqi to McMahon, 4 August 1916, FO 141/461/3 (and see Clayton's marginal notes thereon); Clayton to McMahon, 7 August 1916, FO 141/461/3 (quoted).

33 Wilson (Jeddah) to Arbur, 29 October 1916, WP, SAD 141/2/180; Clayton to Wilson, 9 November 1916, CP, SAD 693/10/75.

34 Lawrence, 'Personal Notes on the Sharifial Family', 27 October 1916, *Arab Bulletin* No. 32, FO 882/25, fo. 482.

35 Lawrence to Wilson, 16 April 1917, FO 882/6; substantially reproduced in Brown, ed., *Lawrence Letters*, pp. 107–110.

36 Lawrence, 'Personal Notes on the Sharifial Family, 27 October 1916, *Arab Bulletin* No. 32, FO 882/25, fo. 482; Wilson to Wingate, 5 October 1916, WP, SAD 141/3/15.

37 Storrs Report, 10 June 1916, Ronald Storrs Papers, box II, file 4, Pembroke College, Cambridge.

38 *Arab Bulletin* No. 41, 6 February 1917, FO 882/26.

39 Lawrence, 'Personal Notes on the Sharifial Family', 27 October 1916, *Arab Bulletin* No. 32, FO 882/25, fo. 482.

40 Wingate to Wilson, 10 November 1916, WP, SAD 143/5/14; Clayton to Wingate, 20 November 1916, CP, SAD 694/4/47.

41 Graves and Liddell Hart, eds., *Lawrence to his Biographers*, II, p. 188.

42 Clayton to Wingate: 9 October, WP, SAD 141/3/35; 18 October 1916, WP, SAD 141/2/36.

43 Newcombe Note, 1927, quoted in Wilson, *Lawrence of Arabia*, p. 169.

44 *See, e.g.*, 'Syria. The Raw Material', *c.* early 1915, reproduced in *Arab Bulletin* No. 44, 12 March 1917, FO 882/26; Wilson, *Lawrence of Arabia*, pp. 183–6.

45 Hogarth, 'T.E. Lawrence', quoted in Wilson, *Lawrence of Arabia*, p. 213.

46 Clayton to Hall (Admiralty), 2 February 1916; Clayton to Beach (Mesopotamia), 17 April 1916, CP, SAD 693/10/1 and 19; Clayton to Wingate, 9 October 1916, WP, SAD 141/3/34 (sending Lawrence); Clayton to Wilson (Jeddah), CP, SAD 693/10/75; Clayton to Wingate, 16 November 1916, WP, SAD 160/5/74 (three greatest experts).

47 Patience Marshall (née Clayton, 1913–2009), Note, 28 October 1988, Clayton family papers. Patience noted that Lawrence's visits to Clayton's house occurred when she was about six years old. This would have been in 1919, during which Lawrence spent only a few days in Cairo. Jane Clayton died in June 1920, so Patience's recollection could not have related to subsequent periods. Most likely her remembrance dates to the period 1916–18.

48   Lawrence, *Seven Pillars* (1935 edn.), p. 63. Lawrence later described his low regard for Holdich's Intelligence work: 'Holdich was excellent in O[perations] and fatal in I[ntelligence].' Graves and Liddell Hart, eds., *Lawrence to his Biographers*, II, p. 92.

49   Wingate to Wilson, 12 November 1916, WP, SAD 143/5/18 (sending Lawrence; Clayton will object); Clayton to Wingate, 4 December 1916, WP, SAD 160/6/30 (hopes Lawrence will return); Lawrence to Wilson, 6 December 1916, in Garnett, ed., *Letters of T.E. Lawrence*, pp. 211–13 (Clayton's orders).

50   Clayton to Pearson, 2 March 1917, FO 882/6; Lawrence to Newcombe, 17 January 1917, quoted in Brown, ed., *Lawrence Letters*, pp. 102–3.

51   These points are well-made by Wilson, *Lawrence of Arabia*, pp. 355–7. Lawrence held that 'handling' the Bedouin was 'an art, not a science' and his practical advice on the subject was set forth in his famous 'Twenty-Seven Articles', appearing in FO 882/7, and reproduced *in toto* in Wilson, *Lawrence of Arabia*, pp. 960–5.

52   Clayton Note, 'Appreciation of possible methods of assisting the Sherif's revolt by means of British Military Action', January 1917, CP, SAD 694/5/17.

53   Lynden-Bell to Maurice, 17 January 1917, Lynden-Bell Papers, ALB 1/4, IWM.

54   Clayton to Sykes, 18 January 1917, CP, SAD 693/12/1.

55   Clayton to Wingate, 20 November 1916, CP, SAD 694/4/47; Clayton memorandum, 20 December 1916, CP, SAD 694/4/49 (responding to Wilson's criticisms).

56   *Arab Bulletin* No. 41, 6 February 1917, FO 882/26; *see also*, Wilson, *Lawrence of Arabia*, pp. 346–54; Mohs, *Military Intelligence and the Arab Revolt*, pp. 92–3, 108–114.

57   Lawrence to Clayton, 28 February 1917, FO 882/6.

58   Clayton to Macdonogh, 27 March 1917, FO 882/6.

59   Lawrence to Stirling, 25 September 1917, in Brown, *Letters*, pp. 125–6; Garland, 'Railway Raids' (essay or lecture notes), n.d., but post-war, Herbert Garland Papers, IWM.

60   Wingate to Robertson, 19 March 1917, FO 882/6; Clayton to Macdonogh, 27 March 1917, FO 882/6 ('all information points to a general concentration on Medina . . . with a view to withdrawal of a considerable portion of the Medina garrison, if not of complete evacuation'.)

61   Bruce, *Last Crusade*, p. 92.

62   Murray to Robertson, 11 March 1917, Murray Papers, box 79/48/3, folder 6, IWM; Clayton to Wigram, 8 April 1917, King George V Papers, RA: PS/PSO/GV/C/Q/2521/102, Royal Archives, Windsor.

63   Clayton to Macdonogh, 15 April 1917, FO 882/6.

64   Grainger, *The Battle for Palestine*, pp. 35, 37–9.

65   Bruce, *Last Crusade*, p. 109.

66   Hardinge to Wingate, 1 April 1917, WP, SAD 145/4/1.

67   Wingate to Hardinge: letter, 'rather tired'; telegram, 'very suitable', both, 2 April 1917, WP, SAD 145/4/5 and 10.

68   Storrs diary, entries for 2, 9 and 23 May 1917, Ronald Storrs Papers, box II, file 5, Pembroke College, Cambridge.

69   Clayton to Sykes, 30 July 1917, FO 882/3; Storrs diary, entry for 14 July 1917, Storrs Papers, box II, file 5, Pembroke College, Cambridge.

70   Clayton to Graham, 22 June 1917, CP, SAD 693/12/20.

71   Notes of a Conference held at 10 Downing Street, 3 April 1917 (describin[g] December 1916 Anglo-French conference), Mark Sykes Papers, box 1, file 3, M[

Sykes to Wingate, 22 February 1917, FO 882/16 (describing Sykes' appointment as CPO).

72 Robertson to Murray, 21 February 1917, FO 882/16.

73 *See* 'Proceedings of Conference held on February 6, 1917', FO 141/654/1. Comprised of Macdonogh, Graham and Lt. Col. Bartholomew of the War Office, the Conference drafted the CPO's instructions, a description of his status and functions, and instructions to the EEF commander to whom the CPO would be attached.

74 'Draft Instructions to Chief Political Officer attached to General Officer Commanding, Egypt', n.d., Sykes Papers, box 1, file 3, MECOX; 'Status and Functions of Chief Political Officer and French Commissioner', n.d., FO 882/16.

75 'Notes of a Conference held at 10 Downing Street . . . on April 3, 1917', Sykes Papers, box 1, file 3, MECOX.

76 Clayton Memorandum, 3 April 1917, FO 882/16; Clayton to Wilson (Jeddah), 28 April 1917, FO 882/12.

77 The arguments supporting this conclusion are well developed in Wilson, *Lawrence of Arabia*, pp. 362–3, 1052–4.

78 Clayton to Wingate: 14 April 1916, WP, SAD 136/4/49; 20 November 1916, WP, SAD 143/6/1. Copies of the 'resume' appear in WO 158/624 and FO 882/5.

79 Wilson to Clayton, 21 March 1917, FO 882/12; Clayton memorandum, 3 April 1917, FO 882/16.

80 Clayton to Wilson: 18 April (Syria will not welcome); and 28 April 1917 (cuts no ice in Mesopotamia), both in FO 882/12, fos. 214, 242; Clayton to Ronnie (Graham), 7 May 1917, CP, SAD 693/12/13.

81 Lawrence to Wilson, 30 July 1917, in Brown, *Letters*, p. 112: Hussein 'is extremely pleased to have trapped M. Picot into the admission that France will be satisfied in Syria with the position that Britain desires in Iraq. That he says means a temporary occupation of the country for strategical and political reasons (with probably an annual grant to the Sherif in compensation and recognition)'.

82 Lloyd Note, n.d., *c.* May/June 1917; Newcombe Note, 20 May 1917; Clayton to Symes (Residency), 27 May 1917 ('same footing'); Clayton to Sykes, 22 July 1917, all in FO 882/16.

83 Sykes, 'Recommendations', 17 May 1917; Sykes 'Observations on Arabian Policy as result of visit to Red Sea ports, Jeddah, Yembo, Wejh, Kamaran and Aden', 5 June 1917, both in FO 141/734/1.

84 Clayton, 'Notes on Draft Report of Mission . . .', 8 June 1917, FO 141/734/1 (original emphasis); Clayton memorandum, 1 July 1917, FO 882/3, fo. 58 (essential); Clayton to Sykes, 22 July 1917, FO 882/16, fo. 143 (vital); Clayton to Sykes, 30 July 1917, CP, SAD 693/12/28, making the same point; Clayton to Wigram, 31 July 1917, King George V Papers, RA: PS/PSO/GV/C/Q/2521/103, Royal Archives, Windsor.

85 Wingate: 'Note of a Meeting at the Residency, Cairo May 12th 1917', FO 141/734/1; Lloyd: 'Note on Draft Report of Sykes–Picot Mission', n.d., *c.* June 1917, Lloyd Papers, GLLD 9/9, Churchill College, Cambridge; Hogarth: Note to Clayton, 7 June 1917, FO 141/734/1.

86 Clayton to Lawrence, 20 September 1917, CP, SAD 693/12/36.

87 Wingate to Murray, 4 June 1917, WP, SAD 145/8/14 (Clayton to replace Sykes); Wingate to Graham, 11 June 1917, WP, SAD 145/8/50 (cannot spare Clayton for

Mesopotamia); Wingate to FO, 11 June 1917, FO 371/3051; Wingate to FO, 18 June 1917, FO 371/3051 (Clayton disposed to refuse appointment).

88 Sykes to Clayton, 22 July 1917, Sykes Papers, box 2, file 6, MECOX; FO minutes of Graham and Hardinge, 13 June 1917, FO 371/3051 (resist appointment); Sykes to Wingate, 18 June 1917 (will explain 'Clayton's importance in Egypt to the high authorities'); Balfour to Wingate, 26 July 1917, WO 158/633; Clayton to Sykes, 30 July 1917, CP, SAD 693/12/28; FO to Wingate, 3 August 1917, FO 371/3043 (confirms appointment).

89 Clayton to Macdonogh, 23 April 1917, FO 882/6.

90 Clayton to Macdonogh, 15 April 1917, FO 882/6; Clayton Memoranda, 14 May, FO 882/6, and 29 May 1917, Sykes Papers, box 2, file 5, MECOX.

91 Lloyd to Clayton, 20 May 1917, Lloyd Papers, GLLD 9/9, Churchill College, Cambridge.

92 The taking of Akaba has rightly been regarded as an important event in modern Arab history and Arab writers have generally denigrated or ignored the participation of Lawrence in the expedition. Some, like Suleiman Musa, have even denied that Lawrence made the northern journey. *Lawrence: An Arab View*, pp. 70–9. In a recent biography, Ali A. Allawi, *Faisal I*, p. 95, fails to even mention the northern reconnaissance and omits any treatment of the period 9 May – 2 July 1917, when it took place, thus leaving a significant gap in his chronology. Wilson, *Lawrence of Arabia*, pp. 395–417, 1069–72, reviews the evidence, including Lawrence's contemporary notebooks and pocket diaries, and has no doubt that Lawrence devised the land-based assault on Akaba and that the northern journey took place. *See also*, Lawrence to Clayton, 10 July 1917, in Garnett, ed., *Letters*, pp. 225–30, in which Lawrence described the northern trip in some detail.

93 Wingate to Sykes, 16 July 1917, WP, SAD 146/1/17; Sykes to Clayton, 22 July 1917, Sykes Papers, box 2, file 6, MECOX; Clayton to Wigram, 31 July 1917, King George V Papers, RA: PS/PSO/GV/C/Q/2521/103, Royal Archives, London.

94 *London Gazette*, 7 August 1917, Third Supp., p. 8103; WO to Wingate, 11 August 1917, WP, SAD 165/2/59.

95 Clayton memoranda: 10 July 1917, Sykes Papers, box 2, file 6, MECOX, and 15 July 1917, FO 882/16, fo. 253. *See also* Clayton to Sykes, 22 July 1917, FO 882/16, fo. 143: '[N]othing definite can be laid down while the Turks actually occupy the soil of Palestine and Syria'.

18 A Very Deep Game: Anglo-French Rivalry in the Middle East

1 Lawrence to Hogarth, 22 March 1915, in Garnett, ed., *Letters of Lawrence*, pp. 195–6.

2 Hogarth to Clayton, 20 July 1917, David G. Hogarth Papers, file 2, MECOX.

3 Clayton to Sykes, 20 August 1917, Mark Sykes Papers, box 2, file 7, MECOX.

4 Clayton, 'Note on the Arab Question', 5 July 1916, CP, SAD 694/4/4.

5 McMahon to FO, 14 August 1916, WP, SAD 139/3/79.

6 Clayton to Wingate, 4 September 1916, WP, SAD 140/1/110.

7 'Notes of a Conference held at the Commander-in-Chief's House on September 5 [1916] . . .' CP, SAD 694/4/8; Clayton to Wingate: 7 September 1916, WP, SAD 140/2/72; 20 September 1916 (tgm), WP, SAD 140/5/5.

8 Grey to McMahon, 14 September 1916, WP, SAD 140/3/28.

9   Wingate to Murray, 12 October 1916, WP, SAD 141/3/40; *and see* Wingate to Clayton: 17 September 1916, CP, SAD 470/3/74; 16 October 1916, CP, SAD 470/4/7.

10   Lawrence, Note, 18 [or 17] November 1916, CP, SAD 694/4/42; Brémond to Defrance (repeated to Paris), 16 October 1916, quoted in Wilson, *Lawrence of Arabia*, p. 309.

11   Brémond to Quai d'Orsay [French Foreign Office], 28 October 1916, quoted in Barr, *A Line in Sand*, p. 35 (partisans of Arab kingdom); *see also* Anderson, *Lawrence in Arabia*, p. 198.

12   Murray to Robertson, 28 November 1916, Archibald Murray Papers, box 79/48/3, folder 6, IWM.

13   Murray to Robertson, 11 February 1917, *ibid.*

14   Wilson to Clayton, 5 March 1917, CP, SAD 470/6/18.

15   Anderson, *Lawrence in Arabia*, pp. 260–5, 268–72; Wilson, *Lawrence of Arabia*, pp. 360–1.

16   Three Notes on the formation of the Arab Legion, n.a., n.d., WO 158/633; 'Notes of a Meeting at the Residency, Cairo, on 12th May 1917, FO 141/734/1; *Arab Bulletin* No. 53, 14 June 1917.

17   Sykes, 'The Arab Legion', 1 June 1917, G.T. 1229, CAB 24/18; Lynden-Bell to Maurice, 20 May 1917, Arthur Lynden-Bell Papers, ALB 1/4, IWM.

18   Hogarth to Clayton, 7 June 1917, FO 141/734/1; Lloyd, 'Notes on Draft Report of Sykes–Picot Mission', n.d., *c.* June 1917, George Lloyd Papers, GLLD 9/9, Churchill College, Cambridge; Clayton, 'Notes of Draft Report of Mission', 8 June 1917, FO 141/734/1; FO Minutes of Balfour, Hardinge and Robert Cecil, n.d., attached to Sykes, 'The Arab Legion', 1 June 1917, G.T. 1229, CAB 24/18.

19   Sykes to Clayton, 22 July 1917, Sykes Papers, box 2, file 6, MECOX; Hogarth to Clayton, 11 July 1917, David G. Hogarth Papers, file 2, MECOX (Curzon rejects 'co-operation in the Arab Legion'); Balfour to Wingate, 26 July 1917, WO 158/633.

20   Clayton to Sykes, 30 July 1917, FO 882/3; *see also* Clayton to Wigram, 31 July 1917, King George V Papers, RA: PS/PSO/GV/C/Q/2521/103, Royal Archives, Windsor (noting the difficulty of dual Anglo-French control of the Legion).

21   Clayton to Sykes, 20 August 1917, Sykes Papers, box 2, file 7, MECOX.

22   Capt. A. W. Lake, 'A brief history of the raising of the Aden detachment of the Arab Legion', 10 September 1917, WO 158/633.

23   Pearson to Clayton, 17 September 1917, WO 158/633 (quoted); Clayton to Sykes, 20 September 1917, Sykes Papers, box 2, file 7, MECOX.

24   Wingate (for Clayton) to FO (for Sykes), 30 September 1917, FO 371/3043.

25   Clayton to Wigram, 10 October 1917, King George V Papers, RA: PS/PSO/GV/C/Q/2521/106, Royal Archives, Windsor (original emphasis).

26   Wingate (for Clayton) to FO (for Sykes), 16 October 1917, FO 371/3043; Sykes' message, 9 October 1917, *ibid.*

27   Lawrence to Clayton, 24 October 1917, CP, SAD 693/11/13 (Faisal anxious to have Legion at Akaba); Clayton to Joyce, 30 October 1917, FO 882/7, fo. 187 (French may want to use Legion); Clayton to Sykes, 18 October 1917, FO 882/16, fo. 151.

28   Clayton to Joyce, 24 October 1917, FO 882/7, fo. 174.

29   Wingate (for Clayton) to FO (for Sykes), 2 November 1917, FO 371/3043; Tauber, *Arab Movements*, pp. 117–21.

30   'Report on the Arab Legion at Ismailia', 19 November 1917, WO 158/633. The report is signed only 'Lt. Col', but was almost certainly written by Lt. Col. Pearson. *Arab*

Bulletin No. 71, 27 November 1917, FO 882/26, also contains the substance of Pearson's report.

31 Joyce to Clayton, 23 November 1917, FO 882/7, fo. 215.

32 Clayton to Sykes, 15 December 1917, Sykes Papers, box 2, file 8, MECOX.

33 Joyce to Clayton: 13 September 1917, FO 882/7, fo. 113 (absolutely essential); 17 September 1917, Pierce Joyce Papers, H/72/73, LHCMA; 27 September 1917, Joyce Papers, I/H 77–78, LHCMA (Faisal not a very strong character).

34 Joyce to Rees-Mogg, 21 December 1916 (rottenest fight); Joyce to Clayton, 14 September 1917 (not sent), both in Joyce Papers, I/H, LHCMA.

35 Clayton to Lloyd, 5 November 1917, Lloyd Papers, GLLD 9/10, Churchill College, Cambridge.

36 Lloyd to Clayton, 5 November 1917, *ibid.*

37 Clayton to DMI, 2 November 1917, FO 141/456/3.

38 Clayton to Wigram, 10 October 1917, King George V Papers, RA: PS/PSO/GV/C/Q/2521/106, Royal Archives, Windsor.

39 Joyce to Clayton, 27 September 1917, Joyce Papers, I/H 77–78, LHCMA.

40 Wilson, *Lawrence of Arabia*, pp. 397–8.

41 Clayton to Lawrence, 20 September 1917, CP, SAD 693/12/36 (original emphasis).

42 Clayton to General Staff Operations, 1st Echelon, 7 September 1917, FO 882/7, fo. 98.

43 Clayton, handwritten Note on a telegram from Mecca to Sheikh Fuad al-Khatib, 3 November 1917, FO 141/456/3; Clayton to Sykes, 20 September 1917, Sykes Papers, box 2, file 7, MECOX.

44 Clayton to Joyce: 18 September, 24 October (quoted), 30 October, and 12 November 1917, FO 882/7, fos. 123, 174, 187 and 200.

45 Clayton to Joyce, 12 November 1917, FO 882/7, fo. 200 (Faisal overrates Arab irregulars); Clayton to Lloyd, 12 November 1917, Lloyd Papers, GLLD 9/10, Churchill College, Cambridge (Faisal and Lawrence underrate Turks in Syria).

46 Wavell, *Allenby*, p. 47.

47 *Ibid.*, pp. 252, 254.

48 *Ibid.*, p. 198, note (fine character); Wavell to B.H. Liddell Hart, 15 March 1934, Basil Liddell Hart Papers, LH1/733/49, LHCMA (shrewdest head).

49 Wavell, *Allenby*, p. 249 (mental superiority). One day in the summer of 1917, Lynden-Bell accompanied Allenby on an inspection when they saw a fire lit in the middle of an ammunition depot. Allenby told Lynden-Bell to issue an order that any similar offense would be punished by court-martial. Lynden-Bell forgot, or failed, to issue the order and 'it was after an interview with Allenby following the incident . . . that he decided his eyesight was beginning to suffer' and was soon on his way home. Wavell to Chetwode, 27 February 1939, Edmund Allenby Papers, 6/8, LHCMA.

50 Wavell, *Allenby*, p. 164.

51 Money, Notes, 27 December 1936, Allenby Papers, 6/9, 10, LHCMA.

52 Wavell, *Allenby*, p. 198.

53 From Lloyd George's *War Memoirs*, quoted in Hughes, *Allenby and British Strategy*, p. 23.

54 Hughes, *Allenby and British Strategy*, pp. 46–7 (*Official History* estimate; actual number 20,000); Bullock, *Allenby's War*, p. 73 (overall strengths); Grainger, *Battle for Palestine*, p. 113 (8 to 1 superiority at Beersheba).

55 Clayton to Bell, 8 December 1917, CP, SAD 693/13/10.

56 Wingate to Balfour, 24 and 25 November 1917; Balfour to Wingate, 26 November 1917, all in FO 141/654/1. The order of entry into Jerusalem appears in Philip Chetwode Papers, PWC 1, folder 6, IWM.

57 Lawrence, *Seven Pillars* (1935 text), ch. 82.

58 Clayton to Bell, 8 December 1917, CP, SAD 693/13/10 (Laws and Usages of War); Clayton to Sykes, 15 December 1917, CP, SAD 693/13/13 (commitments).

59 Wingate (for Clayton) to FO (for Sykes), 28 November 1917; FO (for Sykes) to Wingate (for Clayton), 26 November 1917, both in FO 141/734/1.

19 Jacob and Esau: Arabs and Jews in Palestine, 1918–1919

1 Huretwitz, *A Documentary Record* , vol. II, p. 106.

2 Among the many studies of the antecedents of the Balfour Declaration are, Stein, *The Balfour Declaration*; Sanders, *High Walls of Jerusalem*; and Schneer, *The Balfour Declaration*.

3 Fraser, *Chaim Weizmann*, p. 19.

4 Macmillan, *Paris 1919* ('what is to become'); Dockrill and Goold, *Peace without Promise* (hewers and drawers). No official census was conducted in Palestine until 1922. However, an informal count in late 1918 disclosed that there were 612,000 Muslims, 61,000 Christians and 66,000 Jews in the country, for a total of 739,000. So, the Jews formed 8.9% of the population at that time, according to this count. Clayton to Balfour, 6 December 1918, FO 371/3386, fos. 255–6.

5 Sanders, *High Walls of Jerusalem*, p. 120.

6 Macmillan, *Paris 1919*, p. 413.

7 Schneer, *The Balfour Declaration*, pp. 343–5; Segev, *One Palestine, Complete*, p. 48.

8 Reinharz, *Chaim Weizmann*, pp. 40–72; Chaim Weizmann, *Trial and Error*, pp. 171–5.

9 Schneer, *The Balfour Declaration*, p. 12; Segev, *One Palestine, Complete*, p. 22.

10 Clayton to Wingate, 3 August 1916, WP, SAD 139/1/58; original emphasis. Clayton's underscoring of 'Salonica' was probably meant to suggest that the Committee of Union and Progress, which had its Near Eastern origins in that city, had been influenced by the large Jewish population there. Indeed, many people in the first decades of the twentieth century believed, as Clayton expressed in this letter, that Jews formed the 'mainspring' of the CUP.

11 Schneer, *Balfour Declaration*, pp. 271–4.

12 Clayton memorandum, 29 June 1917, WP, SAD 145/8/12. Clayton's memorandum appears to have been prompted by a Foreign Office telegram to Wingate (23 June 1917, WP, SAD 145/8/108), in which it was reported that Morgenthau planned to secretly get in touch with the CUP 'for the purpose of detaching Turkey from [the] Central Powers'.

13 Sheffy, *Palestine Intelligence*, p. 77.

14 *Ibid.*, pp. 82–3, 145–7, and 159–66.

15 Clayton to Symes, 20 June 1917; Clayton to Sykes, 22 June 1917, both in FO 141/805/1.

16 Clayton to Mervyn Herbert, 10 July 1917, *ibid.*; Florence, *Lawrence and Aaronsohn*, pp. 268–9.

17 Clayton to Symes, 16 August 1917, and Wingate (for Clayton) to FO (for Graham), 18 August 1917 (quoted), FO 141/805/1.

18 Clayton to Sykes, 20 August 1917, Mark Sykes Papers, box 2, file 7, MECOX.

19 Lawrence to Clayton, 7 September 1917, enclosing Lawrence to Sykes, 9 September 1917, CP, SAD 693/11/3, 4–8.

20 Clayton to Lawrence, 20 September 1917, CP, SAD 693/12/36.

21 Sykes to Clayton, 16 November 1917, Sykes Papers, box 2, file 7, MECOX.

22 Clayton to Wilson (Jeddah), 17 December 1917, CP, SAD 693/13/18 (Sykes 'right in principle'); Wingate (for Clayton) to FO, 12 December 1917, Sykes Papers, box 2, file 8, MECOX.

23 Clayton to Bell, 8 December 1917, CP, SAD 693/13/10.

24 Wingate to Allenby, 16 December 1917, WP, SAD 166/3/108.

25 Clayton to Sykes, 15 December 1917, CP, SAD 693/13/13.

26 Wingate (for Clayton) to FO (for Sykes), 28 November 1917, FO 141/734/1.

27 *Ibid.*; original emphasis.

28 Wingate (for Clayton) to FO, 19 December 1917, Sykes Papers, box 2, file 8, MECOX.

29 FO to Wingate (for Clayton), 11 December 1917, *ibid*. In his book *Orientations*, p. 340, Storrs claims that he and Clayton 'could hardly believe our eyes' when Clayton showed him a telegram in early March 1918, informing him of the impending arrival of the Zionist Commission. But, if Storrs is correct on the date, Clayton could hardly have been surprised; he had been informed three months earlier that such a Commission would be sent.

30 Clayton to Sykes, 15 December 1917, CP, SAD 693/13/13.

31 Wingate (for Clayton) to FO, 14 December 1917, file 379, WA (quoted); Wingate (for Clayton) to FO, 7 January 1918, FO 371/3391 (Arab proposal rejected).

32 Clayton to Wingate, 12 October 1917, file 368, WA.

33 Yale to Harrison (U.S. State Department), 24 December 1917, enclosing Report No. 9 of same date, William Yale Papers, box 1, file 2, MECOX.

34 Yale to Harrison, 17 December 1917, enclosing Report No. 6, *ibid*.

35 Wingate (for Clayton) to FO, 30 December 1917, Sykes Papers, box 2, file 8, MECOX; Syria Welfare Committee to Sykes, 17 January 1918, FO 371/3398 (deduce); Wingate (for Clayton) to FO, 5 January 1918, FO 141/654/1.

36 FO to Wingate (for Clayton), 24 January 1918, FO 141/654/1; Wingate (for Clayton) to FO, 27 January 1918, FO 371/3388.

37 Clayton to Sykes, 4 February 1918, CP, SAD 693/13/39.

38 Hogarth Message, January 1918, in Hurewitz, *Documentary Record*, vol. II, p. 111; *and see* Kedourie, *Labyrinth*, pp. 187–93.

39 Antonius, *Arab Awakening*, pp. 267–9.

40 See Clayton to FO: 14 January (WP, SAD 167/1/173; Arabs 'uneasy' and 'fear a Jewish Government of Palestine'); 29 January (FO 371/3393; 'uneasiness' and 'distrust'); 25 February (FO 371/3391; Muslims 'much disturbed' at 'preferential treatment of Jews'); 10 March (FO 371/3391; Muslims 'nervous' and think British 'intend to set up a Jewish Government'); 14 March (FO 371/3391; 'fear and dislike' by Arabs); Clayton to Balfour, 16 March 1918, FO 371/3405 (quoted in text).

41 War Cabinet, 'Report by General Smuts on his Mission to Egypt', 1 March 1918, G-199, WO 106/1545; Leo Amery Diary, entry for 21 February 1918, Leo Amery Papers, AMEL 7/14, Churchill College, Cambridge.

42 Weizmann to Brandeis, 25 April 1918, FO 371/3395.

43 Weizmann, *Trial and Error*, p. 228, and generally, pp. 220–8; Segev, *One Palestine Complete*, p. 90 (Jabotinsky).

44 Clayton to Sykes, 18 April 1918, Sykes Papers, box 2, file 8, MECOX.

45 Clayton to Wigram, 18 June 1918, King George V Papers, RA: PS/PSO/GV/C/Q/2521/108, Royal Archives, Windsor. An undated copy also appears in CP, SAD 693/13/53.

46 Clayton to Wingate, 29 January 1918, WP, SAD 167/1/422.

47 Bell to Clayton, 22 January [1918], CP, SAD 470/14/21; Clayton to Bell, 17 June 1918, CP, SAD 693/13/55.

48 Clayton to Wilson, 17 December 1917, CP, SAD 693/13/18.

49 Clayton to Lord Edward Cecil, 31 December 1917, CP, SAD 693/13/25; Clayton to Wingate, 5 January 1918, CP, SAD 693/13/27.

50 Hogarth to Wingate, 3 February 1918, WP, SAD 167/2/59.

51 Middle East Committee, Minutes, 12 January 1918, FO 371/3394.

52 *Ibid.*; and Hardinge, Note to Lord Robert Cecil, 4 January 1918, FO 371/3388; FO to Wingate, 12 January 1918, FO 141/738/1.

53 Middle East Committee, Minutes, 12 January 1918, FO 371/3394.

54 Wingate to FO, 15 January 1918, FO 371/3388. Allenby's concurrence is reflected on a draft of this telegram in WP, SAD 167/1/168.

55 Wingate to Graham, 13 January 1918, WP, SAD 167/1/144.

56 Minutes of Sykes (16 January 1918) and Hardinge (n.d.), filed with Wingate to FO, 15 January 1918, FO 371/3388. Reporting from the Middle East, George Lloyd also proposed that Clayton should give up his OETA work. Lloyd, 'Arab Bureau Reorganisation', 24 January 1918, Lloyd Papers, GLLD 9/10, Churchill College, Cambridge.

57 FO to Wingate, 13 December 1917, FO 141/654/1 (Clayton to report weekly to FO); Middle East Committee, Minutes, 19 January 1918, FO 371/3394; FO to Wingate, 23 January 1918, FO 141/738/1.

58 Clayton to Wingate, 28 February 1918, file 400, WA; Clayton to Lloyd, 2 March 1918, Lloyd Papers, GLLD 9/3, Churchill College, Cambridge (Clayton 'glad' to give up OETA).

59 Clayton to Sykes, 26 January 1918, FO 371/3398 (permanent work in Palestine); Clayton to Lloyd, 2 March 1918, Lloyd Papers, GLLD 9/3, Churchill College, Cambridge.

60 Clayton to Sykes, 4 April 1918, FO 371/3391.

61 Clayton to Ormsby-Gore, 20 April 1918, file 414, WA.

62 Reinharz, *Chaim Weizmann*, p. 234.

63 Clayton to Balfour, 18 April 1918, FO 371/3394.

64 Clayton to Wingate, 21 April 1918, file 414, WA.

65 Clayton to FO: 10 April (FO 371/3397); 14 April (FO 371/3394); and 19 April 1918 (FO 371/3391).

66 Clayton to FO, 1 May 1918, FO 371/3394, repeating Weizmann's speech of 27 April.

67 Knox, *British Palestine Policy*, pp. 64–70.

68 Ormsby-Gore to Sykes, 9 April 1918, Sykes Papers, box 2, file 8, MECOX.

69 Money, diary entry for 5 July 1918, Arthur Money Papers, 9211-19-223, National Army Museum, London.

70 Clayton to Sykes, 18 April 1918, Sykes Papers, box 2, file 8, MECOX ('unjustified';

objects to Sykes–Ormsby-Gore direct communication); Clayton to Balfour, 3 May 1918, FO 371/3395 ('every effort').

71 Ormsby-Gore to Balfour, 19 May 1918 (Report No. 5), CP, SAD 694/6/11, enclosed in Ormsby-Gore to Clayton, 17 May 1918, CP, SAD 694/4/10.

72 Clayton, Notes, including a list of ten points favourable to Zionists, n.d.; Weizmann to Ormsby-Gore, n.d., appended to the latter's letter to Clayton of 17 May 1918; Clayton, Notes, n.d., attached to foregoing, all in CP, SAD 694/4/20, 22.

73 Money, draft autobiography (unpublished), c. 1944, p. 53, Money Papers, 9211-19-224, National Army Museum, London.

74 Richard Allen Bennett, 'the Anglo-Egyptian Sudanese influence' (Ph.D. dissertation), p. 194; see also Clayton to Wingate, 7 March 1918, file 404, WA: 'Men with a knowledge of administration and also of Arabic are almost impossible to lay hands on.'

75 Clayton to Balfour, 18 April 1918, FO 371/3394.

76 Yale to Harrison, 27 May 1918, report no. 29, Yale Papers, box 2, MECOX.

77 Transcript of conversation between Mr. Alsberg of the Israeli State Archives and Major R.F.P. Monckton, September 1968, R.F.P. Monckton Papers, file 1, MECOX.

78 Money diary, entry for 23 April 1918, Money Papers, 9211-19-223, National Army Museum, London.

79 Money to Hills, 29 March 1919, ibid.; original emphasis.

80 Money diary, entries for 23 April (level headed fellow), and 19 May 1918, Money Papers, 9211-19-223, National Army Museum, London.

81 Clayton memorandum, 19 May 1918, CP, SAD 694/6/30. The points made in this memorandum were repeated in Clayton to Balfour, 16 June 1918, FO 371/3395.

82 Clayton to FO, 26 May 1918, FO 371/3398; Clayton to Faisal, 27 May 1918, FO 882/14, fo. 363.

83 Joyce, Notes of 'Interview between Dr. Weizmann and Sherif Faisal on 4th June 1918 at Wahaida', Faisal ibn Hussein Papers, box 1, MECOX; Joyce to Clayton, 5 June 1918, FO 882/14, fo. 366; Clayton to FO, 12 June 1918, FO 371/3398.

84 Weizmann to Balfour, 17 July 1918, FO 371/3398.

85 Clayton to Balfour, 16 June 1918, FO 371/3395.

86 Clayton to Bell, 17 June 1918, CP, SAD 693/13/55.

87 Ormsby-Gore wrote in June 1918: 'Faisal and his regulars are real men and even the Bedawi stand for something real, self-reliant and free. The Arabic-speaking Effendi of the Mediterranean littoral is really a parasite who has subsisted for generations on successive alien civilisations from which there is no vice which he has not learnt.' Clayton to Ormsby-Gore, 29 June 1918, describing Clayton's deletions from the Minutes of the 17th meeting of the Zionist Commission, including Ormsby-Gore's description of the Palestinian Arabs, FO 371/3395, fo. 200. On the same point, see Wasserstein, British in Palestine, pp. 12–13.

88 Clayton to Balfour, 1 July 1918, FO 371/3398.

89 Weizmann to Clayton, 5 November 1918, file 459, WA.

90 Clayton to Balfour, 8 November 1918, FO 371/3385 (tact and discretion); Clayton to FO, 25 November 1918, ibid. (defer further declarations); Clayton to FO, 29 June 1918, FO 371/3388 (gradual development; no striking developments); Clayton to Balfour, 5 December 1918, FO 371/3386; and Clayton to FO, 5 December 1918, FO 371/3385 (submit further statements to him).

91 FO to Clayton, 11 and 30 April 1918, and Clayton to FO, 23 April 1918, FO 371/3406

(enemy Jews in Egypt); Clayton to FO, 6 May 1918, FO 371/3398 (Stein); Clayton to Balfour, 16 June 1918, FO 371/3395 (Hebrew University); Clayton to FO, 25 September 1918, FO 371/3388 (censors anti-Zionist articles); Clayton to FO, 25 May and 7 June 1918, FO 371/3391 (Syrian Delegation); Clayton to FO, 20 November 1918, FO 371/3395 (Hebrew language).

92 Clayton to Balfour, 16 June, 31 August and 1 October 1918, FO 371/3395.

93 Clayton to Balfour, 29 June 1918, FO 371/3380.

94 Clayton to Balfour, 16 June 1918, FO 371/3395.

20 A Nest of Intrigue: Allied Disputes in the Levant

1 Storrs, *Orientations*, pp. 274–5.

2 Wyndham Deedes to his mother, 20 October 1918, Wyndham Deedes Papers, box 1, file 3, MECOX.

3 J. Loder to his father, 18 December 1917, John deVere Loder Papers, box 1, MECOX (bumption); A. Keown-Boyd to his parents, 3 September 1918, Alexander Keown-Boyd Papers, box 1, file 3, MECOX (orientalized).

4 Storrs diary, entry for 19 December 1917, Ronald Storrs Papers, box 2, folder 5, Pembroke College, Cambridge. Storrs' diary entry may be compared with his edited and uncritical description of Clayton appearing in *Orientations*, p. 275.

5 Storrs, *Orientations*, pp. 291–2. Compare this description with Lawrence's in *Seven Pillars of Wisdom*, quoted in Chapter 12 above.

6 *Ibid.*, p. 403.

7 Money to Hills, 29 April 1918, Arthur Money Papers, 9211-19-223, National Army Museum, London.

8 Storrs, *Orientations*, p. 403.

9 Report by Political Intelligence Officer, Jerusalem, 13–19 May 1918, enclosed in Clayton to Balfour, 13 June 1918, FO 371/3400 (Jews buying up Greek debt); Clayton to FO, 13, 24 and 25 August 1918, FO 371/3400 (Greek debt; stop of judgment executions).

10 Storrs, *Orientations*, pp. 408–9.

11 *Ibid.*, p. 409.

12 *Ibid.*, p. 304.

13 *Ibid.*, pp. 304–7; *and see* Clayton to FO, 5 May 1918, FO 371/3400.

14 From a Note by Lady Clayton to Robert O. Collins, n.d., described in Clayton, *Arabian Diary*, ed. by Robert O. Collins, p. 70.

15 FO to Wingate (for Clayton), 24 January 1918; Clayton to FO, 27 January 1918, FO 141/654/1.

16 Clayton to FO, 25 February 1918, FO 371/3400; Clayton to Balfour, 2 March 1918, enclosing Pearson (Jerusalem) to Clayton, 16 February 1918, FO 371/3383 (Picot dispute with Franciscans); Clayton to Mervyn Herbert, 2 March 1918, FO 141/654/1 (Italians); Clayton to Graham (FO), 3 February 1918, FO 371/3389.

17 Graham to Wingate, 14 January 1918, WP, SAD 167/1/237.

18 Clayton to Sykes, 4 February 1918, CP, SAD 693/13/39 (D'Agostino); Sykes (FO) to Clayton, 21 February 1918, FO 371/3389 (Senni); Clayton to Sykes, 25 February 1918, FO 371/3389 (objects to Senni's return); Balfour to Clayton, 10 March 1918, FO 141/665/2 (Rome informed).

19 FO to Clayton, 2 telegrams of 8 February 1918, FO 371/3397, fos. 493, 496.

20 Clayton to Balfour, 21 March 1918, FO 371/3403 (French and Italians petition Vatican); Clayton to FO, 28 March 1918, FO 371/3391, and Clayton to Balfour, 28 March 1918, FO 371/3403 (Vatican decides for France on 22 March).

21 Clayton to FO, 11 February 1918, FO 371/3389; Clayton to Wingate, 28 February 1918, file 400, WA.

22 Clayton to FO, 28 January 1918, and FO to Wingate (for Clayton), 30 January 1918, FO 371/3403; Storrs, *Orientations*, p. 289.

23 Clayton to Wigram, 27 February 1918, King George V Papers, RA: PS/PSO/QV/C/Q/2521/107, Royal Archives, Windsor.

24 Amery diary, entry for 21 February 1918, Leo Amery Papers, AMEL 7/14, Churchill college, Cambridge; Smuts Report, 1 March 1918, G-199, WO 106/1545, p. 10.

25 Sykes, 'Memorandum on the Asia-Minor Agreement', 14 August 1917, Mark Sykes Papers, box 2, file 7, MECOX.

26 Sykes to Clayton, 3 March 1918, Mark Sykes Papers, FO 800/221/106, TNA.

27 Clayton to Sykes, 26 January 1918, FO 371/3398.

28 Clayton to Sykes, 4 April 1918, FO 371/3391.

29 Hurewitz, *Documentary Record*, vol. II, pp. 111–12; FO to Wingate, 11 June 1918, FO 371/3381 (sends Declaration). On the background of the Declaration, *see* Tauber, *Arab Movements*, pp. 180–9.

30 Antonius, *Arab Awakening*, p. 273.

31 To his credit, Sykes tried to draw Picot into agreeing to a joint Anglo-French pronouncement along the lines of the Declaration to the Seven. But Picot would not agree that the Sykes–Picot Agreement could be abolished and, since the Declaration was in obvious conflict with it, the joint statement proposed by Sykes was never adopted. *See* Sykes Memorandum, 3 July 1918, and attachments 'A' and 'B' thereto, FO 371/3381.

32 Wingate to FO, 23 March 1918, FO 371/3403.

33 Sykes Minute, 25 March 1918, FO 371/3403, fo. 355.

34 Sykes Minute on paper no. 38817, n.d., but *c.* 2 March 1918, FO 371/3380, fo. 491.

35 Minutes of Graham (26 March) and Hardinge, n.d., FO 371/3043, fos. 357–8; Minutes of Eastern Committee, 28 March 1918, CAB 27/24; FO to Clayton, 30 March 1918, FO 371/3403.

36 Clayton to FO, 2 April 1918, FO 371/3403. The idea that Faisal's authority should be confirmed in the area east of the Jordan 'then occupied' by the EEF had been suggested by the Foreign Office (FO to Clayton, 30 March 1918, FO 371/3403). But Clayton removed the qualification 'then occupied' by the EEF. He considered Arab sovereignty in Trans-Jordan as consistent with the policy 'we have always laid down in our dealings with him . . . that we regard the country east of the Jordan as his sphere so far as he is able to make good in it'. Clayton to Sykes, 4 April 1918, FO 371/3391.

37 Wingate to FO, 8 April 1918 (telegram at fo. 372) and Wingate to Balfour, same date (letter at fos. 397–402), both in FO 371/3403. Wingate's letter enclosed a letter from Jemal dated 10 February 1918).

38 Allawi, *Faisal I*, p. 112, and generally, pp. 108–13, 131.

39 *Ibid.*, pp. 113, 131; Graves ed., *T.E. Lawrence to his Biographers*, p. 142 (selling us); Wilson, *Lawrence of Arabia*, pp. 511–12.

40 Sykes, 'Memorandum on General Clayton's Telegram', __ April 1918, Sykes Papers, FO 800/221/121, TNA; FO to Clayton, 14 April 1918, FO 371/3403; *see also* Wingate

to Clayton, 26 April 1918, paraphrasing FO to Wingate, n.d., WP, SAD 168/2/134.

41 Clayton to FO, 19 April 1918, FO 371/3403.

42 Clayton to Ormsby-Gore, 29 June 1918, enclosing extracts from Appendix 105 to the Minutes of the 17th Meeting of the Zionist Commission, redacted by Clayton. *See* FO 371/3395, at fo. 204, where Weizmann stated that the eastern boundary of Palestine should be defined by 'a line more than halfway between the Jordan and the Hedjaz Railway'. The railway was, at most points, at least fifty miles east of the Jordan.

43 Zionist proposal, quoted in part in Ingrams, *Palestine Papers*, pp. 52–3.

44 Arnold Toynbee (FO) Memorandum of October 1918, and Minute of 2 December 1918, *Ibid.*, pp. 40–3; *and see* Minutes of Eastern Committee meeting, 5 December 1918, CAB 27/24 (comments of Lord Curzon).

45 Clayton o FO, 18 November 1918, FO 371/3385.

46 Allenby to Wingate, 2 September 1918, FO 141/738/1.

47 Wingate to Allenby, 4 September 1918 and Wingate to FO, 5 September 1918, *ibid*.

48 Clayton, 'Secret Note', 8 September 1918, FO 141/734/1.

49 *Ibid.*, and Clayton to Symes, 13 and 18 September 1918, FO 141/734/1.

50 A detailed treatment of the post-war support of the Hashemites and the eventual deterioration of Britain's 'Hussein policy' appears in Paris, *Sherifian Solution.*

51 Bruce, *Last Crusade*, pp. 171–268.

52 Clayton to FO, 8 October 1918, FO 371/3383; *and see* Kedourie, 'The Capture of Damascus' in Kedourie, *Chatham House Version*, pp. 33–51.

53 Clayton to Wingate, 30 September 1918, WP, SAD 170/1/153.

54 Clayton to FO, 6 October 1918, FO 371/3383. Clayton's instructions were consistent with a draft *modus vivendi* of 30 September 1918, negotiated by Lord Robert Cecil of the Foreign Office. Under that arrangement, ratified by the French and British governments in mid-October, Allenby was to recognize a representative of the French Government as his 'Chief Political Adviser' in Area A, who would be the commander's 'sole intermediary on political and administrative questions involving any Arab Government'. The Adviser would also establish 'provisional civil administration in the towns of the Syrian littoral in the blue area . . . as may be necessary'. British-French Draft Modus Vivendi, 30 September 1918, reproduced in Hurewitz, *Documentary Record*, vol. II, pp. 120–1.

55 Clayton to FO, 8 October 1918 (Faisal afraid); 6 October 1918 (Arabs turn to British), both in FO 371/3383.

56 Clayton to FO, 11 October 1918, FO 371/3384.

57 William Yale, *It Takes So Long*, unpublished book manuscript, 1938, William Yale Papers, box 1, file 7, MECOX.

58 Yale to Elizabeth Monroe, 9 June 1970, *ibid*.

59 Clayton to FO, 12 October 1918, FO 371/3384.

60 Allenby Assurance, 17 October 1918, Hurewitz, *Documentary Record*, vol. II, p. 112.

61 Clayton to FO, 18 October 1918, FO 371/3384.

62 Clayton to FO, 12 October 1918, *ibid*.

63 Clayton to FO, 12, 14, 15, 18 and 19 October 1918, *ibid*.

64 British-French draft modus vivendi, 30 September 1918, in Hurewitz, *Documentary Record*, vol. II, pp. 120–1; Minute of Eyre Crowe (FO), 18 October 1918, FO 371/3384, fo. 186 (Declaration being prepared).

65 Balfour to Clayton, 14 October 1918, FO 371/3384.

66   Descriptions of Clayton's promotions and honours appear in CP, SAD 473/2 and 473/4.

67   Yapp, *Making of the Modern Near East*, p. 293.

68   Hurewitz, *Documentary Record*, vol. II, p. 112.

69   Clayton to FO, 16 November 1918, FO 371/3385.

70   Clayton to FO, 4 December 1918, *ibid.*

71   Eastern Committee Minutes, 5 December 1918, CAB 27/24. Lord Hardinge took a more moderate view, writing that the Declaration would only 'effectively prevent [French] annexation' of Syria, not repudiate Sykes–Picot. Hardinge to Bell, 6 December 1918, Hardinge Papers, vol. 39, Cambridge University Library.

72   Cambon to FO, 22 October and 18 November 1918, in Hurewitz, *Documentary Record*, vol. II, pp. 125–7.

73   Eastern Committee Minutes, 5 December 1918, CAB 27/24.

74   Clayton to Balfour, 21 September 1918, FO 141/654/1.

75   Clayton to Wingate, 29 January 1918, WP, SAD 167/1/422.

21   The Shadow and the Substance: The Egyptian Revolution, 1919

1   Hopwood, *Tales of Empire*, pp. 99–102; Young, *A Little to the East: Experiences of an Anglo-Egyptian Official, 1899–1925*, chapter 13, unpublished book MS, *c.*1945, J. W. A. Young Papers, MECOX.

2   Thomas Russell to his father, *c.*April 1919, Thomas Russell Papers, file 1/13, MECOX.

3   Mansfield, *The British in Egypt*, p. 225; Long, *British Pro-Consuls in Egypt*, p. 87.

4   Long, *British Pro-Consuls in Egypt* , pp. 204–5.

5   Terry, *The Wafd*, p. 103.

6   Marlowe, *History of Modern Egypt*, pp. 216–17; 'Report of the Special Mission to Egypt, 1920', Cmd. 1131 (1921) ('Milner Mission Report'), pp. 7–8.

7   Young, *Egypt*, p. 210; Terry, *The Wafd*, p. 26; Grafftey-Smith, *Bright Levant*, p. 56.

8   Mansfield, *The British in Egypt*, p. 209; Elgood, *Egypt and the Army*, p. 244, claims that over the course of the war 170,000 Egyptians served in the Camel Transport Corps.

9   Young, *Egypt*, p. 223; Marlowe, *History of Modern Egypt*, p. 223.

10   Terry, *The Wafd*, pp. 27–8; Marlowe, *History of Modern Egypt*, p. 224 (rise in cotton prices); Milner Mission Report, p. 12 (quoted).

11   Marlowe, *History of Modern Egypt*, pp. 224–5; Grafftey-Smith, *Bright Levant*, p. 57; Milner Mission Report, pp. 11–12.

12   Terry, *The Wafd*, p. 53; Milner Mission Report, footnote, p. 30.

13   Terry, *The Wafd*, p. 32; Milner Mission Report, Cmd. 1131, p. 10; Gertrude Bell, diary entry for 29 September 1919, describing Clayton as saying that 'the Egyptian government had (without any pressure) spontaneously contributed £E4,000,000 to war expenses', Gertrude Bell Archive, Newcastle University Library at: http://gertrude bell.ncl.ac.uk/diary (hereafter, 'Gertrude Bell Online'). The Wafd put the amount at £E3,500,000. Badrawi, *Isma'il Sidqi*, p. 17.

14   Vatikiotis, *History of Modern Egypt*, pp. 257–60; Long, *British Pro-Consuls in Egypt*, pp. 177–81, 205; Terry, *The Wafd*, pp. 73–4.

15   Wingate to FO, 17 November (supports Egyptian request to come to London); FO to Wingate, 27 November (no useful purpose); FO to Wingate, 14 November (Native aspirations); FO to Wingate, 2 December 1918 (unfortunate), all quoted in part in Daly, *The Sirdar*, pp. 281–3.

16 Kedourie, 'Sa'd Zaghlul and the British', in Kedourie, *Chatham House Version*, pp. 93–6.

17 *Ibid.*, pp. 108–110; Daly, *The Sirdar*, pp. 257–8, 283–4, 287.

18 Kedourie, 'Zaghlul and the British', pp. 109–110; Leo Amery diary, entry for January 1, 1919, Leo Amery Papers, AMEL 7/15, Churchill College, Cambridge.

19 Wingate, 'Main Points which Have Given Rise to the Present Situation', n.d., but likely autumn 1919, WP, SAD 175/1/100. My thanks to Jane Hogan of the Sudan Archive, Durham University, for bringing this document to my attention.

20 Kedourie, 'Zaghlul and the British', p. 101.

21 Enid Clayton, 'A Week in Palestine', March 1919, Clayton Family Papers.

22 'Notes taken at the meeting of the Egyptian Nationalist Delegation and a Subsequent Interview with General Clayton', 16 March 1919, CP, SAD 470/9/2.

23 Clayton, 'Memorandum of Egyptian Situation', dated 18 March 1919, but a concluding note by Clayton states that it was given to Cheetham on 17 March 1919, CP, SAD 470/9.

24 *Ibid.* In an addendum to his 17 March memo Clayton also provided the names of those Egyptians he thought should be approached to form a new Ministry.

25 Clayton to Wavell, 20 March 1919, CP, SAD 473/3/4.

26 Cheetham to FO, 17 March 1919, FO 371/3714.

27 Terry, *The Wafd*, p. 106; Kedourie, 'Zaghlul and the British', p. 100 (Cheetham panics); Clayton to Wavell, 20 March 1919, CP, SAD 473/3/4, and Wavell, *Allenby*, p. 272 (Bulfin agrees with Clayton).

28 Clayton to Wavell, 22–23 March 1919, CP, SAD 473/3/7.

29 Clayton to Wingate, 23 April 1919, WP, SAD 162/2/45.

30 Kedourie, 'Zaghlul and the British', p. 115.

31 Dorothea Russell to her father, n.d., *c.* late March or early April 1919, Russell Papers, file 1/14, MECOX.

32 Kedourie, 'Zaghlul and the British', pp. 114–15; Graham to Cheetham, 16 April 1919, Milne Cheetham Papers, file 5, MECOX.

33 Lady Enid Clayton to General A.P. Wavell, 18 January 1937, CP, SAD 473/3/14. This letter was written in response to a request by Wavell for letters that might be useful in the preparation of his biography of Allenby. In fact, there are three other letters extant between Allenby and Clayton, but they deal only with the issue of Clayton's Egyptian pension. Clayton to Allenby, 22 September 1922, and 6 October 1924, and Allenby to Clayton, 17 November 1924, CP, SAD 472/12/74, 86 and 100.

34 Allenby to Clayton, 27 August 1920, CP, SAD 473/3/13.

35 Wingate to Graham, 13 January 1918, WP, SAD 167/1/144.

36 Long, *British Pro-Consuls in Egypt*, p. 108; Lord (George) Lloyd, *Egypt Since Cromer*, vol. I, pp. 305–7, 351.

37 GHQ to WO, 7 June 1919, WO 106/192 (Clayton's duties as CPO to include Egypt); Allenby to FO, 22 June 1919, FO 371/3727 (offers Clayton job of Adviser to Egyptian Interior Ministry); Wavell to Residency (Cairo), 9 August 1919, and Major General L. Bols, Circular Memorandum, 22 August 1919, both in FO 141/738/1 (Clayton to take control of Political Officers in Egypt); First Secretary (Cairo Residency) to Clayton, 2 May 1919, Clayton to Chancery (Residency), 3 May 1919, and Clayton to Residency, 3 May 1922, all in FO 141/473/3 (Clayton's martial law powers); FO to Allenby, 18

December 1919, and Minute of J. Murray (FO), 18 December 1919, FO 371/3721, fos. 433, 435 (Clayton to deal direct with MI1(c) in Italy).

38 Kedourie, 'Zaghlul and the British', pp. 113 and 146 (quoted).

39 Gertrude Bell diary, entry for 30 September 1919, Gertrude Bell Online.

40 Gertrude Bell diary, entry for 29 September 1919, *ibid*.

41 Terry, *The Wafd*, p. 84.

42 Wavell, *Allenby*, p. 278; Thomas Russell to his father, 20 April 1919, Russell Papers, file 1/13, MECOX; Carman and McPherson, eds., *The Man who Loved Egypt*, pp. 211–17.

43 Ronald Lindsay (FO), Minute of 3 July 1919, FO 371/3727, fo. 208.

44 Clayton to Wingate, 23 April 1919, WP, SAD 162/2/45; Allenby to Maxwell, 4 May 1919, John Maxwell Papers, box 2, folder 4, Princeton University Library.

45 Quoted in Kedourie, 'Zaghlul and the British', p. 115.

46 Churchill to Shuckburgh, 12 November 1921, Winston Churchill Papers, 17/15, Churchill College, Cambridge; Macmillan, *Paris 1919*, pp. 183, 404–5.

47 Gertrude Bell diary, entry for 29 September 1919, Gertrude Bell Online.

48 Clayton to his father, __ September 1919, Robert O. Collins Papers, SAD 930/9.

49 Darwin, *Britain, Egypt and the Middle East*, pp. 62–5.

50 Clayton, 'The Future Political Status of Egypt', 22 July 1917, CP, SAD 470/7/6. A copy also appears in the Foreign Office files at FO 371/3722.

51 See Gertrude Bell diary, entry for 30 September 1919, Gertrude Bell Online, where Bell describes Clayton's earlier preference for annexation.

52 *Ibid.*; Wavell to Dawnay, 23 November 1919, Guy Dawnay Papers, 69/21/5, IWM.

53 Young, *Egypt*, p. 214; Marlowe, *Modern Egypt*, p. 216.

54 Eastern Committee, meeting minutes, 18 December 1918, CAB 27/24.

55 In the separate Treaty of Sèvres (10 August 1920), Turkey renounced 'all rights and title in or over Egypt' and, at the same time, recognized the British protectorate over Egypt (Article 101).

56 'Meeting Note', Allenby, Clayton, Bulfin and Bols with Hussein Rushdi, 14 April 1919, FO 371/3716.

57 Terry, *The Wafd*, p. 54.

58 Allenby to FO, 22 June 1919, FO 371/3727 (Clayton offered Interior and accepts); FO, Minutes of Graham and Curzon, July 1919, *ibid.*, fos. 208–210 (Allenby anticipates Curzon); FO to Allenby, 7 July 1919, *ibid.*, fo. 213 (appointment approved); Allenby to Curzon, 10 July 1919, FO 371/3718 (Haines shows lack of judgment).

59 Clayton to Wingate, 23 April 1919, WP, SAD 162/2/45.

22   Peace and Empire: The Middle Eastern Settlement

1 Weizmann, *Trial and Error*, p. 244. There are different versions of Weizmann's response. One describes him as saying he hoped that Palestine would become 'as Jewish as America was American or England was English (Fraser, *Chaim Weizmann*, p. 82). In another, he says that Palestine would be 'as Jewish as the French Nation was French and the British Nation British' (Reinharz, *Chaim Weizmann*, p. 229.

2 Clayton to Balfour, 8 November 1918 (FO 371/3385), and 6 December 1918 (FO 371/3386); Clayton to FO, 25 November 1918 and 5 December 1918, FO 371/3385.

3 Young, *A Little to the East: Experiences of an Anglo-Egyptian Official, 1899–1925,* ch. 12, unpublished book MS, *c*.1945, J. W. A. Young Papers, MECOX.

4   Money to Hills, 29 March 1919, Arthur Money Papers, 9211-19-223, National Army Museum, London.

5   Clayton to FO, 26 March 1919, WO 106/190.

6   Clayton to FO, 28 March 1919, sending telegram of Christian Moslem Society of Jerusalem, *ibid.*; *and see* Clayton to FO, 2 June 1919, FO 371/4181, repeating a circular issued by the 'Moslem-Christian Society of Jerusalem'.

7   Clayton to FO, 5 December 1918, repeating Weizmann to Eder, 28 November 1918, FO 371/3385.

8   Curzon Minute, 26 January 1919, quoted in Ingrams, *Palestine Papers*, pp. 56–7.

9   Curzon to Balfour, 26 January 1919, *ibid.*, pp. 57–8.

10   Balfour memorandum, 11 August 1919, in Hurewitz, *Documentary record*, vol. II, pp. 185–91.

11   Letters of 3 and 9 April 1919, quoted in Dockrill and Goold, *Peace Without Promise*, p. 161.

12   Lloyd George, *The Truth about the Peace Treaties*, vol. II, p. 1038.

13   Dockrill and Goold, *Peace Without Promise*, p. 145.

14   Article 22 of the Covenant of the League of Nations, approved 28 April 1919, in Hurewitz, *Documentary Record*, vol. II, pp. 179–80. *And see* Northedge, *The League of Nations*, pp. 34–8, 64–5.

15   Paris, *Sherifian Solution*, pp. 52–4.

16   *Ibid.*, pp. 53–4, 61.

17   *Ibid.*, pp. 55–6.

18   Clayton Memorandum, 11 March 1919, David Lloyd George Papers, F/205/3/9, Parliamentary Archives, London.

19   Paris, *Sherifian Solution*, pp. 60–1.

20   Kerr, Note to Lloyd George, 16 July 1919, Lloyd George Papers, F/89/3/4, Parliamentary Archives, London.

21   McNamara, *The Hashemites*, p. 95.

22   Faisal, Memorandum to the Supreme Council, 1 January 1919, in Hurewitz, *Documentary Record*, vol. II, pp. 130–2.

23   Allawi, *Faisal I*, p. 201. Support for the notion that Faisal was the first to suggest an international commission to the Middle East also appears in Meinertzhagen to CIGS, 23 May 1919, WO 106/192, where it was reported that President Wilson stated that the commission was being sent 'to fulfil a pledge made to Feisal'. McNamara, in *The Hashemites*, pp. 96–7, suggests that the commission was proposed by Howard Bliss, President of the Syrian Protestant College in Beirut.

24   Record of Meeting of the Supreme Council at Paris, 20 March 1919, in Hurewitz, *Documentary Record*, vol. II, pp. 158–66.

25   Clayton to Curzon, 1 June 1919, DBFP, 1st ser., vol. IV, no. 181, p. 263.

26   George Kidston, minute, 3 June 1919, FO 371/4180, fo. 412.

27   Clayton to Curzon, 8 June 1919, FO 371/4181.

28   Clayton to Curzon, 20 June 1919, DBFP, 1st ser., vol. IV, no. 198, pp. 285–6 (meets Commission); Yale, *It Takes So Long*, unpublished draft book MS, *c*.1938, and Yale to Elizabeth Monroe, 9 June 1970, William Yale Papers, box 1, file 7, MECOX.

29   Clayton to FO, 24 June 1919, FO 371/4181.

30   Clayton to FO, 2 May 1919, enclosing Money Report (quoted), FO 371/4180.

31   *Ibid.*

32 Minutes of Kidston, Graham and Curzon, June 1919, FO 371/4180, fo. 176.

33 MI2 to DDMI, 5 May 1919, WO 106/190. On Meinertzhagen's Zionism *see* Meinertzhagen to Curzon, 26 September 1919, FO 371/4184.

34 Mallett (for Balfour) to Curzon, 18 May 1919, FO 371/4180; FO to Clayton, 27 May 1919, repeating same, *ibid.*

35 Clayton to Curzon, 19 June 1919, DBFP, 1st ser., vol. IV, no. 196, pp. 281–2.

36 Knox, *British Palestine Policy*, p. 132.

37 Clayton to FO, 9 June 1919, FO 371/4181.

38 Balfour to Curzon, 24 June 1919; FO to Balfour, 10 July 1919; and Clayton Minute, 8 July 1919 (at fo. 230), all in FO 371/4181.

39 Balfour to Clayton, 19 June 1919, DBFP, 1st ser., vol. IV, no. 200 (enclosure), p. 295. Brandeis had offered to go to Palestine to influence Zionist opinion 'in [the] direction of moderation'. British Delegation (Paris) to FO, 26 May 1919, WO 106/192.

40 Tyrrell (FO) to Samuel, 31 May 1919, WO 106/192.

41 Samuel to Tyrrell, 5 June 1919, FO 371/4181.

42 Curzon minute, 27 July 1919, FO 371/4181, fo. 292.

43 Kidston (FO) minute, 12 June 1919, FO 371/4181, fos. 33–4.

44 Graham minute, 2 July 1919, FO 371/4181, fos. 344–7.

45 Storrs to Money, n.d., but likely July 1919, Ronald Storrs Papers, box III, file 4, Pembroke College, Cambridge.

46 Weizmann to Clayton, 8 September 1918, CP, SAD 693/14/8.

47 Minutes of a meeting, 8 July 1919, in DBFP, 1st ser., vol. 4, pp. 330–35; Clayton minute, 8 July 1919, FO 371/4181, fo. 343.

48 O.A. Scott minute, 6 August 1919, FO 371/4223, fo. 319; *and see* Knox, *British Palestine Policy*, p. 141.

49 Money to his wife, 1 November 1918, Arthur Money Papers, 9211-19-212, National Army Museum, London.

50 Weizmann to Balfour, 23 July 1919, FO 371/4233; Crowe (for Balfour) to Curzon, 1 August 1919, *ibid.*

23   A Witch's Cauldron: Egypt, 1920–1922

1 Biographical Notes on Gilbert Falkingham Clayton, Clayton Family Papers; Cromer (Buckingham Palace) to Clayton, 7 and 9 August 1919, *ibid.*; diary of King George V, entry for 15 August 1919, RA: GV/PRIV/GVD/1919: 15 Aug., Royal Archives, Windsor.

2 Allenby to FO, 4 August 1919, FO 371/3727; Allenby to his wife, 14 August 1919, Edmund Allenby Papers, 1/10, LHCMA.

3 Clayton to the Residency (Cairo), 5 April 1922, enclosing Report of the Ministry of the Interior for 1921, FO 141/586/4.

4 Hogarth to Clayton, 19 May 1919, David G. Hogarth Papers, file 4, MECOX. Hogarth was responding to a letter from Clayton, not preserved, in which Clayton must have described his devolution policy to Hogarth. This suggests that Clayton may have had in mind his move to the Ministry of the Interior as early as May 1919.

5 Ronald Lindsay minute, 15 October 1921, FO 371/6305, fo. 178.

6 Clayton to Bell, 31 July 1919, Percy Cox Papers, box 2, file 5, MECOX.

7 Clayton to the Residency, 29 May 1920, CP, SAD 470/10/9.

8 *Ibid.*

9   Young, *A Little to the East: Experiences of an Anglo-Egyptian Official, 1899–1925*, unpublished draft memoir, *c.*1945, J.W.A. Young Papers, MECOX; Clayton desk diary, entries for 7–25 March 1920, private collection.

10   Gertrude Bell diary, entry for 29 September 1919, Gertrude Bell Diaries, Newcastle University, online at http://gertrudebell.ncl.ac.uk/diary (hereafter 'Bell Online').

11   From an undated Note by Miss E. M. Clayton, in the author's possession [original emphasis]. The story is also recounted by Collins in his Introduction to Clayton, *Arabian Diary*, pp. 72–3.

12   Extract of a letter from Waley to Murray (FO), 27 November 1919, FO 371/3721.

13   Clayton desk diary, entries for January – June 1920, private collection. Clayton's diary for 1919, if he kept one, has not been preserved; so it is uncertain whether Lady Clayton was in contact with Egyptian ladies in 1919 as well.

14   Clayton to FO (for Deedes), 22 September 1919, Wyndham Deedes Papers, box 2, file 10, MECOX; FO (for Deedes) to Cheetham (for Clayton), 24 September 1919, FO 371/3727; FO to Cheetham, 29 September 1919 (MacMichael), *ibid.*; FO minute, 3 October 1919 (MacMichael sails for Port Said on 4 October), *ibid.*, at fo. 230.

15   Gertrude Bell diary, entry for 29 September 1919, Bell Online.

16   Darwin, *Britain, Egypt and the Middle East*, p. 84.

17   McIntyre, *Boycott of the Milner Mission*, pp. 48–53.

18   Gertrude Bell diary, entry for 29 September 1919, Bell Online; Cheetham to FO, 25 September 1919, FO 141/522/6.

19   Darwin, *Britain, Egypt and the Middle East*, p. 89.

20   Kedourie, 'Sa'd Zaghlul and the British', in Kedourie, *Chatham House Version*, p. 123.

21   Clayton to the Residency, 13 October 1919, FO 371/3720.

22   Darwin, *Britain, Egypt and the Middle East*, p. 87.

23   Testimony of Brigadier General Sir Gilbert Clayton, 18–19, 23 December 1919, FO 848/6; *and see* Clayton Note, 21 December 1919, *ibid.*

24   Extract from a letter from an anonymous inspector in the Egyptian Interior Ministry to Murray (FO), 11 November 1919, FO 371/3721.

25   Extract from a letter from an anonymous inspector to FO, 28–29 November 1919, *ibid.*

26   Gertrude Bell diary, entry for 30 September 1919, Bell Online.

27   Clayton testimony before Milner Mission, 23 December 1919, FO 848/6.

28   Milner Mission report, 9 December 1920, p. 20, Cmd. 1131.

29   *See* footnote 10 of Milner report, *ibid.* Before the war, fifteen countries held Capitulatory rights in Egypt. But Germany and Austria-Hungary were compelled to relinquish their rights by the treaties of Versailles and St. Germain, respectively.

30   Annual report of the Egyptian Ministry of the Interior for 1926, FO 141/586/4.

31   Milner's private diary, entries for 16, 18, 19, 23 and 28 December 1919, FO 848/5, Part A.

32   Maxwell diary, entries for 13 and 19 December 1919, John Maxwell Papers, box 1, folder 3, Princeton University Library.

33   Clayton to his father, 17 January 1920, Robert O. Collins Papers, SAD 930/9.

34   Milner to Lloyd George, 28 December 1919, quoted in part in Darwin, *Britain, Egypt and the Middle East*, p. 97, and in Bishku, 'British Empire and Egypt's Future' (Ph.D. dissertation), p. 59.

35   Clayton desk diary, entry for 27 February 1920, private collection. The Missions' General Conclusions are dated 3 March 1920.

36 *Report of the Special Mission to Egypt: General Conclusions*, 3 March 1920, C.P. 1960, CAB 24/112.

37 Hurst's memo of 24 February 1920 appears in FO 848/8 and is described in Kedourie, 'Zaghlul and the British', pp. 122–3, and Bishku, 'British Empire and Egypt's Future', pp. 59–60.

38 Spender's undated memo is in FO 848/8.

39 Clayton's desk diary, entries for 28 July (Spender) and 31 July1920 (Milner), private collection. His diary entry for 24 August 1920 describes Clayton's commencement of work at the Foreign Office, and he left England for Egypt on 25 October 1920, *ibid.*

40 E. E. Waley to Murray (FO), 27 November 1919, extracts in FO 371/3721.

41 Clayton desk diary, entries for 4 April, 18 May 1920; Iltyd Clayton, unpublished partial memoir, *c.*1946, Iltyd Clayton Papers, box 1, file 5, MECOX.

42 *Ibid.*

43 Clayton desk diary, entry for 14 June 1920, private collection; Gilbert F. Clayton bible, in the possession of the Clayton family.

44 Enid to her mother-in-law, 23 June 1920, Collins Papers, SAD 930/9 [original emphasis].

45 Annual Report of the Ministry of the Interior for 1919, 12 May 1920, pp. 21–22, FO 141/586/4. During the same year – 1918 – 140,000 persons died from influenza and 27,000 from typhus in Egypt.

46 Clayton desk diary, entries for 26–27 June and 5 July 1920, private collection.

47 Enid to her mother-in-law, 23 June 1920, Collins Papers, SAD 930/9.

48 Clayton to Harvey, 21 June 1920, CP, SAD 472/12/47; Clayton to Wingate, 6 September 1920, WP, SAD 251/6/64.

49 Milner to Maxwell, 21 May 1920 (invitation to Zaghlul), and 24 June 1920 (quoted), Maxwell Papers, box 4, folder 27, Princeton University Library.

50 Memorandum, n.d., but mid-August 1920, C.P. 1960, CAB 24/112, fos. 310–11.

51 Churchill Memorandum, 24 August 1920, C.P. 1803, CAB 24/111; Curzon Memorandum, 11 October 1920, C.P. 1960, CAB 24/112; Montagu Memorandum, 19 October 1920, C.P. 2000, CAB 24/112.

52 Clayton minute, 20 September 1920, FO 371/4980; Clayton to Wingate, 12 October 1920, WP, SAD 251/7/33.

53 Terry, *The Wafd,* p. 85.

54 Clayton desk diary, entry for 24 August 1920, private collection; Clayton to Wingate, 6 September 1920, WP, SAD 251/6/64 (Palestine and Arabia).

55 Paris, *Sherifian Solution*, pp. 108–23; Helmut Mejcher, 'British Middle East Policy, 1917–1922, pp. 81–101.

56 Curzon Memorandum, 16 August 1920, C.P. 1777, CAB 24/110.

57 Allenby to Selby, 27 August 1920, Walford Selby Papers, Eng. c.6592, Bodleian Library, Oxford.

58 Clayton minute, describing conversation with Gabriel Haddad, 20 September 1920, FO 371/5040.

59 *Ibid.*; and Clayton minute, 10 September 1920, *ibid.*, fo. 23; *and see generally*, Paris, *Sherifian Solution,* pp. 124–49.

60 The phrase was Curzon's: minute, 5 July 1919, FO 371/4146, fo. 352; Paris, *Sherifian Solution*, pp. 249–362.

61 Clayton Note, 9 September 1920, FO 371/5063.

62 Quoted in Paris, *Sherifian Solution,* 163.

63 Clayton minute, 1 September 1920, FO 371/5122, fos. 63–4.

64 IDCE Minutes, 24 August 1920, CP, SAD 694/9/38.

65 Clayton minute, 20 September 1920, FO 371/5123, fo. 33.

66 Young to Clayton, __ October; Young to Deedes, 15 October; and Clayton to Young, 24 October 1920, all in Hubert W. Young Papers, file 3, MECOX.

67 Kerr to Lloyd George, 31 December 1920, David Lloyd George Papers, F/90/1/30, Parliamentary Archives, London.

68 Clayton to Allenby, 16 November 1920, CP, SAD 470/10/14; Allenby to FO, 18 November 1920, FO 141/431/1 (sending memo); *and see* Clayton to Residency, 26 January 1921, CP, SAD 470/11/8 (warning against failure to adopt Milner proposals).

69 Clayton desk diary, entries for 2 and 4 November 1920, and 5 March 1921 (meetings with Tawfiq), and 2 December 1920 (with Adli), private collection; Allenby to Curzon, 18 March 1921, FO 371/6294; draft manuscript, 'British Policy in Egypt, 1919–1922', n.d., n.a., with annotations by Walford Selby in Selby Papers, MS Eng. c. 6582, Bodleian Library, Oxford.

70 Milner to Maxwell, 23 January 1921, Maxwell Papers, box 4, folder 27, Princeton University Library.

71 Allenby to Sultan Fu'ad, 26 February 1921, FO 371/6294.

72 Clayton desk diary, entry for 7 March 1921, private collection; Allenby to Curzon, 18 March 1921, FO 371/6294.

73 Clayton minute, 18 October 1921, FO 141/791/1.

74 Russell to his father, 5 April 1921, Thomas Russell Papers, 1/13, MECOX.

75 Harry Boyle, Memorandum on his visit to Egypt, April 14th to May 26th 1921, dated 11 June 1921, Harry Boyle Papers, box D, file 1, MECOX.

76 Scott to Curzon, 28 September 1921, FO 371/6305.

77 Lindsay to Scott, 25 August 1921, CP, SAD 470/12/6; Scott to Clayton, 3 September 1921, *ibid.*, at 1–5; Clayton to Scott, 5 September and Scott to Lindsay, 14 September 1921, FO 371/6305.

78 Kedourie, 'Zaghlul and the British', p. 143.

79 Allenby to Curzon, 17 June 1921, enclosing Hayter, 'Memorandum on a Political Settlement in Egypt', 5 June 1921, FO 371/6298.

80 Clayton Memorandum, 8 October 1921, G .N. Curzon Papers, FO 800/153, fos. 114–20, TNA.

81 Scott to Curzon, 10 October 1921, FO 371/6306.

82 Egyptian Delegation Statement, 15 November 1921, quoted in Kedourie, 'Zaghlul and the British', p. 142.

83 Clayton Memorandum, 8 October 1921, Curzon Papers, FO 800/153, TNA.

84 Allenby Note, 22 October 1921, FO 371/6306, fos. 95–7 (endorsing plan); Minutes of Murray and Lindsay, 19 October 1921, *ibid.*, fos. 34–5 (objecting).

85 From Notes by Gerald C. Delany (Reuter's correspondent in Egypt in the 1920s) to A.P. Wavell (for his biography of Allenby), n.d., *c.*1940–43, in Edmund Allenby Papers, 7/3/11, LHCMA; Selby to Allenby, 26 September 1921, Selby Papers, MS. Eng. c.6592, Bodleian Library, Oxford.

86 Selby to Allenby, 26 September 1921, *ibid.*; Scott to FO, 4 September 1921, FO 371/6304.

87 Curzon to Scott, 10 September 1921; FO to Swan (Labour MP), 10 September 1921, both in FO 371/6304.

88 Scott to Curzon, 29 September (FO 371/6305, quoted), and 14 October 1921 (FO 371/6306).

89 Scott to Lindsay (FO), 14 October 1921, enclosing Note by Hassan Rifaat of interview of Labour MPs, FO 371/6306.

90 Scott to Curzon, 21 and 23 September 1921, FO 371/6305, fos. 3, 10; Scott to Curzon, 23 September 1921, *ibid.*, fos. 97–101, enclosing letters between Clayton and William Lunn, MP of 22 September 1921.

91 Curzon to Scott, 3 October 1921, *ibid.*

92 Notes of Gerald C. Delany for A.P. Wavell, n.d., *c.* 1940–43, Allenby Papers, 7/3/11, LHCMA.

93 J. W. A. Young Note to Clayton, 17 October 1921, FO 141/791/1.

94 Clayton to Residency, 21 October 1921, enclosing reports from Sohag and Girga, and 19 October 1921, including requests of the Mudirs, both in FO 141/791/1.

95 Clayton to Residency, 19 October 1921 (handwritten note), *ibid.*; Scott to Curzon, 20 October 1921, CP, SAD 470/13/6.

96 Allenby to FO, 17 November 1921, repeating Advisers' Memorandum, FO 371/6307.

97 Allenby to Curzon, 6 and 11 December 1921, Cmd. 1592.

98 Curzon to Allenby, 18 November and 8 December 1921, *ibid.*

99 Annotations of Selby on draft MS 'British Policy in Egypt, 1919–1922', n.d., in Selby Papers, MS. Eng. c.6582, Bodleian Library, Oxford; original emphasis.

100 Selby, draft book MS, *The Foreign Office, A Perspective of Thirty Years*, n.d., *c.*1940s, Selby Papers, MS. Eng. c.6609, Bodleian Library, Oxford.

101 Clayton to Zaghlul, 22 December 1921, FO 141/791/1; Allenby to Curzon, four telegrams of 23 December 1921, Cmd. 1592.

102 Selby annotations on 'British Policy in Egypt, 1919–1922', Selby Papers, MS. Eng. c.6582, Bodleian Library, Oxford; Allenby to Curzon, 12 January 1922, (no. 17), C.P. 3614, CAB 24/132 (new government formed).

103 Allenby to Curzon, 12 January 1922 (no. 18), C.P. 3614, CAB 24/132.

104 Allenby to Curzon, 12 January 1922 (no. 19), *ibid.* Reference to the Sudan was omitted from telegram no. 19 of 12 January, but added in a cable from Allenby the next day.

105 Selby, draft MS, *The Foreign Office*, Selby Papers, MS. Eng. c.6609, Bodleian Library, Oxford; *and see* Allenby to Curzon, 15 January 1922, C.P. 3614, CAB 24/132.

106 Curzon to Allenby, 18 January, and Allenby to Curzon, 20 January 1922, Cmd. 1592.

107 Long, *British Pro-Consuls in Egypt*, pp. 121–22.

108 Curzon to Allenby, 28 January, and Allenby to Curzon, 29 January 1922, Cmd. 1592.

109 Wavell, *Allenby*, p. 302.

110 Diary of General Sir Henry Wilson (CIGS), entry for 11 February 1922, recounting conversation with Allenby, extracts in Allenby Papers, 7/1/31, LHCMA. Clayton's son, John, also remembered his mother recounting the story of Allenby causing Curzon to dissolve in tears at the meeting of February 10. Dr. John P. Clayton, C.V.O., to the author, 9 April 2011. The phenomenon was not unusual; on other occasions Curzon was reported to have been frustrated to the point of tears. On 29 October 1918, while attending an Eastern Committee meeting, Lawrence had turned on Curzon: 'You people don't yet understand the hole you have put us all into.' According to Lawrence, this caused the Foreign Secretary to promptly burst into tears (Graves and Liddell Hart,

eds., *T.E. Lawrence to his biographers*, p. 108). On another occasion, in September 1922, Curzon had a run-in with the French Premier, Raymond Poincaré, who exploded after a remark made by the Foreign Secretary. Curzon was later discovered, laying on a sofa, tears pouring down his face, a brandy bottle by his side. (Gilmour, *Curzon*, p. 544).

111 Clayton to Curzon, 12 February 1922, CP, SAD 470/14/54.

112 Memorandum of a Conversation held at 10 Downing Street, February 15th 1922, at 11.00 a.m., CAB 23/35.

113 Curzon Memorandum, 16 January 1922, C.P. 3616, CAB 24/132. On the widespread press criticism of the Government's Egyptian policy *see* Bishku, 'British Empire and Egypt's Future', pp. 124–135.

114 Henry Wilson diary extracts, entry for 12 February 1922, Edmund Allenby Papers, box 1, file 2, MECOX.

115 Wavell, *Allenby*, p. 303; Memorandum of a conversation held at 10 Downing Street, February 15th, 1922, at 6.00 p.m., CAB 23/36.

116 Murray to Selby, 26 November 1936, Selby Papers, MS. Eng. c.6592, Bodleian Library, Oxford.

117 Curzon to Allenby, 21 February 1922, enclosing 'Declaration to Egypt', Cmd. 1592.

118 Clayton to Wingate, 26 February 1922, WP, SAD 240/2/72.

119 Clayton Memorandum, 1 January 1922, CP, SAD 470/14/4.

120 Clayton to Residency, 13 April 1922, enclosing two memos regarding post of Adviser to the Interior, CP, SAD 470/15/5-10; Clayton to Sarwat Pasha, 8 May 1922, *ibid.*, SAD 470/15/11.

121 Public Security Department, Situation Report for 11–17 May 1922, FO 371/7742.

24 Palestine Revisited: Chief Secretary in the Mandate, 1923–1925

1 Clayton desk diary, entries for 25–26 August 1924, private collection; interview, Dr. John P. Clayton, C.V.O., 17 January 2010. The daggers remain a prized possession of the Clayton family.

2 Paris, *Sherifian Solution*, p. 154.

3 *Ibid.*, pp. 156–8.

4 Lawrence statement, as later reported to Liddell Hart in Graves and Liddell Hart, eds, *T.E. Lawrence to his Biographers*, p. 131.

5 Paris, *Sherifian Solution*, pp. 153–183.

6 *Ibid.*, pp. 167–72.

7 Allenby to FO, 10 January 1922, and FO to Allenby, 9 March 1922, FO 141/436/1.

8 CO to FO, 9 March 1922, Clayton family papers; Bell to [her family?], 14 March 1922, Gertrude Bell Papers, Newcastle University Library, http://gertrudebell. ncl.ac.uk/letters; ('Bell Online'); Philby diary, entry for 28 April 1922, Harry St.John Bridger Philby Papers, box 1, file 2(a), MECOX (refuses Iraq offer).

9 Clayton to Samuel, 4 July 1922, Herbert Samuel Papers, box 1, MECOX.

10 Minutes of Churchill (5 August) and Young (3 August 1922); Samuel to Shuckburgh (CO), 20 July 1922, CO 733/39.

11 Palestine Arab Delegation to Churchill, 16 March 1922, in *Correspondence with the Palestine Arab Delegation and the Zionist Organisation*, Cmd 1700, no. 3.

12 Deedes to Weizmann, 30 May 1920, quoted in Wasserstein, *The British in Palestine*, p. 86.

13 Knox, *British Palestine Policy*, p. 169; Huneidi, *A Broken Trust*, p. 109.

14 *British Policy in Palestine*, Cmd. 1700.

15 Clayton to Deedes, 29 January 1923, CP, SAD 472/12/127.

16 WO to Clayton, 29 January 1921; Egyptian Ministry of Finance to Clayton, 18 October 1922; and Clayton to Financial Adviser, Cairo, __ September 1922, CP, SAD 472/12/15, 110, 82.

17 Patterson to Clayton, 16 November 1924, and Clayton to Clark-Kerr, 18 December 1924, CP, SAD 472/12/99, 101; interview, Dr. John P. Clayton , C.V.O., 16 September 2011, Windsor, England (university education).

18 Clayton to Deedes, 29 January 1923, CP, SAD 472/12/127; Shuckburgh (CO) to Clayton, 6 and 21 March 1923; Clayton to Shuckburgh, 8 and 23 March 1923, CP, SAD 472/12/138, 140, 141, 143.

19 Florence Caroline Clayton diary, entries for 23 February, 11 May, 7 and 21 July and 4 September 1922, private collection.

20 T. E. Lawrence, *Seven Pillars of Wisdom* (1935 edn.), facing page 112.

21 Lawrence to Clayton, 19 August 1922, T. E. Lawrence Papers, MS Eng. c. 6737, Bodleian Library, Oxford.

22 Young minute, 3 October 1922; Young to Clayton, 6 October 1922, CO 733/35.

23 Paris, *Sherifian Solution*, pp. 184–204.

24 Transjordan Report no. 6, 1 August 1921, CO 733/5.

25 League of Nations, minutes of meetings of 22, 24 July 1922, C.P. 4125, CAB 24/138; minutes of 16 September 1922 meeting, C.P. 4223, CAB 24/139.

26 Paris, *Sherifian Solution*, p. 209.

27 Philby diary, entry for 25 July 1922, Philby Papers, box I, file 2(a), MECOX.

28 Clayton note, 18 October 1922, CO 733/37.

29 Colonial Office outline of points for discussion, n.d., *c.* mid-October 1922, CP, SAD 471/3/39-50.

30 Meinertzhagen, *Middle East Diary*, p. 130; Paris, *Sherifian Solution*, pp. 211–12.

31 Wilson, *King Abdullah, Britain and the making of Jordan*, p. 75; Paris, *Sherifian Solution*, pp. 212–13.

32 FO note, n.d., on draft agreement dated 1 December 1922, FO 371/7792.

33 Paris, *Sherifian Solution*, pp. 212–16; Dann, *Studies in the History of Transjordan*, pp. 47–65.

34 Samuel to J .H. Thomas, 18 July 1924, Samuel Papers, box 1, MECOX.

35 Samuel to Deedes, 31 May 1920, Wyndham Deedes Papers, box 2, file 7, MECOX.

36 Wasserstein, *British in Palestine*, pp. 122–3.

37 Clayton to CO, 12 July 1923; Clayton to Shuckburgh, 13 July 1923 (quoted), both in CP, SAD 694/2/25, 29.

38 CO: *Policy in Palestine*, 16 February 1923, C.P. 106(23), CAB 24/159 (somewhat strained); Devonshire: diary, entry for 27 March 1923, quoted in Paris, *Sherifian Solution*, p. 212 (Balfour Declaration 'quite inconsistent' with pledges to Arabs); Curzon: Eastern Committee minutes, 5 December 1918, CAB 27/24 (Palestine included in October 1915 pledge of Arab independence); Shuckburgh: record of conversation with S. Moody of CO, 13 April 1923, quoted in Friesel, 'British Officials on the Situation in Palestine, 1923', pp. 194–210.

39 CO, *Policy in Palestine,* 16 February 1923, C.P. 106(23), CAB 24/159, quoting Clayton note at pp. 12–13. Clayton also argued that the current British policy concerning Egypt

would never have been 'recommended or accepted' had it not appeared certain that British control of Palestine would be maintained.

40 Clayton to Devonshire, 6 July 1923, CO 733/47. The House of Lords debate which prompted Clayton's dispatch appears in Hansard (5th series), 27 June 1923, cols. 54–82.

41 Meinertzhagen diary, entry for 24 July 1923, vol. 24, p. 36, Bodleian Library, Oxford. The Meinertzhagen diaries must be viewed with circumspection, as it has been shown that, in many respects, they are *ex post facto* fabrications. However, while one may question the correctness of Meinertzhagen's views of Clayton's attitude, there is little reason to doubt his belief that Clayton was anti-Zionist. *See also* his diary entry for 27 August 1919, vol. 21, p. 100, *ibid.*

42 Meinertzhagen to Samuel, 18 July 1923, Herbert Samuel Papers, SAM/H/5/87, Parliamentary Archives, London.

43 Clayton to Shuckburgh, 13 July 1923, CP, SAD 694/2/29. In this letter Clayton stated he had given his views in a private letter to Samuel before sending his July 6 despatch.

44 Samuel to Clayton, 29 July 1923, CP, SAD 694/2/34.

45 Samuel, note on Clayton's despatch of 6 July 1923, CO 733/47.

46 Cabinet, Palestine Committee Report, *The Future of Palestine*, 27 July 1923, C.P. 351(23), CAB 24/161.

47 *Ibid.*

48 *Ibid.* The Palestine Mandate is reproduced in Ingrams, *Palestine Papers*, pp. 177–83.

49 CO to Clayton, 27 July 1923, CO 733/47.

50 Clayton to CO, 1 and 3 August 1923, CO 733/48.

51 Shuckburgh minute, 3 August, and Devonshire to Clayton, 3 August 1923, *ibid.*

52 Clayton to Devonshire, 7 September 1923, CO 733/49; *and see* Palestine Political Report for July 1923, CO 733/48.

53 C.P. 433(23), CAB 24/162; Samuel to CO, 11 October 1923, CO 733/50.

54 Devonshire memorandum, 'Future of Palestine', 27 October 1923, *ibid.*; Devonshire to Samuel, 17 October 1923, *ibid.*

55 Samuel to Shuckburgh, 12 October 1923; Devonshire to Samuel, 8 November 1923, *ibid.*

56 Kedourie, 'Sir Herbert Samuel and the Government of Palestine', in Kedourie, *Chatham House Version*, pp. 52–81, at 77–8.

57 Samuel to Clayton, 23 August 1923, CP, SAD 694/2/50.

58 Clayton to Devonshire, 24 August 1923; Devonshire to Samuel, 29 September 1923, CO 733/48.

59 Clayton to Shuckburgh, 3 August 1923, and CO minutes at CO 733/60, fos. 44–6; Wasserstein, *British in Palestine*, p. 208.

60 CO, minutes of Keith-Roach (14 August 1924) and Clauson (19 August 1924), CO 733/71, fos. 15–24; Clayton to Thomas (CO), 9 July 1924, *ibid.*, fos. 25–7; Wasserstein, *British in Palestine*, pp. 210–11.

61 Clayton to Devonshire, 31 August 1923; Devonshire to Samuel, 2 October 1923, CO 733/48.

62 Clayton to Shuckburgh, 12 July 1924 (in sympathy; Mandate government objects); Pinhas Rutenberg to Vernon (CO), 15 July 1924 (Clayton favours scheme), CO 733/85; Clayton to Thomas (CO), 5(6) August 1924, CO 733/72 ('unsound').

63 Mavrogordato to Clayton, 13 May and 17 November 1924, CO 733/76; Wasserstein, *British in Palestine*, p. 137, n.5.

64 Samuel to Devonshire, 8 December 1922, C.P. 4379, CAB 24/140; Middle East Department memorandum, 12 February 1924, C.P. 121(24), CAB 24/165. There was also a 500-man Palestine gendarmerie, paid for from local funds.

65 Clayton to Shuckburgh, 27 July 1923, CO 733/60.

66 Clayton to Thomas (Colonial Secretary), 1 August and 22 August 1924, CO 733/72.

67 Clayton to Devonshire, 24 July 1923, CO 733/47.

68 Vernon (CO) minute, 15 May 1924, CO 733/68, fos. 38–9; Thomas to Samuel, 20 May 1924, *ibid.*, fo. 80.

69 Clayton to Thomas, 1 and 22 August 1924, CO 733/72.

70 Clayton to Thomas 25 July (telegram) and 26 July (despatch) 1924, CO 733/71.

71 *See generally*, Clayton to Shuckburgh, 9 May 1924 (CO 733/85); Clayton to Thomas, 16 July 1924 (CO 733/71); Bentwich note, n.d., *c.* June 1924 (CO 733/70); Shuckburgh to Clayton, 3 July 1924 (CO 733/85); Shuckburgh to Amery, 29 March 1925 (CO 733/91); and Amery to Symes, 13 August 1925, *ibid.*

72 The complex issues surrounding the Orthodox debt, and Clayton's positions on them, are detailed in documents appearing in CO 733/46, 49, 52, 67, 68, 71, 74 and 76.

73 Weizmann, *Trial and Error*, pp. 225–6.

74 Bentwich, *Mandate Memories*, pp. 48–9.

75 Council (Waad Hair) of the Ashkenasic Jewish Community, Jerusalem, to the League of Nations, 1 October 1924, CO 733/74.

76 Clayton to Thomas, 15 July 1924, CO 733/71.

77 Goodman to Keith-Roach (CO), 6 January 1925, CO 733/74.

78 Minutes of Young and Keith-Roach, 16 June 1924, CO 733/85, fos. 204–5.

79 Monckton to his father, 17 August 1923, R. F. P. Monckton Papers, file 3, MECOX, describing the tour of Clayton and Enid to Haifa, Zichron, Ludd and Tulkaram.

80 Shuckburgh to Clayton, 19 June 1923, CP, SAD 472/12/147 (Treasury will not approve allowance); Clayton desk diary, entries for 16 May 1923 (Enid arrives Port Said); 16 November 1923 (Phyllis arrives Jerusalem with Patience and Sam); and 23 April 1924 (Ellinor and John arrive Port Said), private collection.

25 Trouble in Transjordan: Clayton and Abdullah, 1923–1925

1 Shuckburgh minute, 25 April 1924, CO 733/67, fo. 327; Young minute, 14 September 1921, CO 733/38, fo. 800.

2 Clauson minute, 13 September 1922, CO 733/38, fo. 799; Vernon minute, 8 November 1922, CO 733/37, fo. 490.

3 Clayton to Devonshire, 20 July 1923, CO 733/47.

4 Clayton to Young, 11 May 1923, CO 733/60.

5 Middle East Department memorandum, 12 February 1924, C.P. 121(24), CAB 24/165; Clayton to Samuel, 1 February 1924, DBFA, II, B, 4, pp. 102–4 (quoted).

6 Clayton to Samuel, 5 April 1924, CO 733/67.

7 Shuckburgh minute, 25 April 1924, *ibid.* at fo. 327 (CO not consulted); Samuel to Thomas, *ibid.*, at fo. 329 (Clayton informs Abdullah no grant for 1924–25).

8 Paris, *Sherifian Solution*, pp. 228–32.

9 Kirkbride, *A Crackle of Thorns*, p. 29.

10 Clayton to Phily, 19 October 1923; Samuel to Devonshire, 7 December 1923, CO

733/51 (Abdullah subsidizing Bedouin tribes); Philby to Samuel, 3 November 1923, *ibid.* (disagrees).

11 Clayton to Samuel, n.d., but enclosed in Samuel to CO, 18 May 1923, CO 733/45.

12 Clayton to Devonshire, 13 July 1923, CO 733/47; Devonshire to Clayton, 2 August 1923, *ibid.*

13 Cox to Churchill, 6 July 1921, CO 537/822.

14 Churchill to Cox (draft), 6 August 1921, CO 730/3.

15 Letter of Reader Bullard, October 1920, quoted in Hodgkin, ed., *Two Kings in Arabia*, p. 48, n. 1.

16 Philby to Bell, 17 February 1922, Philby Papers, box XVII, file 1, MECOX (riding off); Philby, *Stepping Stones* (unpublished book manuscript, *c.*1956–7), p. 115, *ibid.*, box VII (conflict).

17 Peake to Philby, [2?] December 1923, Frederick Peake Papers, 78/3/3, IWM, London.

18 Philby, *Stepping Stones*, p. 229.

19 Clayton to Devonshire, 29 June 1923, CO 733/46.

20 Clayton to Shuckburgh, 13 July 1923, CP, SAD 694/2/29.

21 Philby to Clayton, 1 July 1923, CO 733/47.

22 Clayton to Shuckburgh, 13 July 1923, CP, SAD 694/2/29.

23 Philby to Samuel, 22 January 1922, CO 733/18.

24 CO to Samuel, 8 February 1922, *ibid.*

25 Quotes in Paris, *Sherifian Solution*, p. 233.

26 Philby diary, entry for 11–12 January 1922, Philby Papers, box I, file 1, MECOX.

27 CO to Samuel, 17 August 1922, CO 733/24.

28 Paris, *Sherifian Solution*, p. 234.

29 CO to Samuel, 22 August 1922, CO 733/24.

30 Cox (Baghdad) to Devonshire, 6 December 1922, CP, SAD 471/2/11.

31 Paris, *Sherifian Solution*, p, 235.

32 Clayton to Samuel, n.d., but enclosed in Samuel to Devonshire, 18 May 1923, CO 733/45.

33 Clayton to Young, 11 May 1923, *ibid.*

34 Clayton to Devonshire, 29 June 1923, CO 733/46 (quoted); *and see* Clayton to Devonshire, 20 July 1923, CO 733/47.

35 Clayton to Thomas, 23 August 1924, CO 733/72.

36 Samuel to Shuckburgh, 5 October 1923, CO 537/860.

37 Shuckburgh to Samuel, 21 November 1923, CO 733/50

38 Samuel to Shuckburgh, 7 December 1923, CO 537/861.

39 Philby diary, entry for 14–15 January 1924, Philby Papers, 1/5/3/4, MECOX.

40 Clayton to Devonshire, 31 August 1923, CO 733/48.

41 Clayton to Devonshire, 6 July 1923, CO 733/47.

42 Clayton to Samuel, 5 April 1924, CO 733/67.

43 Dann, *Studies in the History of Transjordan*, p. 86.

44 Cox to Clayton, 1 July 1924, CO 733/71.

45 Cox to Clayton, 3 July 1924, *ibid.*

46 Clayton to Thomas, 24 July 1924, *ibid.*

47 CO minutes of Young and J. H. Thomas, 7 August 1924, *ibid.*, fos. 451–2; D. G. O. (FO) to Young, *c.* 12 August 1924, *ibid.*, fo. 480 (Prime Minister concurs); Thomas to Clayton, 12 August 1924, CO 733/72.

48 Clayton to Abdullah, 14 August 1924, FO 371/1012.

49 Uriel Dann, in *Studies in the History of Transjordan*, pp. 81–92, states that the cavalry squadron was sent to Amman as a security measure in the wake of a large Wahhabi attack near Amman on 14 August. But Mary Wilson, in *King Abdullah, Britain and the Making of Jordan*, p. 235, n. 96, shows that the squadron was sent in connection with the political crisis.

50 Cox to Clayton, 20 August 1924, CO 733/72.

51 Dann, *Studies in the History of Transjordan*, p. 91.

52 Philby, *Stepping Stones*, p. 163. Philby describes this discussion as having occurred during a visit of Samuel and Clayton to Amman on 9–11 November 1923. However, Clayton's desk diary entries for those dates disclose that Clayton was in Jerusalem during Samuel's November visit. Clayton's diary does reflect a trip to Amman on 10–11 December 1923, and that may be when the talk described by Philby occurred.

53 Philby, *Stepping Stones*, p. 165. Clayton's diary (private collection) records this visit as occurring on 21–22 January 1924, as does Philby's diary, Philby Papers, 1/5/3/4, MECOX.

54 Philby, *Stepping Stones*, p. 229.

55 Bowman diary, entry for 3 February 1924, Humphrey Bowman Papers, box 3B(g), MECOX.

56 Wasserstein, *The British in Palestine*, pp. 142–5.

57 Samuel to Shuckburgh, 28 September 1923, CO 733/60.

58 Bowman diary, entry for 4 March 1924, Bowman Papers, box 3B(g), MECOX; *see also*, Wasserstein, *British in Palestine*, p. 148.

59 Richmond to Samuel, 13 March 1924, Herbert Samuel Papers, SAM/H/6, vol. 6, 1924, Parliamentary Archives, London.

60 Clayton to Selby, 3 March 1924, Curzon Papers, FO 800/156/177, TNA.

61 Philby memorandum, 26 June 1924, Herbert Samuel Papers, box 1, MECOX.

62 Clayton to Shuckburgh, 13 June 1924 (draft), Clayton family papers.

63 G. C. Delany (Reuter's correspondent, Cairo), Notes prepared for A. P. Wavell's biography of Allenby, n.d., Allenby Papers, 7/3/2, LHCMA, London.

64 Samuel to Shuckburgh, 21 November 1924, Austen Chamberlain Papers, FO 800/256/317, TNA; Edgcumbe (CO) to Selby (FO), 3 December 1924, *ibid.*, at 316.

65 Extract of Cabinet Conclusions of 24 November 1924, Cab. 63(24), in FO 371/10045; Chamberlain to Allenby, 1 December 1924, FO 407/199.

66 Clayton desk diary, entry for 29 November 1924, private collection.

67 *Ibid.*, entries for 2, 7, 8 and 14 December 1924.

68 Clayton to Leonard Stein, 27 December 1924, file 972, WA.

69 Clayton desk diary, entries for 20, 30–31 December 1924, private collection; Angus McNeil diary, entry for 7 February 1925, Angus McNeil Papers, diaries, 1922–1926, MECOX (Clayton 'told me he was asked whether he would accept the High Comm'r if offered to him. So he is certainly in the running.').

70 Wasserstein, *British in Palestine*, p. 147, n. 5.

71 *Ibid.*, pp. 108–12.

72 Bowman diary, entry for 29 September 1923, Bowman Papers, box 3B(g), MECOX.

73 Weizmann to Samuel, 6 February 1924, Herbert Samuel Papers, SAM/H/6, Parliamentary Archives, London.

74 Bowman diary, entry for 26 October 1924, box 3B(g), Bowman Papers, MECOX.

75 *Ibid.*, *and see* Angus McNeil diary, entry for 19 April 1925, MECOX; and Rosamund Templeton to Balfour, 13 April 1925, Clayton family papers ('There is a consensus of opinion that . . . Sir Gilbert Clayton would make "an ideal High Commissioner".').

76 Samuel to Amery, 29 January 1925, Leo Amery Papers, AMEL 2/4/16, Churchill College, Cambridge.

77 Amery to Samuel, 13 February 1925, *ibid.*

78 Samuel to Amery, 27 February 1925, *ibid.*

79 Wasserstein, *British in Palestine*, pp. 149–150.

80 *Ibid.*

81 Weizmann to Kisch, 4 June 1925, WA, file 1006.

82 Weizmann to Moshe Beilinson, 29 June 1925, *ibid.*, file 1011.

83 Samuel to Amery, 23 April 1925, Amery Papers, AMEL 2/4/16, Churchill College, Cambridge.

26 Desert Diplomat: The Arabian Treaties, 1925–1926

1 Paris, *Sherifian Solution*, pp. 249–76.

2 Minute, 9 March 1922, FO 371/7711, fo. 236.

3 Minute, 13 October 1920, FO 371/5065, fo. 64–5.

4 Paris, *Sherifian Solution*, pp. 299–319.

5 *Ibid.*, pp. 277–98.

6 Darlow and Bray, *Ibn Saud*, pp. 226–7.

7 Paris, *Sherifian Solution*, p. 264.

8 Kostiner, *Making of Saudi Arabia*, pp. 83–6.

9 Dickson, *Kuwait and Her Neighbours*, pp. 274–5; Vasiliev, *History of Saudi Arabia*, pp. 257–8.

10 Paris, *Sherifian Solution*, pp. 343–6; Kostiner, *Making of Saudi Arabia*, pp. 87–92.

11 Samuel to CO, 7 March 1924, FO 371/10217.

12 Musa, *Al-Husayn Ibn Ali wa al-thawra al-'Arabiyya al-kubra*, p. 200; Paris, *Sherifian Solution*, pp. 346–8.

13 Jeddah Report, 1–29 March 1924, DBFA, pt. II, ser. B, vol. 4, p. 87.

14 CO to FO, 12 September 1924, CO 727/9.

15 Paris, *Sherifian Solution*, pp. 348–53.

16 Clayton desk diary, entry for 22 July 1925, private collection.

17 Vernon (CO) to Clayton, 4 September 1925, Clayton family papers.

18 Clayton desk diary, entries for 22–23 July 1925; Dr. John P. Clayton, C.V.O., to the author, 16 November 2010 (chummy car).

19 Cabinet conclusions, 27(25), 28 May 1925, CAB 23/50.

20 CID sub-committee report, 4 June 1925, and Minutes of CID meeting, 29 June 1925, both in C.P. 315(25), CAB 24/174; Cabinet conclusions, 32(25), 1 July 1925, CAB 23/50.

21 Young note to Amery, 7 July 1925, CO 727/10, fo. 415.

22 Young to Clayton, 31 July 1925, CP, SAD 471/6/1.

23 Clayton to Young, 1 August 1925, CO 727/10.

24 Young to Clayton, 6 August 1925, CP, SAD 471/6/3.

25 Clayton desk diaries, entries for 19 August and 10 and 23 September 1925, private collection.

26 Instructions in CO to Clayton, 10 September 1925, DBFA, pt. B, ser. II, vol. 4, pp. 369–73.

27 High Commissioner, Iraq to CO, 5 and 8 September, and CO to High Commissioner, 7 September 1925, CP, SAD 471/6/6,7 and 8.

28 Plumer to Amery, 4 September 1925, CP, SAD 471/6/11; Antonius, Memorandum on the Eastern Frontiers of Trans-Jordan, 22 September 1925, *ibid.*, SAD 471/6/38-45.

29 Clayton, *Arabian Diary*, p. 89.

30 *Ibid.*, p. 128. Another British acquaintance of Ibn Saud, Robert Brooke-Popham, considered that his face was 'neither cruel nor deceitful . . , but he has a very cynical, almost contemptuous smile'. R. Brooke-Popham, Notes on the Meeting of King Faisal and King Ibn Saud, February 1930, Robert Brooke-Popham Papers, 2/2, LHCMA.

31 Clayton to Wingate, 21 October 1925, CP, SAD 471/7/30; Clayton, *Arabian Diary*, pp. 99–103; Clayton desk diary, entries for 11–13 October 1925.

32 Report by Sir Gilbert Clayton . . . on his Mission to negotiate certain Agreements with the Sultan of Nejd, p. 17, CP, SAD 471/7/56 ('Report').

33 Report, pp. 25–8.

34 Clayton to Wingate, 21 October 1925, CP, SAD 471/7/30 (spirit-breaking); Clayton, *Arabian Diary*, p. 104 (both feet); Report, pp. 7 (abatement), 25–8.

35 The Bahra Agreement appears in Report, Annexure 11, pp. 68–71; *see also* Helms, *Cohesion of Saudi Arabia*, pp. 219–21.

36 Report, pp. 8–9.

37 Clayton to Wingate, 21 October 1925, CP, SAD 471/7/30; Clayton, *Arabian Diary*, pp. 107–13; Clayton desk diary, entries for 24–25 October 1925, private collection.

38 Clayton, *Arabian Diary*, pp. 116–17; Clayton desk diary, entry for 25 October 1925, private collection.

39 Report, p. 32.

40 *Ibid.*, pp. 5–6.

41 *Ibid.*, pp. 6–7, 31–42; Clayton, *Arabian Diary*, pp. 111–12, 116–21. The text of the Hadda Agreement appears in Report as Annexure 7, pp. 57–62. Darlow and Bray, *Ibn Saud*, p. 314, incorrectly state that Ibn Suad 'ceded' Akaba to Transjordan at Bahra. He did not; no part of the Transjordan-Hijaz boundary was settled at Bahra.

42 Clayton desk diary, entry for 1 November 1925, private collection.

43 Clayton, *Arabian Diary*, pp. 127–8.

44 Clayton to CO, 2 telegrams of 4 November 1925, DBFA, ser. II, pt. B, vol. 4, p. 385; Amery to Clayton, 16 November 1925, CP, SAD 471/7/46. Leatherdale, in *Britain and Saudi Arabia*, p. 58, n. 104, states that the Clayton mission was haled in Britain 'as a considerable success'.

45 Report, p. 11; *and see* Clayton, *Arabian Diary*, p. 120 (27 October 1925): 'I am quite convinced that I could not have succeeded without him.'

46 Clayton, *Arabian Diary*, p. 137 (9 November 1925).

47 *Ibid.*, pp. 142–8 (15–22 November 1925).

48 Clayton to CO, 4 November 1925, CP, SAD 471/7/43; Chamberlain (for Amery) to Lloyd (for Clayton), 18 November 1925, DBFA, ser. II, pt. B, vol. 4, p. 390; Lloyd (for Clayton) to Chamberlain (for Amery), 20 November 1925, *ibid.*, pp. 390–1.

49 Clayton, *Arabian Diary*, pp. 147–52.

50 *Ibid.*, pp. 151–8; Bell to her father, 2 December 1925, Gertrude Bell Papers, Newcastle University, online at http://gertrudebell.ncl.ac.uk.

51 Clayton to Amery, 10 December 1925, CP, SAD 471/7/50; Clayton, *Arabian Diary*, pp. 159–63.

52 Clayton to CO, 26 November 1925, CP, SAD 471/4/27; Clayton to Amery, 10 December 1925, *ibid.*, SAD 471/7/50 (quoted).

53 Stewart to Clayton, 5 (far from easy) and 19 (under CO) December 1925, CP, SAD 471/4/29; Clayton, *Arabian Diary*, pp. 170–1 (postpone).

54 Clayton, *Arabian Diary*, pp. 176–86.

55 Dresch, *History of Modern Yemen*, p. 6. The Anglo-Turkish Convention was not ratified until 1914.

56 CO to Resident, Aden, 24 December 1925, CP, SAD 471/4/33.

57 Collins, introduction to part II of Clayton, *Arabian Diary*, pp. 198–99.

58 Report by Sir Gilbert Clayton on his Mission to the Imam of San'a, 6 April 1926, pp. 6–7, CP, SAD 471/1/4 ('Sanaa Report').

59 *Ibid.*, p. 7.

60 Clayton, *Arabian Diary*, pp. 216–23.

61 *Ibid.*, pp. 227–8.

62 *Ibid.*, pp. 237–8; Sanaa Report, p. 9 (quoted).

63 Draft treaty, 10 February 1926, in Clayton, *Arabian Diary*, Appendix VI, pp. 290–1.

64 Clayton, *Arabian Diary*, p. 242.

65 *Ibid.*, pp. 231–42.

66 Sanaa Report, p. 51; Clayton to CO, 4 March 1926, CP, SAD 471/4/41.

67 Clayton, *Arabian Diary*, pp. 244, 247.

68 Sanaa Report, p. 15.

69 Dresch, *History of Modern Yemen*, p. 34; Wilkinson, *Arabia's Frontiers*, pp. 158–65.

70 Clayton, *Arabian Diary*, pp. 248–61; Clayton desk diary, entry for 24 February 1926, private collection (fever, pleurisy).

27   Rome and Jeddah: Eastern Diplomacy, 1927–1928

1 Clayton desk diary and pocket diary, entries for 21–24 March, 21 May-5 June, and 28 July 1926, private collection.

2 Florence Caroline Clayton diary, vol. 13, entry for 16 July 1926 (Apple Porch), private collection.

3 Clayton desk diary, entry for 8 May 1926 (John); entries for 27 October, 11 and 25 November, and 12 December 1926; 27 March and 28 June 1927 (lectures).

4 Clayton desk diary, entry for 23 April (Windsor Castle); King George V Diary, entry for Friday, 23 April 1926, RA:GV/PRIV/GVD/1926:23 Apr., Royal Archives, Windsor.

5 Edgcumbe (CO) to Lord Stamfordham, 28 June 1926, RA:PS/PSO/GV/C/J/2063, and Stamfordham note to Clive Wigram, same date, RA:PS/PSO/GV/C/J/2063/61, Royal Archives, Windsor. At the bottom of Stamfordham's note, Wigram wrote: 'The King approves. CW 29/6'.

6 Report by Sir Gilbert Clayton on his Mission to negotiate certain Agreements with the Sultan of Nejd, 25 November 1925, CP, SAD 471/7/56, p. 44; Clayton to Amery, 16 December 1925, CP, SAD 471/7/52.

7 Almana, *Arabia Unified*, p. 75.

8 CO Memorandum, 'British Interests in Arabia', 26 November 1926, C.P. 415(26), CAB 24/182.

9 Minutes of a Conference at the Colonial Office on the 12th of March 1926, CP, SAD 472/1/2.

10 Baldry, 'Anglo-Italian Rivalry in Yemen', pp. 155–193, 162.

11 Quoted in Tripodi, 'Anglo-Italian Involvement in the Red Sea', pp. 209–234, 217.

12 Baldry, 'Anglo-Italian Rivalry in Yemen', p. 167; Tripodi, 'Anglo-Italian Involvement in the Red Sea', p. 216.

13 Steiner, *The Lights That Failed*, pp. 314–48.

14 Tripodi, 'Anglo-Italian Involvement in the Red Sea', p. 219.

15 Cabinet Conclusions, 47(26), 21 July 1926, CAB 23/53.

16 Minute, 7 October 1926, quoted in Tripodi, 'Anglo-Italian Involvement in the Red Sea', p. 215, n. 15.

17 CO Memorandum, 18 October 1926, describing 5 August 1926 interdepartmental conference, C.P. 377(26), CAB 24/182.

18 Tripodi, 'Anglo-Italian Involvement in the Red Sea', p. 223.

19 CID, Report of Chiefs of Staff Sub-Committee, 'Position in South-West Arabia', 8 November 1926, C.P. 377(26), CAB 24/182. The Army concluded that a military expedition against the Imam would require a division, at a cost of £6–10 million, while the RAF noted that it could maintain a bombing squadron at Aden for £12,000 per month.

20 Oliphant (FO) to Clayton, 1 November 1926, CP, SAD 471/1/36.

21 Minutes of CID Meeting, 25 November 1926, C.P. 401(26), CAB 24/82 (Chamberlain quote); Cabinet Conclusions, 1 December 1926, 61(26), CAB 23/53.

22 Chamberlain to Clayton, 28 December 1926, DBFP, ser. IA, vol. II, pp. 841–4.

23 Oliphant to Clayton, 21 December 1926, CP, SAD 471/1/41.

24 Lloyd (Cairo) to Chamberlain, 12 January 1927, DBFP, ser. IA, vol. II, p. 845.

25 Guariglia was then Director-General of the Department of Political, Commercial and Private Affairs of Europe and the Levant.

26 Notes of First Meeting, 11 January 1927, DBFA, pt. II, ser. B, vol. 5, pp. 260–2.

27 Notes of Second Meeting, 12 January 1927, *ibid.*, pp. 263–4; Graham to Chamberlain, 13 January 1927, *ibid.*, p. 259 (quoted).

28 FO to Graham, 11 January 1927, CP, SAD 471/9/12; Graham to Chamberlain, 13 January 1927, DBFA, pt. II, ser. B, vol. 5, p. 259. Notes of Third Meeting, 14 January 1927, *ibid.*, pp. 264–5. The Ibn Saud–Idrisi treaty, called 'The Mecca Agreement', is printed in *ibid.*, pp. 266–7.

29 Note of a Private Conversation between Signor Gasparini and Sir Gilbert Clayton, 15 January 1927, *ibid.*, pp. 265–6.

30 Notes of Third meeting, 14 January 1927, *ibid.*, p. 265. The Italian decision not to pursue a position in Kamaran was fortunate, for the 'juridical status' of the Island was far from clear. By the Treaty of Lausanne (July 1923), the Turks formally relinquished any claim to their former Arab lands and sovereignty over Kamaran was to be 'settled by the parties concerned', although no mention was made of who those parties were. Britain had occupied the island in 1915, and was still there, and, owing to its strategic importance, had no intention of allowing the place to revert to any Arab ruler, or its status to be decided by any other Power. *See* Tripodi, 'Anglo-Italian Involvement in the Red Sea', p. 270, n. 37.

31 Clayton Note, 14 January 1927, marked 'not sent', CP, SAD 471/9/21.

32 Graham to Chamberlain, 14 January 1927, DBFA, pt. II, ser. B, vol. 5, p. 259; Chamberlain to Graham, 15 January 1927, DBFP, ser. IA, vol. II, p. 847.

33 Chamberlain to Clayton, 27 January 1927, DBFA, pt. II, ser. B, vol. 5, pp. 278–9 (instructions); CO Memorandum, 'British Interests in Arabia', 26 November 1926, C.P. 415(26), CAB 24/182.

34 *See* note 30, above, regarding Kamaran. Instructions: DBFA, pt. II, ser. B, vol. 5, pp. 278–9.

35 Chamberlain to Lord Birkenhead (Secretary of State for India), 27 January 1927, DBFP, ser. IA, vol. II, p. 850.

36 Notes of a Meeting held at the Palazzo Chigi on January 31, 1927, DBFA, pt. II, ser. B, vol. 5, pp. 283–5.

37 The agreed record appears in DBFA, *ibid.*, pp. 280–1. The British and Italian drafts are in CP, SAD 471/9/42 and 52, respectively. Tripodi, in 'Anglo-Italian Involvement in the Red Sea', pp. 225–8, concludes that both sides felt 'they had more or less achieved their objectives'.

38 Chamberlain to Clayton, 9 March 1927, CP, SAD 471/9/82; Clayton desk diary, entry for 7 February 1927, private collection; Dr John P. Clayton, C.V.O., to the author, 25 January 2013 (describing Mussolini meeting).

39 Government of India to Secretary of State for India, 12 July 1926, and IO to CO, 26 July 1926, CP, SAD 471/8/19 and 16.

40 Clayton to Shuckburgh, 21 April 1926, CP, SAD 472/1/15; minutes of inter-departmental conference of 6 October 1926, CP, SAD 471/8/77 (Young).

41 Clayton to Shuckburgh, 21 April 1926, CP, SAD 472/1/15.

42 Minutes of inter-departmental conference of 11 August 1926, CP, SAD 471/8/31 (recommends Antonius); Antonius to Clayton, 11 September 1926, *ibid.*, at 55.

43 Antonius to Clayton, 21 November 1926, CP, SAD 471/8/97.

44 Minutes of inter-departmental conference, 6 October 1926, CP, SAD 471/8/77.

45 Jordan and Antonius to Chamberlain, 26 January 1927 (report of mission), DBFA, pt. II, ser. B, vol. 5, pp. 268–77; Silverfarb, 'The Treaty of Jiddah', pp. 276–85; Leatherdale, *Britain and Saudi Arabia*, p. 70.

46 Clayton to Shuckburgh, 21 April 1926, CP, SAD 472/1/15; minutes of inter-departmental conference, 11 August 1926, CP, SAD 471/8/31.

47 Notes and minutes of Colonial Office conferences of 13 January (CP, SAD 471/10/10); 19 January (*ibid.*, at 15; CO suggests discontinuing talks, Antonius objects); 4 February (*ibid.*, at 57; IO wishes to terminate talks); and 7 February 1927 (*ibid.*, at 57).

48 Oliphant (FO) to Clayton, 18 February 1927, CP, SAD 471/10/47.

49 Chamberlain to Clayton, 14 April 1927 (instructions, with draft treaty and protocol), DBFA, pt. II, ser. B, vol. 5, pp. 299–303.

50 Clayton to Chamberlain, 6 June 1927, *ibid.*, pp. 310–329 ('Mission Report').

51 Mission Report, at pp. 311, 312 (indented quote), 324–5; Record of private and personal interview between Ibn Saud and Sir G. Clayton, n.d., but describing conversation of 16 May 1927, marked 'secret', CP, SAD 471/11/55.

52 Mission Report, at pp. 316–18; Leatherdale, *Britain and Saudi Arabia*, p. 71.

53 That was not the British intent; London had intended to abandon capitulatory rights in Ibn Saud's domains without expressly so stating only because there was no wish to prejudice the claims of other Powers still holding capitulation rights in former Ottoman territories or to encourage other Eastern countries in which Britain still retained capitulation rights from demanding abandonment of those rights in light of the concession given in Arabia.

54 Clayton diary, entries for 10 June and 25 July 1927, private collection (stallions); Dr. John P. Clayton, C.V.O., to the author, April 2010 (toy trains).

55 Silverfarb, 'The Treaty of Jiddah', p. 281.

56 Chamberlain to Clayton, 23 July 1927, DBFA, pt. II, ser. B, vol. 5, p. 344.

57 Clayton to FO, 24 June 1927, CP, SAD 471/11/64-5; FO to Clayton, 22 August 1927, CP, SAD 472/12/14.

28 The Attack of the Ikhwan: The Arabian Threat to Iraq, 1928

1 Charts of Ikhwan raids, December 1927 – March 1928, CP, SAD 472/2/1, 59.

2 Silverfarb, 'Revolt of the Ikhwan', pp. 222–48.

3 The literature on the Ikhwan revolt of 1927–30 is substantial. This account relies primarily on Silverfarb, 'Revolt of the Ikhwan'; Habib, *Ibn Saud's Warriors of Islam*; Helms, *Cohesion of Saudi Arabia*; Kostiner, *Making of Saudi Arabia*; Vasiliev, *History of Saudi Arabia*; and al-Rasheed, *History of Saudi Arabia*.

4 Esposito, *Islam, The Straight Path*, p. 118.

5 Vasiliev, *History of Saudi Arabia*, pp. 269–70; Darlow and Bray, *Ibn Saud: The Desert Warrior*, pp. 309–10, 319.

6 Vasiliev, *History of Saudi Arabia*, pp. 268–8; Almana, *Arabia Unified*, p. 80.

7 Helms, *Cohesion of Saudi Arabia*, pp. 137–9.

8 *Ibid.*, pp. 143–4.

9 Vasiliev, *History of Saudi Arabia*, p. 275 (contrary to orders); Kostiner, *Making of Saudi Arabia*, p. 125 (agrees to Ikhwan raids).

10 Clayton diary, entries for June – December 1927, private collection.

11 *Ibid.*, entries for 7, 9 March 1928.

12 Lloyd to Chamberlain: 14 January (CP, SAD 472/2/8), 17 February (DBFA, pt. II, ser. B, vol. 6, pp. 9–10), and 25 February 1928, *ibid.*, p. 11; Dobbs to Amery, 9 March 1928, CP, SAD 472/2/32; Haworth (Resident, Bushire) to CO, CP, SAD 472/2/35; Stonehewer-Bird (Jeddah) to Chamberlain, 26 February 1928, DBFA, pt. II, ser. B, vol. 6, p. 11 (Ibn Saud rejects Haworth).

13 Cabinet Conclusions, 13(28), 7 March 1928, CAB 23/57.

14 Silverfarb, 'Revolt of the Ikhwan', pp. 234–6; Trenchard Note, 'Akhwan Raids – The Effect of Air Action in Stopping Raiding', 10 April 1928, CP, SAD 472/3/29.

15 Silverfarb, 'Revolt of the Ikhwan', pp. 238–9.

16 Chamberlain to Amery, 11 April 1928, Lancelot Oliphant Papers, FO 800/253/29, TNA.

17 Clayton to Ibn Saud, 19 May 1927, DBFA, pt. II, ser. B, vol. 5, p. 318.

18 Cabinet Conclusions, 20(28), 4 April; 21(28), 18 April; and 28(28), 9 May 1928, all in CAB 23/57; Oliphant (FO) to Clayton, 4 April 1928, CP, SAD 472/3/6 (does Clayton adhere to his view on arms embargo?); Shuckburgh to Clayton, 4 April 1928, *ibid.*, at 8; Note, n.a., n.d., *c.* 5–15 April 1928, *ibid.*, at 10 ('well nigh disastrous').

19 Clayton to Shuckburgh, 12 April; CO to Dobbs, 14 April; Shuckburgh to Clayton, 14 April; CO to Dobbs, 14 April 1928, CP, SAD 472/3/26, 36, 39; Oliphant to Shuckburgh, 26 April 1928, Oliphant Papers, FO 800/252, TNA.

20 Clayton diary, entries for 2, 7, 8 and 16 May 1928, private collection; Clayton to Lloyd (Cairo), 17 May 1928, CP, SAD 472/5/3 ('[I]t looks as if I am going to fail').

21 Article 3 of the Uqair Protocol is quoted in Shuckburgh to Clayton (Instructions), 17

April 1928, DBFA, pt. II, ser. B, vol. 6, pp. 28–35; Clayton to Chamberlain, 15 May 1928, *ibid.*, p. 40 (Ibn Saud's position).

22   Clayton to Chamberlain, 15 May 1928, DBFA, pt. II, ser. B, vol. 6, p. 40.

23   Clayton to CO, 10 July 1928 (First Report), *ibid.*, p. 63.

24   Glubb, *War in the Desert*, pp. 212–13.

25   Glubb Note, 17 May 1928, John Bagot Glubb Papers, box 5(2), MECOX. In his book, *War in the Desert*, p. 214, Glubb modified this language: 'It was pathetic to hear such a speech [from Ibn Saud], so obviously sincere, and Clayton's vague reply that he was sure that the friendship would always continue between His Majesty and Britain.'

26   Glubb, *War in the Desert*, pp. 215–16.

27   Glubb, manuscript draft of chapter 21 of *War in the Desert*, p. 39, Glubb Papers, box 1(3), MECOX ('liked and admired'); published version of *War in the Desert*, pp. 216, 220.

28   Glubb, *War in the Desert*, pp. 216–17.

29   Chamberlain to Clayton, 19 May, and Clayton to Chamberlain, 21 May 1928, DBFP, ser. IA, vol. VII, pp. 677–9.

30   Clayton to Dobbs, 22 May 1928, CP, SAD 472/5/11.

31   Clayton memorandum, 18 June 1928, CP, SAD 472/6/8.

32   Agent, Jeddah to Chamberlain, 12 June 1928, DBFA, pt. II, ser. B, vol. 6, p. 46.

33   Henry Cox (Amman) to Plumer, 27 June, 4 and 22 July 1928, CP, SAD 472/7/1, 7, 90; Plumer to Clayton, 24 July 1928, *ibid.*, at 97.

34   Minutes of CID meeting of 22 May 1928, C.P. 163(28), CAB 24/195.

35   *Ibid.*; Cabinet Conclusions, 30(28), 23 May 1928, CAB 23/57.

36   Chamberlain to Amery, 11 April 1928, FO 371/12992.

37   Chamberlain to Amery, 19 May 1928, Oliphant Papers, FO 800/253/30, TNA.

38   Sir Samuel Wilson (permanent under-secretary, CO) to Amery, 17 December 1927, Leo Amery Papers, Churchill College, Cambridge, AMEL 2/1/14; Alawi, *Faisal I*, p. 487.

39   Ormsby-Gore to Amery, 8 December 1927, Amery Papers, AMEL 2/1/14.

40   Chamberlain minutes, 1 and 21 June 1928; Oliphant minute, 8 June 1928, Oliphant Papers, FO 800/252, TNA.

41   Edgcumbe (CO) to Lord Stamfordham, __ June 1928; Stamfordham to Edgcumbe, 26 June 1928, King George V Papers, RA:PS/PSO/GV/C/L/2168A1, 2, Royal Archives, Windsor. When King George learned that Clayton had been proposed for the post of High Commissioner for Iraq, he was reported to have said, 'Oh good; now I shall get some of those lovely Arabian stamps from Baghdad.' Dr. John P. Clayton, C.V.O. to the author, 9 April 2011. It will be recalled that King George was a keen stamp collector and that Clayton had sent the King a set of the first issue of Hijaz stamps in 1916 (Chapter 15).

42   Amery Memorandum, 'Akhwan Situation', 15 June 1928, C.P. 187(28), CAB 24/195; Cabinet Conclusions, 33 (28), 20 June 1928, CAB 23/58.

43   Clayton's 26 June testimony is contained in Annexure 'D' to the Report of the CID sub-committee on 'The Akhwan Situation', 10 July 1928, C.P. 217(28), CAB 24/196. In the India Office, it was observed that for the phrase 'in the vicinity of the border' Cox more accurately could have used '*fi jiwar al-hudud*' [in the neighbourhood of, in the vicinity of, near or close to the border], or '*bi al-qurb min al-hudud*' [in the proximity of, or in the vicinity of, near to the border]. Helms, *Cohesion of Saudi Arabia*, pp. 232–33, 247, n. 15; *see also* Kostiner, *Making of Saudi Arabia*, p. 120.

44　Chamberlain to Clayton, 1 August 1928, DBFA, pt. II, ser. B, vol. 6, p. 82 (reporting Cox's interpretation).

45　CID sub-committee Report, 10 July 1928, C.P. 217(28), CAB 24/196. The Note by the Air Staff agreeing to a reduction in the number of posts from eight to six appears in the Report as Annexure 'A'.

46　Cabinet Conclusions, 37(28), 11 July 1928, CAB 23/58.

47　Clayton to Trenchard, 22 June 1928, CP, SAD 472/6/40.

48　*Ibid.*

49　Shuckburgh (CO) to Clayton (instructions), 19 July 1928, DBFA, pt. II, ser. B, vol. 6, pp. 76–80. The copy in DBFA bears no date, but that appearing in Clayton's papers reflects a date of 19 July 1928, CP, SAD 472/7/81.

50　Dobbs to CO, 11 March 1928, CP, SAD 472/2/37.

51　Dobbs to CO, 14 March 1928, *ibid.*, SAD 472/2/41.

52　Dobbs to CO, 30 March 1928, *ibid.*, SAD 472/2/60; Iraq Minister of the Interior, Memorandum, 17 April 1928, *ibid.*, SAD 472/4/40; Dobbs to CO, 18 April 1928, *ibid.*, SAD 472/4/75.

53　Dobbs to CO, 17 April 1928, CP, SAD 472/4/47; Abdul Muhsin al-Sadun (Iraq Prime Minister) to Dobbs, 21 April 1928, *ibid.*, SAD 472/4/75.

54　Clayton notes, n.d., *c.*June-July 1928, CP, SAD 472/5/23.

55　Clayton diary, entries for 19–20, 30 July, and 2 August 1928, private collection; Clayton to Chamberlain, 7 August 1928, DBFP, ser. IA, vol. VII, p. 684.

56　Clayton to FO, 9 August 1928, DBFP, ser. IA, vol. VII, pp. 685–6.

57　Clayton diary, entries for 2–3 August 1928; Clayton to Amery, 3 September 1928 (Report of second 1928 mission to Ibn Saud), DBFA, pt. II, ser. B, vol. 6, pp. 87–91. Clayton had been authorized to inform Ibn Saud that Transjordan would also recognize his 'Kingdom of Hijaz and Najd'.

58　Clayton to Dobbs, 9 August 1928, CP, SAD 472/8/6 ('throwing away'); Clayton diary, entry for 3 August 1928 ('nothing doing').

59　In any event, it was unclear whether Iraq would have agreed to the extradition of 'political refugees'. Glubb recorded during the May 1928 negotiations that Iraq was not willing to agree to this and that, for his part, Ibn Saud had no interest in the extradition of anyone *except* political refugees. *See* Glubb, *War in the Desert*, p. 213.

60　Clayton diary, entries for 4–8 August 1928; Clayton to Dobbs, 9 August 1928, CP, SAD 472/8/6.

61　Vasiliev, *History of Saudi Arabia*, pp. 216–17.

29　Final Posting: High Commissioner for Iraq, 1929

1　Clayton diary, entries for September – December 1928, private collection.

2　The Colonial Office's formal offer of the High Commissionership appears in Amery to Clayton, 6 October 1928, and Clayton's acceptance in Clayton to Amery, 8 October 1928, CO 323/1016/6; T. E. Shaw (Lawrence) to Clayton, 9 October 1928, in Brown, ed., *Lawrence Letters*, p. 383.

3　Florence Caroline Clayton diary, entry for 21 December 1928, vol. 16, private collection.

4　Clayton to Percy Cox, 27 November 1928, CP, SAD 472/13/13.

5　Clayton, 'Arabia and the Arabs', pp. 8–20. Forty years later Professor Robert O. Collins published portions of Clayton's 1925–26 diary, detailing his negotiations at Bahra and Sanaa, as *An Arabian Diary.*

6 Clayton to Seymour (FO), 15 January and Clayton to Monteagle (FO), 18 January 1929, FO 371/13766; *and see* Chapter 1.

7 Clayton to Shuckburgh, 16 February 1929, FO 371/13769 (nightmare); Dr. John P. Clayton to the author, 16 November 2010.

8 Clerk to Chamberlain, 15 February, and Clayton Memorandum, 14 February 1929, FO 371/13769; Rendel (FO) Minute, 20 February 1929, *ibid.*

9 Tripp, *History of Iraq*, p. 43.

10 Sluglett, *Britain in Iraq*, p. 252, n. 81.

11 *Ibid.*, p. 80. The districts were Arbil, Kirkuk and Sulaymaniya.

12 *Ibid.*, pp. 49–64; Dodge, *Inventing Iraq*, pp. 19–22.

13 Treaty of Alliance between Great Britain and Irak, 10 October 1922, and Subsidiary Agreements, Cmd. 2370, CO 730/167/1.

14 *Ibid.*

15 Treaty of 13 January 1926, and attached 'Explanatory Note', Cmd. 2587, CO 730/167/1.

16 Dobbs to Amery, 24 March 1927, C.P. 173(27), CAB 24/187.

17 Amery memorandum, 'Entry of Iraq into the League of Nations', 9 June 1927, C.P. 178(27), CAB 24/187.

18 Memoranda of Dobbs and Ormsby-Gore, 20 and 21 November 1927, respectively, both in C.P. 288(27), CAB 24/189.

19 Chamberlain note, 29 November 1927, C.P. 300(27), CAB 24/189.

20 Ormsby-Gore memorandum, 5 December 1927, and draft Anglo-Iraqi treaty, C.P. 304(27), CAB 24/190. The signed treaty appears as Cmd. 2998, in CO 730/148/8.

21 Sluglett, *Britain in Iraq*, p. 108.

22 Alawi, *Faisal I*, pp. 507–8.

23 Dobbs to Amery, 15 September 1928, Leo Amery Papers, AMEL 2/4/13, Churchill College, Cambridge.

24 Dobbs to his wife, 29 December 1928, quoted in Alawi, *Faisal I*, p. 508.

25 G. Jebb (FO) minute, 18 October 1928, quoted in Sluglett, *Britain in Iraq*, pp. 113–14.

26 Clayton to Amery, 14 March 1929 (No. 110), C.P. 103(29), CAB 24(203).

27 Clayton to Amery, 14 March 1929 (No. 111); *and see* Amery memorandum, 28 March 1929, *ibid.*

28 Amery to Clayton, 25 March 1929, *ibid.*

29 Cabinet Conclusions, 17(29), 17 April 1929, CAB 23/60.

30 Clayton to Amery, 13 May 1929, cited in Sluglett, *Britain in Iraq*, p. 118.

31 Taylor, *English History, 1914–1945*, pp. 26–7.

32 Clayton to Amery, 16 March 1929, CO 732/37/1.

33 Ibn Saud to Clayton, two letters of 24 April 1929, DBFA, pt. II, ser. B, vol. 6, pp. 212–13.

34 Clayton to Ibn Saud, 19 April 1929, Robert Brooke-Popham Papers, 2/1/3, LHCMA.

35 Clayton to Ibn Saud, 25 May 1929, and Ibn Saud to Clayton, 26 June 1929, DBFA, pt. II, ser. B, vol. 6, pp. 214–15; Jakins (Jeddah) to Henderson (FO), 12 June 1929, DBFP, ser. IA, vol. VII, pp. 778–9. The correspondence relating to arbitration of the desert posts dispute appears in CO 730/140/5.

36 Clayton to Shuckburgh, 6 May 1929, CO 730/142/8; *and see* generally, correspondence and papers in that file.

37 Papers relating to the extradition treaty appear in CO 730/143/4.

38 Papers relating to the proposed abrogation of the 1924 Judicial Agreement appear in CO 730/140/6 and 7.

39 Sluglett, *Britain in Iraq*, pp. 74–5.

40 Extracts of a letter from Clayton to Shuckburgh, 20 May 1929; Colonial Office minutes of Bigg (13 June), Hall and Shuckburgh (14 June); and Shuckburgh to Clayton, 31 July 1929, all in CO 730/147/4.

41 Clayton to Passfield, 22 July 1929, CO 730/148/8.

42 Clayton to Shuckburgh, 22 July 1929, *ibid*.

43 Clayton to his sons, Sam and 'Squinch' (John), both 4 September 1929, Clayton family papers.

44 Sluglett, *Britain in Iraq*, p. 118; Clayton to Passfield, 1 September 1929, CO 730/148/8.

45 Clayton to Passfield, 31 August 1929, CO 730/149/5.

46 Memorandum, 'Disturbances in Palestine', n.a., n.d., but early September 1929, *ibid*.

47 Clayton to Faisal, 3 September 1929; Clayton to Passfield, 2 and 5 September 1929, *ibid*.

48 Clayton to Passfield, 1 September 1929, CO 730/148/8.

49 CO Minutes of Hall, 27 August, and Williams, 2 September 1929, *ibid*.

50 Passfield memorandum, 'Policy in Iraq', 3 September 1929, C.P. 239(29), CAB 24/205.

51 Hall (CO) minute, 16 August 1929, CO 730/148/8. Hall's minute was repeated, with few changes, in the Colonial Office's memorandum, 'Future Policy in Iraq', 31 August 1929, C.P. 239(29), CAB 24/205.

52 A. Cadogan (FO) minute, 6 September 1929, CO 730/148/8; Passfield memorandum, 'Policy in Iraq', 3 September 1929, C.P. 239(29), CAB 24/205. However, the Air Ministry welcomed Clayton's proposal; anything to conciliate Iraq was 'all to the good'. Trenchard comment at inter-departmental conference at the Colonial Office, n.d., *c.*1–8 September 1929, CO 730/149/5.

53 CO memorandum, 'Future Policy in Iraq', 31 August 1929, C.P. 239(29), CAB 24/205.

54 Cabinet Conclusions, 32(29), CAB 23/61.

55 Lindsay (FO) to MacDonald, 10 September 1929; Hankey to Passfield, 9 September 1929, both in CO 730/148/8;

56 Clayton to Enid Clayton, 9 September 1929, Clayton family papers.

57 Brooke-Popham to Passfield, 16 September 1929, Brooke-Popham papers, 2/2, LHCMA; Dr John P. Clayton to the author, June 2010. Dr. Clayton learned the details of his father's death years later from his brother-in-law, Dr A. G. Marshall who, during the Second World War, met the young RAF physician who attended Sir Gilbert at his death in 1929.

30 Conclusion: Friend of the Arabs

1 From a Note by Clayton's daughter, Patience Marshall, 28 October 1988, Clayton Family papers. Lawrence was aware that his former chief had only a small estate to leave to his wife and three children. When Clayton's will was proved on 8 January 1930, it disclosed a net value of only £1130. (Clayton will, 29 January 1929, copy provided by D. S. Thorne). Lawrence worked quietly behind the scenes to augment this: 'Lady

Clayton's income will be made up to about £1000 by Government. This seems to me (and I hope to you) satisfactory. Do not give the news any <u>extended</u> currency, as people dislike having their good deeds anticipated . . . and don't whisper my name, anyhow, please.' T.E.S. (Lawrence) to Alan Dawnay, 31 October 1929, in Brown, ed., *Lawrence Letters*, p. 431, original emphasis.

2   Florence Caroline Clayton diary, vol. 17, entry for 12 September 1929, private collection.

3   *Baghdad Times*, 12 September 1929, copy in Robert O. Collins Papers, SAD 930/12.

4   Faisal to Brooke-Popham, 12 September 1929, Robert Brooke-Popham Papers, 2/2, LHCMA.

5   *Al 'Iraq*, 18 September 1929, copy in Collins Papers, SAD 930/12.

6   Ibn Saud to Dickson (Kuwait), 27 September 1929, Collins Papers, SAD 930/12.

7   Faris Nimr to Lady Clayton, 28 November 1929, Clayton Family papers.

8   *Al Ahrar* (Beirut), 14 September 1929, copy in Collins Papers, SAD 930/12.

9   *See* Chapters 21 and 23.

10 Lawrence to Curzon, 27 September 1919, in Garnett, ed., *Letters of Lawrence*, p. 291.

11 Wigram to Wingate, 31 July 1916, CP, SAD 470/3/20; Keith-Roach, unpublished appreciation of Clayton entitled 'What Shall it Profit', n.d., Clayton Family papers; Storrs, *Orientations*, pp. 292–3; Lawrence, *Seven Pillars of Wisdom*, quoted above, in Chapter 12.

12 Brooke-Popham to Passfield, 16 September 1929, Brooke-Popham papers, 2/2/, LHCMA; *The Times* (London), 12 September 1929.

13 T. E. Shaw (Lawrence) to Lady Clayton, 14 September 1929, Clayton Family papers.

Bibliography

UNPUBLISHED SOURCES

I Archives

The National Archives, Kew, London

AIR Air Ministry
   AIR 5, AIR 20 Air Ministry, Air Historical Branch
Army Lists, 1896–1929
CAB Cabinet
   CAB 17 Committee of Imperial Defence
   CAB 21 Cabinet Office, Registered Files
   CAB 23 Cabinet Minutes, Conclusions
   CAB 24 Cabinet Memoranda
   CAB 27 Cabinet, Miscellaneous Committees
   CAB 42 War Council, 1914–1916
CO Colonial Office
   CO 323 Colonies, General: Original Correspondence
   CO 537 Supplemental General Correspondence
   CO 727 Arabia
   CO 730 Iraq
   CO 732 Middle East
   CO 733 Palestine
   CO 935 Colonial Office Confidential Print
   CO 959 Private Collections
CSC Civil Service Commission Records
FO Foreign Office
   Foreign Office Lists, 1915–1929
   FO 141 Records of British Agency/Residency, Cairo
   FO 371 Political Correspondence
   FO 407 Foreign Office Confidential Print
   FO 608 Paris Peace Conference: British Delegation, 1918–1920
   FO 624 Records of the High Commission and Embassy, Iraq
   FO 668 Jeddah Agency Papers
   FO 848 Records of the Milner Mission to Egypt
   FO 867 *Sudan Gazettes*
   FO 882 Records of the Arab Bureau, Cairo
KV Records of the Security Service (MI5)
WO War Office
   WO 32 Registered Files

WO 33 Reports, Memoranda and Papers
WO 106 Directorate of Military Operations and Military Intelligence
WO 149 Woolwich, Register of Cadets (*see* 'websites', below)
WO 157 Intelligence Summaries, First World War
WO 158 Military Headquarters, Corresp. and Papers, First World War

Private Paper Collections at TNA:
FO 800
Chamberlain, Austen
Curzon, George N
Grey, Edward
Oliphant, Lancelot
Sykes, Mark
PRO 30
Kitchener, H. H.
WO
Murray, Archibald (WO 79)
Macdonough, George (WO 106)

Royal Artillery Museum, Woolwich

Records of the Royal Military Academy, 1741–1892

Alphabetical List of the Officers of the Royal Regiment of Artillery (Woolwich: Royal Artillery Institution, January 1896)

Carisbrooke Castle Museum, Isle of Wight

Teesdale, K. J. M., *Historical Record of Isle of Wight College*, (unpublished, n.d.)

Middle East Centre, St. Antony's College, Oxford University

Private Papers of:
Allenby, Edmund H. H.
Antonius, George
Bowman, Humphrey
Boyle, Harry
Cheetham, Milne
Clayton, Iltyd N.
Cox, Percy
Deedes, Wyndham
Faisal ibn Hussein
Furness, Robin
Glubb, John Bagot
Herbert, Mervyn
Hogarth, David G.
Keown-Boyd, Alexander
Loder, John de Vere
Luke, Harry
McNeil, Angus
Monckton, R.F.B
Philby, H. St. J. B.

Rowlatt, Frederick
Russell, Thomas
Samuel, Herbert
Sykes, Mark
Yale, William
Young, Hubert
Young, J.W.A.

Sudan Archives, University of Durham

Private Papers of:
Clayton, Gilbert F.
Collins, Robert O.
Wingate, F. R.

National Army Museum, London

Private Papers of:
Money, Arthur

Imperial War Museum, London

Private Papers of:
Chetwode, Philip
Dawnay, Guy
Garland, Herbert
Kirke, Walter
Lynden-Bell, Arthur
Murray, Archibald
Peake, Frederick

Liddell Hart Centre for Military Archives, King's College, University of London

Private Papers of:
Allenby, Edmund H. H.
Brooke-Popham, Robert
Liddell Hart, Basil
Joyce, Pierce
Robertson, William

St. Cecilia's Abbey, Ryde, Isle of Wight

Isle of Wight, College Ground Plan, *c.* 1905
Map of the Apley House Property, *c.* 1905–6

Churchill Archives, Churchill College, Cambridge University

Private Papers of:
Amery, Leo
Churchill, Winston
Lloyd, George
Wemyss, Rosslyn

British Library, London

Private Papers of:
    Curzon, George N.
Oriental and India Office Collections:
L/P&S/10 Letters, Political & Secret, Political Department
L/P&S/11 Letter, Political and Secret, Annual Files, 1912–1930

Cambridge University Library

Private Papers of:
    Hardinge, Charles

Birmingham University Library

Private Papers of:
    Chamberlain, Austen

Weston Library, Oxford University

Diaries of:
    Meinertzhagen, Richard

Bodleian Library, Oxford University

Private Papers of:
    Lawrence, T.E.
    Selby, Walford

Firestone Library, Princeton University

Private Papers of:
    Maxwell, John

Parliamentary Archives, London

Private Papers of:
    Lloyd George, David
    Samuel, Herbert

Pembroke College, Cambridge University

Private Papers of:
    Storrs, Ronald

Royal Archives, Windsor

Papers and Diaries of H.M. King George V

Weizmann Archive, Rehovot, Israel

Papers of Chaim Weizmann (copies kindly provided by Prof. M. W. Daly)

University of Newcastle Library

Private Papers of:
Bell, Gertrude (some online at: http://gertrudebell.ncl.uk/)

II Interviews

Dr. John P. Clayton, C.V.O.:
  January 2010, Shepperton, England
  April 2010, Market Lavington, England
  August 2010, York, England
  September 2011, Windsor, England
Mrs Margaret Gosling (neé Clayton):
  September 2011, Abingdon, England

III Clayton Family Papers

W. L. N. Clayton, Unpublished partial family history (The "Green Book")
Clayton Family, 'Biographical Notes' (n.a., n.d.)
Gilbert F. Clayton, Bible
Lady Enid Clayton, 'A Week in Palestine', 1919 (unpublished MS)
Ellinor M. Clayton, Notes, n.d., *c.*1960s
Miscellaneous correspondence, 1914–1929

IV Miscellaneous

Gilbert F. Clayton Diaries, Desk Diaries and Pocket Diaries (private collection)
Isle of Wight College Prospectus, *c.*1880s (provided by Mr R. E. Brinton, Isle of Wight)
Isle of Wight College Advertisement, *c.*1885 (provided by Mr R. E. Brinton, Isle of Wight)
Correspondence, Dr. John P. Clayton, C.V.O. to the author, 2010–2015
Diaries of Florence Caroline Clayton (née Schuster) (private collection)

PUBLISHED SOURCES

I Document Collections

Bourne, Kenneth and D. Cameron Watt, (eds.), *Documents on British Foreign Affairs: Reports and Papers from the Foreign Office Confidential Print* (London, 1985).
Hurewitz, J. C., (ed.), *The Middle East and North Africa in World Politics: A Documentary Record*, 2 vols.(Yale Univ. Press, 2nd edn., 1979).
Woodward, E. L. and Rohan Butler, et al., (eds.), *Documents on British Foreign Policy, 1919–1939* (London, 1947–67).

II Books

Adelson, Roger, *Mark Sykes: Portrait of an Amateur* (London: Jonathan Cape, 1975).
Alawi, Ali A., *Faisal I of Iraq* (Yale Univ. Press, 2014).
Almana, Mohammed, *Arabia Unified: A Portrait of Ibn Saud* (London: Hutchinson Benham, 1980).
al-Rasheed, Madawi, *A History of Saudi Arabia* (Cambridge Univ. Press, 2nd edn., 2010).
Anderson, Scott, *Lawrence in Arabia: War, Deceit, Imperial Folly and the Making of the Modern Middle East* (N.Y.: Doubleday, 2013).

Andrew, Christopher, *Her Majesty's Secret Service: The Making of the British Intelligence Community* (New York: Viking, 1985).

———, *Defend the Realm: The Authorized History of MI5* (New York: Vintage, 2009).

Antonius, George, *The Arab Awakening* (London, 1938).

Badrawi, Malak, *Isma'il Sidqi: Pragmatism and Vision in Twentieth Century Egypt* (Richmond: Curzon Press, 1996).

Baker, Randall, *King Husain and the Kingdom of the Hejaz* (Cambridge: The Oleander Press, 1979).

Bardell, Mark, *The Isle of Wight, Portsmouth & the Solent: A Cultural History* (Oxford: Signal Books, Ltd., 2012).

Barr, James, *A Line in the Sand: The Anglo-French Struggle for the Middle East, 1914–1948* (N.Y.: W.W. Norton & Co., 2012).

Beesly, Patrick, *Room 40: British Naval Intelligence, 1914–1918* (New York: Harcourt Brace Jovanovich, 1982).

———, *Very Special Intelligence: The Story of the Admiralty's Operational Intelligence Centre, 1939–1945* (London: Hamish Hamilton, 1977).

Bentwich, Norman and Helen, *Mandate Memories, 1918–1948* (N.Y.: Schocken Books, 1965).

Boyle, Susan Silsby, *Betrayal of Palestine: The Story of George Antonius* (Boulder, CO: Westview Press, 2001).

Brown, Malcolm, ed., *T.E. Lawrence: The Selected Letters* (New York: W.W. Norton & Co., 1989).

———, ed., *Secret Despatches from Arabia and other writings by T.E. Lawrence* (London: Bellew, 1991).

Bruce, Anthony, *The Last Crusade: The Palestine Campaign in the First World War* (London: John Murray, 2002).

Bullock, David L., *Allenby's War: The Palestine-Arab Campaigns, 1916–1918* (London: Blandford Press, 1988).

Busch, B.C., *Britain, India and the Arabs, 1914–1921* (Univ. of California Press, 1971).

Carman, Barry and McPherson, John, eds., *The Man Who Loved Egypt, Bimbashi McPherson* (London: Ariel Books, 1985 edn.).

Caws, Sheila, *The Isle of Wight, A Pictorial History* (Chichester: Phillimore & Co., 1989).

Cecil, Lord Edward, *The Leisure of an Egyptian Official* (London: Hodder and Stoughton, 1921).

Charmley, John, *Lord Lloyd and the Decline of the British Empire* (New York: St Martin's Press, 1987).

Churchill, Winston S., *My Early Life: A Roving Commission* (N.Y.: Manor Books, 1972 edn.).

———, *The River War* (London, 1902; 2007 reprint).

Clayton, Gilbert F., *An Arabian Diary*, ed. by Robert O. Collins (Univ. of Claifornia Press, 1969).

Cleveland, William L., *A History of the Modern Middle East* (Boulder, CO: Westview Press, 1994).

Clutterbuck, Robert, *History and Antiquities of the County of Hertford* (1815–27).

Collins, Robert O., ed., *An Arabian Diary*, by Gilbert F. Clayton (Univ. of California Press, 1969).

———, *Land Beyond the Rivers: The Southern Sudan, 1898–1918* (New Haven, CT: Yale Univ. Press, 1971).

Collins, Robert O., and Robert L. Tignor, *Egypt and the Sudan* (Englewood Cliffs, N.J.: Prentice Hall, 1967).

Cromer, Earl of, *Modern Egypt* (N.Y.: The Macmillan Company, 1908).

Daly, M.W., *Empire on the Nile: The Anglo-Egyptian Sudan, 1898–1934* (Cambridge Univ. Press, 1986).

———, *The Sirdar: Sir Reginald Wingate and the British Empire in the Middle East* (Philadelphia, PA.: American Philosophical Society, 1997).

———, *Darfur's Sorrow: The Forgotten History of a Humanitarian Disaster*, 2nd edn. (Cambridge Univ. Press, 2010).

Dann, Uriel, *Studies in the History of Transjordan, 1920–1949: The making of a State* (Boulder, CO: Westview Press, 1984).

Darlow, Michael and Bray, Barbara, *Ibn Saud: The Desert Warrior and his Legacy* (London: Quartet Books, 2010).

Darwin, John, *Britain, Egypt and the Middle East: Imperialism and policy in the aftermath of war* (N.Y.: St. Martin's Press, 1981).

Dickson, H.R.P., *Kuwait and Her Neighbours* (London: Allen & Unwin, 1956).

Dockrill, Michael, and Goold, J. Douglas, *Peace Without Promise: Britain and the Peace Conferences, 1919– 1923* (London: Bratsford Academic, 1981).

Dodge, Toby, *Inventing Iraq: The Failure of Nation Building and a History Denied* (Columbia Univ. Press, 2003).

Drayson, A.W., *The Gentleman Cadet: His Career and Adventures at the Royal Military Academy*, Woolwich (London: Griffith and Farran, 1875).

Dresch, Paul, *A History of Modern Yemen* (Cambridge Univ. Press, 2000).

Elgood, P.G., *Egypt and the Army* (Oxford Univ. Press, 1924).

Esposito, John L., *Islam, the Straight Path* (Oxford Univ. Press, 3rd edn., 1998).

Falls, Cyril and George MacMunn, *Military Operations, Egypt and Palestine, vol. I: From The Outbreak of War with Germany to June 1917* (London, 1928).

Farwell, Byron, *Mr. Kipling's Army: All the Queen's Men* (London: W.W. Norton & Co., 1981).

Featherstone, Donald, *Omdurman, 1898* (London: Praeger, 2005).

Fergusson, Thomas G., *British Military Intelligence, 1870–1914* (London: Arms and Armour Press, 1984).

ffrench Comyn, D.C.E., *Service and Sport in the Sudan, a record of administration in the Anglo-Egyptian Sudan* (London: John Lane, 1911).

Finkel, Caroline, *Osman's Dream* (N.Y.: Basic Books, 2005).

Fisher, John, *Curzon and British Imperialism* (London: Frank Cass, 1999).

FitzHerbert, Margaret, *The Man who was Greenmantle: A Biography of Aubrey Herbert* (London: John Murray, 1983).

Florence, Ronald, *Lawrence and Aaronsohn: T.E. Lawrence, Aaron Aaronsohn and the Seeds of the Arab–Israeli Conflict* (New York: Viking, 2008).

Fothergill, Edward, *Five Years in the Sudan* (New York: D. Appleton & Co., 1911).

Fraser, T.G., *Chaim Weizmann: The Zionist Dream* (London: Haus Publishing, 2009).

Friedman, Isaiah, *The Question of Palestine: British–Jewish–Arab Relations: 1914–1918* (New Brunswick, N.J.: Transaction Publishers, 2nd edn. 1992).

Fromkin, David, *A Peace to End All Peace: Creating the Modern Middle East, 1914–1922* (New York: Henry Holt, 1989).

Garnett, David, ed., *The Letters of T.E. Lawrence of Arabia* (London: Spring Books, 1964 edn.).

Gerolymatos, Andre, *Castles Made of Sand: A Century of Anglo-American Espionage and Intervention in the Middle East* (New York: St Martin's Press, 2010).

Gilmour, David, *Curzon* (London: John Murray, 1994).

Glubb Pasha, (John Bagot), *War in the Desert* (New York: W.W. Norton, 1960).

Goldschmidt, Arthur, *Modern Egypt*, (Boulder, CO: Westview Press, 2nd edn., 2004).

Gooch, John, *The Plans of War: The General Staff and British Military Strategy, 1900–1916* (London: Routledge and Kegan Paul, 1974).

Grafftey-Smith, Laurence, *Bright Levant* (London: John Murray, 1970).

Graham, C.A.L., *The Story of the Royal Regiment of Artillery* (Woolwich: Royal Artillery Institution, 1962).

Grainger, John D., *The Battle for Palestine, 1917* (Woodbridge: The Boydell Press, 2006).

Graves, Robert and Liddell Hart, B.H.,eds., *T.E. Lawrence to his Biographers Robert Graves and B.H. Liddell Hart* (New York: Doubleday & Co., combined edn., 1963).

Gudgin, Peter, *Military Intelligence, the British Story* (London: Arms and Armour Press, 1989).

Guggisberg, Frederick Gordon, *"The Shop": The Story of the Royal Military Academy* (London: Cassell & Co., 1900).

Haag, Michael, *Alexandria, City of Memory* (New Haven, CT: Yale Univ.Press, 2004).

Habib, J. S., *Ibn Saud's Warriors of Islam: The Ikhwan of Najd and their Role in the Creation of the Saudi Kingdom* (Leiden: Brill, 1978).

Harrington, Peter, and Frederick A. Sharf, *Omdurman 1898: The Eyewitnesses Speak* (London: Greenhill Books, 1998).

Hedrick, Daniel R., *The Tools of Empire: Technology and European Imperialism in the Nineteenth Century* (Oxford Univ. Press, 1981).

Helms, Christine Moss, *The Cohesion of Saudi Arabia: Evolution of Political Identity* (London: Croom Helm, 1981).

Hill, Roderic, *The Baghdad Air Mail* (London: 1929; Nonsuch Publishing edn., 2005).

Hodgkin, E.C., ed., *Two Kings in Arabia: Sir Reader Bullard's Letters from Jeddah* (Reading: Ithaca Press, 1993).

Holt, P.M., *The Mahdist State in the Sudan, 1881–1898* (Oxford Univ. Press, 1958).

Hope Moncrieff, A. R., *Isle of Wight* (London: Adam and Charles Black, 1908).

Hopkirk, Peter, *Like Hidden Fire: The Plot to Bring Down the British Empire* (N.Y.: Kodansha, 1994).

Hopwood, Derek, *Tales of Empire: The British in the Middle East* (London: I.B. Tauris, 1989).

Hughes, Matthew, *Allenby and British Strategy in the Middle East, 1917–1919* (London: Frank Cass, 1999).

Huneidi, Sahar, *A Broken Trust: Sir Herbert Samuel, Zionism and the Palestinians* (London: I.B. Tauris, 2001).

Ingrams, Doreen, *Palestine Papers, 1917–1922: Seeds of Conflict* (London: Eland, 2009 paperback edn.).

Jarvis, C.S., *Desert and Delta* (London: John Murray, 1938).

Jeffery, Keith, *MI6: The History of the Secret Intelligence Service, 1909–1949* (London: Bloomsbury, 2010).

Jenkins, Roy, *Churchill: A Biography* (N.Y.: Farrar, Straus & Giroux, 2001).

Jones, Jack and Johanna, *The Isle of Wight, an Illustrated History* (Stanbridge: The Dovecote Press, Ltd., 1987).

Judd, Alan, *The Quest for C: Mansfield Cumming and the Founding of the British Secret Service* (London: Harper Collins, 2000 edn.).

Karsh, Efraim and Inari, *Empires of the Sand: The Struggle for Mastery in the Middle East, 1789–1923* (Harvard Univ. Press, 1999).

Kayali, Hasan, *Ottomanism, Arabism and Islamism in the Ottoman Empire, 1908–1918* (Univ. of California Press, 1997).

Kedourie, Elie, *The Chatham House Version and other Middle Eastern Studies* (Chicago: Ivan R. Dee, 1984 edn.).

———, *In the Anglo-Arab Labyrinth: The McMahon–Husayn Correspondence and its Interpretations, 1914–1939* (Cambridge Univ. Press, 1976).

———, *England and the Middle East: The Destruction of the Ottoman Empire, 1914–1921* (Boulder, CO: Westview Press, 1987 edn.).

Keith-Roach, Edward (Paul Eedle, ed.), *Pasha of Jerusalem: Memoirs of a District Commissioner under the British Mandate* (London: The Radcliffe Press, 1994).

Keown-Boyd, Henry, *A Good Dusting: A centenary review of the Sudan campaigns, 1883–1899* (London: Leo Cooper, 1986).

Khalidi, Rashid, et al., eds., *The Origins of Arab Nationalism* (Columbia Univ. Press, 1991).

Kirkbride, A., *A Crackle of Thorns: Experiences in the Middle East* (London: John Murray, 1956).

Knox, Edward, *The Making of a New Eastern Question: British Palestine Policy and the Origins of Israel, 1917–1925* (Catholic Univ. of America Press, 1981).

Kostiner, Joseph, *The Making of Saudi Arabia: From Chieftaincy to Monarchical State* (Oxford Univ. Press, 1993).

Lawrence, A. W., ed., *T. E. Lawrence by his Friends* (New York: Gordian Press, 1980).

———, ed., *Oriental Assembly* (London: Williams and Norgate, 1939).

Lawrence, T. E., *Seven Pillars of Wisdom, A Triumph: The Complete 1922 Text* (Blacksburg, Va.: Wilder Publications, 2011).

———, *Seven Pillars of Wisdom, a triumph* (N.Y.: Doubleday, Doran & Co., 1935).

Leatherdale, Clive, *Britain and Saudi Arabia, 1925–1939: The Imperial Oasis* (London: Frank Cass, 1983).

Lloyd, Lord (George), *Egypt Since Cromer*, 2 vols (London: Macmillan, 1933).

Lloyd George, David, *The Truth about the Peace Treaties*, 2 vols. (London: 1938).

Long, C.W.R., *British Pro-Consuls in Egypt, 1914–1929: The challenge of nationalism* (London: RoutledgeCurzon, 2005).

Macmillan, Margaret, *Paris 1919: Six Months that Changed the World* (N.Y.: Random House, 2001).

Manchester, William, *The Last Lion: Winston Spencer Churchill; Visions of Glory: 1874–1932* (Boston: Little Brown & Co., 1983).

Mangan, J. A., *The Games Ethic and Imperialism* (New York: Viking, 1985).

Mansfield, Peter, *The British in Egypt* (New York: Holt, Rinehart & Winston, 1972).

Marlowe, John, *A History of Modern Egypt and Anglo-Egyptian Relations, 1800–1956* (Hamden, CT: Archon Books, 1965).

———, *The Seat of Pilate* (London: The Cresset Press, 1959).

McGregor, Andrew, *A Military History of Modern Egypt from the Ottoman Conquest to the Ramadan War* (Westport, CT: Praeger Security International, 2006).

McGuirk, Russell, *The Sanusi's Little War* (London: Arabian Publishing, 2007).

McIntyre, John D., *The Boycott of the Milner Mission: A Study in Egyptian Nationalism* (N.Y.: Peter Lang, 1985).

McKale, Donald, *War by Revolution: Germany and Great Britain in the Middle East in the Era of World War I* (Kent State Univ. Press, 1998).

McMeekin, Sean, *The Berlin–Baghdad Express: The Ottoman Empire and Germany's Bid for World Power* (Cambridge, Mass.: The Belknap Press of Harvard Univ. Press, 2010).

McNamara, Robert, *The Hashemites: The Dream of Arabia* (London: Haus Pub., 2009).

Meinertzhagen, Richard, *Middle East Diary, 1917–1956* (London: The Cresset Press, 1959).

Mohs, Polly A., *Military Intelligence and the Arab Revolt: The First Modern Intelligence War* (London: Routledge, 2008).

Morris, James (Jan), *Pax Britannica: The Climax of Empire* (London: Harcourt Brace Jovanovich, 1968).

Mostyn, Trevor, *Egypt's Belle Epoque: Cairo and the Age of the Hedonists* (London: Tauris Paperbacks, 2006).

Musa, Suleiman, *T.E. Lawrence: An Arab View* (Oxford Univ. Press, 1966).

————, *Al-Husayn Ibn Ali wa al-thawra al-'Arabiyya al-kubra* [*Husayn ibn Ali and the great Arab revolt*] (Amman, 1957).

Northedge, F.S., *The League of Nations, its Life and Times, 1920 – 1946* (Leicester Univ. Press, 1988).

Occleshaw, Michael, *Armour Against Fate: British Military Intelligence in the First World War* (London: Columbus Books, 1989).

Omissi, David E., *Air Power and Colonial Control: The Royal Air Force, 1919–1939* (Manchester Univ. Press, 1990).

Pakenham, Thomas, *The Scramble for Africa: White Man's Conquest of the Dark Continent from 1876 to 1912* (New York: Avon Books, 1991).

Pappe, Ilan, *A History of Modern Palestine* (Cambridge Univ. Pess, 2nd edn., 2006).

Paris, Timothy J., *Britain, the Hashemites and Arab Rule, 1920–1925: The Sherifian Solution* (London: Frank Cass, 2003).

Pollock, John, *Kitchener: Architect of Victory, Artisan of Peace* (N.Y.: Carroll & Graf Publishers, Inc., 2001).

Reninharz, Jehuda, *Chaim Weizmann: The Making of a Statesman* (Brandeis Univ. Press, 2001 edn.).

Robbins, Simon, *British Generalship on the Western Front* (London: Routledge, 2005).

Roberts, Andrew, *Salisbury: Victorian Titan* (London: Weidenfeld & Nicolson, 1999).

Robinson, Ronald, and John Gallagher with Alice Denny, *Africa and the Victorians: The Official Mind of Imperialism* (London: The Macmillan Press, 1961).

Rodger, N.A.M., *The Command of the Ocean: A Naval History of Britain, 1649–1815* (London: Norton, 2004).

Rogan, Eugene, *The Arabs, A History* (London: Allen Lane, 2009).

————, *The Fall of the Ottomans: The Great War in the Middle East* (N.Y.: Basic Books, 2015).

Russell, Thomas, *Egyptian Service, 1902–1946* (London: John Murray, 1949).

Sa'id, Amin, *Al-Thawra al-'Arabiyya al-kubra* [*The Great Arab Revolt*] (Cairo, 1934).

Salibi, Kamal, *The Modern History of Jordan* (London: I.B. Tauris, 1993).

Sanders, Ronald, *The High Walls of Jerusalem: A History of the Balfour Declaration and the Birth of the British Mandate for Palestine* (N.Y.: Holt, Rinehart & Winston, 1983).

Sattin, Anthony, *Lifting the Veil: British Society in Egypt, 1768–1956* (London: J.M. Dent & Sons, 1988).

Schneer, Jonathan, *The Balfour Declaration: The Origins of the Arab Israeli Conflict* (N.Y.: Random House, 2010).

Segev, Tom, *One Palestine, Complete: Jews and Arabs Under the British Mandate* (N.Y.: Henry Holt, 1999).

Sheffy, Yigal, *British Military Intelligence During the Palestine Campaign, 1914–1918* (London: Frank Cass, 1998).

Shepherd, Naomi, *Ploughing Sand: British Rule in Palestine, 1917–1948* (New Brunswick, N.J.: Rutgers Univ. Press, 2000).

Sikainga, Ahmad, *The Western Bahr al-Ghazal Under British Rule, 1898–1956* (Athens, OH: Ohio Univ. Press, 1991).

Sluglett, Peter, *Britain in Iraq: Contriving King and Country* (Columbia Univ. Press, 2nd edn., 2006).

Smith, Charles D., *Palestine and the Arab–Israeli Conflict* (N.Y.: St. Martins Press, 3rd edn., 2006).

Spiers, Edward M., *The Late Victorian Army, 1868–1902* (Univ. of Manchester Press, 1992).

Steevens, G.W., *Egypt in 1898* (N.Y.: Dodd Mead & Co., 1899).

———, *With Kitchener to Khartoum* (N.Y.: Dodd Mead & Co., 1900).

Stein, Leonard, *The Balfour Declaration* (N.Y.: Simon & Schuster, 1961).

Steiner, Zara, *The Lights that Failed: European International History, 1919–1933* (Oxford Univ. Press, 2005).

Stirling, *Safety Last* (London: Hollis and Carter, 1953).

Storrs, Sir Ronald, *Orientations* (London: Nicholson & Watson, 1943 edn.).

Strachey, Lytton, *Eminent Victorians* (London, 1918).

Symes, Stewart, *Tour of Duty* (London: Collins, 1946).

Tauber, Eliezer, *The Arab Movements in World War I* (London: Frank Cass, 1993).

Taylor, A. J. P., *English History, 1914–1945* (Oxford Univ. Press, ppbk edn., 1992).

Teitelbaum, Joshua, *The Rise and Fall of the Hashimite Kingdom of Arabia* (New York Univ. Press, 2001).

Terry, Janice, *The Wafd, 1919–1952* (London: Third World Centre, 1982).

Thomas, Martin, *Empires of Intelligence: Security Services and Colonial Disorder after 1914* (Univ. of California Press, 2008).

Toms, Jan, *Isle of Wight Villains, Rogues, Rascal and Reprobates* (Stroud, Gloucester: The History Press, 2012).

Trench, Charles Chevenix, *The Road to Khartoum: A Life of General Charles Gordon* (New York: Dorset Press, 1987 edn.).

Tripp, Charles, *A History of Iraq* (Cambridge Univ. Press, 2000).

Twigg, Stephen, Hampshire, Edward and Macklin, Graham, *British Intelligence: Secrets, Spies and Sources* (Kew: The National Archives, 2008).

Vasiliev, Alexei, *The History of Saudi Arabia* (New York Univ. Press, 2010).

Vatikiotis, P.J., *The History of Modern Egypt*, 4th edn. (Baltimore, MD: John Hopkins Univ. Press, 1991).

Warburg, Gabriel, *The Sudan Under Wingate* (London: Frank Cass & Co., 1971).

Wasserstein, Bernard, *The British in Palestine: The Mandatory Government and the Arab–Jewish Conflict, 1917–1929* (London: Royal Historical Society, 1978).

———, *Herbert Samuel, A Political Life* (Oxford Univ. Press, 1992).

Wavell, Field-Marshal Viscount, *Allenby: Soldier and Statesman* (London: Harrap, 1946).

Weekes, Davis, *The Origins of Lexham Gardens and Lee Abbey in London* (Leominster: Gracewing, 1996).

Weizmann, Chaim, *Trial and Error: The Autobiography of Chaim Weizmann* (N.Y.: Harper, 1949).

West, Nigel (pseud., Rupert Allison), *MI5* (New York: Military Heritage Press, 1981).

———, *MI6: British Secret Intelligence Service Operations, 1909–1945* (New York: Random House, 1983).

Westrate, Bruce, *The Arab Bureau: British Policy in the Middle East, 1916–1920* (Pennsylvania State Univ. Press, 1992).

Wilkinson, John C., *Arabia's Frontiers: The Story of Britain's Boundary Drawing in the Desert* (London: I.B. Tauris, 1991).

Wilson, Jeremy, *Lawrence of Arabia: The Authorized Biography of T.E. Lawrence* (New York: Atheneum, 1990).

Wilson, Mary C., *King Abdullah, Britain and the Making of Jordan* (Cambridge Univ. Press, 1987).

Wingate, Ronald, *Wingate of the Sudan* (London: John Murray, 1955).

Winstone, H.V.F., ed., *The Diaries of Parker Pasha* (London: Quartet Books, 1983).

———, *The Illicit Adventure: The Story of Political and Military Intelligence in the Middle East from 1898 to 1926* (London: Jonathan Cape, 1982).

———, *Woolley of Ur: The Life of Sir Leonard Woolley* (London: Secker & Warburg, 1990).

Winter, C.R.W., *The Enchanted Isle: An Island History* (London: Cross Publishing, 1900).

Woodward, David R., *Hell in the Holy Land: World War I in the Middle East* (The University Press of Kentucky, 2006).

Yapp, Malcolm, *The Making of the Modern Near East, 1792–1923* (London: Longman, 1987).

Young, George, *Egypt* (London: Ernest Benn, 1927).

Zeine, Zeine N, *The Struggle for Arab Independence: Western Diplomacy & the Rise and Fall of Faisal's Kingdom in Syria* (Beirut: Khayat's, 1960).

Ziegler, Philip, *Omdurman* (Barnsley: Pen and Sword Books, 2003 edn.).

III Articles.

'Appley House', *The Gardener's Chronicle*, 30 Dec. 1876, 838–9.

Alon, Yoav, 'Tribal Shaykhs and the Limits of British Imperial Rule in Transjordan, 1920–1946', *Journal of Imperial and Commonwealth History*, 32, 1 (2004), 69–92.

Baldry, John, 'Anglo-Italian Rivalry in Yemen and 'Asir', *Die Welt des Islams*, XVII, 1–4 (1976–1977), 155–193.

Clayton, Gilbert F., 'Arabia and the Arabs', *Journal of the Royal Institute of International Affairs*, 8, 1 (January 1929), 8–20.

Dann, Uriel, 'The Political Confrontation of Summer 1924 in Transjordan', *Middle Eastern Studies*, 12, 2 (1976), 159–68.

Eldar, Dan, 'French Policy Towards Husayn, Sharif of Mecca', *Middle Eastern Studies*, 26, 3 (July, 1990), 329–50.

Fisher, John, 'The Rabegh Crisis, 1916–17: "A Comparatively Trivial Question" or "A Self-Willed Disaster"', *Middle Eastern Studies*, 38, 3 (2002), 73–92.

Friesel, Evyatar, 'British Officials on the Situation in Palestine, 1923', *Middle Eastern Studies*, 23, 2 (April, 1987), 194–210.

Johnson, Maxwell, 'The Arab Bureau and the Arab Revolt: Yanbu' to Aqaba', *Military Affairs*, 46, 4 (1982), 194–201.

McGregor, Alan, 'Flying the Furrow', *Saudi Aramco World*, 52, 2 (March/April, 2001), 24–31.

McKale, Donald, 'Germany and the Arab Question in the First World War', *Middle Eastern Studies*, 29, 2 (1993), 236–253.

————, 'German Policy Towards the Sherif of Mecca', *The Historian*, 55, 2 (1993), 303–314.

Mejcher, Helmut, 'British Middle East Policy, 1917–1922: The Inter-Departmental Level', *Journal of Contemporary History*, 8 (1973), 81–101.

Sheffy, Yigal, 'British Intelligence and the Middle East, 1900–1918: How Much Do We Know?', *Intelligence and National Security*, 17, 1 (2002), 33–52.

Shipman, John, 'The Clayton Mission to Sana'a, 1926', *British-Yemeni Society* (2001) .

Silverfarb, Daniel, 'The Treaty of Jiddah of May 1927', *Middle Eastern Studies*, 18, 3 (1982), 276–285, .

————, 'Great Britain, Iraq, and Saudi Arabia: The Revolt of the Ikhwan, 1927–1930', *The International History Review*, IV, 2 (1982), 222–248.

Slight, John, 'British Perceptions and Responses to Sultan Ali Dinar of Darfur, 1915–1916', *Journal of Imperial and Commonwealth History*, 38, 2 (2010), 237–260.

Tripodi, Christian W. E., 'The Foreign Office and Anglo-Italian Involvement in the Red Sea and Arabia, 1925–1928', *Canadian Journal of History*, XLII (Autumn, 2007), 209–234.

IV Newspapers

Isle of Wight County Press
Isle of Wight Observer
Manchester Guardian
The Times (London)
The Hamsphire Telegraph
London Gazette

V Parliamentary Debates

Hansard, House of Commons (1921–9)
  House of Lords (1921–9)

VI Websites

Isle of Wight Family History Society (http://www.isle-of-wight-fhs.co.uk)

David S. Thorne (http://dsthorne.com/tree)

Sandhurst Collection (http://archive.sandhurst.org.uk) (containing Woolwich Register of Cadets, WO 149/7)

University of Newcastle Library, Gertrude Bell Papers (http://gertrude bell.ncl.uk)

VII Dissertations

Bennett, Richard Allen, 'The Anglo-Egyptian Sudanese Influence in the Occupied Enemy Territory Administration, South, 1917–1920' (Florida State University, Ph.D., 1992)

Bishku, Michael, 'The British Empire and the Question of Egypt's Future, 1919–1922' (New York University, Ph.D., 1981)

Knox, Dennis Edward, 'The Development of British Policy in Palestine, 1917–1925: Sir Gilbert Clayton and the "New Eastern Question"' (Michigan State University, Ph.D.)

Scoville, Sheila Ann, 'British Logistical Support to the Hashemites of the Hejaz: Ta'if to Ma'an, 1916–1918' (Univ. of California at Los Angeles, Ph.D., 1982)

Stoddard, Philip H., 'The Ottoman Government and the Arabs, 1911 to 1918: A Preliminary Study of the *Teşkilat-ı Mahsusa*' (Princeton Univ., Ph.D., 1963)

Index